THE COMPLETE
COOKERY
MANUAL

THE COMPLETE
COOKERY
MANUAL

Anthony O'Reilly

Pitman Publishing
128 Long Acre, London WC2E 9AN

A Division of Longman Group UK Limited

© Longman Group UK Limited 1993

First published in Great Britain 1993

British Library Cataloguing-in-Publication Data
A catalogue record for this book is available
from the British Library

ISBN 0-273-03387-5

Typeset in 9 on 12 Frutiger by
Mathematical Composition Setters Ltd, Salisbury, Wiltshire

Printed in England by Clays Ltd, St Ives plc

CONTENTS

13

Baking and sweet preparations

14

Cold preparations

15

Microwave cookery

PART THREE
SPECIALIST COOKERY

19

Farinaceous cookery

20

Vegetarian cookery

21

Traditional British and Irish cookery

22

Eastern cookery

23

African-Caribbean cookery

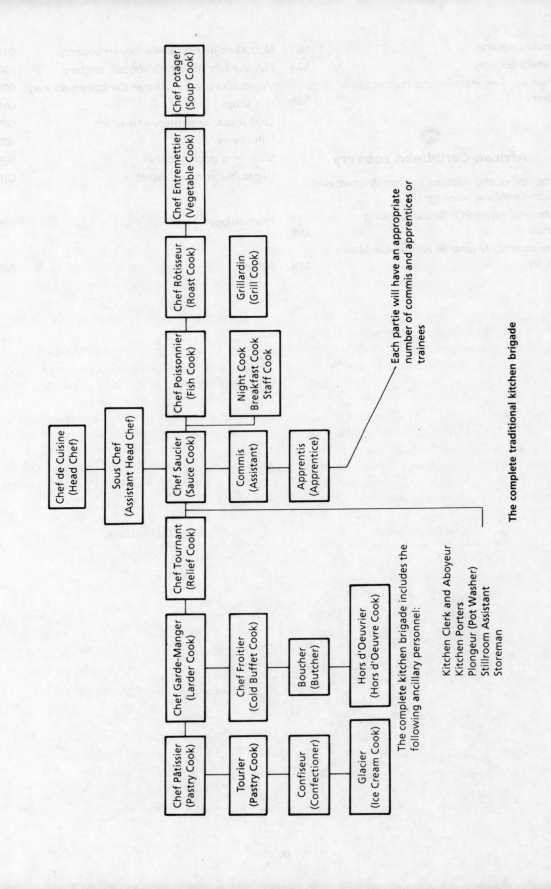

The complete traditional kitchen brigade

INTRODUCTION

In order to use this book properly one must first read the introductory information in each chapter. Each chapter has its own associated terminology which is repeated in a complete directory on p 625–44. Chapter 3 helps identify the necessary equipment required, while chapter 2 Commodities not only identifies the different foods, but suitable cuts of meat and fish for each process.

The recipes have been formatted using a more natural way of reading, from left to right and down the page – making it more 'user-friendly'.

Basic recipes are followed by derivatives or variations. The base recipes are in most cases one portion and ten portions so the user can multiply for any amount required no matter now little or how great. It will be necessary to adjust the quantities of certain recipes when increasing by large numbers.

Useful information on who would be responsible for carrying out the process in a large kitchen under the traditional partie system is also provided.

This text has been designed for trainee catering students studying on a range of BTEC and City and Guilds courses. Although the book covers all aspects of the City and Guilds 706-1 and 706-2, due to finish in 1994, it is specifically written to cover the new NVQ schemes at Levels 1, 2 and units of 3.

The Complete Cookery Manual contains both the theory and practice of food preparation in one volume. The information contained in the book looks ahead to developments in the more knowledge-based approach to Catering at GNVQ Level 3.

Offering a vast range of recipes and packed full of information, this book can be used in industry as well as college. The text will also be useful long after the individual has completed his or her training programme.

ABBREVIATIONS

g	gramme
kg	kilogramme (1000 grammes)
ml	millilitre
mm	millimetre
cm	centimetre
°C	Celsius (Centigrade)
°F	Fahrenheit
tsp	teaspoon
tbsp	tablespoon
⌣	preparation time
♨	cooking time
☰	baking time
≋	temperature

OVEN TEMPERATURES

°C	°F	Regulo No.	Definition
130	266	1/2	Very cool
140	284	1	Cool
150	302	2	Warm
170	338	3	Moderate
180	356	4	Moderate
190	374	5	Moderate
200	392	6	Hot
220	428	7	Hot
230	446	8	Very hot
240	464	9	Very hot
300	575	10	Extremely hot

ACKNOWLEDGEMENTS

I would like to thank the following organisations for kindly allowing me to use copyright material in this book:

- East Midlands Electricity
- M Gilbert (Greenford) Limited
- The Electricity Council
- The Fresh Fruit and Vegetable Information Bureau
- The Meat and Livestock Commission
- Merrychef Limited
- The National Dairy Council
- The Sea Fish Industry Authority
- Zanussi CLV Systems Limited.

I would like to dedicate this book to my wife, Julie, and my children, Terry, Kelly and Lisa, for all their devotion, encouragement and support; to Frank Bond of Lewisham College for his professional guidance; and to my Mum, for always believing in me.

In memory of Dad, Thomas Anthony O'Reilly,
died 1 June 1991.

PART ONE

INTRODUCTION

HEALTH AND SAFETY

Health and safety at work legislation

Every year thousands of people are killed and many more suffer serious injury at work. Industrial accidents are responsible for the loss of millions of working days every year and legislation is in operation to miminise them.

The Health and Safety at Work Act, 1974 was passed in order to protect both the employer and the employee, and make them more aware of safety in the workplace.

The law states that the employer 'must as far as is reasonably practicable ensure ... the health, safety and welfare at work of all his/her employees', and that the employee must 'take reasonable care for the health and safety of him/herself and other persons who may be affected by his or her actions or omissions at work'. The employee must also 'co-operate with the employer so far as is necessary to meet or comply with any requirements concerning health and safety and not to interfere with, or misuse anything provided in the interests of health, safety and welfare'.

The Prescribed Dangerous Machines Order, 1964

Under this Act certain machinery should be tested by a qualified fitter before being used by employees. The manufacturer's advice regarding servicing should be followed and a record book kept, showing when and what relevant maintenance the machinery is receiving. The Prescribed Dangerous Machines Order covers the following machinery:

(a) worm type mincing machines;
(b) bone chopping machines;
(c) dough mixers;
(d) food mixing machines;
(e) pie making machines;
(f) gravity feed slicing machines;
(g) potato chipping machines.

The responsibilities of the employer

The employer must:

1 provide and maintain the premises and equipment ensuring that they are safe and free from health hazards;
2 provide supervision and training in health and safety aspects;
3 produce and provide the employees with a copy of the company's Health and Safety policy.

The responsibilities of the employee

The employee must:

1 take reasonable care to avoid injury to themselves and to others by their actions;
2 co-operate with the employer and others so as to comply with the law;
3 refrain from misusing or interfering with anything provided for health and safety.

Enforcement

The Health and Safety Act is enforced by health and safety officers and the local environmental

3

health officers. They have the power to:

1 issue a prohibition notice preventing a business from trading until corrective action is taken;
2 issue an improvement notice to employees and/or employers, who must act upon the recommendations within a given time scale.
3 prosecute an employee or employer for breaking the law as laid down in the Act.
4 seize, render harmless or destroy anything that they might consider to be the cause of imminent danger.

Accidents – legal requirements of notification

All accidents must be reported to the employer or to their representative (internal safety officer) and recorded in an official accident book. If an accident causes either a major injury or a death, it must be reported to the Environmental Health Department.

Accident prevention

Accidents don't happen, they are caused. They may be caused by:

1 excessive haste, charging around the kitchen because of disorganisation;
2 distraction, not concentrating on the 'job in hand';
3 failure to apply the safety rules.

Accidents are an inconvenience, they cause pain to individuals and cause a loss of time. There are two main types of accidents in kitchens – cuts and burns/scalds.

Cuts are caused by:

1 using blunt knives;
2 not concentrating on the job;
3 using the incorrect knife for the job;
4 misuse of slicing machinery. Under the 1964 Prescribed Dangerous Machines Order, only persons above the age of 18 who have been properly trained may use this equipment.

Burns result from exposure to dry heat and scalds from boiling liquids or steam. To prevent burns and scalds always:

1 wear the appropriate uniform, with sleeves rolled down and aprons worn to below the knees.
2 use a good, thick, dry oven cloth to remove hot objects from the stove – a damp one can cause a scald.
3 ensure that the handles of saucepans are not protruding over the edge of the stove where they might be knocked.

4 make sure that you have the strength to lift saucepans from and to the stove. Ask a fellow worker to help if necessary.
5 place filled saucepans below eye level – never above.
6 take care when frying to regulate the temperature as required. Never place your hand in the hot fat. Always make sure that hot fat is properly and clearly marked.
7 always stand away and behind the door of a steamer before opening. With pressure steamers make sure that the pressure has equalised to atmosphere before attempting to open them.

Other accidents

Other less commonly-occurring accidents are related to the use of machines, e.g. operators turning mixing machines on, trapping a person's hand and breaking fingers or an arm. Dirty, greasy and wet floors are also dangerous. Always check that spillages are mopped up and dried immediately they happen. There are industrial washer/dryer machines that will carry out this task effectively.

Explosions can occur if safety measures are not adhered to when using gas-fed cooking equipment. Always make sure that pilot lights are lit and that the main jet has ignited from the pilot. Always check before lighting a taper that the main switch is off and that you cannot smell gas.

First aid

Since 1982 it has been a legal requirement that employers must have adequate first aid equipment, facilities and trained personnel to administer first aid in the workplace. First aid training is a useful employee skill and there are many nationally recognised first aid courses available at local colleges, and through the St John Ambulance Association and The Red Cross. First aid, as the term implies, is only temporary and if the injury warrants it the person must be treated by professionals (a doctor or nurse) as quickly as possible.

A first aid box should be situated in an accessible area and contain the following minimum pieces:

1 An accident report book
2 Cotton wool   4 × 25 g packs
3 Safety pins   12
4 Triangular bandages   2
5 Sterile eye pads with attachments   2
6 Sterile unmedicated dressings   4 medium
7 Sterile unmedicated dressings   2 large
8 Sterile unmedicated dressings   2 extra large
9 Disposable gloves
10 Scissors
11 Sterile, waterproof dressings   20 individually wrapped of various sizes
12 Card with general first aid advice   1

A QUICK GUIDE TO FIRST AID

For cuts. Wash the cut and the skin around the cut, dry and cover with a waterproof dressing. If bleeding does not stop, try controlling it by direct pressure. This application should not be used for more than 15 minutes. For nose bleeds, sit the person down with the head forward, loosen clothing around the neck. Pinch the soft part of the nose at 10 minute intervals until the bleeding stops. If it has not stopped after 30 minutes contact professional medical help.

Burns and scalds. Immerse the burned or scalded area in slow running cold water or immerse in cold water for 10 minutes, or until the pain ceases. Allow blisters to form as they are a natural protective barrier. Never use adhesive dressings, lotions or ointments.

Fractures. Keep the person still; do not move. Obtain professional medical help.

Electric shock. Switch off the power at the source. If this is not possible, try to free the victim from the power source using a dry insulating object – take care not to touch either the source or the victim with the bare hand.

Gassing. Carry the person out into the fresh air.

Artificial respiration. If the person has stopped breathing, mouth-to-mouth resuscitation may be administered by a trained first aider.

Shock and fainting. The signs of shock are sickness, clamminess, pale face and faintness. If a person is in shock he or she should be laid down and kept warm with a blanket or clothing. If a person faints, the patient should be laid down with the legs slightly raised. When they recover they should be allowed into the fresh air.

Fires

Fires are easily started in a catering establishment and can cause injury or even death if the right action is not taken. It is important that you are aware of the correct procedures in the event of a fire and that you know what steps to take should you have to tackle it.

The procedures in the event of a fire are:

1 Do not panic. Raise the alarm. Warn other people in the vicinity.
2 Contact the fire brigade. Do not wait for the fire to get out of control before calling them.

3 Follow the fire instructions of the establishment.

4 If the fire is small, use the appropriate extinguisher to put it out.

5 Close (not lock) all doors and windows, and if possible turn off the gas and electricity.

Fire needs three components to spread:

1 Fuel – Something to burn

2 Air – Oxygen to sustain combustion.

3 Heat – a source, i.e. gas or electricity

To put out a fire, one or all of the above elements must be removed. The most effective way to do this is by using either a fire blanket or a fire extinguisher. However, the correct extinguisher must be used for the specific type of fire. All fire extinguishers are manufactured in accordance with British Standards specifications and are colour coded to indicate their type and instructions on their use (*see* the table, right).

FIRE HOSES

These may be used to put out some fires, but are limited because water conducts electricity. Suitable for wood, fabric or paper fires.

WATER SPRINKLER SYSTEMS

A sprinkler system consists of an array of sprinkler heads at ceiling level that release water when the ceiling temperature level rises above a pre-set level. Such systems are not always practicable in a hot kitchen.

FIRE EXTINGUISHERS

Colour	Contents	Type of fire
Red	Water	Used on wood, fabrics, paper, etc. and eliminates heat. Must not be used on electrical fires as it is a conductor or on fat fires as it will most certainly cause the fat to ignite and spread.
Blue	All purpose powder	Used on fat fires, it extinguishes oxygen and does not conduct electricity.
Cream	Foam	Used to form a blanket over a fat fire thus eliminating oxygen. Foam is a conductor of electricity and must not be used on electrical fires.
Green	BCF Halons	BCF is short for bromochlorodifluoro-methane. It does not conduct electricity, so is used in extinguishing electrical fires.
Black	Carbon dioxide (CO_2)	Used on inflammable liquids it cools, removing heat and does not conduct electricity.

Kitchen safety and hygiene

Kitchen premises need to be a safe and hygienic working environment to minimise accidents and cross-contamination of food poisoning bacteria.

WALLS AND CEILINGS

Walls and ceilings should be light in colour, and free from cracks and flaking paint. Walls especially should be washable and the joins between the ceiling and walls, and walls and floors should be rounded for ease of cleaning. Tiling is best for walls, but not compulsory.

Maintenance Report any broken or chipped tiles. Clean with hot detergent water and dry.

FLOORS

Kitchen floors need to be laid properly and evenly, and be strong and durable to withstand the constant use. The surface must be smooth without being slippery, be impervious and easy to clean. They must be free from cracks or open joints. Quarry tiles or a good strong industrial vinyl flooring meet all the above requirements and are most suitable.

Maintenance Report any cracks or lifting of the floor covering. Floors should be swept regularly throughout the shift, and spills should be mopped up and dried at once. The floors should be cleaned thoroughly with hot detergent water and dried after each shift.

EQUIPMENT

Kitchen equipment is usually designed to be easily cleaned and maintained. Failure to do so will result in the equipment being unhygienic and dangerous to use.

NOTE: Always remember to isolate electrical items from the main supply before attempting to clean them or around them. Take care when cleaning gas appliances that gas pilots are not extinguished.

Maintenance Fixed equipment (stoves, sala-manders, tables, etc.) should have all food and grease scraped off or in the case of salamanders brushed off with a wire brush. The equipment should then be thoroughly cleaned with hot detergent water, rinsed and dried immediately.

NOTE: Abrasives should only be used in moderation as the scratches caused make the item more difficult to clean and are an ideal breeding ground for bacteria.

All moveable equipment should be washed thoroughly in hot detergent water immediately after use. Some items may have to be soaked to remove food particles and grease. Rinse in water above 75°C and allow to drain on wire racks.

Always follow the manufacturer's instructions when cleaning.

SINKS AND PLUMBING

There should be an adequate supply of sinks with hot and cold running water for three specific purposes:

1 to keep the kitchen and equipment clean;
2 to be used for food preparation only;

3 special 'hand washing only' sinks supplied with nail brush, bacterial soap and hygienic drying facilities (paper towels, hot air dryer or roller towel).

Maintenance All cracked or damaged sinks and hand basins should be reported. Sinks and hand basins should be cleaned thoroughly and rinsed well.

LIGHTING

Poor lighting causes eye strain. Proper lighting is also necessary in kitchens to enable staff to see dirt and clean the kitchen properly.

Maintenance Strip lighting is desirable in a kitchen environment and can be cleaned by removing the tubes and light diffusing covers and wiping with a damp cloth. Dry well before replacing.

VENTILATION

It is important to have a good ventilation system in a kitchen. Ventilation extraction systems have fans fitted that extract cooking fumes and heat from the kitchen and also help to keep staff cool by facilitating the evaporation of sweat from the body.

Maintenance Ventilation systems need to be cleaned regularly as grease and dirt accumulate quickly in the filters and hoods. If not removed the build up of greasy dirt might cause a fire.

KNIVES

Always select the correct knife for the particular job. Never misuse knives, keep handles free from grease, and never have more than one knife on the work surface at any one time. Always carry knives by the side and pointed down. A blunt knife is more likely to cause harm than a sharp one, so knives should be kept sharp at all times. Never place knives in a sink; they should always be cleaned and put away immediately after use. Wipe clean with a damp cloth, blade facing away from you. Always replace in the knife case.

A set of knives should consist of:

1 Chef's knife 25 cm	Use for slicing, chopping and shredding.
2 Carving knives	For carving meats.
3 Boning knife	For general butchery work.
4 Filleting knife 15 cm	For skinning and filleting fish.
5 Palette knife	Spreading, turning and lifting food items.
6 Vegetable knife 10 cm	General use.
7 Vegetable peeler	Peeling vegetables and fruit.
8 Trussing needle	Trussing meat and poultry.
9 Fork	Lifting and holding joints of meat and poultry.
10 Steel	Sharpening knives.

NOTE: A meat chopper is optional, but is necessary if chopping bones. Always keep sharp and clean.

Personal appearance and hygiene

Food handlers must have a more than average interest in appearance and hygiene because of the nature of the profession. The general public expects us to uphold the highest standards to ensure that they are not poisoned by our cooking.

Caterers tend to work long hours and split shifts and it is important to be self-disciplined. How we appear to people is a clear sign of our commitment to these standards of hygiene. It is essential to bath or shower daily, to brush teeth regularly and keep ears clean. Keep cosmetics to a minimum. Fingernails should be kept short and men should be clean shaven. Cover cuts, burns and sores with waterproof dressings. Hair should be washed regularly, never scratched and kept well covered in kitchens to prevent loose hairs falling into food. Chef's or cook's clothing should not only be clean and free from germs, but starched lightly and well ironed.

Hands and fingernails should be washed thoroughly and frequently with bacterial soap, hot water and a nail brush. This should be done before commencing work, after using the toilet and in between tasks to avoid cross-contamination of food. Women should avoid nail varnish; chipped varnish indicates general sloppiness.

Watches, earrings, jewellery and rings, except for wedding rings, should not be worn as food particles become trapped on these items and germs can multiply and be transferred to foods. Also, earrings, especially sleepers, might come off and fall into food.

Never smoke in the kitchen – it is an offence against the law. Also ash may fall into food and food may be contaminated by the action of putting your hands to your mouth or lips and coming into contact with saliva and then touching the food. Never cough or sneeze over food as it will become contaminated with harmful germs. Never pick or touch your nose as harmful bacteria can be passed onto food through this action. If you sneeze and have to blow your nose with a handkerchief, always wash your hands thoroughly afterwards. Disposable handkerchiefs are preferable to cloth ones.

PROTECTIVE CLOTHING

Food handlers must wear clothing that not only protects the body from the excessive heat but is adequate to protect from burns or scalds. White or light-coloured clothing should be worn as it both reflects the heat and also shows up the dirt. Sleeves should be long and it is advisable that jackets or overalls should be starched to give additional protection against hot liquids. Aprons should be worn to below the knees and again should be adequately starched to protect the trunk area and legs against scalds and burns.

The chef's traditional check trousers are made from a light cotton. A chef's hat is designed to enable the air to circulate around the top of the head and keep it cool. A neck tie acts as a band to soak up sweat. Footwear should be safe with non-slip soles and sturdy tops to protect the toes. It is important that they are big enough so as not to harm the feet (which may swell in the heat of the kitchen). Clogs are ideal for kitchens because they allow air to circulate around the feet and give the appropriate support and protection.

Food poisoning and bacteria

Food poisoning is an illness which can cause stomach pains, acute diarrhoea and vomiting between one and 36 hours after eating the infected food. There are a few foods that are resistant to food poisoning, i.e. sterilised foods (canned), preserved foods with a high concentration of sugar, salt or vinegar and irradiated foods (foods that have been treated with X-rays).

Some bacteria produce the toxins or poisons outside their own bodies and thus the food itself is poisonous causing very rapid symptoms of food poisoning. Other bacteria produce the toxins within their own bodies and these are not released until the bacteria die. In some circumstances food poisoning is delayed until the bacteria die in sufficient numbers.

Foods may be infected by two major types of contamination: chemicals and bacteria.

CHEMICALS

Chemicals may enter the food accidentally during processing and/or cooking, or may occur naturally in certain plants:

(a) Arsenic. This is sometimes found in fruit after it is treated by special sprays during growth.
(b) Copper, antimony or zinc. Acid foods can sometimes become contaminated by these substances if stored in poor quality enamelled, galvanized containers or copper containers.
(c) Lead. Water in contact with lead for long periods can become contaminated.
(d) Poisonous plants, certain fungi, rhubarb leaves.

BACTERIA

Bacteria contaminating food derive from animal, human, or other sources and are the most common cause of food poisoning. Bacteria are microscopic single cell organisms which are present practically everywhere, but can only be brought into contact with foods by outside agents, e.g. humans, animals, air movements, insects and vermin (flies, cockroaches, mice, rats).

Under no circumstances should pets be allowed into the kitchen. Care must be taken not to encourage vermin by leaving foods out in the kitchen. Never leave food uncovered. Flies settle on foods and contaminate food with their own excreta or that of others and/or saliva. Since flies breed in rubbish and filth and feed from mostly from rubbish and waste the most effective method of eradication should be taken. The most hygienic is the use of a special electric fly exterminator with a collection tray. Insecticides (fly sprays) should not be used on or near surfaces or foods.

Food handlers who feel ill, are suffering from diarrhoea or vomiting, have septic cuts, weeping sores, cold or sore throats must under no circumstances work with foods. Only when they have been given a clear bill of health by a doctor may they return to work. Some people are food poisoning carriers and it is the responsibility of employee and the employer to inform the Public Health Inspector/Medical Officer of Health if this is the case or is suspected.

Bacteria need the correct conditions to multiply:

(a) The right type of food – stocks, sauces, gravies, soups; meat and meat products (i.e. cooked meats, pies, etc.); egg and egg products (i.e. quiches, custards, mayonnaise, etc.); cream and cream products (trifles, mousses, etc.); jellies and coconut.
(b) The right temperature – rapid growth occurs around body temperature, 37°C. Below this temperature the rate of growth slows down, but does not cease until the temperature falls below 3°C. At this temperature the bacteria are dormant. At 76°C and above the bacteria begin to die, though there are some bacteria that produce heat resistant spores that require

1

between one and five hours cooking above this temperature to die.

(c) Moisture – foods such as sauces, mayonnaise, custards and creams are ideal breeding grounds for bacteria. It should be noted that bacteria cannot grow in dry foods.

(d) Time – the longer the food is left at the right temperature for bacterial growth, the more poisoning bacteria will be present. Given the right conditions, a single cell can multiply to over 16 million cells in five hours.

Salmonella

These bacteria occur in the intestines of many animals, humans, flies, cockroaches, rodents and pets and can be passed on through raw meat, poultry, fish, meat and meat products such as sausages. The salmonella group includes the bacteria which cause typhoid and paratyphoid fevers. In some circumstances people who are already ill, very young or very old can die.

Salmonella poisoning is usually caused by infected excreta from vermin or a person not washing their hands after going to the toilet cross-contaminating raw foods. Symptoms appear between 6 to 72 hours after eating the infected food and can last for up to seven days, or even longer.

Staphylococcus

Staphylococci bacteria secrete food poisoning toxins. Infection is caused by poor personal hygiene, and the bacteria occur in infected cuts, sores and boils around the face and hands and in inflamed throat conditions. Symptoms appear one to six hours after eating the infected food and include nausea, diarrhoea and vomiting.

Clostridium botulinum (welchii)

Clostridium welchii bacteria are found in the intestines and excreta of humans and animals, and in the soil. They are usually found in meat products and these types of foods have to be thoroughly cooked as the spores can survive light cooking.

The prevention of food poisoning
1 Wash hands regularly – have adequate washing and cleaning facilities.
2 Handle food as little as possible.
3 Shower daily and wear only clean clothes.
4 Cover cuts and burns with the appropriate dressings.
5 Protect foods from vermin and insects.
6 Store food correctly – have ample cold storage facilities.
7 Cook meat, poultry and eggs thoroughly.
8 Cook and serve foods on the same day – try not to cook more food than is required.
9 Provide spacious, well-lit and well-ventilated premises.
10 Use only suitable washing-up facilities.

COMMODITIES

Dairy products

MILK

Milk is one of the most complete foods, and makes a valuable contribution to a healthy diet, providing protein, vitamins and minerals, especially calcium. The main nutrients are as follows:

1 **Calcium**. This is vital for children in forming strong teeth and bones, and also throughout life for the prevention of osteoporosis (brittle bones) in the elderly.
2 **Protein**. The three principal milk proteins are casein, lactoglobulin and lactalbumin which provide high quality protein.
3 **Vitamins**. Milk is a good source of vitamin A and vitamin B_2 (riboflavin). Vitamin B_2 is destroyed gradually by UV light. Milk should, therefore, be stored out of direct sunlight.
4 **Carbohydrate**. Lactose, the carbohydrate found in milk, is thought to aid the absorption of calcium.
5 **Fat**. Milk fat contains tiny fat globules surrounded by a protein membrane, which protects and keeps the fat globules separate. It also enables the fat to exist as an emulsion in the milk, therefore making it easily digestible. The fat is lighter than the rest of the milk so can easily be separated for cream and butter production.

Processing

Milk is designated according to its fat content and the heat treatment it receives. Heat treatment ensures the destruction of pathogenic bacteria, ensuring the milk is safe to drink, and improves the keeping qualities.

1 **Pasteurised** (silver top) 3.9% fat. Pasteurisation is a mild heat treatment of 72°C (161°F) for 15 seconds followed by rapid cooking to not more than 10°C (50°F).
2 **Homogenised** (red top) 3.9% fat. Milk is homogenised by forcing it through a fine aperture to break down the fat globules. These do not rise to the surface but remain distributed throughout the milk. The milk is then pasteurised.

Composition

	Quality (g)	Energy (kcals)	Energy (kj)	Protein (g)	Fat (g)	Carbohydrate (g)	Calcium (mg)	Vitamin A (µg) (Retinol equiv)	Vitamin B_2 (mg) (Riboflavin)
Whole	100	66	275	3.2	3.9	4.8	115	56	0.17
Semi-skimmed	100	46	195	3.3	1.6	5.0	120	23	0.18
Skimmed	100	33	140	3.3	0.1	5.0	120	1	0.18

3 **Semi-skimmed** (red/silver striped top) 1.5%–1.8% fat. This milk contains half the fat content of whole milk. The milk is homogenised and pasteurised.
4 **Skimmed** (blue/silver checked top) less than 0.3% fat. Virtually all the fat is removed. The milk is homogenised and pasteurised.
5 **Channel Islands** (gold top) 4.9% fat. This milk comes from Jersey and Guernsey breeds of cow. The milk has a very marked cream line. The milk is pasteurised.
6 **Sterilised** (crown cap for long neck bottles, blue cap for plastic bottles). The milk is homogenised, bottled and sealed, then heated to at least 100°C (212°F) for 20–30 minutes then cooled. Sterilised milk is also available.
7 **Ultra heat treated** (UHT) 'Long Life'. The milk is homogenised, heated to not less than 132°C (270°F) for 1 second then rapidly cooked and aseptically packed in polythene and foil-lined containers. Whole, semi-skimmed and skimmed are available.

Uses

1 Fresh milk is often served on its own ice cold as a **drink**, but can be flavoured using bottled syrup, powdered flavouring or thick milk shake mixes. Milk cocktails, both alcoholic and non-alcoholic, can also be prepared using flavourings, milk and alcohol if desired.
2 Milk is also the basis of many **sauces**, both sweet and savoury, for example Mornay, bechamel, chocolate and butterscotch. It is the foundation of custard which can be flavoured and thickened to achieve different results, such as trifle, pouring custard and egg custard. Milk is also used in soup preparation where it can enrich the soup and bring out the flavour of the other ingredients.
3 **Pancakes**, in which milk is a major ingredient, can be filled with a variety of sweet and savoury fillings to be served for any course.

Freezing

Homogenised milk freezes successfully for up to 1 month. It should be packed in polythene or plastic containers of one pint capacity. Other types of milk do not freeze successfully unless incorporated into a recipe.

Microwaving

When heating milk, whether on its own or as a part of another dish, a large enough container should always be used to prevent the milk or sauce from boiling over. To prevent milky drinks from frothing during heating, the flavouring powder should be added to hot milk. Egg custards and souffles can be cooked in some ovens on defrost where the microwave energy is reduced. However, if this facility is not available, the container holding the mixture should be placed in a dish of water and cooked as normal.

DRIED MILK POWDER

Dried milk powders are sometimes added to recipes to increase the protein content. The most common varieties used are:

1 Whole milk powder;
2 Skimmed milk powder; and
3 Filled milk powder, i.e. skimmed milk powder to which vegetable fat has been added.

All milk powders should be kept cool and dry in an airtight container and out of direct light.

CHEESE

Cheese is made from milk, usually cow's milk, but some cheeses are made from goats, ewes and yaks.

The production process (for cheddar cheese)

1 The milk is first made sour by the addition of a bacteria which produces lactic acid.
2 Rennet (made from calf's stomach) is then added: this causes the milk to curdle and 'clot'.
3 The curd is then cut. The curd is already set solid, so has to be cut into half inch cubes by mechanical cheese knives.
4 Scalding, i.e. the heating of the curd for one hour, the purpose of which is to help remove the whey liquid from the curd solids. The curd is stirred continuously, even for 20 minutes after cooking to prevent the outside from cooking.

Stilton

Derby and Sage Derby

Caerphilly

Red Leicester

A range of English and Welsh cheeses

2

5 Settling: the whey is run off and curd particles allowed to settle.
6 Cheddaring: the curd is cut into blocks and piled on top of each other. This helps to run off the last of the whey and gives the curd a silky texture.
7 Milling: the curd is mixed with fine dairy salt and well milled.
8 Moulding: the curd is poured into hoops lined with cloth and placed into powerful presses sprayed with steam and left for 24–36 hours. (The spraying of steam produces a thin, hard rind so keeps better.)
9 Ripening: the cheese is removed from the hoops and date stamped and placed in a humid ripening room. Cheeses are frequently turned to ensure they all ripen evenly, and are then left for about 3 months to mature.

Variations in types

The main variations in cheese are as follows:

1 Texture: hard, soft, etc. The greater the temperature during the scalding process, the harder the cheese is likely to be.
2 The percentage of fat affects the texture of the cheese. A low percentage will produce a hard leathery cheese, and a high percentage produces a soft, smoother type.
3 Moisture. The lower the moisture content left in the curd, the firmer the cheese, the milder the flavour, and the longer it keeps.
4 Moulds. The less pressing the cheese has, the more open the texture, giving more chance for moulds to develop.
5 Salt. Cheeses made without salt tend to have a shorter shelf life.

Types of cheeses

French	Brie, Camembert, Port Salut (Saint-Paulin), Gervais, Neufchatel, Gerome, Gruyere, Bondon, Roquefort, Cantal, Pont L'Eveque, Carre de l'Est.
German	Munster, Sapsago
Dutch	Edam, Gouda
Italian	Gorgonzola, Parmesan, Provoline, Bel Paese
Swiss	Emmenthal, Schabzieger, Pommel Demi-Suisse (Petit Suisse)
USA	Brick, Jack
Danish	Danish Blue

The main British and Irish cheeses

Cheese	Type
ENGLAND	
Blue Cheshire	Mild, firm, creamy textured version of traditional Cheshire cheese.
Blue vinny (vinew) and Dorset Blue	Sharp tasting cheese made with skimmed milk. The blue mould is developed naturally.
Cheddar	A fine waxy texture with tangy, nutty flavour. Suitable for cooking.
Cheshire	The oldest known British cheese. Crumbly texture with a salty tang.
Cotherstone	Rare cheese with semi-soft texture with rich flavour.
Derby	Traditionally made in large cartwheels. Mild flavour, suitable for cooking.
Gloucester and Double Gloucester	Full cream cheese with a mellow flavour. Ideal in sandwiches and salads.
Lancashire	A white semi-hard cheese with a rich, mellow flavour.
Leicester	Traditionally made in large, flat cartwheels. Mild flavoured with granular texture. Suitable for cooking.
Melbury	Mild tasting, loaf-shaped, soft full fat cheese.
Sage Derby	Celebration cheese, traditionally available at Christmas. Produced by colouring curds with chlorophyll and adding powdered sage.
Stilton	A rich, creamy, open-textured blue cheese with orange-brown rind.
Wensleydale	Yorkshire cheese, originally made from sheep or goat's milk. Firm texture with a mellow flavour.

Cheese	Type
SCOTLAND	
Caboc	Rich and delicate flavour, made with double cream. Rolled in toasted oatmeal.
Cheddar	Similar to English cheddar but orange coloured.
Crowdie	Low fat cheese with slight lemony flavour. Produced without rennet. Made from unpasteurised skimmed milk.
Dunlop	A distinctive hard cheddar type cheese from Ayrshire and Orkney.
Highland soft	Full fat soft cheese from Ayrshire.
Hramsa	Similar to crowdie with wild garlic and pepper. Rolled in mixed nuts.
Lothian	Soft cheese similar to French brie.
Pentland	Soft cheese similar to French brie.
WALES	
Caerphilly	Mild, crumbly cheese from South Wales.
Llangloffan	Hard skin, traditional style cheese with a creamy texture.
Waun Gron	A cheddar-like cheese from West Wales.
IRELAND	
Abban	Octagonal, brie-type cheese from Co Wexford.
Beara	Mild gouda-type cheese. Flat, wheel-shaped, produced in Eyeries.
Bonane	Full fat, hard pressed cheese from Co Kerry.
Coisceam	Hard goat's cheese from Co Clare.
Gigginstown	Natural stilton-type with firm, crumbly texture from Co Westmeath.
Gubbeen	Round, firm cheese with assertive flavour. Produced in Co Cork.
Lavistown	Open textured, mild-flavoured, round cheese produced in Kilkenny.

Cheese	Type
IRELAND (*continued*)	
Lough Caum	Hard goat's cheese from Co Clare.
Milleens	New style farmhouse cheese. Soft, ripe with a natural orange rind. Produced in Eyeries.
Scivog	Hard, farmhouse cheese.
St Killians	Rich full fat cheese produced from unpasteurised cow's milk. Hexagonal shaped, comes from Co Wexford.

Soft cheeses

Type	Commonly known names	% fat	% moisture
Cream cheese	Cream Cheese	min 45%	Not more than 40
Full fat soft cheese	Full fat soft cheese, full fat fromage frais	min 20%	Not more than 60
Medium fat soft cheese	Medium fat soft cheese, curd cheese	10–20%	Not more than 70
Low fat soft cheese	Low fat soft cheese, low fat cottage cheese, low fat fromage frais	2–10%	Not more than 80
Skimmed milk soft cheese	Skimmed milk soft cheese, very low fat fromage frais	2%	Not more than 80

Curd cheese

This can either be a medium fat or low fat soft cheese.

1 **Cream cheese** Made from single or double cream producing a cream cheese with a rich buttery taste.
2 **Fromage frais** A soft cheese made from pasteurised skimmed milk and produced to a

traditional French recipe which is not left to mature hence the term 'fresh'.

3 **Quark** Quark or Quarg originated from Germany. Made from pasteurised skimmed milk with cream added for a creamy texture and rich taste.

4 **Cream fraiche** A slightly soured and cultured cream with all the qualities but only half the fat of double cream.

5 **Ripened soft cheese** Ripened soft cheeses are characterised by their white outer rind – their flavours and textures develop as the cheese matures with age to give a soft pliable cheese with a mellow flavour.

To accelerate ripening, store in a warm place, otherwise keep refrigerated.

Uses

All the soft cheeses are suitable for use in recipes such as cheesecakes. The flavour and texture will vary according to the type of cheese used. Cream cheese will give a richer continental type cheesecake, whereas cottage cheese is more suitable for the uncooked citrus flavoured cheesecakes.

Cottage or curd cheeses are also suitable for Yorkshire curd tarts, or as part of the filling for sweet and savoury flans. Cottage cheese served on its own or mixed with other ingredients can form the basis of a summer salad, which is particularly suitable for those on a slimming diet. It can also form a basis for many different jacket potato fillings. Cream and curd cheese form the ideal basis for party dips and spreads.

Fromage frais may be spooned onto fruit or swirled into soups.

Quark may be stirred into sauces to enrich them. It can be boiled as it is stable at boiling temperatures.

Tips on using soft cheese

● Add a little fresh milk to curd or cream cheese if fromage frais unavailable.

● Sweeten Quark with icing sugar to taste and use to fill cakes, gateaux or choux pastries – a healthy alternative to fresh cream.

● To soften soft cheese before mixing, cook 225 g (8 oz) on HIGH in a microwave for 20–30 seconds to make it easier to use.

Freezing

Medium or full fat soft cheese can be frozen in their cartons. Full fat soft cheese should be used within 1 month, medium fat within 3 months.

The range of flavoured cheeses has increased rapidly over recent years; most of them are combinations of the traditional English cheeses, some of which are listed below:

Cotswold: a tangy blend of Double Gloucester with chopped chives and onions.
Cheviot: a mild cheese consisting of a mixture of cheddar and chopped chives.
Charnwood or Applewood: smoked cheddar with a coating of paprika.
Windsor Red: cheddar marbled with elderberry wine.
Huntsman: layers of Double Gloucester and Stilton.
Nutwood: a blend of cheddar, roasted hazelnuts, raisins and cider.
Whirl: Red Leicester and full fat cheese, onions and chives, celery or ham.
Sherwood: a blend of Double Gloucester and sweet mixed pickle.
Rutland: a mixture of cheddar, beer, garlic and parsley.

Storage of cheese

Whole cheeses will keep for a considerable time in a cool place. If a large number of cheeses are stored, it is important that stock rooms are airy, non-draughty and well lit. Racks should be cleaned at regular intervals to prevent mite infestation, and strict stock control should be exercised to ensure that cheeses are used in rotation. If only a small number of cheeses are to be stored, the bottom shelf of a cold room or larder is ideal.

1 **Waxed or wrapped cheese**. Cheese blocks are waxed or film wrapped to protect them and prevent them from drying out. They are best kept at similar temperatures to traditional cheeses, but as the coating makes them impervious to water, humidity control is necessary.

2 **Vacuum-packed cheese**. This cheese will keep

longer than loosely wrapped cheese; the date code will indicate its keeping qualities.

3 **Cut cheese**. To prevent drying, cheese that has been cut should be closely wrapped with polythene, foil or cling film and stored in a cool place.

4 **Traditional cylindrical cheese**. These cheeses are best kept at a temperature of 5°C (40°F) and a relative humidity of 85%. They should be placed at intervals on a shelf and turned regularly.

5 **Blue cheeses**. These keep better at a slightly lower temperature of 4°C (38°F) and a higher relative humidity of 90%.

Serving cheese

Before cheese is served, it should be brought to room temperature to bring out its full flavour (about 1 hour before serving). Do not remove too much cheese from storage at any one time as a good quality cheese does not improve with constant changes of temperature.

Cheeseboards

When preparing a cheeseboard, at least three good sized wedges rather than several small pieces of cheese should be used. Cheese should be chosen to present a good variety of colour, texture and flavours. Where possible, the cheeseboard should be kept in a cool part of the dining room and should be covered to prevent the cheese from drying out. It can be garnished with fresh fruit (especially grapes) and vegetables and biscuits.

Freezing

As cheese keeps well in a cool place, it is not necessary to freeze supplies. If there is an excess of cheese in stock, it can be frozen successfully in 450 g (1 lb) blocks, although it does tend to go crumbly on thawing.

Hard cheeses can be frozen for up to 4 months and some, particularly cheddar, can be kept for up to 6 months. Each piece of cheese should be well wrapped in freezer polythene or freezer foil to prevent drying out. Cheese purchased in vacuum packs of up to 450 g (1 lb) can be frozen without repacking. Grated or crumbled cheese can be frozen in small portions of 225 g (8 oz). It should be packed into plastic containers or preferably freezer bags where all the air can be excluded.

When **thawing**, best results are achieved if cheese is thawed for 24 hours in a refrigerator, or microwave using the defrost/lowest setting. Grate hard cheese for a smooth result.

Microwaving

Cooking in a microwave takes seconds rather than minutes, and low to medium power should be used. To bring the flavour out of the cheese, the defrost setting should be used to bring cheese up to room temperature from the refrigerator.

CREAM

Cream is produced from whole milk by mechanical centrifugal separation. For the majority of people, it is used to enhance food on special occasions. It makes an insignificant contribution – less than 1% – to our total fat intake.

Additives

The use of food additives is illegal in pasteurised, in half, single, whipping and double cream when such creams are sold by retail. However, there is a restricted number of additives allowed in certain creams:

1 Up to 13% sugar may be added to cream intended for use in flour confectionery; to whipping cream sold to manufacturers or caterers and whipped cream; and in particular cream in aerosol containers. They may also contain the stabilisers, sodium algmate, sodium carboxymethyl cellulose, carrageenan and gelatine, used singly or in combination but which should not exceed 0.3%.

2 Aerosol cream may also contain glycerol monostearate to improve foam stiffness and nitrous oxide is permitted as a propellant.

3 Calcium chloride, sodium and potassium salts of carbonic, citric and orthophosphoric acids are permitted in sterilised and UHT cream at levels not exceeding 0.2%. They are necessary to restore mineral balance in cream that is to undergo this type of heat treatment. The mineral content of milk is subject to slight seasonal variation.

4 Clotted and canned cream may contain nisin as a preservative.

Cream substitutes

These are mainly based on vegetable fats or oils which are emulsified in water with other permitted substances. A variety of these products are available under descriptions such as 'imitation cream', 'non-dairy cream' and 'dessert topping'. These are the terms that must be used to describe the product if used in catering establishments as these are not fresh and natural products.

Types of fresh cream

Type of cream	Colour codes	Legal minimum fat%	Processing and packaging
Half cream	Brown	12	Homogenised, and then pasteurised or ultra heat treated.
Cream or single cream	Red	18	Homogenised and pasteurised by heating to at least 72°C (161°F) for not less than 15 seconds then cooled to 4.5°C (40°F).
Soured cream	Purple	18	Homogenised, pasteurised cream is 'soured' by the addition of 'starter' bacterial culture to produce a piquant acid flavour.
Whipped cream	Green	35	Rarely homogenised, but pasteurised or ultra heat treated.
Double cream	Blue	48	Slightly homogenised, then pasteurised and packaged. This cream is best for piping.
Double cream 'thick'		48	Heavily homogenised, then pasteurised and packaged. Does not whip.
Spoonable cream		35	Usually only available in domestic quantities. This cream will not whip, it is designed to be spooned.
Clotted cream	Gold	55	Heated to 82°C (180°F) and cooled for about 4½ hours. The cream crust is then skimmed off. Usually packed in cartons by hand. Bulk quantities available according to local suppliers.
Sterilised half cream		12	Homogenised, filled into cans, sealed and heated to 108°C (226°F) for at least 45 minutes or equivalent time/temperature combination. It is then cooled rapidly.
Sterilised cream		23	Processed as above. This cream can be spooned but will not whip.
Ultra heat treated cream		12 18 35	Half single or whipping cream is homogenised and heated to 140°C (248°F) for at least 2 seconds and cooled immediately. Aseptically packed in polythene and foil lined containers.
Aerosol cream			UHT cream is filled into aerosol cans under sterile conditions. Nitrous oxide is used as the propellant. This cream starts to collapse soon after applying but can be used on milk shakes, iced coffee etc.

Uses

1 **Double cream** is the most versatile. It will float on soups and coffee, can be poured onto fruit salad or whipped and piped for decorating.

2 **Whipping cream** will whip to at least double its volume; the light and fluffy texture makes it ideal for trifles, in sponge cakes or folded into dips and vol-au-vent fillings.

3 **Single cream** will add an extra special something poured onto sweets, into coffee, added to soups, sauces and casseroles.

4 **Soured cream** is ideal for use in savoury dishes and salad dressings. It enhances the flavour by adding a refreshing piquant taste. Good in dips, salads and curries.

5 **Clotted cream** has a distinctive nutty flavour. It is traditionally served with scones and jam. Is suitable for spooning or spreading.

The whipping of cream

The optimum fat content for whipping cream is 35–40%. If the fat content is too low, there will not be enough fat to enclose air bubbles and form the foam. If the fat content is too high, the fat globules come into contact too easily and form butter granules before sufficient air can be incorporated. Double cream does not give as great an increase in volume (usually 80%) as whipping cream (which may be over 100%). Four tablespoons of milk may be added to each 600 ml (1 pint) of double cream before whipping to increase the volume and give a softer consistency.

Before whipping, cream should be aged for at least 24 hours at 5°C (40°F) to help improve viscosity and whipping properties. This usually takes place at the dairy. Cream should be whipped quickly at first until it takes on a matt finish then slowly until it stands in peaks. Care should be taken to prevent over-whipping as this will turn the cream into butter. If the cream is not required immediately, it should be covered and stored under refrigeration.

Storage

Fresh cream should always be kept cool, clean and covered. It will store successfully unopened for 10 days under refrigeration and is always date-stamped. Sterilised cream will store for up to 2 years. UHT cream is also always date-stamped: individual portions of UHT cream will have a date stamp on the box, so the box should not be discarded and should be used in rotation. Once sterilised or UHT cream has been opened it should be treated as fresh cream and kept away from any food which might taint it.

Freezing

Half and single and soured cream do not freeze successfully. Double and whipping creams can be frozen in quantities up to 300 ml (½ pint).

Caterers are not recommended to freeze fresh cream in bulk, unless commercially frozen, there is some reduction in whipping properties due to crystallisation damaging the emulsion.

For both whipping and double cream, better results are obtained by semi-whipping before freezing. The cream can then be whipped to the desired consistency after thawing but care must be taken not to overwhip.

10% sugar by weight can be added to unwhipped cream before freezing. It acts as a stabiliser but does limit the use of the cream to sweet dishes. There is very little advantage in adding sugar to whipped or semi-whipped cream before freezing.

Whipping Cream will whip satisfactorily after storage of up to two months. The longer the cream is stored in the freezer the more buttery it becomes on thawing.

Double cream tends to become buttery more readily than whipping cream when frozen, therefore only one month freezer storage is recommended.

Clotted Cream may be frozen but tends to become buttery after one month.

Made-up dishes

Most dishes containing cream will freeze successfully. Desserts with a high proportion of cream should only be frozen for one month as longer storage leads to the development of a granular texture.

Microwaving

Having made soups, sauces and savoury dishes in the microwave, add cream during the standing time to prevent curdling and allow the cream to heat through. Dishes which contain cream such as quiches and souffles can be cooked successfully on low.

Commercial frozen cream

Commercially frozen cream is available to the caterer in 2 kg and 10 kg slabs – single, whipping, double and clotted.

Commercially frozen dairy cream products

Some of the most useful products for the caterer are frozen dairy cream gateaux and cheesecakes. Look for fresh dairy cream logo as a sign that fresh cream has been used.

Storage. Frozen dairy cream gateaux and cheesecakes should be stored at below 18°C (0°F) for 1 month only otherwise the texture of the cream becomes granular.

Thawing. Rapid thawing will spoil the appearance of the cake. Remove any vacuum-sealed packaging before defrosting. This can cause condensation and spoil the top of the cake. Thaw a large gateaux on the top shelf of the refrigerator overnight, or in a cool room for about 5½ hours. The best portion can be obtained by cutting each slice when partially thawed. Use a long sharp knife dipped in hot water. For easier handling, place a small square of greaseproof paper between each slice.

Tips on using cream

Fresh cream enhances the flavour of the most basic of foods. A little cream will make ordinary dishes into something special. Remember when storing fresh cream to keep it cool, preferably in a refrigerator, clean and covered.

1 Mix equal quantities of fresh double cream and natural yoghurt for a salad dressing.
2 Swirl a little fresh cream into soups just before serving.
3 After grilling or frying steaks or chops, add a little cream to the juices and serve.

4 Don't waste cream in the bottom of the carton, use it to enrich sauces and soups.
5 Toss cooked vegetables or pasta in a little seasoned cream for a luxury touch.
6 Always add wine before the cream in hot dishes. Do not reboil after adding cream or it will separate.
7 Fresh double cream whips more easily and will go further when a tablespoon of milk is added per 150 ml, (5 fl.oz), carton.
8 When whipping cream, be sure to chill the cream and all the utensils, including piping bags and nozzles before you start.
9 Whipped cream thickens with the pressure used to force it through a piping nozzle, so do not whip cream too stiff for piping.
10 If there is any whipped cream left in the piping bag, pipe rosettes onto a non-stick baking tray and open freeze. Use them when still frozen to decorate cakes and trifles. Allow about 30 minutes to defrost.
11 Freeze leftover whipping or double cream in ice-cube trays ready to add to dishes.
12 Equal quantities of whipped cream and cream or fromage frais cheese mixed with chopped fruit makes a quick dessert.

YOGHURT

Yoghurt is a soured milk product thought to have originated among the nomadic tribes of Eastern Europe. Traditionally it was a drink made by allowing the natural milk flora to ferment the milk sugar, lactose, to lactic acid. Without refrigeration to limit acid production, a very sour yoghurt will result.

In this country we are not accustomed to such sharp taste and prefer yoghurt with a semi-solid consistency and a mild acid flavour. By inoculating pasteurised milk with a specific bacterial culture and controlling the conditions of incubation, yoghurt with the desired flavour and texture can be produced.

Processing

Most yoghurt is made from a skimmed milk base to which extra skimmed milk powder is added.

This improves the consistency of the final product.

1 Milk is pasteurised and cooled at 38°C (100°F).
2 It is inoculated with a mixed culture of *Lactobacillus bulgaricus* and *Streptococcus thermophilus* and incubated at 43°C (109°F). About half of the lactose is fermented to lactic acid.
3 Incubation is continued until the acidity increases to the point where the milk protein, casein, is precipitated and the product thickens.
4 Bacterial growth is arrested by cooling to 4.5°C (40°F).
5 If the yoghurt is to be flavoured before packaging, fruit puree or flavoured syrups are stirred in.

There are two distinct variations in the final processing:

1 'Stirred-type' yoghurts. Incubation takes place at 43°C (109°F) in large tanks, the yoghurt is continually stirred to give a smooth cream-like consistency and then transferred to pots.
2 'Set-type' yoghurts. Incubation takes place in the carton to give a junket-like texture and can be natural or fruit flavoured.

'Live' yoghurt

Most commercially produced yoghurt, unless it has been pasteurised after manufacture will contain 'live' bacteria which remains dormant when kept at low temperature. If stored at room temperature or above, the dormant bacteria become active and produce more acid. Too high an acidity kills the bacteria and impairs the flavour and causes the yoghurt to separate. Pasteurised yoghurt will have a longer shelf life.

Special cultured yoghurts

A new type of yoghurt is now available containing lactic acid and 'bifidus and acidophilus' bacteria. These differ from other yoghurts in that the culture used is organically produced which is said to aid efficient digestion.

The yoghurt is still a natural and live product available in natural and fruit flavours, some having wheatgerm flakes added to provide extra vitamins and add dietary fibre.

Varieties of yoghurt

Low fat yoghurt is the most popular, but there is currently a range of products available with varying fat contents.

1 'Very low fat yoghurt' or 'skimmed milk' yoghurt should contain less than 0.5% fat. These are often available as 'diet' yoghurts sweetened with artificial sweeteners.
2 'Low fat yoghurt' should contain between 0.5–2.0% fat.
3 There are now some 'creamier' yoghurts available. These are often based on whole milk (3.8% fat). The fat content will be declared on the label.
4 Greek-style yoghurt – a creamy yoghurt with a thicker consistency. Either made from sheep's or cows' milk with a fat content of 1.8%–10.5%.

Natural yoghurt

These yoghurts should contain no colour, preservatives, stabilisers or thickeners and may be fortified with vitamins A and D.

Natural yoghurt may be fortified with fruit juice, honey, chocolate, nuts, sugar or natural flavourings.

Flavoured yoghurts

Fruit yoghurt should contain at least 5% of the whole fruit as pieces or purée. If colours, stabilisers, thickeners or preservatives are used they will be declared on the label.

Frozen commercial yoghurt

Ready frozen yoghurt can be purchased. A stabiliser may have been added to prevent separation on thawing, but usually sufficient sugar has been added as flavouring to prevent this happening.

To thaw, leave for 24 hours in a refrigerator.

Storage

Keep all yoghurt under refrigeration, and use within the period recommended by the date stamp.

2

Freezing

Fruit yoghurt may be frozen for 3 months, natural for 2 months.

Uses

Individual cartons of yoghurt make a quick dessert, but yoghurt can enhance the flavour of many sweet or savoury dishes, such as cheesecakes, salad dressings or soups. It can also make a good topping, flavoured or unflavoured for fresh fruit or as a filling for gâteaux. Provides a refreshing piquant flavour to salad dressings and dips.

Some dairy companies supply yoghurt in one gallon containers. This way the yoghurt can be portioned or added to dishes.

Although yoghurt can be made in domestic quantities, it is not advisable to make it in bulk for catering purposes.

OTHER CULTURED MILK PRODUCTS

Cultured buttermilk

Traditionally this is a by-product of butter manufacture. Today it is made commercially by adding a buttermilk culture to skimmed milk to give a refreshing drink with a slightly acidic flavour. The bacteria in this culture differ from those used in yoghurt manufacture and convey their own characteristic flavour to the product. Can be used when making scones and bread.

BUTTER

Butter is made simply by churning fresh cream. A little salt may be added but no preservatives or artificial flavourings are allowed. Most of the butter produced in the UK is of the 'sweet cream' variety made from fresh cream with a mild taste and smooth texture. Choose between salted and unsalted varieties. Welsh butter is famous for its salty taste. Like hard and soft margarine, butter contains 81% fat so has the same number of calories.

Uses

1 **Grilling**. Brushing with butter gives an appetising glaze. It moistens and enhances the flavour of grilled meats and fish.
2 **Sauté**. Butter is ideal for sautéing meat and vegetables adding flavour and succulence.
3 **Sauces**. Butter is an excellent base for a white or hollandaise sauce, giving a richly flavoured accompaniment to many simple dishes.
4 **Baking**. Butter provides special qualities of flavour, shortening and enriching when making cakes, pastry, shortbread and puddings.
5 **Spreading**. Butter is delicious on biscuits or bread.
6 **Flavoured butter**. Butter flavoured with garlic or herbs is delicious stirred through pasta or cooked vegetables or add spices to butter to accompany scones, pancakes or Christmas puddings and mince pies.
7 **Unsalted butter**. This type is preferable for using in butter icing and brandy butter.
8 **Concentrated butter**. Especially made for cooking and baking containing less water than ordinary butter. Has a minimum fat content of 96%. Ideal for stir frying and general baking but has its limitations especially when making shortbread, for deep frying or spreading.
9 **Clarified butter or ghee**. This is often used when frying and grilling. Simply melt salted butter over a gentle heat. Cook without stirring until butter begins to foam. Continue until the foaming stops but do not brown. Allow the milky deposit to sink to the bottom and pour the clear yellow liquid through muslin. Store in the refrigerator.

Storage

Foil packaging keeps butter in peak condition. Buy it regularly and rotate stocks to ensure freshness. Use before the 'best before' date. Salted will keep longer than unsalted, up to one month in the refrigerator.

Salted butter will freeze for up to 3 months. Unsalted for 6 months.

Butter is available for caterers in individual portions.

Note: butter absorbs other flavours easily, so keep away from strong smelling foods.

Microwaving

For easy spreading, soften 225 g (8 oz) butter on defrost for 15 secs (using a 600 watt oven).

Use unsalted butter when cooking meat and fish. Salt has a dehydrating effect in the microwave which can toughen food.

DAIRY ICE CREAM

Dairy ice cream is one of the oldest desserts in the world and is made by the blending and freezing of milk and cream products to which sugar, emulsifiers, stabilisers and flavourings are added.

Legislation

The Ice Cream Regulations 1961 state that ice cream in the UK should have a minimum requirement of:

1 not less than 5% milk fat; and
2 not less than 7.5% milk solids other than fat.

To be legally defined as dairy ice cream, the minimum requirement is:

1 not less than 5% milk fat;
2 no fat other than milk fat; and
3 not less than 7.5% milk solids other than fat.

To qualify for membership to the Milk Marketing Board's quality mark, each litre of finished ice cream must contain at least 56 g of milk fats, with at least 28 g of this being derived from double cream (48% fat). This equates to 10% and 5%

respectively. The maximum overrun should not exceed 100%, and the recipe must be released to the Milk Marketing Board for verification.

Non-dairy ice cream is often made from skimmed milk and vegetable fat.

Storage and handling

Ice cream will keep in the freezer for up to 3 months, provided the temperature is kept constant.

Once the air gets to ice cream, it develops ice crystals which spoil the texture. Therefore, once the carton is opened, greaseproof paper or cling film should be placed over the surface of the ice cream to exclude air. Containers should always be kept well sealed to prevent the ice cream from absorbing other flavours.

Before serving, ice cream needs to be softened in the refrigerator; it is then easier to serve and the flavour will be more pronounced. 1.1 litres (2 pints) will need about 30 minutes in the refrigerator.

Uses

Ice cream can be served as a dessert on its own or accompanied by topping such as crushed ginger nuts, coconut, toasted brown breadcrumbs, chocolate, candied peel, glace fruits, nuts, praline or raisins. Sweet syrups and sauces, such as chocolate, butterscotch, fruit purees, peppermint, hot fudge, or even brandy, rum or rose wine, are also often used over ice cream.

2

Fresh fruit and vegetables

Note: Where it is indicated that produce is available all year, this does not necessarily mean that the season for each of the countries listed is all year. For example, strawberries are available all year, but the British season is from June–October.

FRUIT

Fruit	Country	Availability
Avocado	Spain, Greece, Canary Islands, Israel, Mexico, Brazil, South Africa, USA, Kenya	All year
Apricots	Spain, France, Turkey, Greece, Hungary Chile, South Africa	June–Aug Dec–Feb
Apples	Britain, Belgium, South Africa, Italy, Hungary, Germany, Denmark, Chile, Bulgaria, Australia, New Zealand, Argentina, British Columbia, Holland, France, Canada, USA, Spain	All year
Asian pears	Japan, New Zealand	Nov–Feb
Babaco	Israel, Guernsey, New Zealand	Nov–March
Bananas	Windward Isles, West Indies, Central America, Canary Islands	All year
Bilberries/ Blueberries	Britain, Holland, USA, Canada	July–Oct
Blackberries	Britain	July–Oct
Carambola	South East Asia, China, India, South America, Israel	All year
Cherries	Britain, France, Spain, Italy, Turkey, Cyprus, USA, Canada, Chile, Australia, New Zealand	All year
Coconuts	West Indies, Sri Lanka, Malaysia, Ivory Coast, Philippines, Indonesia, Papua New Guinea	All year
Cranberries	USA	Dec–Jan
Damsons	Britain	Aug–Oct
Dates	USA, Tunisia, Iraq Israel	Sept–March All year
Figs	Spain, Greece, France, Turkey, Brazil	All year
Ginger	Thailand, Brazil, West Indies, Australia, Fiji	All year
Greengages	Britain, Italy, Spain, France	June–Aug
Grapes	Israel, Greece, Italy, USA, Spain, Lebanon, South Africa, Australia, Chile	All year
Grapefruit	South Africa, Israel, Cyprus, USA, South America, West Indies, Spain	All year
Gooseberries	Britain	May–Aug
Guava	Brazil, South Africa	Aug–Feb
Kiwifruit	New Zealand, Greece, France, Italy	All year
Kumquats	Israel, France, Brazil, Morocco	Oct–March
Lemons	South Africa, Spain, Turkey, Cyprus, South America, USA, Greece, Israel, Italy	All year
Limes	USA, Mexico, West Indies, South Africa, Israel	All year
Loganberries	Britain	July–Aug
Lychees	Israel, Madagascar, South Africa, Mauritius, USA, South East Asia	Nov–March
Mangoes	Israel, South America, Africa, Mexico, Kenya, Brazil, India	All year

Fruit (*continued*)

Fruit	Country	Availability
Mangosteens	Indonesia, Thailand, West Indies, South East Asia	March–Oct
Melons	Spain, Greece, Brazil, Argentina, Chile, Canary Islands, Cyprus, France, South Africa, Holland, Israel	All year
Nectarines	Spain, Italy, South Africa, France	June–Sept/ Nov–Feb
Oranges	South Africa, South America, Spain, Morocco, Israel, USA, Australia, Italy, Cyprus	All year
Passion fruit	Kenya, West Indies, Brazil	All year
Paw Paws (Papaya)	Brazil, West Indies, Bahamas, Kenya, Hawaii, South Africa, West Africa	All year
Peaches	Spain, Italy, France, South Africa	June–Sept/ Nov–Feb
Pears	Britain, Holland, Belgium, Chile, USA, Spain, Italy, Argentina, South Africa, Australia, France, New Zealand	All year
Physalis	Colombia, Kenya, India, South Africa	Sept–Feb
Pineapples	Ivory Coast, Uganda, Ghana, Kenya, South Africa	All year
Plums	Spain, Italy, USA, Britain, South Africa, France	June–Oct
Pomegranates	Spain, Israel, Cyprus	Sept–Nov
Pomelo	Israel	Dec–Mar
Raspberries	Britain, South Africa, New Zealand	June–Dec
Redcurrants	Britain	June–Aug
Rhubarb	Britain (forced) Britain (outdoor)	Dec–March March–June
Sharon fruit	Israel	Nov–Jan
Soft citrus	South Africa, Israel, USA, Italy, Israel, Morocco	All year
Clementines	Spain, Corsica, Morocco, Cyprus	Nov–Feb
Minneolas	Israel, USA, South Africa, Cyprus	Jan–March
Satsumas	Spain, Argentina, South Africa	Oct–Feb
Tangarines	Israel	Feb–March
Topaz	Israel	March–May
Strawberries	Britain, Holland, Belgium, Spain, France, USA, Portugal, Italy, Chile, Israel, South America, Cyprus, Greece, Guernsey, Jersey, Kenya, New Zealand	All year
Sweeties	Israel	Nov–Feb
Tamarillos	Colombia, New Zealand, Kenya	Feb–Oct
Ugli	Jamaica	Jan–April
Water melon	Spain, France, Greece, Italy, South Africa	May–Oct

2

A range of fruit and vegetables

VEGETABLES

Vegetable	Country	Availability
Artichokes	Globe: Egypt, France, Italy, Cyprus, Spain	All year
	Jerusalem: Britain	Oct–Feb
Asparagus	Britain, France, Israel, Spain, Cyprus, Chile, South Africa, USA, Kenya, Australia	All year
Aubergines	Holland, Canary Islands, Cyprus, Israel, Italy, Kenya, South Africa	All year
Baby sweetcorn	Thailand, Kenya	All year
Beans	Britain, Kenya, Spain, Jersey, Guernsey, Italy, Canary Islands, France	All year
Beansprouts	Britain, Holland	All year
Broccoli	Britain, Spain, Italy, Jersey, Holland, France	All year
Brussel sprouts	Britain, Holland	Aug–Apr
Cabbage	Britain, Holland, France	All year
Carrots	Britain, Holland, France, Italy, Israel, Cyprus, USA, Canada	All year
Cauliflower	Britain, France, Jersey	All year
Chillies	Spain, France, Cyprus, Canary Islands, Kenya	March–Feb
Courgettes	Britain, Spain, France, Italy, Jersey, Canary Islands, Israel, Cyprus, East Africa, Ethopia, Mexico	All year
Fennel	Italy, Holland, France, Spain	All year
Garlic	Britain, Italy, Portugal, Spain, France, South America	All year
Kale	Britain	Nov–May

Vegetables (continued)

Vegetable	Country	Availability
Kohl-Rabi	Britain, Holland	July–Feb
Leeks	Britain, Holland, France, Italy, Ireland	All year
Mangetout	Zambia, Guatemala, South Africa, Morocco, Israel, Spain, USA, France, Kenya	All year
Marrows	Britain, Italy, Cyprus	Apr–Oct
Mushrooms	Britain, Holland, Belgium, Ireland	All year
Okra	Kenya, India, Morocco, Cyprus, West Indies, South America	All year
Onions	Britain, Holland, Italy, France, Spain, Egypt, Canary Islands, Chile, Poland, South Africa, Israel, Canada, Hungary, USA	All year
Parsnips	Britain	Aug–Apr
Peas	Britain	May–Oct
Peppers	Holland, Spain, Britain, Canary Islands	All year
Potatoes	Britain, Majorca, Italy, Cyprus, Israel, Morocco, Guernsey, Jersey, Belgium, Greece (For more detailed information on potato varieties see pp 28–9)	All year
Pumpkin	Britain	Oct–Nov
Salsify	Britain, Belgium, France	Oct–April
Spinach	Britain, France, Italy, Cyprus	All year
Squash	Britain, Italy, France, Spain, Canary Islands, Malta, Egypt	Oct–Nov
Swedes	Britain	Sept–May
Sweetcorn	Britain, France, Spain, Israel, USA	Feb–Oct
Sweet potatoes	Canary Islands, Israel, Spain, USA, South Africa, Egypt, Mexico, Brazil	All year
Turnips	Britain, France	All year

Salads

Salad item	Country	Availability
Beetroot	Britain, Holland, Cyprus, Italy	All year
Celeriac	Holland, Britain, France	Sept–Apr
Celery	Britain, Holland, Spain, Italy, USA, Israel	All year
Chicory	Holland, Belgium, France	All year
Chinese leaves	Britain, Holland, Israel	All year
Chives	Britain	All year
Cucumber	Britain, Holland, Spain, Canary Islands, Cyprus	All year
Lettuce	Britain, Holland, Belgium, France, Spain, Italy	All year
Parsley	Britain, France, Jersey	All year
Radish	Britain, Holland, Guernsey, Israel, USA	All year
Spring onions	Britain, Spain, Egypt, Italy, Holland, Mexico	All year
Salad cress	Britain	All year
Tomatoes	Britain, Holland, Guernsey, Jersey, Spain, France, Cyprus, Israel, Morocco, Canary Islands	All year
Watercress	Britain	All year

2

Potatoes

All potatoes grown for retail through reputable high street shops are grown by registered potato growers, and it is compulsory for them to show the name of the varieties of the sacks.

1 **Early potatoes (May–August)**. These should be bought in quantities which can be used immediately, ensuring the potatoes are fresh and full of flavour. Potatoes can be tested for freshness by making sure skins rub off easily and are damp to touch.
2 **Maincrop potatoes (August–May)**. As soon as the potatoes have firmly set skins they can be bought in large quantities (brown skins), which is considerably cheaper. They should be stored in a cool, dry and dark place.

Potatoes should be properly graded for size:

'Ware'   80 × 40 × 165 mm length
'Mid'   Extra small
'Bakers'   Extra large

Registered potato growers should avoid the following:

1 Potatoes affected by common scab on more than a quarter of the surface;
2 Tainted, damaged, diseased potatoes;
3 Badley mis-shapen or shrivelled potatoes;
4 Potatoes that are bruised or damaged by frosts or pests (wire worms, flies);
5 Potatoes affected by greening (caused by too much exposure to the light, i.e. blighted) hollow heart or waterlogging;
6 Unclean potatoes.

An allowance of 5% in respect of these faults is permitted.

Preparation: Peel thinly, preferably with a peeler. Thick peeling is wasteful and also means the loss of nutrients, many of which are concentrated immediately under the skin. May be served in skins, Pomme au Robe de Chambre.

Cooking: Boil gently, consider steaming if they tend to break up. If they show a tendency to go black during cooking add a teaspoonful of vinegar or lemon juice.

British early varieties

Usually available in late May, June, July and August, at their most flavourful when fresh, try not to store for more than 48 hours to serve at their best. Early potatoes are rich in Vitamin C.

The varieties' usage ratings (out of 4)

1 **Home guard**. Creamy white flesh, of a generally good cooking quality. Best quality early in the season, though has a tendency to blacken later. Medium soft, slightly dry texture. Not as waxy as some early varieties.
Boiling 4, roast 2, chipped and sauté 2, salad 3.
2 **Maris peer**. Creamy white flesh, of good cooking quality. Rarely disintegrates during cooking. Slightly dry, moderately waxy texture.
Boiling 4, jacket (august only) 1, roast 3, chipped and sauté 3, salad 3.
3 **Pentland javelin**. A very white fleshed potato of good shape. Keeps well for early potato texture, moderately waxy.
Boiled 3, roast 2, chipped and sauté 2, salad 3.
4 **Ulster sceptre**. White fleshed, rarely discolours before or after cooking. Soft waxy texture. One of the earliest varieties available in the shop.
Boiled 3, roast 2, chipped and sauté 3, salad 3.
5 **Wilja**. Pale yellow flesh. Rarely disintegrates, soft slightly dry texture and not as waxy as some varieties.
Boiled 3, jacket (august) 1, roast 2, chipped and sauté 2, salad 2.
6 **Other good varieties**. Epicure (Scotland); Maris Bard, Estima, Ulster Prince, Craigs, Alliance and Red Craigs Royal, (Pink skin); Arran Comet. Jersey Royals and Micks Cypres, Egyptian – light soils.

British main crop

Usually available from September. In the autumn the flesh is waxy, but tends to become floury after storage. Although there is a loss of Vitamin C during storage, potatoes still remain a valuable source of Vitamin C.

The varieties' usage ratings (out of 4)

1 **Desirée**. A pink skin variety, pale yellow flesh, rarely disintegrates or discolours after cooking. Moderately soft texture, not as dry as most types of main crop potatoes, shape may be variable.
Boiling 3, mashed 3, jacket 3, roast 4, chipped and sauté 4, salad 1.

2 King Edward. A particoloured pink skin, cream flesh of good cooking quality. A moderately dry, floury texture, a very high quality potato.
Boiled 4, mashed 4, jacket 4, roast 3, chipped and sauté 4, salad 1.

3 Maris piper. Creamy white flesh, soft dry floury texture, uniform shape.
Boiled 3, mashed 3, jacket 4, roast 3, chipped 4 and salad 1.

4 Pentland crown. Soft and with a tendency to have a wet texture, creamy white flesh.
Boiling 2, mashed 2, jacket 3, roast 2, chipped and sauté 2, salad 0.

5 Pentland dell. White to cream flesh, of moderate cooking quality. A tendency to distintegrate during cooking. Soft, moderate texture, long oval shape.
Boiled 2, mashed 2, jacket 3, roast 2, chipped and sauté 2, salad 1.

6 Pentland hawk. Creamy flesh, moderate cooking quality. Medium firm, slightly dry texture.
Boiled 3, mashed 3, jacket 3, roast 2, chipped and sauté 2, salad 1.

7 Pentland ivory/Pentland squire. Cream white flesh, firm texture.
Chipped and saute 3, boiled 3, roast 2, salad 1, jacket 0.

Storage of potatoes

Potatoes are such an accepted part of any caterer's stock that very little thought is given to exactly how they should be stored in order to keep them in good condition.

There are certain points to remember when planning potato storage e.g.

1 Cleanliness – freedom from dirt and earth means that any potato disease is not spread.

2 Dryness – potato tubers will go mouldy and rotten if they are kept in the damp. Damp potatoes are also more susceptible to frost damage.

3 Good ventilation and air circulation – this is necessary to keep potatoes fresh, dry and free from contact with strong smelling foodstuffs or chemicals.

4 Correct temperature – between 40°F to 50°F is ideal in order to avoid frosting or sprouting through warmth.

5 Minimum handling – potatoes bruise easily and then turn black during cooking. Potatoes should be checked on receipt and surplus soil removed. Sacks are best stored on slats raised a few inches from the ground to allow air to circulate. Close sacks after use. Ideally, sacks should be emptied into trolley filled with slatted trays for easy transport to the preparation area.

6 Strong light should be avoided – potatoes turn green in even a moderately strong light.

NOTES. Potatoes which have been washed to remove dirt rather than dry brushed do not keep so long.

Potato stocks should be turned round every week, if possible.

2

Herbs and spices

Name	What it is	Where it comes from	How it is used	How to remember
Allspice (Whole ground) (*le piment*)	Berry	Caribbean area only	Whole – in pickling, stews. Ground – in almost all food especially cakes, puddings	Named because flavour is blend of cinnamon, nutmeg
Aniseed (*la graine d'anis*)	Seed	Eastern Mediterranean, Turkey, Spain, Syria	Cakes, bread	Liquorice flavour
Apple pie spice	Blend of sweet spices	China, Ceylon and West Indies	Apple pie, cooked apples, sprinkled on ham to glaze	Perfect blend for apples
Arrowroot (*le arrow-root*)	Rhizome	Caribbean, West Indies	Ground root of maranta plant produces fine starch for thickening, glazing	Bland starch
Basil (*le basilic*)	Herb	Italy, France, Hungary, Belgium	Tomato and egg dishes, stews, fish, pasta	Affinity with Italian dishes
Bay (*le laurier*)	Leaf of Bay Laurel tree	Turkey, Greece, Portugal, Yugoslavia	Meat and fish stock, boiled ham, beef, lamb, tongue, fowl, soused herrings, tomato dishes, savoury sauces, puddings	One of the flavours in classic bouquet garni
Bouquet garni	Sachet of herbs	France, Greece	Add to meat soups, stews, casseroles, sauces, poultry and game, court bouillon for fish	Sprigs of thyme, parsley and bay leaf. Do not forget to remove before serving!
Caraway seed (*le carri*)	Seed	Originally Asia Minor. Netherlands, Denmark, Poland, Russia, Syria	Rye breads, coffee cakes, seed cake, cheese spreads, ghoulash, sauerkraut	Crescent-shaped seeds. Distinctive liquorice-like flavour
Cardamom (*le cardomome*)	Seed	Native of India. Guatemala, Ceylon	Ground in curries, beef and pork, sausages. Danish pastries, cakes, some stewed fruit	Aromatic, slightly lemony flavour
Celery seed (*la graine de céleri*)	Seed	India, France	Pickles, meat stews, casseroles, salads, e.g. cole slaw	Slightly bitter celery flavour
Chili seasoning	Pod of chilli pepper	Originally South America. Tropical and temperate climates, e.g. Hungary, Mexico, India and Japan	Whole in pickling spice. Ground in Mexican dishes, baked beans, seafood cocktails, barbecue sauces	Fiery, spicy flavour. Orange/red colour

Herb and spices (continued)

Name	What it is	Where it comes from	How it is used	How to remember
Chives (Freeze dried) (*la ciboulette*)	Leaves of grass-like onion plant	Freeze dried, produced in USA	Garnish to cream soups, salads, mashed and baked potatoes, omelettes, stuffed eggs, etc.	Mild onion flavour looks like fresh green grass
Cinnamon (*la cannelle*)	Dried bark of evergreen tree of laurel family	Far East – India, Ceylon, Indonesia, South Vietnam	Most important baking spice. Ground in cakes, puddings, Christmas pudding, pumpkin pie. Stick – Pickling, mulled drinks	Sweet aromatic flavour. Ground cinnamon looks like cocoa powder
Cloves (*le clou de girofle*)	Flower bud of tropical evergreen	Malagasy and Tanzania, Madagascar	Whole in pickling, hot spiced wines, stuck in whole onion for stews, sauces, in apple pie. Ground in fruit cake, mincemeat, puddings, gingerbread, meat stews	Strong, spicy flavour. Whole cloves look like small black four-sided twigs – pungent
Coriander seed (*la coriandre*)	Seed	Native of Mediterranean, Morocco, Rumania, Argentine and France	Crushed in curries, pea soup, roast pork casseroles. Tea-cakes, apple pie.	Round white ridged seed
Cumin seed	Seed	Mediterranean origin, native of Egypt, India	Curries, Mexican dishes, minced beef, beef loaf, pickles and chutneys, cream cheese dips, cabbage and sauerkraut dishes.	Seed similar to caraway but different aroma
Dill seed (*l'aneth odorant*)	Seed	Native of Europe, India	Dill pickles, fish, salads, cole slaw, sauerkraut	Look like caraway. Slight anise flavour
Fennel seed (*la fenauil*)	Seed	Native to Europe but imported from India and Argentina	Court Bouillon for fish, sausages, breads, rolls	Similar to Dill. Slight anise flavour
Fenugreek	Seed	Native of Europe, grown in Egypt, India and Morocco	Ground in curries, pickles, chutneys	Strong, slightly bitter flavour
Fine herbs (*les fines-herbes*)	Mixture of culinary herbs	Blended product	Soups, stews casseroles, meat loaves, omelettes, spaghetti dishes, salads	Omelette Finas Herbs – Classic French use of Parsley, Thyme, Chives, Chervil and Tarragon

(continued)

2

Herbs and spices (*continued*)

Name	What it is	Where it comes from	How it is used	How to remember
Garlic (*l'ail*)	Bulb	Warm climates. Native of ancient world, Greece, Egypt, USA, Indonesia	Garlic salt – Garlic Flakes product of USA. Roast lamb, pork, meat and fish stews, French dressing, salads, cheese dishes, garlic bread	Intensified onion flavour and aroma
Ginger (*le gingembre*)	Root (rhizome) of tropical plant	Indonesia, India, Nigeria	Whole – pickling, preserving, confectionery. Ground – curries, baked goods, ginger ale, Indian, Chinese, West Indian dishes	Hot and peppery
Mace and nutmeg (*la macis et la muscade*)	Outer shell and nut of tropical tree	Indonesia, West Indies, Granada	Mace – blade (outer shell) in stews, court bouillon, sauces. Ground in baking. Nutmeg – Whole nut freshly grated on milk puddings, egg-nog, mulled drinks, in baking, on carrots, spinach. Ground in baked goods, seasoned meats.	Spicy brown specks on baked custard, rice pudding, egg-nog
Marjoram (*la marjolaine*)	Herb	Western Asian origin. France, Portugal, Greece and Rumania	Lamb, poultry, stuffings (one of ingredients of Italian seasoning), also used in bologna, liverwurst, lima and green beans, peas	Similar to oregano

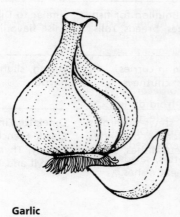

Garlic

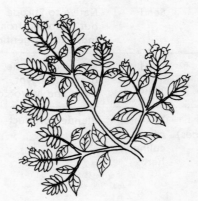

Marjoram

Herbs and spices (*continued*)

Name	What it is	Where it comes from	How it is used	How to remember
Minced onion	Vegetable	Product of USA	Dehydrated pieces of pure onion to be used as fresh onions in recipes	Peeled onions without tears
Mint (*la menthe*)		USA, Argentina, UK, France, Morocco, Bulgaria, the UAE, South Africa, Romania, CIS, England	Add to potatoes	
Oregano	Herb	Italy, Greece	Add to meats, salads, soups stuffings, pasta, sauces	Similar to marjoram
Parsley (*le persil*)	Plant	Britain	Flavouring and garnish	
Poppy seeds	Seed		Topping for bread and cakes, etc.	
Rosemary (*le romarin*)	Herb	Britain	Fresh or dried for flavouring sauces, stews, salads, and stuffings. Sprinkled on roast and grills of meat, poultry and fish.	
Saffron (*le safron*)	Stigmas from saffron crocus	Spain	Add to soups, sauces and particularly rice dishes.	Bright yellow
Sesame seeds	Seed		Topping for bread and cakes, and used in Chinese and vegetarian cookery.	
Surmac seeds	Seed	Middle East	Used in Middle Eastern cookery for for their acidic lemon peppery flavour.	Deep red maroon colour
Tarragon (*l'estragon*)	Plant		Used to decorate chaud-froid dishes. Used in sauces (e.g. sauce Béarnaise). One of the fine herbs used for omelettes, salads, fish and meat dishes.	

2

(*continued*)

Name	What it is	Where it comes from	How it is used	How to remember
Thyme (*le thym*)	Plant	Britain	Used fresh or dried for flavouring soups, sauces, stews, stuffings, salads and vegetables.	
Turmeric (*le curcuma*)	Root (rhizome) of tropical plant		Used for colouring curry powder. Ground – used in pickles, relishes and as colouring in cakes and rice.	

Tarragon

Thyme

Farinaceous products

PASTA

There are over 200 different shapes and sizes of pasta. The most commonly used ones are:

- cannelloni
- lasagne
- macaroni
- noodles
- spaghetti
- tagliatelle
- vermicelli.

All pasta is made from flour dough and the particular flour used is produced from durum wheat as this has excellent binding qualities. The dough is kneaded and rolled and then pressed into

Cannelloni

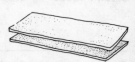

Lasagne

Macaroni

Spaghetti

Tagliatelle

Vermicelli

moulds or through cutters to give the required shape.

The flavour can be varied by adding egg or spices to the dough or coloured at this stage, too, e.g. adding spinach to make lasagne verdi.

Use pasta for:

- hors d'oeuvres, hot or cold
- main meals
- accompaniments to fish, meat or poultry dishes.

RICE

It is estimated that there may be 7000 different varieties of rice produced throughout the world, but the rice produced in the USA may be divided into three broad groupings:

1 **Long-grain rice**. The length of the rice is four to five times its width. The grains are clear and translucent with very little chalkiness. They remain separate and distinct after cooking. Varieties grown in the United States include Blue Bonnet, Rexoro and Belle Patna.

2 **Medium-grain rice**. The length of the rice is about three times as long as the width. The separation characteristics are not quite as distinct after cooking as that of long-rice. It is, therefore, slightly less expensive. Varieties grown in the United States include Calrose and Nato.

3 **Short-grain**. The length of the rice is only one-and-a-half to two times as long as the width. When cooked, the grains may be slightly more glutinous. Because of the shorter growing season and high yields per acre, this is a popular priced variety on the market. The best known short grain variety grown in the USA is Pearl.

Kinds of rice on the market

Because recipes call for different kinds of rice, it is important to understand the difference.

1 **Milled rice**. This is the white rice usually referred to in a recipe calling for 'rice'. It is the rice from which hulls, germ, outer bran layers, and most of the inner bran layers are removed in the milling process.

2 **Brown rice**. This is the rice from which only the hulls have been removed. It still retains the bran layers and most of the germ.

3 **Par-boiled rice**. This is rice which has been subjected to steam or water treatment prior to milling. It retains more vitamins and minerals because of the process.

4 **Pre-cooked rice**. This is milled rice which has been completely cooked and the water removed. Consequently it requires a shorter time for preparation.

NOTE: Cooked or uncooked rice in a recipe means **white milled rice**. Where another type of rice is called for, it should be stated in full; for example, 1 cup of **uncooked brown rice** or 2 cups cooked **par-boiled rice**.

Products and by-products of rice

1 **Rice bran** is the first major by-product removed from the rice kernel during the milling process. It is relatively high in protein and is primarily used for livestock feed.

2 **Rice polish** is the final layers removed from the rice kernel during the polishing process. It is finer and heavier than bran and is high in fat and carbohydrate. It is blended in various process foods. Rice polish is also used as livestock feed.

3 **Rice oil** is the oil extracted from rice bran and polish. It is a stable neutral oil which is adaptable to the manufacture of some margarine, cooking oil, salad oil, industrial oil, soap and a wide range of other products.

4 **Rice flour** is milled rice which is ground into flour. It is used in place of wheat flour in cakes and breads for those who have an allergy to wheat. It is also used in face powders and similar cosmetics. Rice flour is also used in frozen pies and other commercial baked goods.

5 **Rice cereal** is rice that has been converted into various forms. There are rice flakes or puffs that may be eaten cold, or pulverised rice which may be cooked in boiling water and served as a hot cereal.

2

Fish

(Text and photographs reproduced with kind permission of the Sea Fish Industry Authority).

SEA FISH

Fish is classified into three main groups: **white fish**, where the oil is concentrated in the liver; **oily fish**, where the oil is dispersed throughout the flesh; and **shellfish**. White fish are divided into two groups: round and flat. The large round species, such as coley and cod, are usually sold by the fishmonger as steaks, fillets (which can be skinned if desired) or cutlets. The small round species, such as whiting and haddock, are sold in fillets and, again, can be skinned. The fishmonger will also clean and trim the whole fish, removing head, fins and tail ready for cooking, if required.

The larger flat fish varieties, such as halibut and turbot, are sold whole and in fillets and steaks, and are trimmed as required. The small flat fish, such as plaice, lemon sole and Dover sole, are usually sold by the fishmonger whole, trimmed or filleted as required.

All fish are important sources of essential nutrients, but the oily fish species such as herring and mackerel are particularly good sources of vitamins A and D. The fat contained in oily fish is mainly polyunsaturated; in fact, the fatty acids in fish oils are believed to assist in preventing heart disease.

Most shellfish are cleaned and sometimes cooked (e.g. crab and prawns) ready for use, and if required, the fishmonger will clean and dress cooked crab.

Shown below are listed the different species of fish available. It should be noted that the illustrations are not to scale.

Key

BK	Baking	G	Grilling
BR	Braising	P	Poaching
DF	Deep frying	ST	Steaming
SF	Shallow or stir frying	MW	Microwaving

White fish: flat species

1 Brill
Season: June–February
Preparation: Whole fish; fillets
Cooking: BK, BR, G, P, SF, ST, MW

Brill

2 Dab
Season: September–May
Preparation: Whole fish, fillets, pocketing, trimming
Cooking: BK, DF, G, P, SF, ST, MW

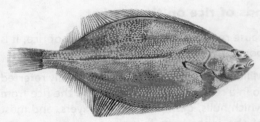

Dab

3 Flounder
Season: March–November
Preparation: Whole fish, fillets
Cooking: BK, BR, G, P, SF, ST, MW, DF

Flounder

4 Halibut
Season: June–March
Preparation: Fillets, steaks, trimming
Cooking: BK, BR, G, P, SF, ST, MW

5 Megrim
Season: May–March
Preparation: Fillets, steaks, skinning and/or scaling
Cooking: BK, DF, G, P, SF, ST, MW

Megrim

6 Plaice
Season: May–February
Preparation: Whole fish, fillets, pocketing, skinning and/or scaling, trimming
Cooking: BK, DF, G, P, SF, ST, MW

Plaice

7 Skate
Season: May–February
Preparation: Fillets, skinning and/or scaling
Cooking: DF, G, P, SF, ST, BR, BK, MW

Skate

8 Lemon sole
Season: May–March
Preparation: Whole fish, fillets, pocketing, skinning and/or scaling, trimming
Cooking: BK, DF, G, P, SF, ST, MW

Lemon sole

9 Dover sole
Season: May–February
Preparation: Whole fish, fillets, pocketing, skinning and/or scaling, trimming
Cooking: BK, DF, G, P, SF, ST, MW

10 Turbot
Season: April–February
Preparation: Whole fish, fillets, steaks, trimming
Cooking: BK, BR, G, P, SF, ST, MW

Turbot

11 Witch
Season: May–February
Preparation: Whole fish, fillets, pocketing, skinning and/or scaling, trimming
Cooking: BK, DF, G, P, SF, ST, MW

White fish: round species

12 Bass
Season: August–March
Preparation: Whole fish, fillets, skinning and/or scaling, trimming
Cooking: BK, BR, G, P, SF, ST, MW

Bass

13 Catfish (rockfish)
Season: February–July
Preparation: Whole fish, fillets, skinning and/or scaling, trimming
Cooking: BK, BR, DF, G, P, SF, ST, MW

Catfish

14 Cod
Season: June–February
Preparation: Whole fish, fillets, cutlets, steaks, skinning and/or scaling
Cooking: BK, BR, G, P, SF, ST, DF, MW

Cod

15 Conger eel
Season: March–October
Preparation: Cutlets, steaks
Cooking: BK, BR, G, P, SF, ST, MW

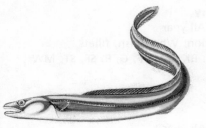

Conger eel

16 Coley (saithe, coalfish)
Season: August–February
Preparation: Whole fish, fillets, cutlets, steaks, skinning and/or scaling
Cooking: BK, DF, G, BR, P, SF, MW

Coley

17 Red gurnard
Season: July–February
Preparation: Whole fish, fillets, trimming
Cooking: BK, DF, P. BR, SF, MW, ST

Red gurnard

18 Haddock
Season: May–February
Preparation: Whole fish, fillets, cutlets, steaks
Cooking: BK, BR, DF, G, P, SF, ST, MW
NB: Available cold smoked as smoked haddock fillets, golden cutlets and Finnan haddock. Available hot smoked as Arbroath smokies.

Haddock

19 Hake
Season: June–March
Preparation: Whole fish, fillets, cutlets, trimming
Cooking: BK, BR, DF, G, P, SF, ST, MW

20 Huss (dogfish, flake, rigg)
Season: All year
Preparation: Whole fish, fillets, cutlets, trimming
Cooking: BK, BR, DF, G, P, SF, MW
NB: Shark is similar to huss and is available all year – fresh or frozen.

Huss

2

21 John Dory
Season: All year
Preparation: Whole fish, fillets
Cooking: BK, BR, DF, G, P, SF, ST, MW

22 Ling
Season: All year
Preparation: Fillets, cutlets
Cooking: BK, BR, DF, G, P, SF, ST, MW

Ling

23 Monkfish (anglerfish)
Season: All year
Preparation: Whole fish, fillets, skinning and/or scaling, trimming
Cooking: BK, BR, DF, G, P, SF, ST, MW

Monkfish

24 Grey mullet
Season: September–February
Preparation: Whole fish, fillets, skinning and/or scaling
Cooking: BK, BR, G, P, ST, MW, SF

25 Red mullet
Season: May–November
Preparation: Whole fish, fillets, skinning and/or scaling
Cooking: BK, BR, G, P, ST, MW, SF

Red mullet

26 Pollack
Season: May–September
Preparation: Fillets, cutlets, trimming
Cooking: BK, BR, DF, G, P, SF, ST, MW

Pollack

27 Redfish (ocean perch, Norway haddock)
Season: All year
Preparation: Fillets, trimming
Cooking, BK, BR, G, P, SF, ST, MW, DF

Redfish

28 Black Sea bream
Season: July–December
Preparation: Whole fish, fillets, cutlets
Cooking: BK, BR, G, P, SF, ST, MW

Black Sea bream

29 Red Sea bream
Season: June–February
Preparation: Whole fish, fillets, cutlets
Cooking: BK, BR, G, P, SF, ST, MW

Red Sea bream

30 Whiting
Season: June–February
Preparation: Whole fish, fillets, trimming
Cooking: BK, BR, DF, G, P, SF, ST, MW
NB: Occasionally available cold smoked.

Oily fish

31 Anchovy
Season: June–December
Preparation: Whole fish, fillets, trimming
Cooking: BK, SF, DF, P, G, MW

Anchovy

32 Herring
Season: May–December
Preparation: Whole fish, fillets, trimming, boning
Cooking: BK, BR, DF, SF, G, MW
NB: Available cold smoked as kippers, bloaters, red herring. Available hot smoked as buckling.

Herring

33 Mackerel
Season: All year
Preparation: Whole fish, fillets, trimming, boning
Cooking: BK, BR, DF, SF, G, MW
NB: Available hot smoked, occasionally cold smoked.

Mackerel

2

34 Pilchard/sardine

Season: January, February, April, November, December

Preparation: Whole fish, trimming

Cooking: BK, BR, G, SF, MW, DF

NB: Small young pilchards are known as sardines.

Pilchard/sardine

35 Sprat

Season: October–March

Preparation: Whole fish, trimming

Cooking: BK, DF, G, SF, MW

NB: Small sprats, herring or mackerel are often sold as whitebait. Occasionally available smoked.

36 Tuna

Season: All year – fresh or frozen

Preparation: Fillets, cutlets, steaks

Cooking: BK, BR, G, P, SF, ST, MW

Tuna

Shellfish

37 Cockles

Season: May–December

Cooking: BK, BR, DF, SF, ST, MW

38 Clams

Season: All year

Cooking: BK, BR, DF, SF, ST, MW, P

NB: The photograph shown here is of the Manila clam.

Clams

39 Brown crab

Season: April–December

Cooking: BK, SF

NB: Crab is available cooked, whole or dressed

Brown crab

42

40 Spider crab
Season: April–December
Cooking: BK, SF

Spider crab

41 Crawfish (spiny lobster, rock lobster)
Season: April–October
Cooking: P, SF, G, ST

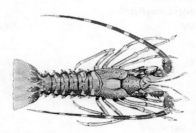

Crawfish

42 Dublin Bay prawn (Norway lobster, langoustines, nephrops or scampi)
Season: April–November
Cooking: BK, BR, P, SF, ST, DF, MW, G

Dublin Bay prawn

43 Lobster
Season: April–November
Cooking: BK, P, SF, G
NB: Live lobster is dark blue, it turns red during cooking.

44 Mussels
Season: September–March
Cooking: BK, BR, DF, P, SF, ST, MW
NB: Mussels should be purchased tightly closed or close when tapped; discard any open ones before cooking.

Mussels

45 Octopus
Season: May–December
Cooking: BR, P

Octopus

46 Native oyster
Season: September–April
Cooking: BK, DF, G, P, SF, ST, MW

Native oyster

47 Pacific oyster
Season: All year
Cooking: BK, DF, G, P, SF, ST, MW

Portuguese Oysters
Season: September–April
Cooking: MW

Portuguese oysters

48 Prawn
Season: All year
Cooking: BK, BR, DF, P, SF, ST, MW, G
NB: Usually sold cooked.

49 Scallop
Season: September–March
Cooking: BK, BR, DF, G, P, SF, ST, MW
NB: The scallop commonly seen in fishmongers is known as the king scallop. Another species, smaller than the king, known as queen scallop is also available. Young queen scallops are known as princess scallops.

Scallop

50 Shrimp
Season: February–October
Cooking: BK, BR, DF, P, SF, ST, MW
NB: Usually sold cooked. The terms 'shrimp' and 'prawn' are often used to describe the same species. The brown and pink shrimp are the most common in the UK.

51 Squid
Season: May–October
Cooking: BR, DF, SF, P, MW
NB: Small squid are often known as 'calamari'.

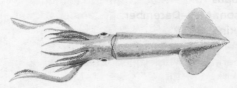

Squid

52 Whelk

Season: February–August
Usually sold cooked

53 Winkle

Season: September–April
Cooking: BK, SF, MW
Usually sold cooked.

Exotic species

Exotic fish are imported from many tropical regions, including the west coast of Africa, the Seychelles, the Pacific Ocean and the Indian Ocean. The following are just a few examples of the wide range available:

54 Croakers or drums (includes black drum and red drum)

Season: All year – fresh or frozen
Preparation: Whole fish, fillets, skinning and/or scaling, trimming
Cooking: BK, BR, G, P, SF, ST, MW
NB: Illustrated is the black drum.

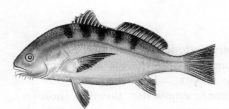

Croaker/drum

55 Emperors or emperor breams (includes capitaine rouge, capitaine blanc, Madame Berrie, gueule longue and Lascar)

Season: All year – fresh or frozen
Preparation: Whole fish, steaks, skinning and/or scaling, trimming
Cooking: BK, BR, G, P, SF, ST, MW

Emperor/emperor bream

56 Groupers (includes vielle platte, vielle maconde and croissant or coral trout)

Season: All year – fresh or frozen
Preparation: Whole fish, steaks, trimming
Cooking: BK, BR, G, P, SF, ST, MW

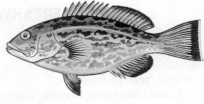

Grouper

57 Jacks (includes horse mackerel, yellowtail, rainbow runner, blue runner, carangue, pompano, trevally, crevally, amberjack and kingfish)

Season: All year – fresh or frozen
Preparation: Whole fillets, steaks, trimming
Cooking: BK, BR, G, P, SF, ST, MW

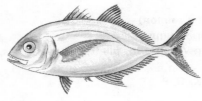

Jack

58 Parrotfish
Season: All year – fresh or frozen
Preparation: Whole fish, skinning and/or scaling, trimming
Cooking: BK, BR, G, P, ST, MW, SF, DF

Parrotfish

59 Pomfret
Season: All year – fresh or frozen
Preparation: Whole fish, skinning and/or scaling, trimming
Cooking: BK, BR, G, P, ST, MW, SF, DF

Pomfret

60 Snappers (includes red snapper, bourgeois, job jaune, job gris, Therese and vara vara)
Season: All year – fresh or frozen
Preparation: Whole fish, skinning and/or scaling, trimming
Cooking: BK, BR, G, ST, MW

Snapper

61 Swordfish
Season: All year – fresh or frozen
Preparation: Cutlets, steaks
Cooking: BK, BR, G, P, SF, MW
NB: Marlin is available from some fish-mongers, related to the swordfish, but it has a stronger flavour.

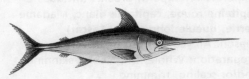

Swordfish

FRESHWATER FISH

Salmon

1 Farmed Atlantic salmon
Season: All year – fresh or frozen
Preparation: Whole fish, fillets, cutlets, steaks, trimming
Cooking: BK, G, P, ST

2 Grilse (young salmon)
Season: April–August
Preparation: Whole fish, fillets, cutlets, steaks, trimming
Cooking: BK, G, P, ST

3 Wild Atlantic salmon
Season: (Irish, Scottish and English) February–August
Preparation: Whole fish, fillets, cutlets, steaks, trimming
Cooking: BK, G, P, ST

4 Pacific salmon
Season: July–November
Preparation: Whole fish, fillets, cutlets, steaks, trimming
Cooking: BK, G, P, ST
NB: Salmon can also be marinaded or cured (gravadlax)

5 Rainbow trout
Season: All year – fresh or frozen
Preparation: Whole fish, fillets, trimming, boning
Cooking: BK, SF, G, ST

6 Brown, wild trout
Season: February–September
Preparation: Whole fish, fillets, trimming, boning
Cooking: BK, G, P.

Meat and poultry

PURCHASING

The purchasing of meat is a large expense for the caterer. It is essential when buying meat to consider carefully:

- the correct amount to use
- the right joint or cut for a particular dish, to give the required flavour and texture
- the quality of meat required
- the amount of waste that is likely to occur due to trimming during preparation and shrinkage during cooking.

Meat can be bought:

- on the carcass and butchered in the kitchen, provided that the staff, equipment and chiller storage are adequate (the overall purchase price will be cheaper, but some parts of the carcass meat will be difficult to use up economically and the cost of the butcher's time must also be taken into account).
- ready jointed and then prepared for a particular dish by the chefs or cooks (the meat purchase price will be slightly higher but most of the meat purchased will be used)
- ready-portioned, trimmed and cut to a stated weight, size and dimensions, e.g., steaks, chops, cutlets, pre-diced for stews or pre-sliced for braising ensuring uniform size and appearance, portion and cost control (the purchase price will be greater but the labour cost and trimming waste will have already been calculated into the portion purchase price).

This latter form is becoming the most usual way to buy large quantities of meat for immediate use or deep freeze storage.

Whichever method of buying or preparation is used it is still most important for the cook or chef to recognise the cuts of meat and signs of quality and good condition.

As the price of fresh meat rises, substitutes are being developed and introduced. In manufactured products 'meat extenders' or 'fillers' are being used.

The product textured vegetable protein (TVP) is a manufactured product made from the natural materials of soya beans or in some cases wheat, oats and other vegetable sources. It is manufactured to take on the appearance and flavour of minced, chunked or sliced beef, pork, lamb or poultry.

A 2 kg (approximately 4½ lb) pack yields 6 kg (13½ lb) when reconstituted by adding stock or water according to the instructions on the pack. Soya protein can be substituted for animal protein up to between 25 and 50 per cent to give a satisfactory effect in a prepared meat dish.

THE RIGHT CUT OF MEAT FOR THE RIGHT DISH

(See ✓ on meat charts)

Good cuts – suitable for roasting, frying, grilling and barbecueing.

Medium cuts – suitable for slow roasting, steam roasting, pot roasting and braising.

Poorer cuts – suitable for stewing, braising, pickling, stock making and chopped, minced, processed, manufactured items.

POULTRY

Good quality poultry will have:

- plump breast and legs
- creamy white flesh without bruises or blood marks
- cleanly plucked flesh
- a fresh smell.

2

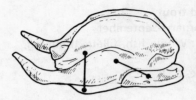

Roasting

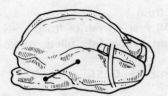

Boiling and poêle

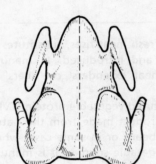

Grilling (crapaudine)

Grilling (spatchcock)

Drumsticks (pilon de cuisse)

Thigh (gras de cuisse)

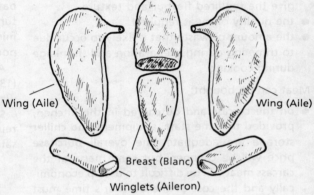

Wing (Aile)

Wing (Aile)

Breast (Blanc)

Winglets (Aileron)

Sauté

Preparation of poultry for cooking

Poultry

	Approximate weight		Use	Number of portions	Season
CHICKEN					
Baby (le poussin)	0.25–0.5 kg	(12 oz–1 lb)	Grilling and pot roasting	1	Spring
Small (le poulet de grain)	1–1.5 kg	(2–3 lb)	Roasting and sautéing	6–8	Spring and early summer
Medium (le poulet reine)	1.5–2 kg	(3–4 lb)	Roasting, sautéing	6–8	Spring, summer
Large (la poule)	2–3 kg	(4–6 lb)	Boiling	8–12	All year round

	Approximate weight		Use	Number of portions	Season
Fat hen (la poularde)	2–3.5 kg	(4–8 lb)	Roasting, boiling and pot roasting	8–16	All year round
TURKEY Hen (la dinde)	3.5–6 kg	(8–14 lb)	Roasting	25–40	Sept–Mar
Cock (le dindon)	5.5–11 kg	(12–24 lb)	Roasting	35–70	September
DUCK Duckling (le caneton)	1.5–2 kg	(3–4 lb)	Braising and roasting	4–6	Mar–Sept
Duck (le canard)	2–3 kg	(4–6 lb)	Braising and roasting	6–12	Aug–Feb
GOOSE Gosling (l'oison)	2–3 kg	(4–6 lb)	Braising and roasting	12–18	Aug–Oct
Goose (l'oie)	3.5–6 kg	(8–14 lb)	Braising and roasting	25–40	Sept–Feb

BEEF

A carcass weighs approximately 163 kg (360 lb).

Fresh, quality beef should have:

- bright red flesh with small white flecks of fat (the flesh should not feel 'slimy')
- creamy yellow-coloured fat that is firm, brittle and fresh-smelling.

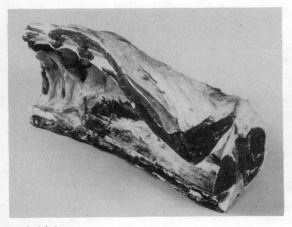

Beef sirloin

Beef rump

Beef

	Approximate weight	Use	Good cuts	Medium cuts	Poorer cuts
Forequarter					
1 Neck or clod and sticking (le talon du collier)	8 kg (18 lb)	Sausages and prepared meat dishes			✓
2 Chuck ribs (les côtes du collier)	13.5 kg (30 lb)	Stewing and braising		✓	
3 Middle ribs (les côtes découvertes)	9 kg (20 lb)	Roasting and braising		✓	
4 Fore ribs (les côtes)	7.25 kg (16 lb)	Roasting and braising	✓		
5 Shank or shin (le jarret)	5.5 kg (12 lb)	Consommé and beef tea			✓
6 Leg of mutton cut (l'épaule)	10 kg (22 lb)	Braising and stewing			✓
7 Brisket (la poitrine)	17.25 kg (38 lb)	Pickled, boiled and pressed			✓
8 Plate (le plat)	9 kg (20 lb)	Stewing and sausages			✓
Hindquarter					
9 Wing ribs (la côte d'aloyau)	5 kg (10 lb)	Roasting, grilling, frying and steaks	✓		
10 Sirloin (l'aloyau)	9 kg (18 lb)	Roasting, grilling, frying and steaks	✓		
11 Rump (la culotte de boeuf)	10 kg (20 lb)	Grilling, frying and steaks	✓		
12 Silverside (la gite à la noix)	14 kg (28 lb)	Pickled and boiled		✓	
13 Topside (la tranche tendre)	10 kg (20 lb)	Braising, stewing and roasting	✓		
14 Leg or shin (le jarret)	7 kg (14 lb)	Consommé and stewing			✓

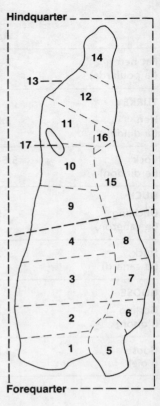

Hindquarter

Forequarter

	Approximate weight	Use	Good cuts	Medium cuts	Poorer cuts
15 Thin flank (la bavette)	9 kg (20 lb)	Stewing, boiling and sausages			✔
16 Thick flank (la tranche grasse)	11 kg (24 lb)	Braising, stewing		✔	
17 Fillet (le filet de boeuf)	3 kg (6 lb)	Roasting, grilling, frying and steaks	✔		

Offal

Heart (le coeur)	1–2 kg (2–4 lb)	Braising			
Kidney (le rognon)	1+ kg (2–3 lb)	Stewing and soup			
Liver (le foie)	5.5–6 kg (12–14 lb)	Braising and frying			
Sweetbreads (young animals only) (le ris de veau)		Braising and frying			
Tongue (la langue)	1.5–2 kg (3–4 lb)	Pickled, boiling and braising			
Tripe (la tripe)	3.5–5.5 kg (8–12 lb)	Boiling and braising			

PORK

A carcass weighs approximately 20 kg (44 lb).
   Fresh, quality pork will have:

- a firm non-slimy texture to the flesh
- white, smooth and firm fat
- smooth skin and rind
- a clean, inoffensive smell.

Pork

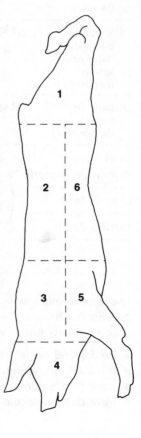

	Approximate weight	Use	Good cuts	Medium cuts	Poorer cuts
1 Leg: knuckle or fillet (le cuissot)	4.5 kg (10 lb)	Boiling and roasting	✔		
2 Loin (la longe)	5.5 kg (12 lb)	Frying, grilling and roasting	✔		

(continued)

Loin of pork

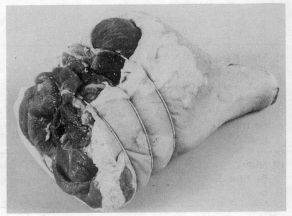

Leg of pork

	Approximate weight		Use	Good cuts	Medium cuts	Poorer cuts
3 Spare rib (la basse côte)	2 kg	(4 lb)	Pies and roasting	✔		
4 Head (la tête)	3.5 kg	(8 lb)	Brawn			✔
5 Shoulder-blade or hand or spring (l'épaule)	3 kg	(6 lb)	Pies, roasting and sausages		✔	
6 Belly or breast (la poitrine)	2 kg	(4 lb)	Boiling and pickling		✔	

Offal

Kidneys (le rognon)	⎫	Grilling and sautéing
Liver (le foie)	⎬ Approximately 3 kg (6 lb)	Frying and pâté
Trotters (le pied)	⎭	Boiling and grilling

BACON

The approximate weight of a side of bacon is 23.5 kg (52 lb).

Good-quality bacon will:

● be dry and not at all sticky
● have a fresh, appetising smell
● have firm, smooth, white fat
● have clear pink-coloured flesh.

All bacon comes from the cured flesh of pigs. Curing is done by dry-salting or soaking it in salt solution to produce unsmoked bacon.

Further curing by smoking then takes place to turn 'green' bacon into the more strongly flavoured smoked product. Smoked bacon keeps well, being slow to deteriorate.

52

Bacon

Item	Approximate weight		Use	Good cuts	Medium cuts	Poorer cuts
1 Gammon – corner, middle	6.3 kg	(14 lb)	Boiling, frying or grilling	✓		
2 Back, loin	7.25 kg	(16 lb)	Frying or grilling	✓		
3 Collar, shoulder	3 kg	(7 lb)	Boiling or grilling		✓	
4 Hock	3 kg	(7 lb)	Boiling			✓
5 Streaky thick	3.5 kg	(8 lb)	Frying and grilling	✓		
6 Streaky thin				✓		

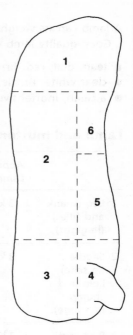

Gammon cut into pieces

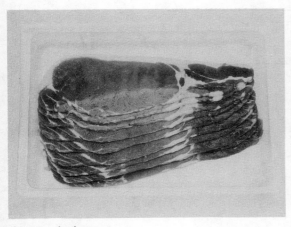

Thin streaky bacon

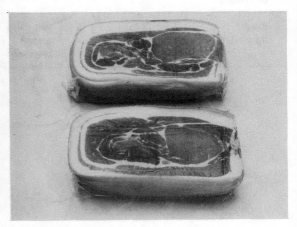

Thick streaky bacon

LAMB AND MUTTON

A lamb carcass weighs 14.5 kg (32 lb). A mutton carcass weighs 22.5 kg (50 lb).
  Good-quality lamb will have:

- lean, dull, red, firm flesh
- clear white, brittle, flaky and hard fat
- a clean, inoffensive smell.

Lamb and mutton

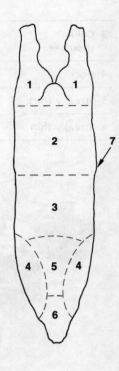

	Approximate weight		Use	Good cuts	Medium cuts	Poorer cuts
	Lamb	Mutton				
1 Leg (shank and fillet) (le gigot)	3 kg (7 lb)	5 kg (11 lb)	Boiling and roasting	✔		
2 Saddle (la selle) Loin and chump (la longe)	3 kg (7 lb)	5 kg (11 lb)	Grilling, frying, roasting	✔		
3 Best end (le carré)	2 kg (4 lb)	3 kg (6 lb)	Grilling, frying, roasting	✔		
4 Shoulder (l'épaule)	3 kg (6 lb)	4 kg (9 lb)	Roasting and stewing	✔		
5 Middle neck (le cou)	2 kg (4 lb)	3 kg (6 lb)	Stewing		✔	
6 Scrag end (le collier or collet)	0.5 kg (1 lb)	1 kg (2 lb)	Stewing			✔
7 Breast (la poitrine)	1.5 kg (3 lb)	2 kg (5 lb)	Roasting and stewing			✔

	Approximate weight		
	Lamb	Mutton	Use
Lamb offal			
Heart (le coeur)			Braising
Kidney (le rognon)			Grilling or sautéing
Liver (le foie)	Approximately 1.5–2 kg (3–5 lb)		Braising or frying
Sweetbreads (le ris)			Braising or frying
Tongue (la langue)			Braising or boiling

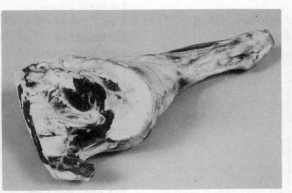

Leg of lamb

Loin of lamb

General guide to portion control

Portion size depends upon several factors:

- whether the portion be Table d'Hôte or à la Carte
- the portion size policy of the management
- the type of customer
- portion size and cost must be such as to allow the required amount of profit.

NB: Weight given indicates raw weight of commodities.

The following is a general guide to portion size though it is by no means a conclusive or exhaustive list.

1 Hors d'oeuvre

(a) Various (variés)	– 100 g per portion
(b) Oysters	– 6 per portion
(c) Smoked Salmon	– 30–40 g per portion
(d) Fish cocktails (Prawn, Shrimp, Crab, Lobster)	– 50 g fish per portion 15 g lettuce per portion 50 mls sauce per portion
(e) Pâté	– 50 g per portion
(f) Fresh fruit cocktail	– 100 g per portion
(g) Fruit juices	– 100 g per portion
(h) Caviare	– 25 g per portion

2 Soups

300 mls per portion

Croûtons and courtes	– 15–20 g per portion
Grated cheese	– 8–10 g per portion

3 Fish

As an extremely general guide, allow	– 150 g off the bone per portion 170 g on the bone per portion

As for other commodities the size of portions of fish depends mainly upon:

- the type of menu
- the number of courses either before or to follow the fish course
- the cost in relation to the selling price.

It is fair to assume the following:

(a) Dover soles – a sole weighing 150–200 g is called a Slip Sole. Soles weighing a pound or over are usually filleted, those weighing less are usually served whole.

(b) Place and sole can lose as much as 45%–50% of its total weight in bone, skin and trimming when filleted.

(c) Cod, haddock, turbot and whiting similarly lose up to 40% of their total weight, also hake and halibut.

(d) Herring and mackerel lose approximately 20% of their total weight.

4 Eggs

(a) Omelettes	– 3 eggs per portion for main course.
(b) Hard boiled	– 1 or 2 per portion for breakfast.
Egg mayonnaise	– 1 for first course 2 for main course
Various oeufs Dur	– 1 egg per portion as they are invariably a hot Hors d'Oeuvre, an egg course or occasionally a savoury
(c) Scrambled eggs	– 1–2 eggs per first course 3 eggs per main course
(d) Poached	– 1 egg per portion first course
(e) En cocotte sur plat	– 1 egg per portion

5 Farinaceous

Spaghetti Macaroni Noodles }	– 15–20 g per portion as a garnish 50 g or more for main course

Ravioli	– Approximately 6–8 pieces per first course
Canneloni	– 2–3 pieces per first course
Riz Pilaff	– 30 g rice per portion as garnish
Risotto	– 30 g rice per first course

6 Meat

A very general guide to ordering	– 125 g meat off the bone per portion
	– 150 g meat on the bone per portion

NB Roasting:
Lamb and mutton lose 30–35% of their total weight in bone and cooking loss.
Beef – 40–45% of its total weight in bone and cooking loss.
Pork – 30% of its total weight in bone and cooking loss.

Boiling:
Mutton loses 25% of its total weight in bone and cooking loss.
Ham loses 25% of its total weight in bone and cooking loss.
Beef = 20% cooking loss (no bone)

The size of steaks, chops, cutlets etc. will depend entirely upon the individual caterer's policy.

Beef

Roast on the bone	4–6 portions per kg
Roast boneless	6–8 portions per kg
Boiled or Braised	6–8 portions per kg
Stews, pudding and pies	8–10 portions per kg
Steaks: Rump	120 g–¼ kg per one portion
Sirloin	120 g–¼ kg per one portion
Tournedos	90–120 g per one portion
Fillet	120–180 g per one portion

Offal

Ox liver	8 portions to the kg
Sweetbreads	6–8 portions to the kg
Sheep's kidneys	2 per portion
Oxtail	4 portions per kg
Ox tongue	4–6 portions per kg

Lamb

Leg	6–8 portions to the kg
Shoulder boned and stuffed	6–8 portions to the kg
Loin and best end	6 portions to the kg
Stewing lamb	4–6 portions to the kg
Cutlet	90–120 g
Chop	120–180 g

Pork

Leg	8 portions to the kg
Shoulder	6–8 portions to the kg
Loin on the bone	6–8 portions to the kg
Pork chop	180 g–¼ kg

Ham

Hot	8–10 portions to the kg
Cold	10–12 portions to the kg
Sausages are obtainable	12, 16 or 20 to the kg
Chipolatas yield approx	32, 48 to the kg
Cold meat	16 portions to the kg
Streaky bacon	32–40 rashers to the kg
Back bacon	24–32 rashers to the kg

7 Poultry

(a) Chicken

Single poussin = 350–450 g	= 1 portion
Double poussin = 450–600 g	= 2 portions
Roasting chickens = 900–1800 g	= 4–6 portions
Large roasting chickens = 1800–2700 g	= 6–8 portions
Capon = 2700–4500 g	= 8–12 portions
Boiling fowl = 2300–3800 g	= 6–10 portions

2

(b) Duck   = 1800–2700 g   = 6–8 portions
Duckling   = 1300–1800 g   = 4–6 portions

NB: All of the above lose 25% of their total weight through drawing and 50% of the remaining weight through bone and cooking loss.

Turkey) Allow 240 g undrawn weight per
Goose) portion e.g. 9 kg turkey = 40 portions.

8 Game

Venison	= 13 kg	= 15–20 portions
Hare	= 2½–3½ kg	= 6–8 portions
Rabbit	= 1 kg	= 4 portions
Pheasant	= 1½–2 kg	= 4 portions
Partridge	= 250–450 g	= 1–2 portions
Woodcock	= 250–350 g	= 1 portion
Snipe	= 120 g	= 1 portion
Grouse	= 350 g	= 1–2 portions
Plover	= 220 g	= 1 portion
Quail	= 130–180 g	= 1 portion
Wild duck	= 1–1½ kg	= 2–4 portions
Teal	= 420–600 g	= 1–2 portions
Wood pigeon	= 350 g	= 1 portion

9 Vegetables

Old potatoes	= 150 g per portion
New potatoes	= 125 g per portion
Globe artichoke	= 1 per portion
Jerusalem artichoke	= 180 g per portion
Asparagus	= 6–8 good sized pieces per portion
Egg plant/ aubergine	= ½ per portion
Carrots	= 100 g per portion
Celery	= ½ medium head per portion
Mushrooms	= 60–80 g per portion
Cabbage	= 3–4 portions per ½ kg
Brussel Sprouts	= 3–4 portions per ½ kg
Cauliflower	= 1 medium sized gives 4 portions
Sea kale	= 3 portions per ½ kg
Marrow	= 2–3 portions per ½ kg
Endive	= 3 portions per ½ kg
Spinach	= 2 portions per ½ kg
Broad beans	= 2 portions per ½ kg
French beans	= 3–4 portions per ½ kg
Haricot beans	= 6–8 portions per ½ kg
Corn on the cob	= 1 per portion

Turnip or swede	= 3–4 portions per ½ kg
Onions	= 2–3 portions per ½ kg (for sauté allow 2 portions per ½ kg)
Peas	= 2 portions per ½ kg
Pimento	= 1 per portion
Salsify	= 2–3 portions per ½ kg
Tomatoes	= 100 g per portion
Leeks	= 150 g per portion
Parsnips	= 3–4 portions per ½ kg

10 Sweets

Milk puddings	= 140 mls milk per portion
Flans-pastry	= 45 g flour per portion
Pastry cream for flans	= 70 mls milk per portion

Fruit for flans

Apple	= 100 g per portion
Cherry (fresh)	= 50–80 g per portion
Gooseberry	= 50–80 g per portion
Rhubarb	= 80 g per portion
Strawberry	= 50 g per portion – slightly more if frozen
Raspberry	= 50 g per portion – slightly more if frozen
Banana	= ½ banana per portion
Tinned fruit	= 50 g per portion

Other sweets using short or sweet pastes

	= 100–150 g per portion
Steamed pudding	= 100–130 g per portion
Fruit fools	= 100 g per portion NB ½ kg = 2½ dl purée
Bavarois	= 100 g per portion
Rum Baba	= 30 g flour per portion
Savarin	= 15 g flour per portion
Melbas	= 100–130 g per portion (50 g ice cream, 40–50 g fruit sauce, cream)
Ice cream	= Graded according to server
Trifle	= 100 g
Choux paste fritters	= 50 g choux paste per portion
Fruit fritters	= 50–70 g fruit per portion
Pancakes (batter)	= 25 g flour per portion
Fresh fruit salad	= 100 g raw fruit per portion

11 Sauces

Cocktail sauce for seafood
= 50 mls per portion
Fish sauces – coating
= 75 mls per portion
Fish sauces – accompanying
= 40 g per portion
Fish butters – cold
= 15 g per portion
Fish butters – hot = 25 mls per portion
Poultry, game and meat sauces (e.g. demi glacé, velouté, béchamel-based)
= 50–70 mls per portion
Rich sauce Béarnaise
= 24–40 mls per portion
Gravy   = 25 mls per portion

Sweet sauces

(Jam, custard)   = 50 g per portion
Those accompanying main courses (apple, cranberry)   = 40 g per portion

Dressings (salad)   = 25 g per portion
Mayonnaise   = 25–40 g per portion

12 Bread

1 kg loaf   = 25 slices for bread and
12 hours old   butter or sandwiches
1 kg loaf   = 28 slices for bread and
24 hours old   butter or sandwiches
1 kg loaf   = 14 slices for toast
24 hours old

NB: Using 2 kg loaves proves more economical as there are 2 less end crusts than in 2 × 1 kg loaves. Bread fried absorbs approximately half its own weight in fat.

13 Butter

Pats   = 7 g each
170 g will butter 28 slices of bread for bread and butter
250 g will butter 14 slices of toasted bread.

2

③ EQUIPMENT

Large-scale catering equipment

BAINS-MARIE

Bains-marie are used to keep soups, sauces and cooked foods hot prior to, or during, service. There are two principal types:

1 Open, in which pots or containers holding sauces and foods are placed in hot water to retain their heat; and
2 those with filler plates and containers, which are either heated directly by a gas burner or indirectly by hot water or steam.

HOTCUPBOARDS

These are cabinets which are directly heated either by a burner sited below a baffle plate, or indirectly by hot gases conducted round the cabinet through channels, or by steam generated in a well in the base.

Hotcupboards are used to heat plates and to keep cooked food hot during the delay between cooking and service. They are available with fitted or open bains-marie.

GENERAL PURPOSE AND ROASTING OVENS

These are used for all oven work (roasting and baking). There are two principal methods of heating them:

1 Internal heating, with visible flames inside the oven, similar to the domestic cooker, and with

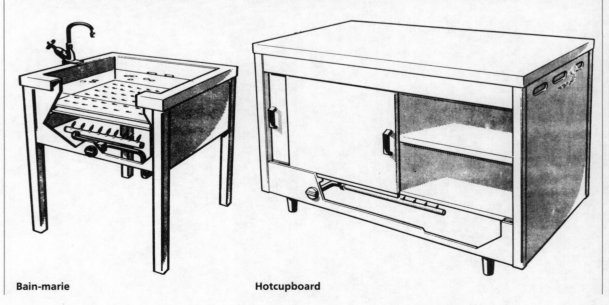

Bain-marie   Hotcupboard

a temperature gradient rising from the bottom to the top of the oven. Roasting ovens are usually of this type.

2 Semi-internal heat, with the burners or burners placed under a metal plate called the sole. The hot gases enter the oven round the edges of the sole plate or through vents in and over the tops of the inner walls of the oven which is evenly heated.

Heavy-duty ovens are usually fitted with drop-down doors, and medium-duty and roasting ovens have side-hinged single or double doors according to the width. Both types can be mounted in tiers one above the other or on a stand.

BOILING TABLES AND STOCKPOT STOVES

Boiling tables can be used for all boiling of top operations; stockpot stoves by virtue of their low height are more suitable for larger utensils.

Boiling tables are available in two types:

1 Open-top with a series of ring burners.
2 Solid-top heated by single or multiple ring burner or jet burner.

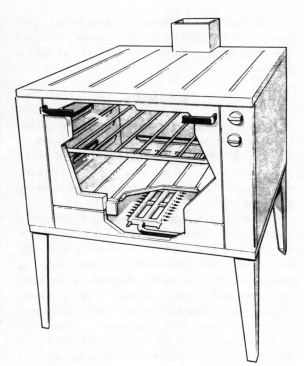

General purpose oven

Stockpot stove

Open top boiling table

Stockpot stoves are low-level boiling tables, generally 610 mm (24 in) high, usually with an open-ring burner, although a solid-top version is available.

RANGES

A range is a composite unit made up of a boiling table (hot plate) and a general purpose oven occasionally with the addition of a grill fitted in the pot-rack at eye-level. A range is found in nearly every kitchen and can be used for all cooking purposes.

Medium-duty ranges usually have open-ring burners, and sometimes include a grill. Solid tops are also available. Ovens are normally internally heated with side-hinged doors, either single or double according to width. Basically, these units are larger and stronger versions of the domestic cooker. Heavy-duty ranges may have a solid top, open-ring burners, griddle plate or a combination of the last two with a semi-externally heated oven with drop-down doors. Heavy-duty appliances are designed for continuous use under severe conditions with weighty utensils, such as the kitchen of a hotel, large restaurant or hospital. A single-oven range will normally cater for up to 50 persons and a double-oven unit from 50–100.

Because of their comparatively lighter construction, medium-duty ranges are more suitable for small establishments such as cafés, public house kitchens and schools and in similar situations where use is moderate or intermittent.

Where only one oven is in use, the internally heated type may be preferred as the temperature gradient will permit the cooking of different dishes at the same time.

Solid top range with semi-externally heated oven

Open top range with direct heated oven

BRAT PANS OR TILTING FRYERS

Brat pans are shallow tilting frying pans approximately 762 × 610 × 178 mm deep (30 × 24 × 7 in). They may be of cast iron or stainless steel. The tilting mechanism can be lever or hand-wheel operated.

Brat pans are mainly used as a multi-purpose appliance for shallow and dry frying or boiling. The versatility of the pan makes it invaluable for bulk cooking in a kitchen with limited space. They are capable of handling up to 200 average portions an hour, as shown below:

Shallow frying
Trout: 36 in 4 minutes

Dry frying
Eggs: 30 at a time, about 600 an hour
Bacon: 100 portions in 10 minutes

Poaching
Eggs: 800 an hour
Fish: 200 portions an hour

Stewing
27–32 litres (6–7 gallons)

Sautéing
27 kg (60 lb) of meat an hour

FORCED CONVECTION OVENS

A forced convection oven is suitable for all normal roasting and baking. With its even temperature distribution the full capacity of the oven may be

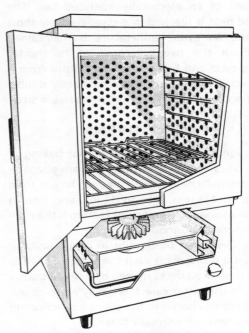

Convection oven (semi-externally heated)

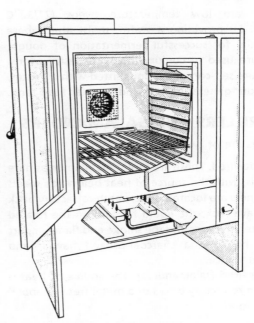

Convection oven (externally heated)

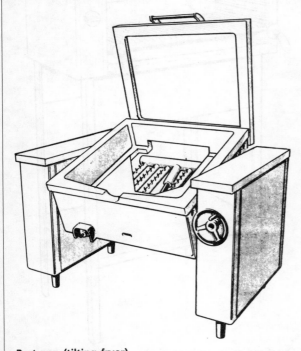

Brat pan (tilting fryer)

used and cooking times reduced. The unit is especially suitable for rapid re-heating and end-cooking of frozen foods.

These ovens may be externally or semi-externally heated, the hot air being recirculated by means of an electrically operated fan. The required heat is reached in a comparatively short time and an even temperature is maintained throughout the oven. Because of its shorter cooking cycle and higher use, the output from a forced convection oven is approximately double that of a conventional oven of comparable size.

PASTRY OVENS

These ovens are used for large output baking of pastry, cakes and plate goods. They are purpose-built, externally heated with an oven height from 127 mm to 135 mm (5 in to 12 in), and have a drop-down door. An important feature is the even temperature throughout the oven.

Pastry ovens can be bought in single units or tiered on a stand, with each oven independently heated or with all decks heated by a single burner system. In the latter case there may be temperature differences between the ovens but indicating thermometers are normally fitted.

Proving ovens

These are low temperature ovens (27/32°C (80/90°F)) providing a warm, moist atmosphere essential for successful fermentation of dough, and are used in conjunction with pastry ovens. They are self-contained units fitted with a heater, a vapour-generating pan and a water feed tank.

GRILLERS AND SALAMANDERS

Grillers are of two main types:

1 **Underfired**. These are sometimes known as flare grills, with the source of heat below the meat. Burners are located underneath refractory brick or lava rock, the liquid fat falls on the heated material, flares and the smoke and flame impart to the meat a charcoal-cooked flavour and appearance.
2 **Overfired (salamanders)**. The source of heat — from refractory bricks or a metal fret — is above the food.

Grillers are used to cook food by radiant heat.

Underfired grillers are mainly used for chops and steaks but overfired grills can also be used for making toast and for quick heating of dishes before service. Overfired grills are more versatile

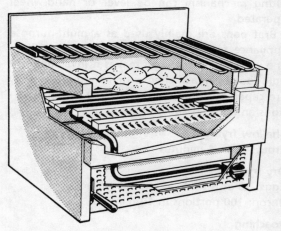

Countertop underfired grill (flare)

Overfired griller (salamander)

because of the extra uses to which they can be put. Underfired grills with their 'flare' effect are often used when cooking is carried out in the public view. Grills are available with wall brackets, as free standing units, or fitted to the pot rack on a range except over a solid top. Some models may be tiered or have a counter stand.

GRIDDLE PLATES

These are sometimes known as dry plates, and are solid plates usually provided with a drain channel, and heated from below by a gas bar burner. They are used for fast or continuous frying of eggs, bacon, liver, steak, chops, etc. or hamburgers and pancakes.

Griddles are chosen according to menu requirements but are particularly useful for call-order cooking in snack bars and grill rooms. A 610 × 457 mm (24 × 18 in) plate can accommodate:

- 30 eggs (2–4 minutes cooking time)
- 80 rashers of bacon cooking time (3–5 minutes cooking time)
- 12 × 113 g (4 oz) minute steaks (2–3 minutes cooking time)
- 32 × 113 g (4 oz) hamburgers for 1½–3 minutes at one time.

Proper ventilation hoods with grease filters are essential.

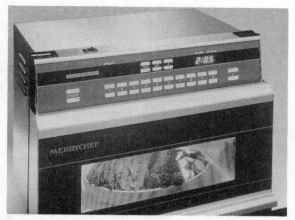

A commercial microwave oven

An electric convection/microwave combination oven

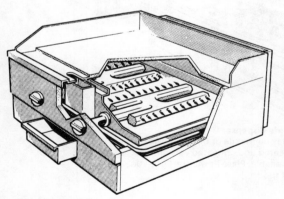

Countertop griddle

Reproduced by kind permission of Merrychef Ltd

A gas/microwave combination oven

MICROWAVES

(See Chapter 15 Microwaving, p 416)

A range of microwave ovens

FOOD COUNTERS

In recent years there has been an increasing tendency towards assisted and/or self-help counter-service operations which has developed because of the need to serve large numbers of people quickly and efficiently. Almost any type of food can be displayed on an electrically controlled service counter: soups, casseroles, roasts, vegetable dishes and cooked desserts, along with a choice of cold meats, salads, fruits and pastries, etc.

Food counters may be:

- a comprehensive combination of units catering for the needs of a staff restaurant or large canteen
- small counter-top units for the display of a limited menu, particularly useful in pubs and clubs
- refrigerated, ambient and heated display cupboards and back bar cooking equipment in small cafés and fast food operations

- mobile, heated, ambient or refrigerated for function catering
- salad bards and carveries
- refrigerated hors d'oeuvre or sweet trolleys in a restaurant
- insulated mobile cabinets to transport hospital food from the kitchen to patients.

When selecting and arranging counter equipment, it is important to bear in mind the number of people to be served over a particular time. Where large numbers of people need to be served over a short period of time, it may be necessary to concentrate each type of food, i.e. hot dishes, salads, snacks, beverages in separate areas or in echelon style with each menu clearly indicated. This means people can go directly to the sort of food they require. Gravies, sauces, napkins and cutlery could be made available on mobile self-help units away from the main counter.

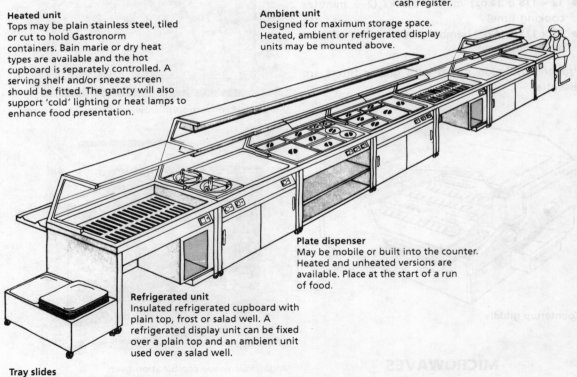

Heated unit
Tops may be plain stainless steel, tiled or cut to hold Gastronorm containers. Bain marie or dry heat types are available and the hot cupboard is separately controlled. A serving shelf and/or sneeze screen should be fitted. The gantry will also support 'cold' lighting or heat lamps to enhance food presentation.

Ambient unit
Designed for maximum storage space. Heated, ambient or refrigerated display units may be mounted above.

Cashier unit
Incorporates locking drawer and foot rest and comes in right – or left-handed versions. Fitted with 13 amp socket for cash register.

Refrigerated unit
Insulated refrigerated cupboard with plain top, frost or salad well. A refrigerated display unit can be fixed over a plain top and an ambient unit used over a salad well.

Plate dispenser
May be mobile or built into the counter. Heated and unheated versions are available. Place at the start of a run of food.

Tray slides
Available in different styles and in widths to suit standard sizes of unit.

Modular food service units

DISHWASHERS

A complete range of heavy duty, automatic dishwashers are available, from front loading smaller machines, right through to the large capacity, side loading machines. These feature a conveyor belt which carries the dirty dishes into the machine and the clean ones back out.

A pass-through dishwasher for corner or straight-line installation

An undercounter dishwasher with pumped waste

A conveyor dishwasher

REFRIGERATORS

THE MOST effective planning begins with initial handling and storage of food and takes you right through cooking, presentation, serving and cleaning up afterwards. In this brochure we demonstrate how each stage in this catering chain can be carried out most effectively using electricity.

The basic units for the refrigerated storage of chilled or frozen foods are reach-in cabinets which make economical use of floor space. They also ensure that food is stored at the correct temperature, thus substantially reducing waste whilst providing hygienic storage capacity. The cabinets are designed to give easy access to the contents which allows for good stock rotation again minimising waste. Built-in features include adjustable shelves to allow for large items and glass panel doors for display of goods if required.

A variety of cabinets are available to suit every need and every temperature requirement from storing wine to chilled meat, fish, frozen food, general use and even dual temperature cabinets for the most versatile storage.

Chest freezer cabinets are also available for bulk storage of frozen food with low running costs, whilst walk-in cabinets and cold rooms are the ideal answer to food storage for larger catering needs, with visual and audible alarms available for the protection of the food and your staff.

Refrigerated preparation units allow food to be stored on site at point of use where it is most convenient.

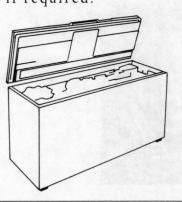 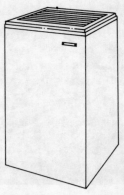 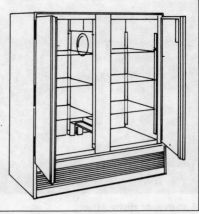

Pots and pans

1 Sauteuse

This is a shallow, long-handled vessel with sloping sides and a wide surface area, made of tin-lined copper. It is predominantly used in the preparation of sauces in which reductions or rapid reducing (evaporation) is required. The wide surface area ensures a speedy evaporation. It is also used for re-heating vegetables in butter as the sloping sides facilitate 'tossing' of vegetables during this process and may be used for stove top stewing. It is available in various sizes, e.g. 20 cm (8 in) diameter, 7 cm (2¾ in) deep.

Sauteuse   Plat à sauter/sauté pan

2 Plat à sauter (sauté pan)

This is a shallow, long-handled vessel, made of tin-lined copper or aluminium with straight sides and a wide surface area. It is ideal for use when preparing meat sautés where the food's juices are incorporated as an integral part of the finished product. It is available in various sizes, e.g. 15 cm (6 in) diameter, upwards.

3 Frying pan

Frying pans are solid-based pans, made of iron, steel, aluminium, vitrified iron or stainless steel, with shallow sloping sides and a wide surface area to ensure even heat for frying foods. They are

Frying pans

available in various sizes with long or side handles, e.g. 15 cm (6 in) base diameter, upwards

4 Friture

Whether round or oval, single or double-handled, a friture has a wire basket that fits into the pan. This type of pan can be used for all deep fat frying and batch frying small quantities.

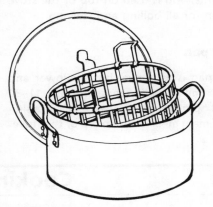

Friture

5 Stockpot

This deep, lidded, double-handled pan has a tap near the bottom for 'letting off' stock and is made from heavy-duty aluminium. Stockpots are used on top of the stove only for making large quantities of stock.

Stockpot

6 Stew pan, or saucepan

This type of aluminium pan is either single or double-handled with a lid. The single-handled type is used on top of the stove only, whereas the double-handled type is also used in the oven. Both types are used for all boiling and stewing.

7 Boiling pan

This aluminium pan has two handles and a lid and is available in a wide range of sizes – 2–65 litres (3½–114½ pints) and is used on top of the stove or in the oven for all boiling and stewing.

8 Braising pan

This type of pan is as above, but shallower and available in a similarly wide range of sizes – 11–30 litres (19–53 pints). It is used for braising vegetables or main meal items on top of the stove.

9 Omelette pan

Made from aluminium, copper or wrought steel, this type of pan is shallow, round and single-handled. It is used only for omelettes and crêpes (very thin pancakes).

Omelette pan

Cooking tins

1 Baking sheets

These are used:

- for bakery and confectionary
- under large and small containers to act as a drip tray
- to assist in the easy handling of batches of individual items.

2 Pie dishes

Usually made from aluminium, these dishes are available in a range of shapes. They are used for all baking of savoury and sweet pies or stewed items.

Pie dish

3 Pudding sleeves

These aluminium cylinders are available in 16–20 portion sizes. These are used for steamed sweets and savoury items.

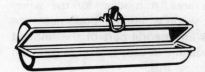

Pudding sleeve

4 Roasting tins

These are used for open oven roasting as they do not have lids. Tin foil covering can be used to protect the meat.

Roasting tin

Kitchen knives

1 Boning knife

This is used for the boning of raw or cooked meat. The carbon steel blade must be sharpened regularly.

Boning knife

2 Cook's knife, vegetable knife (103 or 155 mm/4 or 6 in)

This knife has a small, shaped handle and short carbon steel or stainless steel blade. It is used for fine preparation, vegetable paring and finishing.

Cook's knife, vegetable knife

3 Cook's knife (205 mm/8 in)

Cook's knives are also available with longer and heavier blades (255 or 305 mm/10 or 12 in) and are usually made from carbon steel, but can be of stainless steel. They are used for all preparation and chopping. The knife is rocked, using the whole length of the blade, for effective chopping.

Cook's knife

4 Filleting knife

This knife has a long, flexible carbon steel or stainless steel, 155 mm (6 in) blade. It is used for skinning and filleting fish.

Filleting knife

5 Palette knife

Palette knives have either carbon steel or stainless steel blades, 155, 205, 255 or 305 mm (6, 8, 10 or 12 in) long. They are used for moving prepared food, turning cooked food and lifting cooked food from oven trays.

Palette knife

6 Steel

This is carbon steel bar with either a wooden or a polypropylene handle. It is used for sharpening all steel knives.

Steel

NOTE: **With steel knives, it is possible to achieve a very sharp edge on a steel knife, but it needs to be sharpened regularly, ideally after each use.**

3

METHODS OF COOKERY

4

BOILING AND SIMMERING

Boiling is classified as either

(a) rapid, in a rapidly boiling liquid at 100°C (212°F), or
(b) simmering, at a temperature just below boiling point, 95°C (200°F).

The choice of method will depend on the type of food to be cooked. The food must always be covered by the liquid. The cooking liquid is usually water but can also be meat stock, vegetable stock, court bouillon or milk.

There are two techniques in boiling:

1 Placing the food into cold water and bringing to the boil. This method is used to soften fibrous materials in root vegetables such as potatoes, carrots and parsnips; to extract the flavours in stock making; to remove excess salt from cured and pickled meat and also to aid in the removal of impurities and scum.

2 By placing the food directly into boiling water. This method is used to seal in the flavour of meats and small cuts of fish; to reduce the overall cooking time; to minimise vitamin loss; and to set the protein and colour in green vegetables.

The main advantages of boiling are:

(a) It needs little attention and is, therefore, labour-saving.
(b) Because the liquid is in direct contact with the food being cooked, it is an efficient and cheap method of heat transfer.
(c) Provided sufficient liquid is maintained to cover the food during cooking, there will be little shrinkage or drying out.
(d) In the case of soups and stocks it is a nutritious method because all of the food is served.

The cooking vessel used for boiling will usually be a saucepan, a boiling or bratt pan or a stock pot with a lid. The size is determined by the amount of food to be cooked. In large commercial establishments steam jacket boilers are used.

NOTE: In a traditional kitchen four parties are involved with the preparation and cooking of boiled foods:

(a) chef entremettier
(b) chef garde-manger
(c) chef poissonnier
(d) chef saucier.

Terms associated with boiling	
à la crème Served in or napped with a cream sauce or fresh cream.	*Au gratin* Coated with cheese sauce, sprinkled with grated cheese and breadcrumbs and browned under a salamander.
à la menthe Cooked with fresh mint leaves and garnished with whole or chopped blanched leaves.	*Aux fines herbes* Finished with a sprinkling of fresh fine herbs.
Amandine Garnished with sliced sauted almonds and finely chopped parsley.	*Batch cooking* The technique of cooking in small quantities as required.
Au beurre A light coating of butter.	

Beurre fondu Accompanied by a sauceboat of melted butter.

Beurre manié A paste made from blending equal quantities of butter and flour which is used to thicken liquids.

Beurre noisette Butter cooked to a nut brown colour.

Blanc Cooking in a liquid consisting of water, lemon juice and flour; used to protect the colour and texture of light coloured vegetables and meats.

Blanched (a) a method of partially cooking food for use at a later stage. (b) a method used to remove impurities from meat by placing them in cold water, bringing to the boil, discarding the water and replacing with fresh water.

Bouquet garni Thyme, bay leaf, parsley stalks placed in a small piece of muslin cloth or wrapped in leek leaves and celery, and then tied with string.

Bouquetière A selection of cooked vegetables, usually carrots, cauliflower, French beans and turnips served au beurre.

Brunoise A cut of vegetable, 2 mm dice.

Cartouche A piece of greased greaseproof paper cut to the shape of the saucepan or bowl and used to protect the surface of the food from drying out.

Chauffant Pan of boiling salted water used to reheat foods.

Clouté Usually refers to an onion with a bay leaf placed on the surface and pierced with three cloves.

Concassé Roughly chopped tomato flesh.

Cooked out Usually describes flour that has been cooked to the stage when it loses its starchy taste.

Court bouillon A cooking liquor for fish consisting of water or stock, wine or vinegar and root vegetables.

Croûtons Shaped pieces of fried bread.

Deglacer Swilling out a pan or roasting tray in which food has been cooked with water, wine or stock in order to extract the flavourings from the sediment to make an accompanying sauce or gravy.

Dégraisser The process of skimming fat away.

Jardinière A cut of vegetable, 3 mm × 3 mm × 18 mm (small sticks or bâtons).

Julienne A cut of vegetable, 2 mm × 2 mm × 4 cm (thin strips).

Liaison A mixture of egg yolks and cream whisked together and used to enrich and thicken sauces.

Macédoine A cut of vegetables, ½ cm dice.

Mirepoix Roughly cut vegetables used as an arromat in sauce making.

Monter au beurre The process of incorporating chilled butter pieces into sauces to thicken and improve the glaze.

Nature (au) Served plain.

Panaché A selection of vegetables served au beurre.

Paysanne A cut of vegetable. There are four accepted methods of cutting paysanne: 1 cm sided triangles; 1 cm sided squares; 1 cm rounds; 1 cm rough sided rounds.

Persillé Brushed with melted butter and sprinkled liberally with finely chopped parsley.

Petit pois flamande Flemish style, a combination of half the amount of carrots cut jardinière or macédoine with garden peas.

Polonaise Sprinkled with sieved hard boiled egg white and egg yolk, finely chopped parsley and fried breadcrumbs; napped with beurre noisette.

Primeurs As for bouquetière but using spring vegetables.

Purée A purée of vegetables – carrots, swede, turnip – or fruit (e.g. apple) which is cooked, drained and passed through a sieve or mouli.

Vichy A French mineral water used for cooking vegetables.

Stocks

Stocks are used for the foundation of soups, sauces, stews and gravies, and are made from raw bones, vegetables, herbs and water. The flavours and soluble nutrients of meats, herbs and vegetables are extracted by prolonged and gentle simmering. This usually takes between six and eight hours. The exception to this rule is fish stock which only takes 20 minutes.

There are two basic methods of making meat stocks, either white stock (fond blanc) or brown stock (fond brun). The meat used to flavour the stock will depend on what the final stock is to be used for. Brown beef stock would be used for brown beef stews as white lamb stock would be used for a white lamb stew. Not all meats are suitable to make stock. On the right is a list of meats suitable to be used for stock making.

Meats	The stocks (English)	The stocks (French)
1 Beef bones	white beef stock	fond blanc or fond de marmite
	brown beef stock	fond brun or estouffade
2 Mutton/Lamb bones	white mutton/ lamb stock	fond blanc de mouton
	brown mutton/lamb stock	fond brun de mouton
3 Chicken bones or a boiling fowl	white chicken stock	fond blanc de volaille
	brown chicken stock	fond brun de volaille
4 Veal bones	white veal stock	fond blanc de veau
	brown veal stock	fond brun de veau
5 Game bones	brown game stock	fond de giber

Basic recipe and method of cooking for all white meat stocks

Yield: 4 litres

Step	Commodity	Quantity	
1	Raw bones	2 kg	Chop up and remove any fat or marrow. Place in a suitably sized stockpot.
2	Cold water	5 litres	Add to the bones and bring to the boil.
			NOTE: If the scum is excessive and dirty, wash bones under running cold water, re-cover with the same amount of water and re-boil, then return to a simmer.
3	Carrots, leeks, celery, onions	125 g of each vegetable	Wash, peel and leave whole. Add to the simmering stock.
4	Bouquet garni	1	Add to the vegetables and stock.
5	Peppercorns	12 only	Add and simmer for 6 to 8 hours.

White meat glaze

A white meat glaze is made by steadily boiling the strained white stock until it reduces to a sticky, gelatinous consistency. It can be used to improve the flavour and strength of soups, sauces and stews.

□   □   □

Basic recipe and method of cooking for all brown meat stocks

Step	Commodity	Quantity		Yield: 4 litres
1	Raw bones	2 kg	Chop up and remove any fat or marrow. Place in a roasting pan and brown in a hot oven (220°C/425°F) or place in a frying pan and brown. Drain off the surplus fat and place the bones in a suitably sized stockpot. Retain the oven tray or frying pan.	
2	Carrots, leeks, celery, onions	125 g of each vegetable	Wash, peel and leave whole. Add to the oven tray/frying pan and brown. Drain away any fat. Add ½ litre of boiling water and deglace for a few minutes to extract all the sediment. Pour over the bones.	
3	Cold water	5 litres	Add to the bones and vegetables, then bring to the boil. Reduce the heat to a simmer. Skim any scum or fat.	
4	Bouquet garni	1	Add to the vegetables and bones.	
5	Peppercorns	12 only	Add and simmer for 6 to 8 hours.	

NOTE: In brown stocks washed mushroom trimmings and soft tomatoes can be added to improve the flavour.

Brown meat glaze

A brown meat glaze is made from steadily boiling the strained brown stock till it reduces to a sticky, gelatinous consistency. It can be used to improve the flavour and strength of soups, sauces and stews.

□   □   □

Basic recipe and method of cooking for fish stock

Step	Commodity	Quantity		Yield: 4 litres
1	Margarine or butter	50 g	Melt in a suitably sized, thick-bottomed saucepan.	
2	Onions	200 g	Peel, slice thinly and add to the melted fat.	
3	Raw fish bones — sole, whiting or turbot	2 kg	Wash well, remove any offal and again wash well. Chop up and add to the onions.	
4	Lemon	½	Extract the juice and add to the fish bones. Discard the lemon.	
5	Peppercorns	6	Add to the other ingredients and stir.	
6	Bay leaf	1	Add to the other ingredients.	
7	Parsley stalks	10 g	Add and stir well, cover with greaseproof paper and a lid and sweat for 5 minutes.	
8	Water	4 litres	Add to the other ingredients stirring continuously. Bring to the boil then simmer for 20 minutes before straining for use.	

NOTE: It will be necessary to remove any scum or any other impurities that may settle on the surface during the cooking process. The stock might go cloudy if it is not skimmed regularly during the cooking process. If the incorrect bones are used or the correct bones are left in the stock for longer than required the stock may have a bitter taste and will have to be discarded. Alternatively, bitterness may be caused by an insufficient cooking time.

Fish glaze

A fish glaze is made from steadily boiling the stock till it reduces to a sticky, gelatinous consistency. It can be used to improve the flavour and strength of soups, sauces and stews. For storage purposes the fish glaze should be transferred to a plastic or porcelain container with a tight-fitting lid and kept refrigerated.

☐ ☐ ☐

General rules about the preparation and cooking of stocks

1 Always use fresh bones and vegetables. Never use unsound meat or bones or rotten vegetables.
2 Fats and scum should be skimmed as soon as they form as they give the stock an unpleasant flavour and greasy taste.
3 Stock should always simmer gently – too rapidly and it will evaporate and go cloudy, too slowly and it might go sour.
4 Salt should never be added to stock as it will become too concentrated through the prolonged cooking process and spoil the flavour.
5 Stock for storage should be strained, re-boiled, rapidly cooled (preferably in a blast chiller) then placed in a refrigerator until required.

Sauces and gravies

A basic sauce is made from a liquid (stock or milk) and a thickening agent. Certain starches need to be 'cooked out' in order to disperse the granules before mixing with a liquid. This is achieved by adding the flour to a melted fat/oil to form a roux and cooking to the required stage, depending on the type of sauce being made. Some thickening agents are dissolved in a cold liquid before adding to the boiling stock. Other thickening agents such as blood and egg yolks are added to a simmering liquid and never re-boiled as the sauce will curdle.

A definition of a good sauce is one that has:

(a) a creamy consistency – it must coat the back of a spoon;
(b) a good colour – the colour must be distinct and not dull; and
(c) a smooth texture and bright gloss. This is achieved by passing the sauce through a strainer or a tammy cloth, or by liquidising.

Thickening agents

1 Arrowroot, cornflour and fecule

These thickening agents are diluted in a cold liquid, then stirred into the boiling liquid, allowed to re-boil and simmer. Flour can also be diluted in water and added to a boiling stock for thickening purposes. This method is known as jay zee, but it must be strained carefully before adding.

2 Beurre manié

This is made from equal quantities of softened butter/margarine and flour kneaded to a smooth paste and mixed into a boiling liquid. It is mainly used for fish dishes.

3 Blood

Blood is used in jugged hare.

4 Egg yolks

The egg yolks are whisked to the ribbon stage. This is called a sabayon and is used in hot and cold butter sauces, custard sauce, and in béchamel and velouté extensions.

5 Glazes

Fish or meat glazes can be made into sauces by adding butter and/or cream.

6 A roux

There are three stages of roux:

(a) **Roux blanc** White roux
   Made with butter or margarine and flour and used to thicken béchamel sauce.

Method of preparation

Melt the required amount of fat over gentle heat, add an equal amount of flour and mix thoroughly. Cook for a few minutes without colouring.

(b) Roux blond Sandy roux

Made with butter or margarine and used to thicken velouté, tomato sauce and certain soups.

Method of preparation

Melt the required amount of fat over gentle heat, add an equal amount of flour and mix thoroughly. Cook for a few minutes allowing the roux to change to a sandy colour.

(c) Roux brun Brown roux

Made with dripping, lard or vegetable oil and used to thicken espagnole and certain soups.

Method of preparation

Melt the required amount of fat over gentle heat, add an equal amount of flour and mix thoroughly. Cook until the roux takes on a rich brown colour. Beware of over-cooking the roux as it will create a bitter flavour in the final preparation.

7 Vegetable or fruit purées

A vegetable or fruit puree is known as a coulis and is mainly used in cuisine au natural.

WHITE ROUX (BLANC) SAUCES

White sauce   Sauce béchamel

🍲 20–30 min

Step	Commodity	1 litre	5 litre	
1	Milk	1 litre	5 litre	Place in a saucepan.
2	Onion	1 small	1 large	Peel and leave whole. Place a bayleaf across the centre and pierce with three cloves. This is called an onion clouté and is added to the milk. Bring the milk to the boil gently, allowing the milk and onion clouté to infuse. Remove from the stove and place on a cooling triangle.
	Bay leaf	1	1	
	Cloves	3	3	
3	Butter/margarine	90 g	450 g	Melt gently in a suitably sized thick-bottomed pan.
4	Plain flour	90 g	450 g	Add to the fat and cook to a first stage roux. Place to the side of the stove and allow to cool for a few minutes. Add ¼ of the warm milk to the roux and stir continuously until the two are combined. Add another ¼ of the milk, stirring to the boil. Add the rest of the milk.

Extensions of béchamel

NOTE: The additions are made to the sauce after it has been strained and just before serving, otherwise it might curdle.

Additions

Sauce	Per 1 litre	Per 5 litre	Served with
Anchovy (anchois)	2 tbsp anchovy essence (approximately)	6 tbsp anchovy essence (approximately)	Poached, fried or boiled fish
Cheese (Mornay)	100 g grated cheese	500 g grated cheese	Poached or boiled fish and vegetable dishes
	2 egg yolks	8 egg yolks	
	50 ml double cream	250 ml double cream	

Sauce	Per 1 litre	Per 5 litre	Served with
Cream (crème)	110 ml double cream 10 g butter	400 ml double cream 50 g butter	Poached fish and boiled vegetables
Egg (sauce aux oeufs)	4 hard boiled eggs (finely diced)	12 hard boiled eggs (finely diced)	Poached or boiled fish dishes
Mustard (moutarde)	10 g English mustard diluted to a paste 50 ml double cream	40 g English mustard diluted to a paste 250 double cream	Grilled herrings
Onion (oignon)	150 g thinly sliced sweated onions	500 g thinly sliced sweated onions	Roast mutton
Parsley (persil)	2 tbsp finely chopped parsely 50 ml double cream	6 tbsp finely chopped parsley 250 ml double cream	Poached or boiled fish and vegetable dishes
Shrimp (aux crevettes)	75 g shrimp butter 100 g shrimp tails 50 ml double cream	300 g shrimp butter 400 shrimp tails 250 ml double cream	Poached or boiled fish dishes
Soubise (soubise)	150 g thinly sliced sweated onions passed through a strainer	500 g thinly sliced sweated onions passed through a strainer	Roast mutton

NOTE: With fish dishes a little of the cooking liquor or fish stock can be used to thin the sauce if required.

□　　　□　　　□

SANDY ROUX (BLOND) SAUCES

Sauces made from white meat stock and a blond roux

Velouté

☺ 20 min ♨ 1 hr approx.

Step	Commodity	1 litre	5 litre	
1	Butter or margarine	75 g	375 g	Melt gently in a suitably sized thick-bottomed pan.
2	Flour	75 g	375 g	Add to the fat and cook to a sandy texture. Take care not to over-colour the roux. Allow the roux to cool slightly.
3	White stock	1 litre	5 litre	Warm the stock. Return the roux to the stove. Add ¼ of the stock and mix thoroughly. Add another ¼ of the stock and bring to the boil. Add the remaining stock, bring to the boil and simmer for 1 hour.

NOTE: A velouté sauce is usually finished by enriching with a liaison of egg yolks and cream. Care must be taken not to re-boil as the liaison will curdle and spoil the sauce.

Extensions of velouté

Additions

Sauce	pr 1 litre	per 5 litre	Served with
Aurore (aurore)	1 tbsp tomato purée (mix well)	4 tbsp tomato purée (mix well)	Boiled chicken, poached eggs, chaud froid work
Caper (aux capres)	50 g chopped capers	250 g chopped capers	Boiled leg of mutton
Ivory (ivoire)	2 tsp meat glaze	2 tbsp meat glaze	Boiled chicken
Mushroom (aux champignons)	100 g thin sliced sweated mushrooms	500 g thin sliced sweated mushrooms	Boiled chicken, sweetbreads
Suprême (suprême)	50 g white mushroom trimmings. Strain before using. 1 tsp lemon juice	500 g white mushroom trimmings. Strain before using. 1 tbsp lemon juice	Boiled chicken, vol au vents, chaud froid, stews, soups

Sauces made from fish stock and a blond roux   Velouté de poisson

⏲ 20 min   🍲 1 hr approx

Step	Commodity	1 litre	5 litre	
1	Butter or margarine	75 g	375 g	Melt gently in a suitably sized thick-bottomed pan.
2	Flour	75 g	375 g	Add to the fat and cook to a sandy texture. Take care not to over-colour the roux. Allow the roux to cool slightly.
3	White stock	1 litre	5 litre	Warm the stock. Return the roux to the stove. Add ¼ of the stock and mix thoroughly. Add another ¼ and bring to the boil. Add the remaining stock, bring to the boil and simmer for 1 hour.

NOTES: A velouté sauce is usually finished by enriching with a liaison of egg yolks and cream. Care must be taken not to re-boil as the liaison will curdle and spoil the sauce.

Fish velouté sauces are served with poached fish dishes and the additions to the basic sauce are cooked with the fish. Therefore, velouté extension sauces are to be found in Chapter 7: Poaching.

BROWN ROUX (BRUN) SAUCES

Sauces made from brown meat stock and a brown roux

Espagnole

🥄 30 min ♨ 4–6 hrs

Step	Commodity	1 litre	5 litre	
1	Dripping or oil	50 g	250 g	Melt in a suitably sized, thick-bottomed saucepan.
2	Plain flour	50 g	250 g	Add to the fat and cook out slowly to a light brown colour. Stir frequently to ensure even browning. Place to the side of the stove and allow to cool.
3	Tomato purée	25 g	125 g	Add to the cooled roux and mix well.
4	Brown stock	1 litre	5 litres	Add ¼ and mix well. Add another ¼ and bring to the boil. Add the remaining stock, return to the boil, then simmer.
5	Carrot	100 g	500 g	Peel and cut into mirepoix. Place in a bowl for use later.
6	Onion	100 g	500 g	Peel, slice in half and cut into mirepoix. Add to the carrots.
7	Celery	50 g	250 g	Wash and cut into mirepoix. Place with the other vegetables.
8	Dripping and oil	50 g	250 g	Place in a suitably sized frying pan. Heat and add the mirepoix vegetables. Lightly brown the vegetables. Drain off any surplus fat. Add the vegetables to the sauce. Skim regularly. Simmer for the required time. Strain and store appropriately.

NOTE: Espagnole sauce is not usually used in its basic form. It is usually refined by mixing with an equal amount of brown stock then reduced by half. This is called demi-glace (half-glaze) and is the basis of all brown sauce derivitives. It should also be noted that the modern trend is to move away from such roux-based sauces and replace them with cornflour or arrowroot thickened sauces.

4

Extensions of demi-glace (half-glaze)

Additions

Commodity	per 1 litre	per 5 litre	
Bolognaise (bolognaise)	50 ml cooking oil	200 ml cooking oil	Place in a suitably sized frying pan and heat.
	250 g minced beef	1¼ kg minced beef	Add to the heated oil and fry lightly.
	1 clove garlic	4 cloves of garlic	Peel, crush and chop. Add to the mince.
	150 g onions	500 g onions	Peel, cut in half and finely dice. Add to the mince and allow to cook until the mince becomes soft. Drain off any surplus fat.
	50 g tomato purée	250 g tomato purée	Add and mix thoroughly. Add the appropriate amount of demi-glace, season with salt and pepper, and simmer until the meat is cooked. Skim as necessary.
			Served with: Pasta.

Commodity	per 1 litre	per 5 litre	
Bordelaise (bordelaise)	200 shallots	800 g shallots	Peel and chop finely. Place in a sauteuse.
	500 ml red wine	2 litre red wine	Pour over the shallots.
	1 tsp mignonette pepper	2 tbsp mignonette pepper	Add to the wine.
	1 small sprig thyme	1 large sprig thyme	Add to the other ingredients and place on the heat. Allow to rèduce to a quarter of the initial amount. Add the appropriate amount of demi glace and simmer for 30 minutes. Correct the seasoning. Pass through a fine strainer.
	50 g poached beef marrow or meat glaze	250 poached beef marrow or meat glaze	Add the meat glaze. Combine with the sauce. Poached beef marrow is sliced thinly and served on fried steaks.
			Serve with: Fried and grilled steaks.
Brown onion (lyonnaise)	500 g onions	2½ kg onions	Peel, cut in half and slice thinly.
	25 g butter	125 g butter	Place in a suitably sized frying pan, heat and add the onions. Brown lightly.
	100 ml dry white wine	500 ml dry white wine	Place in a measuring jug.
	50 ml wine vinegar	250 ml wine vinegar	Add to the white wine. Pour the liquid over the browned onions and deglacer. Reduce by two-thirds, then add the appropriate amount of demi-glace. Simmer for 30 minutes. Remove any fat or scum that might form on the surface.
			Serve with: Fried liver, Hamburg or Vienna Steaks.
Charcutiere (charcutière)	50 g butter	250 butter	Melt in a suitably sized sauteuse.
	200 g onions	1 kg onions	Peel, cut in half and finely chop. Add to the butter and cook gently without colouring.
	200 ml white wine vinegar	1 litre white wine vinegar	Add to the softened onions and reduce by two-thirds. Add the appropriate amount of demi-glace and simmer for 20 minutes. Skim as required.
	½ tbsp English mustard diluted to a paste	2 tbsp English mustard diluted to a paste	Dilute with a little water.
	15 g castor sugar	75 g castor sugar	Add to the water and add to the sauce. Correct the seasoning.
	100 g gherkins	500 g gherkins	Slice into julienne and add to the finished sauce.
			Serve with: Pork chops

Commodity	per 1 litre	per 5 litre	
Chasseur (chasseur)	100 g butter	400 g butter	Melt in a suitably sized sauteuse.
	50 g shallots	250 g shallots	Peel, cut in half and finely dice. Add to the melted butter and cook gently without colouring.
	200 g button mushrooms	1 kg button mushrooms	Slice thinly and add to the shallots. Cover and cook gently without colouring for 5 minutes. Drain off any excess fat.
	250 ml dry white	1 litre dry white	Add to the mixture and reduce by two-thirds.
	400 g tomatoes	1½ kg tomatoes	Remove the eyes. Place in a saucepan of boiling water for 10 seconds. Refresh immediately in ice-cold water. Remove the skins and discard. Cut in half, remove the seeds and discard. Chop the flesh into small dice and add to the sauce. Simmer for 30 minutes. Correct the seasoning and skim as required.
	1 small bunch tarragon	1 large bunch tarragon	Remove the leaves and discard the stalks.
	10 g parsley leaves	50 g parsley leaves	Wash, dry and place on a chopping board with the tarragon. Chop finely and add to the sauce.
			Serve with: Chicken, fried steaks and chops.

NOTE: A small amount of garlic can be added with the onions as an optional extra.

Commodity	per 1 litre	per 5 litre	
Devilled (diable)	200 g shallots	800 g shallots	Peel and chop finely. Place in a sauteuse.
	400 ml dry white wine	1½ litre dry white wine	Pour over the shallots.
	100 ml wine vinegar	500 ml wine vinegar	Add to the mixture.
	1 tspn mignonette pepper	2 tbsp mignonette pepper	Pour over the other ingredients.
	10 g cayenne pepper	40 g cayenne pepper	Sprinkle over the liquid. Place on the stove and allow to reduce by three-quarters. Add the appropriate amount of demi-glace and simmer for 30 minutes. Correct the seasoning. Pass through a fine strainer.
			Serve with: fried meats, poultry and fish

Commodity	per 1 litre	per 5 litre	
Italian (Italienne)	100 g butter	500 g butter	Melt in a suitably sized sauteuse.
	50 g shallots	250 g shallots	Peel, cut in half and finely dice. Cook gently in the melted butter for 5 minutes without colouring.
	200 g mushrooms	1 kg mushrooms	Wash and finely dice. Add to the shallots and cook for a further 5 minutes without colouring. Add the appropriate amount of demi-glace.
	400 g tomatoes	1½ kg tomatoes	Remove the eyes. Place in a saucepan of boiling water for 10 seconds. Refresh immediately in ice-cold water. Remove the skins and discard. Cut in half and remove the seeds and discard. Chop the flesh into small dice and add to the sauce.
	100 g lean cooked ham	500 g lean cooked ham	Cut into julienne and add to the sauce.
	1 small bunch tarragon	1 large bunch tarragon	Remove the leaves and discard the stalks. Wash, dry and place on a chopping board.
	1 small bunch chervil	1 large bunch chervil	Remove the leaves and discard the stalks. Mix with the tarragon.
	10 g parsley leaves	50 g parsley leaves	Wash, dry and place on the chopping board with the tarragon and chervil. Chop finely and add to the sauce.
			Serve with: Escalope of veal.
Madeira (Madere)	150 ml Madeira wine	500 ml Madeira wine	Place in a suitably sized sauteuse and heat. Add the appropriate amount of demi-glace and bring to the boil. Correct the seasoning and skim when necessary. Pass through a fine chinois.
	100 g butter	500 g butter	Cut the butter into 1 cm pieces and 'monte' into the sauce.
			Serve with: Braised ox tongue, sweetbreads, veal escalopes and ham.
Marsala (marsala)	150 ml Marsala wine	500 ml Marsala wine	Place in a suitably sized sauteuse and heat. Add the appropriate amount of demi-glace and bring to the boil. Correct the seasoning and skim when necessary. Pass through a fine chinois.
	100 g butter	500 g butter	Cut the butter into 1 cm pieces and 'monte' into the sauce.
			Serve with: Braised ox tongue, sweetbreads, veal escalopes and ham.

Commodity	per 1 litre	per 5 litre	
Piquante (piquante)	200 ml white wine vinegar	1 litre white wine vinegar	Place in a suitably sized sauteuse.
	200 g shallots	1 kg shallots	Peel, cut in half and finely dice. Add to the vinegar. Place on the stove and cook until it has reduced by two-thirds. Add the appropriate amount of demi-glace and simmer for 30 minutes.
	100 g gherkins	500 g gherkins	Cut into fine dice and retain in a bowl for use.
	50 g capers	250 g capers	Chop into small dice. Mix with the gherkins and add to the sauce.
	1 small bunch tarragon	1 large bunch tarragon	Remove the leaves and discard the stalks. Wash, dry and place on a chopping board.
	1 small bunch chervil	1 large bunch chervil	Remove the leaves and discard the stalks. Mix with the tarragon.
	10 g parsley leaves	50 g parsley leaves	Wash, dry and place on the chopping board with the tarragon and chervil. Chop finely and add to the sauce.
			Serve with: Grilled meats.
Poivrade (poivrade)	100 g butter	1 kg butter	Melt in a suitably sized sauteuse.
	200 g carrots	1 kg carrots	Peel, cut into mirepoix and retain for use later.
	200 g onions	1 kg onions	Peel, cut into mirepoix and place with the carrot.
	200 g celery	1 kg celery	Wash and cut into mirepoix. Mix with the other vegetables, add to the butter and allow to cook until a brown colour is achieved.
	1 small sprig thyme	1 large sprig thyme	Discard the stalks and add to the vegetables. Allow to cook for 2–3 minutes to infuse the flavours. Discard the fat.
	200 ml dry white wine	1 litre dry white wine	Pour over the vegetables.
	50 ml white wine vinegar	250 ml white wine vinegar	Add to the other ingredients and reduce by two-thirds. Add the appropriate amount of demi-glace. Correct the seasoning and simmer for 30 minutes. Skim as required. Pass through a fine chinois.
			Serve with: Venison.
Port (porto)	150 ml Port wine	500 ml Port wine	Place in a suitably sized sauteuse and heat. Add the appropriate amount of demi-glace and bring to the boil. Correct the seasoning and skim when necessary. Pass through a fine chinois.
	100 g butter	500 g butter	Cut the butter into 1 cm pieces and 'monte' into the sauce.
			Serve with: Braised ox tongue, sweetbreads, veal escalopes and ham.

4

Commodity	per 1 litre	per 5 litre	
Réform (réforme)	100 g butter	500 g butter	Melt in a suitably sized sauteuse.
	100 g carrots	500 g carrots	Peel, cut into mirepoix and retain for use later.
	100 g onions	500 g onions	Peel, cut into mirepoix and place with the carrot.
	50 g celery	250 g celery	Wash, cut into mirepoix. Mix with the other vegetables and add to the butter. Cook till a golden brown colour is achieved.
	1 small sprig thyme	1 large sprig thyme	Discard the stalks and add to the vegetables. Allow to cook for 2–3 minutes to infuse the flavours. Discard the fat.
	10 g peppercorns	50 g peppercorns	Crush with the back of a knife and sprinkle over the vegetables.
	100 ml white wine vinegar	500 ml white wine vinegar	Add to the mirepoix and reduce by two-thirds. Add the appropriate amount of demi-glace and simmer for 30 minutes. Skim as required.
	100 g redcurrant jelly	500 g redcurrant jelly	Add to the simmering sauce. Pass through a fine chinois.
	50 g cooked beetroot	400 g cooked beetroot	Peel and cut into julienne. Place in a bowl for use later.
	25 g gherkins	125 g gherkins	Cut into julienne and place with the beetroot.
	25 g cooked mushrooms	125 g cooked mushrooms	Cut into julienne add to the other ingredients.
	15 g cooked truffles	75 g cooked truffles	Cut into julienne and add to the other ingredients.
	25 g cooked tongue	125 g cooked tongue	Cut into julienne and add to the other ingredients.
	25 g cooked white of eggs	125 g cooked white of eggs	Wash to remove any trace of yolk. Cut into julienne. Add to the sauce along with the other ingredients just before service.
			Serve with: Lamb cutlets.
Robert (robert)	50 g butter	250 g butter	Place in a suitably sized sauteuse.
	200 g shallots	1 kg shallots	Peel, cut in half and finely dice. Add to the melted butter and cook gently for 5 minutes without colouring.
	250 ml white wine vinegar	1 litre white wine vinegar	Add to the cooked shallots and reduce by two-thirds. Add the appropriate amount of demi-glace. Simmer for 20 minutes.
	½ tbsp English mustard diluted to a paste	2 tbsp English mustard diluted to a paste	Dilute with a little water.
	15 g caster sugar	75 g castor sugar	Add to the water and add to the sauce. Correct the seasoning.
			Serve with: Grilled meats, fish and poultry.

Commodity	per 1 litre	per 5 litre	
Sherry (Xeres)	150 ml dry sherry	500 ml dry sherry	Place in a suitably sized sauteuse and heat. Add the appropriate amount of demi-glace and bring to the boil. Correct the seasoning and skim when necessary. Pass through a fine chinois.
	100 g butter	500 g butter	Cut the butter into 1 cm pieces and 'monte' into the sauce.

Serve with: Braised ox tongue, sweetbreads, veal escalopes and cooked ham.

☐   ☐   ☐

MISCELLANEOUS SAUCES

This section covers all non-conventional hot sauces recipes. Unless otherwise stated, quantities are given for ¼ litre and 1 litre servings.

Commodity	¼ litre	1 litre	
Apple (aux pommes)	400 g cooking apples	1½ kg cooking apples	Wash, peel, core, slice thinly into a bowl of water with a little lemon juice to ensure that they do not discolour.
	25 g butter	100 g butter	Place in a suitably sized sauteuse and heat gently. Drain the water off the apples, place in the sauteuse and cook gently.
	25 g sugar	100 g sugar	Add to the apples and mix in well.
	15 ml water	50 ml water	Pour over the apples. Cover the sauteuse with a tight-fitting lid and cook gently to a purée. Pass through a sieve to serve.

Serve with: Roast pork, duck and goose.

4

Commodity	¼ litre	1 litre	
Bearnaise	15 g shallots	60 g shallots	Peel, cut in half and finely dice. Place in a suitably sized sauteuse.
	6 peppercorns	24 peppercorns	Crush with a rolling pin or the back of a knife. Place with the shallots.
	5 g tarragon	20 g tarragon	Chop the leaves and stalks and add to the shallots.
	5 g chervil	20 g chervil	Chop as for tarragon and add to the other ingredients.
	50 ml tarragon vinegar	250 ml tarragon vinegar	Pour into the sauteuse and place on the heat. Reduce by two-thirds.
	25 ml cold water	100 ml cold water	Add to the sauteuse and allow to cool.
	2 egg yolks	8 egg yolks	Place the egg yolks in a clean bowl and whisk together. Mix into the cooled reduction. Return to a gentle heat, whisking continuously. The cooking of egg yolks to a thickened consistency is called a sabayon. The sabayon is ready when the mixture resembles double cream. Removed from the heat and cool slightly.
	200 g butter	800 g butter	Melt in a suitably sized saucepan. Gradually add the warm melted butter to the sabayon. Whisk thoroughly until all the butter is added. Correct the seasoning. Pass through a chinois and tammy cloth or muslin. Bérnaise is kept in a bain-marie and is served slightly warm.

Serve with: Grilled meat and fish dishes.

NOTE: To stabilise the sauce for service a little thick béchamel can be combined with the sauce before straining. This sauce will curdle if:

(a) the butter has been added too quickly; or
(b) the cooking temperature is too high.

A curdled sauce can be rectified by:

(a) placing a spoonful of boiling water in a clean sauteuse and adding the curdled sauce; or
(b) placing an egg yolk into a clean sauteuse and whisking lightly over a gentle heat. Remove from the heat and add the curdled mixture.

Melted butter (beurre fondu)	200 g butter	800 g butter	This sauce can be made by:
	50 ml dry white wine	200 ml dry white wine	(a) gently simmering the butter and wine till they are combined. Pass through a fine chinois and/or muslin. Or (b) melting the butter and carefully straining off the fat through a muslin and chinois leaving the sediment behind.

Serve with: Salmon, blue trout, sea kale and asparagus.

NOTE: Water may be used instead of wine.

Commodity	¼ litre	1 litre	
Bread (pain)	300 ml milk	1.2 litre milk	Place in a suitably sized saucepan.
	1 small onion	1 medium onion	Peel, leave whole and stud with three cloves. Place on the heat and bring to the boil. Remove from the heat and discard the onion and cloves.
	25 g white breadcrumbs	100 g white breadcrumbs	Mix into the milk and simmer for 5 minutes. Correct the consistency, and season with a little salt and cayenne pepper.
	15 g butter	50 g butter	Melt and pour over the sauce to prevent a skin from forming. Mix the butter in when serving.
			Serve with: Roast chicken and roast game.
Cranberry (airelles)	500 g cranberries	2 kg cranberries	Place in a suitably sized saucepan.
	50 g sugar	200 g sugar	Sprinkle over the cranberries.
	75 ml water	300 ml water	Add to the other ingredients and boil until the berries are soft. Serve warm.
			Serve with: Roast turkey.

NOTE: This sauce may be passed through a sieve for service.

Curry (kari)	15 g butter or oil	60 g butter or oil	Place in a suitably sized saucepan and heat gently.
	50 g onions	200 g onions	Peel, cut in half and finely dice. Add to the saucepan and cook without colouring for 5 minutes.
	10 g curry powder	40 g curry powder	Add to the onions and cook for a further 5 minutes to infuse the flavours.
	15 g flour	60 g flour	Add and gently cook to a brown (brun) coloured roux. Remove from the heat and allow to cool.
	5 g tomato purée	20 g tomatoe purée	Add to the cooled roux. Return to the heat.
	500 ml brown stock	2 litre brown stock	Add a quarter of the stock and mix thoroughly. Add another quarter and bring to the boil. Add the remaining stock, re-boil and return to a simmer.
	25 g apples	100 g apples	Peel, remove the core and chop finely. Add to the sauce.
	15 g chutney	60 g chutney	Chop finely and add to the sauce.
	15 g sultanas	60 g sultanas	Wash, chop finely and add to the sauce.
	10 g fresh ginger	40 g fresh ginger	Grate finely and add to the sauce. NOTE: If using powdered ginger use half the amount stated.
	10 g coconut butter	40 g coconut butter	Chop finely and add to the sauce. Season with salt and black pepper. Simmer for 1 hour. Skim as required. Correct the consistency and seasoning.
			Serve with: Poached or boiled eggs, vegetables, prawns and shrimps.

NOTE: If the sauce is too spicy it may be cooled by adding a small amount of natural yoghurt.

Commodity	¼ litre	1 litre	
Hollandaise (hollandaise)	6 peppercorns	24 peppercorns	Crush with a rolling pin or the back of a knife. Place in a suitably sized sauteuse.
	25 ml cold water	100 ml cold water	
	15 ml vinegar	60 ml vinegar	Pour into the sauteuse and place on the heat. Reduce by two-thirds.
	10 ml water	40 ml water	Add to the sauteuse and allow to cool.
	2 egg yolks	8 egg yolks	Place the egg yolks in a clean bowl and whisk together. Mix into the cooled reduction. Return to a gentle heat, whisking continuously. The cooking of egg yolks to a thickened consistency is called a sabayon. The sabayon is ready when the mixture resembles double cream. Remove from the heat and cool slightly.
	200 g butter	800 g butter	Melt in a suitably sized saucepan. Gradually add the warm melted butter to the sabayon. Whisk thoroughly until all the butter is added. Correct the seasoning. Pass through a chinois and tammy cloth or muslin. Hollandaise sauce is kept in a bain marie and is served slightly warm. *Serve with*: Salmon, trout, turbot, asparagus, broccoli and cauliflower.

NOTE: To stabilise the sauce for service a little thick béchamel may be combined with the sauce before straining. This sauce will curdle if:

(a) the butter has been added to quickly. Or
(b) the cooking temperature is too high.

The curdled sauce can be rectified by:

(a) placing a spoonful of boiling water in a clean sauteuse and adding the curdled sauce; or
(b) placing an egg yolk into a clean sauteuse and whisking lightly over a gentle heat. Remove from the heat and add the curdled mixture.

Unless otherwise stated, quantities are given for ¼ litre and 1 litre servings.

Commodity	¼ litre	1 litre	
Roast gravy (jus roti)	250 g raw bones	1 kg raw bones	Using the appropriate type of bone, i.e. beef bones for roast beef gravy etc., chop up into small pieces and place in a suitably sized roasting tray. Place in an oven pre-heated to 190°C (375°F) for 1½ hours. Remove from the oven and place on top of the stove. Drain any excess oil into a container for use later.
	50 g onions	200 g onions	Peel, cut into mirepoix and retain.
	50 g carrots	200 g carrots	Peel, cut into mirepoix and retain.
	25 g celery	100 g celery	Wash and cut into mirepoix. Mix with the other ingredients. Using the oil from the bones fry the vegetables in a suitably sized frying pan. Add to the bones.
	250 ml suitable stock	1 litre suitable stock	Pour over the bones and vegetables and deglacer. Bring to the boil and simmer for 30 minutes. Remove any fat or scum that may have risen to the surface. Strain through a fine chinois. Correct the seasoning. *Serve with*: All roast meats.

Commodity	¼ litre	1 litre	
Smitaine (smitaine)	15 g butter	60 g butter	Melt in a suitably sized sauteuse.
	25 g onions	100 g onions	Peel, cut in half and finely dice. Add to the butter and cook without colouring.
	50 ml dry white wine	200 ml dry white wine	Add the wine to the onions and reduce by two-thirds.
	¼ litre sour cream	1 litre sour cream	Add to the other ingredients and reduce by another third.
	25 ml lemon juice	100 ml lemon juice	Add to the sauce, correct the seasoning with salt and pepper, and pass through a fine chinois. *Serve with*: Hamburg or Vienna steaks.
Thickened gravy (jus lié)	250 g raw bones	1 kg raw bones	Using the appropriate type of bones, i.e. beef bones for roast beef gravy etc., chop up into small pieces and place in a suitably sized roasting tray. Place in a pre-heated oven, 190°C (375°F), for 1½ hours. Remove from the oven and place on top of the stove. Drain any excess oil into a container for use later.
	50 g onions	200 g onions	Peel, cut into mirepoix and retain.
	50 g carrots	200 g carrots	Peel, cut into mirepoix and retain.
	25 g celery	100 g celery	Wash and cut into mirepoix. Mix with the other ingredients. Using the oil from the bones fry the vegetables in a suitably sized frying pan. Add to the bones.
	250 ml suitable stock	1 litre suitable stock	Pour over the bones and vegetables and deglace. Bring to the boil and simmer for 30 minutes. Remove any fat or scum that may have risen to the surface.
	50 g mushrooms	200 g mushrooms	Wash and add to the boiling gravy.
	10 g cornflour or arrowroot	40 g cornflour or arrowroot	Mix with a little water. When it is completely dissolved, add to the boiling liquid stirring continuously until it returns to the boil. Simmer for a further 30 minutes. Strain through a fine chinois. Correct the seasoning. *Serve with*: Pot roast meats, shallow fried meat dishes and vegetables.

NOTE: Jus lié is sometimes used as an alternative to demi-glace as it has a more subtle taste which appeals to people today.

Commodity	¼ litre	1 litre	
Tomato (tomate)	15 g butter	60 g butter	Melt in a suitably sized sauteuse.
	15 g bacon	60 g bacon	Cut into small pieces and place in a large bowl.
	50 g carrots	200 g carrots	Peel, cut into mirepoix and place with the bacon.
	50 g onions	100 g onions	Peel, cut into mirepoix and add to the carrots.
	25 g celery	100 g celery	Wash, cut into mirepoix, mix with the other vegetables and bacon. Add to melted fat and cook to a light brown colour.
	15 g flour	60 g flour	Add to the vegetables and cook to a sandy coloured roux (blond). Allow to cool.
	25 g tomato purée	100 g tomato purée	Mix into the cooled roux.
	500 ml stock	2 litres stock	Add a quarter and mix thoroughly. Add another quarter and bring to the boil. Add the remaining stock, re-boil, then allow to simmer.
	1 clove garlic	2 cloves garlic	Peel, place on a chopping board. Sprinkle with salt and crush with the back of a knife. Add to the sauce. Season. Simmer for 1 hour. Correct the seasoning. Pass through a fine chinois.

Serve with: Spaghetti, deep fried fish, meats and egg dishes.

NOTE: To extract the maximum amount of flavour, the sauce should be liquidised before straining.

☐   ☐   ☐

SAUCES: WHAT WENT WRONG?

Problem	Caused by	To rectify
There is a starchy flavour.	Insufficient cooking.	Carefully reboil and simmer for a period to remove 'raw' starch flavour.
There is a bitter taste.	Over-browning or burning of roux.	Cannot be rectified.
Sauce is lumpy.	**(1)** Roux was too dry when liquid added; i.e. ratio of fat to flour was incorrect.	Add more fat and alter amount of liquid added to compensate
	(2) Liquid was added too quickly to the roux and the sauce was not stirred sufficiently.	Do not add any more liquid and continue to cook the sauce until the lumps have dissolved. The rest of the liquid can then be added slowly while mixing thoroughly until all the liquid is added and the sauce reaches boiling point.
	(3) A skin has formed on the simmering sauce caused by the surface coming into contact with the cooking air.	Strain the sauce into a clean pan or cover the completed sauce with a cartouche, (traditionally made from a piece of grease-proof paper cut to the correct size and brushed with butter or margarine). A thin film of melted butter or margarine may be used instead.
	(4) Insufficient stirring of the mixture at the bottom and sides of the cooking vessel which thickens and is later stirred into the sauce.	Strain the sauce into a clean saucepan.

Problem	Caused by	To rectify
Sauce has a poor gloss.	Insufficient cooking of the sauce or not straining the sauce correctly.	Cook the sauce for a longer period and/or passing through a tammy cloth. If this does not work, add a few pieces of chilled butter just before service (a technique known as *monter au beurre*), and is used in some fish sauces.
Sauce is too greasy.	Using greasy stock; by an incorrect balance of fat to flour in a roux; or by a failure to remove any surface grease that forms during the cooking process.	Skim the sauce at regular intervals.
Incorrect consistency.	(1) Incorrect ration of roux/thickening: too thick means too much roux and too thin means insufficient roux used.	Return to boil and simmer and correct ratio.
	(2) Insufficient cooking.	Return to boil and simmer.
Sauce has poor/dull colour.	Incorrect cooking of the roux, either too dark or not dark enough; also using dirty or unsuitable utensils and cooking vessels, e.g. using a metal whisk instead of a wooden spoon in an aluminium saucepan will cause white sauces to go grey.	Cannot be rectified.
Sauce has curdled.	Sauce has been retained at too high a temperature.	Cannot be rectified and must be discarded.

Soups

Soups are classified into seven main areas:

1 Consommés — clear soups made from refined stock. They can be garnished with cooked prepared vegetables, meats, cereals or egg preparations.

2 Purée-based soups — soups that are thickened by the main ingredient or by a starched-based additive. The additive can be fresh as in potatoes, or dried as in a pulse vegetable.

3 Broths — unstrained soups made with vegetables, stock and a cereal.

4 Creams — made by either adding béchamel sauce to a vegetable purée and finishing with cream (e.g. green pea soup), or a stock thickened with a blond roux and finished with cream.

5 Veloutés — a stock thickened by a blond roux, passed for service and finished with a liaison.

6 Bisques — shellfish soups thickened with rice or a roux, passed and finished with cream.

7 Miscellaneous — these are soups that do not fit into the other categories because of their unique method of preparation, e.g. French onion, oxtail, and brown roux soups.

In a large kitchen brigade a Chef Potager would be responsible for soups; in smaller kitchens the vegetable section would be expected to prepare soups.

As a rule purées, creams, broths and miscellaneous soups are served for luncheon whereas consommés, creams, veloutés and bisques are normally served at dinner.

THE PREPARATION OF CONSOMMES SOUPS

A consommé is defined as a clear soup made from a good stock – beef, chicken, game or fish – which is flavoured and clarified by a combination of ingredients.

How a stock is clarified

A preparation of egg white, good quality minced beef, carrot and onion is combined and placed in the stock. The mixture is brought to the boil then simmered. The protein in the egg white and minced beef coagulates, flocculates and rises to the surface of the liquid thus clarifying the stock to become a consommé.

Basic consommé preparation

🥄 (per 10 portions): 30 min
🍲 (per 10 portions): 2 hrs approx

Step	Commodity	1 portion	10 portions	
1	Egg whites	1	5	Place in a clean bowl and whisk briskly.
2	Minced beef	125 g	1¼ kg	Add to the egg whites.
3	Thyme	1 small sprig	1 medium sprig	Add to the mixture.
4	Carrots	25 g	250 g	Wash, peel and cut into mirepoix. Add to the mixture.
5	Onions	25 g	250 g	Wash, peel and cut into mirepoix. Add to the mixture.
6	Celery	25 g	250 g	Wash and cut into mirepoix. Add to the minced beef. Season with salt and pepper and mix in well. Place in a suitably sized saucepan.
7	Cold stock	750 ml	7½ litres	Add to the mixture and mix well. Gently bring to the boil. Once the consommé comes to the boil, quickly turn the heat down to a simmer. Allow the crust to form on the surface. Do not allow the mixture to be stirred or disturbed in any way as the consommé will become cloudy and defeat the object of clarification. Cook for the appropriate time. Strain the consommé into a clean saucepan through a fine muslin cloth and conical strainer with the minimum of disturbance to the crust. Return to the heat. Degraisser, garnish accordingly and serve.

Extensions of basic consommés

Name of soup	Garnish or finish (per 10 portions)
Cold clear soup with pasta shapes (consommé alphabetique)	100 g alphabet pasta
Cold clear soup in a cup* (consommé en tasse)	
Clear soup with vegetables* (consommé brunoise)	20 g brunoise of carrots
	20 g brunoise of turnips
	20 g brunoise of leeks
	20 g brunoise of celery
Clear soup with savoury pancake (consommé celestine)	75 g julienne of savoury pancake

96

Name of soup	Garnish or finish (per 10 portions)
Clear soup with vegetables* (consommé julienne)	20 g julienne of carrots 20 g julienne of turnips 20 g julienne of leeks 20 g julienne of celery
Consommé with celery and tomato* (consommé madrilene)	75 g tomato concasse 75 g cooked celery batons 75 g cooked diced pimento 50 g cooked vermicelli 1 sprig sweated shredded sorrel
Clear soup with port wine* (consommé au porto)	150 ml port wine
Clear soup with vermicelli (consommé vermicelle)	100 g cooked vermicelli
Clear soup with sherry* (consommé au xeres)	150 ml dry sherry
Clear soup with turtle flavour (consommé tortue)	1 sachet of turtle herbs bouquet garni 100 g cooked diced turtle meat 150 ml dry sherry
Clear soup, savoury egg custard (consommé royale)	100 g cooked egg custard cut into julienne.

NOTE: The consommés marked with an asterisk can also be served cold, omitting any pasta as this may cause the soup to go cloudy. These consommés are called jellied consommés. They are prepared by adding gelatine to the simmering liquid and allowing the liquid to go cold in the serving cup. Jellied consommés are usually served during the summer months.

☐   ☐   ☐

THE PREPARATION OF BROTH SOUPS

Broths are derived from peasant style meals. They are made from a meat stock and usually contain a variety of vegetables, a small amount of meat, either diced or minced, and a cereal. The meat used will depend on the type of broth being made. Beef for beef broths, chicken for chicken broths, etc. The vegetables in unsweated broths are usually diced whereas in sweated broths the cut of vegetable will depend on the soup.

Broths are sub-divided into three groups: those in which the vegetables are sweated, those in which they are not and fish broths.

Unsweated broths

Step	Commodity	1 portion	10 portions	
1	Appropriate meat	50 g	500 g	Mince or dice the meat finely. Place in a suitably sized saucepan and cover with cold water. Bring to the boil. Remove any impurities that may form on the surface. Boil for 10 minutes then refresh by placing under cold water and allowing the meat to go cold. Drain away the water and return the meat to a suitably sized clean saucepan.
2	White stock	250 ml	2½ litres	Pour over the meat, bring to the boil then simmer.
3	Bouquet garni	1 sm	1 lg	Place in the simmering stock.
4	Barley	5 g	50 g	Wash the barley under cold running water. Add to the stock. Season with salt and pepper. Allow to simmer.
5	Carrots	10 g	100 g	Peel, cut into fine dice (brunoise) and place in a bowl.
6	Onions	10 g	100 g	Peel, cut in half and finely dice. Place with the carrots.
7	Leeks	10 g	100 g	Wash, cut in half and finely dice. Add to the onions.
8	Turnips	10 g	100 g	Peel, cut into fine dice (brunoise) and place with the other vegetables.
9	Swedes	10 g	100 g	Peel, cut into fine dice (brunoise). Collect the other vegetables and add to the soup. Simmer until the vegetables and meat are cooked. Remove the bouquet garni. Correct the seasoning.

NOTE: If there is excessive evaporation of stock, add sufficient to compensate.

Extensions of unsweated broths

Name of soup	Garnished or finished with (per 10 portions)
Beef broth (bouillon de boeuf)	15 g finely chopped parsley
	500 g cooked minced/diced beef
Chicken broth (bouillion de volaille)	15 g finely chopped parsley
	500 g cooked diced/minced chicken
Game broth (bouillion de giber)	15 g finely chopped parsley
	500 g cooked diced/minced game meat
Scotch broth (potage Eccossais)	15 g finely chopped parsley
	500 g cooked diced/minced lamb/mutton

Sweated broths

☺ (per 10 portions): 30 min

☼ (per 10 portions): 45 min–1 hr approx

Step	Commodity	1 portion	10 portions	
1	Vegetables	100 g	1 kg	Wash and prepare the vegetables. Cut into the required shape. Place in a bowl.
2	Butter	10 g	100 g	Place in a suitably sized, thick-bottomed saucepan and gently heat. Add the prepared vegetables and sweat, ensuring that they do not colour.
3	White stock	250 ml	2½ litres	Pour over the vegetables, bring to the boil then simmer. Skim off any impurities that may rise to the surface.
4	Boquet garni	1 sm	1 lg	Place in the simmering soup and simmer until the vegetables are almost cooked.
5	Appropriate garnish	15 g	150 g	Add to the soup and complete the cooking process. Season and correct the consistency.

NOTE: If there is excessive evaporation of stock, add sufficient to compensate.

Extensions of sweated broths

Name	Base (per 10 portions)	Garnished or finished with (per 10 portions)
Cockie-leekie	1 kg leeks cut julienne	150 g cooked chicken cut into julienne 75 g cooked prunes cut into julienne 15 g finely chopped parsley
Leek and potato (potage bonne femme)	500 g of leek and potato cut paysanne	15 g finely chopped parsley 150 ml single cream
Minestrone (minestroni)	125 g of carrots, leeks, onions, swedes, turnips, potatoes and 75 g cabbage	75 g 1 cm lengths of spagehtti 75 g blanched tomatoes with skin and seeds removed, and cut into fine dice to make a concassé. 50 g tomato purée 50 g french beans cut paysanne 50 g garden peas 50 g fine diced bacon, parsley and garlic rolled into pea size pellets and added near completion of cooking time.
Peasant broth (potage paysanne)	125 g of carrots, leeks, onions, swedes, turnips, potatoes and 75 g cabbage	50 g french beans cut paysanne 50 g garden peas 15 g finely chopped parsley

Shellfish broths/chowders

NOTE: This type of soup is always made from bi-valve shellfish.

⌣ (per 10 portions): 1 hr
♨ (per 10 portions): 45 min approx

Step	Commodity	1 portion	10 portions	
1	Butter	10 g	100 g	Place in a suitably sized thick bottomed saucepan and heat gently.
2	Belly pork	25 g	250 g	Wash, cut into small dice and place in the saucepan.
3	Leeks	25 g	250 g	Wash, cut into paysanne and add to belly pork.
4	Potatoes	25 g	250 g	Peel, wash, cut into paysanne and place with the leeks. Cook gently without colouring until the vegetables are soft.
5	Fish stock	250 ml	2½ litre	Pour over the vegetables and pork. Season with salt and pepper.
6	Prepared shellfish	50 g	500 g	Add to the soup and bring to the boil. Return to a simmer.
7	Bouquet garni	1 sm	1 lg	Place in the simmering soup and simmer until the vegetables are almost cooked.
8	Tomatoes	40 g	400 g	Remove the 'eye' of each tomato and score. Place in boiling water for 10 seconds then refresh immediately. Remove the skins and discard. Cut in half and discard the seeds. Cut the flesh into fine dice and add to the soup. Correct the seasoning. Remove the bouquet garni.

NOTE: Chowders are traditionally thickened by adding crushed water biscuits just prior to service. Some establishments use fresh white breadcrumbs or beurre manié as an alternative.

Extensions of shellfish broths

Name of soup	Base (per 10 portions)	Garnished or finished with (per 10 portions)
Clam chowder	500 g clams	15 g finely chopped parsley
		150 ml cream
Mussel chowder	500 g mussels	15 g finely chopped parsley
		150 ml cream
Oyster chowder	500 g oysters	15 g finely chopped parsley
		150 ml cream
Scallop chowder	500 g scallops	15 g finely chopped parsley
		150 ml cream
Seafood chowder	500 g assorted shellfish	15 g finely chopped parsley
		150 ml cream

☐   ☐   ☐

THE PREPARATION OF PURÉE SOUPS

Purée soups are sub-divided into two groups: those made from pulse vegetables and those from aqueous vegetables. Apart from potato soup, aqueous preparations need an added starch in the form of rice to achieve the required consistency.

Pulse-based purée recipe

Potage purée

🥄 (per 10 portions): 30 min   Soaking time 12 hrs
🍲 (per 10 portions): 1½ hrs approx

Step	Commodity	1 portion	10 portions	
1	White stock	500 ml	5 litres	Place in a suitably sized saucepan.
2	Pulse vegetables	50 g	500 g	Add to the stock (pre-soaked).
3	Carrots	50 g	500 g	Wash, peel and cut into mirepoix. Place in the stock.
4	Onions	50 g	500 g	Peel, cut into mirepoix and add to the carrots.
5	Scrap bacon	10 g	100 g	Roughly cut and add to the other ingredients. Season with salt and pepper and place on the heat. Bring to the boil, skim and simmer.
6	Bouquet garni	1 sm	1 lg	Place in the simmering soup and cook for the required time. Remove the bouquet garni and bacon. Liquidise then pass through a conical strainer. If there is no liquidiser available, pass through a medium sieve then a conical strainer. Return to the heat and re-boil. Correct the consistency and seasoning. Garnish as required.

NOTE: Purée soups are usually served with croûtons.

4

Extensions of pulse purées

Name of soup	Garnished or finished with (per 10 portions)
Purée of haricot bean (potage soisonnaise)	15 g finely chopped parsley
Purée of red bean (potage conde)	150 ml dry red wine 15 g finely chopped parsley
Purée of lentil (a) (potage de lentilles)	15 g finely chopped parsley
Purée of lentil (b) (potage conti)	15 g finely chopped parsley 150 g diced cooked bacon pinch of chopped chervil
Purée of lentil (c) (potage esau)	50 g boiled rice
Purée of green pea soup (potage St Germain)	15 g chopped parsley
Purée of yellow split pea soup (potage Egyptienne)	15 g chopped parsley

☐   ☐   ☐

Aqueous-based purée recipe

Potage purée

🍲 (per 10 portions): 30 min
🍲 (per 10 portions) 1½ hrs approx

Step	Commodity	1 portion	10 portions	
1	Butter	10 g	100 g	Melt gently in a suitably sized thick-bottomed saucepan.
2	Main vegetable	75 g	750 g	Peel, slice thinly and add to the melted butter.
3	Carrots	15 g	150 g	Peel, cut into mirepoix and add to the butter.
4	Onions	15 g	150 g	Peel, cut into mirepoix and add to the carrots. Cook without colouring (sweat) and season with salt and pepper.
5	White stock	500 ml	5 litres	Add to the softened vegetables. Bring to the boil and skim as required.
6	Patna rice	10 g	100 g	Add to the soup and stir in well.
7	Bouquet garni	1 sm	1 lg	Add to the simmering soup. Cover with a lid to avoid excessive evaporation. Cook for the required time. Remove the bouquet garni. Liquidise then pass through a conical strainer. If there is no liquidiser available, pass through a medium sieve then a conical strainer. Return to the heat and re-boil. Correct the consistency and seasoning. Garnish as required.

NOTE: Purée soups are usually served with croûtons.

Extensions of aqueous purées

Name of soup	Garnished or finished with (per 10 portions)
Purée of carrot (purée de carotte)	15 g finely chopped parsley
Purée of cauliflower (purée Dubarry)	100 g cooked small sprigs of cauliflower 15 g finely chopped parsley
Purée of celery (purée de celeri)	15 g finely chopped parsley
Purée of Jerusalem artichoke (purée de Palestine)	15 g finely chopped parsley
Purée of leek (purée de poireaux)	15 g finely chopped parsley
Purée of onion (purée d'oignon)	15 g finely chopped parsley
Purée of potato (purée of parmentier)	15 g finely chopped parsley
Purée of pumpkin (purée de potiron)	15 g finely chopped parsley
Purée of swede (purée de rutabaga)	15 g finely chopped parsley
Purée of brussels sprout (purée flamande)	10 g finely chopped parsley
Purée of vegetable (purée de legumes)	10 g finely chopped parsley
Purée of watercress*	* As for potato soup, but cooked with a bunch of watercress. 10 blanched watercress leaves to garnish.

Veloute-based soup recipes

🥄 (per 10 portions): 30 min
🍲 (per 10 portions): 1½ hrs approx

Step	Commodity	1 portion	10 portions	
1	Butter	10 g	100 g	Melt in a suitably sized, thick bottomed saucepan. Do not allow the butter to burn.
2	Appropriate vegetable	25 g	250 g	Wash, peel and cut into thin slices. Sweat in the butter without colouring.
3	Flour	10 g	100 g	Add to the cooked vegetables and cook to a second stage (blond) roux. Allow to cool.
4	Appropriate white stock	250 ml	2½ litres	Warm the stock. Return the cooled roux to the stove. Add a quarter of the stock to the roux and thicken. Add another quarter and bring to the boil. Add the remaining stock and return to the boil. Lower the heat and allow the velouté to simmer. Season with salt and white pepper.*
5	Bouquet garni	1 sm	1 lg	Add to the velouté. Cover with a lid to avoid excessive evaporation. Cook for 1 hour. Remove the bouquet garni. Liquidise and pass through a conical strainer. Return to the heat and re-boil. Correct the consistency and seasoning. Garnish appropriately.
6	Cream	10 ml	100 ml	Place in a clean bowl.
7	Egg yolks	½	5	Add to the cream and whisk together. Add to the soup just prior to serving. Do not allow to re-boil.

*NOTE: It must be white pepper as black pepper leaves flecks in the soup.

Extensions of velouté soups

Name of soup	Type of stock	Garnished or finish (per 10 portions)
Velouté Agnes Sorel	chicken	75 g cooked tongue cut into julienne
		75 g cooked chicken cut into julienne
		75 g cooked mushrooms cut into julienne
Velouté d'asperges (asparagus velouté)	chicken	20 cooked asparagus tips
Velouté de volaille (chicken velouté)	chicken	100 g cooked chicken cut into julienne
		15 g finely chopped parsley
Velouté de poisson (fish velouté)	fish	15 g finely chopped parsley
Velouté Dieppoise (mussel velouté)	fish/mussel	100 g prepared cooked mussels
		100 g prawns
		15 g finely chopped parsley
Velouté aux hûitres (oyster velouté)	fish/oyster	20 poached oysters
		15 g finely chopped parsley

CREAM SOUP RECIPES   Crèmes

Cream soups can be made in a variety of ways. Either as a velouté-based soup or a pulse-based purée soup enriched with cream (see pulse-based purées and veloutés) or yoghurt. Alternatively, a combination of five parts aqueous vegetable purée to one part béchamel sauce may be used.

Boiling meats

Because of their tougher structure, pickled meats such as hams, bacon joints, beef joints, some offal, mutton and boiling fowl are ideal for boiling. Pickled meats need to be soaked overnight in cold water to remove excess salt.

Before cooking it is important to ensure that the meat is properly prepared. All meats should have the sinew removed and any excess fat trimmed. Mutton and hams have the pelvic bone removed and all meats are tied with string to prevent them falling apart during the cooking process.

Fresh meats are immersed completely in boiling water and cooked for 50 minutes per kilo plus 25 minutes over. Pickled meats are placed in the cooking vessel, completely covered with cold water, brought to the boil and then simmered for 40 minutes per kilo plus 20 minutes over. (These times are only a guide and the meat should always be checked to ensure it is cooked thoroughly.) It is important that the meats are always completely covered by the liquid throughout the cooking process. The liquid will have to be skimmed regularly to remove any scum or grease that may form on the surface. Once cooked, the meat and poultry must be allowed to stand and set before portioning.

Boiled fresh red meats

Viande bouilli

🥄 (per 10 portions): 30 min
🍲 (per 10 portions): 2–2¼ hrs approx

Step	Commodity	1 portion	10 portions	
1	prepared meat	150 g	1½ kg	Place in a saucepan of boiling water. Return to boil.
2	mirepoix—carrots, onions, leeks and celery	50 g	500 g	Wash, peel, roughly cut and add to the meat.
3	Bouquet garni	1 small	1 large	Add to the meat. Season with salt and pepper, cover with a lid and cook for the required time.

☐   ☐   ☐

Boiled pickled meats

🥄 (per 10 portions): 30 min
🍲 (per 10 portions): 1¾–2¼ hrs approx

Step	Commodity	1 portion	10 portions	
1	Prepared meat	150 g	1½ kg	Place in a saucepan and completely cover with cold water. Bring to the boil then simmer.
2	Mirepoix—carrots, onions, leeks and celery	50 g	500 g	Wash, peel, roughly cut and add to the meat.
3	Bouquet garni	1 small	1 large	Add to the meat. Season with salt and pepper, cover with a lid and cook for the required time.

☐   ☐   ☐

Boiled chicken

Poulet bouilli

🥄 (per 10 portions): 30 min
🍲 (per 10 portions): chicken 2 hrs approx
boiling fowl 2½–3 hrs

Step	Commodity	1 portion	10 portions	
1	Prepared bird	500 g	2 × 2½ kg	Place in a saucepan and completely cover with water or chicken stock. Bring to the boil then simmer gently.
2	Mirepoix—carrots, onions, leeks and celery	50 g	500 g	Wash, peel, roughly cut and add to the poultry.
3	Bouquet garni	1 small	1 large	Add to the meat. Season with salt and pepper, cover with a lid and cook for the required time.

Extensions of boiled meat and poultry dishes

Dish	Garnished or finished with (per 10 portions)
Boiled pickled beef, English style (boeuf bouilli à l'anglaise)	500 g turned carrots 20 × shallots or small onions 20 × 25 g suet dumplings (see Chapter 14: Baking)

NOTE: The above ingredients are boiled in the cooking liquor then arranged alongside the meat. A sauceboat of the strained cooking liquor is also served.

Boiled beef French style (boeuf bouilli à la francaise)	500 g turned carrots and turnips 1 kg cabbage, washed, quartered, stalk removed and tied. 500 g of celery and leeks tied in ten small separate bundles.

NOTE: The above ingredients are boiled in the cooking liquor then arranged alongside the meat. A sauceboat of the strained booking liquor is also served.

Boiled chicken with rice and suprême sauce (poulet poche au riz et sauce suprême)	Dress on 10 × 50 g riz pilaff beds (see Chapter 9: Braising). Napper with 1½ litres of suprême sauce.
Boiled chicken with rice and asparagus sauce (poulet poche Argenteuil)	Garnish with 20 asparagus tips. Dress on 10 × 50 g riz pilaff beds (see Chapter 9). Add 250 g of cooked asparagus purée to 1½ litres of suprême sauce. Pass and napper.

4

Dish	Garnished or finished with (per 10 portions)
Boiled chicken with rice and mushroom sauce (poulet poché au riz et sauce champignons)	Dress on 10 × 50 g riz pilaff beds (see Chapter 9: Braising). Garnish with 250 g of button mushrooms cooked glacés à blanc (see Chapter 11: Shallow frying). Napper with 1½ litres of mushroom sauce.
Boiled chicken with rice and curry sauce. (poulet poché à la Stanley)	Dress on 10 × 50 g riz pilaff beds (see Chapter 9: Braising). Garnish with 100 g of cooked tongue, 100 g mushrooms cooked glacés à blanc and 50 g of truffle of garnishing paste cut into julienne. Napper with 1½ litres of curry sauce.

NOTE: As an alternative to beds, the rice may be cooked and placed in buttered dariole moulds then turned out and placed around the portioned chicken.

Boiled ham with parsley sauce (jambon bouilli au sauce persil)	1½ litres of parsley sauce served in a sauceboat.

NOTE: Gammon may be used in place of the ham.

Boiled leg of mutton with caper sauce (gigot de mouton sauce aux capres)	1½ litres of caper sauce made with the cooking liquor and served in a sauceboat.
Boiled pickled ox tongue, English style (langue de boeuf bouilli à l'anglaise)	500 g turned carrots 20 × shallots or small onions. 20 × suet dumplings (see Chapter 14: Baking)
Boiled pickled ox tongue with Madeira sauce (langue de boeuf bouilli au sauce Madère)	1½ litres of Madeira sauce served in a sauceboat.
Boiled ox tongue with spinach and Madeira sauce (langue de boeuf bouilli Florentine)	500 g of boiled leaf spinach, portioned, heated and placed on a serving dish to form a bed. The sliced ox tongue is then dressed on top. 1½ litres of Madeira is served in a sauceboat.

Boiling eggs

There are five types of egg that can be cooked by boiling: chicken or hen, quail, duck, turkey and goose. The eggs should be clean and well-shaped. When broken, there should be a high proportion of thick to thin white, and the yolk should be rounded and of a good colour.

When eggs cook the protein hardens. This hardening is called coagulation. In chicken eggs the white coagulates at 65°C and the yolk at 70°C.

Hen eggs are graded in 7 sizes:

Size 1	70 g	Size 5	50 g
Size 2	65 g	Size 6	45 g
Size 3	60 g	Size 7	44 g and below
Size 4	55 g		

Cooking times

À la Coque	3 minutes
Mollet	6 minutes. Serve out of the shell
Dur	10 minutes

Hard boiled eggs with mushroom and cheese sauce

Oeuf chimey

⌣ (per 10 portions): 30 min
♨ (per 10 portions): 1½ hrs approx

Step	Commodity	1 portion	10 portions	
1	Mornay sauce	50 ml	500 ml	Prepare as per recipe. Keep warm in a bain-marie.
2	Eggs	1	10	Hard boil the eggs. Allow to cool until cold. Cut in half lengthwise. Remove the yolk and pass through a sieve. Place the egg whites in an earthenware serving dish.
3	Mushrooms	25 g	250 g	Wash, peel if necessary and dice finely.
4	Shallots	5 g	50 g	Peel and dice finely.
5	Butter	5 g	25 g	Place in a suitably sized saucepan and heat gently. Add the chopped mushrooms and shallots and sweat for 2–3 minutes. This mixture is called a duxelle. Drain off excess fat. Add the sieved egg yolks and correct the seasoning.
6	Chopped parsley	½ tsp	1 tbsp	Add to the duxelle and mix thoroughly. Allow the mixture to cool. Place the cooled mixture into a piping bag with a No. 3 duchess nozzle and pipe into the egg whites. Napper with the warm Mornay sauce.
7	Parmesan cheese	5 g	50 g	Sprinkle over the sauce, brown slowly under a salamander and serve.

☐　　☐　　☐

4

Boiling vegetables

The vitamins and minerals in vegetables are water-soluble and are easily lost during the preparation and cooking process. The emphasis in cooking is on a minimum amount of cooking time and liquid use. Over-cooking of vegetables will result in low nutritive value, poor colour and flavour.

Most vegetables can be cooked by boiling. Whether they are placed in cold water and brought to the boil to cook, or placed into boiling salted water then returned to the boil will depend in principle on whether they are grown below or above the ground.

Some vegetables need to be cooked in a *blanc* preparation or acidulated water in order to keep their colour. A *blanc* is made as below:

1 litre cold water	Combine the ingredients
25 g flour	using a whisk, stir to the
½ lemon juice	boil, strain and use
pinch of salt	accordingly

For catering purposes vegetables grown below the ground are referred to as Green (G) vegetables and those grown below the ground are known as Root (R) vegetables. The proper classification of vegetables is given below:

Leaf: Chicory, lettuce, spinach, sorrel, watercress, radiccio

Root: carrots, swedes, parsnips, turnips, beetroot, celeriac, horseradish, mooli, radish, salsify

Brassicas: Cabbage, cauliflower, broccoli, calabrese, curly kale, spring greens, brussel sprouts

Pod and seeds: Peas, haricot beans, broad beans, okra, sweetcorn

Fungi: Mushrooms, truffles, ceps, morels'

Tubers: Jerusalem artichokes, potatoes, yams

Bulb: Onions, garlic, shallots, leeks, spring onions

Blanched stem and shoots: Celery, asparagus, beans, endive, sea kale, globe artichokes, kohlrabi

Fruiting: Aubergine, avocado, marrow, tomato, pumpkin, courgette, cucumber, peppers

THE PREPARATION AND COOKING OF DRIED PULSE VEGETABLES

Pulses are vegetables grown in pods. Dried vegetables often need to be soaked overnight in cold water to reduce the cooking time. To cook the pulses, cover with cold water, and gradually bring to the boil. Then simmer gently till cooked. Correct the seasoning, drain well and serve.

Name	Cooking instructions	
Butter beans	Simmer for 1½ to 2 hours	
Menu examples	au beurre	with butter
	à la menthe	with blanched fresh mint leaves
	nature	plain
Haricot beans (haricot blanc)	Simmer for 1½ to 2 hours	
Menu examples	au beurre	with butter
	nature	plain
	Bretonne	with a cohere of tomato sauce
Kidney beans, green (haricot flageolets)	Simmer for 1½ to 2 hours	
Menu examples	au beurre	with butter
	nature	plain
Kidney beans, red (haricot rouge)	Simmer for 1½ to 2 hours	
Menu examples	au beurre	with butter
	nature	plain
Lentils (lentilles)	Simmer for 1½ to 2 hours	
Menu examples	purée	cooked, drained of the cooking liquor and passed through a sieve or mouli
	purée à la créme	cooked, drained of the cooking liquor and passed through a sieve or mouli, finished with fresh cream, or cream sauce
Marrowfat peas	Simmer for ¼ to 1 hour	
Menu examples	au beurre	with butter
	à la menthe	with blanched fresh mint leaves
	nature	plain

THE PREPARATION AND COOKING OF FRESH VEGETABLES

Name	Preparation	Cooking instructions
Artichoke, globe— cooked whole (fonds d'artichauts)	Cut across the top removing between a quarter and a third of the leaves. Remove the stem at the base. Place a slice of lemon on the base and tie with string.	Place in boiling, salted water for between 40 and 50 minutes. When cooked remove the string, lemon, heart and the choke (inner fibrous section). Serve on a napkin.
Menu examples	au beurre fondu	with a sauceboat of melted butter
	hollandaise	with hollandaise sauce

Name	Preparation	Cooking instructions
Artichoke, globe— bottoms	Cut off the stalk. Pluck away the underneath leaves until the bottom is clearly visible. Immediately rub the base with lemon then place in acidulated water until cooking commences.	Place in a simmering blanc for between 20 and 25 minutes. When cooked remove the choke (inner fibrous section) using a stainless steel spoon. Serve whole, halved or quartered.
Menu examples	au beurre	with butter
	à la crème	with fresh cream, or cream sauce
	aux fine herbs	with fine herbs
	hollandaise	with hollandaise sauce
	Mornay	with cheese sauce
	nature	plain
	persillés	with melted butter and finished with finely chopped parsley
Artichoke Jerusalem (topinambours)	Wash, peel and wash again. Cut to the required size. Place in a bowl of acidulated water until cooking commences.	Place in boiling, salted water with a drop of lemon juice and cook for between 20 and 25 minutes.
Menu examples	au beurre	with butter
	à la crème	with fresh cream, or cream sauce
	aux fine herbs	with fine herbs
	nature	plain
	persillés	with melted butter and finished with finely chopped parsley
	purée	cooked, (the cooking liquor drained) and passed through a sieve or mouli
Asparagus (asperges)	Remove the tips of the leaves. Scrape the stems lightly and wash. Remove excess stem and tie into even bundles of 6–12.	Place in boiling, salted water for approx. 15 minutes. Test by pressing the green part of the stem, which should be tender. Remove and drain to serve.

NOTE: Young thin asparagus (Pointes d'asperges) are known as sprew or sprue and are cooked similarly to mature asparagus, but in bundles of up to 50 pieces and the leaves are not removed for cooking. They can be served as a vegetable or used as a garnish for soups, egg and fish dishes and in salads and buffet work.

Menu examples	au beurre	with butter
	au beurre fondu	accompanied by a sauceboat of melted butter
	amandines	sauted almonds
	hollandaise	with hollandaise sauce
	nature	plain
	purée	cooked, drained of the cooking liquor and passed through a sieve or mouli.
Beetroot	Trim the stalk and root. Wash well.	Place in cold water, bring to the boil and cook for 1½ hours from boiling.
Menu examples	au beurre	with butter
	à la crème	with fresh cream, or cream sauce
	nature	plain

4

Name	Preparation	Cooking instructions
Broad beans (feves)	Remove from the pods and wash. In some cases it may be necessary to remove the inner shells if they are too tough.	Cook in boiling salted water for 15 minutes.
Menu examples	au beurre	with butter
	à la crème	with fresh cream
	à sauce persil	with parsley sauce
	nature	plain
Broccoli (broccoli)	Remove any rotten leaves, trim the base of the stem and make an incision in the shape of a cross. Rinse under cold running water.	Place in the minimum amount of boiling salted water and cook for 10–15 minutes.
Menu examples	au beurre	with butter
	amandine	with sauted almonds
	hollandaise	with hollandaise sauce
	Milanaise	sprinkled with parmesan cheese, gratinate and finished with beurre noisette
	Mornay	with cheese sauce
	nature	plain
	Polonaise	sprinkled with hard boiled egg whites sieved, hard boiled egg yolks sieved, finely chopped parsley, fried breadcrumbs and finished with beurre noisette
Brussels sprouts (choux de bruxelles)	Remove any rotten leaves, trim the base of the stem and make an incision in the shape of a cross. Rinse under cold running water.	Place in the minimum amount of boiling salted water and cook for 10 minutes.
Menu examples	au beurre	with butter
	limousine	cooked, peeled, with chopped chestnuts
	Milanaise	sprinkle with parmesan cheese, gratinate and finish with beurre noisette
	nature	plain
	Polonaise	sprinkled with hard boiled egg whites sieved, hard boiled egg yolk sieved, finely chopped parsley, fried breadcrumbs and finished with beurre noisette
Cabbage (chou)	Trim any rotten leaves. Cut into quarters and remove all the stalk. Wash well in salted water.	Place in the minimum amount of boiling salted water and cook for 10 minutes
Menu examples	au beurre	with butter
	nature	plain
Spring Cabbage — (chou de printemps)	Trim any rotten leaves. Cut into quarters and remove all the stalk. Wash well in salted water.	Place in the minimum amount of boiling salted water and cook for 10 minutes.
Menu examples	au beurre	with butter
	nature	plain

Name	Preparation	Cooking instructions
Carrots (carrottes)	Remove the stalk and stem, wash and cut into the selected shape.	Use just enough cold water to cover the carrots. Bring to the boil, season and cook for 15 minutes from boiling.
Menu examples	au beurre	with butter
	à la crème	with fresh cream, or cream sauce
	glace	glace with sugar and butter
	Mornay	with cheese sauce
	nature	plain
	à sauce persil	with parsley sauce
	persillées	with melted butter and finished with finely chopped parsley
	purée	cooked, drained of the cooking liquor and passed through a sieve or mouli
	vichy	cooked in vichy water and glazed with sugar and butter
Cauliflower (choufleur)	Remove the green leaves and the stalk. Hollow out the core and wash well in salted water.	Place in plenty of boiling salted water, return to the boil and cook for 15 minutes.
Menu examples	au beurre	with butter
	amandine	with sauted almonds
	aux fine herbs	with fine herbs
	à la crème	with fresh cream, or cream sauce
	hollandaise	with hollandaise sauce
	Milanaise	sprinkle with parmesan cheese, gratinate and finish with beurre noisette
	Mornay	with cheese sauce
	nature	plain
	Polonaise	sprinkled with hard boiled egg whites sieved, hard boiled egg yolks sieved, finely chopped parsley, fried breadcrumbs, and finished with beurre noisette.
Celeriac (celeri-rave)	Wash, peel and cut into the required shape. Place in acidulated water until cooking commences.	Place in boiling salted water with a drop of lemon juice and cook for between 20 and 25 minutes.
Menu examples	au beurre	with butter
	à la crème	with fresh cream, or cream sauce
	aux fine herbs	with fine herbs
	nature	plain

4

Name	Preparation	Cooking instructions
Chicory (endive)	Remove any damaged leaves and wash thoroughly.	Place in plenty of boiling salted water and cook for 20–25 minutes.
Menu examples	nature	plain
	au beurre	with butter
	à la crème	with fresh cream, or cream sauce
	Mornay	with Mornay sauce
	purée	cooked, drained of the cooking liquor and passed through a sieve or mouli
Corn on the cob **Sweetcorn** (mais)	Remove the outer leaves and any fibres, trim the ends and wash well.	Place in plenty of boiling salted water and cook for 15 minutes.
Menu examples	au beurre fondu	with a sauceboat of melted butter
	nature	plain
Corn off the cob **Sweetcorn** (mais)	Remove the outer leaves and any fibres, trim the ends and wash well.	Place in plenty of boiling salted water for 10 minutes. Remove from the boiling water and allow to cool. Remove the corn from the cob with a spoon. Cook for a further 5 minutes in the boiling water and serve.
Menu examples	au beurre	with butter
	à la crème	with fresh cream, or cream sauce
	nature	plain

NOTE: Frozen sweetcorn can be used in place of fresh. It is already par cooked and usually takes 5–10 minutes to cook in boiling salted water for off the cob and 15–20 minutes on the cob.

Name	Preparation	Cooking instructions
Courgette (courgette)	Wash well, trim the stalks, peel. To cook, leave whole or slice.	Place in the minimum amount of boiling salted water and cook for 8 minutes.
Menu examples	au beurre	with butter
	à la crème	with fresh cream, or cream sauce
	aux fine herbes	with herbs
	Mornay	with cheese sauce
Cucumber (concombre)	Wash, remove the outer skin. Remove the seeds. Cut into slice, wedge or barrel shape.	Place in the minimum amount of boiling salted water and cook for 5 minutes approximately.
Menu examples	au beurre	with butter
	à la crème	with fresh cream, or cream sauce
	glace	glazed with sugar and butter
	Milanaise	sprinkle with parmesan cheese, gratinate and finish with beurre noisette
	nature	plain
	persillé	with parsley

Name	Preparation	Cooking instructions
Fennel (fenouil)	Trim the bulb, removing the stalks and leaves and wash well. Fennel can be cooked whole, halved or quartered according to the size.	Place in a simmering blanc for between 1 and 1½ hours approximately, depending on the size.
Menu examples	au beurre	with butter
	amandine aux fine herbs	with almonds and fine herbs
	hollandaise	with hollandaise sauce
	Milanaise	sprinkle with parmesan cheese, gratinate and finish with beurre noisette
	Mornay	with cheese sauce
	nature	plain
	Polonaise	sprinkled with hard boiled egg whites sieved, hard boiled egg yolks sieved, finely chopped parsley, fried breadcrumbs and finished with beurre noisette
French beans (haricot verts)	Remove the top and tail. Wash in cold running water.	Place in boiling salted water and cook for 8 minutes. Use immediately or refresh. Reheat by plunging into boiling salted water for 1 minute or toss small amounts in melted butter.
Menu examples	amandine aux fine herbs	with almonds and fine herbs
	au beurre	with butter
	hollandaise	with hollandaise sauce
	nature	plain
Kohlrabi	Remove the leaves from the bulb and trim the roots. Wash well in cold water and remove the thick peel. Kohlrabi can be cooked whole, sliced or cut into the required shape.	Place in cold water, bring to the boil, season and cook for approximately 45 minutes from boiling.
Menu examples	au beurre	with butter
	à la crème	with fresh cream, or cream sauce
	nature	plain
	persillés	with melted butter and finished with finely chopped parsley
Leeks (poireaux)	Trim the root and remove any dark or damaged leaves. Trim the top. Cut in half lengthwise. Wash well and tie into bundles for cooking.	Place in boiling salted water and cook for 20 minutes.
Menu examples	au beurre	with butter
	à la crème	with fresh cream, or cream sauce
	Mornay	with cheese sauce
	nature	plain

4

Name	Preparation	Cooking instructions
Marrow (courge)	Peel the outer skin. Cut in half lengthwise. Remove the seeds. Cut into 5 cm dice.	Place in boiling salted water and cook for 10 minutes.
Menu examples	au beurre	with butter
	à la crème	with fresh cream, or cream sauce
	au fine herbs	with fine herbs
	Mornay	with cheese sauce
	nature	plain
	persillée	with parsley
Onions (oignon)	Peel, trim the root and leave whole. Wash well.	Place in cold water, bring to the boil, season and cook for 30 minutes approximately from boiling.
Menu examples	à la crème	with fresh cream, or cream sauce
	nature	plain
Okra — gumbo, ladies' fingers	Wash well. Trim the stem, but do not remove.	Place in boiling salted water for 15 minutes.
Menu examples	au beurre	with butter
	à la crème	with fresh cream, or cream sauce
	hollandaise	with hollandaise sauce
	nature	plain
Parsnips (panais)	Wash well, peel and trim the stalk. Wash again. Cut into quarters. Remove the centre root if it is tough. Cut into neat 5 cm pieces.	Place in cold water, bring to the boil, season and cook for approximately 30 minutes from boiling.
Menu examples	au beurre	with butter
	à la crème	with fresh cream, or cream sauce
	hollandaise	with hollandaise sauce
	nature	plain
	persillés	with melted butter and finished with finely chopped parsley
	purée	cooked, drained of the cooking liquor and passed through a sieve or mouli
Peas, fresh (petit pois)	Remove from the pod and wash well.	Place in boiling salted water for 15–20 minutes.

NOTE: Peas can be cooked with fresh mint leaves.

Menu examples	au beurre	with butter
	à la menthe	with blanched fresh mint leaves
	nature	plain
	persillés	with parsley

NOTE: Frozen peas can be used in place of fresh. They are par-cooked already and usually take 5–10 minutes to cook in boiling salted water. The time difference will depend on the quality. It is advisable to check the instructions on the packet before cooking.

Name	Preparation	Cooking instructions
Peas, snow (mangetout)	Top and tail. Leave in the pod wash well.	Place in boiling salted water and cook for 5 minutes. Serve immediately.
Menu examples	au beurre	with butter
	glace	glazed with sugar and butter
	hollandaise	with hollandaise sauce
	nature	plain
Runner beans	Remove the top, tail and the stringy piece from the side of the bean. Wash well and cut into 1 cm pieces at an angle.	Place in boiling salted water and cook for 15 minutes.
Menu examples	au beurre	with butter
	nature	plain
Salsify (salsifis)	Wash, peel and cut into 5 cm slices. Place in acidulated water until cooking commences.	Place in a simmering blanc for between 40 and 45 minutes. When cooked remove from boiling liquid.
Menu examples	au beurre	with butter
	à la crème	with fresh cream, or cream sauce
	aux fine herbs	with fine herbs
	nature	plain
	persillés	with melted butter and finished with finely chopped parsley
	tourangelle	cream sauce flavoured with garlic
Seakale (chou de mer or chou marin)	Trim away any damaged stalks and roots. Wash well in plenty of cold water. Tie into bundles.	Place in boiling salted water and cook for 25 minutes.
Menu examples	au beurre	with butter
	à la crème	with fresh cream, or cream sauce
	hollandaise	with hollandaise sauce
	nature	plain
Spinach (epinards en branch)	Remove leaves from the stems. Wash well in plenty of cold water.	Place in boiling salted water and cook for 8 minutes.
Menu examples	au beurre	with butter
	à la crème	with fresh cream, or cream sauce
	Mornay	with cheese sauce
	nature	plain
	purée	cooked, drained of the cooking liquor and passed through a sieve or mouli

4

Name	Preparation	Cooking instructions
Swedes (rutabaga)	Wash, trim the stalk and root. Remove the thick peel. Swede can be sliced or cut into the required shape.	Place in cold water, bring to the boil, season and cook for 20 minutes approximately from boiling.
Menu examples	au beurre	with butter
	nature	plain
	persillés	with melted butter and finished with finely chopped parsley
	purée	cooked, drained of the cooking liquor and passed through a sieve or mouli
Sweetcorn— see corn on the cob		
Turnips (navets)	Wash, trim the stalk and root. Remove the thick peel. Turnip can be sliced or cut into the required shape.	Place in cold water, bring to the boil, season and cook for 20 minutes approximately from boiling.
Menu examples	au beurre	with butter
	nature	plain
	persillés	with melted butter and finished with finely chopped parsley
	purée	cooked, drained of the cooking liquor and passed through a sieve or mouli

NOTE: Some vegetables can be combined to form a speciality dish. Such dishes are served as an accompaniment to meat or fish or as part of a vegetarian menu. These dishes can be found in Chapter 20: Vegetarian cookery, for example courgettes with walnut and sage, stuffed baked aubergine, broccoli fritters and hot potatoes with dill.

THE BOILING OF POTATOES

The correct method of boiling of potatoes will depend on whether they are old crop or new crop. The rule is that old potatoes are placed into *cold* water, seasoned with salt and pepper, brought to the boil, then cooked for 20 minutes. New potatoes are placed into *boiling* seasoned water then cooked for 15 minutes. Both new and old crop potatoes can be boiled in their skins (jackets), but take care not to over-cook or to allow the potatoes to stand in hot water as they will fall apart and be unfit for use. The average weight per portion allowed is 100 g with skins on or 150 g if the skins are removed. For new potatoes allow 100 g per portion.

Potatoes, new (peeled)

pommes nouvelles nature

⏲ 20 min   ♨ 15–20 min

Step	Commodity	
1	New potatoes	Wash the potatoes with a scrubbing brush. Scrape the skin off. Rinse in cold running water. Place in boiling salted water and cook for 15 minutes. Serve immediately.

Extensions

Pommes nouvelles à la menthe	Add washed mint leaves during cooking. Brush with melted butter and garnish with blanched mint leaves.
Pommes nouvelles, persillés	Cook as for nature, brush with melted butter and sprinkle with finely chopped parsley.

□   □   □

Potatoes, new (skins on)

🥄 20 min   🍲 15–20 min

Step	Commodity	
1	New potatoes	Wash the potatoes with a scrubbing brush. Rinse in cold running water. Place in boiling salted water and cook for 15 minutes. Serve immediately

☐   ☐   ☐

Potatoes, old (peeled)

Pommes nature

🥄 20 min   🍲 20 min approx

Step	Commodity	
1	Old potatoes	Wash the potatoes with a scrubbing brush. Peel and cut into evenly sized pieces. Rinse in cold running water. Place in cold water and season. Bring to the boil and cook for 20 minutes. Serve immediately.

Extensions

Pommes à la neige   Cook as for pommes nature. Drain away the cooking liquid through a colander. Allow to stand in a saucepan over a warm stove for 5 minutes. Pass through a ricer into the service dish.

Pommes Biarritz   Cook as for pommes nature. Drain away the cooking liquid through a colander. Allow to stand in a saucepan over a warm stove for 5 minutes. Pass into a clean saucepan. Finely dice 100 g of pimento, 150 g of cooked ham and 1 tablespoon of finely chopped parsley per 10 portions and add to the potato. Pour in 100 ml of warm milk per 10 portions and 50 g of melted butter. Season and mix thoroughly. Serve dome-shaped in the dish.

Pommes duchesse   Cook as for pommes nature. Drain away the cooking liquid through a colander. Allow to stand in a saucepan over a warm stove for 5 minutes to dry out. Pass through a ricer and/or mouli. Add approximately 3 egg yolks and 50 g of butter per 10 portions*. Stir vigorously with a wooden spoon. Correct the seasoning. Place in a piping bag with a large star nozzle. Pipe into 2 cm diameter × 5 cm high spirals on a lightly greased baking tray (2–3 per portion). Place in a hot oven 230°C for 5 minutes to harden. Remove and brush with egg wash. Finish the browning process in the oven or under a preheated salamander.

*If the mixture is too wet reduce the amount of egg yolk used. There are other pommes duchesses extensions (see Chapter 12: Deep frying).

Pommes persillés   Cook as for pommes nature. Brush with melted butter and sprinkle with finely chopped parsley.

Pommes purée   As for pommes à la neige, but instead of passing into a service dish pass into a clean saucepan. Add 100 ml of warm milk per 10 portions and 50 g of melted butter. Season and mix thoroughly. Serve dome shaped in the dish.

Pommes purée, à la créme   As for pommes purée. Finish with a cordon of cream (100 ml approximately per 10 portions).

Pommes purée au gratin   As for pommes purée. Finish by sprinkling with grated cheese and gratinating (100 g of cheese, per 10 portions).

☐   ☐   ☐

Potatoes, old (skins on)

Pommes en robe de chambre

Pommes en robe de chambre

⏱ 20 min   ♨ 20 min approx

Step	Commodity	
1	Old potatoes	Select even-sized, small to medium potatoes. Clean the potatoes with a scrubbing brush. Rinse in cold running water.
2		Place in cold water and season. Bring to the boil and cook for 20 minutes. Serve immediately.

Extensions

Pommes à la crème	Cook as for pommes en robe de chambre. Allow to cool and peel. Cut into ½ cm roundels. Place in a clean saucepan and cover with 150 ml of single cream. Season with salt and pepper. Add 50 g of butter. Return to the boil, simmer for 5 minutes and serve.
Pommes maître d'hôtel	As for pommes à la crème. Sprinkle with finely chopped parsley and serve.

□   □   □

5

POACHING

Poaching is defined as gently cooking delicate foods in the minimum amount of simmering liquid. The liquid should never be allowed to boil, but should reach a temperature that is as near to boiling point as possible without actually boiling, 75°–95°C.

Terms associated with poaching

Carry over cooking This is when whole poached fish prepared for cold buffets are usually allowed to cool in the cooking liquor to avoid damage and drying out while cooling. The carry over cooking time must be taken into account when calculating the cooking times.

Cisalaying Making shallow incisions on the skin side of the filleted fish to prevent it from curling during cooking.

Cartouche A piece of greaseproof paper cut to the circumference of the cooking vessel. It is brushed with butter, seasoned and placed butter-side down on the food being cooked. It has the effect of generating steam and aiding the complete cooking of the food in the shortest time.

Compote de cassis Poached blackcurrants.

Compote de cerises Poached cherries.

Compote de fraises Poached strawberries.

Compote de framboises Poached raspberries.

Compote de fruits Poached fruit salad consisting of dried prunes and apricots and fresh apples and pears.

Compote d'abricots Poached apricots.

Compote de groseilles rouges Poached redcurrants.

Compote de groseilles vertes Poached gooseberries.

Compote de pêches Poached peaches.

Compote de poires Poached pears.

Compote de pommes Poached apples.

Compote de pruneaux Poached prunes.

Compote de prunes Poached prunes.

Compote de reines-claude Poached greengages.

Compote de rhubarbe Poached rhubarb.

Court bouillon A vegetable stock made with water and vinegar or wine, used as a cooling liquor for fish.

Cutting and tying Cutting of foods into even pieces and tying them up to retain the shape and give ease of handling.

Darne A steak cut from a round fish.

Délice A cut of fish with either ends folded underneath itself for cooking and presentation.

Draining Draining or drying off all the cooking liquor from the food before coating with sauce, usually done by placing the poached food onto a clean cloth or absorbent paper. This is important as the undrained liquor mixing with the masking sauce will spoil both its appearance and consistency.

Duchess potatoes Boiled potatoes, dried, sieved and bound with egg yolk, butter and seasoning and piped into serving dishes to garnish poached fish dishes.

Fish forcemeat Minced fish, sieved twice, combined with a panada, eggs and cream seasoned with salt, pepper and nutmeg.

Fleurons Small crescent shaped pieces of puff pastry that are brushed heavily with egg wash and used to garnish poached fish dishes.

Fumet A concentrated fish stock used to give more flavour to the finished dishes.

Glazed Coated with an enriched sauce and evenly cooked under a salamander until brown.

Gratinate To nappe with sauce, sprinkle with

parmesan cheese and/or breadcrumbs and brown under a hot salamander.

Panada A binding agent made from either white breadcrumbs and milk; butter, water and flour; or eggs, butter and flour.

Paupiette A fillet of fish filled with a fish stuffing and rolled with the skin side innermost.

Quenelles Finely sieved fish forcemeat, the forcemeat used will depend on the fish being used. Seasoned and flavoured accordingly, and whisked egg whites and shipping cream added.

Reducing The cooking liquor is strained after use and rapidly boiled. It is then added to the accompanying or coating sauce.

Sabayon A mixture made from whisked egg yolks and a little water used to enrich and aid colouring of glazed dishes.

Suprême This is a cut from the fillet of a large fish.

Tronçons This is a steak cut of fish on the bone, from a flat fish.

FOODS SUITABLE FOR POACHING

Poaching is used to cook fish, eggs, gnocchi and white meat, particularly poultry. In practice poached whole poultry, usually boiling fowl, is very similar to – and is classed by many as being boiled. Suprêmes of chicken are shallow poached in the traditional manner.

In some cases the foods being poached are only partly submerged in the cooking liquor. It is, therefore, necessary to use a lid or a cartouche to cover the food to ensure that even heat is maintained within the cooking vessel.

There are two methods of poaching: shallow poaching and deep poaching.

(a) **Shallow poaching** is carried out on smaller items of food such as cuts of fish and poultry. The cooking liquor is brought to the boil, then simmered. The item is then placed in the liquid to cook. It used to be practice to place the item into the liquid and return to the boil before simmering, this was 'to set the surface protein'. This practice is not common nowadays. It is usual practice when shallow poaching to complete the cooking process in a moderate oven (180°C). This prevents the liquid from boiling and ruining the food.

(b) **Deep poaching** is used to cook eggs and whole fish. It should be noted that what the English refer to as boiled fish, the French refer to as *poisson poché*.

POACHED FRUITS

Apples and pears are peeled, quartered, the core removed and placed into a shallow poaching pan of simmering stock syrup. A cartouche is placed over the pan and the fruit cooked until tender, around 20 minutes. Allow 100 g of unprepared fruit per portion. Served cold as a lunchtime sweet with cream or custard, or use as the base of another preparation.

Blackcurrants, gooseberries and redcurrants are prepared by carefully washing, removing the stalks and in the case of gooseberries the top which is not edible. They are then placed into a suitably sized shallow poaching pan and covered with boiling stock syrup and a cartouche. Simmer gently for 8 minutes. Allow 75 g of unprepared fruit per portion. Serve cold as a lunchtime sweet with cream or custard, or use as the base of another preparation.

Figs and prunes are soaked overnight and cooked in a suitably sized shallow poaching pan covered with boiling stock syrup and a cartouche. Simmer gently for 8 minutes. Allow 75 g of unprepared fruit per portion. Served cold on a breakfast menu or as a sweet with cream or custard, or use as the base of another preparation. A mixture of figs, prunes, apples and pears served together is called a compote of fruit and can be offered on a breakfast menu.

Rhubarb is prepared by trimming the stalk and leaves. The branch is then washed and cut into 4 cm lengths, placed in a suitably sized shallow poaching pan, covered with boiling stock syrup and a cartouche and simmered gently for 8–10 minutes. Allow 100 g of unprepared fruit per portion. Serve cold as a sweet with cream or custard, or use as the base of another preparation.

Stone fruit such as fresh apricots, cherries, damsons, greengages and plums are carefully selected and washed before cooking. Then are then placed into a suitably sized shallow poaching pan and covered with boiling stock syrup and a cartouche. Simmer gently for 8 minutes. Peaches are blanched in boiling water for approximately 10 seconds and then plunged into cold water to loosen the skin. They are then peeled and cooked in the same way as other stone fruit. Allow 100 g of unprepared fruit per portion. Serve cold as a sweet with cream or custard, or use as the base of another preparation.

> **Staff associated with the preparation and cooking of poached dishes**
>
> *Chef Poissonier* Fish products and fish sauces
> *Chef Saucier* Entrées

COOKING VESSELS USED IN POACHING

Shallow poaching can be carried out in a sauteuse or a plat à sauter. Special fireproof china dishes called sole dishes or enamelled, cast iron dishes can also be used.

Deep poaching can be carried out in a large saucepan or bratt pan. Saucepans need to be wide enough for the item to fit into them and leave space for the food to be removed when it is cooked.

Poached whole fish are normally cooked in a special 'fish kettle'. A fish kettle has a perforated drainer that fits into the bottom of the kettle with handles at both ends for ease of removal and has a tight-fitting lid. Fish kettles can be made form stainless steel, aluminium or tin-lined copper.

There are special egg poachers that look like frying pans with small shaped moulds for the eggs to fit into and a lid to cover. However, it is argued that, as the egg never comes in contact with the cooking liquor, only the steam, this is not true poaching. A more correct term is oeuf moules, moulded eggs.

TESTS FOR COOKING

Eggs

Eggs are the simplest to test for over/under-cooking. If under-cooked the white is translucent and sloppy; when properly cooked it is white and firm. Poached eggs that are over-cooked have a cloudy looking yolk and are hard to the touch.

Fruit

The texture of poached fruit should be firm, retaining their natural shape but tender to eat. Over-cooking will cause the fruit to become mishapen and soft.

Fish

To test whether a whole fish is cooked completely, apply a little pressure with the thumb on the flesh – if it is cooked, it should yield with no sign of sponginess. With portioned fish, the skin and bone should leave the cooked flesh with ease. If the fish is over-cooked it will fall to pieces and disintegrate into flakes.

Poultry

To test whether poultry is cooked, make an incision with a knife into the thickest part of the breast. Apply pressure with your thumb on the flesh: if it is cooked the juice will run clear. If not, return to the oven and cook for a further few minutes.

Factors that may affect the cooking time

The addition of an acid to the cooking liquor has a tenderising effect on the food being cooked and helps the setting or coagulation of the protein, thus speeding up the cooking process.

The cooking liquor

The choice of cooking liquor is determined by the food being prepared and its size. Vinegar is added to some cooking liquors to aid coagulation of the protein. Although it is traditional to strain court bouillon prior to use, many chefs leave the liquor unstrained for maximum flavour.

When poaching eggs the quantity of vinegar used will depend on the condition of the eggs; fresh eggs need little or none because they hold firm and do not spread like older or stale eggs.

Fruits are poached in a liquor made with water, sugar, lemon juice and an additional flavour of a wine or liquor depending on the finished dish.

Red wine court bouillon

Used to cook freshwater fish.

Step	Commodity	1 litre	10 litres	
				⏱ 15 min
1	Fish stock	1 litre	10 litres	Place in a suitably sized poaching pan and bring to the boil, then simmer.
2	Onions	50 g	500 g	Peel, cut in half and slice thinly. Add to the stock.
3	Thyme, sprig	1 small	1 large	Add to the cooking liquor.
	Bay leaf	2	6	
	Parsley stalks	5 g	20 g	
	Peppercorns	5	20	
4	Lemon juice	25 ml	250 ml	Add to the fish stock.
5	Red wine	250 ml	2½ litres	Pour over the other ingredients. Add salt to season. Cook for 5 minutes before using.

□   □   □

Stock syrup

Used to cook fruits, this stock syrup may also be used cold for fruit salads.

Step	Commodity	½ litre	5 litres	
				⏱ 5 min
1	Water	½ litre	5 litres	Place in a suitably sized saucepan and heat.
2	Castor sugar	200 g	1 kg	Add and dissolve.
3	Lemon	1	5	Extract the juice and add.
4	Cinnamon stick	¼	1	Add and bring the liquid to the boil and simmer for 20–30 minutes. This is now a basic stock syrup.

□   □   □

Vinegar court bouillon

Used to cook calves' and lambs' brains, shellfish and oily fish such as salmon, trout and skate.

Step	Commodity	1 litre	10 litres	
				⏱ 15 min
1	Water	1 litre	10 litres	Place in a suitably sized poaching pan. Bring to the boil.
2	Carrots	50 g	500 g	Wash, peel and cut into thin slices. Place in the cooking liquor.
3	Onions	50 g	500 g	Peel, cut in half and slice thinly.
	Leeks	25 g	250 g	
4	Peppercorns	5	20	Add.
	Bay leaf	2	6	Add.
	Parsley stalks	5 g	20 g	Wash and add.
5	White vinegar	50 ml	500 ml	Pour over the other ingredients. Add salt to season. Cook for 20 minutes before using.

□   □   □

White court bouillon (fish)   Court bouillon blanc

Used to cook white fish, cod, halibut and turbot.

Step	Commodity	1 litre	10 litres	⤵ 15 min
1	Water	1 litre	10 litres	Place in a suitably sized poaching pan. Bring to the boil, then simmer.
2	Onions	50 g	500 g	Peel, cut in half and slice thinly. Add to the water.
3	Peppercorns	5	20	Add to the onions.
	Bay leaf	2	6	
4	Parsley stalks	5 g	20 g	Wash and add.
5	Lemon juice	50 ml	500 ml	Pour over the other ingredients. Add salt to season. Cook for 5 minutes before using.

☐   ☐   ☐

White court bouillon (Meat)   Court bouillon blanc

Used to cook whole poultry.

Step	Commodity	1 litre	10 litres	⤵ 15 min
1	Chicken stock	1 litre	10 litres	Place in a suitably sized poaching pan. Bring to the boil, then simmer.
2	Onions	50 g	500 g	Peel, cut in half and slice thinly. Add to the wine.
3	Carrots	50 g	500 g	Add to the onions and stock. Bring to the boil before adding the meat to be cooked.
	Celery	25 g	250 g	
	Leeks	25 g	250 g	
	Parsley stalks	5 g	20 g	
	Bay leaves	1	5	

☐   ☐   ☐

White wine court bouillon (fish)   Court bouillon au vin blanc

Used to cook white fish, cod, halibut, turbot and freshwater fish.

Step	Commodity	1 litre	10 litres	⤵ 15 min
1	Fish stock	1 litre	10 litres	Place in a suitably sized poaching pan. Bring to the boil, then simmer.
2	Onions	50 g	500 g	Peel, cut in half and slice thinly. Add to the wine.
3	Thyme, sprig	1 small	1 large	Add to the onions and fish stock.
	Bay leaf	2	6	
	Parsley stalks	5 g	20 g	
	Peppercorns	5	20	
4	Lemon juice	25 ml	250 ml	Add to the fish stock.
5	Dry white wine	250 ml	2½ litres	Pour over the other ingredients. Add salt to season. Cook for 5 minutes before using.

☐   ☐   ☐

5

White wine court bouillon (meat)

Court bouillon au vin blanc

Used to cook suprêmes of poultry

🥄 15 min

Step	Commodity	1 litre	10 litres	
1	Chicken stock	1 litre	10 litres	Place in a suitably sized poaching pan and bring to the boil, then simmer.
2	Shallots/ onions	50 g	500 g	Peel, cut in half and slice thinly. Add to the stock.
3	Dry white wine	250 ml	2½ litres	Pour over the other ingredients. Add salt to season. Cook for 5 minutes before using.

NOTE: Lemon juice can be used in place of white wine, 10 ml per portion.

☐   ☐   ☐

Sauces and preparations associated with poaching

FISH FORCEMEAT

Beurre fondu

Step	Commodity	1 portion	10 portions	
1	Butter	50 g	500 g	Place in a suitably sized saucepan.
2	Dry white wine	1 tsp	5 tbsp	Add to the butter and heat. Bring to the boil gently. When the two ingredients are combined pass through a muslin cloth and fine strainer.

☐   ☐   ☐

FISH VELOUTÉ

Classically, fish sauce was made from the strained cooking liquor which was simmered until it reduced in volume to become a glaze. This was allowed to cool slightly. Small pieces of butter that had been kept in chilled water were briskly whisked in to create an emulsion. The sauce was seasoned and used immediately. A variation on this method was to add 1 part of lightly whisked double cream to 2 parts of fish glaze. This method of preparation is rarely used these days.

Sandy roux (blond) and white stock sauces

🥄 20 min   ♨ 1 hr

Step	Commodity	1 litre	5 litres	
1	Butter/ margarine	75 g	375 g	Melt gently in a suitably sized thick-bottomed pan.
2	Flour	75 g	375 g	Add to the fat and cook to a sandy texture. Take care not to over colour the roux. Allow the roux to cool slightly.
3	White stock	1 litre	5 litres	Warm the stock. Return the roux to the stove. Add a quarter of the stock and mix thoroughly. Add another quarter and bring to the boil. Add the remaining stock, bring to the boil and simmer for 1 hour.

NOTE: A velouté sauce is usually finished by enriching with lightly whipped cream – 1 part cream to 10 parts of sauce. The resulting sauce is called suprême sauce.

Extensions of suprême sauce

Additions

Sauce	per 1 litre	per 5 litres	
Tomatoed suprême sauce (Sauce aurore)	1 litre tomato sauce	5 litres tomato sauce	Combine equal quantities of supreme with tomato sauce, season and flavour accordingly.

NOTE: Aurore sauce may be made by adding 100 g of tomato purée per 1 litre of supreme sauce.

Sauce	per 1 litre	per 5 litres	
Curried suprême sauce (Sauce Indienne)	40 g butter	200 g butter	Place in a saucepan and melt.
	75 g onions	325 g onions	Peel, cut into brunoise and add to the butter.
	25 g curry powder	125 g curry powder	Add to the butter and sweat for 3 minutes.
	25 g cream coconut	125 g cream coconut	Add to the curry powder. Add the appropriate amount of sauce and simmer for 30 minutes. Correct the seasoning and pass through a chinois.
Paprika sauce (Sauce hongroise)	25 g butter	125 g Butter	Place in a suitably sized saucepan and melt.
	50 g onions	250 g onions	Peel, cut in half and finely dice. Add to the butter and sweat for 2–3 minutes.
	150 ml white wine	750 ml white wine	Pour over the onions and reduce by half.
	25 g paprika	125 g paprika	Add to the onions. Add the suprême sauce, correct the seasoning and strain through a chinois.
Mushroom sauce (Sauce champignons)	25 g butter	125 g butter	Place in a suitably sized saucepan and melt.
	200 g button mushrooms	1 kg button mushrooms	Wash, peel, slice and add to the butter. Sweat for 2–3 minutes. Add the appropriate amount of sauce. Season with salt and pepper. Degraisser and serve.
German sauce (Sauce Germain)	4 egg yolks	20 egg yolks	Whisk with a little cold water. Combine with the hot suprême sauce. Correct the seasoning. Do not allow to re-boil.
Poulette sauce (Sauce poulette)	4 egg yolks	20 egg yolks	Whisk with a little cold water. Combine with the hot suprême sauce.
	100 ml mushroom essence	500 ml mushroom essence	Add to the sauce. Correct the seasoning. Do not allow to re-boil.

NOTE: If in the case of some fish dishes the finished item is glazed, a sabayon made from egg yolks and a little water (4 egg yolks to 1 litre of sauce) whisked over a gentle heat until it reaches the consistency of double cream is added to the sauce. The sabayon is used to assist the glazing of sauces. The finished sauce should be tested for consistency by placing a small amount of sauce on a flat dish and glazing under a salamander. Any problems can be analysed and rectified before the fish is coated. Do not re-boil the sauce after the cream and sabayon have been added as it will curdle and spoil.

☐   ☐   ☐

Poached fish dishes

SHALLOW POACHED FISH DISHES

The dish used to shallow poach is always buttered and seasoned with salt and pepper before adding the fish. During cooking the fish is always covered with a buttered and seasoned cartouche.

Care must be taken to drain all the cooking liquor from the cooked fish when presenting, otherwise the remaining cooking liquor will seep and spoil the appearance of the finished dish. Shallow poached fish dishes are always served coated with a sauce. The majority of these sauces are made from the reduced cooking liquor, usually with a béchamel or velouté base, though on occasion shellfish flavour or a red wine sauce may be used. There are three ways of finishing these dishes for service: gratinating, glazing under a salamander or serving unglazed.

(a) Gratinated fish dishes: napper with sauce, sprinkle with grated parmesan cheese and brown under a hot salamander.
(b) Glazed fish dishes: napper with a sauce enriched with a sabayon and glaze under a hot salamander.
(c) Unglazed fish dishes: just napper with a sauce and serve with small crescent-shaped pieces of puff pastry called fleurons.

GRATINATED OR GLAZED FISH DISHES

Poached fish Cubat

Poisson Cubat

🥘 1 hr (per ten portions)
🍲 10 min ≋ 205°C (400°F)

Step	Commodity	1 portion	10 portions	
1	Butter	5 g	50 g	Lightly brush on to the base of the poaching dish. Season with salt and pepper.
2	Shallots	5 g	50 g	Chop finely and sprinkle into the dish.
3	Fillet of fish	1 × 150 g	10 × 150 g	Fold and lay on top of the onions.
4	Fish stock	150 ml	1½ litres	Pour over the fish. Cover with a buttered cartouche. Place on top of a hot stove and bring to the boil. Place directly into the oven and cook for the required time. Once cooked remove from the cooking liquor and drain. Strain the cooking liquor into a clean saucepan and reduce to a glaze. Clean the poaching dish and heat.
	Dry white wine	50 ml	500 ml	
5	Warm béchamel	75 ml	750 ml	Heat through and keep warm in a bain-marie.
6	Egg yolks	¼ equiv	2½	Whisk and add to the sauce. Do not allow to re-boil.
7	Cheddar cheese	15 g	150 g	Grate and add to the béchamel.
8	Duxelle	25 g	250 g	Divide into portions and arrange in a decorative manner on the heated serving dish. Place the cooked fish on top of the duxelle. Napper with the sauce, sprinkle with parmesan cheese and gratinate under a hot salamander.
9	Truffles	2 slices	20 slices	Use to decoratively garnish the finished dish.

NOTE: This dish can also be glazed, omitting the parmesan cheese.

□　　　□　　　□

Poached fish Florentine

Poisson Florentine

⤵ 1 hr (per 10 portions)
🍲 10 min ≋ 205°C (400°F)

Step	Commodity	1 portion	10 portions	
1	Butter	5 g	50 g	Lightly brush onto the base of the poaching dish. Season with salt and pepper.
2	Shallots	5 g	50 g	Chop finely and sprinkle into the dish.
3	Fillet of fish	1 × 150 g	10 × 150 g	Fold and lay on top of the onions.
4	Fish stock	150 ml	1½ litres	Pour over the fish. Cover with a buttered cartouche. Place on top of a hot stove and bring to the boil. Place directly into the oven and cook for the required time. Once cooked remove from the cooking liquor and drain. Strain the cooking liquor into a clean saucepan and reduce to a glaze. Clean the poaching dish and heat.
	Dry white wine	50 ml	500 ml	
5	Warm béchamel	75 ml	750 ml	Heat through and keep warm in a bain-marie.
6	Egg yolks	¼ equiv	2½	Whisk and add to the sauce. Do not allow to re-boil.
7	Cheddar cheese	15 g	150 g	Grate and add to the béchamel.
8	Cooked spinach	50 g	500 g	Divide into portions and arrange in a decorative manner on the heated serving dish. Place the cooked fish on top of the spinach. Napper with the sauce, sprinkle with parmesan cheese and gratinate under a hot salamander.

NOTE: This dish can also be glazed omitting the parmesan cheese.

☐　　☐　　☐

Poached fish Walewska

Poisson Waleswka

⤵ 1½ h (per 10 portions)
🍲 10 min ≋ 205°C (400°F)

Step	Commodity	1 portion	10 portions	
1	Butter	5 g	50 g	Lightly brush onto the base of the poaching dish. Season with salt and pepper.
2	Shallots	5 g	50 g	Chop finely and sprinkle into the dish.
3	Fillet of fish	1 × 150 g	10 × 150 g	Fold and lay on top of the onions.
4	Fish stock	150 ml	1½ litres	Pour over the fish. Cover with a buttered cartouche. Place on top of a hot stove and bring to the boil. Place directly into the oven and cook for the required time. Once cooked, remove from the cooking liquor and drain. Strain the cooking liquor into a clean saucepan and reduce to a glaze. Clean the poaching dish and heat.
	Dry white wine	50 ml	500 ml	
5	Warm béchamel	75 ml	750 ml	Heat through and keep warm in a bain-marie.
6	Egg yolk	¼ equiv	2½	Whisk and add to the sauce. Do not allow to re-boil.
7	Cheddar cheese	15 g	150 g	Grate and add to the bechamel. Place the cooked fish in the serving dish.
8	Cooked lobster tails	2 slices	20 slices	Place decoratively with the fish.
9	Truffles	2 slices	20 slices	Napper with the sauce, sprinkle with parmesan cheese and gratinate under a hot salamander.

NOTE: This dish can also be glazed omitting the parmesan cheese.

☐　　☐　　☐

UNGLAZED FISH DISHES

Poached fish in white wine sauce

Poisson au sauce vin blanc

🥄 1½ hr (per 10 portions)
🍲 10 min ≋ 205°C (400°F)

Step	Commodity	1 portion	10 portions	
1	Butter	5 g	50 g	Lightly brush onto the base of the poaching dish. Season with salt and pepper.
2	Shallots	5 g	50 g	Chop finely and sprinkle into the dish.
3	Fillet of fish	1 × 150 g	10 × 150 g	Fold and lay on top of the onions.
4	Fish stock	150 ml	1½ litres	Pour over the fish. Cover with a buttered cartouche. Place on top of a hot stove and bring to the boil. Place directly into the oven and cook for the required time. Once cooked, remove from the cooking liquor and drain. Keep warm. Strain the cooking liquor into a clean saucepan and reduce to a glaze. Clean the poaching dish and heat.
	Dry white wine	50 ml	500 ml	
5	Warm velouté	75 ml	750 ml	Heat through and keep warm in a bain-marie. Place the cooked fish into the serving dish. Napper with the sauce.
6	Fleurons	2	20	Garnish and serve.

☐   ☐   ☐

Poached fish Suchet

Poisson Suchet

🥄 1½ hrs (per 10 portions)
🍲 10 min ≋ 205°C (400°F)

Step	Commodity	1 portion	10 portions	
1	Butter	5 g	50 g	Lightly brush onto the base of the poaching dish. Season with salt and pepper.
2	Shallots	5 g	50 g	Chop finely and sprinkle into the dish.
3	Fillet of fish	1 × 150 g	10 × 150 g	Fold and lay on top of the onions.
4	Fish stock	150 ml	1½ litres	pour over the fish. Cover with a buttered cartouche. Place on top of a hot stove and bring to the boil. Place directly into the oven and cook for the required time. Once cooked, remove from the cooking liquor and drain. Keep warm. Strain the cooking liquor into a clean saucepan and reduce to a glaze. Clean the poaching dish and heat.
	Dry white wine	50 ml	500 ml	
5	Warm velouté	75 ml	750 ml	Heat through and keep warm in a bain-marie. Place the cooked fish into the serving dish. Napper with the sauce.
6	Celery	10 g	100 g	Wash, cut into julienne and boil. Refresh and drain.
	Carrots	10 g	100 g	
	Leeks	10 g	100 g	
7	Truffles	5 g	50 g	Cut into julienne and add to the cooled vegetables. Add to the sauce and mix in. Napper over the sauce.
8	Fleurons	2	20	Garnish and serve.

☐   ☐   ☐

GLAZED FISH DISHES

Poached fish Bercy

Poisson Bercy

🍲 20 min (per 10 portions)
🍳 10 min   ≋ 205°C (400°F)

Step	Commodity	1 portion	10 portions	
1	Butter	5 g	50 g	Lightly brush onto the base of the poaching dish. Season with salt and pepper.
	Shallots	5 g	50 g	Chop finely and sprinkle into the dish.
	Fillet of fish	1 × 150 g	10 × 150 g	Fold and lay on top of the onions.
	Fish stock	150 ml	1½ litres	Pour over the fish. Cover with a buttered cartouche. Place on top of a hot stove and bring to the boil. Place directly into the oven and cooked for the required time. Once cooked, remove from the cooking liquor and drain. Keep warm. Strain the cooking liquor into a clean saucepan and reduce to a glaze. Clean the poaching dish and heat.
	Dry white wine	50 ml	500 ml	
2	Fish velouté	75 ml	750 ml	Heat to just below boiling point.
	Parsley	5 g	50 g	Wash, chop finely and dry. Add to the sauce. Place the cooked fish in the serving dish. Napper with the sauce and glaze.

☐   ☐   ☐

Poached fish good woman

Poisson bonne femme

🍲 20 min (per 10 portions)
🍳 10 min   ≋ 205°C (400°F)

Step	Commodity	1 portion	10 portions	
1	Butter	5 g	50 g	Lightly brush onto the base of the poaching dish. Season with salt and pepper.
	Shallots	5 g	50 g	Chop finely and sprinkle into the dish.
	Fillet of fish	1 × 150 g	10 × 150 g	Fold and lay on top of the onions.
	Butter	5 g	50 g	Place in a suitably sized sauté pan and heat.
	Button mushrooms	20 g	200 g	Wash, cut into slices and add to butter. Cook without colouring for 2–3 minutes. Remove and sprinkle over the fillets.
	Fish stock	150 ml	1½ litres	Pour over the fish. Cover with a buttered cartouche. Place on top of a hot stove and bring to the boil. Place directly into the oven and cook for the required time. Once cooked, remove from the cooking liquor and drain. Keep warm. Strain the cooking liquor into a clean saucepan and reduce to a glaze. Clean the poaching dish and heat.
	Dry white wine	50 ml	500 ml	
2	Fish velouté	75 ml	750 ml	Heat to just below boiling point.
	Parsley	5 g	50 g	Wash, chop finely and dry. Add to the sauce. Place the cooked fish in the serving dish. Napper with the sauce and glaze.

☐   ☐   ☐

5

Poached fish Bréval/d'Antin

Poisson Bréval/d'Antin

Step	Commodity	1 portion	10 portions	
1	Butter	5 g	50 g	Lightly brush onto the base of the poaching dish. Season with salt and pepper.
	Shallots	5 g	50 g	Chop finely and sprinkle into the dish.
	Fillet of fish	1 × 150 g	10 × 150 g	Fold and lay on top of the onions.
	Butter	5 g	50 g	Place in a suitably sized sauté pan and heat.
	Tomatoes	1	10	Remove the eye and score the bottom. Place in a pan of boiling water for 10 seconds, refresh immediately. Remove the skin, cut in half, discard the skin and seeds. Dice the flesh in brunoise and sprinkle over the fish fillets.
	Button mushrooms	20 g	200 g	Wash, cut into slices and add to butter. Cook without colouring for 2–3 minutes. Remove and sprinkle over the fillets.
	Fish stock	150 ml	1½ litres	Pour over the fish. Cover with a buttered cartouche. Place on top of a hot stove and bring to the boil. Place directly into the oven and cook for the required time. Once cooked, remove from the cooking liquor and drain. Keep warm. Strain the cooking liquor into a clean saucepan and reduce to a glaze. Clean the poaching dish and heat.
	Dry white wine	50 ml	500 ml	
2	Fish velouté	75 ml	750 ml	Heat to just below boiling point.
	Parsley	5 g	50 g	Wash, chop finely and dry. Add to the sauce. Place the cooked fish in the serving dish, napper with the sauce and glaze.

☐   ☐   ☐

DEEP POACHED FISH DISHES

The cooking liquor for deep poaching will depend on the type and cut of fish being cooked. Oily fish, such as Mackerel, Salmon, Salmon Trout, Skate and Trout are cooked in a vinegar court bouillon, (bouillon ordinaire). White fish, including Brill, Cod, Coley, Haddock, Halibut and Turbot are cooked in a white court bouillon (court bouillon blanc). Smoked fish, such as Coley, Haddock and Kippers are cooked in a milk and water liquor. Cooking times will depend on the portion or fish's size. As a rule a portion of fish steak should weigh between 150–180 g and this should take between 8–10 minutes to cook. To test if the fish is cooked: using the tip of a knife, try to loosen the bone. If the bone comes away with ease the fish is cooked. It is important to remove the fish as soon as it is cooked as it is liable to fall apart if left in the cooking liquor. To test filleted portions, light pressure should be applied to the flesh; if it feels firm with no sign of sponginess it is cooked. Whole fish should be brought to the boil and simmered for 15 minutes, then the heat is turned off and the fish is allowed to cool and set in the cooking liquor.

Whole fish for poaching are prepared by removing the skin on both sides, cutting off the head and the side bones, and cleaning the gut, thoroughly removing all traces of blood. Once cooked the remaining side bones are removed and the fillets are loosened and folded. The back bone is removed and the fillets returned to give the impression of a whole fish.

Blue trout

Amount per portion: 1 whole fish

Truit au bleau

⏱ 8 min

Trout used for this dish are kept alive right up to the time they are ordered by the customer. A fish is then removed from the fish tank, stunned by hitting it on the back of the head and then gutted. The trout is cooked and served in a special fish kettle garnished with sprigs of parsley. The term blue trout comes from the action of the vinegar on the outer mucus of the fish turning it blue.

NOTE: serve with beurre fondu.

☐   ☐   ☐

Poached brill steak

Tronçon de barbue poche

🥄 40 min (per 10 portions)   ⏱ 20–25 min

Step	Commodity	1 portion	10 portions	
1	Small turned potatoes	2	20	Place in boiling salted water and cook for 15–20 minutes.
2	White court bouillon	½ litre	5 litres	Place in a suitably sized poaching pan. Bring to the boil.
3	Brill steaks	170 g	10 × 170 g	Wash well in salted water to remove any blood. Place in the boiling liquor. Return to the boil then simmer immediately. Skim the surface. Poach gently for 8–10 minutes. Remove from the cooking liquor. Drain and place the fish on a chopping board. Remove the centre bone and the skin. Place a little of the strained cooking liquor into a heated earthenware dish. Carefully place the darne on top.
4	Lemon	1	2	Flute with a canalle cutter and cut into slices. Garnish with a slice of lemon on top of each steak, picked parsley and the cooked potatoes.

NOTE: Serve with beurre fondu.

☐   ☐   ☐

Poached cod steak (1)

Darne de cabillaud pochee

🥄 20 min (per 10 portions)   ⏱ 40 min (per 10 portions)

Step	Commodity	1 portion	10 portions	
1	Small turned potatoes	2	20	Place in boiling salted water and cook for 15–20 minutes.
2	White court bouillon	½ litre	5 litres	Place in a suitably sized poaching pan. Bring to the boil.
3	Cod steaks	170 g	10 × 170 g	Wash well in salted water to remove any blood. Place in the boiling liquor. Return to the boil then simmer immediately. Skim the surface. Poach gently for 8–10 minutes. Remove from the cooking liquor. Drain and place the fish on a chopping board. Remove the centre bone and the skin. Place a little of the strained cooking liquor in a heated earthenware dish. Carefully place the darne on top.
4	Lemon	1	2	Flute with a canalle cutter and cut into slices. Garnish with a slice of lemon on top of each steak, picked parsley and the cooked potatoes.

NOTE: Hake, haddock, halibut, or tubot can be used instead of cod. This dish can be served with sauce à la crème, aux oeufs, hollandaise, homard and persille.

5

Poached cod steak Portugaise (2)

Darne de cabillaud Portugaise

🥄 20 min (per 10 portions)

♨ 40 min (per 10 portions)   ≋ 175°C (350°F)

Step	Commodity	1 portion	10 portions	
1	Tomato	100 g	1 kg	Remove the eye of the tomato and make a slight incision in the other end. Place into a pan of boiling water for 10 seconds. Remove and plunge into a bowl of cold water. Remove the skin and discard, cut in half. Remove the seeds and discard. Wash the tomato flesh and cut into small dice. Store for use later.
2	Cod steaks	170 g	10 × 170 g	Wash well in salted water to remove any blood. Place in a suitably sized buttered and seasoned poaching dish. Sprinkle with the tomato concassé.
3	Butter	10 g	100 g	Melt gently into a sauteuse.
	Onions	20 g	200 g	Cut into fine dice (brunoise). Add to the butter and begin to cook.
	Garlic	¼ clove	1 clove	Peel, cut small. Sprinkle some salt over the garlic and crush with the side of a knife. Add the onion and cook without colouring. Sprinkle over the fish.
	Finely chopped parsley	½ tsp	1 tbsp	Sprinkle over the onion.
4	Dry white wine	25 ml	250 ml	Pour over the fish. Cover with a buttered cartouche and place in the oven for 10–15 minutes. Remove the steaks carefully and place on a chopping board. Remove the centre bone and the skin. Place in the prepared serving dish and keep covered and warm. Pour the complete cooking liquor into a pan and allow to reduce slightly on the side of the stove. Season with salt and pepper.
	Fish stock	25 ml	250 ml	
5	Butter	10 g	100 g	Cut into small pieces and add to the cooking liquor piece by piece shaking the pan gently (monter). This has the effect of lightly thickening the liquor to produce a sauce. The sauce is carefully ladled over the warm fish. Sprinkle with a little chopped parsley and serve.

NOTE: Hake, haddock, halibut, or turbot can be used instead of cod.

☐   ☐   ☐

Mackerel, fillet of

Filet de macquereau

🥄 30 min (per 10 portions) ♨ 6 min

Step	Commodity	1 portion	10 portions	
1	Small turned potatoes	2	20	Place in boiling salted water and cook for 15–20 minutes.
2	Vinegar court bouillon	½ litre	5 litres	Place in a suitably sized poaching pan and bring to the boil.
3	Mackerel fillets	125 g	10 × 125 g	Wash well in salted water to remove any blood. Place in the boiling liquor. Return to the boil then simmer for 6–8 minutes. Remove from the cooking liquor and drain well. Place on a chopping board and carefully remove the skin. Pour a little of the strained cooking liquor onto a heated serving dish. Carefully place the cooked mackerel fillet on top. Garnish with the boiled potatoes.

NOTE: This fish dish is usually accompanied with a sauceboat of parsley sauce (75 ml per portion of fish).

☐   ☐   ☐

Salmon with hollandaise sauce

Darne de saumon poche, sauce hollandaise

🥄 30 min (per 10 portions) ♨ 20–25 min

Step	Commodity	1 portion	10 portions	
1	Small turned potatoes	2	20	Place in boiling salted water and cook for 15–20 minutes.
2	Vinegar court bouillon	½ litre	5 litres	Place in a suitably sized poaching pan and bring to the boil.
3	Salmon steaks	170 g	10 × 170 g	Wash well in salted water to remove any blood. Place in the boiling liquor. Return to the boil then simmer for 6–8 minutes. Remove from the cooking liquor and drain well. Place on a chopping board and carefully remove the skin and the centre bone. Pour a little of the strained cooking liquor onto a heated serving dish. Carefully place the cooked salmon on top.
4	Lemon	1	2	Flute with a canalle cutter and cut into slices. Garnish with a slice of lemon on top of each steak, picked parsley and the cooked potatoes.

NOTE: Cod, hake, haddock, halibut, or turbot can be used instead of salmon. This dish is usually served with hollandaise sauce.

☐   ☐   ☐

Skate with black butter

Raie au beurre noir

🥄 30 min (per 10 portions)   ♨ 8 min

Step	Commodity	1 portion	10 portions	
1	Vinegar court bouillon	½ litre	5 litres	Place in a suitably sized poaching pan and bring to the boil.
	Skate wing	200 g	10 × 200 g	Wash well in salted water to remove any blood. Place in the boiling liquor. Return to the boil then simmer for 10–12 minutes. Remove from the cooking liquor and drain well. Place on a serving dish and keep in a hot plate for use later.
	Butter	15 g	150 g	Place in a frying pan and heat until almost black.
	Capers	½ tsp	5 tsp	Add.
	Vinegar	½ tsp	5 tsp	Add and pour over the fish.
2	Lemon	1	2	Flute with a canalle cutter and cut into slices. Garnish with a slice of lemon on top of each steak, picked parsley and the cooked potatoes.
3	Parsley	5 g	50 g	Wash, chop finely, dry and sprinkle over the fish. Serve immediately.

□   □   □

Shallow poached ham and poultry dishes

Poached chicken breast

Suprême de volaille poché

🥄 30 min (per 10 portions)
♨ 15 min approximately   ≋ 175°C (350°F)

Step	Commodity	1 portion	10 portions	
1	Chicken suprêmes	1 × 150 g	10 × 150 g	Prepare by trimming any fat and loose meat. Scrape the bone clean. Lightly season with salt and pepper. Place in a suitably sized, buttered cooking vessel.
2	White wine court bouillon	250 mls	2½ litres	Pour, just covering the suprêmes. Place on the side of the stove and steadily bring to the boil. Cover with a buttered cartouche and place in the pre-heated oven for the required time. Once cooked, remove from the cooking liquor and drain thoroughly. Serve accordingly.

NOTE: A thin layer of sauce is usually placed on the bottom of the heated serving dish to prevent the suprêmes from sticking.

□   □   □

Chicken mousselines Alexandra style

Mousselines de volaille Alexandra

⏱ 3 h   🍲 15 min   ≋ 180°C

Step	Commodity	1 portion	10 portions	
1	Minced lean raw chicken	75 g	750 g	Place in a blender and season with salt and paprika.
	Egg whites	¼	3 equiv	Add and liquidise until light and fluffy. Pass through a fine sieve twice and chill thoroughly.
2	Double cream	50 ml	500 ml	Beat lightly and gradually add to the mixture. Correct the seasoning.
	Butter	2 g	20 g	Melt and use to butter a deep-sided tray. Using two tablespoons dipped in hot water, shape the mousseline mixture into egg shapes, two to a portion and place on the buttered tray.
3	White chicken stock	100 ml	1 litre	Bring to the boil, season and pour over the mousselines. Cover with a cartouche and place in a pre-heated oven for the appropriate time. Remove, drain well. Place in a suitably sized earthenware dish.
5	Mornay sauce	50 ml	500 ml	Napper over the top of the mousselines.
	Grated parmesan cheese	5 g	50 g	Sprinkle over the top and gratinate under a pre-heated salamander. Garnish with sliced truffles and asparagus tips.

☐   ☐   ☐

Ham mousselines Florentine style

Mousselines de jambon florentine

⏱ 3 h   🍲 15 min   ≋ 180°C

Step	Commodity	1 portion	10 portions	
1	Minced lean raw ham	75 g	750 g	Place in a blender and season with salt and paprika.
	Egg whites	¼	3 equiv	Add and liquidise until light and fluffy. Pass through a fine sieve twice and chill thoroughly.
2	Double cream	50 ml	500 ml	Beat lightly and gradually add to the mixture. Correct the seasoning.
	Butter	2 g	20 g	Melt and use to butter a deep-sided tray. Using two tablespoons dipped in hot water, shape the mousseline mixture into egg shapes, two to a portion and place in the buttered tray.
3	White chicken stock	100 ml	1 litre	Bring to the boil, season and pour over the mousselines. Cover with a cartouche and place in a pre-heated oven for the appropriate time. Remove, drain well.
4	Cooked spinach	25 g	250 g	Drain well, season, portion and place on the bottom of a suitably sized earthenware dish. Place the mousselines on top.
5	Suprême sauce	50 ml	500 ml	Napper over the top of the mousselines and gratinate under a pre-heated salamander.

5

Extensions to shallow poached chicken dishes

Suprême sauce (150 ml per portion) with: Suprême de volaille poché

Dish	1 portion	10 portions	
Asparagus (*Princesse*)	3 asparagus tips	30 asparagus tips	Warm, but do not over-heat.
	1 slice of bread	1 slice of bread	Cut into two triangles and shape each piece into a heart. Toast under a salamander or shallow fry till golden brown. Dip one edge of the crouton in the finely chopped parsley for a different effect.
	1 slice of truffle	10 slices of truffle	Napper the breasts with the suprême sauce. Garnish with the asparagus tips and sliced truffle. Finish off with the croûtons.
Mushroom sauce (*aux sauce champignons*)	50 g button mushrooms	500 g button mushrooms	Wash and cut into thin slices.
	10 g butter	75 g butter	Place in a suitably sized sauté pan and heat gently. Add the sliced mushrooms and cook without colouring. Remove the mushrooms from the fat and stir into the sauce. Degraisser as required.
	3 button mushrooms	30 button mushrooms	Cook in a blanc (*see* Chapter 5: Boiling). Napper the cooked suprêmes with the sauce. Garnish with the button mushrooms. Finish with finely chopped parsley.
Spinach and cheese (*Florentine*)	50 g cooked spinach	500 g cooked spinach	Squeeze dry, divide into portions and lay on the base of the service dish. Place a portion of chicken on top.
	25 g cheddar cheese	250 g cheddar cheese	Grate and stir into the sauce. Napper the chicken with the sauce.
	10 g parmesan cheese	100 g parmesan cheese	Sprinkle over the sauce and gratinate.
Vegetables (*Polignac*)	25 g cooked carrots, leeks, celery, mushrooms	250 g cooked carrots, leeks, celery, mushrooms	Add to the sauce and stir in well. Pour over the chicken and serve.

Deep poached poultry dishes

Poached chicken, petite-mariée

Poularde petite-mariée

⤵ 30 min (per 10 portions)   ♨ 2 hr approximately

Step	Commodity	1 portion	10 portions	
1	Chicken stock	½ litre	6 litres	Place in a large saucepan, and bring to the boil and season.
2	Chicken	300 g	3 × 1½ kg	Prepare the chicken by removing the wishbone, cleaning the inside of the carcass and trussing the chicken as for roasting. Place into the boiling stock. Ensure there is sufficient stock to cover the bird(s). Simmer for 1½ hours.
3	Chicken velouté	100 ml	1 litre	Place in a saucepan and heat. Strain to remove any lumps. Keep hot in a bain-marie.
4	New potatoes	3 sm	30 sm	Clean thoroughly and add to the stock.
	Button onions	3	30	Peel and add to the potatoes.
	Carrots	100 g	1 kg	Peel and turn small. Add.
5	Garden peas	15 g	150 g	Remove from the shell. Wash and add to the other vegetables. Cook for 30 minutes. Remove the chicken when cooked. Discard the string and skin. Place on a suitably warmed earthenware dish. Decorate with the cooked vegetables and keep warm. Allow the cooking liquor to reduce and strain. Add 50 ml per portion of the liquor to the velouté to strengthen the flavour. Strain through a fine chinois.
6	Butter	10 g	100 g	Cut into small pieces and monte into the sauce.
7	Double cream	25 ml	250 ml	Add to the finished sauce. Do not allow to re-boil. Napper over the chicken. Sprinkle with finely chopped parsley and serve.

☐   ☐   ☐

Poached chicken with suprême sauce

Poularde poché au riz, sauce suprême

⤵ 30 min (per 10 portions)   ♨ 2 hr approximately

Step	Commodity	1 portion	10 portions	
1	Chicken stock	½ litre	6 litres	Place in a large saucepan, and bring to the boil and season.
2	Chicken	300 g	3 × 1½ kg	Prepare the chicken by removing the wishbone, cleaning the inside of the carcass and trussing the chicken as for roasting. Place into the boiling stock. Ensure there is sufficient stock to cover the bird(s). Simmer for 1½ hours.
3	Chicken velouté	100 ml	1 litre	Place in a saucepan and heat. Strain to remove any lumps. Keep hot in a bain-marie. Remove the chicken when cooked. Discard the string and skin and place on a suitably warmed earthenware dish. Allow the cooking liquor to reduce and strain. Add 50 ml per portion of the liquor to the velouté to strengthen the flavour. Strain through a fine chinois.
4	Butter	10 g	100 g	Cut into small pieces and monte into the sauce.
5	Double cream	25 ml	250 ml	Add to the finished sauce. Do not allow to re-boil. Napper over the chicken. Sprinkle with finely chopped parsley and serve with braised rice (riz pilaff), 25 g raw weight per portion.

☐   ☐   ☐

5

Poached Eggs

Oeuf Poche

Step	Commodity	1 portion	10 portions		
				⏲ 2 min	♨ 4–5 min
1	Water	250 mls	2 litres	Place in a suitably sized plat à sauter.	
2	Vinegar	25 mls	200 mls	Add to the water. Bring to the boil and reduce to a simmer. The vinegar assists in making the whites contract tightly around the yolk so it dose not fall apart.	
3	Egg	1–2	10–20	Break into the simmering liquid and poach gently for 4–5 minutes until the egg white is firm and the yolk still soft. The eggs are carefully removed from the cooking liquor with a perforated spoon and the egg white trimmed with a knife or a pastry cutter before serving. The egg is then reheated in a pan of simmering water to remove the taste of vinegar. If they are to be stored for use later the eggs are placed in a bowl of cold water and reheated as required in a plate a saute of simmering salted water for approximately 1–1½ minutes. Serve on rounded pieces of buttered toast on an egg dish.	

☐   ☐   ☐

WHAT WENT WRONG

Problem	Caused by	To rectify
Eggs		
Eggs are misshapen.	Poaching at too low a temperature.	Discard the mis-shapen eggs and cooking liquid. Start again with a clean cooking vessel and ensure that the correct temperature is achieved.
Eggs are stuck to the bottom of the cooking vessel.	Poaching at too low a temperature.	Discard the mis-shapen eggs and cooking liquid. Start again with a clean cooking vessel and ensure that the correct temperature is achieved.
Fruit		
Fruit is discoloured.	(1) Allowing the fruit to come into contact with air during preparation.	Fruits such as apples and pears discolour if they are not submerged in an acidulated solution. Once discoloured, the only thing to do is to carefully remove the affected area with a knife.
	(2) By not immersing in enough cooking liquid.	Once affected, the only solution is to carefully remove the affected area with a sharp knife. Care should be taken to keep the fruit submerged during cooking and also to cover with a cartouche.
Fish		
Fish curls/distorts during cooking.	Not removing skin or not cissalaying.	Use a palette knife to flatten the filleted fish as far as possible.
Cooked fish has distorted shape.	Over-cooking.	Cannot be rectified.
Fish dark in colour.	Over-cooking.	Cannot be rectified.

Problem	Caused by	To rectify
Fish has dry texture.	Over-cooking.	Cannot be rectified.
Cooked white fish is discoloured.	Using the wrong kind of cooking liquid.	Cannot be rectified.
Cooked fish has oily flavour and smell.	Over-using the cooking liquid.	Cannot be rectified. Ensure cooking liquid is changed regularly.
Cooked fish seeps liquid into finishing sauce.	Insufficient draining of fish and not drying on kitchen paper before presenting.	Remove as much liquid as possible on kitchen paper. All subsequent fish should be drained and dried sufficiently
Fish sticks to dish while cooking.	Cooking dish was not buttered before adding the fish.	With a fish slice, try to remove the fish from the dish without breaking it.
Cartouche sticks to fish while cooking.	Grease-proof paper was not buttered sufficiently before being placed on top of fish.	Carefully remove the paper with a dampened knife, or moisten another sheet of grease-proof paper and place directly on top of the dry grease-proof paper. This should loosen the bottom paper.
The surface of the cooked fish has a dry appearance.	Grease-proof paper was not buttered sufficiently, causing it to lift off during cooking.	Cannot be rectified. The fish will be too dry.
The surface has a raw flour flavour.	Insufficient cooking of the velouté.	Continue cooking until the flavour subsides.
The sauce runs off the fish when placed under the grill.	(1) The sauce being too thin;	Allow the sauce to cook longer and napper with the thicker sauce.
	(2) The grill temperature was too low; or	Wait until the salamander has reached the correct temperature then napper and glaze.
	(3) The fish was not dried sufficiently before coating with the sauce.	Wipe the fish dry with a piece of kitchen paper, napper and glaze.
The sauce appears discoloured.	(1) Using poor quality fish stock to poach the fish or make the sauce with;	Discard the stock and begin again.
	(2) Cooking the sauce in an aluminium saucepan; or	Discard the sauce and begin again.
	(3) Insufficient cream added.	Add more cream, ensuring the cream does not become too thin.
The glaze on the fish is uneven.	(1) The sauce being too thin;	Correct the thickness, either by adding to a sauce that is thicker or, if the sabayon has not been added, by cooking for longer until the required thickness is achieved.
	(2) The sauce being too thick;	Correct the thickness, either by adding additional sabayon cream, strained fish stock or a thinner sauce.
	(3) Insufficient dispersal of the sabayon;	Cannot be rectified once the fish is glazed.
	(4) Insufficient liaison;	Cannot be rectified once the fish is glazed.
	(5) Incorrect proportion of egg yolk to cream in the liaison.	Cannot be rectified once the fish is glazed.

5

6

STEWING

The word stew comes from the French verb *étuver*, meaning 'to cook in its own juices'. A definition of stewing would be, the cooking of the prepared food by a moderate heat in the minimum amount of liquid. The liquid can be water, wine, beer, stock or sauce. It should be noted that meat is always cut into pieces for stewing. The temperature used in stewing is just below boiling point and during cooking the slow, gentle process aids the extraction of flavours from the stewed food. Once cooked, the food and liquid are almost always served together.

Stewing usually takes place on top of the stove, simmering gently on a low heat setting with a tight-fitting lid covering the cooking vessel. Condensation forms on the inside of the lid and acts as a self-basting process keeping the food moist. Cooking on top of the stove with a small amount of usually thickened liquid means stewed foods are prone to burn. Stewing can also be 'started off' on top of the stove, then transferred to the oven in an appropriate cooking vessel with a tight-fitting lid. It is easier to maintain an even gentle heat setting in the oven and this method of stewing may suit beginners as the cooking process is easier to control.

Because the slow cooking process in stewing converts the connective tissue of meat into a gelatinous substance causing the fibres to fall apart easily and become digestible, cheaper cuts of meat and poultry can be used – making this an economical method of cooking. It is also nutritional because, even though vitamins are at risk from the lengthy cooking process, the liquid which will contain any water soluble vitamins is served with the stewed food.

Terms associated with stewing

Blanc A cooking liquor made from flour, water and lemon juice. Used to cook vegetables that discolour when boiled.

Blanching Placing in cold water and bringing to the boil.

Blanquette White stew.

Bouquet garni A blend of parsley stalk, bay leaf, thyme and peppercorns wrapped in a leek or a muslin cloth and secured with string.

Browned flour Flour that has been browned in the oven or under the grill to assist in the colouring of brown stews.

Browning Cooking in hot fat till brown in colour (a brun).

Cook out This refers to the cooking of flour to release the starch granules in order to thicken the sauce.

Flashing Sealing the meat at a very high temperature, usually in an oven.

Fricassée White stew.

Glace au brun Cooked in butter till it becomes brown and has a glazed finish.

Jaysee A mixture of sieved flour and water, whisked to a smooth paste. Used for thickening sauces and soups.

Liaison A basic mixture of egg yolks and cream whipped to the ribbon stage.

Mirepoix Roughly cut vegetables, usually carrots, celery, onions and leeks.

Navarin Brown stew.

Onion clouté An onion studded with bay leaf and cloves.

Ragoût Brown stew.

The cooking vessel

This can be a copper (tin-lined), stainless steel, or aluminium saucepan. A suitable roasting tray (heavy bottomed, with deep sided walls) or a braising pan can be used for stewing in the oven. In large establishments bratt pans are used for catering for large numbers.

Additional ingredients

Before fridges, additional ingredients used to be added to stews to mask the strong flavour of mortified meat. Now they are usually added to enhance the flavour of the main stewed item. The herbs parsley, thyme and bayleaf can be used, as may vegetables like celery, carrot, onion and leek, to increase the flavour. Usually all these additional ingredients are removed from the stew before service.

Some contemporary stews contain spices such as chilli powder, cayenne, paprika or curry powder, giving the stews a distinct hot flavour.

METHODS OF STEWING

Stewing is divided into three main categories: brown stews, white stews, and miscellaneous stews.

Brown stews

Brown stews are further divided into two areas: ragoûts and navarins.

1 Ragout

A ragoût is usually associated with brown beef stews though it is possible to have a ragoût of veal, rabbit or ox kidney.

2 Navarin

A navarin can either be a lamb or veal stew. These stews are usually always thickened with a brown roux at the beginning of the cookery process. The browning effect is created by shallow frying or briefly cooking (flashing) the meat in a hot oven. The flour used to thicken the liquid may also be browned, either under the grill or in the oven. This has the effect of browning the sauce. Cooking time is usually 2 hours.

White stews

White stews are also split into two categories: fricassée and blanquette.

1 Fricassée

A fricassée is only suitable for tender cuts of either veal, chicken, pork or rabbit. The meat is cooked in a white sauce made with a sandy (blond) roux and appropriate white stock. The resulting sauce is called a velouté. If you are making a chicken fricassée a white chicken stock would be used.

The cooking time is usually no more than 1 hour, any longer and there is a chance that the sauce will discolour and spoil the appearance of the finished item.

2 Blanquette

A blanquette is normally made with lesser quality, tougher cuts of meat. The nature of the meat used has a direct effect on the cooking time which is longer than a fricasée, approximately 1½ hours. The meat is first brought to the boil in water, once boiled it is then cooled down. This process is called blanching and refreshing and is used to remove impurities and excess blood which form as a scum on the top of the liquid. The meat is then placed into stock and the cooking process takes place. The strained cooking liquor (the liquid the meat was cooked in) is thickened using a blond roux to make a velouté and is used as the serving sauce.

Although not called a blanquette, tripe can be cooked by the above method.

6

Both blanquettes and fricassées are finished off with a liaison of lightly whisked egg yolk and cream. Care must be taken not to re-boil the stew once the liaison has been added, otherwise the sauce will curdle and spoil the appearance of the dish.

NOTE: Stews can also be thickened with cornflour, arrowroot, beurre maniée and blood.

Miscellaneous stews

These are stews that cannot be classified into the other two main areas.

Miscellaneous meat stews

All types of curry, goulash, chilli con carne, osso-buco, coq au vin, feathered game stews (salmis), furred game stews (gibiers) and all unthickened stews, lamb chop champvallon, Irish stew and Lancashire hot pot.

Fish stews

Bouillabaisse, lobster Américain, lobster Newburg and mussels in white wine, better known moules marinière.

Stewed vegetable dishes

Peas, marrow and pumpkin.

Stewed fruits

Apples, apricots, figs, peaches, pears, plums and prunes.

NOTE: Working in a traditional kitchen brigade, six different parties would be involved with the preparation and cooking of stewed foods:

The Breakfast Chef – Le Chef du Petit Déjeuner – fruit dishes.

The Pastry Chef – Le chef Pâtissier – fruit dishes.

The Fish Chef – Le Chef Poissonnier – stewed fish dishes.

The Larder Chef – Le Garde-Manger – initial preparation of all meat and fish.

The Sauce Chef – Le Chef Saucier – all butchers' meats, offal, poultry and game.

The Vegetable Chef – Le Chef Entremettier – vegetable and potato dishes.

THE SERVICE OF STEWS

Stews are usually garnished for service with toasted or fried heart-shaped croûtons that have been partly dipped in the sauce then into finely chopped parsley.

Stews are served in either an earthenware or metal entrée dish that is placed on an appropriate serving flat.

Stewed vegetables are served in a vegetable dish and stewed fruits in a fruit bowl.

CUTS OF MEAT SUITABLE FOR STEWING

Type	Cut	Amount per portion (raw)
Beef	Thick flank	125 g
	Topside	125 g
Lamb	Shoulder	125 g
	Middle neck	175 g
Poultry	Chicken	125 g
	Turkey	125 g
Pork	Shoulder	125 g
Game	Hare	150 g
	Pheasant	1 whole Pheasant
	Venison	100 g
Veal	Shoulder	125 g
	Middle neck	175 g

Brown stews

Navarin

🍲 30 min approximately (per 10 portions)
🍲 2 hr (per 10 portions)   ≋ 150°C (300°F)

Step	Commodity	1 portion	10 portions	
1	Fat (lard, dripping or cooking oil).	6 g	60 g	Melt in a suitable cooking vessel.
2	Prepared stewing meat	125 g	1.25 kg	Season, add to the hot fat and brown on all sides.
3	Mirepoix of carrots	15 g	150 g	Place in the frying pan along with the meat and brown accordingly.
	Mirepoix of onions	15 g	150 g	
4	Browned flour	6 g	60 g	Add to the ingredients in the cooking vessel and mix to form a roux. Cook out. Allow to cool slightly.
5	Tomato purée	6 g	60 g	Add and stir in thoroughly.
6	Brown stock	150 ml	1½ litres	Add a quarter and mix in thoroughly, add another quarter and bring to the boil, add the remaining stock, bring to the boil then simmer.
7	Bouquet garni	1 small	1 large	Place in the simmering liquid, secure the string to the handle. Complete the process.
8	Final seasoning (salt and pepper)	A pinch	To taste	Carefully adjust the seasoning. Correct the colour and consistency of the stew accordingly. Place in a serving dish.
9	Finely chopped parsley	A pinch	2 tsp	Sprinkle over the top and serve.

Suitable garnishes for Navarin

	English term	French term	Commodities
1	Brown lamb stew with vegetables.	Navarin d'agneau printanier.	Spring season vegetables. Button onions, glace à brun, turned carrot and turnips. Finished by sprinkling with finely chopped parsley.
2	Brown lamb stew with vegetables.	Navarin d'agneau paysanne.	Vegetables cut in the style of paysanne and glazed. Paysanne – thin sliced roundels, ½ rounds, ¼ rounds, squares or triangles. Finely chopped parsley.
3	Brown lamb stew with vegetables.	Navarin d'agneau julienne.	Vegetables cut in the style of julienne and glazed. Julienne – thin strips ¼ cm square by 3 cms long. Finely chopped parsley.
4	Brown lamb stew with vegetables.	Navarin d'agneau jardinière.	Vegetables cut in the style of jardinière. Jardinière – ½ cm square by 1½ cms long.
5	Brown lamb stew Bourgeoise.	Navarin d'agneau bourgeoise.	Button onions and turned carrots, glace à brun, lardons of bacon. Finely chopped parsley.

The quantities for the above vegetable garnishes should be 60 g in total per portion.
The same garnishes can be used for navarin de veau (veal) dishes.

□   □   □

6

Ragoût

Suitable meats: Beef, rabbit and veal

⏱ 30 min approximately (per 10 portions)
🍲 2 h (per 10 portions)   ≋ 150°C (300°F)

Step	Commodity	1 portion	10 portions	
1	Fat (lard, dripping or cooking oil).	6 g	60 g	Melt in a suitable cooking vessel.
2	Prepared stewing meat	125 g	600 g	Season, add to the hot fat and brown on all sides.
3	Mirepoix of carrots	15 g	150 g	Place in the frying pan along with the meat and brown accordingly.
	Mirepoix of onions	6 g	150 g	
4	Browned flour	6 g	60 g	Add to the ingredients in the cooking vessel and mix in to form a roux. Cook out. Allow to cool slightly.
5	Tomato purée	6 g	60 g	Add and stir in thoroughly.
6	Brown stock	150 ml	1½ litres	Add a quarter and mix in thoroughly, add another quarter and bring to the boil, add the remaining stock, bring to the boil then simmer.
7	Bouquet garni	1	1	Place in the simmering liquid, secure the string to the handle. Complete the process.
8	Final seasoning (salt and pepper)	A pinch	To taste	Carefully adjust the seasoning.
9				Correct the colour and consistency of the stew accordingly.

Suitable garnishes for ragoût

English term	French term	Commodities
Savoury minced beef	Hachis de boeuf	As for the basic recipe, mincing the beef instead of dicing. Usually served with a border of duchesse potato and a fried heart-shaped croûton.
Brown beef stew	Ragoût de boeuf	As for the basic recipe, with stewing beef.
Brown beef stew with dumplings	Ragoût de boeuf à l'anglaise	As above, garnished with suet dumplings.
Brown beef stew with vegetables	Ragoût de boeuf printanier	Spring season vegetables. Button onions, glace à brun, turned carrots and turnips. Finished by sprinkling with finely chopped parsley.
Brown beef stew with vegetables	Ragoût de boeuf paysanne	Vegetables cut in the style of paysanne and glazed. Paysanne – thin sliced roundels, half rounds, quarter rounds, squares or triangles. Finely chopped parsley.

English term	French term	Commodities
Brown beef stew with vegetables	Ragoût de boeuf julienne	Vegetables cut in the style of julienne and glazed. Julienne – thin strips ¼ cm square of 3 cms long. Finely chopped parsley.
Brown beef stew with vegetables	Ragoût de boeuf jardinière	Vegetables cut in the style of jardinière. Jardinière – ½ cm square by 1½ cms long.
Brown beef stew bourgeoise	Ragoût de boeuf bourgeoise	Button onions and turned carrots, glace à brun, lardons of bacon. Finely chopped parsley.
Brown beef stew with red wine	Ragoût de boeuf au vin rouge	The basic recipe replacing approximately half the stock with red wine.
Beef stew Burgundy style	Boeuf bourguignonne	As for the above recipe with the inclusion of 50 g per portion of each of the following: glazed button mushrooms à brun, glazed button onions à brun and lardons of bacon. These items are cooked separately and are added to the stew just prior to service. Each portion of the stew is finished off with toasted heart shaped croûtons part dipped in finely chopped parsley.
Brown rabbit stew	Ragoût de lapin	Rabbit stews can be garnished as for recipes 2 to 9.
Brown veal stew	Ragoût de veau	As for the basic ragoût recipe.
Brown veal stew with white wine	Ragoût de veau au blanc	As for the basic recipe, replacing half the stock with white wine.
Veal Marengo	Ragoût de veau marengo	As for the above recipe with the inclusion of 50 g per portion of each of the following: glazed button mushrooms à brun, glazed button onions à brun and tomato concassé. These items are cooked separately and are added to the stew just prior to service. Each portion of the stew is finished off with toasted heart-shaped croûtons, part dipped in finely chopped parsley.
Stewed oxtails	Ragoût de queue de boeuf	As for the basic recipe using 250 g of oxtail per portion.

□   □   □

White stews

Fricassée

Suitable meats: chicken, rabbit and veal

🥄 40 min approximately (per 10 portions)
♨ 1½ hr maximum (per 10 portions)   ≋ 180°C (350°F)

Step	Commodity	1 portion	10 portions	
1	Butter or margarine	10 g	100 g	Heat the fat in a suitable cooking vessel. Be careful not to apply too much heat otherwise it will burn.
2	Prepared stewing meat	125 g	1.25 kg	Season and place in the cooking vessel and set it.
3	Plain flour, sieved	10 g	100 g	Sprinkle the flour over the meat. To avoid the meat breaking up stir gently with a wooden spatula to form a roux. Cook out to a blond (second stage) roux.
4	Appropriate stock	200 ml	2 litres	Add a quarter and mix thoroughly, add another quarter of the stock and bring to the boil. Add the remaining stock, bring to the boil and then simmer. Skim and season accordingly.
5	Bouquet garni	1 small	1 large	Place in the simmering liquid. Complete the cooking process. Skim off any surplus fat and any scum that may form on the surface. Once the meat is cooked, remove the bouquet garni, strain the sauce into a pan and place the meat in a cooking vessel.
6	Egg yolks	½	3	Place in a mixing bowl.
7	Whipping cream	25 ml	250 ml	Add the cream to the egg yolks and whisk to the ribbon stage. Using a wooden spatula, a little of the warm sauce is added to this. The liaison is then blended into the stew, stirring continuously so as not to curdle it. Pour this over the meat, re-heat, but do not allow to boil.
8	Slices of bread	1	10	Cut into heart-shaped pieces and toast or fry until a golden brown.
9	Parsley	5 g	20 g	Finely chop. Dip the tips of the croûtons into the sauce and then into the parsley. Garnish and serve accordingly.

Suitable garnishes for fricassée

English term	French term	Commodities per portion
Ancient style	à l'ancienne	Garnish with 25 g of button onions and 25 g of button mushrooms that have first been cooked in a blanc and then finished in melted butter.
Carel style	Carel	Garnish with 15 g of peanuts and 15 g pimentos that have been cut into julienne and blanched in butter.
With asparagus	argenteuil	Garnish basic recipe with 3 cooked asparagus tips per portion.
With mushrooms	aux champignons	Garnish basic recipe with glazed button mushrooms.
With cucumber	doria	Garnish basic recipe with poached turned/shaped cucumber.

☐   ☐   ☐

Blanquette

Suitable meats: chicken, lamb, mutton, pork, rabbit and veal

🥄 40 min approximately (per 10 portions)
🍲 1½ hr (per 10 portions)　　≋ 180°C (350°F)

Step	Commodity	1 portion	10 portions	
1	Prepared stewing meat	125 g	1¼ kg	Place in a cooking vessel. Cover with water and blanch. Boil for approximately 5 minutes then refresh. Drain off the water when the meat is cold. This is done to remove any impurities in the form of scum that will taint the flavour or finished appearance.
2	Suitable stock	200 ml	2 litres	Place the meat in a clean cooking vessel and pour the stock over it. Bring to the boil, simmer and remove any fat or scum.
3	Studded onion	1 small	1 large	Add to the meat and stock.
4	Carrots	5 g approx	50 g approx	Add to the meat and stock.
5	Bouquet Garni	1 small	1 large	Add to the meat and stock. Complete the cooking process. When the meat is cooked, strain the cooking liquor into a jug. Discard the studded onion, carrot and bouquet garni. Place the meat into a clean pan. Cover with a little stock to keep it moist.
6	Butter	10 g	100 g	Melt the butter in a thick-bottomed pan.
7	Flour	10 g	100 g	Add to the butter and cook to a blond (second stage) roux. Allow to cool.
8	Cooking liquor/stock	150 ml	1½ litres	Add a quarter to the roux and mix thoroughly. Add another quarter and bring to the boil. Add the remainder, bring to the boil, simmer and cook for 1 hour. Correct the seasoning and consistency accordingly. Pass the sauce through a conical strainer onto the meat. Re-heat, but do not re-boil.
10	Single cream	20 ml	200 ml	Place in a clean bowl.
11	Lemon juice	¼ tsp	2 tsp	Mix well with the cream then pour over the stew just before service. Do not attempt to re-boil. Season to taste.

NOTE: Tripe is also cooked by this process using half stock and half milk omitting the carrots and using extra onions instead. The onion is sliced and served with the tripe. Garnish and serve accordingly.

□　　□　　□

6

Miscellaneous stews

Curried meat

Suitable meats: all meats and poultry

🥄 30 min approximately (per 10 portions)
♨ 1½ hr (per 10 portions) ≋ 150°C (300°F)

Step	Commodity	1 portion	10 portions	
1	Fat (dripping or oil)	10 g	100 g	Melt in a suitable frying pan.
2	Prepared stewing meat	125 g	1.25 kg	Add to the fat and seal quickly.
3	Onions	25 g	250 g	Add to the meat and fry off.
4	Curry powder	7.5 g	75 g	Add to the meat and onions and cook slowly so as not to burn the curry powder.
5	Flour	7.5 g	75 g	Add to the meat and brown lightly. Allow the mixture to cool on the side of the stove.
6	Tomato purée	5 g	50 g	Add and mix in well.
7	Appropriate brown stock	150 ml	1½ litres	Add a quarter of the stock and mix well, add another quarter and bring to the boil. Add the remaining stock, bring to the boil then simmer. Allow the stew to cook for approximately one hour.
8	Finely chopped chutney	7.5 g	75 g	Add to the stew.
9	Finely chopped apples	15 g	150 g	Add to the stew.
10	Coconut milk	15 ml	150 ml	Add to the stew. If there is no coconut milk available, desiccated coconut can be used (½ tsp per portion). This must be boiled in water than strained before use. The resulting liquid is used and the coconut used as an accompaniment for service. Complete the cooking process. Remove any fat or scum that may arise. If the curry is too hot in flavour, a little yoghurt or cream can be added to tone down its strength.

NOTE: Curried meat is usually served with a boiled rice (see Chapter 5: Boiling) and accompanied by a selection of the following: fried or grilled poppadums; mango chutney; grilled Bombay duck; lime pickle; lemon wedges; sliced tomato, cucumber or onion; mint yoghurt; diced apple, pineapple, sliced banana or plantain in cream or desiccated coconut. The above dishes can be served in a hors d'oeuvres roundel or individual ravier dishes.

☐   ☐   ☐

Goulash

Suitable meats: beef, lamb, mutton, pork and veal

🥘 30 min approximately (per 10 portions)
♨ 1½–2 hr (per 10 portions)   ≋ 180°C (350°F)

Step	Commodity	1 portion	10 portions	
1	Lard or dripping	6 g	60 g	Heat the fat in a suitable cooking vessel.
2	Prepared stewing meat	150 g	1½ kg	Season the meat and add it to the hot fat, lightly fry the meat until it is golden brown on all sides.
3	Finely chopped onions	50 g	500 g	Add the onions to the meat and cook for a few minutes.
	Garlic (optional)	¼ clove	1 clove	Crush with a little salt and add to the meat.
4	Paprika	10 g	100 g	Place in a clean bowl.
5	Plain flour – sieved	5 g	50 g	Using a wooden spoon, mix in well with the paprika then add to the remainder of the ingredients in the cooking vessel. Cook to a brun roux (third stage roux). This will take approximately 15 minutes in a pre-heated oven. When the roux is ready, remove it from the oven.
6	Tomato purée	5 g	50 g	Add to the roux and stir thoroughly.
7	Appropriate white stock	200 ml	2 litres	Add a quarter of the stock and mix thoroughly. Add another quarter and bring to the boil. Add the remaining stock bring back to the boil and then simmer. Season to taste.
8	Bouquet garni	1 small	1 large	Place in the simmering liquid. Complete the cooking process. Skim off any surplus fat or scum accordingly.
9	Small or turned potatoes	2 each	20 each	Add to the goulash 15 minutes before serving.
10	Final seasoning	To taste		Carefully adjust the seasoning.
11	Finely chopped parsley	5 g	50 g	Sprinkle over the goulash before serving.

Suitable garnish for goulash

English term	French term	Commodities
Hungarian	Hongroise	Goulash is served with thinly piped pieces of poached gnocchi parisienne or buttered noodles.

□   □   □

Osso-bucco

☞ 40 min approximately (per 10 portions)
〰 2 hr (per 10 portions) ≋ 180°C (350°F)

Step	Commodity	1 portion	10 portions	
1	Onions	50 g	500 g	Cut into brunoise (finely chopped).
2	Carrots	10 g	100 g	Cut into brunoise.
3	Garlic	½ clove	3 cloves	Finely crush and add to the onions and garlic.
4	Dripping, oil or lard	5 g	50 g	Melt in a suitable frying pan. When the required temperature is reached the onions, carrots and garlic are added and sweated off.
5	Tomatoes	100 g	1 kg	Blanch and refresh. Discard the skins and the seeds. The flesh of the tomatoes is the cut into brunoise and then added to the other vegetables.
6	Flour, plain	15 g	150 g	Place on a tray, season with salt and pepper.
7	Prepared knuckle of veal (sectioned)	2 pieces	20 pieces	Pass through the seasoned flour.
8	Dripping, oil or lard	10 g	75 g	Place the fat in a clean cooking vessel and heat. When the correct temperature is reached, add the veal and brown it on all sides. Discard the excess fat. The vegetables are then placed in the cooking vessel with the veal.
9	Dry white wine	50 ml	500 ml	Add to the veal and reduce by half.
10	White veal stock	200 ml	2 litres	Add to the mixture and bring to the boil. Simmer and remove and excess fat or scum that might form.
11	Bouquet garni	1 small	1 large	Add to the stew and complete the cooking process. Check the stew on a regular basis. If the consistency is too dry, add more stock.
12	Lemon juice	½ tsp	2 tsp	Add to the stew just before serving.

Suitable garnish for Osso-bucco

English term	French term	Commodities
Milanaise style	Milanaise	Osso-bucco may be accompanied by maize or flour dumplings, polenta, braised rice or noodles.

□   □   □

Chilli con carne

Suitable meats: Usually minced beef or lamb

🍲 30 min approximately* (per 10 portions)

♨ 1½ hr (per 10 portions)   ≋ 180°C (350°F)

Step	Commodity	1 portion	10 portions	
1	Oil or lard	5 ml	50 ml	Heat in a suitable frying vessel.
2	Onions	25 g	250 g	Peel and finely chop the onions. Add to the hot fat and cook without colouring.
3	Chilli peppers	1 each	5 approx.	Finely chop and add to the onions.
4	Coarse minced meat	125 g	1¼ kg	Season with salt and pepper. Add to the onions and peppers, seal and colour.
5	Tomato purée	5 g	50 g	Add and mix in well.
6	Prepared red kidney beans	25 g	250 g	Add to the mince.
7	Tomatoes	100 g	1 kg	Blanch and refresh. Remove the skin and the seeds and discard them. Finely dice the flesh and add to the stew.
8	Brown stock	50 ml	500 ml	Use enough stock to cover the meat. Bring to the boil, remove any scum or fat that may form. Complete the cooking process. Correct the seasoning.

NOTE: Chilli con carne is usually served with plain boiled rice or pilaff (braised rice).

* The dried red kidney beans must be soaked for 12 hours and boiled vigorously for a minimum of 10 minutes prior to use. Alternatively, tinned or frozen may be used immediately.

□   □   □

6

Chicken in red wine

Coq au vin

🍲 20 min approximately (per 10 portions)
♨ 1 hr (per 10 portions)   ≋ 150°C (300°F)

Step	Commodity	1 portion	10 portions	
1	Flour	7.5 g	75 g	Place on a tray. Season with salt and pepper.
2	Chicken	250 g	2½ kg	Cut as for sauté, pass and coat the chicken in the seasoned flour.
3	Fat (½ oil/ ½ butter)	7.5 g	75 g	Heat in a suitable frying vessel. When the correct temperature is obtained add the chicken and seal it in the hot fat. Remove the chicken and place it into an appropriate stewing vessel. Keep the fat and the frying pan for use later.
4	Button onions	3 only	30 only	Peel, trim and leave whole.
5	Button mushrooms	3 only	30 only	Peel, trim and leave whole.
6	Back bacon	15 g	150 g	Cut into lardon pieces. Place the onions into the frying pan and cook for two minutes, add the bacon and the mushrooms and brown for another two minutes until lightly brown. When this is done, remove them from the heat and, using a perforated spoon, place the onions, mushrooms and bacon on top of the chicken. Discard the excess fat, but do not throw away the sediment in the bottom of the frying pan. Place the pan on the stove.
7	Red wine	75 ml	750 ml	Pour into the frying pan and bring to the boil, stirring so as to loosen the sediment.
8	Brown stock	25 ml	250 ml	Add to the wine and re-boil. When it has re-boiled pour it over the chicken. Place the chicken into the oven and complete the cooking process.

NOTE: As for other stews, coq au vin is garnished with heart-shaped croûtons, traditionally though these croûtons are spread with a purée of cooked chicken livers and the sauce thickened with the blood.

☐   ☐   ☐

Feathered game stews

Salmis de gibier

Suitable meats: Pheasant, wild duck, grouse or partridge

It should be noted that the game birds are roasted before completing the cooking process (*see* Chapter 10: Roasting) by stewing. They are then skinned and jointed into the appropriate portions depending on the bird. The carcass is retained for use in the finishing sauce

> 20 min approximately (per 10 portions)
> 45 min to 1 h   180°C (350°F)

Step	Commodity	1 portion	10 portions	
1	Game bird	¼–½ bird	2½–5 birds	Remove the skin and joint into portions. Place in a suitable stewing vessel.
2	Butter	15 g	150 g	Heat in a frying pan. Add the chopped up carcass and brown.
3	Shallots	15 g	125 g	Dice into brunoise and add to the butter and carcass.
4	Peppercorns	2 only	10 only	Add to the chopped shallots.
6	Bayleaves	½	3	Add to the peppercorns.
7	Brandy	10 ml	100 ml	Add with due care to the frying pan and flame.
8	Red wine	70 ml	700 ml	Déglacé with the red wine and reduce the liquid to half as much.
9	Demi-glace	125 ml	1 litre	Add to the mixture and simmer until the required consistency is achieved. Season with salt and pepper. Strain the sauce over the portioned game bird. Cover with a lid and complete the cooking process.

NOTE: Traditionally salmis is served in a cocotte serving dish, garnished with glazed button mushrooms 25 g per portion and heart shaped croûtons spread with game stuffing (farce de gibier).

☐   ☐   ☐

Farce de gibier

Step	Commodity	1 portion	10 portions	
1	Butter	10 g	100 g	Melt in a suitable frying pan.
2	Game livers	25 g	240 g	Season with salt and pepper and quickly toss in the butter.
3	Finely chopped onions	7.5 g	75 g	Add and continue to toss.
4	Pinch of thyme and bayleaf			Add to the liver. Pass the mixture through a sieve.
5	Butter	5 g	50 g	Add to the sieved mixture. Correct the seasoning and allow to cool. Use accordingly.

☐   ☐   ☐

Furred game stews

Suitable meats: hare and venison

Initial preparation time is approximately 8 hours for marinading. The marinade impregnates the meat with flavours and also helps to tenderise the meat during this period. The blood from the animal is kept and used later to thicken the stew.

Red wine marinade

Step	Commodity	1 portion	10 portions	⏲ 10 min approximately
1	Red wine	125 ml	1.25 litres	Place in a suitable bowl.
2	Mirepoix of onions	25 g	250 g	Add to the wine.
3	Mirepoix of carrots	25 g	250 g	Add to the onion and wine.
4	Salt	To taste		Add to the mixture.
5	Crushed peppercorns	2	10	Add to the mixture.
6	Bouquet garni	1 small	1 large	Add to the other ingredients.
7	Garlic – optional	1 clove	4 cloves	Add to the mixture. The meat is then placed in the marinade. Ensure that it is completely covered by the marinade. If it is not, then more wine can be added. Place the marinading meat into the fridge and leave for 8 hours.

The cooking process

Step	Commodity	1 portion	10 portions	⏲ 30 min approximately (per 10 portions) ♨ 2½–3 h (per 10 portions) ≈ 150°C (300°F)
1	Meat and marinade	125 g	1.25 kg	Drain the marinading liquor into a jug, place it to one side. Remove the bouquet garni and discard it. Keep the meat, vegetables and peppercorns.
2	Fat (dripping or oil)	10 g	100 g	Place in a frying pan and heat. Add the meat and vegetables. Seal and colour.
3	Flour	7.5 g	75 g	Add to the meat and mix in well. Singe in a hot oven for 10 minutes. Remove and place on the side of the stove and allow to cool.
4	Tomato purée	7.5 g	75 g	Add to the cooled mixture.
5	Appropriate game stock	100 ml	1 litre	Place in a measuring jug.
6	Marinade	25 ml	250 ml	Add to the stock. Return the roux to the heat. Add a quarter of the stock and mix well, add another quarter and bring to the boil. Add the remaining liquid and bring to the boil. Simmer and remove any fat or scum. Cover with a tight-fitting lid and place in the pre-heated oven. Complete the cooking process checking occasionally to ensure that sufficient liquid is covering the meat. Replenish with the marinade or stock. When the meat is cooked it is removed and placed in the serving dish and kept warm. The cooking liquor is allowed to simmer on top of the stove.

Step	Commodity	1 portion	10 portions	
7	Blood from the animal	25 ml	250 ml	Place in a clean bowl.
8	White wine vinegar	¼ tsp	2 tsp	Add to the blood.
9	Cold water	1 tsp	4 tsp	Add to the blood and mix in well; this is now called a blood liaison. This mixture is then added to the simmering sauce. The sauce cannot be allowed to re-boil as the blood will curdle and spoil the finished appearance. The sauce is strained and poured over the meat for service.

Suitable garnishes for civets

English style	French term	Commodities
English style	À l'anglaise	Forcemeat balls made from game liver and a little sausage meat. They are panéd and deep fried. 2 balls per portion. Heart-shaped croûtons.
Burgundy style	À la bourguignonne	25 g of glazed button mushrooms, 25 g of glazed button onions and 15 g of bacon cut into lardons and gently fried per portion. Heart-shaped croûtons.

NOTE: All civets are accompanied by redcurrant jelly.

☐ ☐ ☐

Fish stews

Fish stew

Bouillabaisse is a type of soup that is prepared by the process of stewing. It originated in the Mediterranean where there are many varieties of this dish.

Bouillabaisse

⤵ 50 min approximately (per 10 portions)

♨ 1 hr (per 10 portions)

Step	Commodity	1 portion	10 portions	
1	John Dory	60 g	600 g	Clean and cut into 5 cm pieces on the bone.
2	Red Mullet	60 g	600 g	As above.
3	Mackerel	60 g	600 g	As above.
4	Mussels	60 g	600 g	Scrape and wash the mussels. Leave them in the shell.
5	Oil (Olive/vegetable)	10 ml	100 ml	Place in a suitable stewing pan, heat and add the fish. Gently cook for 5 minutes.
6	Onions	25 g	250 g	Slice into paysanne and add to the stew.
7	Leeks	25 g	250 g	Cut into julienne and add to the stew.
8	Garlic	¼ clove	2 cloves	Peel the skin and discard. Crush the garlic with a little salt and chop finely using a large chef's knife. Add to the stew.
9	Fennel seed	small pinch	pinch	Place in a clean bowl.
10	Bayleaf	½	2	Mix with the fennel seed.
11	Thyme	small pinch	pinch	Add to the above ingredients.
12	Saffron	small pinch	pinch	As above.
13	Finely chopped parsley	pinch	1 tbsp	Mix with the other ingredients and then add to the stew.
14	Tomatoes	75 g	750 g	Remove the eyes of the tomatoes, blanch in boiling water for 10 seconds and refresh. Remove and discard the skin. Cut in half, remove and discard the seeds. Chop the flesh into small dice and add to the stew.
15	Dry white wine	50 ml	500 ml	
16	Water	50 ml	500 ml	Add the water to the wine and pour over enough to cover the fish. Continue to cook.
17	Whiting	60 g	600 g	Add to the stew 10 minutes before it is cooked. Correct the seasoning and complete the cooking process.

NOTE: The bouillabaisse is served in a soup tureen accompanied with slices of plain or toasted French bread flavoured with garlic.

□   □   □

Stewed mussels in white wine

Moules marinière

🥄 30 min approximately (per 10 portions)
🍲 15 min maximum (per 10 portions)

Step	Commodity	1 portion	10 portions	
1	Mussels	250 g	2½ kg	Scrape and wash the mussels well. Put to one side for the moment.
2	Dry white wine	50 ml	500 ml	Place in a suitable cooking vessel.
3	Shallots	25 g	200 g	Chop finely and add to the wine. Add the mussels.
4	Parsley	pinch	1 tbsp	Add to the mussels, season with salt and pepper and cover with a lid. Cook for 5–8 minutes until the shells are wide open. Remove the mussels from the cooking liquor. Discard the shell tops and the beards as well as any mussels whose shells remain unopened. Loosen the mussel from the bottom shell for service. Place in a suitable serving dish, cover and keep warm. Bring the cooking liquor to the boil.
5	Butter	10 g	100 g	Place in a bowl and soften.
6	Flour	5 g	50 g	Add to the butter and mix to a paste to make a buerre manié. Whisk the beurre manié into the cooking liquor. Return to the boil and pass through a fine chinois into a clean saucepan.
7	Double cream	10 ml	100 ml	Add to the sauce being careful not to re-boil the sauce. Correct the seasoning with salt and pepper.
8	Lemon juice	1 tsp	2 tbsp	Add to the sauce and pour the sauce over the mussels.
9	Finely chopped parsley	1 tsp	2 tbsp	Sprinkle over the sauce.

6

157

Lobster American

Homard Américain

NOTE: Hen lobsters are selected for the following dishes because of their coral, which acts to flavour and colour the sauce.

🥄 30 min approximately (per 10 portions)
♨ 30 min maximum (per 10 portions)

Step	Commodity	1 portion	10 portions	
1	Live hen Lobster	1 × 325 g	5 × 650 g	Prepare the lobster by washing in a weak salt water solution. Place the live lobster on a chopping board. Pierce the middle of the head with the point of the knife and split it in two lengthwise, leaving the tail section whole. Wash and keep the head and the fan tail for decoration. Discard the stomach (sac). Remove the coral and liver (cream of lobster) and place in a clean bowl. Separate the tail from the head section and cut the meat into thick slices (tronçons) using the lobster's natural sections as a thickness. Remove the claws and crack them open. Season the lobster with salt and pepper.
2	Cooking oil	25 ml	100 ml	Heat the oil in a suitable cooking vessel.
3	Butter	15 g	150 g	Add to the oil and melt. Add the lobster and cook until the shell turns red.
4	Shallots	10 g	100 g	Finely chop and add to the lobster.
5	Garlic	¼ clove	2 cloves	Remove the skin and discard. Add a pinch of salt and chop finely. Add to the lobster.
6	Brandy	25 ml	200 ml	Add and ignite (flambé).
7	Dry white wine	50 ml	400 ml	Add to the lobster and bring to the boil, then simmer. Season with salt and pepper. Cover with a lid and cook for 20 minutes. Remove any excess fat or scum.
8	Tomatoes	75 g	750 g	Remove the eye of the tomatoes, blanch in boiling water for 10 seconds and refresh. Remove and discard the skin. Cut in half, remove and discard the seeds. Chop the flesh into small dice and add to the lobster.
9	Tomato purée	15 g	100 g	Add to the tomato concassé. Remove the lobster and pick the meat from the shell. Place the meat in a suitable serving dish. Cover and keep warm. Reduce the cooking liquor by half.
10	Finely chopped parsley	pinch	1 tbsp	Add to the stew.
11	Butter	15 g	150 g	Add to the coral and creamy parts and mix thoroughly. Shake this mixture into the sauce, allow to thicken. Correct the seasoning and add a little cayenne pepper. Pass the sauce through a coarse chinois over the lobster. Decorate the serving dish with the tops of the head.
12	Finely chopped parsley	pinch	1 tbsp	Sprinkle over the sauce.

NOTE: Homard Américain is served with Riz Pilaff (braised rice).

☐   ☐   ☐

Stewed fruits

Stewed fruits

Compote des Fruits

Suitable fruits: apples, apricots, figs, peaches, pears, plums, prunes

NOTE: Stewed fruits are usually served for breakfast and in certain pastry products. They can also be utilized in savoury preparations. Fruits for stewing are prepared in the following way. Apples are peeled and quartered. Pears can be peeled and quartered or left whole. Apricots and plums are washed, and left whole. Peaches are blanched and skinned. Figs and prunes are soaked overnight.

⏲ 15 min approximately (per 10 portions)   ♨ see individual chart (per 10 portions)

Apples	10–12 minutes
Apricots	12–15 minutes
Figs	12–15 minutes
Peaches	12–15 minutes
Pears	20 minutes
Plums	8–10 minutes
Prunes	10–12 minutes

Step	Commodity	1 portion	10 portions	
1	Water	150 ml	1½ litres	Place in a pan and boil.
2	Cinnamon stick	¼	1	Add to the water.
3	Sugar	150 g	1½ kg	Place in the boiling water.
4	Lemon juice	1 tsp	1 tbsp	Add to the sugar and simmer the ingredients for 15 minutes to form a stock syrup. Place the prepared fruit in the stock and stew gently until the fruit is tender.

NOTE: Allow the fruit to cool in the cooking liquor. The stewed fruit is served in a little of the cooled cooking liquor.

□   □   □

6

Stewed vegetables

Etuvés style

Légumes etuvés

Suitable vegetables: peas

15 min approximately (per 10 portions)
30 min maximum for fresh peas,
15 min for frozen peas (per 10 portions)

Step	Commodity	1 portion	10 portions	
1	Shelled fresh peas	50 g	500 g	Wash the peas and place in a suitable pan.
2	Button onions	25 g	250 g	Peel and wash. Place with the peas.
3	Lettuce leaves	15 g	150 g	Wash and shred to a chiffonade and place with the peas. Season with salt, sugar and pepper. Pour boiling water over the ingredients and cover with a lid. Stew the vegetables until they are cooked.
4	Butter	10 g	100 g	Place in a bowl and soften.
5	Flour	5 g	50 g	Add to the butter and mix to a paste to make a buerre manié. Whisk the beurre manié into the cooking liquor, taking care not to add too much and over-thicken the stewed peas. Correct the seasoning and serve in a suitable serving dish.

Extensions of etuvés

English term	French term	
French style	À la française	As for etuvés
Good woman (housewife)	Bonne femme	As for etuvés with the addition of 25 g of cooked lardons of bacon per portion.

□   □   □

Provençale style vegetables

Suitable vegetables: courgettes, marrows and pumpkins

Cooking vegetables for provençale is done in two stages. The first stage is the tomato concassé and the second the actual vegetable to be cooked.

🥄 30 min approximately (per 10 portions)
♨ 1 hr maximum (per 10 portions)

Step	Commodity	1 portion	10 portions	
1	Cooking oil	15 ml	100 ml	Heat the oil in a suitable pan.
2	Thinly sliced onions	25 g	200 g	Add to the oil and sweat off.
3	Garlic	¼ clove	2 cloves	Peel and finely chop. Add to the onions.
4	Prepared sliced vegetable	100 g	1 kg	Season with salt and pepper and add to the onions and garlic. Cook quickly until it is transparent.
5	Tomato concassée	75 g	750 g	Add the tomato concassée to the vegetables and heat gently. Correct the seasoning. Place in a suitable serving dish.
6	Parsley, finely chopped	1 tsp	1 tbsp	Sprinkle over the vegetable just before serving.

□   □   □

Tomato concassées (cuites)

🥄 30 min approximately (per 10 portions)
♨ 10 min (per 10 portions)

Step	Commodity	1 portion	10 portions	
1	Tomatoes	75 g	750 g	Remove the eyes from the tomatoes. Blanch them (see Chapter 5: Boiling). Peel them, cut them in half and remove the seeds. Cut the flesh into large dice. Place to the side to use later.
2	Butter	10 g	100 g	Melt the butter in a suitable pan.
3	Onions	10 g	100 g	Finely chop and add to the butter.
4	Garlic clove	⅕ clove	1 small clove	Finely chop and add to the onion. Cook without colouring. Add the diced tomatoes. Season with salt, pepper and a pinch of sugar. Cook gently until most of the liquid has evaporated. Place in a clean container and store for later use.

6

Ratatouille style   Ratatouille

Suitable vegetables: courgettes, aubergine, green and red peppers, tomatoes

NOTE: Ratatouille is a peasant dish made from a selection of stewed vegetables.

⏱ 45 min approximately (per 10 portions)
🍲 1 h maximum (per 10 portions)

Step	Commodity	1 portion	10 portions	
1	Courgettes	50 g	500 g	Peel and slice.
2	Aubergines	50 g	500 g	Peel and slice.
3	Red peppers	25 g	250 g	Cut into rough julienne.
4	Green peppers	25 g	250 g	Cut into rough julienne.
5	Onions	25 g	250 g	Cut into small dice.
6	Garlic	¼ clove	1 clove	Peel and finely chop.
7	Butter	25 g	250 g	Melt in a suitable cooking vessel. Add the onions and garlic and cook without colouring. Add the aubergines, courgettes and peppers and season accordingly.
8	Tomato concassée	50 g	500 g	Add the tomato concassée, cover with a tight-fitting lid and cook until the vegetables are tender.
9	Parsley, finely chopped	1 tsp	1 tbsp	Sprinkle over the vegetables just before serving.

☐   ☐   ☐

WHAT WENT WRONG?

Problem	Caused by	To rectify
Rapid evaporation.	Cooking at too high a temperature.	Add more liquid, and adjust and control temperature.
Meat is stringy and breaks up.	Cooking at too high a temperature and for too long.	Cannot be rectified.
Discolouration.	Cooking at too high a temperature and for too long.	Drain the sauce away and add fresh sauce to finished item.
Bitter/spoilt flavour.	Roux and stew over-cooked.	Cannot be rectified.
Sauce too thin.	Too much liquid, too low a cooking temperature.	Return to the heat and reduce accordingly; or thicken with cornflour or jaysee.
Sauce too thick.	Not enough liquid or too much thickening agent.	Add more liquid and reduce the temperature accordingly.
Sauce has curdled.	Stew was boiled after liaison was added to finished item.	Drain the sauce away and add fresh sauce or pass through a fine sieve or muslin cloth.
Brown stew was not dark enough.	Meat/vegetables or roux were not coloured enough. Stock was too pale.	Add gravy browning to sauce.
White stew is dark brown.	Poor quality stock or the roux was over-cooked.	Add extra cream to the finished product.
White stew is grey.	Type or quality of mushrooms.	Add extra cream to the finished product.
Meat is tough and chewy.	Meat not cooked enough.	Cook for a longer period until tender.
Vegetables are hard.	Not cooked for long enough.	Cook for a longer period until tender.

7

BRAISING

Braising is a combination of pot roasting and stewing. Pot roasting, because it is carried out in an oven and stewing because it is cooked in a minimum amount of liquid in an enclosed container.

It is a suitable method of cookery for items of meat, poultry and game that are of a tough nature.

The technique of braising is long and slow. The highly flavoured liquor or sauce becomes an integral part of the completed dish.

There are two techniques used in braising: white braising and brown braising.

(a) **White braising** is used to cook white meats such as veal, poultry and offal such as sweetbreads. White braising is rarely used today for cooking joints. More acceptable results are achieved by pot roasting.
(b) **Brown braising** is used to cook meats such as beef, veal, mutton, duck and offal such as heart, tongue and oxtail.

In brown braising the process is initially started by browning the meat by shallow frying or flash roasting at 250°C (480°F) to seal the flavour of the meat and give it its distinct colour and flavour. The flavour of braised items is additionally enhanced by a mirepoix of vegetables and a bouquet garni.

The main advantages of braising

(a) Tougher, less expensive meats and poultry can be made digestable and palatable by the long, slow process.
(b) Maximum flavour and nutritional value are retained.

The cooking vessel

Braising can be carried out in copper, stainless steel, enamelled, cast iron, ovenproof earthenware and porcelain dishes, the stipulation being that they must all have a tight-fitting lid to prevent evaporation and be thick bottomed.

A 'daubière' is a special earthenware, stoneware or tin-lined copper casserole, traditionally used for cooking 'en daube'.

NOTE: In a traditional kitchen three parties would be involved with the preparation and cooking of braised items.

Chef Entremettier – vegetable and potato dishes.

Chef Garde Manger – the preparation of meats, offal, poultry and game to be braised.

Chef Saucier – butchers meats, offal, poultry and game.

Terms associated with braising

Barding Placing a thin layer of fat over and around the surface of a piece of meat.

Basting Frequently spooning the cooking liquor over the cooking meat to prevent the item from becoming too dry during the cooking process.

Blanching Par cooking of a food item, then arresting the process by refreshing in cold water until completely cold.

Blending Bringing together different flavours and textures in a marinade.

En daube Braising with wine, stock and herbs.

Fine herbs A mixture of fresh herbs, usually chervil, tarragon and parsley.

Flash roasting Placing the joint of meat into a pre-heated oven 250°C (500°F) for up to 10 minutes to brown the surface and seal in the flavour.

Glazing The process of creating an attractive, shiny appearance to the surface of braised meats by basting with the cooking liquor.

Larding The practice of inserting thin strips of pork fat through meat and fish by means of a special larding needle enabling the food item to remain moist during cooking and reducing excess shrinkage.

Marinading Soaking of raw food items in a rich spiced pickling liquor to tenderise and give flavour.

Mirepoix Roughly cut root vegetables used as aromats in the braising process.

Pique The practice of inserting thin strips of pork fat through meat and fish by means of a special larding needle.

Refreshing The process of cooling par cooked food items by placing in a sink under cold running water and leaving till completely cold.

Sealing Applying heat to the surface of the meat to seal in the natural juices.

Sweating The practice of extracting flavour without colourisation.

Brown braised cuts of meat and poultry

Braised Beef steaks

Biftecks braises

Step	Commodity	1 portion	10 portions		30 min		1½–2 h		160°C (325°F)
1	Beef steaks	1 × 125 g	10 × 125 g	Lightly season the meat with salt and pepper.					
2	Oil or dripping	10 g	100 g	Melt in a suitably sized frying pan and heat. Add the seasoned steaks and seal quickly until brown. Remove and place in the braising pan. Place the frying pan to the side of the stove. Do not discard.					
3	Carrots	50 g	500 g	Wash, peel and cut into mirepoix.					
4	Onions	50 g	500 g	Peel, cut in half and into mirepoix. Heat the fat in the frying pan and add the vegetables and brown.					
5	Flour	10 g	100 g	Add to the vegetables and cook to a third stage roux (brown). Allow to cool.					
6	Tomato purée	5 g	50 g	Add to the roux and mix well.					
7	Brown stock	150 ml	1½ litres	Add quarter and mix. Add another quarter and bring to the boil. Add the remainder of the stock, bring to the boil then simmer. Season with salt and pepper, skim. Pour over the meat in the braising pan.					
8	Bouquet garni	1 small	1 large	Add to the liquid. Cover the braising pan with a tight-fitting lid. Place in the pre-heated oven for the required time. Check periodically to ensure that the liquid has not evaporated. When the steak is cooked remove and place in a warm clean vessel. Pass the cooking liquor through a fine chinois. Correct the consistency and season with salt and pepper. Re-boil and pour over the warm meat. Garnish as required.					

□   □   □

Braised lamb chops

Chops d'Agneau braises

Step	Commodity	1 portion	10 portions	🥘 30 min · 🍲 1½–2 h · ≋ 160°C (325°F)
1	Lamb chops	1 × 150 g	10 × 150 g	Lightly season the meat with salt and pepper.
2	Oil or dripping	10 g	100 g	Melt in a suitably sized frying pan and heat. Add the seasoned chops and seal quickly until brown. Remove and place in the braising pan. Place the frying pan to the side of the stove. Do not discard.
3	Carrots	50 g	500 g	Wash, peel and cut into mirepoix.
4	Onions	50 g	500 g	Peel, cut in half and into mirepoix. Heat the fat in the frying pan and add the vegetables and brown.
5	Flour	10 g	100 g	Add to the vegetables and cook to a third stage roux (brown roux). Allow to cool.
6	Tomato purée	5 g	50 g	Add to the roux and mix well.
7	Brown stock	150 ml	1½ litres	Add one quarter and mix. Add another quarter and bring to the boil. Add the remainder of the stock, bring to the boil then simmer. Season with salt and pepper, skim. Pour over the meat in the braising pan.
8	Bouquet garni	1 small	1 large	Add to the liquid. Cover the braising pan with a tight-fitting lid. Place in the pre-heated oven for the required time. Check periodically to ensure that the liquid has not evaporated. When the steak is cooked remove and place in a warm clean vessel. Pass the cooking liquor through a fine chinois. Correct the consistency and season with salt and pepper. Re-boil and pour over the warm meat. Garnish as required.

Braised veal chops

⏱ 30 min ♨ 1½–2 h ≋ 160°C (325°F)

Step	Commodity	1 portion	10 portions	
1	Veal chops	1 × 150 g	10 × 150 g	Lightly season the meat with salt and pepper.
2	Oil or dripping	10 g	100 g	Melt in a suitably sized frying pan and heat. Add the seasoned chops and seal quickly until brown. Remove and place in the braising pan. Place the frying pan to the side of the stove. Do not discard.
3	Carrots	50 g	500 g	Wash, peel and cut into mirepoix.
4	Onions	50 g	500 g	Peel, cut in half and into mirepoix. Heat the fat in the frying pan and add the vegetables and brown.
5	Flour	10 g	100 g	Add to the vegetables and cook to a third stage roux (brown roux). Allow to cool.
6	Tomato purée	5 g	50 g	Add to the roux and mix well.
7	Brown stock	150 ml	1½ litres	Add one quarter and mix. Add another quarter and bring to the boil. Add the remainder of the stock, bring to the boil then simmer. Season with salt and pepper, skim. Pour over the meat in the braising pan.
8	Bouquet garni	1 small	1 large	Add to the liquid. Cover the braising pan with a tight-fitting lid. Place in the pre-heated oven for the required time. Check periodically to ensure that the liquid has not evaporated. When the steak is cooked remove and place in a warm clean vessel. Pass the cooking liquor through a fine chinois. Correct liquor through a fine chinois. Correct the consistency and season with salt and pepper. Re-boil and pour over the warm meat. Garnish as required.

□ □ □

Braised beef olives

⏱ 30 min ♨ 1½–2 h ≋ 160°C (325°F)

Step	Commodity	1 portion	10 portions	
1	Trimmed beef topside	125 g	1¼ kg	Cut thin slices across the grain of the meat allowing two escalopes per portion. Flatten with a cutlet bat and trim into rectangles. Lightly season the meat with salt and pepper.
2	Forcemeat	50 g	500 g	Divide the forcemeat into the required amount of portions. Place each portion of forcemeat in the centre of each escalope. Roll each one, ensuring that the forcemeat does not protrude and secure each paupiette with a piece of string on either end.
3	Oil or dripping	10 g	100 g	Melt in a suitably sized frying pan and heat. Add the paupiettes and seal quickly until brown. Remove and place to the side. Place the frying pan to the side of the stove. Do not discard.
4	Carrots	40 g	400 g	Wash, peel and cut into mirepoix.
5	Celery	10 g	100 g	Wash and cut into mirepoix.
6	Onions	50 g	500 g	Peel, cut in half and into mirepoix. Heat the fat in the frying pan and add the vegetables and brown. Place the browned vegetables in the bottom of the braising pan and carefully place the paupiettes on top.

7

Step	Commodity	1 portion	10 portions	
7	Espagnole	75 ml	750 ml	Place in a suitably sized jug.
8	Brown stock	75 ml	750 ml	Add to the espagnole and stir. Pour over sufficient liquid to cover a good two thirds of the paupiettes in the braising pan.
9	Bouquet garni	1 small	1 large	Add to the cooking liquor. Place on the stove and bring to the boil. Cover with the tight-fitting lid and place in a pre-heated oven for the required time. Check periodically to ensure that the liquid has not evaporated. When the paupiettes are cooked, remove and discard the string. Arrange the paupiettes in a warm, clean earthenware dish. Pass the cooking liquor through a fine chinois. Correct the consistency and season with salt and pepper. Re-boil and pour over the warm paupiettes. Sprinkle with finely chopped parsley. Garnish as required. Serve with boiled noodles.

☐   ☐   ☐

Braised beef in beer   Carbonnade de boeuf

Step	Commodity	1 portion	10 portions	⏲ 40 min 🍲 1½–2 h ♨ 160°C (325°F)
1	Trimmed beef topside	125 g	1¼ kg	Cut thin slices across the grain of the meat allowing two escalopes per portion. Flatten with a cutlet bat. Pass the meat through seasoned flour.
2	Oil/butter	10 g	100 g	Melt in a suitably sized frying pan and heat. Add the slices of beef and seal quickly until brown. Remove and place to the side. Place the frying pan to the side of the stove. Do not discard.
3	Onions	75 g	750 g	Peel, cut in half and slice finely. Heat the fat in the frying pan, add the onions and brown. Layer the onions and meat in a suitably sized braising pan.
4	Demerara sugar	5 g	50 g	Sprinkle over the beef and onions.
5	Brown ale	75 ml	750 ml	Pour over the meat.
6	Brown stock	25 ml	250 ml	Add sufficient stock to just cover the beef. Cook for the required time. Serve in an earthenware dish. Sprinkle with finely chopped parsley.

☐   ☐   ☐

Braised chicken ballotines

Step	Commodity	1 portion	10 portions
				⌣ 1 h 　 ⌣⌣⌣ 1½–2 h 　 ≋ 160°C (325°F)
1	Chicken legs	1 × 150 g	10 × 150 g	Bone out the chicken legs ensuring that the skin and flesh are left intact. Leave a small amount of the end bone in place.
2	Forcemeat	50 g	500 g	Divide the forcemeat into the required amount of portions. Place each portion of forcemeat into the boned out leg in place of the bone. Tie the end off to ensure that the forcemeat is secure and does not protrude.
3	Oil or dripping	10 g	100 g	Melt in a suitably sized frying pan and heat. Add the ballotines and seal quickly until brown. Remove and place to the side. Place the frying pan to the side of the stove. Do not discard.
4	Carrots	40 g	400 g	Wash, peel and cut into mirepoix.
5	Celery	10 g	100 g	Wash and cut into mirepoix.
6	Onions	50 g	500 g	Peel, cut in half and into mirepoix. Heat the fat in the frying pan and add the vegetables and brown. Place the browned vegetables in the bottom of the braising pan and carefully place the ballotines on top.
7	Espagnole	75 ml	750 ml	Place in a suitably sized jug.
8	Brown stock	75 ml	750 ml	Add to the espagnole and stir. Pour over sufficient liquid to cover a good two-thirds of the ballotines in the braising pan.
9	Bouquet garni	1 small	1 large	Add to the cooking liquor. Place on the stove and bring to the boil. Cover with the tight-fitting lid and place in the pre-heated oven for the required time. Check periodically to ensure that the liquid has not evaporated. When the ballotines are cooked, remove and discard the string. Arrange the ballotines in a warm, clean earthenware dish. Pass the cooking liquor through a fine chinois. Correct the consistency and season with salt and pepper. Re-boil and pour over the warm ballotines. Sprinkle with finely chopped parsley. Garnish as required. Serve with braised rice.

□　　□　　□

7

GARNISHES SUITABLE FOR BRAISED CUTS OF MEAT AND POULTRY

Spring vegetables

Printanier

🥣 45 min   🍲 20 min approximately

Step	Commodity	1 portion	10 portions	
1	Carrots	50 g	500 g	Wash, peel and cut into 4 cm pieces then barrel shape with an office knife.
2	Turnips	50 g	500 g	Wash, peel and cut into 4 cm pieces then barrel shape with an office knife. Place in a suitably sized saucepan. Just cover with water and season with salt and pepper. Place on the stove, bring to the boil and cook for 15 minutes approximately. Refresh and drain.
3	Butter	10 g	100 g	Melt in a suitably sized sauteuse and heat gently.
4	Button onions	50 g	500 g	Peel and add to the butter. Cook to a light brown colour. Add to the other vegetables. Reheat in melted butter as required.

☐   ☐   ☐

Peasant style

Paysanne

🥣 45 min   🍲 20 min approximately

Step	Commodity	1 portion	10 portions	
1	Carrots	50 g	500 g	Wash, peel and cut into 4 cm pieces then barrel shape with an office knife.
2	Turnips	50 g	500 g	Wash, peel and cut into 4 cm pieces then barrel shape with an office knife. Place in a suitably sized saucepan. Just cover with water and season with salt and pepper. Place on the stove, bring to the boil and cook for 15 minutes approximately. Refresh and drain.
3	Butter	10 g	100 g	Melt in a suitably sized sauteuse and heat gently.
4	Button onions	50 g	500 g	Peel and add to the butter. Cook to a light brown colour. Add to the other vegetables. Reheat in melted butter as required.

☐   ☐   ☐

Gardener's style

Jardinière

🥣 45 min   🍲 20 min approximately

Step	Commodity	1 portion	10 portions	
1	Carrots	50 g	500 g	Wash, peel and cut into 4 cm pieces then barrel shape with an office knife.
2	Turnips	50 g	500 g	Wash, peel and cut into 4 cm pieces then barrel shape with an office knife. Place in a suitably sized saucepan. Just cover with water and season with salt and pepper. Place on the stove, bring to the boil and cook for 15 minutes approximately. Refresh and drain.
3	Butter	10 g	100 g	Melt in a suitably sized sauteuse and heat gently.
4	Button onions	50 g	500 g	Peel and add to the butter. Cook to a light brown colour. Add to the other vegetables. Reheat in melted butter as required.

☐   ☐   ☐

Brown braised joints of meat and suitable garnishes

Braised joint of meat

Pièce de viande braises

Step	Commodity	1 portion	10 portions	
		⏲ 30 min	♨ 3 h approximately	≋ 160°C (325°F)
1	Oil or dripping	10 g	100 g	Melt in a suitably sized frying pan and heat.
2	Prepared topside	125 g	1¼ kg	Ensure that the meat is larded. Season with salt and pepper and fry until brown on all sides. Remove and place in a suitably sized braising pan. Place the frying pan to the side of the stove. Do not discard the fat.
3	Carrots	25 g	250 g	Wash, peel and cut into mirepoix.
5	Onions	25 g	250 g	Peel, cut in half and into mirepoix. Heat the fat in the frying pan and add the vegetables and brown. Drain away the fat and place the browned vegetables around the meat in the braising pan.
6	Espagnole	100 ml	1 litre	Pour over the beef.
7	Brown stock	100 ml	1 litre	Add sufficient liquid to cover a good two-thirds of the beef in the braising pan. Place on the stove and bring to the boil.
8	Bouquet garni	1 small	1 large	Add to the boiling stock. Correct the seasoning. Cover with a tight-fitting lid. Place in the oven for 2½ hours. To test if cooked, pierce the beef with a trussing needle. This should penetrate without a pronounced resistance. When the beef is cooked remove the string, cover and keep warm. Place the cooking liquor in a saucepan. Bring to the boil. Degrasse and correct the seasoning, colour and consistency. Pass through a fine strainer. Carve the beef into 3 mm thick slices. Dress on an oval serving dish.

Suitable for cooking beef (piece de Boeuf Braise), braised cushion of veal (Noix de veau Braisee), braised stuffed shoulder of veal* (L'Epaule de Veau Farcie Braisee) and braised stuffed breast of veal* (Poitrine de Veau Farcie Braisee).

* Use lemon, parsley and thyme stuffing.

Bourgeoise

Bourgeoise

Step	Commodity	1 portion	10 portions	
				🥣 45 min ♨ 20 min approximately
1	Carrots	50 g	500 g	Wash, peel and cut into 4 cm pieces then barrel shape with an office knife.
2	Turnips	50 g	500 g	Wash, peel and cut into 4 cm pieces then barrel shape with an office knife. Place in a suitably sized saucepan. Just cover with water and season with salt and pepper. Place on the stove, bring to the boil and cook for 15 minutes approximately. Refresh and drain.
3	Butter	10 g	100 g	Melt in a suitably sized sauteuse and heat gently.
4	Bacon	15 g	150 g	Cut into thin strips (lardons) and add to the butter. Cook to a light brown colour. Add to the vegetables. Reheat in melted butter as required.

Suitable for cuts of beef (pièce de boeuf bourgeoise) and cushion of veal (noix de veau braise bourgeoise).

▫   ▫   ▫

In the fashion

à la mode

Step	Commodity	1 portion	10 portions	
				🥣 45 min ♨ 20 min approximately
1	Calves' feet	¼	2	Split in half lengthwise and blanch in boiling water for 5 minutes. Refresh, drain and add to the cooking beef.
2	Carrots	50 g	500 g	Wash, peel and cut into 4 cm pieces then barrel shape with an office knife.
3	Turnips	50 g	500 g	Wash, peel and cut into 4 cm pieces then barrel shape with an office knife. Place in a suitably sized saucepan. Just cover with water and season with salt and pepper. Place on the stove, bring to the boil and cook for 15 minutes approximately. Refresh and drain.
4	Butter	10 g	100 g	Melt in a suitably sized sauteuse and heat gently.
5	Bacon	15 g	150 g	Cut into thin strips (lardons) and add to the butter. Cook to a light brown colour. Add to the vegetables. Reheat in melted butter as required.

Suitable for cuts of beef (pièce de boeuf à la mode).

▫   ▫   ▫

Braised beef Burgundy style

Pièce de boeuf bourguignonne

Step	Commodity	1 portion	10 portions	
				🥣 45 min ♨ 20 min approximately
1	Red wine	100 ml	1 litre	Replace the stock with the equivalent amount of wine.
2	Butter	10 g	100 g	Melt in a suitably sized sauteuse and heat gently.
3	Button onions	50 g	500 g	Peel and add to the butter. Cook to a light brown colour. Remove and place aside for use later.
4	Button mushrooms	50 g	500 g	Wash, remove the stalk. Dry on kitchen paper and add to the butter. Cook to a light brown colour. Remove and add to the onions.
5	Bacon	15 g	150 g	Cut into thin strips (lardons) and add to the butter. Cook to a light brown colour. Add to the vegetables. Reheat as required. Garnish around the cooked beef.

Step	Commodity	1 portion	10 portions	
6	Slices of bread	1	10	Cut into heart shapes and toast.
7	Parsley	10 g	100 g	Wash, dry, remove the stalks and chop finely. Dip half of each of the croûtons into the sauce and then into the parsley.

☐   ☐   ☐

Beef 'en daube'   Daube de boeuf

Step	Commodity	1 portion	10 portions	🥄 4 hr ♨ 3 hr approximately ≋ 160°C (325°F)
1	Piece of topside	125 g	1¼ kg	Cut the meat into thick slices. Lard each individual piece of meat with lardons of pork fat. Season with salt and pepper.
2	Garlic	¼ clove	1 clove	Chop finely, sprinkle with salt and crush. Place in a bowl.
3	Fine herbs	pinch	10 g	Prepare a mixture of fine herbs, chop finely and add to the garlic. Spread over the braising steaks. Place the steaks in a daubière.
4	Streaky bacon	50 g	500 g	Cut into large lardons and blanch for 2–3 minutes in boiling water. Strain and add to the meat.
5	Carrots	25 g	250 g	Wash, peel and cut into mirepoix.
6	Onions	25 g	250 g	Peel, cut in half and into mirepoix and place over the steaks.
7	Brandy	15 ml	150 ml	Pour into a measuring jug.
8	Red wine	125 ml	1¼ litres	Add to the brandy.
9	Tomato purée	1 tsp	30 g	Mix into the liquor and pour over the meat ensuring to cover the steaks completely. If not, use some brown stock. Allow to marinade for 3 hours minimum.
10	Flour	20 g	200 g	Place into a bowl.
11	Baking powder	1 g equiv	10 g	Add.
12	Salt	small pinch	large pinch	Add and sieve all the ingredients into a clean bowl.
13	Beef suet	10 g equiv	100 g	Add to the other ingredients.
14	Water	12 ml	125 ml	Mix lightly to a stiff paste. Allow to rest for 20 minutes. Roll out and place over the daubière to seal. Cover with a tight-fitting lid and place in a pre-heated oven for the required time. Serve the steaks in the daubière. The crust is only removed at the table.

NOTE: This dish can be made with a whole piece of beef.

☐   ☐   ☐

7

Braised offal dishes

Braised oxtail
Queue de boeuf braise

Step	Commodity	1 portion	10 portions	
				⏲ 45 min　🍲 3–4 hr　≋ 160°C (325°F)
1	Oxtail	250 g	2½ kg	Wash and section the oxtail. Season with salt and pepper.
2	Dripping	10 g	100 g	Melt in a suitably sized sauteuse and heat. Add the oxtail and seal quickly till light brown.
3	Carrots	25 g	250 g	Wash, peel and cut into mirepoix.
4	Onions	25 g	250 g	Peel, cut in half and into mirepoix. Add to the oxtail and continue cooking.
5	Flour	15 g	150 g	Sprinkle over the oxtail and singe. Allow to cool slightly.
6	Tomato purée	1 tsp	30 g	Add to the cooled roux.
7	Brown stock	150 ml	1½ litres	Add one quarter and mix well. Add another quarter and bring to the boil. Add the remainder of the stock, re-boil and skim.
8	Bouquet garni	1 small	1 large	Add to the stock. Season with salt and pepper and allow to simmer. Place in a suitably sized braising pan. Cover with a tight-fitting lid and place in the oven for the required time. Stir periodically to ensure even cooking. Once the oxtail is cooked remove and place in a clean vessel. Keep warm. Return the sauce to the heat, re-boil. Correct the seasoning and consistency of the sauce. Strain and pour over the oxtail. Serve as required. Garnish as for braised meats.

Braised lambs' hearts
Coeur d'agneau braisé

Step	Commodity	1 portion	10 portions	
				⏲ 45 min　🍲 2½ hr　≋ 160°C (325°F)
1	Prepared hearts	1	10	Wash and season with salt and pepper.
2	Dripping	10 g	100 g	Melt in a suitably sized sauteuse and heat. Add the hearts and seal quickly till light brown.
3	Carrots	25 g	250 g	Wash, peel and cut into mirepoix.
4	Onions	25 g	250 g	Peel, cut in half and into mirepoix. Add to the oxtail and continue cooking.
5	Flour	15 g	150 g	Sprinkle over the oxtail and singe. Allow to cool slightly.
6	Tomato purée	1 tsp	30 g	Add to the cooled roux.
7	Brown stock	150 ml	1½ litres	Add one quarter and mix well. Add another quarter and bring to the boil. Add the remainder of the stock, re-boil and skim.

Step	Commodity	1 portion	10 portions	
8	Bouquet garni	1 small	1 large	Add to the stock. Season with salt and pepper and allow to simmer. Place in a suitably sized braising pan. Cover with a tight-fitting lid and place in the oven for the required time. Stir periodically to ensure even cooking. Once the oxtail is cooked, remove and place in a clean vessel. Keep warm. Return the sauce to the heat, re-boil. Correct the seasoning and consistency of the sauce. Strain and pour over the oxtail. Serve as required. Garnish as for braised meats.

NOTE: The lambs' hearts may be filled with sage and onion stuffing before braising (coeur d'agneau braisé farci). This dish may be done with prepared ox heart steaks.

☐   ☐   ☐

Braised lambs' tongues

Langues d'agneau braisées

🥄 45 min   ♨ 2½ hr   ≋ 160°C (325°F)

Step	Commodity	1 portion	10 portions	
1	Prepared tongues	1	10	Wash and blanch in boiling water to seal then refresh. Place in a suitably sized braising pan.
2	Brown lamb stock	125 ml	1¼ litres	Pour over the tongues, bring to the boil, skim, season with salt and pepper, cover with a tight-fitting lid and cook in the oven for 1 hour. Remove the tongues and refresh in water. Retain the cooking liquor for use later. Skin and trim the tongues. Place in a suitably sized braising pan.
2	Dripping	10 g	100 g	Melt in a suitably sized sauteuse and heat.
3	Carrots	25 g	250 g	Wash, peel and cut into mirepoix.
4	Onions	25 g	250 g	Wash, peel and cut into mirepoix. add to the hot fat and onions.
5	Flour	15 g	150 g	Sprinkle over the mirepoix and singe. Allow to cool slightly.
6	Tomato purée	1 tsp	30 g	Add to the cooled roux.
7	Cooking liquor	125 ml	1¼ litres	Add ¼ and mix well. Add another ¼ and bring to the boil. Add the remainder of the cooking liquor, re-boil and skim.
8	Bouquet garni	1 small	1 large	Add, season with salt and pepper and re-boil. Strain and pour over the tongues. Cover with a tight-fitting lid and place in the oven for the required time. Stir periodically to ensure even cooking. Once the tongues are cooked remove and place in a clean vessel. Keep warm. Return the sauce to the heat and re-boil. Correct the seasoning and consistency of the sauce. Strain and pour over the tongues. Serve as required. Garnish as for braised meats.

NOTE: The lambs' tongues may also be served on a bed of cooked leaf spinach (langues d'agneau braisées florentines). This dish can be made with ox tongue (langues de boeuf braisées) and garnished accordingly.

☐   ☐   ☐

7

Braised beef liver with onions

Foie de boeuf braisée lyonnaise

🍲 30 min   🍲 2 hr   ≋ 160°C (325°F)

Step	Commodity	1 portion	10 portions	
1	Slices of ox liver	125 g	1¼ kg	Pass through seasoned flour.
2	Dripping/ lard	10 g	100 g	Melt in a suitably sized sauteuse and heat. Add the liver and brown quickly. Remove and place in a suitably sized braising pan. Retain the fat.
3	Onions	50 g	500 g	Peel, cut in half and slice thinly. Add to the hot fat and brown quickly as before.
4	Flour	5 g	50 g	Add to form a roux. Cook to the third stage (roux brun).
5	Brown stock	150 ml	1½ litres	Add one quarter and mix well. Add another quarter and bring to the boil. Add the remainder of the stock, re-boil and skim. Pour over the liver. Cover with a tight-fitting lid and place in the oven for the required time. Once the liver is cooked remove and place in a clean vessel. Keep warm. Return the cooking liquor to the heat. Correct the seasoning and consistency. Remove the fat (degraisser) and pour the completed sauce over the liver.
6	Parsley	3 g	30 g	Chop finely and sprinkle over the liver and onions. Serve accordingly.

☐   ☐   ☐

Braised duck with orange

Canard braisé a l'orange

🍲 30 min   🍲 2 hr   ≋ 160°C (325°F)

Step	Commodity	1 portion	10 portions	
1	Prepared duck	500 g	3 × 2 kg	Season the duck with salt and pepper.
2	Butter/ margarine	15 g	150 g	Melt in a suitably sized sauteuse and heat. Add the duck and brown quickly on all sides. Remove, drain off the excess fat and place in a braising pan.
3	Brown stock	50 ml	500 ml	Pour over the duck.
4	Demi-glace	50 ml	500 ml	Pour over the duck.
5	Bouquet garni	1 small	1 large	Add to the liquid, cover with a tight-fitting lid and cook for the appropriate time. Remove the duck. The duck can either be served whole or cut into the appropriate portions. Place in a serving dish and keep warm. Pour the cooking liquor into a clean saucepan, degraisse and simmer.
6	Lemon juice	10 ml	100 ml	Add to the sauce.
7	Orange juice	40 ml	400 ml	Add to the sauce and continue to simmer.
8	Orange	¼ equiv	3	Remove the zest and retain. Squeeze the juice into the sauce.
9	Lemon	equiv	1	Remove the zest and retain. Squeeze the juice into the sauce. Pass through a fine chinois and cook the sauce to a coating consistency. Cut the zest of the orange and lemon into julienne. Blanch in boiling water for 3 minutes and refresh. Add to the sauce and mix in well.
10	Butter	10 g	100 g	Cut into small pieces. Monte into the sauce and napper over the whole/portioned duck.
11	Parsley	3 g	30 g	Chop finely and sprinkle over the duck. Serve accordingly.

☐   ☐   ☐

White braised dishes

Braised meat (white)

Piece de viande braise à blanc

🥣 45 min   ♨ 2 hr   ≋ 160°C (325°F)

Step	Commodity	1 portion	10 portions	
1	Prepared meat	150 g	1½ kg	Season with salt and pepper.
2	Butter/ margarine	10 g	100 g	Melt in a suitably sized sauteuse and heat gently. Add the meat and sweat.
3	Celery	10 g	100 g	Wash and cut into mirepoix.
4	Carrots	25 g	250 g	Wash, peel and cut into mirepoix.
5	Onions	25 g	250 g	Peel, cut in half and into mirepoix. Add to the meat and continue cooking without colouring. Place in a suitably sized braising pan.
6	White meat stock	150 ml	1½ litres	Pour over the meat, covering two-thirds. Bring to the boil and skim.
7	Bouquet garni	1 small	1 large	Add to the stock. Season with salt and pepper. Cover with a buttered cartouche and a tight-fitting lid. Cook for the appropriate time, basting frequently to effect a glaze. Test to ensure that the meat is cooked. Remove the meat and allow to cool for 15 minutes. Carve into portions, place in a serving dish and keep warm. Pour the cooking liquor into a clean saucepan. Bring to the boil. Add the appropriate amount of arrowroot (diluted with a little water) to thicken to a pouring consistency. Correct the seasoning and strain. Garnish accordingly.

Suitable for cushion of veal and veal/lamb sweetbreads.

NOTE: When using veal the meat can be served whole, lightly napper with the cooking sauce.

☐   ☐   ☐

GARNISHES FOR WHITE BRAISED DISHES

Braised meat with cream

Pièce de viande à la créme

Step	Commodity	1 portion	10 portions	
1	Single cream	25 ml	250 ml	Add to the finished sauce just before serving. Do not allow to re-boil.

☐   ☐   ☐

Ancienne style

Step	Commodity	1 portion	10 portions	
				⏲ 45 min 🍲 30 min approximately
1	Button onions	25 g	250 g	Wash and peel. Place in a pan of simmering blanc (*see* Chapter 4: Boiling) and cook for 10 minutes.
2	Button mushrooms	25 g	250 g	Wash and remove the stalks. Place the mushroom caps in the blanc with the onions after 6 minutes, allowing the mushrooms to cook for 4 minutes. Drain and keep warm.
3	Slices of bread	1	10	Cut in half to form two triangles. Cut each piece into the shape of a heart and toast on both sides.
4	Parsley	3 g	30 g	Wash and pick from the stalks. Chop finely. Dip a corner of each croûton into the sauce and then into the chopped parsley.
5	Single cream	25 ml	250 ml	Add to the finished sauce just before serving. Do not allow to re-boil. Arrange the mushrooms and onions around the meat. Place the croûtons on top.

☐　　☐　　☐

With vegetables
Bonne maman

Step	Commodity	1 portion	10 portions	
				⏲ 30 min 🍲 15 min approximately
1	Carrots	15 g	150 g	Wash, peel and cut into julienne. Place in a suitably sized saucepan of cold salted water. Bring to the boil and cook for 5 minutes.
2	Celery	15 g	150 g	Wash and cut into julienne. Add to the carrots and continue cooking for another 2 minutes.
3	Leeks	15 g	150 g	Wash, cut in half then into julienne. Add to the other vegetables and cook for another 3 minutes. Drain and serve around the finished dish.
4	Parsley	3 g	30 g	Wash and pick from the stalks. Chop finely and sprinkle over the finished sauce.

☐　　☐　　☐

Demidoff style
Demidoff

Step	Commodity	1 portion	10 portions	
				⏲ 30 min 🍲 15 min approximately
1	Carrots	15 g	150 g	Wash, peel and cut into paysanne. Place in a suitably sized saucepan of cold salted water. Bring to the boil and cook for 5 minutes.
2	Celery	15 g	150 g	Wash and cut into paysanne. Add to the carrots and continue cooking for another 2 minutes.
3	Leeks	15 g	150 g	Wash, cut in half then into paysanne. Add to the other vegetables and cook for another 2 minutes.
4	Truffle	5 g	50 g	Cut into julienne and add to the vegetables for 1 minutes. Drain and serve around the dish.
5	Parsley	3 g	30 g	Wash and pick from the stalks. Chop finely and sprinkle over the finished sauce.

☐　　☐　　☐

Braising vegetables

Braised vegetables

Legumes braisés

Step	Commodity	1 portion	10 portions	
				⏲ 30 min 🍲 1½–2 hr ≋ 160°C (325°F)
1	Vegetable selected/ base vegetable	100 g	1 kg	Prepare the vegetables accordingly.
2	Carrots	15 g	150 g	Wash, peel and cut into mirepoix.
3	Onions	15 g	150 g	Wash, peel and cut in half.
4	Butter/ margarine	5 g	50 g	Melt in a suitably sized saucepan. Add the mirepoix and sweat without colouring. Place in a braising vessel and lay the selected vegetable on top. Season with salt and pepper.
5	White stock	100 ml	1 litre	Pour over the vegetables, covering just half. Cover with a buttered cartouche and a tight-fitting lid and braise for the appropriate time or until tender. Once the vegetable is cooked, remove and keep warm. Drain the sauce into a clean saucepan and boil. Add the appropriate amount of arrowroot (diluted with a little water) to thicken to a pouring consistency. Correct the seasoning and strain. Garnish accordingly. Pour over the warm vegetable. Serve accordingly.

☐   ☐   ☐

7

THE PREPARATION AND COOKING OF VEGETABLES FOR BRAISING

	Preparation	Cooking instructions
Celery (celeri)	Trim the root and remove any decaying leaves. Wash thoroughly. Cut off the celery top to leave hearts. Cut in half lengthwise.	Blanch in boiling water for 10 minutes before braising. Refresh and drain. Cook as for the method above.

Menu example and extensions	Served
Celeri braiśe au Jus Braised celery in juice	Coated lightly with the thickened cooking liquor.
Celeri braisé Mornay Braised celery in cheese sauce	Coated with Mornay sauce. Sprinkled with parmesan cheese and gratinated under a salamander.
Celeri braisé au Parmesan Braised celery with parmesan cheese	Coated with demi-glace sauce and sprinkled with grated parmesan cheese and gratinated.
Celeri Braisé à la Moelle Braised celery with poached beef marrow	Coated lightly with the thickened cooking liquor. Garnished with poached slices of beef marrow. Sprinkled with finely chopped parsley.

	Preparation	Cooking instructions
Belgium endive (chicorée)	Remove any damaged leaves. Trim the top and wash thoroughly.	Blanch in boiling salted water for 10 minutes. Refresh and drain. Braise and garnish as for celery.
Leeks (poireaux)	Remove any damaged leaves. Remove the minimum amount of stalk. Trim the tops and split in half lengthwise. Fold in half and tie securely.	Blanch in boiling salted water for 5 minutes. Refresh and drain. Braise and garnish as for celery.
Onions (oignons)	Lightly trim the root and stalk. Remove the skin.	Blanch in boiling salted water for 10 minutes. Refresh and drain. Braise and garnish as for celery.
Fennel (fenouil)	Trim the stem and top. Wash thoroughly.	Blanch in boiling salted water for 10 minutes. Refresh and drain. Serve and garnish as for celery.
Cabbage, braised (chou braisé)	Remove the root, discard any decaying and coarse outer leaves. Cut the cabbage in quarters and remove the centre stalk. Retain 1 large leaf per portion and remove the centre stalk. Shred the remaining cabbage.	Blanch for 8 minutes in boiling salted water. Refresh. Season the cabbage. Divide the shredded cabbage into the appropriate portions and wrap each portion in a large leaf. Place in a clean cloth and squeeze firmly into the shape of a ball. Cook as for the basic recipe (see p 179).

Menu example	Served
Chou braisé Braised cabbage	with the strained, thickened cooking liquor. Finished with finely chopped parsley.

	Preparation	Cooking instructions

Cabbage, braised stuffed
(chou farci braisé)

Preparation

Remove the root, discard any decaying and coarse outer leaves. Cut the cabbage in quarters and remove the centre stalk. Retain 1 large leaf per portion and remove the centre stalk. Shred the remaining cabbage.

Cooking instructions

Blanch in boiling water for 8 minutes in boiling salted water. Refresh. Season the cabbage. Divide the shredded cabbage into the appropriate portions, place 25 g sausage meat in the centre ball, and lay each portion in a large leaf. Place in a clean cloth and squeeze firmly into the shape of a ball. Cook as for the method above.

Menu example

Chou farci braisé
Braised stuffed cabbage

Served

with the strained cooking liquor. Finished with finely chopped parsley.

Peppers, stuffed braised

Preparation

Carefully trim the stalk. Remove the skins by placing the peppers on a tray in a hot oven, in a deep fryer at 180°C or under a hot salamander until the skin blisters.

Cooking instructions

One pepper per portion. Cut across the top and remove the seeds. Fill each pepper with 50 g plain pilaff rice or extension. Place on a bed of mirepoix, half cover with white stock and season with salt and pepper. Add a bouquet garni. Cover with a cartouche and a tight-fitting lid and braise for 1 hour or until tender. Remove and serve on an earthenware dish finished with picked parsley.

☐   ☐   ☐

Braised potatoes Berrichonne

Pommes Berrichonne

➐

👐 30 min   ♨ 1½ hr   ≋ 180°C (350°F)

Step	Commodity	1 portion	10 portions	
1	Potatoes	125 g	1¼ kg	Wash, peel and barrel shape.
2	Butter	5 g	50 g	Melt in a suitably sized sauteuse.
3	Onions	15 g	150 g	Peel and dice finely, add to the butter and cover with a lid. Cook for 3 minutes without colouring.
4	Streaky bacon	25 g	250 g	Remove the rind, cut into lardons and add to the other ingredients. Replace the lid and cook for a further 3 minutes without colouring. Place the potatoes in a suitably sized earthenware dish. Sprinkle over the onions and bacon.
5	White stock	25 ml equiv	250 ml	Pour over sufficient stock to half cover the potatoes. Season with salt and pepper.
6	Butter	5 g	50 g	Melt and brush over the potatoes. Place in the pre-heated oven for the required time or until tender and most of the stock has been absorbed. The top layer of potatoes must also be cooked to a golden brown colour.
7	Chopped parsley	1 tsp	1 tbsp	Sprinkle over the cooked potatoes.

NOTE: Berrichonne potatoes are cooked and served in the same dish. If the dish is dirty, clean the edges with a damp cloth dipped in salt.

Extensions of Berrichonne

Brittany style potatoes
Pommes bretonnes

Hungarian-style potatoes
Pommes hongroises

Potatoes with bacon and onions
Pommes au lard

Preparation

Replace the bacon with 25 g of tomato concassé per portion and dice the potatoes instead of turning.

As for Berrichonne potatoes, excluding the bacon, and with garlic, 5 g of tomato purée and 1 tsp of paprika pepper per portion.

As for Berrichonne potatoes, replacing the diced onions with button onions.

☐ ☐ ☐

Savoury potatoes

Pommes boulangères

🥘 30 min

🍲 1½ hr   ≋ 220°C (425°F)–180°C (350°F)

Step	Commodity	1 portion	10 portions	
1	Potatoes	125 g	1¼ kg	Wash, peel and slice into 2 mm rounds on a mandolin. Choose one-third of the best slices for the top layer.
2	Onions	15 g	150 g	Peel and slice thinly add to the other two-thirds of potatoes. Season lightly with salt and pepper. Place the potatoes and onions in a suitably sized earthenware dish. Lay the remaining potatoes neatly on top.
3	White stock	25 ml equiv	250 ml	Pour over sufficient stock to three-quarters of the potatoes. Season with salt and pepper.
4	Butter	5 g	50 g	Melt and brush over the potatoes. Place in the pre-heated oven for 20 minutes until the top layer is lightly coloured. Reduce the heat to 180°C and cook until tender and most of the stock has been absorbed.
5	Chopped parsley	1 tsp	1 tbsp	Sprinkle over the cooked potatoes.

NOTE: **To prevent the potatoes from curling and drying out during cooking, the potatoes must be pressed down firmly from time to time with a fish slice or palette knife. Savoury potatoes are cooked and served in the same dish. If the dish is dirty clean the edges with a damp cloth dipped in salt.**

☐ ☐ ☐

Fondant potatoes

Pommes fondantes

🥄 30 min

Step	Commodity	1 portion	10 portions	🍲 1½ hr ≋ 220°C (425°F)–180°C (350°F)
1	Potatoes	125 g	1¼ kg	Wash, peel and turn into barrel shapes 5 cm long. Place in a suitably sized earthenware dish.
2	White stock	25 ml equiv	250 ml	Pour sufficient stock to three-quarters cover the potatoes. Season with salt and pepper.
3	Butter	5 g	50 g	Melt and brush over the potatoes. Place in the pre-heated oven for 20 minutes until the top layer is lightly coloured. Reduce the heat to 180°C (350°F) and cook until tender and most of the stock has been absorbed. Brush frequently with melted butter to encourage browning and prevent the potatoes from drying out.
4	Chopped parsley	1 tsp	1 tbsp	Sprinkle over the cooked potatoes.

NOTE: Fondant potatoes are cooked and served in the same dish. If the dish is dirty, clean the edges with a damp cloth dipped in salt.

Extensions of fondant potatoes

Cretan potatoes
Pommes cretanes

Preparation
As for fondant potatoes with the addition of thyme in the stock.

Champignol potatoes
Pommes champignoles

As for fondant potatoes with the addition of 15 g of gruyere cheese and 5 g of parmesan cheese per portion sprinkled over the top and gratinated.

□   □   □

Dauphinoise potatoes

Pommes dauphinioses

Step	Commodity	1 portion	10 portions	🥄 30 min 🍲 1½ hr ≋ 180°C (350°F)
1	Potatoes	125 g	1¼ kg	Wash, peel and slice into 2 mm rounds on a mandolin.
2	Gruyère cheese	25 g	250 g	Grate and add half to the potatoes.
3	Garlic	⅛ clove	1 clove	Peel, chop, sprinkle with salt and crush. Add to the other ingredients. Season lightly with salt and pepper. Place in a suitably sized earthenware dish.
4	Milk	25 ml equiv	250 ml	Place in a saucepan and bring to the boil. Pour sufficient milk to three-quarters cover the potatoes. Season with salt and pepper.
5	Butter	5 g	50 g	Melt and brush half over the potatoes. Sprinkle the remaining cheese over the top. Place in the pre-heated oven until the potatoes are tender and all of the milk has been absorbed. Remove from the oven and brush with the remaining butter.
6	Chopped parsley	1 tsp	1 tbsp	Sprinkle over the cooked potatoes.

NOTE: To prevent the potatoes from curling and drying out during cooking, the potatoes must be pressed down firmly from time to time with a fish slice or palette knife. Savoury potatoes are cooked and served in the same dish; if the dish is dirty, clean the edges with a damp cloth dipped in salt.

□   □   □

Delmonico potatoes

Pommes Delmonico

🍲 45 min   ♨ 1½ hr   ≋ 180°C (350°F)

Step	Commodity	1 portion	10 portions	
1	Potatoes	125 g	1¼ kg	Wash, peel and cut into 6 mm dice. Place in a suitably sized earthenware dish.
2	Milk	25 ml equiv	250 ml	Season with nutmeg. Place in a saucepan and bring to the boil. Pour over sufficient milk to just cover the potatoes. Season with salt and pepper.
3	Butter	5 g	50 g	Melt and brush half over the potatoes. Place in the pre-heated oven until the potatoes are almost cooked and most of the milk has been absorbed.
4	Breadcrumbs	15 g	150 g	Remove from the oven and sprinkle over the potatoes together with the remaining butter. Return to the oven and continue cooking until the potatoes are cooked and the breadcrumbs browned.

NOTE: Delmonico potatoes are cooked and served in the same dish. If the dish is dirty, clean the edges with a damp cloth dipped in salt.

☐   ☐   ☐

Braised red cabbage Flemish style

Chou rouge flamand

🍲 30 min   ♨ 2½ hr   ≋ 160°C (325°F)

Step	Commodity	1 portion	10 portions	
1	Red cabbage	100 g	1 kg	Remove the root, discard any decaying and coarse outer leaves. Cut the cabbage in quarters and wash in cold salted water. Remove the centre stalk and shred the cabbage.
2	Butter	5 g	50 g	Soften and use to butter a suitably sized earthenware braising dish. Add the cabbage and season with salt and pepper.
3	Wine vinegar	15 ml	150 ml	Pour over the other ingredients. Cover with a butter cartouche and a tight-fitting lid. Place in the pre-heated oven and cook for 1½ hours, stirring occasionally.
4	Cooking apples	25 g	250 g	Wash, peel and cut into slices. Add to the cabbage and mix well. Continue cooking for the required time or until tender. Correct the seasoning and serve accordingly.

NOTE: An earthenware dish must always be used when cooking this dish as the acid present in the wine and applies will react with metal dishes and cause the cabbage to discolour.

☐   ☐   ☐

Braised sauerkraut with garnish

Choucroute garniture

Step	Commodity	1 portion	10 portions	
				🥣 30 min ♨ 3 hr ≋ 160°C (325°F)
1	Butter	5 g	50 g	Soften and use to butter a suitably sized earthenware braising dish.
2	Sauerkraut	100 g	1 kg	Season the sauerkraut and place in the dish.
3	Streaky bacon	50 g	500 g	Remove the rind and cut into slices. Blanch in boiling water for 5 minutes. Drain and add to the sauerkraut.
4	Carrots	25 g	250 g	Wash, peel, leave whole and add to the sauerkraut.
5	Onions	25 g	250 g	Trim the stalk and root. Remove the skin, leave whole and add.
6	Bouquet garni	1 small	1 large	Prepare.
7	Juniper berries	2	10	Sprinkle into the bouquet garni and secure. Add to the sauerkraut.
8	White stock	50 ml	500 ml	Pour over the ingredients. Cover with a buttered cartouche and a tight-fitting lid. Cook for 2½ hours.
9	Frankfurters	2	20	Add to the sauerkraut and continue cooking until tender. Correct the seasoning. Remove from the oven and discard the bouquet garni and onion. Dress the sauerkraut on a dish to form a bed. Place the sliced bacon, carrots and frankfurters on top. Serve with boiled potatoes.

☐   ☐   ☐

Braised sauerkraut (pickled white cabbage)

Choucroute braisée

Step	Commodity	1 portion	10 portions	
				🥣 30 min ♨ 3 hr ≋ 160°C (325°F)
1	Butter	5 g	50 g	Soften and use to butter a suitably sized earthenware braising dish.
2	Sauerkraut	100 g	1 kg	Season the sauerkraut and place in the dish.
3	Carrots	25 g	250 g	Wash, peel, leave whole and add to the sauerkraut.
4	Onions	25 g	250 g	Trim the stalk and root. Peel off the skin, leave whole and add. Season with salt and pepper.
5	Bouquet garni	1 small	1 large	Prepare.
6	Juniper berries	2	10	Sprinkle into the bouquet garni and secure. Add to the sauerkraut.
7	White stock	50 ml	500 ml	Pour over the ingredients. Cover with a buttered cartouche and a tight-fitting lid. Cook until tender. Correct the seasoning. Remove from the oven and discard the bouquet garni and onion. Cut the carrot into slices and use to garnish the finished dish.

☐   ☐   ☐

7

Braised rice

Braised rice

Riz pilaff

Step	Commodity	1 portion	10 portions	
				⌣ 15 min ⌣ 20–25 min ≋ 200°C (400°F)
1	Butter/ margarine	5 g	50 g	Melt in a suitably sized sauteuse.
2	Onions	10 g	100 g	Peel, cut in half and finely dice. Add to the butter and sweat without colouring.
3	Long grain rice	50 g	500 g	Wash, drain and add to the onions.
4	Bay leaves	¼	2	Add to the other ingredients.
5	White stock	100 ml equiv	1 litre	Bring to the boil and pour over the rice. Season with salt and pepper. Cover with a buttered cartouche and a tight-fitting lid. Place in the pre-heated oven until the rice is cooked and all the stock absorbed. Stir occasionally with a fork to keep the rice grains separated.
6	Butter/ margarine	10 g	100 g	Remove the rice from the oven. Cut the butter/margarine into knobs and stir into the rice.
7	Chopped parsley	1 tsp	1 tbsp	Sprinkle over the cooked rice.

NOTE: If all the stock is absorbed before the rice is cooked just add more.

Extensions of braised rice

Preparation

Braised rice with chicken
Riz pilaff a Volaille

As for braised rice with the addition of 50 g of cooked chicken per portion.

Braised rice with ham
Riz pilaff au Jambon

As for braised rice with the addition of 50 g diced cooked ham per portion.

Braised rice with chicken liver
Riz pilaff au foie de Volaille

As for braised rice with the addition of 50 g of diced sautéd chicken livers per portion.

Braised rice with mushrooms
Riz pilaff aux Champignons

As for braised rice with the addition of 50 g of sliced sautéd mushrooms per portion.

Braised rice with Prawns
Riz pilaff aux Crevettes Rose

As for braised rice with the addition of 50 g of cooked prawns per portion.

Braised rice Creole
Riz pilaff Creole

As for braised rice with the addition of 25 g of sliced sautéd mushrooms, 10 g cooked pimento and 10 g of tomato concassé per portion.

Braised rice Piemontaise
Riz pilaff Piemontaise

As for braised rice Creole with the addition of 15 g of grated parmesan cheese and 5 g diced truffle per portion.

Braised rice Italian style
Riz pilaff Italienne

As for braised rice with the addition of 15 g of grated parmesan cheese per portion.

Braised rice Milan style
Riz pilaff Milanaise

As for braised rice with the addition of saffron in the stock to flavour and colour, 25 g of sliced sautéd mushrooms, 15 g tomato concassé and 15 g of grated parmesan cheese per portion.

□   □   □

WHAT WENT WRONG?

Problem	Caused by	To rectify
Marinade turns grey.	The container used to hold the marinade was made of aluminium.	Place the meat in a suitable container and replenish with fresh marinade.
Marinaded meat is uneven in colour.	Not covering all the meat with marinade and not turning the meat in the marinade.	Continue to marinade covering all the meat and turning regularly.
Severe loss of liquid or over-thickening during cooking.	(1) Too high an oven temperature; or	Add more cooking liquid and reduce the oven temperature.
	(2) Lid was not tight-fitting.	Add more cooking liquor and replace the lid. Aluminium foil can be placed over the braising pan and the lid placed on top.
Meat has shrunk too much.	(1) The sealing temperature was too high; or	Cannot be rectified.
	(2) The meat has been cooked for too long.	Cannot be rectified.
Meat is dry and stringy.	(1) The meat has been over-cooked; or	Cannot be rectified.
	(2) Holding for too long a period before serving.	Cannot be rectified.
Sauce is too thick.	(1) Reducing too much; or	Add more stock to correct the consistency.
	(2) Not enough liquid has been added originally.	Add more stock to correct the consistency.
Sauce is too thin.	Incorrect ratio of stock to sauce.	Drain the sauce from the braising pan into a saucepan. Bring to the boil and reduce to the correct consistency.
Sauce is too dark/pale	The meat and vegetables were either browned too much or not enough.	Use gravy browning or tomato purée to darken a sauce. Replace the dark sauce with a light coloured sauce.
Meat does not have a rich appearance.	Poor quality stock, jus lié or espagnole.	Drain the sauce into a pan. Add tomato purée and gravy browning. Bring to the boil, skim and return to the braising dish.
Meat will not glaze	(1) Too low an oven temperature; or	Raise the oven temperature.
	(2) Not basting often enough.	Baste more frequently.
Vegetables have a dry or shrivelled appearance.	(1) The braising pan was not covered with a cartouche; or	Cannot be rectified.
	(2) Not basting the vegetables during cooking.	Cannot be rectified.
Vegetables have a bitter taste.	Not blanching thoroughly before braising.	Cannot be rectified.

8

STEAMING

Steaming is the cooking of food in vapourised water under varying degrees of pressure. The water is heated to 100°C and above to produce steam. When the steam touches the food it condenses, heat is transferred from the steam to the surface of the food. The steam cools and reverts back to water, repeating the cycle. Steaming causes the food structure and texture to change by chemical action.

Terms associated with steaming

Atmospheric steaming The cooking of foods in a steam cooking compartment at atmospheric pressure.

Covering and water proofing The protection of prepared foods with greaseproof paper and foil to prevent the product from becoming soggy.

High pressure steaming Cooking of food by steam with a pressure greater than atmospheric and at a water temperature of 121°C.

Low pressure steaming As for atmospheric steaming.

Moulding The placing of prepared food items into moulds.

Sleeves Specially designed moulds used to cook steamed sponge puddings and suet puddings.

METHODS AND TYPES OF STEAMING

There are four methods and types of steaming:

(a) In a saucepan
(b) In an atmospheric steamer
(c) In a pressureless convection steamer
(d) In a high pressure steamer

In a saucepan

A small amount of water is placed in a saucepan and the food is placed in a hanging wire basket or on a metal trivet above the water line and a tight fitting lid applied. There are special steaming saucepans available with 2–3 compartments that sit one on top each other above the saucepan. Care must be taken to replenish any water lost by evaporation. In Chinese cookery, wooden skillets with lids sitting on a trivet in a wok are used to steam the food parcels called dim sum. There is no pressure build-up with this method and the water temperature is 100°C.

In an atmospheric steamer

An atmospheric steamer uses a water bath in the bottom of a sealed cooking compartment. Water is replenished by means of a reservoir fed by a ball valve. Although called a pressureless steamer, there is a little pressure built up (17 kN/m$_2$) when the door of the steamer seals. This in turn raises the boiling temperature of water to 103°C.

In a pressureless convection steamer

Pressureless convection steamers use an external generator to produce and replenish steam in the oven. A fan forces the air around the cooking compartment at 100°C.

Combination ovens are based on pressureless steamers and are used in roasting to keep the meats moist and to minimise the loss of natural juices.

In a high pressure steamer

High pressure steamers use water heated to between 115°C and 121°C in a sealed cooking compartment at a steam pressure of between 70 kN/m² and 105 kN/m². A mechanism on the door prevents it from being opened while in operation and before the pressure on the inside has equalled atmospheric pressure. To prevent the pressure from continuously building up a safety valve allows steam to escape once the required pressure is achieved. In some models the steam is sprayed at very high speed from jets onto the food, enabling a much more rapid transfer of heat.

Steamers must be cleaned regularly with a mild solution of hot water and detergent and then rinsed as they are an ideal breeding ground for bacteria.

NOTE: Atmospheric pressure is the pressure produced by the weight of air at any one point on the earth's surface. Pressure is measured in force units of one thousand Newtons per square metre (kN/m²).

The advantages of steaming

Steaming, especially high pressure steaming, is rapid thus cutting down on time and energy bills. Steamed sponges and puddings are lighter in texture than baked ones. It is ideal for cooking vegetables with strong smells (caused by the release of hydrogen sulphide and ammonia), such as cauliflower, broccoli, turnip, cabbage and sprouts. Steaming requires little attention during the cooking process and providing the cooking times are correct there is better retention of colour and water soluble vitamins. Low pressure steaming reduces the risks of over-cooking the protein in fish.

The long and moist conditions of steaming are excellent for tough meats such as the diced steak used in steak and kidney puddings.

The disadvantages of steaming

Steamed foods lack some of the colour and flavour associated with other methods of cookery and foods cooked by this method have to be highly flavoured and seasoned and/or served with a sauce.

Foods have a tendency to 'pick up' flavours if the steamer is not cleaned properly.

Condensation forming a layer on the surface of the cooking food insulates the food, acting as a barrier to efficient heat transfer from further steam.

Unless vegetables are cooked by high pressure steaming there is a tendency for the vegetables to retain their acidity and with green vegetables this causes a dulling of the colour making them unattractive.

NOTE: In a traditional kitchen five parties would be involved with the preparation and cooking of steamed items:

(a) Chef Garde Manger – the preparation of meats, poultry and fish
(b) Chef Saucier – butcher's meats and poultry dishes
(c) Chef Poissonnier – steamed fish dishes
(d) Chef Entremettier – steamed vegetables
(e) Chef Patissier – preparation and steaming of suet and sponge puddings

Cooking times and temperatures

The temperature of the steam is governed by the type of steamer used. Cooking times vary according to the manufacturer's instructions.

Steak pudding

Step	Commodity	1 portion	10 portions		⏲ 30 min 🍲 1–1½ hr
1	Topside of beef*	125 g	1¼ kg		Remove any gristle or fat and cut into 1 cm cubes. Place in a bowl.
	Onions	25 g	250 g		Peel, cut in half, dice finely and add to the meat.
	Chopped parsley	pinch	25 g		Add.
	Worcester sauce	½ tsp	5 tsp		Sprinkle over the meat.
	Brown beef stock	50 ml	500 ml		Pour over the other ingredients. Season with salt and pepper and place to the side for use later.
2	Plain flour	40 g	400 g		Place in a clean bowl. Add a pinch of salt.
	Baking powder	2 g	20 g		Sprinkle over the flour and sieve together three times.
	Prepared suet	20 g	200 g		Add to the flour and mix in.
	Water	25 ml	250 ml		Add and lightly mix together to form a paste. Lightly grease the correct amount of pudding bowls. Portion off the paste allowing a quarter for the lids. Fill the basins with the remaining paste and add the meat. Allow a small gap at the top for spillage. Dampen and edges and place on the lid. Seal the edges, trim off any excess paste and cover with greaseproof paper and foil.

NOTE: A pleat is made in the paper and foil to allow for expansion of steam during cooking. Cook in a low pressure steamer or atmospheric steamer for the appropriate time. Serve garnish with a sprig of parsley.

* Thick flank of beef may be used instead.

Extensions

Steak and kidney pudding

As for steak pudding with the addition of:

Step	Commodity	1 portion	10 portions		⏲ 30 min 🍲 1–1½ hr
1	Ox or lamb kidney	25 g	250 g		Remove any core or pipe and cut into ½ cm dice. Add to the prepared steak.

Steak and mushroom pudding

As for steak pudding with the addition of:

Step	Commodity	1 portion	10 portions		⏲ 30 min 🍲 1–1½ hr
1	Button mushrooms	25 g	250 g		Wash, peel, cut into quarters and add to the prepared steak.

Steak, kidney and oyster pudding

As for steak and kidney pudding with the addition of:

Step	Commodity	1 portion	10 portions		⏲ 30 min 🍲 1–1½ hr
1	Prepared oysters	2	20		Wash, remove from shell and re-wash. Add to the steak.

NOTE: This dish can be made substituting half of the stock with Guiness stout to make steak, oyster and Guiness pudding.

Christmas pudding

Step	Commodity	1 portion	10 portions	
1	Mixed peel	5 g	50 g	Place in a bowl.
	Carrots	5 g	50 g	Peel, grate and add.
	Raisins	10 g	100 g	Add.
	Currants	15 g	150 g	Add.
	Sultanas	10 g	100 g	Add.
	Lemon	1/5	2	Grate the zest into the bowl. Cut in half and squeeze the strained juice into the fruit.
	Orange	1/5	2	Grate the zest into the bowl. Cut in half and squeeze the strained juice into the fruit.
	Chopped suet	15 g	150 g	Add.
	Demerara sugar	15 g	150 g	Add.
	Ground nutmeg	pinch	1/4 tsp	Add.
	Mixed spice	1 g equiv	10 g	Add.
	Ground ginger	pinch	1/2 tsp	Add.
	Brandy	5 ml	50 ml	Add.
	Stout	15 ml	150 ml	Add, cover, place in the fridge and allow to marinade overnight.
2	White breadcrumbs	10 g	100 g	Add to the mixture.
	Ground almonds	5 g	50 g	Add.
	Plain flour	15 g	150 g	Add and stir together.
	Eggs	1/4 equiv	2 approx.	Add and mix the ingredients together. If the mixture is too dry add extra eggs or a little milk. If too wet, add breadcrumbs. Place in prepared steaming basins or sleeves. Cook for the appropriate time. Serve with a rum or brandy sauce (see hot sweet sauces, Chapter 13: Baking and sweet preparations).

NOTE: Once cooked the pudding may be reheated either by microwaving or by re-steaming for 1½–2 hours.

☐   ☐   ☐

Steamed suet pudding

Suitable for use with poached or raw apples and/or blackberry and/or rhubarb.

Step	Commodity	1 portion	10 portions	⏲ 25 min ♨ 2 hr approximately
1	Plain flour	50 g	500 g	Place in a bowl.
	Baking powder	2 g	20 g	Add and sieve together 3 times.
	Suet	25 g	250 g	Add and made a well.
	Water	30 ml approx.	300 ml approx.	Add and mix well together to produce a fairly stiff paste. Allow to rest for 5 minutes before using. Grease the pudding moulds or sleeves. Line with three-quarters of the paste, saving the remaining paste for the lids.
2	Prepared fruit	250 g	2½ kg	Place in the lined mould. Add a sprinkle of water. Moisten the edges of the paste. Cover with the remaining paste and seal well. Cover with greaseproof paper and foil or a pudding cloth. Cook for the appropriate time. Serve with a custard sauce.

☐   ☐   ☐

Steamed jam roll

Use whatever jam you require.

Step	Commodity	1 portion	10 portions	⏲ 15 min ♨ 2 hr approximately
1	Plain flour	50 g	500 g	Place in a bowl.
	Baking powder	2 g	20 g	Add and sieve together 3 times.
	Suet	25 g	250 g	Add and make a well.
	Water	30 ml approx.	300 ml approx.	Add and mix well together to produce a fairly stiff paste. Allow to rest for 5 minutes before using. Roll out into a 32 cm × 16 cm rectangle.
2	Jam	25 g	250 g	Spread over the paste allowing a clear edge of 1 cm on all sides. Moisten the edge closest to yourself. Fold over the short sides by 1 cm and roll the pastry from the top towards yourself. Seal and wrap in buttered greaseproof paper and foil or pudding cloth. Place in a pudding sleeve and cook for the required time. Serve with a custard sauce.

☐   ☐   ☐

Steamed fruit pudding

Suitable for use with sultanas, dates, raisins or currants

⟍ 30 min   2 hr approximately

Step	Commodity	1 portion	10 portions	
1	Plain flour	20 g	200 g	Place in a bowl.
	Baking powder	2 g	20 g	Add to the flour and sieve together 3 times, add a pinch of salt.
	Breadcrumbs	20 g	200 g	Add.
	Suet	20 g	200 g	Add.
	Castor sugar	20 g	200 g	Add.
	Selected fruit	20 g	200 g	Add.
2	Egg	¼ equiv	2½ approx.	Add and mix in well.
	Milk	20 ml	200 ml	Add and place in a greased pudding bowl or sleeve. Cover and steam for the appropriate time. Serve with a custard or vanilla sauce.

☐ ☐ ☐

Golden syrup or treacle pudding

⟍ 20 min   2 hr approximately

Step	Commodity	1 portion	10 portions	
1	Plain flour	30 g	300 g	Place in a bowl.
	Baking powder	3 g	30 g	Add to the flour and sieve together 3 times, add a pinch of salt.
	Suet	20 g	200 g	Add.
	Castor sugar	20 g	200 g	Add.
	Lemon	¼	2	Grate the zest into the flour and pour in the strained juice.
2	Egg	¼ equiv	2½ approx.	Add.
	Milk	20 ml	200 ml	Add, mix well into a dough.
3	Golden syrup/ treacle	25 ml	250 ml	Pour into the prepared pudding bowls or sleeves. Place the pudding mixture on top. Cover and steam for the appropriate time. Serve with lemon sauce.

☐ ☐ ☐

Steamed sponge pudding – basic recipe

⟍ 30 min   2 hr approximately

Step	Commodity	1 portion	10 portions	
1	Butter/ margarine	20 g	200 g	Place in a bowl and soften.
	Castor sugar	20 g	200 g	Add and cream until fluffy and almost white.
	Eggs	½ equiv	3	Beat and gradually add to the creamed butter and sugar, mixing vigorously.
2	Plain flour	30 g	300 g	Place in a bowl.
	Baking powder	3 g	30 g	Add to the flour and sieve together 3 times, add a pinch of salt. Gradually incorporate into the mixture taking care not to knock the air out of the mixture. Place in a prepared pudding bowl. Cover with greaseproof paper and foil. Steam for the appropriate time.

NOTE: If the mixture is too thick add a little milk to achieve 'dropping' consistency.

8

Extensions of steamed sponge pudding

Vanilla sponge pudding

As for the basic recipe with the addition of vanilla essence.

Step	Commodity	1 portion	10 portions			
1	Vanilla essence	Few drops	2 tsp	Add to the creamed butter.	✋ 30 min	🍲 1½–2 hr

NOTE: Serve with a vanilla flavoured sauce (see hot sweet sauces, Chapter 13: Baking and sweet preparations.

Chocolate sponge pudding

As for the basic recipe with the addition of cocoa powder in place of the same amount of flour.

Step	Commodity	1 portion	10 portions			
1	Cocoa powder	5 g	50 g	Add to the flour.	✋ 30 min	🍲 1½–2 hr

NOTE: Serve with a chocolate flavoured sauce (see hot sweet sauces, Chapter 13: Baking and sweet preparations.

Lemon sponge pudding

As for the basic recipe with the addition of lemon flavouring.

Step	Commodity	1 portion	10 portions			
1	Lemons	½	2	Grate the zest and add to the flour and baking powder. Add the strained lemon juice to the sponge mixture.	✋ 30 min	🍲 1½–2 hr

NOTE: Serve with a lemon flavoured sauce (see hot sweet sauces, Chapter 13: Baking and sweet preparations.

Orange sponge pudding

As for the basic recipe with the addition of orange flavouring.

Step	Commodity	1 portion	10 portions			
1	Oranges	½	2	Grate the zest and add to the flour and baking powder. Add the strained orange juice to the sponge mixture.	✋ 30 min	🍲 1½–2 hr

NOTE: Serve with an orange flavoured sauce (see hot sweet sauces, Chapter 13).

Cherry sponge pudding

As for the basic recipe with the addition of 15 g chopped glace cherries, per portion.

✋ 30 min 🍲 1½–2 hr

Sultana sponge pudding

As for the basic recipe with the addition of 15 g sultanas, per portion. ✋ 30 min 🍲 1½–2 hr

Currant pudding

As for the basic recipe with the addition of 15 g currants, per portion. ✋ 30 min 🍲 1½–2 hr

Raisin sponge pudding

As for the basic recipe with the addition of 15 g raisins, per portion. ✋ 30 min 🍲 1½–2 hr

NOTE: Serve with a custard sauce (see hot sweet sauces, Chapter 13).

☐   ☐   ☐

WHAT WENT WRONG

Problem	Caused by	To rectify
Steamed food has an unpleasant flavour.	Not cleaning the steamer properly.	Cannot be rectified.
Vegetables are not evenly cooked.	Batch cooking vegetables of different sizes.	Re-distribute the vegetables accordingly, removing those that are cooked sufficiently, and steaming the vegetables that need further cooking.
Puddings are soggy.	Poor insulation of the pudding from the steam.	Remove and re-cover with grease-proof paper and foil
Puddings have a heavy texture.	(1) Using the wrong proportions of ingredients, e.g. not enough baking powder.	Cannot be rectified.
	(2) Not giving the baking powder sufficient time to aerate the product, e.g. by using a high pressure steamer.	Cannot be rectified.
The sponge or paste is dark in colour.	Over-cooking or holding for service too long.	Cannot be rectified.
The sponge is tough.	Over-handling or over-cooking.	Cannot be rectified.

9
ROASTING

Traditionally roasting was carried out over an open fire on a rotating spit, hence the term spit-roasting (à la broche). Today roasting is defined as the cooking of good quality whole or joints of meat, whole game or poultry, potatoes and parsnips in an oven by convected heat which is either circulated naturally by air or forced round by an electrical fan. The dryness within the oven is modified by the presence of steam. Originally the steam was only generated by the action of heat upon the moisture content within the food. Now modern ovens are equipped with steam generators to produce the required amount of moisture. Items for roasting are never covered with a lid while cooking. This would be known as pot roasting (poêler).

Roasting temperatures will depend on the food being cooked but usually they range from 180°C (400°F) to 230°C (450°F). This high temperature has the effect of drying the surface of the food quickly creating a rich brown crust. The browning effect can be enhanced by initially sealing the food in hot fat at the start of cooking. This process is called searing. It was thought that searing had the effect of sealing in the juices of the meat during the cooking process but this has since been proved to be wrong. Although most meat juices are retained, some escape into the roasting tray and are used in the accompanying gravies.

Searing can also be carried out by having a higher initial oven temperature. Items of meat and poultry should be cooked at 220°C for the first 15 minutes. The temperature is then reduced to the usual cooking temperature.

Meat consists of fat, protein and water. The proportion of fat on meat varies depending on the type of animal and its age. Some meats do not have a natural coating of fat. With the exception of chicken and turkey all should either be larded (inserting strips of fat through the meat) or barded (wrapping thin slices of fat around the exposed parts of the meat). This acts to provide extra moisture throughout the cooking process.

The protein comes in the form of numerous bundles of long fibres known as muscle. The younger the animal and the less exercised the muscle, the more tender the meat – the older the animal the more tough the meat will be. For this reason meat is usually hung at a temperature of between 1°C (34°F) and 3°C (36°F) in order for it to relax and become tender. The water content of meat accounts for 75 per cent of its make-up and it is this water/moisture that will aid the cooking process by producing steam.

Before roasting the oven must first reach the required temperature (see chart on p 200).

Terms associated with roasting

Barding This involves layering thin pieces of fat (usually pork fat) over lean meat so as to prevent drying out.

Basting Pouring melted fat over the item being roasted at regular intervals, improving the colour and flavour.

Larding This involves threading small strips of fat through the meat using a special larding needle. The extra fat helps keep the meat moist and improves the roasting quality of lean meat.

Meat glaze Meat stock reduced to a gelatinous paste concentrated in flavour.

Mirepoix Also known as a matignon, this is a collective term used to describe roughly chopped root vegetables used to flavour and protect roast joints from burning during the cooking process.

Searing Placing the meat in the oven at a high temperature to encourage the browning and produce a roasting flavour in the crust.

Singeing (1) To place over an open flame to remove feathers and down. (2) To brown over an open flame.

Spit roasting (à la broche). Fixing the meat on a rotating spit to roast.

Trivet A trivet is used to raise the food out of the fat in the roasting tray preventing it from frying. A trivet can be made with roughly chopped onions and carrots and/or chopped bones. Alternatively a special metal trivet can be used.

Trussing Securing a joint of meat or a whole item with string to retain its shape during the cooking process.

THE COOKING VESSEL

The cooking vessel is a metal roasting tray with tall sides. Always ensure that the tray is just large enough to hold the item to be cooked comfortably. Too small and fat might spill over the walls of the tray and cause a fire, too large and fat in the tray will burn ruining the finished taste.

Joints for roasting are first seared in hot fat and then placed in a roasting tray on a trivet. A trivet can come in the form of either a special metal rack or chopped bones and roughly chopped carrot and onion known as a bed of root vegetables. The vegetables will add flavour to the final gravy. The purpose of a trivet is to raise the items being cooked out of the fat which lies on the base of the roasting tray thus preventing it from burning. Cooking foil or damp greaseproof paper can also be placed over the meat to prevent burning and stop the food from drying out. The disadvantage of using foil is that moisture is trapped between the food and foil, slowing down the cooking process and stopping colour development.

For hygiene reasons there is a need for the internal temperature of the meat being cooked to be a minimum of 63°C. Between 63°C and 65°C the degree of cooking is classed as being rare, 65°C to 70°C is underdone, and 80°C to 85°C is medium and there should be no trace of blood (*see* the table on p 200).

ADDITIONAL INGREDIENTS

Traditionally all items to be roasted are first seasoned with salt and a little pepper and some roast dishes can be cooked with a range of herbs and/or spices to create a unique taste. The problem with using salt is that it attracts the juices of the meat to the surface and slows down the browning process. To get around this problem the meat may be salted before it is rolled up. Most roast meats can be served with a stuffing. The practice used to be to fill the cavity of poultry and game with these stuffings but this does not occur now because of hygiene reasons.

THE PROCESS OF ROASTING

After the item is properly prepared and placed into the pre-heated oven it is checked at regular intervals and turned to ensure even cooking and colouring. Fat and cooking juices from the bottom of the roasting tray are spooned over the food to moisten it. The technical term used to describe this action is basting. Basting with fat is important in roasting because it prevents the surface of the food from drying out and it also helps to flavour the roasting item.

Roasting temperatures

Initially items of meat and poultry should be cooked at 225°C (440°F) for approximately the first 15 minutes. The high cooking temperature quickly sets the surface protein, creating the required colour. The heat is then reduced to 180°C (360°F) until the item is cooked.

Once the cooking process is completed the food should be removed from the roasting tray and placed on a wire rack, above a tray to collect the cooking juices. These juices are retained to make the roast gravy. Further flavourings and juices can be collected from swilling out the roasting tray with the appropriate stock and straining into an appropriate receptacle.

9

How to test if cooked

There are several ways of testing the food.

1 **Thermo-needle** – This is the most accurate and hygienic method of testing a joint. The food is pierced with the special needle and the internal temperature is recorded. This is important when cooking meats that have been stuffed. The stuffing has to reach the required temperature so as to kill harmful bacteria and moulds. Using the table on p. 200 the correct degree of cooking can be achieved.

2 **Pressure test** – Press the meat with the hand. A general rule is that the less resilient the meat is to pressure, the more cooked (well done) it is.

3 **Appearance** – This can usually only be done by experienced chefs, and even then it is not an accurate test and should be done in conjunction with one or other of the other tests.

Staff associated with the preparation and cooking of roast items

In a traditional kitchen party the **Chef Garde Manger** prepares meats for roasting. The **Chef Entremettier** prepares the vegetables and the **Chef Rotisseur** roasts all meats, game and poultry.

JOINTS OF MEAT, GAME AND POULTRY SUITABLE FOR ROASTING

Meat	English term	French term	
Beef	Filletheart	Coeur de filet de boeuf	First class
	Fore rib	Les côtes premières	First class
	Middle rib	Les côtes decouvertes	Second class
	Sirloin	Aloyau de boeuf	First class
	Strip loin	Contrefilet de boeuf	First class
Lamb	Breast	Poitrine d'agneau	Second class
	Best end	Carre d'agneau	First class
	Crown	Curonne d'agneau	First class
	Loin	Longe d'agneau	First class
	Saddle	Selle d'agneau	First class
Game (feathered)	Guinea fowl	Pintade	First class
	Grouse	Tétras	First class
	Partridge	Perdreau	First class
	Pheasant	Faisan	First class
	Plover	Pluvier	First class
	Quail	Caille	First class
	Snipe	Becassine	First class
	Teal	Sarcelle	First class
	Wild duck	Canard sauvage	First class
	Woodcock	Becasse	First class
Game (furred)	Saddle of hare	Rable de lievre	First class
	Haunch of venison	Hanche de venaison	First class
	Saddle of venison	Selle de venaison	First class
Pork	Leg	Cuissot de porc	First class
	Loin	Longe de porc	First class
	Shoulder	Epaule de porc	Second class
	Spare rib	Echine de porc	Second class

Meat	English term	French term	
Poultry	Capon	Chapon	First class
	Chicken (baby)	Poussin	First class
	(small)	Poulet au gratin	First class
	(medium)	Poulet reine	First class
	(large)	Poularde	First class
	Duck	Canard	First class
	Duckling	Caneton	First class
	Goose	Oie	First class
	Gosling	Oison	First class
	Turkey	Dinde	First class
	Turkey (young)	Dindonneau	First class
Veal	Best end	Carre de veau	First class
	Breast	Poitrine de veau	Second class
	Leg	Cuissot de veau	First class
	Loin	Longe de veau	First class

Factors that may affect the cooking time

1 The type of oven used

Conventional/general purpose ovens rely on convected heat circulating around the oven. With constant use the heat circulation can be poor. Every time the oven door is opened the temperature drops and the time taken for the temperature to rise has to be taken into account when calculating the optimum cooking time. Forced air ovens are more effective as the heat is pushed around the oven by a fan, ensuring a consistent temperature throughout the oven.

2 The oven temperature

Using a higher temperature will shorten the cooking time, buy may affect the quality of the finished item. If the temperature is too high, the meat will tighten and be tough; if it is too low, the meat's natural juices will escape and the meat will be very dry when it is eventually done.

3 The size and shape of the item

Some meats are cooked with the bone in (on the bone), because bones conduct heat faster than meat. This type of joint will cook faster than boned and rolled or stuffed joints.

OVEN TEMPERATURES

	Gas mark	°C	°F
Very cool	¼	115	240
	½	120	250
Cool	1	135	275
	2	150	300
Warm	3	160	325
Moderate	4	175	350
	5	190	375
	6	200	400
Hot	7	215	425
	8	230	450
Very hot	9	245	475

9

Ideal degree of cooking

Meat	Degree of cooking	Final internal temperature
Beef	Underdone	63°C–65°C
Chicken	Cooked through	80°C–85°C
Duck	Well done	80°C–85°C
Goose	Well done	80°C–85°C
Lamb	Underdone	63°C–65°C
Lamb	Cooked through	63°C–65°C
Mutton	Cooked through	63°C–65°C
Partridge	Just done	80°C–85°C
Pheasant	Just done	80°C–85°C
Plover	Just done	80°C–85°C
Pork	Well done	80°C–85°C
Saddle of hare	Underdone	63°C–65°C
Turkey	Cooked through	80°C–85°C
Veal	Cooked through	80°C–85°C
Venison	Underdone	63°C–65°C
Wild duck	Underdone	80°C–85°C
Woodcock	Just done	80°C–85°C

Approximate roasting times

Meat	Cooking time
Beef	15 minutes per ½ kg (1 lb) and 15 minutes over
Chicken	15 minutes per ½ kg (1 lb) and 15 minutes over
Duck	20 minutes per ½ kg (1 lb) and 20 minutes over
Goose	20 minutes per ½ kg (1 lb) and 20 minutes over
Lamb	15 minutes per ½ kg (1 lb) and 15 minutes over
Lamb	20 minutes per ½ kg (1 lb) and 20 minutes over
Mutton	20 minutes per ½ kg (1 lb) and 20 minutes over
Partridge	15–25 minutes per partridge
Pheasant	30–50 minutes per pheasant
Plover	15–20 minutes per plover
Pork	25 minutes per ½ kg (1 lb) and 25 minutes over
Saddle of hare	25–30 minutes per saddle
Turkey	20 minutes per ½ kg (1 lb) and 20 minutes over
Veal	25 minutes per ½ kg (1 lb) and 25 minutes over
Venison	15 minutes per ½ kg (1 lb) and 15 minutes over
Wild duck	20–25 minutes per wild duck
Woodcock	15–25 minutes per woodcock

ROASTING TIMES

The cooking time will depend on the size and shape of the joint or cut. The table opposite will give approximate cooking times and should be used in conjunction with the table above and on p 199.

Garnishes and accompaniments for roasts

All joints of meat, game and poultry have a traditional accompaniment and garnish that should always be served with it. These accompaniments might include a stuffing and always include a sauce, and some are specific to certain dishes e.g. wild duck is served with an orange salad and Yorkshire puddings with roast beef English style. Below is a list of roast meats with appropriate accompaniments. This is followed by the recipes and methods of preparing such accompaniments.

TRADITIONAL GARNISHES FOR ROAST MEATS AND POULTRY

English term	French term	Garnish
Roast beef	Boeuf rôti à l'anglaise	Yorkshire pudding, roast gravy, horseadish sauce, watercress.
Roast lamb	Agneau rôti	Mint sauce, or redcurrant jelly, watercress and roast gravy.
Roast mutton	Mouton rôti	White onion sauce, redcurrant jelly, watercress and roast gravy.
Roast pork	Porc rôti	Sage and onion stuffing, apple sauce, roast gravy and watercress.

English term	French term	Garnish
Roast veal	Veau rôti	Thickened roast gravy, lemon parsley and thyme stuffing, watercress.
Roast chicken (English style)	Poulet rôti à l'anglaise	Roast gravy, bread sauce, grilled bacon, game chips, watercress.
Roast chicken with stuffing	Poulet rôti farci	Roast gravy, parsley and thyme stuffing, watercress.
Roast chicken with stuffing, English style	Poulet rôti farci á l'anglaise	Roast gravy, parsley and thyme stuffing, bread sauce, grilled bacon, game chips and watercress.
Roast duck/duckling	Canard/caneton rôti	Sage and onion stuffing, apple sauce, roast gravy and watercress.
Roast goose/gosling	Oie/oison rôti	Sage and onion stuffing, apple sauce, roast gravy and watercress.
Roast turkey (young) Roast turkey (female)	Dindonneau rôti Dinde rôtie	Bread sauce, grilled bacon, chestnut stuffing, grilled chipolata sausages, cranberry sauce, roast gravy and watercress.
Roast guinea fowl, (English style)	Pinade rôtie à l'anglaise	Roast gravy, bread sauce, grilled bacon, game chips and watercress.

TRADITIONAL GARNISHES FOR ROAST GAME MEATS

English term	French term	Garnish
Grouse	Grouse rôtie	Brown breadcrumbs, bread sauce, grilled bacon, roast gravy, game chips and watercress.
Hare, saddle of	Rable de lievre rôti	Forecmeat balls, redcurrant jelly, roast gravy and watercress.
Partridge	Perdreau rôti	Brown breadcrumbs, bread sauce, grilled bacon, roast gravy, game chips and watercress.
Plover	Pluvier rôti	Brown breadcrumbs, bread sauce, grilled bacon, roast gravy, game chips and watercress.
Pheasant	Faisan rôti	Brown breadcrumbs, bread sauce, grilled bacon, roast gravy, game chips and watercress.
Quail	Caille rôti	Brown breadcrumbs, bread sauce, grilled bacon, roast gravy, game chips and watercress.
Snipe	Becassine rôtie	Brown breadcrumbs, bread sauce, grilled bacon, roast gravy, game chips and watercress.
Teal	Sarcelle rôtie	Orange salad, roast gravy and watercress.
Venison	Venaison rôti	Redcurrant jelly, roast gravy, watercress. NOTE: Sauce poivrade is often served, *see* Chapter 4: Boiling.
Wild duck	Canard sauvage	Orange salad, roast gravy and watercress.
Woodcock	Becasse rôtie	Brown breadcrumbs, bread sauce, grilled bacon, roast gravy, game chips and watercress.

NOTE: Roast game is either presented on:

(a) a fried croûton of appropriate size spread with game farce, or
(b) the croûtes are offered as an accompaniment.

STUFFINGS

Sage and onion stuffing

Farce de sauge et oignon

🍲 30 min approximately (per 10 portions)
🔥 20 min ≈ 150°C (300°F)

Step	Commodity	1 portion	10 portions	
1	Fat (dripping or lard)	15 g	150 g	Melt the fat in a suitable pan.
2	Onions	25 g	250 g	Finely dice (brunoise) the onions and add to the fat. Cook gently without colouring.
3	Sage	pinch	15 g	Add the sage to the onions.
4	Parsley	pinch	5 g	Add to the onions.
5	White breadcrumbs	50 g	500 g	Add the breadcrumbs to the pan to form the stuffing. Season accordingly with salt and pepper. Lay the stuffing on a sheet of greased greaseproof paper and shape into a cylinder. Wrap the stuffing in tin foil and bake accordingly. Allow to cool slightly before slicing, otherwise it might fall apart.

☐ ☐ ☐

Chestnut stuffing

Farce de marrons

🍲 30 min approximately (per 10 portions)
🔥 45 min ≈ 150°C (300°F)

Step	Commodity	1 portion	10 portions	
1	Chestnuts	50 g	500 g	Slit the shell of the chestnut on both sides. Plunge into boiling water and simmer for 10 minutes. Remove the chestnuts from the water and remove the shells and the inner skins. Chop the chestnuts up coarsely. Place them in a clean bowl.
2	Pork sausagemeat	30 g	300 g	Add the sausagemeat to the chestnuts and mix together carefully. Lay the stuffing on a sheet of greased greaseproof paper and shape into a cylinder. Wrap the stuffing in foil and bake accordingly. Allow to cool slightly before slicing. Serve accordingly.

☐ ☐ ☐

Forcemeat

🍲 15 min

Step	Commodity	1 portion	10 portions	
1	Pork sausage-meat	25 g	250 g	Place in a suitably sized bowl.
2	White breadcrumbs	10 g	100 g	Add to the sausagemeat and mix well.
3	Prepared suet	10 g	100 g	Add to the other ingredients.
4	Mixed herbs	pinch	½ tsp	Sprinkle over the ingredients. Season with salt and pepper.
4	Egg	¼	1	Add and combine all the ingredients to form a stuffing.

☐ ☐ ☐

Parsley and thyme stuffing

Farce de persil et thym

🥄 30 min approximately (per 10 portions)
🍲 20 min 〰 150°C (300°F)

Step	Commodity	1 portion	10 portions	
1	White breadcrumbs	25 g	250 g	Place in a clean bowl.
2	Chopped suet	15 g	150 g	Add to the breadcrumbs.
3	Thyme, rubbed	¼ tsp	1 tsp	Sprinkle the thyme over the breadcrumbs.
4	Parsley, fine chopped	½ tsp	2 tsp	Combine the parsley with the rest of the ingredients.
5	Suet, finely chopped	15 g	150 g	Add the suet and mix in well. If the mixture is too dry add a little water or milk to bind. Lay the stuffing on a sheet of greased greaseproof paper and shape into a cylinder. Wrap the stuffing in foil and bake accordingly. Allow to cool slightly before slicing. Serve accordingly.

☐ ☐ ☐

Parsley, thyme and lemon stuffing

Farce de persil et thym au citron

🥄 30 min approximately (per 10 portions)
🍲 20 min 〰 150°C (300°F)

As for the basic recipe with the addition of ¼ lemon per portion. Grate the zest and add. Squeeze the juice, strain and add to the stuffing.

☐ ☐ ☐

Sausagemeat stuffing (also known as a plain forcemeat)

🥄 30 min approximately (per 10 portions)
🍲 20 min 〰 150°C (300°F)

Step	Commodity	1 portion	10 portions	
1	Pork sausagemeat	25 g	250 g	Place the sausagemeat in a clean bowl.
2	Suet, finely chopped	10 g	125 g	Sprinkle the suet over the sausagemeat.
3	White breadcrumbs	10 g	125 g	Add the breadcrumbs with the rest of the ingredients.
4	Mixed herbs	pinch	1 tsp	Add to the other ingredients.
5	Eggs	¼	2	Beat the eggs and combine with the other ingredients. Mix well. Season with salt and pepper to taste. Lay the stuffing on a sheet of greased greaseproof paper and shape into a cylinder. Wrap the stuffing in foil and bake accordingly. Allow to cool slightly before slicing. Serve accordingly. Alternatively the forcemeat can be shaped into the desired sized ball, passed through seasoned flour, egg wash and breadcrumbs and deep fried.

☐ ☐ ☐

9

SAUCES

Mint sauce
Sauce menthe

🥄 20 min approximately   🍲 5 min

Step	Commodity	2 portions	20 portions	
1	Water	20 ml	200 ml	Place in a saucepan and bring to the boil.
2	Mint leaves	25 g	250 g	Remove any stalks. Wash well. Place on a clean chopping board.
3	Castor sugar	10 g	100 g	Sprinkle over the mint leaves and chop. The sugar works as an abrasive and helps to chop the mint more finely. Add to the boiling water and return to the boil, remove from the heat immediately and allow to cool.
4	Malt vinegar	50 ml	500 ml	Add to the cooled liquid.

☐   ☐   ☐

Horseradish sauce
Sauce raifort

🥄 45 min–1 hr approximately

Step	Commodity	2 portions	20 portions	
1	Breadcrumbs, white	15 g	150 g	Place in a clean bowl.
2	Milk	30 ml	300 ml	Pour over the breadcrumbs and allow to soak for 30 minutes.
3	Whipping cream	70 ml	700 ml	Lightly whip.
4	Horseradish	15 g	150 g	Grate the horseradish finely and add to the cream. Squeeze the milk from the breadcrumbs and fold them into the horseradish.
5	Vinegar	1 tsp	1 tbsp	Add to the sauce. Season with salt and pepper. A little mustard can also be added for flavour.

☐   ☐   ☐

Redcurrant jelly sauce
Sauce de groseilles rouges jelli

🥄 45 min–1 hr approximately   🍲 30–40 min

Step	Commodity	2 portions	20 portions	
1	Redcurrants	75 g	750 g	Wash the redcurrants and place them in a suitable saucepan.
2	Castor sugar	15 g	150 g	Add to the redcurrants.
3	Water	50 ml	500 ml	Place in the saucepan with the rest of the ingredients, bring to the boil, then simmer until tender. Pass through a sieve or liquidise. Allow to cool. Use as required.

☐   ☐   ☐

ACCOMPANIMENTS

Game farci

Farce de giber

Step	Commodity	2 portions	20 portions	
				🥄 15 min approximately · 🍲 10 min approximately
1	Butter or margarine	10 g	100 g	Gently heat the butter in a suitable frying pan.
2	Onions	10 g	100 g	Add to the butter.
3	Game livers	50 g	500 g	Chop finely and add to the butter.
4	Thyme	pinch	sprig	Add to the livers.
5	Bay leaf	½	1	Add to the liver and brown well. Remove the bay leaf and pass through a fine sieve.
6	Butter or margarine	15 g	150 g	Mix into the sieved liver. Correct the seasoning.
7	Slices of bread	1	10	Cut into heart shapes and shallow fry in a little butter. Spread with the liver.

Orange salad
Salade d'orange

Step	Commodity	2 portions	20 portions	
				🥄 15 min approximately
1	Oranges	1	10	Remove the skin and pith and cut into segments. Pour the juice over the segments.
2	Lettuce	2 leaves	20 leaves	Lay a lettuce leaf in a salad dish, arrange the segments on top, pour over a little juice.
3	Parsley	5 g	50 g	Finely chop and sprinkle over the orange segments.

Game chips
Pommes chips

Step	Commodity	2 portions	20 portions	
				🥄 15 min approximately · 🍲 5–8 min approximately
1	Potatoes	50 g	500 g	Wash, peel and rewash the potatoes. Cut them into thin slices on a mandolin. Wash to remove the starch and dry well in a cloth. Cook in hot deep fat 185°C (365°F) until they are golden brown and crisp. Drain well, season with salt.

THE CARVING OF ROAST MEATS, GAME AND POULTRY

The first rule of carving is to ensure that the knife used is kept sharp at all times. All meat, poultry and game must be allowed to set before carving. To 'set' means to allow the meat to stand for 20 minutes after removal from the oven. This allows the meat muscle to relax, which in turn makes carving easier. The easier the meat is to carve, the better the yield of portions. Removing the wishbone in poultry and feathered game before roasting also facilitates carving. All strings must be removed before attempting carving.

Carving requires a high level of skill to ensure that the meats are attractively presented to the customer. The correct way to carve is to cut across the grain of the meat, ensuring a short-fibred, tender cut. When carving poultry and feathered game it is usual to serve a combination of leg and breast meat per portion. Some poultry and feathered game are small enough to serve as one portion or may need only be cut in half.

Storage of cooked meats

All cooked meats should be stored away from raw meats and at a temperature of no higher that 3°C. They should be placed on a wire rack standing on a tray so as to allow the meat juices to drain away. These juices can be used in the production of gravies.

Roasting vegetables

There are few vegetables that can be roasted successfully, among the lesser known are sweet potatoes, onions and Jerusalem artichokes. Potatoes and parsnips are the most common vegetables to be roasted and either or both of these vegetables will usually accompany an English style roast meal.

ROAST VEGETABLES RECIPES

Jerusalem artichokes

Topinambours

🥄 15 min approximately (per 10 portions)
♨ 1 hr approximately ≋ 240°C (464°F)

Step	Commodity	1 portion	10 portions	
1	Jerusalem artichokes	150 g	1½ kg	Wash, peel and trim into large even-sized shapes and place into a bowl of water.
2	Lemon juice	¼ lemon	1 lemon	Pour over the artichoke to prevent discoloration.
3	Fat or oil	20 g	200 g	Melt in a suitable roasting tray. Drain the water off the artichokes and add to the hot fat. Season with salt and pepper and baste the artichokes in the hot fat. Place in the pre-heated oven and cook for 1 hour or until cooked.

☐   ☐   ☐

Sweet potatoes

🥄 15 min approximately (per 10 portions)
♨ 1 hr approximately ≋ 240°C (464°F)

Step	Commodity	1 portion	10 portions	
1	Sweet potatoes	150 g	1½ kg	Wash, peel and cut into large even-sized pieces. Place in a bowl of water to prevent discoloration.
2	Cooking fat or oil	20 g	200 g	Melt in a suitably sized roasting tray. Drain the water off the sweet potatoes and add them to the hot fat. Baste the potatoes in the hot fat. Place them in the pre-heated oven and cook for approximately 1 hour or until they are a golden brown and tender. Serve accordingly.

☐   ☐   ☐

Onions

🥄 15 min approximately (per 10 portions)
♨ 1 hr approximately ≋ 240°C (464°F)

Step	Commodity	1 portion	10 portions	
1	Onions	150 g	1½ kg	Wash and peel leaving the onion whole.
2	Fat or oil	20 g	200 g	Melt and heat in a suitable roasting tray. Add the onions to the hot fat. Season with salt and pepper and baste the onions in the hot fat. Place in the pre-heated oven and cook for 1 hour or until cooked.

☐   ☐   ☐

Parsnips

Panais rôtis

🥄 15 min approximately (per 10 portions)
♨ 45 min approximately ≋ 240°C (464°F)

Step	Commodity	1 portion	10 portions	
1	Parsnips	150 g	1½ kg	Wash, peel and trim into large even-sized shapes and place into a bowl of water.
2	Lemon juice	¼ lemon	1 lemon	Pour over the parsnips to prevent discoloration.
3	Fat or oil	20 g	200 g	Melt in a suitable roasting tray. Drain the water off the parsnips and add them to the hot fat. Season with salt and pepper and baste the parsnips in the hot fat. Place in the pre-heated oven and cook for 45 minutes or until cooked.

NOTE: Take care not to cut the parsnips too small and that they are all about the same size, otherwise they will burn quickly.

☐   ☐   ☐

Potatoes

Pommes rôties

There are six different ways of cutting potatoes for roasting. The basic recipe below is followed by a description of each cut.

🥄 15 min approximately (per 10 portions)
♨ 1 hr approximately ≋ 240°C (464°F)

Step	Commodity	1 portion	10 portions	
1	Potatoes	150 g	1½ kg	Wash, peel and trim into large even-sized shapes and place into a bowl of water.
2	Fat or oil	20 g	200 g	Melt in a suitable roasting tray. Drain the water off the potatoes and add them to the hot fat. Season with salt and pepper and baste the potatoes in the hot fat. Place in the pre-heated oven and cook for 1 hour or until cooked.

Roast potatoes preparations

Chateau potatoes
(Pommes château)
Select small even-sized potatoes and turn into barrel-shaped pieces 5 cm (2 in) long, with a centre diameter of 2½ cm (1½ in) and an end diameter of 1½ cm (¾ in). NOTE: pommes chateau can be part-boiled for 2–3 minutes and refreshed before roasting.

Noisette potatoes
(Pommes noisettes)
Select even-sized potatoes and using a special noisette spoon cutter turn into hazel-nut sized balls and cook in butter until golden brown. Finish cooking in the oven.

Parisienne potatoes
(Pommes Parisienne)
Select even-sized potatoes and using a special Parisienne spoon or scoop shape accordingly. Cook in butter until golden brown. Complete cooking in the oven. Finish off by rolling in a little meat glaze and sprinkle with parsley.

Rissolee potatoes (Pommes rissolée)	Select small even-sized potatoes and turn into barrel-shaped pieces 3 cm (1½ in) long, with a centre diameter of 1½ cm (¾ in) and an end diameter of 1 cm (½ in).
	NOTE: pommes rissolee can be par-boiled for 2–3 minutes and refreshed before roasting.
Roast potatoes (Pommes rôties)	Wash, peel and cut into even-sized pieces. Allow 2–3 medium-sized pieces per portion. Cover the bottom of a suitably sized roasting tray with oil or fat and heat fiercely. Drain and dry the potatoes and add to the hot oil or fat. Season lightly and coat the potatoes in the hot fat. Place in a pre-heated oven and roast until golden brown.

☐   ☐   ☐

Pot roasting (poêler)

Poêler is similar to roasting in that it involves the cooking of joints of meat, poultry and game in an oven and the food is basted with a fat. Traditionally, pot roasting (poêler) is carried out in a cast iron pot (cauldron) over an open fire, and where it differs from roasting is that the food is placed in a cooking vessel with a tight-fitting lid on a bed of vegetables and herbs and the fat used to baste is always butter. The cooking vessel used can be a cocotte, casserole or braising pan. The cooked item is sometimes served to the customer in the cooking vessel.

Another term used when cooking à la poêle is cocotte and is usually used when referring to chicken cooked by this method.

Chicken cooked in casserole or cocotte   Poulet en cocotte

🥄 1 h   🍲 1½ h   〰 210°C

Step	Commodity	1 portion	10 portions	
1	Butter	7½ g	75 g	Soften and brush the inside of the casserole/cocotte dish.
	Carrots	30 g	300 g	Peel, roughly dice and place in the dish.
	Onion	30 g	300 g	Peel, roughly dice and place in the dish.
	Celery	25 g	250 g	Wash, trim the root and roughly dice.
	Bacon trimmings	15 g	150 g	Roughly cut and add.
2	Oven ready chicken	400 g equiv	4 kg	Wash, remove the wishbone and secure with string. Place on its back on top of the vegetables.
	Bouquet garni	1 small	1 large	Add.
	Butter	25 g	250 g	Melt and pour over the chicken. Season with salt and pepper. Cover with a lid and place in a pre-heated oven allowing 40 minutes per kilo and 20 minutes over. Baste occasionally. Remove the lid and continue cooking until the chicken is golden brown. To test if cooked insert a fork into the leg. If the juices run out clear the chicken is cooked. Remove from the oven and discard the string and bouquet garni. Keep the chicken warm. Pour the cooking juices and vegetables into a suitably sized saucepan and place on top of the stove and simmer. Wipe the cocotte/casserole dish clean and place the chicken inside. Cover with the lid and keep warm.
3	Brown stock	25 ml	250 ml	Add to the cooking juices and vegetables.
	Jus lié	75 ml	750 ml	Add, bring to the boil and simmer for 10 minutes. Degrasser and correct the seasoning. Pass through a fine sieve. Pour over the chicken. Sprinkle with finely chopped parsley and serve in the cocotte dish.

NOTE: This dish may be made with capon, duck, guinea fowl, poussins (baby chickens) or poularde (young fattened fowl), and pheasant may be used in place of chicken.

Extensions of pot roasting of poultry and game

1 Chicken cooked in a cocotte, bonne femme   Poulet en cocotte bonne femme

As for basic recipe with the addition of cocotte potatoes, lardons of bacon and glazed button onions.

Step	Commodity	1 portion	10 portions	
1	Potatoes	100 g	1 kg	Peel, wash and turn into 2½ cm barrels.
	Lard	7 g	70 g	Place in a thick bottomed frying pan and heat. Add the potatoes, season with salt and pepper and fry until golden brown. Toss from side to side to prevent uneven cooking. Remove and keep warm. Wipe the frying pan clean.
2	Button onions	60 g	600 g	Peel and trim the root.
	Butter	5 g	50 g	Place in the clean frying pan and heat gently. Add the onions, season with salt and pepper and cover with a lid. Toss from side to side to prevent burning and uneven cooking. Cook for 20 minutes.
	Castor sugar	2 g	20 g	Add and toss to ensure that the onions take on the required brown glaze. Remove and place with the potatoes. Wipe the frying pan clean.

9

Step	Commodity	1 portion	10 portions	
3	Streaky bacon	1 slice	10 slices	Remove the rind and any bones, and cut into thin slices. Place in a saucepan of boiling water and blanch for 2–3 minutes. Remove, drain and dry. Add a little fat to the clean pan and heat. Add to the hot fat and fry until golden brown, remove, drain and place with the potatoes and onions. Use to garnish the chicken in the cocotte dish. Sprinkle with finely chopped parsley and serve hot.

NOTE: Pheasant may be used in place of chicken.

2 Chicken cooked in a cocotte, champeaux   Poulet en cocotte champeaux

As for basic recipe replacing the brown stock with dry white wine and with the addition of cocotte potatoes and glazed button onions.

Step	Commodity	1 portion	10 portions	
1	Potatoes	100 g	1 kg	Peel, wash and turn into 2½ cm barrels.
	Lard	7 g	70 g	Place in a thick-bottomed frying pan and heat. Add the potatoes, season with salt and pepper and fry until golden brown. Toss from side to side to prevent uneven cooking. Remove and keep warm. Wipe the frying pan clean.
2	Button onions	60 g	600 g	Peel and trim the root.
	Butter	5 g	50 g	Place in a clean frying pan and heat gently. Add the onions, season with salt and pepper and cover with a lid. Toss from side to side to prevent burning and uneven cooking. Cook for 20 minutes.
	Castor sugar	2 g	20 g	Add and toss to ensure that the onions take on the required brown glaze. Remove and place with the potatoes. Use to garnish the chicken in the cocotte dish. Sprinkle with finely chopped parsley and serve.

NOTE: Pheasant may be used in place of chicken.

3 Chicken cooked in a cocotte, fermière

Poulet en cocotte fermière

As for basic recipe with the addition of paysanne of vegetables (carrots (25 g), turnips (15 g), swede (15 g), French beans (15 g) and garden peas (10 g) per portion) boiled then tossed in butter. Paysannes are thin sliced triangles, squares or rounds. Sprinkle with finely chopped parsley.

Step	Commodity	1 portion	10 portions	
1	Carrots	25 g	250 g	Peel, wash and cut into thin slices. Place in a saucepan and cover with water. Season, bring to the boil and cook for 15 minutes. Refresh and drain.
	Turnips	15 g	150 g	Peel, wash and cut into thin slices. Place in a suitably sized saucepan.
	Swede	15 g	150 g	Peel, wash and cut into thin slices. Place with the turnip, cover with water. Season, bring to the boil and cook for 12 minutes. Refresh and drain. Mix with the carrots.
	French beans	15 g	150 g	Top and tail. Cut into diamond (lozenge) shapes. Place in a saucepan of boiling salted water, return to the boil and simmer for 5 minutes. Refresh immediately and drain. Add to carrots.
	Garden peas	10 g	100 g	Place in a saucepan of boiling salted water, return to the boil and simmer for 2–3 minutes. Refresh immediately and drain. Add to the other vegetables.
	Butter	10 g	100 g	Place in the clean frying pan and heat. Add the mixed vegetables, season with salt and pepper. Toss from side to side, drain and arrange with the chicken. Sprinkle with finely chopped parsley and serve.

NOTE: Pheasant may be used in place of chicken.

4 Chicken cooked in a cocotte, grand'mere

Poulet en cocotte grand'mere

As for basic recipe with the addition of sautéed mushrooms and heart shaped croûtons.

Step	Commodity	1 portion	10 portions	
1	Button mushrooms	75 g	750 g	Wash, trim the roots and dry.
	Butter	5 g	50 g	Place in the clean frying pan and heat. Add the mushrooms, season with salt and pepper, fry quickly tossing from side to side to prevent burning and uneven cooking. Remove, drain and garnish the chicken. Keep warm. Wipe the frying pan clean.
2	Sliced bread	1	10	Remove the crusts and cut into two triangles. Shape into hearts.
	Butter	5 g	50 g	Place in the clean frying pan and heat. Add the croûtons and fry on both sides until golden brown. Remove, dip the tips in finely chopped parsley and use to garnish the chicken.

NOTE: Pheasant may be used in place of chicken.

9

Duckling with cherries

🍲 1 hr   ♨ 2 hr   ≋ 200°C

Step	Commodity	1 portion	10 portions	
1	Butter	7½ g	75 g	Soften and brush the inside of the casserole dish.
	Carrots	30 g	300 g	Peel, roughly dice and place in the dish.
	Onions	30 g	300 g	Peel, roughly dice and place in the dish.
	Celery	25 g	250 g	Wash, trim the root, roughly dice and place in the dish.
	Bacon trimmings	15 g	150 g	Roughly cut and add.
2	Oven ready duckling	400 g equiv	4 kg	Wash, remove the wishbone and secure with string. Place on its back on top of the vegetables.
	Bouquet garni	1 small	1 large	Add.
	Butter	25 g	250 g	Melt and pour over the duckling. Season with salt and pepper. Cover with a lid and place in a pre-heated oven, allowing 40 minutes per kilo and 20 minutes over. Baste occasionally. Remove the lid and continue cooking until the duckling is golden brown. To test if cooked insert a fork into the leg. If the juices run out clear the chicken is cooked. Remove from the oven and discard the string and bouquet garni. Keep the duckling warm. Pour the cooking juices and vegetables into a suitably sized saucepan and place on top of the stove and simmer. Wipe the cocotte/casserole dish clean and place the duck inside. Cover with the lid and keep warm.
3	Madeira	15 ml	150 ml	Add to the cooking juices and vegetables.
	Brown stock	25 ml	250 ml	Add.
	Jus lié	75 ml	750 ml	Add, bring to the boil and simmer for 10 minutes. Degrasser and correct the seasoning. Pass through a fine sieve.
	Stoned cherries	6	60	Add to the simmering sauce and cook for 5 minutes. Carve the duckling into portions. Arrange in the cocotte dish. Napper with the sauce and cherries. Sprinkle with finely chopped parsley and serve.

☐   ☐   ☐

Aiguillettes de caneton bigarrade

Step	Commodity	1 portion	10 portions	
				⏱ 1 hr 🍲 2 hr ≋ 200°C
1	Butter	7½ g	75 g	Soften and brush the inside of the casserole/cocotte dish.
	Carrots	30 g	300 g	Peel, roughly dice and place in the dish.
	Onion	30 g	300 g	Peel, roughly dice and place in the dish.
	Celery	25 g	250 g	Wash, trim the root, roughly dice and place in the dish.
	Bacon trimmings	15 g	150 g	Roughly cut and add.
2	Oven ready duckling	400 g equiv	4 kg	Wash, remove the wishbone and secure with string. Place on its back on top of the vegetables.
	Bouquet garni	1 small	1 large	Add.
	Butter	25 g	250 g	Melt and pour over the duckling. Season with salt and pepper. Cover with a lid and place in a pre-heated oven allowing 40 minutes per kilo and 20 minutes over. Baste occasionally. Remove the lid and continue cooking until the duckling is golden brown. To test if cooked, insert a fork into the leg; if the juices run out clear the duckling is cooked. Remove from the oven and discard the string and bouquet garni. Keep the duckling warm. Pour the cooking juices and vegetables into a suitably sized saucepan and place on top of the stove and simmer. Wipe the cocotte/casserole dish clean and place the duck inside. Cover with the lid and keep warm.
3	Brown stock	100 ml	1 litre	Add, bring to the boil and simmer for 10 minutes. Degrasser and correct the seasoning.
	Arrowroot	3 g	30 g	Dilute in a little water and add to the simmering liquid. Pass through a fine chinois.
4	Oranges	1	10	Remove the zest and blanch in boiling water for 3–4 minutes. Drain, refresh and place to the side.
	Lemons	¼	2	Remove the zest and blanch in boiling water for 4 minutes. Drain and refresh and place with the oranges. Squeeze the juice of the oranges and lemon and strain into the thickened gravy.
	Castor sugar	10 g	100 g	Place in a sauteuse and cook to a light caramel. Add the sauce and mix well. Season with salt and pepper. Pass through a chinois and add the blanched zest. Cut the duck into thin slices and dress the slices overlapping on a serving dish. Napper with the sauce and serve.

☐   ☐   ☐

9

Duckling with orange

Caneton poêlé à l'orange

🍲 1 hr ♨ 2 hr ≋ 200°C

Step	Commodity	1 portion	10 portions	
1	Butter	7½ g	75 g	Soften and brush the inside of the casserole/cocotte dish.
	Carrots	30 g	300 g	Peel, roughly dice and place in the dish.
	Onion	30 g	300 g	Peel, roughly dice and place in the dish.
	Celery	25 g	250 g	Wash, trim the root, roughly dice and place in the dish.
	Bacon trimmings	15 g	150 g	Roughly cut and add.
2	Oven ready duckling	400 g equiv	4 kg	Wash, remove the wishbone and secure with string. Place on its back on top of the vegetables.
	Bouquet garni	1 small	1 large	Add.
	Butter	25 g	250 g	Melt and pour over the duckling. Season with salt and pepper. Cover with a lid and place in a pre-heated oven allowing 40 minutes per kilo and 20 minutes over. Baste occasionally. Remove the lid and continue cooking until the duckling is golden brown. To test if cooked insert a fork into the leg; if the juices run out clear the duckling is cooked. Remove from the oven and discard the string and bouquet garni. Keep the duckling warm. Pour the cooking juices and vegetables into a suitably sized saucepan and place on top of the stove and simmer. Wipe the cocotte/casserole dish clean and place the duck inside. Cover with the lid and keep warm.
3	Brown stock	100 ml	1 litre	Add, bring to the boil and simmer for 10 minutes. Degrasser and correct the seasoning.
	Arrowroot	2½ g	25 g	Dilute in a little water and add to the simmering liquid. Pass through a fine chinois.
4	Oranges	1	10	Remove the zest and blanch in boiling water for 3–4 minutes. Drain, refresh and place to the side.
	Lemons	¼	2	Remove the zest and blanch in boiling water for 4 minutes. Drain and refresh and place with the orange. Segment the oranges and lemons and place to the side. Add the pith and remaining flesh to the sauce and simmer.
	Castor sugar	10 g	100 g	Place in a sauteuse and cook to a light caramel. Add the sauce and mix well. Season with salt and pepper. Pass through a chinois and add the blanched zest. Cut the duck into portions and place in the cocotte dish. Napper with the sauce, garnish with the segments and serve.

☐　　　☐　　　☐

Cushion of veal

Noix de veau poêlé

Step	Commodity	1 portion	10 portions				

Step	Commodity	1 portion	10 portions	
				🥣 1 hr ♨ 2 hr ≋ 200°C
1	Butter	7½ g	75 g	Soften and brush the inside of a braising pan.
	Carrots	30 g	300 g	Peel, roughly dice and place in the dish.
	Onion	30 g	300 g	Peel, roughly dice and place in the dish.
	Celery	25 g	250 g	Wash, trim the root, roughly dice and place in the dish.
	Bacon trimmings	15 g	150 g	Roughly cut and add.
2	Cushion of veal	150 g	1½ kg	Secure with string. Season with salt and pepper and place on top of the vegetables.
	Bouquet garni	1 small	1 large	Add.
	Butter	25 g	250 g	Melt and pour over the veal. Cover with a lid and place in a pre-heated oven allowing 50 minutes per kilo and 25 minutes over. Baste occasionally. Remove the lid and continue cooking until the veal is golden brown. Remove from the oven and discard the string and bouquet garni. Keep the veal warm. Pour the cooking juices and vegetables into a suitably sized saucepan and place on top of the stove and simmer.
3	Madeira	10 ml	100 ml	Add to the cooking juices.
	Tomato purée	2½ g	25 g	Add and mix in well.
	Brown stock	100 ml	1 litre	Add and bring to the boil and simmer for 10 minutes. Degrassé and correct the seasoning.
	Arrowroot	2 g	20 g	Dilute in a little water and add to the simmering liquid. Cook for 5 minutes and pass through a fine chinois. Remove and discard the string. Cut into thin slices and dress the slices overlapping on a serving dish. Napper with the sauce and serve.

NOTE: This dish may be garnished with jardinière of vegetables.
This dish may be made with cushion of pork, and fillet of beef may be used in place of veal.

9

Loin of lamb

Longe d'agneau poêlé

🥄 1 hr 🍲 2 hr ≋ 200°C

Step	Commodity	1 portion	10 portions	
1	Butter	7.5 kg	75 kg	Soften and brush the inside of a deep braising dish.
	Carrots	30 kg	300 kg	Peel, roughly dice and place in the dish.
	Onion	30 g	300 kg	Peel, roughly dice and place in the dish.
	Celery	25 g	250 kg	Wash, trim the root, roughly dice and place in the dish.
	Bacon trimmings	15 g	150 g	Roughly cut and add.
2	Loin of lamb (boned and rolled)	150 kg	1.5 kg	Secure with string. Season with salt and pepper and place on top of the vegetables.
	Bouquet garni	1 small	1 large	Add.
	Butter	25 kg	250 kg	Melt and pour over the lamb. Cover with a lid and place in a pre-heated oven allowing 40 minutes per kilo and 20 minutes over. Baste occasionally. Remove the lid and continue cooking until the lamb is golden brown. Remove from the oven and discard the string and bouquet garni. Keep the lamb warm. Pour the cooking juices and vegetables into a suitably sized saucepan and place on top of the stove and simmer.
3	Brown stock	75 ml	750 ml	Add to the cooking juices. Bring to the boil and simmer for 10 minutes. Degrasser and correct the seasoning.
	Arrowroot	3 g	30 g	Dilute in a little water and add to the simmering liquid. Cook for 5 minutes and pass through a fine chinois. Remove and discard the string. Cut into thin slices and dress the overlapping slices on a serving dish. Napper with the sauce and serve.

NOTE: Fillet of beef may be used in place of lamb.

Extensions of loin of lamb

1 Loin of lamb, Dubarry

Longe d'agneau Dubarry

As for cushion of veal with the addition of small château potatoes and bouquets of cauliflower Mornay.

🥄 1 hr 🍲 50 min ≋ 200°C

Step	Commodity	1 portion	10 portions	
1	Potatoes	100 g	1 kg	Peel, cut into small pieces and parcel shapes 3 cm long.
	Cooking oil/fat	5 g	50 g	Place in a roasting pan, melt and heat. Add the potatoes, season with salt and pepper. Place in a pre-heated oven for the required time or until the potatoes are golden brown. Remove and keep warm.
2	Cauliflower	50 g	500 g	Remove the stalks and cut into small florets. Wash and place in a saucepan of boiling salted water. Bring to the boil and simmer for 10 minutes. Refresh and drain well. Place on a grilling tray.
3	Mornay sauce	50 ml	500 ml	Napper over the drained cauliflower and glaze under a pre-heated salamander. Arrange alternative portions of cauliflower Mornay and château potatoes around the meat. Serve hot.

NOTE: Fillet of beef or cushion of veal may be used in place of lamb.

2 Loin of lamb, Niçoise

Longe d'agneau Niçoise

As for cushion of veal with the addition of small château potatoes, bouquets of French beans and whole skinned cherry tomatoes.

Step	Commodity	1 portion	10 portions	⤵ 1 hr ♨ 50 min ≋ 200°C
1	Potatoes	100 g	1 kg	Peel, cut into small pieces and barrel shapes 3 cm long.
	Cooking oil/fat	5 g	50 g	Place in a roasting pan, melt and heat. Add the potatoes, season with salt and pepper. Place in a pre-heated oven for the required time or until the potatoes are golden brown. Remove and keep warm.
2	French beans	50 g	500 g	Trim the tops and tails and wash. Place in a saucepan of boiling salted water and cook for 5 minutes. Refresh and drain. Place to the side.
3	Cherry tomatoes	2	20	Remove the stalks and make a small incision in the other end. Blanch in boiling water for 8–9 seconds. Remove and refresh. Discard the skins and place on a grilling tray. Brush with melted butter and place under a pre-heated salamander for 5 minutes. Remove and keep warm.
	Butter	5 g	50 g	Melt and heat in a sauté pan. Add the beans and season with salt and pepper. Arrange alternative portions of château potatoes, bouquets of French beans and cherry tomatoes around the meat. Serve immediately.

NOTE: Fillet of beef of cushion of veal may be used in place of lamb.

□   □   □

WHAT WENT WRONG?

Problem	Caused by	To rectify
Meat is dry, tough and has shrunk excessively.	(1) Over-cooking and at too high a temperature.	Cannot be rectified.
	(2) Not basting sufficiently/regularly during the cooking process.	Cannot be rectified.
Meat is under-cooked.	Cooking at too low a temperature or not cooking for sufficient time.	Remove the item from the oven. Re-adjust the temperature before returning the meat to the oven.
The meat yields fewer portions than expected.	(1) Over-cooking or cooking at too high a temperature.	Cannot be rectified.
	(2) Not allowing the meat to rest before carving or not carving properly.	Cannot be rectified.
Surface of the meat has not browned.	Cooking at too low a temperature.	Remove the meat from the oven. Re-adjust the temperature before returning the meat to the oven.
The surface of the potatoes has not browned.	Cooking at too low a temperature.	If they are not too cooked, remove the potatoes from the oven. Re-adjust the temperature before returning them to the oven.

9

⑩
GRILLING

Grilling is the cooking of tender cuts of meat, offal, poultry, fish and vegetables by radiant heat. The process is not suitable for tougher, coarser items that need thorough cooking to become digestible as the extreme heat and dryness of grilling would destroy the food before it was ever cooked. Most grilled foods only take a matter of between 2–15 minutes to cook.

Terms associated with grilling

Au bleu Blue or very rare.

Au gratin To cover with breadcrumbs and/or grated cheese and grill until brown.

à point Just done or medium.

Bien cuit Well cooked or well done.

Blanch Cook without colouring.

Broche (à la) Food cooked on an open fire.

Brochette On a skewer.

Broiling American term for grilling.

Glazing Coating with sugar syrup during cooking.

Porterhouse American term for T-bone steak.

Saignant Underdone or rate.

Searing The action of using fierce heat to create the initial colouring of the food's surface.

Skewers Thin lengths of wood, bamboo or stainless steel used to hold small pieces of meat, vegetables, fish and/or fruit to cook over a grill.

Toasting To brown with 'dry' heat (i.e. without the use of fat).

There are three techniques used to grill foods:

1 Cooking under radiant heat, e.g. over-fired grills such as gas or electric salamanders.

Steaks, cutlets and chops can be cooked on greased salamander bars. Food items such as cuts of fish, sausages, tomatoes, mushrooms, bacon, and kidneys are suited to being cooked this way. Salamanders are also used to brown certain dishes such as macaroni au gratin, cauliflower Mornay, duchesse potatoes and to glaze and gratinate fish dishes.

2 Cooking over radiant heat, e.g. charcoal barbecues or on gas or electrically heated grill bars that sometimes have special fire bricks to simulate real charcoal.

This technique is used to cook larger items such as steaks, chops and cutlets. The wire bars produce an attractive pattern and the open flames on the food create a very distinctive flavour.

3 Cooking between heat, e.g. specially designed electrically heated grill bars or plates, sometimes known as contact or infra grills.

This technique is suitable for smaller items of meat.

NOTE: There are specialised items of grilling apparatus used to cook specific foods, such as continuous/rotary grills. These are specially designed grills used in fast food outlets for cooking burgers and in large hotels and restaurants for cooking toast. The raw food items are placed on a conveyor belt that carries the food past the heat source.

NOTE: The process of grilling should not be mixed up with that of griddling. Griddling is in fact a form of shallow frying carried out on a griddle plate.

PREPARATION FOR GRILLING

Before the grilling process begins the meat must be properly prepared. Some meats are marinaded to improve the flavour and to tenderise them. Others are flavoured with fresh herbs and/or spices, but usually the item for cooking is seasoned with salt and milled pepper just before cooking. Liver, whole fish and cuts of fish are lightly coated with seasoned flour to protect them during cooking and to produce a crisp coating. All items for grilling are brushed with oil and/or butter to keep them moist and prevent them from sticking to the cooking surface or tray.

The grilling appliance is always pre-heated before commencing the cooking process. This is important as it will influence the cooking time and if the grill is not hot enough the food item might stick to the surface and be ruined. The actual cooking process begins with the food being sealed to retain the natural juices and flavour.

DEGREES OF COOKING

Most foods are usually cooked thoroughly for service, but in the case of beef steaks, lamb and offal they may be served according to the customer's wishes. Grilling items will vary according to thickness and quality of the food being cooked. The chart below can be used as a guide.

NOTE: Attention must be paid to the cooking time to ensure that the grilled food is cooked to the correct degree otherwise the customer will return the dish.

Au bleu blue or very rare	Sealed for a matter of seconds on each side. The meat looks nearly raw.
Saignant (bleeding) underdone or rare	The cooked meat has a reddish pink tinge.
à point just done or medium	A slight pinkness of the meat.
Bien cuit well cooked or well done	Thoroughly cooked throughout. No sign of pinkness in the meat.

NOTE: In a traditional kitchen brigade three parties would be involved in the preparation and cooking of grilled foods:

Chef Garde-Manager Larder Chef
Chef Entremettier Vegetable chef
Chef Grillardin Grill cook

The advantages of grilling

1 The speed of the process enables the food to be cooked to order.
2 The speed of the cooking process enables maximum retention of nutrients and flavour.
3 The process can be monitored easily as the food is visible throughout cooking.

10

COOKING GUIDE FOR GRILLED MEAT, POULTRY, OFFAL, FISH AND VEGETABLES

Commodity	Menu example	Weight per portion	Cooking time, medium cooked	Commodity	Menu example	Weight per portion	Cooking time, medium cooked
BEEF				Sirloin	Entrecôte minute grillé Minute steak	200 g	3–4 min
Fillet	Chateaubriand grillé Double fillet steak	250 g	15–18 min	Sirloin	Porterhouse steak (T-bone)	650 g	15–18 min
Fillet	Tournedos	150 g	8–10 min	Rump	Point steak, grilled	200 g	10–12 min
Fillet	Filet grillé Fillet steak	200 g	10–15 min	Rump	Rump steak, grilled	200 g	8–10 min
Sirloin	Entrecôte double grillé Double sirloin steak	400 g	15–18 min				
Sirloin	Entreôte grillé Single sirloin steak	200 g	8–10 min				

NOTE: The above dishes can be garnished:
à la maison: in the style of
bouquetière: bouquet of
Henri IV: Henry IV style
maître d'hôtel: head waiter style
vert pré: green meadow style

Commodity	Menu example	Weight per portion	Cooking time, medium cooked
LAMB			
Chump chop		250 g	15–18 min
Crown chop		400 g	15–18 min
Cutlet		100 g	8–10 min
Double cutlet		200 g	15–18 min
Noisette		100 g	3–5 min
Rosette		100 g	5–8 min
Liver		200 g	5–6 min
Kidneys		75 g	3–8 min
PORK			
Bacon		100 g	3–8 min
Chop		200 g	15–18 min
Gammon steak		150 g	8–10 min
POULTRY			
Chicken, whole portioned		400 g	8–10 min
Spring chicken		400 g	20–25 min
VEAL			
Cutlet		250 g	8–10 min
Escalope		150 g	8–10 min
Liver		200 g	5–6 min
WHOLE FISH			
Herring	Hareng	200 g	15–20 min
Kippers	Craquelot	200 g	15–20 min
Mackerel	Maquereau	200 g	15–20 min
Red mullet	Rouget	200 g	15–20 min
Plaice	Plie	200 g	15–20 min
Sole, Dover	Sole Douvres	250 g	15–20 min
Sole, lemon	Sole limande	250 g	15–20 min
Trout	Truite	200 g	8–12 min
Whiting	Merlan	200 g	8–12 min
CUTS OF FISH			
Cod			
Fillet	Filet de cabillaud	100 g	3–10 min

Commodity	Menu example	Weight per portion	Cooking time, medium cooked
Steak	Darne de cabillaud	150 g	3–10 min
Suprême	Suprême de cabillaud	100 g	3–10 min
Dover sole			
Fillet	Filet de sole	100 g	3–10 min
Haddock			
Fillet	Filet de aigrefin	100 g	3–10 min
Steak	Darne de aigrefin	150 g	3–10 min
Suprême	Suprême de aigrefin	100g	3–10 min
Hake			
Fillet	Filet de Colin	100 g	3–10 min
Steak	Darne de Colin	150 g	3–10 min
Suprême	Suprême de Colin	100 g	3–10 min
Halibut			
Steak	Tronçon de Flétan	150 g	3–10 min
Lemon sole			
Fillet	Filet de sole limande	100 g	3–10 min
Plaice			
Fillet	Filet de Plie	100 g	3–10 min
Salmon			
Steak	Darne de Saumon	150 g	3–10 min
Suprême	Suprême de Saumon	100 g	3–10 min
SHELLFISH			
Lobster	Homard (Lobster butter)	300 g (shell on)	10–15 min
Scampi	Langoustine (Hard butter sauce or sauce diable.)	200 g (shell on)	8–12 min

Grilling fish and shellfish

Fish is usually grilled portioned either in darnes (steaks cut from a round fish), a tronçon (steak cut from a flat fish) or a fillet (fish off the bone, flat or round). Some fish and shellfish can be grilled whole. They include herrings, kippers, mackerel, red mullet, plaice, sole, trout, whiting, lobster and scampi.

PREPARING FISH FOR GRILLING

Remove the scales from the fish with the back of a knife. Remove the heart and clean out the intestines, taking care not to damage the roe. Remove the roe and in the case of herrings keep the roe for further use. Trim off the fins and the tail. Make three 2 mm incisions (to ciseler) on either side of the fish. This reduces curling during cooking. Dover sole, lemon sole and plaice have the dark skin removed before grilling.

Grilled fish (whole, fresh)

Poisson grillé

👐 20 min 🔥 10–15 min approximately

Step	Commodity	1 portion	10 portions
1	Whole prepared fish	1 × 200 g	10 × 200 g

Pass through seasoned flour and shake off any surplus. Brush the fish and the grilling tray with melted butter, margarine or oil. Warm the tray and place the fish on it serving side down. Place under the pre-heated salamander and cook on both sides for the required time. Serve on an oval flat garnished with fluted lemon and picked parsley. Serve with a compound butter.

☐ ☐ ☐

Grilled fish (portioned, fresh)

Poisson grillé

👐 10 min 🔥 3–12 min approximately

Step	Commodity	1 portion	10 portions
1	Prepared fish	1 × 100 g	10 × 100 g

Dry the fish off, make three 2 mm incisions (to ciseler) on either side of the fish to reduce curling and pass through seasoned flour. Shake off any surplus. Brush the fish and the grilling tray with melted butter, margarine or oil. Warm the tray and place the fish on it serving side down. Place under the pre-heated salamander and cook on both sides for the required time. Serve on an oval flat garnished with fluted lemon and picked parsley. Serve with a compound butter.

☐ ☐ ☐

10

Grilled fish (cured/smoked)

Usually served for breakfast.

Kippers (cured whole herring) are prepared by cleaning and trimming them, and cutting off the head and trimming the tail. They are brushed with butter just before cooking. Kippers can also be filleted before cooking. Bloaters (cured and smoked herring) are prepared by cutting off the head and trimming the tail and are brushed with butter just before cooking.

Step	Commodity	1 portion	10 portions
1	Prepared fish	1 × 200 g	10 × 200 g

⏲ 10 min   🍲 3–12 min approximately

Dry the fish off, brush the fish and the grilling tray with melted butter, margarine or oil. Warm the tray and place the fish on it serving side down. Place under the pre-heated salamander and cook on both sides for the required time. Serve on an oval flat garnished with picked parsley. Serve with a compound butter.

☐   ☐   ☐

Grilled shellfish

Step	Commodity	1 portion	10 portions
1	Lobster	1 × 200 g	10 × 200 g

⏲ 10 min   🍲 8–15 min approximately

Cut in half lengthwise and clean. Dry off. Brush the lobster and the grilling tray with melted butter. Warm the tray and place the lobster on the tray. Place under the pre-heated salamander and cook on both sides for the required time. Serve on an oval flat garnished with lobster butter and picked parsley.

☐   ☐   ☐

Grilled scampi on a skewer

Langoustine en brochette

Step	Commodity	1 portion	10 portions
1	Shelled scampi	100 g	1 kg
2	Fresh/dried thyme	pinch	5 g
3	Lemon juice	10 ml	100 ml
4	Onions	30 g	300 g
5	Bayleaves	2	20

⏲ 20 min   🍲 5 min approximately

Place in a bowl.

Sprinkle over the lamb.

Pour over the other ingredients and allow to marinade for 2 hours.

Cut into large dice.

Divide the scampi and onions into equal portions. Arrange alternative pieces of the scampi, onions and bayleaves on the appropriate number of skewers. Cook for the required time. Serve on a bed of braised rice (riz pilaff) and accompany with a devilled sauce or hard butter sauce.

Extensions

Dish	French	Ingredients
Scampi wrapped in bacon	Languoustine en brochette au lard	50 g sliced bacon per portion

Serve on a bed of braised rice (riz pilaff) and accompany with a sweet and sour sauce.

☐   ☐   ☐

Garnishes for meats, offal and fish

In the style of the house
à la maison

Step	Commodity	1 portion	10 portions

🥣 30 min   🍲 20 min approximately

Step	Commodity	1 portion	10 portions	
1	Tomatoes	1	10	Remove the eye from tomatoes and make a shallow cross incision in the other end. Place on a buttered grilling tray and brush with melted butter. Season with salt and pepper.
2	Large mushrooms	25 g	500 g	Wash and remove the stalks. Place the tomatoes under the pre-heated salamander and cook for 10 minutes. Add the mushrooms, brush with melted butter and season with salt and pepper. Continue cooking for 5–8 minutes. When cooking is complete remove from the salamander and keep warm.
3	Straw potatoes (see Chapter 12: Deep frying)	50 g	500 g	Cook and keep warm.
4	French fried onions (see Chapter 12: Deep frying)	50 g	500 g	Cook and keep warm

Use to garnish grilled beef steaks, pork and lamb. Finish off with small bunches of watercress.

□   □   □

Caprice style
Filet de poisson caprice

🥣 30 min   🍲 10 min approximately

Step	Commodity	1 portion	10 portions	
1	Fish fillets	1 × 100 g	10 × 100 g	Dry the fish off, make three 2 mm incisions (to ciseler) on either side of the fish to reduce curling and pass through seasoned flour. Shake off any surplus. Brush the fish and the grilling tray with melted butter, margarine or oil. Place under the pre-heated salamander and cook on both sides for the required time. Serve on an oval flat garnished with picked parsley.
2	Bananas	1	10	Peel, cut in half lengthways. Pass through seasoned flour and brush with butter. Grill for 3 minutes. Arrange by the side of the fish. Serve with Robert sauce.

□   □   □

Fillet of fish Saint Germain

Filet de poisson St Germain
🥄 30 min · 🍲 8 min approximately

Step	Commodity	1 portion	10 portions	
1	Fish fillets	1 × 100 g	10 × 100 g	Dry the fish off, make three 2 mm incisions (to ciseler) on either side of the fish to reduce curling and pass through seasoned flour. Shake off any surplus. Brush the fish and the grilling tray with melted butter, margarine or oil. Place under the pre-heated salamander and cook on both sides for the required time. Serve on an oval flat garnished with picked parsley
2	Potatoes	150 g	1½ kg	Wash and peel. Using a special spoon cutter, cut into hazel-nut size.
3	Butter	20 g	200 g	Melt in a suitably sized frying pan. Add the potatoes and cook until golden brown. Arrange around the cooked fish. Serve with béarnaise sauce.

☐   ☐   ☐

Bouquet of vegetables

Bouquetière de légumes
🥄 30 min · 🍲 20 min approximately

Step	Commodity	1 portion	10 portions	
1	Cauliflower	50 g	500 g	Place in boiling water and cook for 10 minutes. Refresh in cold water.
2	French beans	25 g	250 g	Place in boiling water. Return to the boil and cook for 5 minutes. Refresh in cold water.
3	Carrots	25 g	250 g	Place in cold water. Bring to the boil and cook for 10 minutes. Refresh in cold water.
4	Turnips	25 g	250 g	As for the carrots. Drain the water off the vegetables and mix together. Re-heat au beurre. Serve with a béarnaise sauce.

Use to garnish chateaubriand. Finish with small bunches of watercress.

☐   ☐   ☐

Pont neuf potatoes

Pommes Pont Neuf
🥄 30 min · 🍲 20 min approximately

Step	Commodity	1 portion	10 portions	
1	Large potatoes	300 g	3 kg	Peel, wash and create pommes Pont Neuf by cutting into 5 cm × 2 cm slices. Cut the slices into 5 cm × 2 cm × 2 cm strips. Wash off the starch, dry and blanch in the deep fryer (165°C) to partly cook. To complete the cooking process, heat the fat to 185°C and cook the potatoes until golden brown. Drain off the excess fat. Place on absorbent paper and keep warm until required.

Use to garnish grilled beef steak. Finish with small bunches of watercress.

NOTE: Pont Neuf potatoes were created to resemble the ninth bridge over the river Seine in Paris. Originally prepared by shaping arches on top and three trusses on the bottom of two of the potato strips. They are then placed on the three bottom strips of potato to resemble the bridge.

☐   ☐   ☐

Continental style

Step	Commodity	1 portion	10 portions	⤵ 30 min ⊞ 20 min approximately
1	Large potatoes	300 g	3 kg	Peel, wash and create pommes soufflées by cutting into 6 cm × 4 cm squares, 3 mm thick. Wash off the starch, dry and blanch in the deep fryer (180°C) for 6 minutes to partly cook. Remove and ensure that the potatoes do not stick together. To complete the cooking process, heat the fat to 190°C and cook the potatoes until they have puffed out and are crisp and golden brown. Drain off, place on absorbent paper and keep warm until required.
2	Large mushrooms	2	20	Wash, trim the stalks and season with salt and pepper. Brush with butter and place on a grilling tray. Begin cooking for 2 minutes.
3	Tomatoes	1	10	Remove eyes from tomatoes and make a slight cross-like incision in the other end. Arrange on the grilling tray, brush with butter, season with salt and pepper. Place on the grilling tray with the mushrooms and cook for a further 3 minutes.

Use to garnish grilled beef steak. Finish with small bunches of watercress.

☐   ☐   ☐

Head waiter style (parsley butter)

Step	Commodity	1 portion	10 portions	⤵ 30 min ⊞ 2–3 min approximately
1	Butter	20 g	200 g	Soften the butter.
	Parsley	5 g	50 g	Wash, remove the stalks and chop finely. Add to the softened butter.
2	Lemon juice	5 ml	50 ml	Mix in with the other ingredients. Place on a sheet of greaseproof paper. Mould into a 3 cm diameter cylindrical shape and place in the fridge. Allow to set. Cut into 1 cm slices and store in iced water for service. Place the parsley butter over the hot meat and allow to melt.
3	Straw potatoes (see Chapter 12: Deep frying)	50 g	500 g	Cook and keep warm.

Use to garnish grilled beef steaks, lamb cutlets and pork chops. Finish with small bunches of watercress.

☐   ☐   ☐

10

Mirabeau

Step	Commodity	1 portion	10 portions	
1	Butter	20 g	200 g	Soften the butter.
	Anchovy essence	5 ml	50 ml	Add to the softened butter.
2	Lemon juice	5 ml	50 ml	Mix in with the other ingredients. Place on a sheet of greaseproof paper. Mould into a 3 cm diameter cylindrical shape and place in the fridge. Allow to set. Cut into 1 cm slices and store in iced water for service. Place the anchovy butter over the hot meat and allow to melt.
3	Anchovy fillets	3	30	Cut lengthways into thin strips. Decorate the meat with the anchovy fillets and olives.

Used to garnish grilled entrecôte steak. Finish with small bunches of watercress.

☐   ☐   ☐

With bacon

Step	Commodity	1 portion	10 portions	
1	Middle bacon	2 slices	20 slices	Place on a greased pre-heated tray and grill.

🥄 30 min   ♨ 10 min approximately

Serve with grilled lambs' liver. Finish with small bunches of watercress.

☐   ☐   ☐

Tyrolienne

Step	Commodity	1 portion	10 portions	
1	French fried onions (see Chapter 12: Deep frying)	50 g	500 g	Cook and keep warm.
2	Tomatoes	50 g	500 g	Remove eyes from the tomatoes and make a shallow cross incision in the other end. Place in a pan of boiling water for 10 seconds and refresh immediately in cold water. Remove the skin. Cut in half. Remove the seeds. Cut the flesh into small dice.
3	Butter	5 g	50 g	Melt in a suitably sized sauteusse. Add the tomatoes and cook without colouring for 3–5 minutes. Keep warm in a bain-marie. Place the appropriate amount of tomato concassé on the grilled meat. Surround with the french fried onions.

🥄 30 min   ♨ 20 min approximately

Serve with grilled beef steaks and lamb. Finish with small bunches of watercress.

☐   ☐   ☐

Green meadow style

Vert pré

Step	Commodity	1 portion	10 portions		
				⌣ 30 min	♨ 20 min approximately
1	Straw potatoes (*see* Chapter 12: Deep frying)	50 g	500 g	Cook and keep warm.	

Used to garnish grilled beef steaks, pork chops, lamb cutlets, poultry and offal.

☐   ☐   ☐

Grilled meat dishes

Mixed grill

Panaché grillé

Step	Commodity	1 portion	10 portions	
				⌣ 45 min ♨ 15 min approximately
1	Butter	20 g	200 g	Soften the butter.
2	Parsley	5 g	50 g	Wash, remove the stalks and chop finely. Add to the softened butter.
3	Straw potatoes (*see* Chapter 12: Deep frying)	50 g	500 g	Cook and keep warm.
4	Lamb cutlets	1 × 100 g	10 × 100 g	French trim. Season with salt and pepper. Brush with oil.
5	Lambs' kidneys	1	10	Remove the skin. Cut open and remove the core. Place on skewers, season with salt and pepper. Brush with oil.
6	Chipolata sausages	1	10	Place on a greased grilling tray. Brush lightly with oil.
7	Grilling mushrooms	1	10	Remove the stalks, wash, place on the grilling tray, brush with oil and season with salt and pepper.
8	Tomatoes	1	10	Remove the eyes, make a shallow incision in the form of a cross on the top. Place on the grilling tray, brush with oil and season with salt and pepper.
9	Back bacon	1 slice	10 slices	Place on the grilling tray. Grill all the ingredients under the salamander beginning with the cutlets and then every other item at 3 minute intervals. The bacon takes 2 minutes to cook. The kidneys should be cooked slightly underdone. Serve with small bunches of watercress.

NOTE: The ingredients above are only a basis to which many establishments add – and ommit accordingly.

☐   ☐   ☐

Grilled gammon steak

Jambon grillé vert pré
🥣 30 min 🍲 10 min approximately

Step	Commodity	1 portion	10 portions	
1	Gammon steak	200 g	10 × 200 g	Prepare the gammon steak by nicking the skin every 2 cms. This prevents the gammon from curling up during the cooking process. Place on a greased grilling tray and place under a pre-heated salamander. Cook for the required time.
2	Straw potatoes (*see* Chapter 12: Deep frying)	50 g	500 g	Cook and place on absorbent paper to remove excess fat. Use to garnish the grilled gammon. Serve with small bunches of watercress.

NOTE: Grilled gammon can be served with a shallow-fried glazed pineapple ring or glazed peach halves. The glazing effect is achieved by sprinkling the fruit with sugar and grilling until the sugar has melted.

□ □ □

Grilled Turkish kebabs

Brochette à la Torque
🥣 3 hr 🍲 15 min approximately

Step	Commodity	1 portion	10 portions	
1	Fillet of lamb	150 g	1½ kg	Trim off the fat and sinew and cut into 1 cm slices. Place in a bowl.
2	Fresh/dried thyme	pinch	5 g	Sprinkle over the lamb.
3	Lemon juice	10 ml	100 ml	Pour over the other ingredients and allow to marinade for 2 hours.
4	Onions	30 g	300 g	Cut into large dice.
5	Bayleaves	2	20	Divide the lamb and onions into equal portions. Arrange alternative pieces of the lamb, onions and bayleaves on the appropriate number of skewers. Cook for the required time. Serve on a bed of braised rice (riz pilaff) and accompany with a demi-glace based sauce.

Extensions of Turkish kebabs

Dish	French	Ingredients
Chicken liver kebab Serve with Madeira sauce	Brochette de foie de volaille	150 g chicken livers per portion.
Grilled kidney kebab Serve with devilled or Madeira sauce	Brochette de rognons	100 g of veal kidney or 2 lambs' kidneys per portion.
Kebab, house style Serve with sweet and sour sauce.	Brochette à la maison	Select 125 g of chosen meat, 4 button mushrooms, 30 g red and green pepper and ½ tomato per portion.

□ □ □

Grilled poultry

Grilled chicken with devilled sauce

Poulet grillé diable

👐 30 min   🍲 20 min approximately

Step	Commodity	1 portion	10 portions	
1	Chicken	400 g	10 × 400 g	Prepare the chicken spatchock style. Place the chicken presentation side down on a greased grilling tray and cook for 10 minutes under a pre-heated salamander. Remove and turn the chicken over. Brush the chicken with diluted English mustard.
2	Butter	15 g	150 g	Melt in a saucepan and brush liberally over the chicken.
3	White breadcrumbs	25 g	250 g	Sprinkle over the chicken and return to the salamander. Continue cooking until the chicken is golden brown and cooked through. Place on a suitably sized serving dish.
4	Straw potatoes (see Chapter 12: Deep frying)	50 g	500 g	Cook, place on absorbent paper to remove excess fat. Use to garnish the chicken. Finish with small sprigs of watercress. Serve with the devilled sauce.

☐   ☐   ☐

Grilled chicken spatchcock*

Poulet grillé à l'anglaise

👐 30 min   🍲 20 min approximately

Step	Commodity	1 portion	10 portions	
1	Chicken	400 g	10 × 400 g	Prepare the chicken spatchcock style. Place the chicken presentation side down on a greased grilling tray and cook for 10 minutes under a pre-heated salamander. Remove and turn the chicken over.
2	Butter	15 g	150 g	Melt in a saucepan and brush liberally over the chicken.
3	White breadcrumbs	25 g	250 g	Sprinkle over the chicken and return to the salamander. Continue cooking until the chicken is golden brown and cooked through. Place on a suitably sized serving dish. Keep warm.
4	Large gherkins	2	20	Cut the gherkins to represent a fan. Open out and use to decorate the chicken.
5	Straw potatoes (see Chapter 12: Deep frying)	50 g	500 g	Cook, place on absorbent paper to remove excess fat. Use to garnish the chicken. Finish with small sprigs of watercress. Serve with the devilled sauce.

*NOTE: Spatchcock style is the term used for a raw chicken split down the backbone and spreading for grilling.

☐   ☐   ☐

Grilled chicken American style

Poulet grillé américain

🥄 30 min   ♨ 20 min approximately

Step	Commodity	1 portion	10 portions	
1	Chicken	400 g	10 × 400 g	Prepare the chicken spatchcock style. Place the chicken presentation side down on a greased grilling tray and cook for 10 minutes under a pre-heated salamander. Remove and turn the chicken over. Brush the chicken with diluted English mustard.
2	Butter	15 g	150 g	Melt in a saucepan and brush liberally over the chicken.
3	White breadcrumbs	25 g	250 g	Sprinkle over the chicken and return to the salamander. Continue cooking until the chicken is golden brown and cooked through. Place on a suitably sized serving dish. Keep warm.
4	Large mushrooms	2	20	Wash, trim the stalks and season with salt and pepper. Brush with butter and place on the grilling tray. Begin cooking for 2 minutes.
5	Tomatoes	1	10	Remove the eyes and make slight cross-like incisions in the other ends. Arrange on the grilling tray, brush with butter, and season with salt and pepper. Place on the grilling tray with the mushrooms and cook for a further 2 minutes.
6	Sliced back bacon	1	10	Place on the tray alongside the mushrooms and tomatoes and cook for a further 2 minutes.
7	Straw potatoes (*see* Chapter 12: Deep fat frying)	50 g	500 g	Cook and place on absorbent paper to remove excess fat. Use to garnish the chicken. Finish with small sprigs of watercress. Serve with the devilled sauce.

☐   ☐   ☐

Grilled chicken in the shape of a toad

Poulet grillé crapaudine

🥄 30 min   ♨ 20 min approximately

Step	Commodity	1 portion	10 portions	
1	Chicken	400 g	10 × 400 g	Prepare the chicken crapaudine style.* Place the chicken presentation side down on a greased grilling tray and cook for 10 minutes under a pre-heated salamander. Remove and turn the chicken over.
2	Butter	15 g	150 g	Melt in a saucepan and brush liberally over the chicken.
3	White breadcrumbs	25 g	250 g	Sprinkle over the chicken and return to the salamander. Continue cooking until the chicken is golden brown and cooked through. Place on a suitably sized serving dish. Keep warm.
4	Straw potatoes (*see* Chapter 12: Deep frying)	50 g	500 g	Cook and place on absorbent paper to remove excess fat. Use to garnish the chicken. Finish with small sprigs of watercress. Serve with the devilled sauce.

*NOTE: This is the term used for a raw chicken cut and shaped to represent a toad. The leg joints are dislocated to make them spreadeagle, and the breast is partially cut near the base so it falls forward. When the bird is turned over it should resemble a toad. After cooking, slices of hard boiled eggs and sliced stuffed olives are used to resemble eyes.

☐   ☐   ☐

Grilled vegetables

Grilled tomatoes — Tomates grillées

Step	Commodity	1 portion	10 portions
1	Medium tomatoes	1	10

🥄 5 min 🍲 5 min approximately

Prepare by removing the eyes. Make a shallow incision in the shape of a cross in the other end. Place on a lightly greased grilling tray, brush lightly with melted butter. Season with salt and pepper and place under a pre-heated salamander for the required time. Finish with a small sprig of parsley.

NOTE: Tomatoes for grilling can be skinned, left whole or cut in half.

☐   ☐   ☐

Grilled mushrooms — Champignons grillés

Step	Commodity	1 portion	10 portions
1	Large mushrooms	50 g	500 g

🥄 5 min 🍲 5 min approximately

Prepare by removing the stalks and, if necessary, peel. Place on a lightly greased grilling tray and brush with melted butter. Season with salt and pepper and place under a pre-heated salamander for the required cooking time. Serve immediately.

☐   ☐   ☐

Grilled aubergines (egg plant) — Aubergines grillées

Step	Commodity	1 portion	10 portions
1	Egg plant	100	1 kg

🥄 10 min 🍲 8 min approximately

Remove stalk and wash. Slice ½ cm thick and sprinkle with salt. Place on a lightly greased grilling tray and brush with melted butter. Place under a pre-heated salamander for the required cooking time. Remove and serve immediately.

☐   ☐   ☐

HOT SAUCES SUITABLE FOR SERVING WITH GRILLED FOODS

Chasseur sauce Sauce chasseur
Devilled sauce Sauce diable
Piquant sauce Sauce piquante
Robert sauce Sauce Robert
Béarnaise sauce Sauce béarnaise

COMPOUND BUTTERS SUITABLE FOR SERVING WITH GRILLED FOODS

Parsley butter Beurre Maître d'hôtel
Anchovy butter Beurre d'anchois

English mustard butter Beure moutarde à l'anglaise
French mustard butter Beurre moutarde à la française
Garlic butter Beurre d'ail
Horseradish butter Beurre de raifort
Colbert butter Beurre Colbert
Red wine butter Beurre vin rouge
Wine merchant's butter Beurre marchand de vin
Caviar butter Beurre de caviar
Lobster butter Beurre d'homard

10

WHAT WENT WRONG?

Problem	Caused by	To rectify
Meat dry and flavourless.	Food was not brushed with melted fat during cooking.	If problem is recognised early enough it can be rectified by brushing with melted fat.
Meat has become distorted.	Poor quality of meat used.	Cannot be rectified.
Meat is not browned.	(1) Grilling temperature not high enough.	Remove the meat from the heat. Re-adjust grill temperature then grill meat quickly and serve immediately.
	(2) Salt was put on the meat before cooking.	Cannot be rectified.
Fish is tasteless.	(1) Poor quality.	Cannot be rectified.
	(2) Bad storage.	Cannot be rectified.
Fish is dry and has a poor appearance.	(1) Over-cooking.	Cannot be rectified.
	(2) Cooking temperature was too high.	Cannot be rectified.
	(3) Fish was not adequately coated with flour before cooking.	Cannot be rectified.
Tomatoes are distorted.	(1) Not brushing with oil before cooking.	Cannot be rectified.
	(2) Cooking temperature was too high.	Cannot be rectified.
	(3) Incision was too deep.	Cannot be rectified.
Mushrooms are dry.	(1) Holding for too long before serving.	Cannot be rectified.
	(2) Not brushing with oil before cooking.	Cannot be rectified.
Deep fried food garnish is soggy.	(1) Cooking too far in advance.	Discard and replace.
	(2) Covering the food.	Discard and replace.
Food has broken up.	Bad handling during preparation and cooking.	Discard and replace.

SHALLOW FRYING

Shallow frying, sautéing, is the rapid cooking of foods, on a thin layer of hot fat in a sauteuse, though other flat surfaces can be used. For large amounts of shallow frying a bratt pan is ideal because it has a heavy bottom, a wide surface and the heat is evenly distributed.

The term sauter is used to describe the shallow frying of meat and poultry and the subsequent utilisation of the cooking juices and sediment by déglacé. The sediment and juices are used to enhance the flavour of the finishing sauce.

The traditional term used to describe shallow fried fish is meunière which means in the style of the miller's wife, so named because it is passed through seasoned flour.

As a rule the presentation side of the food is cooked first. The reason for this is that it is easier to turn food over without damage when it is partly cooked as opposed to fully cooked, when the action might damage the food and ruin the appearance of the finished product.

NOTE: Shallow frying should be carried out on an individual or two portion basis as the more items there are in the frying pan, the lower the cooking temperature will drop and the more fat the food will absorb, adversely affecting the quality of the finished product.

Staff associated with shallow frying

In a traditional kitchen brigade there would be five parties associated with shallow frying:

Chef Garde manger Preparation of meats, poultry, game and offal.

Chef Saucier Cooking of meats, poultry, game and offal.

Chef Poissonier Cooking of shallow fried fish dishes.

Chef Entremettier Cooking of shallow fried potatoes and vegetables.

Chef du petit déjeuner Shallow fried breakfast dishes – fried bacon, mushrooms, scrambled eggs, fried eggs, omelettes, pancakes, steaks, potato cakes, sauté potatoes, bubble and squeak, etc.

Terms associated with shallow frying

Bauveuse The term applies to the degree of 'wetness' of cooking eggs in an omelette (the centre of the omelette should be slightly undercooked).

Cartouche Greaseproof paper cut to the shape of the frying pan and used to contain moisture when cooking.

Déglacé Rinsing or swilling out the cooking vessel with wine, stock, spirits or a plain sauce after the food has been fried to extract the food particles and enchance the finishing sauce.

Flamber This means to flame, to set on fire with a spirit, e.g. whisky, brandy, rum etc. Its purpose is to enhance the flavour of the food. The spirit is poured over the food in the pan and set alight.

Griddling Cooking on a solid surface.

Lardons Thin strips of bacon.

Meunière Literally means in the style of the miller's wife and is associated with the shallow frying of fish.

Pané Means to pass through seasoned flour, egg wash and coat with breadcrumbs.

Proving To make a frying pan non-stick by filling with salt and heating till brown. The salt is then removed and the pan is wiped clean with kitchen paper. The pan is then wiped with oil to prevent it from rusting.

Sautéing French term for shallow frying. Literally means to 'jump'. The technique involves moving the pan sharply so that the food hits the edge, jumps in the air and turns over. **Shallow frying** Plain frying as opposed to sautéing.	**Stir fry** Chinese method of quickly frying in the minimum amount of oil. **Sweating** To cover the food with a cartouche and cook/soften the food without browning. **Wok** Specialised Chinese frying pan shaped like a bowl.

THE COOKING MEDIUM USED IN SHALLOW FRYING

There is a wide variety of fats and oils that can be used for frying.

Type	Source	Frying temperature
Sunflower oil	Sunflower seeds.	175°–195°C
Soya oil	Soya bean extract used in vegetarian cookery.	175°–195°C
Corn oil	Obtained from maize. Very economical.	175°–195°C
Rapeseed oil	Obtained from rapeseed.	175°–195°C
Palm oil	Coconut palm.	175°–195°C
Olive oil	Extracted from olives.	150°–175°C
Groundnut oil	Obtained from groundnuts (peanuts).	175°–195°C
Cottonseed oil	Extracted from cotton.	175°–195°C
Ghee (butter)	Made from clarified butter, used in Asian cookery.	150°–175°C
Ghee (oil)	Made from vegetable oil, used in Asian cookery.	175°–195°C
Margarine	Homogenized animal, soya or vegetable fat and milk. Vegetarian margarine is made from vegetable or soya oil and soya milk.	125°–150°C
Grapeseed oil	Extracted from grapeseeds, very aromatic.	150°–175°C
Lard	Made from rendered pigs' fat.	150°–175°C
Butter	Produced from churning fresh cream. For the best results the butter should be clarified. Available salted and unsalted.	125°–150°C
Sesame oil	Made from sesame seeds, it has a distinctive nutty flavour and is used chiefly in Chinese cookery.	125°–150°C
Dripping	Obtained from clarified animal fat.	150°–175°C

EQUIPMENT USED IN SHALLOW FRYING

Bratt pans

An industrial sized, dual fuel (gas and electrical), multi-purpose cooking appliance which is used for frying large amounts of foods.

Crêpe pan

A very shallow pan with sloping sides made from black wrought steel, it is used for making pancakes (crêpes).

Fish slice

A long handled, wide, flat utensil used for turning large items during the frying process.

Frying pans

Frying pans always have a solid base. They have shallow sloping sides and a wide surface area to ensure even heat for frying foods. Frying pans can be made from iron, steel, aluminium, vitrified iron or stainless steel.

Griddle

A thermostatically controlled, heated surface used to fry meats, poultry and eggs. Griddles can have grooved bars to simulate the markings of grilled meats.

Oval frying pans

Used to cook fish meunière style. Made from wrought steel, aluminium or tin-lined copper.

Omelette pans

Made from black wrought steel, aluminium or tin-lined copper. They have a heavy flat base and have shallow sloping sides.

Palette knife

A flat flexible knife with no sharp edges used for turning narrow foods in the frying pan.

Sauté pan

Also called a plat à sauter, this is a shallow long handled pan made from tin-lined copper or aluminium with straight sides and a wide surface. Used for sautéing meats and poultry.

Sauteuse

Shallow, long handled vessel, ideal for tossing vegetables and potatoes because of the sloping sides and wide surface, made from tin-lined copper.

FOODS SUITABLE
FOR SHALLOW FRYING

The types of food suitable for frying are small pieces of good quality, tender meat, cuts of fish, vegetables, fruits and made-up dishes.

Meats and poultry

Only the leanest, most tender cuts of meat are suitable for shallow frying though tougher cuts can be shallow fried if they are minced and shaped before cooking. Some fat is needed to keep the meat moist during cooking. This fat is naturally present in red meats like beef and lamb.

Pork chops and veal cutlets are suitable for shallow frying. Pork, veal and poultry can also be cut into escalopes (thin slices) for cooking. Bacon and gammon can also be shallow fried.

Game

Most game is too tough for shallow frying and is usually only re-heated in a frying pan, though loin of venison marinaded for 24 hours before cooking may be lightly shallow fried.

Offal

Calves', pigs' and lambs' liver and kidneys can be shallow fried, as can the sweetbreads (thyroid glands) of veal and lamb.

Fish and shellfish

Large fish are usually filleted or cut into suprêmes or steaks for shallow frying. Smaller fish may be cooked and served whole. Scallops, lobster, crayfish and Dublin Bay prawns (scampi) may also be shallow fried.

Eggs

Eggs can be plain fried, scrambled, made into omelettes and in special *sur le plat* dishes.

Vegetables and potatoes

Mushrooms, onions, aubergines, courgettes and marrow are shallow fried from raw. Other vegetables are cooked by other methods and re-heated by shallow frying. Potatoes can be shallow fried from raw or part-cooked by boiling or steaming first.

11

Egg dishes

Scrambled eggs

Oeufs brouillés nature

Step	Commodity	1 portion	10 portions	⏲ 3 min 🍳 5 min per portion ≋ 80°–90°C
1	Butter	15 g	150 g	Melt in a suitably sized sauteuse.
	Eggs	2	20	Break into a bowl. Season lightly with salt and pepper. Whisk thoroughly and place in the sauteuse. Cook gently stirring the bottom continuously to avoid it burning. Cook until it has lightly set. The texture should be light and moist. Remove from the heat.
2	Butter	15 g	150 g	Add.
	Single cream	10 ml	100 ml	Add and mix in. Place in a sur le plat dish. Finish with finely chopped parsley.

NOTE: For large quantities of scrambled eggs, the raw mixture may be placed in a container and cooked in a bain-marie of hot water. Cooking time for 10 portions will be approximately 25 minutes.

Scrambled eggs served for breakfast are usually placed on hot buttered toast.

☐ ☐ ☐

Scrambled eggs with mushrooms

Oeufs brouillés aux champignons

Step	Commodity	1 portion	10 portions	⏲ 10 min 🍳 5 min per portion ≋ 80°–90°C
1	Butter	10 g	100 g	Melt in a sauteuse.
	Button mushrooms	25 g	250 g	Wash, slice and add to the hot fat. Cook for 2–3 minutes without colouring. Remove and keep warm.
2	Butter	15 g	150 g	Melt in a suitably sized clean sauteuse.
	Eggs	2	20	Break into a bowl. Season lightly with salt and pepper. Whisk thoroughly and place in the sauteuse. Cook gently stirring the bottom continuously to avoid it burning. Cook until it has lightly set. The texture should be light and moist. Remove from the heat.
3	Butter	15 g	150 g	Add.
	Single cream	10 ml	100 ml	Add and mix in. Place in a sur la plat dish. Place the appropriate amount of cooked mushrooms in the centre of the cooked egg. Sprinkle with finely chopped parsley.

☐ ☐ ☐

Scrambled eggs with chicken livers

Oeufs brouillés aux foie de volaille

⤵ 10 min　♨ 5 min per portion　≋ 80°–90°C

Step	Commodity	1 portion	10 portions	
1	Butter	10 g	100 g	Melt in a sauteuse.
	Chicken livers	25 g	250 g	Wash, remove the bile bag and any fat. Dice and add to the hot fat. Cook for 2–3 minutes without colouring. Remove and keep warm.
2	Butter	15 g	150 g	Melt in a suitably sized clean sauteuse.
	Eggs	2	20	Break into a bowl. Season lightly with salt and pepper. Whisk thoroughly and place in the sauteuse. Cook gently stirring the bottom continuously to avoid it burning. Cook until it has lightly set. The texture should be light and moist. Remove from the heat.
3	Butter	15 g	150 g	Add.
	Single cream	10 ml	100 ml	Add and mix in. Place in a sur la plat dish. Place the appropriate amount of cooked liver in the centre of the cooked egg. Finish with a cordon of madeiria sauce. Sprinkle with finely chopped parsley.

☐　　☐　　☐

Plain omelette

Omelette nature

⤵ 3 min　♨ 4 min per portion　≋ 80°–90°C

Step	Commodity	1 portion	10 portions	
1	Eggs	2/3	20/30	Break the eggs into a bowl ensuring that there is no shell present. Season lightly with salt and pepper. Beat the eggs thoroughly with a fork to combine the white and yellow.
2	Clarified butter or oil	5 ml	50 ml	Heat in a proved omelette pan. Add the beaten eggs. Stir with the fork at the same time as shaking the pan until the egg is lightly set (bauveuse). Loosen the sides of the omelette and tilt the pan forward pushing the omelette partly up the side. Fold one side of the omelette to the centre and then the other over it so it resembles a cigar shape. Remove from the pan and place on a serving dish or on a plate, ensuring that it keeps its shape. Brush with melted butter and garnish with a small sprig of parsley. Serve immediately.

☐　　☐　　☐

11

Cheese omelette

Omelette au fromage

⏲ 3 min 🍲 4 min per portion ≋ 80°–90°C

Step	Commodity	1 portion	10 portions	
1	Eggs	2/3	20/30	Break the eggs into a bowl ensuring that there is no shell present. Season lightly with salt and pepper. Beat the eggs thoroughly with a fork to combine the white and yellow.
2	Clarified butter or oil	5 ml	50 ml	Heat in a proved omelette pan. Add the beaten eggs. Stir with the fork at the same time as shaking the pan until the egg is lightly set (bauveuse).
3	Grated cheese*	25 g	250 g	Sprinkle over the omelette. Loosen the sides of the omelette and tilt the pan forward, pushing the omelette partly up the side. Fold one side of the omelette to the centre and then the other over it so it resembles a cigar shape. Remove from the pan and place on a serving flat or on a plate, ensuring that it keeps its shape. Make a light incision in the omelette and sprinkle with a little grated cheese. Brush with melted butter and garnish with a small sprig of parsley. Serve immediately.

*NOTE: Any cheese may be used to make a cheese omelette once it is specified. If using parmesan, allow only 15 g per portion as it is very strong.

☐   ☐   ☐

Ham omelette

Omelette au jambon/yorkaise

⏲ 3 min 🍲 4 min per portion ≋ 80°–90°C

Step	Commodity	1 portion	10 portions	
1	Eggs	2/3	20/30	Break the eggs into a bowl ensuring that there is no shell present. Season lightly with salt and pepper. Beat the eggs thoroughly with a fork to combine the white and yellow.
2	Clarified butter or oil	5 ml	50 ml	Heat in a proved omelette pan. Add the beaten eggs. Stir with the fork at the same time as shaking the pan until the egg is lightly set (bauveuse).
3	Cooked ham	50 g	500 g	Dice finely and add to the cooked omelette. Loosen the sides of the omelette and tilt the pan forward, pushing the omelette partly up the side. Fold one side of the omelette to the centre and then the other over it so it resembles a cigar shape. Remove from the pan and place on a serving flat or on a plate, ensuring that it keeps its shape. Make a light incision in the omelette and sprinkle with a little diced ham. Brush with melted butter and garnish with a small sprig of parsley. Serve immediately.

NOTE: Fried lardons of bacon may be used in place of cooked ham to give Bacon omelette – Omelet au lard.

☐   ☐   ☐

Kidney omelette

Omelette aux rognons

⌣ 15 min   ♨ 4 min per portion   ≋ 80°–90°C

Step	Commodity	1 portion	10 portions	
1	Lambs' kidneys	50 g	500 g	Remove the core, the outer membrane and any fat. Dice and place to one side.
	Clarified butter	5 ml	50 ml	Place in a frying pan and heat. Add the diced lambs' kidneys and cook for 8 minutes. Remove and keep warm in a bain-marie.
2	Eggs	2/3	20/30	Break the eggs into a bowl ensuring that there is no shell present. Season lightly with salt and pepper. Beat the eggs thoroughly with a fork to combine the white and yellow.
3	Clarified butter or oil	5 ml	50 ml	Heat in a proved omelette pan. Add the beaten eggs. Stir with the fork at the same time as shaking the pan until the egg is lightly set (bauveuse). Loosen the sides of the omelette and tilt the pan forward, pushing the omelette partly up the side. Fold one side of the omelette to the centre and then the other over it so it resembles a cigar shape. Remove from the pan and place on a serving flat or on a plate, ensuring that it keeps its shape. Make a light incision in the omelette and add the cooked kidneys. Serve with a cordon of Madeira sauce and sprinkle with finely chopped parsley.

☐   ☐   ☐

Chasseur style omelette

Omelette chasseur

⌣ 3 min   ♨ 4 min per portion   ≋ 80°–90°C

Step	Commodity	1 portion	10 portions	
1	Chicken livers	50 g	500 g	Remove the bile bag and any fat. Dice and place to the side.
	Button mushrooms	25 g	250 g	Wash and slice.
	Clarified butter	5 ml	50 ml	Place in a frying pan and heat. Add the mushrooms and sweat for 2–3 minutes. Add the diced chicken livers and cook for a further 4 minutes. Remove and keep warm in a bain-marie.
2	Eggs	2/3	20/30	Break the eggs into a bowl, ensuring that there is no shell present. Season lightly with salt and pepper. Beat the eggs thoroughly with a fork to combine the white and yellow.
3	Clarified butter or oil	5 ml	50 ml	Heat in a proved omelette pan. Add the beaten eggs. Stir with the fork at the same time as shaking the pan until the egg is lightly set (bauveuse). Loosen the sides of the omelette and tilt the pan forward, pushing the omelette partly up the side. Fold one side of the omelette to the centre and then the other over it so it resembles a cigar shape. Remove from the pan and place on a serving flat or on a plate, ensuring that it keeps its shape. Make a light incision in the omelette and add the cooked mixture. Brush with melted butter and garnish with finely chopped parsley. Serve immediately. Serve with a cordon of Madeira sauce (see Chapter 5: Boiling).

☐   ☐   ☐

11

Spanish omelette (served flat)   Omelette espagnole

Step	Commodity	1 portion	10 portions			
				🍲 20 min	♨ 6 min per portion	≋ 80°–90°C
1	Onions	25 g	250 g	Peel, cut into thin slices. Place to one side in a bowl.		
	Red peppers (pimentos)	50 g	50 g	Remove the stalk and seeds. Dice finely and add to the onions.		
	Clarified butter	10 ml	100 ml	Place in a frying pan and heat. Add the onions and peppers and sweat for 3–4 minutes. Remove and place in a clean bowl.		
	Tomatoes	25 g	250 g	Remove the eye and make an incision in the bottom. Place in a saucepan of boiling water for 10 seconds. Refresh immediately. Discard the skin and seeds. Dice the flesh and add to the cooked onions and peppers.		
	Parsley	5 g	50 g	Wash, chop finely and dry. Add to the other vegetables.		
2	Eggs	2/3	20/30	Break the eggs into a bowl, ensuring that there is no shell present. Season lightly with salt and pepper. Beat the eggs thoroughly with a fork to combine the white and yellow. Add the cooked vegetables.		
3	Clarified butter	5 ml	50 ml	Heat in a proved omelette pan. Add the beaten eggs. Stir with the fork at the same time as shaking the pan until the egg is lightly set (bauveuse). Loosen with the fork. Brush the sides with melted butter. Shake the pan until the omelette is free. Toss the omelette over and continue cooking. Alternatively, place under a pre-heated salamander to finish off. Slide the omelette onto a serving flat or plate. Brush with melted butter and garnish with a small sprig of parsley. Serve immediately.		

Extension of Spanish omelette

Omelette suissesse. As for Spanish omelette with 25 g (per portion) of grated Gruyère cheese sprinkled over the cooked mixture and gratinated under a pre-heated salamander.

Fermière omelette (served flat)

Omelette fermière

Step	Commodity	1 portion	10 portions

🥄 20 min   🍳 6 min per portion   ≋ 80°–90°C

Step	Commodity	1 portion	10 portions	
1	Cooked ham	50 g	500 g	Dice finely and place to one side in a bowl.
	Parsley	10 g	100 g	Wash, chop finely and dry. Add to the ham.
2	Eggs	2/3	20/30	Break the eggs into a bowl, ensuring that there is no shell present. Season lightly with salt and pepper. Beat the eggs thoroughly with a fork to combine the white and yellow. Add the ham and parsley.
3	Clarified butter or oil	5 ml	50 ml	Heat in a proved omelette pan. Add the beaten eggs. Stir with the fork at the same time as shaking the pan until the egg is lightly set (beuveuse). Loosen with the fork. Brush the sides with melted butter. Shake the pan until the omelette is free. Place under a pre-heated salamander to finish off. Slide the omelette onto a serving flat or plate. Brush with melted butter and garnish with a small sprig of parsley. Serve immediately.

☐   ☐   ☐

Soufflé omelette

Omelette mousseline

🥄 10 min   🍳 6 min per portion   ≋ 80°–90°C

Step	Commodity	1 portion	10 portions	
1	Eggs	2/3	20–30	Break the eggs separating the yolks and whites into separate bowls, ensuring that there is no shell present. Season the yolks lightly with salt and pepper. Beat the yolks thoroughly with a fork. Place in the fridge for use later. Whisk the whites until they are stiff then fold into the egg yolks.
2	Clarified butter or oil	5 ml	50 ml	Heat in a proved omelette pan. when it is very hot add the egg mixture. Stir with the fork at the same time as shaking the pan until the egg is lightly set. Loosen the sides of the omelette. Toss over or place under a pre-heated salamander to set. Tilt the pan forward, pushing the omelette partly up the side. Remove from the pan and place on a serving flat or plate, ensuring that it keeps its shape.

NOTE: This omelette can also be served cigar shaped.

☐   ☐   ☐

Fried eggs

Oeufs frits à la poêle

🥄 2 min   🍳 3–4 min per portion   ≋ 80°–90°C

Step	Commodity	1 portion	10 portions	
1	Clarified butter or oil	5 ml	50 ml	Heat in a proved omelette pan.
2	Eggs	1	10	Break into the frying pan and cook gently. Baste with the hot fat until the egg white is set and the egg yolk has a cooked film over the top. Remove and serve immediately.

☐   ☐   ☐

11

Eggs cooked in a dish
Oeufs sur le plat

Step	Commodity	1 portion	10 portions	⏱ 2 min	〰 3–4 min per portion	≋ 80°–90°C
1	Butter	5 g	50 g	Place in a sur le plat dish. Season lightly with salt and pepper. Heat on the side of the stove.		
2	Eggs	1/2	10/20	Carefully break into the dish and cook gently until the egg white is set. Finish off under a pre-heated salamander. Serve immediately.		

Extensions of oeufs sur le plat

Dish	Additions per portion	Action
With black butter (beurre noir)	25 g butter	Place in a frying pan and heat until well browned. Move to the side of the stove.
	Few drops vinegar	Add to the butter and pour over the egg. Sprinkle with finely chopped parsley.
Bercy style (Bercy)	2 chipolatas	Grill and keep warm. Garnish the egg with a cordon of tomato sauce. Garnish with a sausage either side.
With ham (au jambon)	25 g slice of ham	Cut to the shape and size of the sur le plat dish. Place on the buttered dish and proceed as for oeuf sur le plat.
With bacon (au lard)	2 slices back bacon	Place on a tray under a pre-heated salamander and grill lightly. Place on the bottom of the buttered dish. Add the egg and continue as for oeuf sur le plat. Garnish with a small sprig of parsley.
Lorraine style	2 slices back bacon	Place on a tray under a pre-heated salamander and grill lightly. Place on the bottom of the buttered dish.
	1 × 25 g slice Gruyère cheese	Place on top of the bacon. Add the egg and continue as for oeuf sur le plat. Garnish with a small sprig of parsley.
With chicken liver (aux foie de volaille)	25 g chicken liver	Remove the bile bag and any fat. Dice finely.
	5 g butter	Heat in a frying pan and add the chicken livers. Season with salt and pepper and cook for 3–4 minutes. Drain and keep warm until the egg is cooked. Garnish the cooked egg with the liver. Serve with a cordon of Madeira sauce. Sprinkle with finely chopped parsley.
Opera style As for above with:	50 g cooked aspagagus tips	Arrange in a bouquet. Brush with butter and finish with a sprinkle of chopped parsley.

□   □   □

Shallow-fried fish

Fish and cuts of fish suitable for shallow frying

Fish	F/R*	French	Whole	Fillet	Suprême	Steaks
Brill	F	Barbue			*	Tronçon
Cod	R	Cabillaud		*	*	Darne
Dover sole	F	Sole Douvres	*	*		
Haddock	R	Aigrefin		*	*	Darne
Hake	R	Colin		*	*	Darne
Halibut	F	Flétan			*	Tronçon
Herring	R	Hareng	*			
Lemon sole	F	Sole limande		*	*	
Mackerel	R	Maquereau				
Plaice	F	Plie		*	*	
Red mullet	R	Rouget				
Salmon	R	Saumon			*	*
Salmon trout	R	Truite saumonée			*	*
Trout	R	Truite	*			
Turbot	F	Turbot			*	Tronçon
Whiting	R	Merlan	*			

*F/R = Flat or round fish.
NOTE: Whole fish are cooked in an oval (meunière) pan.

Shallow-fried (gilded) fish

Poisson doré

🥄 20 min   ♨ 3–4 min per 100 g portion for fillet
♨ 8–10 min per 150 g darne or tronçon
≋ 175°–195°C

Step	Commodity	1 portion	10 portions	
1	Plain flour	25 g	250 g	Place on a tray. Season with salt and pepper.
	Fish fillet, or darne or tronçon	1 × 100 g 1 × 150 g	10 × 100 g 10 × 150 g	Pass the fish through the seasoned flour and pat off excess. Place to the side.
	Clarified butter or cooking oil	25 ml	250 ml	Place in the frying pan and heat. Add the fish presentation side down and cook until golden brown on both sides. Remove and place on the serving flat and keep warm.
2	Lemon	¼ equiv	2½ equiv	Cut into wedges. Remove the pips and pith. Place on the cooked fish.

□   □   □

Fish miller's wife's style

Poisson meuniére

🥘 20 min   🍳 3–4 min per 100 g portion for fillet
       🍳 8–10 min per 150 g darne or tronçon
       ≋ 175°–195°C

Step	Commodity	1 portion	10 portions	
1	Plain flour	25 g	250 g	Place on a tray. Season with salt and pepper.
	Fish fillet, or darne or	1 × 100 g	10 × 100 g	Pass the fish through the seasoned flour and pat off excess. Place to the side.
	tronçon	1 × 150 g	10 × 150 g	
	Cooking oil	15 ml	150 ml	
	Clarified butter	15 ml	150 ml	Mix with the cooking oil. Place in the frying pan and heat. Add the fish presentation side down and cook until golden brown on both sides. Remove and place on the serving flat and keep warm.
2	Lemon	¼ equiv	2½ equiv	Peel, remove the pith. Cut into slices. Place on the cooked fish.
3	Butter	25 g	250 g	Place in a pre-heated frying pan and cook until golden brown (noisette).
	Lemon	¼ equiv	2½ equiv	Squeeze the juice into a bowl and strain. Pour into the butter and stir. Pour over the fish.
4	Parsley	5 g	50 g	Wash, chop finely, dry and sprinkle over the fish.

Extensions of fish meuniére

Dish	Commodity	1 portion	10 portions	
Amandine	Almonds	25 g	250 g	Place on a tray and bake in a pre-heated oven or under a pre-heated salamander until brown. Add to the noisette butter.
Bretonne	Button mushrooms	15 g	150 g	Wash, cut into slices. Add to the noisette butter.
	Peeled shrimps	15 g	150 g	Add to the noisette butter and finish as for meunière.
Belle meunière	Button mushrooms	2	20	Wash, remove the stalk.
	Tomatoes	2 slices	20 slices	Remove the eye and make an incision in the bottom. Place in a saucepan of boiling water for 10 seconds. Refresh immediately. Discard the skin, cut into slices and warm gently under a pre-heated salamander. Keep warm in a hot cupboard.
	*Prepared soft herring roe	1	10	Wash.
	Butter	2 g	20 g	Place in a frying pan and heat. Add the mushrooms and cook for 2–3 minutes. Remove, keep warm in a bain-marie, retain the butter. Add the herring roe and cook for 4–5 minutes. Place on the side of the fish. Garnish with the button mushrooms and three slices of tomato. Finish as for meunière.

Dish	Commodity	1 portion	10 portions	
Cleopatra	Clarified butter	10 g	100 g	Place in a frying pan and heat.
	*Prepared soft herring roe	1	10	Add to the pan and cook for 4–5 minutes. Add to the noisette butter.
	Peeled shrimps	15 g	150 g	Add.
	Capers	10 g	100 g	Add and finish as for meunière.

NOTE: * The roe can be pre-cooked and refreshed in cold water for use later.

Doria	Cucumber	25 g	250 g	Peel, cut into turned shapes. Add to the noisette butter and finish as for meunière.
Grenobloise	Capers	10 g	100 g	Add to the beurre noisette and finish as for meunière.

NOTE: With Grenobloise the lemon is peeled, the pith removed and the lemon cut into segments.

Murat	Potatoes	25 g	250 g	Peel, wash and cut into 1 cm dice.
	Clarified butter	5 ml	50 ml	Place in a frying pan and heat. Add the potatoes and sauté until golden brown. Keep warm in the hot cupboard.
	Cooked artichoke bottoms	25 g	250 g	Cut into ½ cm slices and add, along with the potatoes, to the noisette butter. Finish as for meunière.

11

245

Shallow-fried shellfish

Lobster Homard
Scallops Coquilles St Jacques
Scampi Langoustine

With tomatoes and garlic Sautée Provençale

Step	Commodity	1 portion	10 portions	🥄 10 min	🍲 5–10 min per portion	〰 125°–150°C
1	Flour	10 g	100 g	Season with salt and pepper.	
	Prepared shellfish	100 g	1 kilo	Pass through the seasoned flour and place to the side.	
2	Clarified butter	15 ml	150 ml	Place in a suitably sized frying pan and heat.	
	Shallots	20 g	200 g	Peel, cut into fine dice, add to the butter and cook without colouring for 2–3 minutes. Add the shellfish and cook for a further 4–5 minutes until golden brown.	
3	Garlic	¼ clove	2 cloves	Peel, sprinkle salt over the clove, crush to a pulp and add to the frying pan.	
	Dry white wine	20 ml	200 ml	Add and déglacé. Reduce by half.	
	Fine herbs	pinch	1 tsp	Add.	
	Basil	pinch	1 tsp	Add. Season with salt and black pepper.	
	Tomatoes	100 g	1 kg	Remove the eye and make an incision in the bottom. Place in a saucepan of boiling water for 10 seconds. Refresh immediately. Discard the skin and seeds. Dice the flesh, and to the other ingredients and simmer for 5 minutes. Correct the seasoning and serve on a bed of riz pilaff (see Chapter 9: Braising).	

☐   ☐   ☐

Newburg style

Step	Commodity	1 portion	10 portions	🥄 10 min	🍲 5–10 min per portion	〰 125°–150°C
1	Flour	10 g	100 g	Season with salt and pepper.	
	Prepared shellfish	100 g	1 kilo	Pass through the seasoned flour and place to the side.	
	Clarified butter	15 ml	150 ml	Place in a suitably sized frying pan and heat. Add the shellfish and cook for 6–8 minutes.	
2	Brandy	10 ml	100 ml	Add and flame.	
	Madeira wine	20 ml	200 ml	Add and reduce by half.	
	Double cream	75 ml	750 ml	Add and simmer to a coating consistency. Serve on a bed of riz pilaff (see Chapter 9: Braising).	
4	Parsley	5 g	50 g	Wash, chop finely and sprinkle over the shellfish.	

☐   ☐   ☐

Thermidor style

Step	Commodity	1 portion	10 portions			
				⏱ 10 min	🔥 5–10 min per portion	≈ 125°–150°C
1	Béchamel sauce	75 ml	750 ml	Heat.		
	Cheddar cheese	15 g	150 g	Add and cook until all the cheese has melted and blended into the sauce.		
	Double cream	15 ml	150 ml	Place in a bowl.		
	Egg yolks	½	5	Add and whisk over a bowl of warm water until a creamy consistency is achieved (sayabon).		
	English mustard	pinch	½ tsp	Dilute with a little water and add to the sabayon. Add to the béchamel and keep warm in a bain-marie, without re-boiling.		
2	Flour	10 g	100 g	Season with salt and pepper and place on a tray.		
	Prepared shellfish	100 g	1 kilo	Pass through the seasoned flour.		
	Clarified butter	15 ml	150 ml	Place in a suitably sized frying pan and heat. Add the shellfish and cook for 6–8 minutes. Add the hot sauce.		
	Parmesan cheese	5 g	50 g	Sprinkle over the sauce and gratinate under a pre-heated salamander until golden brown.		
	Sliced truffle	1	10	Pass through melted butter or stock and use to garnish the finished item. Serve immediately.		

☐ ☐ ☐

11

Shallow-fried meat

Beef steaks can be plain fried served with grilled tomatoes, fried mushrooms and onions or served with a suitable sauce. Steaks are usually cooked to order and to the degree required by the customer as listed below.

au bleu	Blue	Rare
saignant	Undercooked	Medium rare
à point	Just done	Medium
bien cuit	Well cooked	Well done.

Sirloin of beef (entrecôte de boeuf), minute steak (entrecôte minute), rump (la culotte) and fillet (le filet) may be shallow-fried. A minute steak is a thinly sliced steak, usually 100 g in weight, which takes only a minute to cook.

Plain fried entrecôte/tournedos steak with watercress

Entrecôte/Tournedos vert pré

Step	Commodity	1 portion	10 portions	⏲ 20 min	🍲 5–10 min per portion	≋ 150°–175°C
1	Cooking oil	10 ml	100 ml	Place in the frying pan and heat.		
	Prepared steak	1 × 250 g	10 × 250 g	Add and cook to the required degree. Arrange on a heated oval flat.		
	Straw potatoes*	25 g	250 g	Garnish with the potatoes.		
	Parsley butter†	5 g	50 g	Cut into ½ cm slices and place on top of the steak.		
	Watercress	1 sprig	10 sprigs	Wash, trim and use to garnish the steak.		

* See Chapter 12 Deep frying
† See Chapter 19 Cold preparations

☐ ☐ ☐

Sirloin Steak Bordelaise

Entrecôte Bordelaise

Step	Commodity	1 portion	10 portions	⏲ 5 min	🍲 5–10 min per portion	≋ 125°–150°C
1	Beef marrow	25 g	250 g	Cut the marrow into ½ cm thick slices and place in a pan of simmering white beef stock for 5 minutes. Remove and refresh in cold water until cold. Place in the fridge for use later.		
	Bordelaise sauce	100 ml	1 litre	Heat, keep warm in a bain-marie until required.		
2	Cooking oil	10 ml	100 ml	Place in a heavy frying pan and heat.		
	Sirloin steak	1 × 250 g	10 × 250 g	Season with salt and black pepper. Add to the pre-heated oil and cook to the degree required. Arrange on an oval flat dish. Garnish with the cooked sliced marrow and napper with the hot sauce.		
	Parsley	10 g	100 g	Wash and chop finely. Sprinkle over the steak.		

☐ ☐ ☐

Sauté chicken archiduc

Poulet sauté archiduc

🥄 30 min

♨ 20–25 min per portion: 1½ hr per 10 portions

≋ 150°–175°C

Step	Commodity	1 portion	10 portions	
1	Clarified butter	15 g	150 g	Place in a sauté pan and heat.
	Chicken	200 g	10 × 200 g	Cut as for sauté. Season with salt and pepper. Add to the hot butter and 'set' on all sides without colouring. Remove and keep warm in a hot cupboard. Drain away the excess fat.
2	Shallots	15 g	150 g	Peel and chop finely. Add to the sauté pan and sweat for 2–3 minutes. Replace the chicken, cover with a lid and cook gently without colouring for 20 minutes or until cooked. Remove and arrange in a warm earthenware dish. Discard the fat from the sauté pan.
	Brandy	10 ml	100 ml	Add to the hot pan and flame.
3	Velouté	50 ml	500 ml	Add, bring to the boil then simmer.
	Double cream	25 ml	250 ml	Add and reduce by half.
	Madeira wine	10 ml	100 ml	Add.
	Lemon juice	1 tsp	25 ml	Add, correct the consistency and seasoning. Pass through a chinois and pour over the chicken.
	Truffle	1 slice	10 slices	Pass through melted butter or stock and use to garnish the chicken.

☐   ☐   ☐

Sauté chicken chasseur

Poulet sauté chasseur

🥄 30 min

♨ 20–25 min per portion: 1 hr per 10 portions

≋ 150°–175°C

Step	Commodity	1 portion	10 portions	
1	Clarified butter	15 g	150 g	Place in a sauté pan and heat.
	Chicken	200 g	10 × 200 g	Cut as for sauté. Season with salt and pepper. Add to the hot butter and quickly brown on all sides. Cover with a lid and cook gently for 25 minutes. Remove and keep warm in a hot cupboard. Drain away the excess fat.
2	Dry white wine	25 ml	250 ml	Déglacé the frying pan. Reduce by half.
	Chasseur sauce	50 ml	500 ml	Add, bring to the boil and simmer for 5 minutes. Correct the seasoning. Place the chicken in a warm earthenware dish and napper with the sauce.
3	Parsley	10 g	100 g	Wash and chop finely. Sprinkle over the chicken.

☐   ☐   ☐

11

Sauté chicken Hungarian style   Poulet sauté hongroise

🥄 30 min

🍲 20–25 min per portion: 1½ hr per 10 portions

≋ 150°–175°C

Step	Commodity	1 portion	10 portions	
1	Clarified butter	15 g	150 g	Place in a sauté pan and heat.
	Chicken	200 g	10 × 200 g	Cut as for sauté. Season with salt and pepper. Add to the hot butter and cook without colouring on all sides. Remove and place to the side. Drain away the excess fat. Return the pan to the heat.
2	Onions	15 g	150 g	Peel, cut into fine dice and add to the pan. Cook without colouring for 2–3 minutes. Replace the chicken, cover with a lid and cook gently on the side of the stove for 25 minutes. Remove, place in a warm earthenware dish and keep warm.
	Tomatoes	25 g	250 g	Remove the eye and make an incision in the shape of a cross in the other end. Place in a pan of boiling water for 10 seconds, remove and refresh in cold water. Discard the skin and seeds. Cut the flesh into small dice and place in the pan.
	Paprika	5 g	50 g	Add and mix in well.
	Velouté	30 ml	300 ml	Add, bring to the boil and simmer. Correct the seasoning.
	Cream	40 ml	400 ml	Add, correct the consistency, strain and pour over the chicken.

NOTE: Serve on a bed of braised rice (*see* Chapter 9: Braising).

☐   ☐   ☐

Thin slices of (pork, beef, veal, chicken) with cream   Escalope de (porc, boeuf, veau, poulet) à la crème

🥄 20 min   🍲 5 min approximately per portion

≋ 175°–195°C

Step	Commodity	1 portion	10 portions	
1	Prepared escalopes	1 × 120 g	10 × 120 g	Pass through seasoned flour.
	Clarified butter	25 ml	250 ml	Place in a suitably sized sauté pan and heat gently. Add the escalopes and cook on both sides for the required time. Remove and place in a warmed earthenware dish. Drain away excess fat from the pan and return to the heat.
2	Dry sherry	10 ml	100 ml	Pour into the pan and déglacé.
	Velouté	30 ml	300 ml	Add, bring to the boil and simmer.
3	Cream	50 ml	500 ml	Add, correct the seasoning and simmer gently until the correct consistency is achieved. Pass through a strainer and pour over the escalope(s).
	Parsley	10 g	100 g	Wash and chop finely. Sprinkle over the sauce.

☐   ☐   ☐

Thin slices of (pork, beef, veal, chicken) cordon bleu

Escalope de (porc, boeuf, veau, poulet) cordon bleu

Step	Commodity	1 portion	10 portions	⏱ 1 hr 🍳 20 min per portion ≋ 175°–195°C
1	Prepared escalopes	1 × 120 g	10 × 120 g	Lay on a clean work surface and season lightly.
	Cooked ham, thick	1 slice	10 slices	Place on top of the escalope.
	Gruyère cheese	1 slice	10 slices	Place in the centre of the ham. Fold over the ham and then the escalope to create an envelope. Press the edges firmly together.
	Flour	15 g	150 g	Season with salt and pepper. Place on a tray.
	Eggs	1	8	Break into a bowl, whisk briskly and pour into a deep sided tray.
	White breadcrumbs	40 g	400 g	Place in another tray. Pané the escalope. Flatten and make a trellis pattern on the serving side.
	Clarified butter	25 ml	250 ml	Place in a suitably sized sauté pan and heat gently. Add the escalope serving side down and cook on both sides for the required time. Remove and place on a warmed serving flat on a dish paper and keep warm. Pour away the fat from the frying pan and wipe clean with kitchen paper. Return to stove.
2	Butter	15 g	150 g	Add to the pan and cook until nut brown. Pour over the escalopes.

NOTE: Serve with a jus lié sauce.

☐   ☐   ☐

11

Thin slices of (pork, beef, veal, chicken) with Madeira sauce

Escalope de (porc, boeuf, veau, poulet) au Madère

Step	Commodity	1 portion	10 portions	⏱ 20 min 🍳 5 min approximately per portion ≋ 175°–195°C
1	Prepared escalope	1 × 120 g	10 × 120 g	Pass through seasoned flour.
	Clarified butter	25 ml	250 ml	Place in a suitably sized sauté pan and heat gently. Add the escalope(s) and cook on both sides for the required time. Remove the place in a warmed earthenware dish. Drain away excess fat from the pan and return to the heat.
2	Madeira wine	10 ml	100 ml	Pour into the pan and déglacé.
	Demi-glace	30 ml	300 ml	Add, bring to the boil and simmer. Pass through a strainer and pour over the escalopes.
	Parsley	10 g	100 g	Wash and chop finely. Sprinkle over the sauce.

NOTE: Marsala wine may be added instead of Madeira to create Escalope de (porc, boeuf, veau, poulet) Marsala.

☐   ☐   ☐

Thin slices of (pork, beef, veal, chicken) Escalope de (porc, boeuf, veau, poulet) in breadcrumbs pané

Step	Commodity	1 portion	10 portions	🍲 20 min 🍽 10 min per portion ≈ 175°–195°C
1	Prepared escalope	1 × 120 g	10 × 120 g	Lay on a clean work surface and season lightly.
	Flour	15 g	150 g	Season with salt and pepper. Place on a tray.
	Eggs	1	8	Break into a bowl, whisk briskly and pour into a deep sided tray.
	White breadcrumbs	40 g	400 g	Place in another tray. Pané the escalope. Flatten and make a trellis pattern on the serving side.
	Clarified butter	25 ml	250 ml	Place in a suitably sized sauté pan and heat gently. Add the escalope, serving side down, and cook on both sides for the required time. Remove and place on a warmed serving flat and dish paper. Keep warm. Pour away the fat from the frying pan and wipe clean with kitchen paper.
2	Butter	15 g	150 g	Add to the pan and cook until nut brown. Pour over the escalopes. Serve with a cordon of jus lié.

Extensions of pané

Escalope de (porc, boeuf, veau, poulet) milanaise
With the addition of 100 g of spaghetti milanaise per portion (*see* Chapter 19: Farinaceous cookery).

Escalope de (porc, boeuf, veau, poulet) napolitaine
With the addition of 100 g of spaghetti napolitaine per portion.

NOTE: Any of the above dishes may be made with lamb cutlets (côtelettes d'agneau) or veal cutlets (côtes de veau).

☐   ☐   ☐

Thin slices of (pork, beef, veal, chicken) Escalope de (porc, boeuf, veau, poulet)
Holstein style   Holstein

Step	Commodity	1 portion	10 portions	⬙ 20 min ♨ 10 min per portion ≋ 175°–195°C
1	Prepared escalope	1 × 120 g	10 × 120 g	Lay on a clean work surface and season lightly.
	Flour	15 g	150 g	Season with salt and pepper. Place on a tray.
	Eggs	1	8	Break into a bowl, whisk briskly and pour into a deep sided tray.
	White breadcrumbs	40 g	400 g	Place in another tray. Pané the escalopes. Flatten and make a trellis pattern on the serving side.
	Clarified butter	25 ml	250 ml	Place in a suitably sized sauté pan and heat gently. Add the escalopes serving side down and cook on both sides for the required time. Remove and place on a warmed serving flat and dish paper. Keep warm. Pour away the fat from the frying pan and wipe clean with kitchen paper. Return to stove.
2	Butter	15 g	150 g	Heat gently in the pan.
	Egg	1	10	Break and fry 3–4 minutes. Place one on each escalope.
	Anchovy fillets	2	20	Place in a criss-cross on top of each egg.
3	Butter	10 g	100 g	Add to the pan and cook until nut brown. Pour over the escalopes.

NOTE: Serve with a cordon of jus lié sauce.

□   □   □

Pork chop flamande   Côtes de porc flamandes

Step	Commodity	1 portion	10 portions	⬙ 45 min ♨ 30 min per portion ≋ 175°–195°C
1	Pork chops	1 × 200 g	10 × 200 g	Season lightly.
	Clarified butter	25 ml	250 ml	Place in a suitably sized sauté pan and heat gently. Add the chops and cook on both sides for 15 minutes. Remove and place in a warmed earthenware dish. Keep warm.
2	Cooking apples	100 g	1 kg	Peel, core and cut the apple into slices. Arrange neatly on top of the chops.
	Butter	5 g	50 g	Melt and brush over the apples. Place in a pre-heated oven (185°C) for 15 minutes. Serve in the earthenware dish.

NOTE: Serve with a cordon of jus lié sauce.

□   □   □

Lamb cutlets maintenon style

Côtelettes d'agneau maintenon

☝ 20 min   🍲 15 min per portion   ≋ 175°–195°C

Step	Commodity	1 portion	10 portions	
1	Clarified butter	10 ml	100 ml	Heat in a suitably sized sauté pan.
	Lamb cutlets	2 × 100 g	20 × 100 g	Add to the hot fat and fry quickly on each side for 5 minutes. Remove, place on a tray and keep warm.
2	Soubise sauce	25 ml	250 ml	Using a palette knife, spread neatly in a dome shape on the serving side of the cutlets.
	Breadcrumbs	10 g	100 g	Sprinkle over the soubise sauce.
	Butter	5 g	50 g	Melt and sprinkle over the breadcrumbs. Place in a pre-heated oven (190°C) for 5 minutes to gratinate.
3	Butter	10 g	100 g	Place in a frying pan and cook until nut brown. Pour over the cutlets. Serve with Périgueux sauce (see Chapter 5: Boiling).

☐   ☐   ☐

Veal cutlets papillote style

Côte de veau en papillote

☝ 20 min   🍲 15 min per portion   ≋ 175°–195°C

Step	Commodity	1 portion	10 portions	
1	Veal cutlets	1 × 200 g	10 × 200 g	Season with salt and pepper.
	Clarified butter	25 ml	250 ml	Place in a suitably sized sauté pan and heat gently. Add the cutlets serving side down and cook one each side for 7–8 minutes. Remove and place in a warmed serving flat. Keep warm.
2	Butter	10 g	100 g	Place in a clean frying pan.
	Onions	25 g	250 g	Peel, dice finely and add to the butter. Cook without colouring for 2–3 minutes.
	Button mushrooms	25 g	250 g	Wash, trim the stalks, dice finely and add to the onions. Cook for a further 2–3 minutes.
	Dry white wine	15 ml	150 ml	Add and reduce until almost dry.
	Demi-glace	25 ml	250 ml	Add, correct the consistency and seasoning. Allow to cool and divide into the appropriate portions. Cut a piece of silicon or greaseproof paper into a minimum of twice the size of the cutlet. Butter liberally.
	Cooked ham	2 slices	20 slices	Cut to the size of the cutlet. Place one slice on the paper. Coat with half a portion of the mixture. Place the cutlet on top. Spread the remainder of the mixture on the top. Place the other slice of ham on top. Fold over the paper and seal by pleating the edges tightly. Place on a tray and cook in a pre-heated oven (190°C) for 5 minutes. Place the bags on a serving flat and serve.

☐   ☐   ☐

Veal cutlets bonne femme   Côtes de veau bonne femme

Step	Commodity	1 portion	10 portions	☌ 1 hr ♨ 30 min per portion ≋ 175°–195°C
1	Clarified butter	10 ml	100 ml	Heat in a suitably sized sauté pan.
	Veal cutlets	1 × 250 g	10 × 250 g	Add to the hot fat and fry quickly on each side for 7–8 minutes. Remove, place in an earthenware dish and keep warm.
2	Cooking oil	5 g	50 g	Place in a frying pan and heat.
	Potatoes	75 g	750 g	Peel and cut into cocotte shape, 3 cm in length. Place in the pan and cook on all sides until golden brown. Remove and keep warm.
	Button onions	50 g	500 g	Peel, add to the hot oil and cook until golden brown (glacés à brun). Remove, mix with the potatoes and drain away the excess fat.
	Back bacon	25 g	250 g	Cut into thin strips (lardons) and cook in the fat until golden brown. Remove, drain and add to the potatoes and onions. Sprinkle over the cutlets. Place in a pre-heated oven (190°C) for 5 minutes.
	Parsley	10 g	100 g	Wash and chop finely. Sprinkle over the cutlets.

NOTE: Serve with a cordon of jus lié sauce.

☐   ☐   ☐

Shallow fried venison with port sauce   Sauté de venaison au porto

Noisettes (noisettes) – a slanted cut from the boned out loin.
Cutlets (côtelettes) – a steak on the bone cut from the best end.

Step	Commodity	1 portion	10 portions	☌ 24 h ♨ 30 min per 10 portions ≋ 150°–175°C
1	Prepared venison	125 g	1¼ kg	Place in a deep dish.
	Red wine	100 ml	1 litre	Pour over the venison.
	Bayleaf	1	5	Add.
	Peppercorns	3	15	Crush and add.
	Onions	25 g	250 g	Peel, slice and add.
	Carrots	25 g	250 g	Peel, cut into mirepoix and add. Cover and place in the fridge to marinade overnight.
2	Clarified oil	15 ml	150 ml	Place in a heavy frying pan and heat. Add the drained venison in batches and cook lightly (do not brown) for 8–10 minutes. Do not overcook as the venison will become dry and tough. Place on a serving flat and keep warm in a hot cupboard.
	Port	10 ml	100 ml	Drain away the fat. Swill out (déglacé) the frying pan.
	*Port sauce	50 ml	500 ml	Add, warm, season with salt and pepper and correct the consistency. Napper over the cooked venison and sprinkle with finely chopped parsley. Serve immediately.

* See Chapter 5: Boiling

☐   ☐   ☐

11

Shallow-fried venison with chasseur sauce — Sauté de venaison au sauce chasseur

Step	Commodity	1 portion	10 portions	☺ 24 hr ♨ 30 min per 10 portions ≋ 150°–175°C
1	Prepared venison	125 g	1¼ kg	Place in a deep dish.
	Red wine	100 ml	1 litre	Pour over the venison.
	Bayleaf	1	5	Add.
	Peppercorns	3	15	Crush and add.
	Onions	25 g	250 g	Peel, slice and add.
	Carrots	25 g	250 g	Peel, cut into mirepoix and add. Cover and place in the fridge to marinade overnight.
2	Clarified oil	15 ml	150 ml	Place in a heavy frying pan and heat. Add the drained venison in batches and cook lightly (do not brown) for 8–10 minutes. Do not overcook as the venison will become dry and tough. Place on a serving flat and keep warm in a hot cupboard.
	White wine	10 ml	100 ml	Drain away the fat. Swill out (déglacé) the frying pan.
	Chasseur sauce	50 ml	500 ml	Add, warm, season with salt and pepper and correct the consistency. Napper over the cooked venison and sprinkle with finely chopped parsley. Serve immediately.

☐   ☐   ☐

Shallow-fried sweetbreads English style — Ris sautés a l'ànglaise

Step	Commodity	1 portion	10 portions	☺ 2 hr ♨ 30 min per 10 portions ≋ 150°–175°C
1	Braised sweetbreads	125 g	1¼ kg	Allow to cool. To ensure a close texture and ease of handling press between two trays. Use weights to keep pressed. Place in the fridge for 45 minutes. Slice into thick escalopes and dry.
2	Flour	10 g	100 g	Season with salt and pepper. Pass the sweetbreads through and pat off the excess flour.
	Eggs	½	5	Break into a bowl and whisk thoroughly.
	Breadcrumbs	25 g	250 g	Sieve onto a tray. Pass the floured sweetbreads through the eggwash then through the breadcrumbs.
3	Clarified oil	15 ml	150 ml	Place in a heavy frying pan and heat. Add the sweetbreads in batches and cook to a light brown. Place on a serving flat and keep warm in a hot cupboard.
4	Butter	15 g	150 g	Place in a pre-heated frying pan and cook until golden brown.
	Vinegar	1 tsp	25 ml	Add to the hot butter to make beurre noisette. Pour over the cooked sweetbreads and sprinkle with finely chopped parsley. Serve immediately.

☐   ☐   ☐

Shallow-fried sweetbreads florentine

Ris sautés florentine

Step	Commodity	1 portion	10 portions			
				⏲ 2 hr	🍲 30 min per 10 portions	≋ 150°–175°C
1	Braised sweetbreads	125 g	1¼ kg	Allow to cool. To ensure a close texture and ease of handling press between two trays. Use weights to keep pressed. Place in the fridge for 45 minutes. Slice into thick escalopes and dry.		
	Flour	10 g	100 g	Season with salt and pepper. Pass the sweetbreads through and pat off the excess flour.		
2	Clarified oil	15 ml	150 ml	Place in a heavy frying pan and heat. Add the sweetbreads in batches and cook to a light brown. Place on a serving flat and keep warm in a hot cupboard.		
3	Clarified butter	10 ml	100 ml	Place in a pre-heated frying pan.		
	Cooked leaf spinach	50 g	500 g	Add and warm through. Arrange on the base of the serving dish. Place the cooked sweetbreads on top.		
	Mornay sauce	75 ml	750 ml	Warm, correct the seasoning and consistency. Napper over the sweetbreads.		
	Parmesan cheese	10 g	100 g	Sprinkle over the sauce and place under a pre-heated salamander to gratinate. Serve immediately.		

☐   ☐   ☐

Shallow-fried sweetbreads maréchale

Ris sautés maréchale

Step	Commodity	1 portion	10 portions			
				⏲ 2 hr	🍲 30 min per 10 portions	≋ 150°–175°C
1	Braised sweetbreads	125 g	1¼ kg	Allow to cool. To ensure a close texture and ease of handling, press between two trays. Use weights to keep pressed. Place in the fridge for 45 minutes. Slice into thick escalopes and dry.		
	Flour	10 g	100 g	Season with salt and pepper. Pass the sweetbreads through and pat off the excess flour.		
2	Clarified oil	15 ml	150 ml	Place in a heavy frying pan and heat. Add the sweetbreads in batches and cook to a light brown. Place on a serving flat.		
3	Cooked asparagus tips	3	30	Arrange by the side of the sweetbreads.		
	Sliced truffle	1	10	Place on top of the cooked sweetbreads.		
	Butter	10 g	100 g	Place in a pre-heated frying pan and cook until golden brown.		
	Vinegar	1 tsp	25 ml	Add to the hot butter to make beurre noisette. Pour over the cooked sweetbreads and sprinkle with finely chopped parsley. Serve immediately.		

☐   ☐   ☐

11

Fried lambs' liver

Foie d'agneau sauté

🍲 30 min per 10 portions   🥄 20 min   ≋ 175°–195°C

Step	Commodity	1 portion	10 portions	
1	Flour	15 g	150 g	Place on a tray and season with salt and pepper.
	Prepared lambs' liver	100 g	1 kg	Remove any skin, tubes and gristle. Pass through the seasoned flour.
2	Clarified butter	25 ml	250 ml	Heat in a suitably sized heavy frying pan. Add the liver in batches and cook on both sides for 4–5 minutes. Place on a flat.
	Butter	10 g	100 g	Place in a pre-heated frying pan and brown (beurre noisette).
	Vinegar	¼ tsp	2 tsp	Add and pour over the liver. Sprinkle with finely chopped parsley. Serve with jus lié sauce (see Chapter 5: Boiling).

NOTE: Calves' and pigs' liver may be cooked in this way.

☐   ☐   ☐

Shallow-fried chicken liver in Madeira sauce

Foie de volaille sauté à sauce madère

🍲 20 min per 10 portions   🥄 20 min   ≋ 175°–195°C

Step	Commodity	1 portion	10 portions	
1	Chicken liver	100 g	1 kg	Remove the bile bag, any stained livers, fat and tubes. Season with salt and pepper.
	Clarified butter	25 ml	250 ml	Heat in a suitably sized heavy frying pan. Add the liver in batches and cook on both sides for 3–4 minutes. Keep the frying pan. Place the cooked livers in a serving dish. Pour away the fat.
2	Madeira wine	20 ml	200 ml	Déglacé with the wine.
	*Madeira sauce	50 ml	500 ml	Add, correct the seasoning, dégraisse and strain over the liver. Sprinkle with chopped parsley. Serve with riz pilaff (see Chapter 9: Braising).

* See Chapter 5: Boiling.

☐   ☐   ☐

258

Fried lambs' liver lyonnaise

Foie d'agneau sauté lyonnaise

⌣ 20 min
♨ 30 min per 10 portions
≋ 175°–195°C

Step	Commodity	1 portion	10 portions	
1	Flour	15 g	150 g	Place on a tray and season with salt and pepper.
	Prepared lambs' liver	100 g	1 kg	Remove any skin, tubes and gristle. Pass through the seasoned flour.
	Clarified butter	25 ml	250 ml	Heat in a suitably sized heavy frying pan. Add the liver in batches and cook on both sides for 4–5 minutes. Place on a flat.
2	Onions	100 g	1 kg	Peel, cut into thin slices.
	Clarified butter	15 ml	150 ml	Place enough fat in a frying pan to cover the bottom and heat. Add the onions and season with salt and pepper.
	Sugar*	pinch	1 tsp	Add and cook until light brown. Arrange over the portioned liver.
	Butter	10 g	100 g	Place in a pre-heated frying pan and brown (beurre noisette).
	Vinegar	¼ tsp	2 tsp	Add and pour over the liver. Sprinkle with finely chopped parsley. Serve with jus lié sauce (see Chapter 5: Boiling). Sprinkle with finely chopped parsley.

NOTE: Calves' and pigs' liver may be cooked in this way.
* The sugar helps to brown the onions.

☐　　☐　　☐

Lambs' kidneys chasseur

Rognons d'agneau sautés chasseur

⌣ 20 min
♨ 30 min per 10 portions
≋ 175°–195°C

Step	Commodity	1 portion	10 portions	
1	Lambs' kidneys	2	20	Remove any skin, tubes and gristle. Season with salt and pepper.
	Clarified butter	15 ml	150 ml	Heat in a suitably sized heavy frying pan. Add the kidneys in batches and cook on both sides for 8–10 minutes. Remove and keep warm in a hot cupboard. Discard the fat.
2	Dry white wine	50 ml	500 ml	Déglacer and allow to reduce by half.
3	Chasseur sauce	75 ml	750 ml	Add, correct the seasoning and dégraisser. Add the kidneys.
	Parsley	5 g	50 g	Wash, chop finely and sprinkle over the kidneys. Serve on a bed of riz pilaff (see Chapter 9: Braising).

☐　　☐

Lambs' kidneys turbigo

🍲 20 min
♨ 30 min per 10 portions   ≋ 175°–195°C

Step	Commodity	1 portion	10 portions	
1	Chipolata sausages	2	20	Pierce with a knife and place under a pre-heated salamander for 5–6 minutes until cooked. Keep warm in a hot cupboard.
	Button mushrooms	25 g	250 g	Wash, trim the stalks and dry.
	Clarified butter	10 ml	100 ml	Place in a heavy frying pan and heat. Add the mushrooms and cook until golden brown. Remove and keep warm.
2	Lambs' kidneys	2	20	Remove any skin, tubes and gristle. Season with salt and pepper.
	Clarified butter	15 ml	150 ml	Heat in a suitably sized heavy frying pan. Add the kidneys in batches and cook on both sides for 8–10 minutes. Remove and keep warm in a hot cupboard. Discard the fat.
3	Madeira wine	50 ml	500 ml	Déglacer and allow to reduce by half.
4	Parsley	5 g	50 g	Wash and chop finely.
	Madeira sauce	75 ml	750 ml	Add, correct the seasoning and dégraisser. Add the kidneys.
	Sliced white bread	1 slice	10 slices	Cut in triangles and shape like a heart. Place under a pre-heated salamander and toast on both sides. Dip one corner in melted butter then into finely chopped parsley. Serve on a bed of riz pilaff (see Chapter 9: Braising).

□   □   □

Chicken pojarski

🍲 1 hr   ♨ 45 min per 10 portions   ≋ 175°–195°C

Step	Commodity	1 portion	10 portions	
1	Breadcrumbs	15 g	150 g	Place in a bowl.
	Milk	30 ml	300 ml	Pour over the breadcrumbs and soak for 30 minutes. Squeeze breadcrumbs to remove the milk.
2	Lean minced chicken meat	100 g	1 kg	Add and re-mince.
	Nutmeg	pinch	1 tsp	Add.
	Lemon juice	5 ml	50 ml	Add.
	Parsley	5 g	50 g	Wash, chop finely and add.
	Onions	10 g	100 g	Peel, cut into brunoise and add to the chicken.
	Butter	10 g	100 g	Melt in a saucepan and add to the mixture.
	Double cream	10 ml	100 ml	Add and season with salt and pepper. Mix thoroughly. Refrigerate for 30 minutes. Divide into the appropriate number of pieces, allowing 2 per portion. Refrigerate until ready to use. Roll into a 5 cm cylinder and cut into 1¼ cm pieces. Shape like cutlets.
	Flour	10 g	100 g	Season with salt and pepper and place on a tray.
	Eggs	1	5	Whisk and place in a bowl.
	Breadcrumbs	30 g	300 g	Finely sieve and place on a tray. Pass the pojarskis through the flour, egg wash and breadcrumbs.

Step	Commodity	1 portion	10 portions	
	Clarified butter	15 ml	150	Heat in a suitably sized heavy frying pan. Add the pojarskis and fry on both sides for 5–6 minutes until golden brown. Remove, place in an earthenware dish and keep warm in a hot cupboard.
	Butter	10 g	100 g	Place in a pre-heated frying pan and cook until golden brown.
	Vinegar	½ tsp	10 ml	Add and pour over the pojarskis. Decorate with a small sprig of parsley. Serve with an appropriate sauce – sauce chasseur, smitaine or Reform (see Chapter 5: Boiling).

NOTE: This dish may be made with minced pork (côtelette de porc pojarski) or minced veal (côtelette de veau pojarski).

☐   ☐   ☐

Hamburg steaks   Biftecks de boeuf

⤵ 1 hr 〰 45 min per 10 portions ≋ 175°–195°C

Step	Commodity	1 portion	10 portions	
1	Breadcrumbs	15 g	150 g	Place in a bowl.
	Milk	30 ml	300 ml	Pour over the breadcrumbs and soak for 30 minutes. Squeeze breadcrumbs to remove the milk.
2	Lean topside of beef, minced	100 g	1 kg	Add and re-mince.
	Onions	10 g	100 g	Peel, cut into brunoise and add to the beef.
	Eggs	¼	2	Add, season with salt and pepper. Mix thoroughly. Divide into the appropriate number of pieces allowing 2 per portion. Shape into 5 cm cylinders, 1½ cm thick. Refrigerate until ready to use.
	Flour	10 g	100 g	Season with salt and pepper and pass the steaks through it.
	Clarified butter	15 ml	150 ml	Heat in a suitably sized heavy frying pan. Add the Hamburg steaks in batches and fry on both sides for 5–6 minutes on each. Remove, place in an earthenware dish and keep warm in a hot cupboard. Decorate with a small sprig of parsley. Serve with french fried onion rings (see Chapter 12: Deep frying) and an appropriate sauce, e.g. piquante, smitaine or lyonnaise (see Chapter 5: Boiling).

NOTE: This dish may be made with minced pork (bifteck de porc) or minced veal (bifteck de veau).

Extension of Hamburg steaks

Vienna steaks: As above and garnished with a shallow-fried egg.

☐   ☐   ☐

Shallow-fried vegetables

Galette potatoes
Pommes galette

☝ 20 min
🍲 40 min per 10 portions
≋ 175°–195°C

Step	Commodity	1 portion	10 portions	
1	Duchess potato	100 g	1 kg	Sprinkle a dusting of flour onto the work surface. Mould the mixture into a 4 cm diameter cylinder. Cut into 1½ cm slices allowing 2 per portion. Reshape and mark in a trellis pattern on the presentation side.
2	Clarified butter	15 ml	150 ml	Place enough fat in a heavy frying pan to cover the bottom and heat. Add the potatoes in batches, cooking presentation side first. Cook until golden brown on both sides. Place in a hot cupboard between batches to keep warm. Serve in a vegetable dish brushed with melted butter. Garnish with a small sprig of parsley.

☐   ☐   ☐

Macaire potatoes
Pommes Macaire

☝ 20 min
🍲 40 min per 10 portions
≋ 200°C

Step	Commodity	1 portion	10 portions	
1	Baking potatoes	200 g	2 kg	Wash well, score and place on a salted tray in a pre-heated oven for 1 hour or until soft. Cut in half and scoop out the potato pulp.
	Butter	10 g	100 g	Add to the warm potato. Season with salt and pepper. Mash with a fork or potato masher.
2	Clarified butter	15 ml	150 ml	Select an appropriately sized heavy frying pan for the amount of mixture to be cooked. Place the fat in the frying pan ensuring that there is fat on the sides as well as on the bottom. Heat. Add the potato mixture and press down well. Smooth the surface with a palette knife. Brush the top. Cook for 4–5 minutes on top of the stove. Place in a pre-heated oven 200°C for 30–40 minutes. Remove from the oven and turn out onto a buttered vegetable dish. Cut into the appropriate portions and brush with melted butter. Garnish with a small sprig of parsley.

NOTE: Macaire potatoes may also be shaped like large galette (6 cm diameter).

☐   ☐   ☐

Shallow-fried potatoes

Pommes sautées

🍲 15–20 min per portions   🖐 20 min   ≋ 175°–195°C

Step	Commodity	1 portion	10 portions	
1	Potatoes	150 g	1½ kg	Wash and scrub the potatoes. Do not peel. Steam for 10 minutes. Refresh. Peel the skins and cut into ½ cm slices.
2	Clarified butter	15 ml	150 ml	Place enough fat in a frying pan to cover the bottom and heat. Add the potatoes in batches. Cook until golden brown on both sides. Place in a hot cupboard between batches to keep warm. Serve in a vegetable dish brushed with melted butter.
3	Parsley	5 g	50 g	Wash, chop finely and sprinkle over the cooked potatoes.

☐   ☐   ☐

Shallow-fried potatoes à cru

Pommes sautées à cru

🍲 15–20 min per portions   🖐 20 min   ≋ 175°–195°C

Step	Commodity	1 portion	10 portions	
1	Potatoes	150 g	1½ kg	Wash and scrub the potatoes. Do not peel. Steam for 10 minutes. Refresh. Peel the skins and cut the potatoes into ½ cm even rounded slices.
2	Clarified butter	15 ml	150 ml	Place enough fat in a frying pan to cover the bottom and heat. Add the potatoes in batches. Cook until golden brown on both sides. Place in a hot cupboard between batches to keep warm. Serve in a vegetable dish brushed with melted butter.
3	Parsley	5 g	50 g	Wash, chop finely and sprinkle over the cooked potatoes.

Extensions of à cru

Columbine potatoes   Pommes sautées columbines

As above with the addition of 25 g cooked pimentos cut into julienne per portion. Add to the potato while sautéing.

☐   ☐   ☐

Parmentier style potatoes

Pommes parmentier

🍲 10–15 min per portions   🖐 20 min   ≋ 175°–195°C

Step	Commodity	1 portion	10 portions	
1	Potatoes	150 g	1½ kg	Wash and peel the potatoes. Cut into 1 cm cubes.
2	Clarified butter	15 ml	150 ml	Place enough fat in a frying pan to cover the bottom and heat. Add the potatoes in batches. Cook until golden brown on all sides. Place in a hot cupboard between batches to keep warm. Serve in a vegetable dish brushed with melted butter.
3	Parsley	5 g	50 g	Wash, chop finely and sprinkle over the cooked potatoes.

Extension of parmentier

Sablé style potoates   Pommes sablées

As above with the addition of 10 g of breadcrumbs per portion sprinkled over the potatoes before cooking.

☐   ☐   ☐

11

Noisette style potatoes

Pommes noisette

🍲 10–15 min per portions   🥄 20 min   ≋ 175°–195°C

Step	Commodity	1 portion	10 portions	
1	Potatoes	150 g	1½ kg	Wash and peel the potatoes. Use a parisienne cutter to create the required ball shapes.
2	Clarified butter	15 ml	150 ml	Place enough fat in a frying pan to cover the bottom and heat. Add the potatoes in batches. Cook until golden brown. Place in a hot cupboard between batches to keep warm. Serve in a vegetable dish brushed with melted butter.
3	Parsley	5 g	50 g	Wash, chop finely and sprinkle over the cooked potatoes.

Extension

Parisienne style potoatoes

Pommes parisiennes

As above, but roll in 1 tsp per portion of meat glaze. If meat glaze is not available beef extract may be used.

☐   ☐   ☐

Cocotte style potatoes

Pommes cocotte

🍲 10–15 min per portions   🥄 20 min   ≋ 175°–195°C

Step	Commodity	1 portion	10 portions	
1	Potatoes	150 g	1½ kg	Wash and peel the potatoes. Use a cocotte cutter to achieve the required shape. If a cutter is not available use a knife to cut into small barrel shapes.
2	Clarified butter	15 ml	150 ml	Place enough fat in a frying pan to cover the bottom and heat. Add the potatoes in batches. Cook until golden brown all over. Place in a hot cupboard between batches to keep warm. Serve in a vegetable dish brushed with melted butter.
3	Parsley	5 g	50 g	Wash, chop finely and sprinkle over the cooked potatoes.

☐   ☐   ☐

Shallow-fried mushrooms

Champignons sautés

🍲 10 min per 10 portions   🥄 10 min   ≋ 150°–175°C

Step	Commodity	1 portion	10 portions	
1	Mushrooms	100 g	1 kg	Wash and trim.
2	Clarified butter	15 ml	150 ml	Place enough fat in a frying pan to cover the bottom and heat. Add the mushrooms, season with salt and pepper and cook until light brown. Serve in a vegetable dish brushed with melted butter.
3	Parsley	5 g	50 g	Wash, chop finely and sprinkle over the cooked mushrooms.

☐   ☐   ☐

Shallow-fried onions

Oignons sautés

🥄 10 min
〰 150°–175°C

🍲 10 min per 10 portions

Step	Commodity	1 portion	10 portions	
1	Onions	100 g	1 kg	Peel and cut into thin slices.
2	Clarified butter	15 ml	150 ml	Place enough fat in a frying pan to cover the bottom and heat. Add the onions, season with salt and pepper.
	Sugar*	pinch	1 tsp	Add and cook until light brown. Serve in a vegetable dish brushed with melted butter.
3	Parsley	5 g	50 g	Wash, chop finely and sprinkle over the cooked mushrooms.

* The sugar helps to brown the onions.

☐   ☐   ☐

Shallow-fried aubergine

Aubergine sauté

🥄 20 min
〰 150°–175°C

🍲 15 min per 10 portions

Step	Commodity	1 portion	10 portions	
1	Aubergine	100 g	1 kg	Peel and cut into ½ cm slices.
2	Clarified butter	15 ml	150 ml	Place enough fat in a frying pan to cover the bottom and heat. Add the sliced aubergine in batches and cook until golden brown on both sides. Place in a hot cupboard between batches to keep warm. Serve in a vegetable dish brushed with melted butter.
3	Parsley	5 g	50 g	Wash, chop finely and sprinkle over the cooked aubergines.

NOTE: Courgette or marrow may be cooked in this manner.

☐   ☐   ☐

11

WHAT WENT WRONG?

Problem	Caused by	To rectify
Fried eggs break up during cooking.	(1) Mis-handling during cooking.	Cannot be rectified.
	(2) Using stale eggs.	Cannot be rectified.
Omelettes/pancakes stick to the frying pan.	(1) Pan was not proved properly.	Re-prove the pan.
	(2) Pan was not cleaned in between.	Wipe clean with absorbent kitchen paper, then with oil and begin cooking again.
	(3) Pan was washed in water.	Re-prove the pan.
Omelette appears to be dry and has a tough skin.	Holding for too long after cooking.	Cannot be rectified.
Fried vegetables or potatoes are broken or discoloured.	(1) Frying too fast or too slow.	Cannot be rectified.
	(2) Cooking too many vegetables at once.	Cannot be rectified.
	(3) Vegetables were mis-handled during cooking.	Cannot be rectified.

Problem	Caused by	To rectify
Fried vegetables or potatoes are soggy.	(1) Cooking at too low a temperature.	Cannot be rectified.
	(2) Vegetables or potatoes were over-cooking before sauteing.	Cannot be rectified.
	(3) Holding for too long before serving.	Cannot be rectified.
Meat has not browned.	(1) Cooking at too low a temperature.	Remove the meat, allow the fat to heat to the required temperature and re-start cooking.
	(2) Cooking too many pieces of meat at once.	Remove the meat, allow the fat to heat to the required temperature and re-start cooking.
	(3) Cooking juices from preceding batch were not poured away before beginning.	Remove the meat, discard the cooking juices. Allow the fat to heat to the required temperature and re-start cooking.
Liver or kidneys 'weep' moisture forming specks on the surface.	(1) Cooking at too low a temperature.	Remove the meat, allow the fat to heat to the required temperature and re-start cooking.
	(2) Cooking too many portions at once.	Remove the meat, allow the fat to heat to the required temperature and re-start cooking.
Coated foods have burnt or discoloured before the food is cooked.	Cooking at too high a temperature.	Cannot be rectified.

DEEP FRYING

Deep frying (frire) is the cooking of food by sub-merging in pre-heated oil or clarified fat in a friture or deep fat fryer between 165°C and 190°C. Frying temperatures vary according to the foods being cooked. The fat must be this hot in order to seal the outside of the food and preventing the food from absorbing fat. If it is not hot enough the food will tend to absorb more fat and its surface will become soggy in texture.

Foods cooked by deep frying are usually small, evenly-shaped individual portions of food. Large items would burn well before the food would cook in the centre. Some fish may be cooked whole though these are usually flat fish or weighing no more than 200 g. Other foods need to be pre-cooked before deep frying such as croquette potatoes; cauliflower, broccoli, etc.; rissoles; minced meats; and left-over fish (fish cakes, croquettes). Foods with high fat content, such as sausages,

bacon, mackerel, tuna or salmon should not be fried as they tend to absorb excessive fat from the cooking process and taste 'over greasy'.

NOTE: To ensure that the food is always cooked at the right temperature, always allow the fat or oil to recover its heat before adding another batch of food. Keep holding time, that is the time between cooking and serving, to a minimum otherwise the foods will lose their crispness.

After each frying the fat should be strained through a fine mesh to remove fried particles. The frier must be cleaned thoroughly and the strained oil carefully replaced.

NOTE: Deep fried food is served on a serving flat lined with a paper to absorb fat/oil. The food is never covered with a lid as steam trapped will cause the food to go soggy, thus ruining the appearance.

Terms associated with deep frying

À l'anglaise (pané) To coat English style, with flour, egg wash and breadcrumbs. Served with a quarter of lemon, deep fried picked parsley and a sauceboat of tartare sauce.

À la française To coat French style, moistened with milk and coated with flour. Served with a quarter of lemon and picked parsley.

À l'orly Associated with deep frying fish. The fish is first marinaded in lemon juice, parsley and oil, then passed through seasoned flour and batter. Served with a quarter of lemon, deep fried picked parsley and a sauceboat of hot tomato sauce.

Blanching To par-cook an item of food in advance to ensure it is cooked through, i.e. French fried potatoes.

Clarifying Slow rendering of coarsely minced beef

fat to remove the water content and any impurities so that it may be used for deep frying. The fat is called dripping.

Coating Passing the item to be cooked through seasoned flour and batter, seasoned flour, egg wash and breadcrumbs, and milk and flour, or wrapping in filo or puff pastry.

Colère (en) Angry style – The fish is prepared by cleaning the inside, removing the eyes, gills, fins and skin; and trimming the tail. Finally paner à l anglaise.

Draining Allowing the fat to drain from the food on wire racks or in the raised frying basket. The food can also be placed on absorbent paper to remove the grease.

The main advantages of deep frying are:

(a) Foods are cooked quickly by this process; and
(b) blanching helps time true finishing items that normally take longer to cook during a busy service.

Staff usually associated with deep frying

In a traditional kitchen:

The **Chef Rôtisseur** would handle all items other than pastry goods.

The **Chef Pâtissier** would cook all deep-fried pastry goods.

POINTS OF SAFETY

Deep frying is one of the most dangerous methods of cookery as the fat or oil, if left unattended, can reach flash point and burst into flames.

Always

1 Dry wet foods before frying as water boils on contact with hot fat causing the fat to 'spit' and this may result in a serious burn. Water also causes fat to spill over the side of the friture.
2 Ensure that there is sufficient oil in the fryer before turning it on.
3 Follow the manufacturer's instructions when using the friture.
4 Use a basket, unless the food is coated with a batter – batter almost always sticks to the wire.
5 In the event of a fat or friture fire, extinguish with a foam extinguisher and/or a mineral blanket.

Never

1 Overload the friture as the food will displace the hot fat causing it to overflow and may result in an accident.

2 Never allow water or damp foods to be placed in the fryer.
3 Never fill the fryer past the maximum level indication mark.
4 Never attempt to put your hands into the friture.
5 Never lean over the friture.

FOODS SUITABLE FOR DEEP FRYING

Meat and poultry

Only tender cuts of meat and poultry can be used in deep-fried dishes as this fast process of cookery would not tenderise the meat sufficiently to make it edible. Chicken can be deep fried as suprêmes (a cut from the breast), chicken legs or drumsticks. Turkey and veal are deep fried as escalopes (thin slices). In all cases the food is either coated with breadcrumbs or passed through a batter.

Fish and shellfish

Small whole fish such as Dover sole, lemon sole, whiting and whitebait are suitable for deep frying. Scampi, scallops, oysters, prawns and mussels may be deep fried. There is a wide range of ready prepared frozen fish products that are cooked straight from the freezer.

Eggs

Eggs can be deep fried if they are first hard boiled, coated with sausagemeat and breadcrumbed to make scotch eggs.

Vegetables, potatoes and fruits

Potatoes are cut into a variety of shapes to deep fry them. Very few vegetables can be deep fried from raw because the process would cause considerable damage and make the food unsuitable to eat. Most vegetables have to be par-cooked by boiling or steaming, coated in batter or breadcrumbs before deep frying.

Apples, apricots, bananas, peaches and pineapple are usually deep fried protected by a batter or breadcrumbs and served with an appropriate sauce.

Cheese

Camembert cheese can be coated in breadcrumbs and deep fried as a hot hors d'oeuvre.

Pastry

Choux pastry flavoured with crabmeat or cheese is deep fried and served as a savoury. Doughnuts are also deep fried and coated with sugar.

EQUIPMENT USED IN DEEP FRYING

Small amounts of food can be deep fried in a friture. A friture is usually made from heavy, black wrought steel or aluminium with a wire basket to remove food from the hot oil or fat. Fritures depend on the heat from a stove to cook and are hard to regulate and can also be dangerous if oil is spilt onto the stove top. Deep fat frying is usually carried out in a fryer. Deep fryers can be electrical or gas, but most have the same basic characteristics:

(a) A thermostat and dial that will regulate the heat of the oil or fat for cooking. Some models have a light that stays on until the correct temperature is achieved.
(b) A lip or hook to hang the frying baskets at a safe height so that oil or fat can be drained from the foods back into the fryer. To aid in the safe retrieval of cooked foods.
(c) A 'cool zone' (the area in the fryer below the elements) where cooked food particles and sediment collect and do not burn and taint the fat or oil, thus prolonging the life of the frying medium.
(d) A mark indicating the level to which the oil should reach, to prevent the hot oil from spilling over and at a height that will allow the baskets to hang without the bottom of the foods burning in the hot oil.

(e) Some fryers have built-in filters to ensure the removal of sediment.
(f) A tap to drain the oil from the fryer after use. Specialised fryers have been developed for the fast food industry and have their very own characteristics.

Computerised automatic fryers

These fryers can be programmed to fry a wide range of foods and all the operator need do is place a measured amount of food in the hanging basket, select the option for whatever food is being cooked and the computer lowers the food into the fat, calculates the correct time, raises the food when cooked, and buzzes to inform the operator that the food is ready.

Pressure fryers

In normal fryers the internal temperature of the food never goes above boiling point. Pressure steamers operate at a temperature of $70°-105°$ CkN/m which means that the internal temperature can reach between $115°-112°$ C. This means that they are ideal for cooking chicken and fresh chipped potatoes that normally have to be blanched first but in a pressure fryer can be cooked in one step. Pressure fryers have automatic timers and controls for precise cooking and a safety locking system to prevent the lid from being opened during cooking. Pressurised fryers are also computerised.

Continuous fryers

These were originally designed to be used for frying doughnuts. A doughnut was lowered into the fat and floated along at a controlled rate of speed to cook on one side. When it reached halfway a device turned the doughnut over to cook on the other side. The doughnut travelled on to the end where it was raised into a recovery tray and allowed to drain. Continuous fryers are now used to cook a wide variety of foods in large, busy establishments.

Enclosed fryers

Enclosed fryers are used in small establishments where it is necessary to remove the fumes and

12

cooking smells effectively. The fryer is enclosed in a steel box and has a built in extraction system.

Ventilation systems

It is essential that an effective ventilation system is available because of the cooking smells and fumes generated by the deep frying process.

COATINGS USED FOR DEEP FRYING

All deep fried foods with the exception of potatoes are cooked in a coating of batter, flour, pastry or breadcrumbs. The coating protects the surface of the food from the intense heat and prevents the escape of moisture. It also helps the food develop an attractive golden brown, crisp-textured surface.

Yeast batter
Pâte à frire
1 hr

Step	Commodity	1 portion	10 portions	
1	Flour	100 g	1k g	Sieve into a bowl and add a pinch of salt. Make a well.
2	Yeast	1½ g	15 g	Place in a clean bowl.
	Tepid water	100 ml	1 litre	Add to the yeast and dissolve completely in the water. Gradually add to the flour to form a smooth batter. Cover and allow to ferment in a warm place for 1 hour. The batter is now ready for use. Pass the food through seasoned flour before passing through the batter.

☐   ☐   ☐

Egg batter
Pâte à frire
1 hr

Step	Commodity	1 portion	10 portions	
1	SR flour*	100 g	1 kg	Sieve into a bowl and add a pinch of salt. Make a well.
	Tepid water	100 ml	1 litre	Gradually add to the flour to form a smooth batter.
	Egg	¼ equiv	2	Add and form a smooth batter. Cover and allow to rest in a cool place to thicken up. The batter is now ready for use. Pass through seasoned flour before passing through the batter.

* SR = self raising flour

☐   ☐   ☐

English style
Pané à l'anglaise
30 min

Step	Commodity	1 portion	10 portions	
1	Flour	25 g	250 g	Place on a tray and season with salt and pepper.
	Eggs	½	5	Break into a bowl and whisk together. Pour into a deep-sided tray.
	Breadcrumbs	50 g	500 g	Pass through a sieve and place on a tray. The coating is now ready for use. The food is first lightly passed through the flour, then the egg and finally the breadcrumbs. The food is battered slightly to ensure the breadcrumbs stay on.

☐   ☐   ☐

French style

Step	Commodity	1 portion	10 portions	
1	Milk	25 ml	250 ml	Place in a deep-sided tray.
	Flour	15 g	150 g	Season with salt and pepper and place on a tray. The food is first passed through the milk and then the seasoned flour. Shake well to remove excess flour.

5 min

NOTE: Once coated the food must be cooked immediately as standing allows the flour to absorb moisture from the food and become soggy.

□   □   □

CARE OF THE COOKING MEDIUM

Fats and oils used in deep frying are chosen for their capabilities of reaching high temperatures without burning. Besides the safety factor, fats that are overheated undergo a chemical change which creates an unpleasant flavour, which in turn will taint the food. Fats and oils must be looked after and treated with care. They start to deteriorate the moment they are heated as heating speeds up the process of oxidisation and oxidised fats turn rancid. Salt also speeds up the oxidisation process. Always keep the oil or fat covered when it is not being used as this helps to slow down oxidisation. Many fats and oils have substances added during processing that act as antioxidants. Some are natural substances like tocopherol (vitamin E), others have specially designed synthetic formulas added.

They must be regularly strained or burnt food particles that may harm the oil and spoil the taste and appearance of the food. Uncared for, oils and fats may also lose their ability to withstand high temperatures and become dangerous to use.

There are many fats and oils that can be used to deep fry, most have a neutral flavour that does not interfere with the flavour of the food while traditional establishments still use lard and dripping for deep fried potatoes and fish because of the distinctive flavour and lustre they give. Some expensive branded processed fats and oils are produced to give good coating properties and ensure that the foods develop a good crisp surface, absorbing less fat then cheaper makes.

NOTE: There are saturated fats and polyunsaturated fats. Saturated fats are associated with, and are known to contribute to, high levels of cholesterol in the blood, which in turn increases the risk of heart attacks. Polyunsaturated fats tend to have the reverse effect and help lower blood cholesterol levels.

The sources of various frying media	
Cooking fat	*Obtained from*
Dripping	clarified animal fats such as beef and lamb.
Lard	rendered pig fat. It is odourless and contains almost 100% fat
Corn oil	maize
Rapeseed oil	rapeseed plants
Sunflower oils	sunflower seeds
Groundnut oil	obtained from the ground nut, i.e. peanut olives grown in Mediterranean countries such as Italy, Spain, Greece and France
Soya oils	the soya bean

12

TEMPERATURE AND TIME CONTROL

Frying temperatures vary from between 160°–195°C. As a guide, the fat or oil is ready for use when the surface is quite still and gives off a faint, bluish tinge. Cooking times vary according to the size, structure and nature of the product being fried and the temperature used. The following table gives useful information about the flash-points, smoke points and frying temperatures of various frying media.

Type of frying medium	Approximate flash-point (°C)	Smoke point (°C)	Recommended frying temperature (°C)
Vegetable oil[1]	324	220	180
Vegetable fat[1]	321	220	180
Vegetable oil[2]	324	204	180
Pure vegetable fat	318	215	175
Pure vegetable oil	330	220	170–180
Maize oil[1]	224	215	180
Finest fat	321	202	180
Dripping[1]	300	165	163[3]
Lard	320		190
Finest olive oil	275	148–165	170

NOTE:
[1] Finest quality   [2] High class
[3] Without chemical modification

Deep-fried fish

Deep-fried fish English style

Poisson frit à l'anglaise

🥣 1 hr   ♨ 6 min   ≋ 175°–180°C

Step	Commodity	1 portion	10 portions	
1	Fish fillets	1 × 125 g	10 × 125 g	Remove the skin and any bones.
	Flour	15 g	150 g	Place on a tray and season with salt and ground pepper.
	Eggs	½	5	Break into a jug and whisk together with a little milk and/or water.
2	Breadcrumbs	25 g	250 g	Pass through a fine sieve and place on a tray. Pass the fish through the seasoned flour, egg wash and breadcrumbs. Ensure that the fish is completely and properly coated. Place in the pre-heated oil or fat for the appropriate time or until the fish is golden brown. Place on absorbent paper and dress on a dish in the appropriate manner.
3	Parsley sprig	1	10	Wash, dry and deep fry. Use to garnish the fried fish.
	Lemon wedge	1	10	Remove the pips and pith and place with the fish. Serve accompanied with a sauceboat of tartare sauce (see Chapter 19: Cold preparations).

NOTE: This dish may be made with fillet of cod, plaice, sole, haddock, whiting or hake.

Deep-fried fish French style

Poisson frit à la Française

⏲ 45 min   🍳 6 min   ≋ 175°–180°C

Step	Commodity	1 portion	10 portions	
1	Prepared fish	1 × 125 g	10 × 125 g	Remove the skin and any bones.
	Milk	25 ml	250 ml	Place in a deep-sided tray.
2	Flour	15 g	150 g	Place on a tray and season with salt and ground pepper. Pass the fish through the milk and then the seasoned flour. Place in the pre-heated oil or fat for the appropriate time or until the fish is golden brown. Place on absorbent paper and dress on a dish in the appropriate manner.
3	Parsley sprig	1	10	Wash, dry and use to garnish the fried fish.
	Lemon wedge	1	10	Remove the pips and pith and place with the fish. Serve accompanied with a sauceboat of tartare or rémoulade sauce (see Chapter 19: Cold preparations)

NOTE: This dish may be made with fillet of cod, plaice, sole, haddock, whiting, hake, oysters, scallops or scampi.

☐   ☐   ☐

Dover sole Colbert

Sole Douvière Colbert

⏲ 1½ hr   🍳 8 min   ≋ 175°–180°C

Step	Commodity	1 portion	10 portions	
1	Dover sole	1 × 300 g	10 × 300 g	Remove the skin from both sides. Remove the eye, guts and side fins. Clean and wash well. Make an incision down the backbone on one side. Commence filleting to within 2 cm of the sides, fold the fillets towards the outsides leaving the fillet attached. Using the heel of a heavy knife break the backbone in two to three places. Curl the opened fillets back.
2	Flour	15 g	150 g	Place on a tray and season with salt and ground pepper.
	Eggs	½	5	Break into a jug and whisk together with a little milk and/or water.
	Breadcrumbs	25 g	250 g	Pass through a fine sieve and place on a tray. Pass the fish through the seasoned flour, egg wash and breadcrumbs. Ensure that the fish is completely and properly coated. Place in the pre-heated oil or fat for the appropriate time or until the fish is golden brown. Place on absorbent paper and dress on a dish in the appropriate manner.
3	Parsley butter*	25 g	250 g	Cut into thin slices and place in the open part of the fish.
	Lemon wedge	1	10	Remove the pips and pith and place with the fish.

* See Chapter 19: Cold preparations

NOTE: This dish may also be made with plaice.

☐   ☐   ☐

12

Goujons of fish

Filets de poisson en goujons

🥣 1 hr   ♨ 3 min   ≋ 185°C

Step	Commodity	1 portion	10 portions	
1	Fish fillets	1 × 125 g	10 × 125 g	Remove the skin and any bones. Cut into 5 cm long × ½ cm thick strips.
	Flour	15 g	150 g	Place on a tray and season.
	Eggs	½	5	Break into a jug and whisk with a little milk and/or water.
2	Breadcrumbs	25 g	250 g	Pass through a fine sieve and place on a tray. Pass the fish through the seasoned flour, egg wash and breadcrumbs. Ensure that the fish is completely and properly coated. Place in the pre-heated oil or fat for the appropriate time or until the fish is golden brown. Place on absorbent paper and dress on a dish in the appropriate manner.
3	Parsley sprig	1	10	Wash, dry and deep fry. Use to garnish the fried fish.
	Lemon wedge	1	10	Remove the pips and pith and place with the fish. Serve accompanied with a sauceboat of tartare sauce (*see* Chapter 19: Cold preparations).

NOTES: This dish may be made with fillet of cod, plaice, sole, haddock, whiting or hake.

Tiny thin strips (les goujonettes) are approximately half the dimensions of goujons and are served at buffets.

☐   ☐   ☐

Deep-fried whitebait

Blanchailles frites

🥣 20 min   ♨ 2 min   ≋ 190°C

Step	Commodity	1 portion	10 portions	
1	Whitebait	100 g	1 kg	Pick over the whitebait and remove any damaged ones. Wash carefully and drain well and pat dry with a clean tea towel or absorbent paper.
	Flour	15 g	150 g	Season with salt and ground pepper.
2	Milk	20 ml	200 ml	Pour into a deep-sided tray. Pass the whitebait through the milk and then through the flour. Remove any excess flour and ensure that the fish are not stuck together. Place in the pre-heated oil or fat for the appropriate time or until the fish is golden brown. Place on absorbent paper and dress on a dish in the appropriate manner.
3	Parsley sprig	1	10	Wash, dry and deep fry. Use to garnish the fried fish.
	Lemon wedge	1	10	Remove the pips and pith and place with the fish.

Extensions

Devilled whitebait

Blanchailles diable

As above, but sprinkled with cayenne pepper.

☐   ☐   ☐

Deep-fried scampi

Scampi frit

Step	Commodity	1 portion	10 portions	🍲 30 min ♨ 4 min ≋ 185°C
1	Shelled scampi	100 g	1 kg	Wash and dry on absorbent paper or a clean tea towel.
	Flour	15 g	150 g	Place on a tray and season with salt and ground pepper.
	Eggs	½	5	Break into a jug and whisk together with a little milk and/or water.
2	Breadcrumbs	25 g	250 g	Pass through a fine sieve and place on a tray. Pass the scampi through the seasoned flour, egg wash and breadcrumbs. Ensure that the scampi is completely and properly coated. Place in the pre-heated oil or fat for the appropriate time or until the fish is golden brown. Place on absorbent paper and dress on a dish in the appropriate manner.
3	Parsley sprig	1	10	Wash and dry. Use to garnish the fried fish.
	Lemon wedge	1	10	Remove the pips and pith and place with the fish. Serve accompanied with a sauceboat of tartare sauce.

NOTE: This dish may be done with oysters or scallops

☐   ☐   ☐

Deep-fried seafood

Fritto misto mare

Step	Commodity	1 portion	10 portions	🍲 1 hr ♨ 5 min ≋ 185°C
1	Flour	15 g	150 g	Season with salt and ground pepper.
	Milk	20 ml	200 ml	Pour into a deep-sided tray.
2	Shelled scampi	25 g	250 g	Pass through the milk and seasoned flour. Shake off excess flour and ensure that they do not stick together.
	Prepared scallops	25 g	250 g	As above
	Fish fillets	25 g	250 g	Cut into goujons and prepare as above.
	Mussels	25 g	250 g	Prepare as above. Place in the pre-heated oil or fat for the appropriate time or until the fish is golden brown. Place on absorbent paper and dress on a dish in the appropriate manner.
3	Parley sprig	1	10	Wash, dry and deep fry. Use to garnish the fried fish.
	Lemon wedge	1	10	Remove the pips and pith and place with the dish.

NOTE: This dish may also be prepared by first passing the fish/shellfish through seasoned flour and then a battering before deep frying.

☐   ☐   ☐

12

275

Deep-fried vegetables

Deep fried crisps

Pommes chips

Step	Commodity	1 portion	10 portions
1	Potatoes	150 g	1½ kg

🥣 45 min   ♨ 4 min   ≋ 190°C

Peel, wash and cut into very thin slices on a mandolin. Rinse well in cold running water to remove the starch. Dry in a clean tea towel or absorbent paper. Place in the pre-heated fat or oil for the appropriate time or until golden brown, agitating with a spider to prevent the potatoes from sticking together. Drain well and place on absorbent paper. Sprinkle with salt and serve hot as a garnish.

☐   ☐   ☐

Deep fried wafer potatoes

Pommes gauffrettes

Step	Commodity	1 portion	10 portions
1	Potatoes	150 g	1½ kg

🥣 45 min   ♨ 4 min   ≋ 190°C

Peel and wash. Using the corrugated blade on the mandolin, cut a slice giving a half turn between each slice to obtain a trellis pattern. Rinse well in cold running water to remove the starch. Dry in a clean tea towel or absorbent paper. Place in the pre-heated fat or oil for the appropriate time or until golden brown, agitating with a spider to prevent the potatoes from sticking together. Drain well and place on absorbent paper. Sprinkle with salt and serve hot as a garnish.

☐   ☐   ☐

Straw potatoes

Pommes pailles

Step	Commodity	1 portion	10 portions
1	Potatoes	150 g	1½ kg

🥣 45 min   ♨ 4 min   ≋ 190°C

Peel, wash and cut into very fine julienne either by hand or on a mandolin. Rinse well in cold running water to remove the starch. Dry in a clean tea towel or absorbent paper. Place in the pre-heated fat or oil for the appropriate time or until golden brown, agitating with a spider to prevent the potatoes from sticking together. Drain well and place on absorbent paper. Sprinkle with salt and serve hot as a garnish for steaks or chops.

☐   ☐   ☐

Deep-fried matchstick potatoes

Pommes alumettes

45 min   4 min   190°C

Step	Commodity	1 portion	10 portions
1	Potatoes	150 g	1½ kg

Peel, wash and cut into 5 cm × 3 mm × 3 mm strips. Rinse well in cold running water to remove the starch. Dry in a clean tea towel or absorbent paper. Place in the pre-heated fat or oil for the appropriate time or until golden brown, agitating with a spider to prevent the potatoes from sticking together. Drain well and place on absorbent paper. Sprinkle with salt and serve.

☐   ☐   ☐

Deep-fried chipped potatoes

Pommes frites

Blanching time: 5–6 min   Blanching temperature: 165°C

45 min   4 min   190°C

Step	Commodity	1 portion	10 portions
1	Potatoes	150 g	1½ kg

Peel, wash and cut into 5 cm × 1 cm × 1 cm strips. Rinse well in cold running water to remove the starch. Dry in a clean tea towel or absorbent paper. Blanch in the pre-heated fat or oil for the appropriate time. Remove, drain and lay out on absorbent paper. Cook to order as required. Deep fry for the appropriate time or until golden brown, agitating with a spider to prevent the potatoes from sticking together. Drain well and place on absorbent paper. Sprinkle with salt and serve.

☐   ☐   ☐

Bataille potatoes

Pommes batailles

Blanching time: 5–6 min   Blanching temperature: 165°C

45 min   4 min   190°Cr

Step	Commodity	1 portion	10 portions
1	Potatoes	150 g	1½ kg

Peel, wash and cut into 1 cm cubes. Rinse well in cold running water to remove the starch. Dry in a clean tea towel or absorbent paper. Blanch in the pre-heated fat or oil for the appropriate time. Remove, drain and lay out on absorbent paper. Cook to order as required. Deep fry for the appropriate time or until golden brown, agitating with a spider to prevent the potatoes from sticking together. Drain well and place on absorbent paper. Sprinkle with salt and serve.

☐   ☐   ☐

12

Croquette potatoes

Pommes croquettes

⌣ 45 min   🍲 4–5 min   ≋ 185°C

Step	Commodity	1 portion	10 portions	
1	Flour	15 g	150 g	Place on a tray and season with salt and ground pepper.
	Eggs	½	5	Break into a jug and whisk together with a little milk and/or water.
	Breadcrumbs	25 g	250 g	Pass through a fine sieve and place on a tray.
2	Duchesse potato mix	100 g	1 kg	Place on a floured surface. Using a palette knife roll into a 2 cm diameter cylinder and cut into pieces 5 cm long. Pass the potatoes through the seasoned flour, egg wash and breadcrumbs. Ensure that the potato is completely and properly coated. Remould with the palette knife. Place in the pre-heated oil or fat for the appropriate time or until golden brown. Remove, drain and lay out on absorbent paper. Cook to order as required. Deep fry for the appropriate time or until golden brown. Drain well and place on absorbent paper. Serve garnished with picked parsley.

☐   ☐   ☐

Almond potatoes

Pommes amandines

⌣ 45 min   🍲 4–5 min   ≋ 185°C

Step	Commodity	1 portion	10 portions	
1	Flour	15 g	150 g	Place on a tray and season.
	Eggs	½	5	Break into a jug and whisk with a little milk and/or water.
	Breadcrumbs	25 g	250 g	Pass through a fine sieve and place on a tray.
	Nibbed almonds	10 g	100 g	Mix well with the breadcrumbs.
2	Duchesse potato mix	100 g	1 kg	Place on a floured surface. Using a palette knife roll into a 2 cm diameter cylinder and cut into pieces 5 cm long. Pass the potatoes through the seasoned flour, egg wash and breadcrumbs and almond mixture. Ensure that the potato is completely and properly coated. Remould with the palette knife. Place in the pre-heated oil or fat for the appropriate time or until golden brown. Remove, drain and lay out on absorbent paper. Cook to order as required. Deep fry for the appropriate time or until golden brown. Drain well and place on absorbent paper. Serve garnished with picked parsley.

☐   ☐   ☐

Berny potatoes

Pommes Berney

Step	Commodity	1 portion	10 portions				
				⏲ 45 min	🍲 4–5 min	≋ 185°C	
1	Flour	15 g	150 g	Place on a tray and season with salt and ground pepper.
	Eggs	½	5	Break into a jug and whisk together with a little milk.
	Breadcrumbs	25 g	250 g	Pass through a fine sieve and place on a tray.
	Nibbed almonds	10 g	100 g	Mix well with the breadcrumbs.
2	Duchesse potato mix	100 g	1 kg	Place in a bowl.
	Fresh truffles	10 g	100 g	Finely dice and add. Mix together well. Place on a floured surface. Using a palette knife roll into a 2 cm diameter cylinder and shape in small apricots. Pass the potatoes through the seasoned flour, egg wash and breadcrumbs. Ensure that the potato is completely and properly coated. Remould and decorate the top with a washed parsley stem to represent the stalk. Place in the pre-heated oil or fat for the appropriate time or until golden brown. Remove, drain and lay out on absorbent paper. Serve in the appropriate manner.

☐   ☐   ☐

Royal potatoes
Florentine potatoes

Pommes royale
Pommes Florentin

Step	Commodity	1 portion	10 portions				
				⏲ 45 min	🍲 4–5 min	≋ 185°C	
1	Flour	15 g	150 g	Place on a tray and season with salt and ground pepper.
	Eggs	½	5	Break into a jug and whisk together with a little milk and/or water.
	Breadcrumbs	25 g	250 g	Pass through a fine sieve and place on a tray.
	Vermicelli	5 g	50 g	Break into very small pieces.
2	Duchesse potato mix	100 g	1 kg	Place in a bowl.
	Cooked ham	25 g	250 g	Finely dice and add to the potato. Mix together well. Place on a floured surface. Using a palette knife roll into a 2 cm diameter cylinder and cut into pieces 5 cm long. Pass the potatoes through the seasoned flour, egg wash and breadcrumbs. Ensure that the potato is completely and properly coated. Remould with the palette knife. Place in the pre-heated oil or fat for the appropriate time or until golden brown. Remove, drain and lay out an absorbent paper. Deep fry for the appropriate time or until golden brown. Drain well and place on absorbent paper. Serve in the appropriate manner.

☐   ☐   ☐

Dauphine potatoes

Pommes Dauphine

☋ 45 min   4–5 min   ≋ 175°C

Step	Commodity	1 portion	10 portions	
1	Duchesse potato mix	150 g	1 kg	Place in a bowl and season with salt and ground pepper.
	Choux paste*	50 ml	500 ml	Add to the duchesse potato and mix together thoroughly. Portion, allowing three per portion. Mould into cylinder shapes 5 cm × 2 cm on greased paper. Place in the pre-heated oil or fat for the appropriate time or until golden brown. Remove, drain and lay out on absorbent paper. Cook to order as required, using a spider to move the potatoes around the fryer. Deep fry for the appropriate time or until golden brown. Drain well and place on absorbent paper. Serve garnished with picked parsley.

* No sugar in the pastry (*see* Chapter 14: Baking).

Extension

Lorette potatoes (pommes Lorette) are made using the same mixture and the same quantities but the mixture is moulded into short, cigar-like shapes.

☐   ☐   ☐

Deep-fried soufflé potatoes

Pommes soufflées

Blanching time: 5 min   Blanching temperature: 175°C

☋ 30 min   4 min   ≋ 190°C

Step	Commodity	1 portion	10 portions	
1	Potatoes	120 g	1.2 kg	Peel, wash and cut into 5 cm × 1 cm × 1 cm strips. Cut the raw potatoes into cylindrical shapes. Cut into ¼ cm slices. Rinse well in cold running water to remove the starch. Dry in a clean tea towel or absorbent paper. Blanch in the pre-heated fat or oil, agitating with a spider for the appropriate time or when the potatoes begin to soufflé. Remove and hold until the frier has reached finishing temperature (190°C). Deep fry for the appropriate time or until the potatoes have souffléd completely and are golden brown and crisp. Drain well and place on absorbent paper. Sprinkle with salt and serve hot as a garnish.

☐   ☐   ☐

Deep-fried aubergine (egg plant)

Aubergine frite à la française

🥣 30 min　♨ 3–4 min　≋ 190°C

Step	Commodity	1 portion	10 portions	
1	Aubergine	100 g	1 kg	Remove and trim both ends. Remove the skin and cut the aubergine into ½ cm slices. Season with salt and ground pepper.
2	Flour	15 g	150 g	Place on a tray and season with salt and ground pepper.
	Milk	20 ml	200 ml	Pour into a deep-sided tray. Pass the aubergine through the milk and then through the flour. Remove any excess flour and ensure that the aubergines are not stuck together. Place in the pre-heated oil or fat for the appropriate time or until golden brown and crisp. Remove and place on absorbent paper and dress on a dish in the appropriate manner.

☐　☐　☐

Deep-fried courgettes

Courgettes frites à la française

🥣 30 min　♨ 2–3 min　≋ 190°C

Step	Commodity	1 portion	10 portions	
1	Courgettes	100 g	1 kg	Remove and trim both ends. Peel the skin and cut the courgettes into ½ cm slices. Season with salt and ground pepper.
2	Flour	15 g	150 g	Place on a tray and season with salt and ground pepper.
	Milk	20 ml	200 ml	Pour into a deep-sided tray. Pass the courgettes through the milk and then through the flour. Remove any excess flour and ensure that the courgettes are not stuck together. Place in the pre-heated oil or fat for the appropriate time or until golden brown and crisp. Remove and place on absorbent paper and dress on a dish in the appropriate manner.

12

☐　☐　☐

Deep-fried mushrooms

Champignons frits

🥣 30 min　♨ 2–3 min　≋ 190°C

Step	Commodity	1 portion	10 portions	
1	Button mushrooms	100 g	1 kg	Wash, trim the stalks and peel if necessary.*
2	Flour	15 g	150 g	Place on a tray and season with salt and ground pepper.
	Batter	20 ml	200 ml	Pass the mushrooms through the seasoned flour and batter. Place in the pre-heated oil or fat for the appropriate time or until the mushrooms are golden brown and crisp. Place on absorbent paper and dress on a dish in the appropriate manner.
3	Parsley sprig	1	10	Wash, dry and deep fry. Use to garnish.
	Lemon wedge	1	10	Remove the pips and pith and place with the mushrooms. Serve accompanied with a sauceboat of mayonnaise-based sauce (see Chapter 19: Cold preparations).

* Peel if the skin is damaged or darkened.

☐　☐　☐

Deep-fried parsnips

🥣 1½ hr   ♨ 4 min   ≋ 185°C

Step	Commodity	1 portion	10 portions	
1	Parsnips	100 g	1 kg	Wash, peel and cut in half. Cut into 3 cm batons, trim the stalk and place in a saucepan of boiling salted water. Return to the boil and simmer for 15 minutes. Remove, refresh and drain well.
2	Flour	15 g	150 g	Place on a tray and season with salt and ground pepper.
	Batter	25 ml	250 ml	Pass the parsnips through the seasoned flour and batter. Place in the pre-heated oil or fat for the appropriate time or until the batter is golden brown and crisp. Place on absorbent paper and dress on a dish in the appropriate manner. Sprinkle with salt and serve.

NOTE: This dish may be made with cooked celery, salsify, artichoke hearts, asparagus tips, cauliflower, fennel, carrots, beans, brussel sprouts and cucumber.

☐   ☐   ☐

French fried onions

🥣 30 min   ♨ 2–3 min   ≋ 185°C

Step	Commodity	1 portion	10 portions	
1	Onions	50 g	500 g	Peel, leave whole and cut into 2 mm slices against the grain. Separate into rings.
2	Flour	15 g	150 g	Season with salt and ground pepper.
	Milk	20 ml	200 ml	Pour into a deep-sided tray. Pass the onion rings through the milk and then through the flour. Remove any excess flour and ensure that the fish are not stuck together. Place in the pre-heated oil or fat for the appropriate time or until the fish is golden brown. Place on absorbent paper and dress on a dish in the appropriate manner.

☐   ☐   ☐

Deep-fried meat

Southern style chicken

Step	Commodity	1 portion	10 portions	⏲ 45 min 🍲 10 min ≋ 175°–190°C
1	Chicken cut for sauté	250 g	2½ g	Remove excess skin, dry in kitchen paper and season with salt and ground black pepper.
	Flour	15 g	150 g	Season with salt, milled black pepper, a pinch of curry powder and ground chilli pepper.
	Batter	50 ml	500 ml	Prepare as per recipe. Pass the chicken through the seasoned flour then the batter and deep fry at the correct temperature for the appropriate time or until golden brown. Remove and place on absorbent paper to remove excess oil or fat. Keep warm.
2	Pineapple rings	1	10	Pass through the seasoned flour and the batter. Deep fry for 5 minutes at the same temperature. Place on absorbent paper to remove excess oil or fat and dress on a dish in the appropriate manner. Serve with the chicken.

NOTE: This dish is served with 1 slice of grilled bacon per portion, one sweetcorn fritter (*see* Chapter 11: Shallow frying) and a sauceboat of tomato sauce.

☐   ☐   ☐

Chicken Kiev

Suprême de volaille Kiev

Step	Commodity	1 portion	10 portions	⏲ 2 hr 🍲 15 min ≋ 175°–190°C
1	Chicken supreme	1 × 150 g	10 × 150 g	Trim the bone and flatten the breast lightly, refrigerate.
2	Butter	25 g	250 g	Place in a bowl and soften.
	Garlic	½ clove	5 cloves	Peel, crush to a purée with salt. Add to the butter.
	Chopped parsley	½ tsp	5 tsp	Add and mix together well. Divide into portions and place the appropriate amount in the centre of the chicken breast. Roll the breast up to enclose the garlic butter. Allow to set in the fridge for 30 minutes.
3	Flour	15 g	150 g	Season with salt and milled black pepper.
	Eggs	½	5	Break into a bowl and whisk together with a little water and/or milk. Place in a deep-sided tray.
	Breadcrumbs	25 g	250 g	Finely sieve and place on a tray. Pass the chicken through the flour, egg wash and breadcrumbs. Ensure that each suprême is evenly and fully coated. Cook at the correct temperature for the appropriate time or until golden brown. Place on absorbent paper to remove excess oil or fat and dress on a dish in the appropriate manner. Place a cutlet frill on the end of each bone.

NOTE: This dish may be made using escalope of pork, veal or turkey.

☐   ☐   ☐

12

Chicken cordon bleu

Suprême de volaille cordon bleu

🍲 2 hr　♨ 10 min　≋ 175°–190°C

Step	Commodity	1 portion	10 portions	
1	Chicken suprêmes	1 × 150 g	10 × 150 g	Trim the bone and flatten the breast. Lay each suprême out on a tray.
	Sliced cooked ham	1	10	Place on top of the flattened chicken.
	Gruyère cheese	1 × 25 g	10 × 25 g	Lay in the centre of the ham. Fold the ham around the cheese and the chicken suprême around the ham. Place in the fridge to set.
	Flour	15 g	150 g	Season with salt and milled black pepper.
	Eggs	½	5	Break into a bowl and whisk together with a little water and milk. Place in a deep-sided tray.
	Breadcrumbs	25 g	250 g	Finely sieve and place on a tray. Pass the chicken through the flour, egg wash and breadcrumbs. Ensure that each suprême is evenly and fully coated. Cook at the correct temperature for the appropriate time or until the suprême is golden brown. Place on absorbent paper to remove excess oil or fat and dress on a dish in the appropriate manner. Place a cutlet frill on the end of the bone.

NOTE: This dish may be made using an escalope of pork, veal or turkey instead of chicken.

☐　　☐　　☐

Scotch eggs

🍲 45 min　♨ 15 min　≋ 175°–190°C

Step	Commodity	1 portion	10 portions	
1	Eggs	1	10	Plunge the eggs into boiling water, re-boil and cook for 10 minutes. Refresh and allow to cool. Remove the shell and dry with absorbent paper.
2	Sausage meat	75 g	750 g	Divide into appropriate portions and completely cover each egg.
	Flour	15 g	150 g	Season with salt and pepper.
	Eggs	½	5	Break into a bowl and whisk together with a little milk. Place in a deep-sided tray.
	Breadcrumbs	25 g	250 g	Finely sieve and place on a tray. Pass the egg through the flour, egg wash and breadcrumbs. Ensure that the eggs are evenly and fully coated. Cook at the correct temperature for the appropriate time or until golden brown. Place on absorbent paper to remove excess oil or fat and dress on a dish in the appropriate manner. Serve hot, garnished with fried parsley sprigs and a sauceboat of tomato sauce or cold, garnished with a salad and salad dressing.

☐　　☐　　☐

Deep fried escalope of veal

Wiener Schnitzel

🥣 45 min　🍲 6 min　≋ 175°–190°C

Step	Commodity	1 portion	10 portions	
1	Escalope of veal	1 × 150 g	10 × 150 g	Batten out. Season with salt and pepper.
	Flour	15 g	150 g	Season with salt and milled black pepper.
	Eggs	½	5	Break into a bowl and whisk together with a little water and/or milk. Place in a deep-sided tray.
	Breadcrumbs	25 g	250 g	Finely sieve and place on a tray. Pass the escalopes through the flour, egg wash and breadcrumbs. Ensure that the eggs are evenly and fully coated. Cook at the correct temperature for the appropriate time or until golden brown. Place on absorbent paper to remove excess oil or fat and dress on a dish in the appropriate manner.
2	Sliced roundel of lemon	1	10	Place on the cooked escalopes.
	Parsley sprigs	1	10	Wash, dry and deep fry. Place on absorbent paper to remove excess oil or fat and place one on each lemon slice.

☐　　☐　　☐

Fried pieces of chicken

Fritots de volaille

🥣 45 min　🍲 7 min　≋ 175°–190°C

Step	Commodity	1 portion	10 portions	
1	Diced chicken	150 g	1½ kg	Trim off excess fat and remove and discard any skin.
	Flour	15 g	150 g	Season with salt and milled black pepper.
	Batter	50 ml	500 ml	Prepare as per recipe. Pass the chicken through the seasoned flour then the batter. Deep fry at the correct temperature for the appropriate time or until golden brown. Remove and place an absorbent paper to remove excess oil or fat. Keep warm.
2	Parsley sprigs	1	10	Wash, dry and deep fry. Place on absorbent paper to remove excess oil or fat. Use to garnish the chicken.

NOTE: This dish may be accompanied with a sweet and sour sauce and braised rice. The chicken may also be replaced with pieces of pork, veal, or turkey.

☐　　☐　　☐

12

Meat croquettes

Step	Commodity	1 portion	10 portions	
1	Cooked meat	50 g	500 g	Mince coarsely or dice small. Place in a suitably sized saucepan.
	White sauce*	25 ml	250 ml	Add and bind together. Bring to the boil. Remove from the heat and allow to cool slightly.
	Egg yolks	¼	2	Add and mix in thoroughly.
	Chopped parsley	pinch	2 tsp	Add.
	Nutmeg	pinch	½ tsp	Add and season with salt and ground pepper. Mix well together. Spread the mixture on a buttered tray and allow to cool and set. Divide into the appropriate portions allowing 2 per portion. Shape each piece into a cylinder.
2	Flour	15 g	150 g	Place on a tray and season with salt and ground pepper.
	Eggs	½	5	Break into a jug and whisk together with a little milk.
	Breadcrumbs	25 g	250 g	Pass through a fine sieve and place on a tray. Pass the croquette through the seasoned flour, egg wash and breadcrumbs. Ensure that the croquette is completely and properly coated. Place in the pre-heated fat/oil for the required time or until the croquettes are golden brown. Place on absorbent paper to remove excess oil. Serve on a dish paper on a flat.
3	Parsley sprig	1	10	Wash, dry and deep fry. Use to garnish the croquettes. Serve with a demi-glace based sauce (see Chapter 5: Boiling).

* Velouté or béchamel (see Chapter 4: Boiling).

Extensions of basic meat croquette recipe

Dish	French term	Meat used	Sauce
Beef croquettes	Croquettes de boeuf	Beef	Devilled
Chicken croquettes	Croquettes de volaille	Chicken	Piquant
Chicken and ham croquettes	Croquettes de volaille et jambon	Half chicken and half ham	Chasseur
Chicken and mushroom croquettes	Croquettes de volaille et champignons	Chicken and 10 g of sweated mushrooms per portion	Madeira
Game croquettes	Croquettes de gibier	Cooked pheasant, venison, rabbit	Port wine and redcurrant jelly

☐   ☐   ☐

Meat cutlets

Step	Commodity	1 portion	10 portions	
				⤵ 1 hr ♨ 5 min ≋ 175°–185°C
1	Cooked meat	50 g	500 g	Mince coarsely or dice small. Place in a suitably sized saucepan.
	White sauce*	25 ml	250 ml	Add and bind together. Bring to the boil. Remove from the heat and allow to cool slightly.
	Egg yolks	¼	2	Add and mix in thoroughly.
	Chopped parsley	pinch	2 tsp	Add.
	Nutmeg	pinch	½ tsp	Add and season with salt and ground pepper. Mix well together. Spread the mixture on a buttered tray and allow to cool and set. Divide into the appropriate portions allowing 2 per portion. Shape each piece into a cutlet shape.
2	Flour	15 g	150 g	Place on a tray and season with salt and ground pepper.
	Eggs	½	5	Break into a jug and whisk together with a little milk.
	Breadcrumbs	25 g	250 g	Pass through a fine sieve and place on a tray. Pass the cutlet through the seasoned flour, egg wash and breadcrumbs. Ensure that the cutlet is completely and properly coated. Insert a length of blanched macaroni in the narrow end to imitate a cutlet bone. Place in the pre-heated fat/oil for the required time or until the cutlets are golden brown. Place on absorbent paper to remove excess oil. Serve on a dish paper on a flat. Place a cutlet frill on the end of the 'bone'.
3	Parsley sprig	1	10	Wash, dry and deep fry. Use to garnish the cutlets. Serve with a demi-glace based sauce (see Chapter 4: Boiling).

* Velouté or béchamel (see Chapter 4: Boiling).

Extensions of basic meat croquette recipe

Dish	French term	Meat used	Sauce
Beef cutlets	Côtelettes de boeuf	Beef	Devilled
Chicken cutlets	Côtelettes de volaille	Chicken	Piquant
Chicken and ham cutlets	Côtelettes de volaille et jambon	Half chicken and half ham	Chasseur
Chicken and mushroom cutlets	Côtelettes de volaille et champignons	Chicken and 10 g of sweated mushrooms per portion	Madeira
Game cutlets	Côtelettes de gibier	Cooked pheasant, venison, rabbit	Port wine and redcurrant jelly

□   □   □

12

Kromeskis Russian style

Cromesquis à la russe

Step	Commodity	1 portion	10 portions	
				🍲 1½ hr ♨ 5 min ≋ 175°–185°C
1	Cooked chicken	35 g	350 g	Mince finely and place in a suitably sized saucepan.
	Cooked tongue	15 g	150 g	Mince finely and add.
	White sauce*	25 ml	250 ml	Add and bind together. Bring to the boil. Remove from the heat and allow to cool slightly.
	Egg yolks	¼	2	Add and mix in thoroughly.
	Chopped parsley	pinch	2 tsp	Add.
	Nutmeg	pinch	½ tsp	Add and season with salt and ground pepper. Mix well together. Spread the mixture on a buttered tray and allow to cool and set. Divide into the appropriate portions, allowing 2 per portion. Shape each piece into a cylinder.
	Streaky bacon	1 slice	10 slices	Wrap around the croquette.
2	Flour	15 g	150 g	Place on a tray and season with salt and ground pepper.
	Batter	50 ml	500 ml	Prepare as per recipe. Pass the croquette through the seasoned flour and then the batter. Deep fry at the correct temperature for the appropriate time or until golden brown. Remove and place on absorbent paper to remove excess oil/fat. Keep warm.
3	Parsley sprig	1	10	Wash, dry and deep fry, Use to garnish the croquettes. Serve with a sauceboat of tomato sauce or smitane (see Chapter 5: Boiling).

NOTE: This dish may also be shallow fried.

☐   ☐   ☐

Durham cutlets

Step	Commodity	1 portion	10 portions		🥣 1 hr ♨ 5 min ≋ 175°–185°C
1	Cooked beef	50 g	500 g		Mince finely.
	Mashed potato	25 g	250 g		Add.
	Onions	15 g	150 g		Peel, dice finely and add.
	Chopped parsley	pinch	2 tsp		Add.
	Egg yolks	¼	2		Add and mix in thoroughly. Season with salt and ground pepper. Mix together well. Divide into the appropriate portions, allowing 2 per portion. Shape each piece into a cutlet.
2	Flour	15 g	150 g		Place on a tray and season with salt and ground pepper.
	Eggs	½	5		Break into a bowl and whisk together with a little milk.
	Breadcrumbs	25 g	250 g		Pass through a fine sieve and place on a tray. Pass the cutlet through the seasoned flour, egg wash and breadcrumbs. Insert a length of blanched macaroni in the narrow end to imitate a cutlet bone. Place in the pre-heated fat or oil for the required time or until the cutlets are golden brown. Serve on a dish paper on a flat. Place a cutlet frill on the end of the 'bone'.
3	Parsley sprig	1	10		Wash, dry and deep fry. Use to garnish the cutlets. Serve with a jus lié sauce (*see* Chapter 4: Boiling).

☐   ☐   ☐

12

Miscellaneous deep-fried dishes

Cheese fritters

Beignets soufflés au fromage

🥣 1½ hr   ♨ 6–7 min   ≋ 185°C

Step	Commodity	1 portion	10 portions		
1	Water	25 ml	250 ml		Place in a suitably sized saucepan and boil. Reduce to a simmer.
	Butter	5 g	50 g		Add and allow to melt slowly.
2	Strong flour	16 g	160 g		Add and mix in well. Cook the mixture until it becomes smooth and does not stick to the sides of the saucepan. Allow to cool slightly.
	Eggs	½ equiv	3		Break into a jug and whisk. Add to the flour mixture a little at a time until a smooth pipable mixture is achieved.
	Grated cheese	10 g	100 g		Add and mix in well. Season with salt and cayenne pepper. Shape into ovals between two dessert spoons into walnut sized pieces and place onto oiled silicon paper. Place in the pre-heated oil or fat for the appropriate time or until the fritters soufflé and become crisp and golden brown. Place on absorbent paper. Dress in the appropriate manner.
3	Grated parmesan	5 g	50 g		Sprinkle over the top and serve hot with picked parsley.

☐   ☐   ☐

Crab fritters

Beignets soufflés de crabe

🥄 1 hr   ♨ 6–7 min   ≋ 185°C

Step	Commodity	1 portion	10 portions	
1	Water	25 ml	250 ml	Place in a suitably sized saucepan and boil. Reduce to a simmer.
	Butter	5 g	50 g	Add and allow to melt slowly.
2	Strong flour	16 g	160 g	Add and mix in well. Cook the mixture until it becomes smooth and does not stick to the sides of the saucepan. Allow to cool slightly.
	Eggs	½ equiv	3	Break into a jug and whisk. Add to the flour mixture a little at a time until a smooth pipable mixture is achieved.
	White crabmeat	10 g	10 g	Add and mix in well. Season with salt and pepper. Shape into ovals between two dessert spoons into walnut sized pieces and place onto oiled silicon paper. Place in the pre-heated oil or fat for the appropriate time or until the fritters soufflé and become crisp and golden brown. Place on absorbent paper. Dress in the appropriate manner.
2	Lemon wedges	1	10	Use to garnish the beignets.

☐   ☐   ☐

Jam doughnuts

🥄 2½ hr   ♨ 6–7 min   ≋ 175°C

Step	Commodity	1 portion	10 portions	
1	Strong flour	25 g	250 g	Sieve into a suitably sized bowl and add a pinch of salt.
	Sugar	3 g	30 g	Add and mix in well.
	Butter or margarine	2.5 g	25 g	Add and rub in well to achieve a breadcrumb-like consistency.
	Egg	⅛	1	Break into a bowl and beat. Add to the flour mixture.
2	Tepid water	10 ml	100 ml	Place in a jug.
	Yeast	1 g	10 g	Add to the water and dissolve completely. Leave to ferment until bubbles appear on the top (10–15 minutes). Add and knead (10–15 minutes) to a smooth pliable dough. Cover and place in a warm place until the mixture has doubled in size (45 minutes). Remove and knock the air out of the dough by pressing firmly down with the knuckles of both hands. This process is known as 'knocking back'. Cover and allow to rest for a further 15 minutes. Divide into the appropriate portions, allowing 1 per portion. Roll up in the palm of the hands to form a smooth round ball.
3	Raspberry jam	10 g	100 g	Smooth with a palette knife and place in a piping bag with a fine nozzle. Insert a little jam into the centre of each doughnut. Dampen the edges of the hole and reseal. Place the doughnuts on a baking tray and allow to double in size (40 minutes). Place in the pre-heated deep frier for the appropriate time. Turn each doughnut over halfway through cooking. Cook until the doughnuts are golden brown. Remove and drain well.
4	Castor sugar	15 g	150 g	Place on a tray and season with ground cinnamon. Roll each freshly cooked doughnut through the sugar and place on a serving dish.

NOTE: Doughnuts can be cooked and served plain without the jam filling.

Deep-fried banana fritters

Beignets de banane

Step	Commodity	1 portion	10 portions			
				⌣ 30 min	≋≋≋ 4 min	≋ 185°C
1	Bananas	1	10	Peel bananas as required. Cut lengthwise and then in half widthwise.		
2	Flour	15 g	150 g	Place on a tray.		
	Batter	25 ml	250 ml	Pass the banana quarters through the flour and batter. Place in the pre-heated oil or fat for the appropriate time or until the batter is golden brown and crisp. Place on absorbent paper and dress on a dish in the appropriate manner. Serve with apricot, raspberry or strawberry sauce (*see* Chapter 13: Baking and sweet preparations).		

NOTES: This dish may be made with apricot halves, peach halves or pineapple rings. Beignets may be coated with breadcrumbs instead of batter.

☐ ☐ ☐

WHAT WENT WRONG?

Problem	Caused by	To Rectify
Potatoes stick together during cooking	(1) Not washing the starch off the potatoes before frying.	Cannot be rectified.
	(2) Blanching at too low a temperature.	Cannot be rectified.
	(3) Not shaking the basket during cooking.	Cannot be rectified.
Fried potatoes are soggy after cooking.	Cooking at too low a temperature.	Cannot be rectified.
The oil starts to smoke or foam at cooking temperature.	(1) Using oil or fat that has been contaminated by frying foods with a high starch or sugar content.	Discard the oil or fat. Clean the fryer thoroughly and re-fill with fresh oil or fat.
	(2) A fault in the thermostat and the oil or fat is actually over-heating	Discard the oil or fat. Clean the fryer thoroughly and re-fill with fresh oil or fat. Have the thermostat checked.
Cooked food is covered with black specks.	The oil or fat has not be strained of cooked food particles before use.	Cannot be rectified.
Croquettes or rissoles burst open during cooking.	(1) Not coating properly.	Cannot be rectified.
	(2) Cooking at too low a temperature.	Cannot be rectified.
Breadcrumbs/batter will not colour and are soggy.	(1) Fat was not hot enough.	Cannot be rectified.
	(2) Deep frying too many items at once.	Cannot be rectified. Batch cook items to prevent the fat temperature from falling too low. Always allow enough time for the fat or oil to regain the correct cooking temperature between batches.

(Continued)

Problem	Caused by	To Rectify
Breadcrumbs/batter will not colour and falls off the item.	Not using strong flour for the batter.	Cannot be rectified.
Food breaks up during cooking.	(1) Cooking at too low a temperature.	Cannot be rectified.
	(2) Too many items are cooked at once, reducing the temperature.	Cannot be rectified.
	(3) Using a frying basket and the item has stuck to the wire.	Cannot be rectified.
Batter runs off during cooking/breadcrumbs come away during cooking.	(1) The batter is too thin.	Cannot be rectified.
	(2) Food was not dried before cooking.	Cannot be rectified.
	(3) Cooking at too low a temperature.	Cannot be rectified.
Finished item has a doughy layer	Batter was too thick.	Cannot be rectified.
Batter over-colours before the item is cooked.	(1) Cooking at too high a temperature.	Cannot be rectified.
	(2) Food pieces are too thick.	Cannot be rectified.
Food browns before the item is cooked.	Using contaminated oil or fat.	Cannot be rectified.
Cooked item lacks flavour.	(1) Using poor quality, stale commodities.	Cannot be rectified.
	(2) Batter and/or flour was not seasoned correctly.	Cannot be rectified.

BAKING AND SWEET PREPARATIONS

Baking is the cooking of food in an oven by dry convected heat. The heat is usually generated by electric elements or gas burners, though other fuels are sometimes used, for example charcoal or wood. The natural moisture within the food is heated sufficiently to produce steam which in turn modifies the dry air. The heat produced changes the structure of raw foods and makes it edible. In the case of sponges it is the chemical action caused by the heat that gives aeration.

In baking the food never comes into contact with liquid and usually the only moisture present is in the form of steam given off by the cooking foods. During baking the dry brown crusty surface formed on food can be achieved by one or more factors:

(a) The high temperature of baking;
(b) The natural sugars present in some foods, or sugar added to the recipe;
(c) Amino acids present in foods such as eggs;
(d) Nitrogen compounds in foods such as milk.

NOTES: Some baked foods benefit by the introduction of steam which helps to form a desirable surface crust, as in bread or choux pastry, or give a more gently heating effect with sponges and pastries. Baking is normally associated with cakes, doughs and pastries, though a wide variety of other foods can be baked including prepared meats, poultry, offal, game, some vegetables, potatoes and fish items.

Always ensure that the oven is preheated to the correct temperature before commencing to bake, as insufficient heat will cause the finished baked items to be inferior. It is also advisable to have the necessary tins or moulds prepared when baking sponge items, as 'raw' sponge mixtures deteriorate in the warm kitchen environment.

Accurate weighing and measuring is essential when preparing doughs and pastes as the wrong proportions can also cause the product to be inferior.

Terms and commodities associated with baking

Arrowroot A thickening agent obtained from the roots of the West Indian maranta plant.

Baking powder Produced by combining 2 parts cream of tartar to 1 part bicarbonate of soda.

Batch cooking Used when needs or oven space are insufficient to cope with demand. Cooking in batches.

Brushing To brush the food stuff with a wash before, during and/or after baking.

Bandied peel Dried orange, lemon and lime. Mixed together to form mixed peel.

Cape gooseberry Also known as physalis peruviana which is similar in appearance to a ground cherry. Dipped in fondant and served as a petit four.

Cornflour A white powder milled from maize and consisting mainly of starch. Used for thickening and in certain cake mixtures.

Currants A dried grape used in puddings and cakes.

Dried fruits Currants, sultanas, raisins, glacé cherries, peel, figs, dates, apricots, peaches, apples, pears and prunes.

Dusting To lightly sprinkle food items with flour or icing sugar.

Finishing To finish a baked good for presentation, i.e. to coat with a glaze or a dusting of icing sugar, returning to a very hot oven for caramelising to give a gloss finish.

General purpose flour A combination of hard and soft flour most suitable for general purpose items.

Ginger The ginger rhizome preserved in a heavy syrup.

Glacé cherries Cherries packed in a thick syrup.

Glaze A liquid made from sugar and water and used to brush some baked items that have a gloss finish.

Greasing To lightly coat baking tins or trays with oil or fat to prevent foods from sticking to them.

High ratio fats Specially prepared fats that will absorb more than usual moisture.

High ratio flour A special flour that is milled to a very fine particle size in order that it will absorb more moisture. It contains 40 per cent of the whole grain. Combined with a high ratio fat it can produce very economical cakes.

Knocked back The process of conditioning the dough by removing the gases after bulk fermentation time.

Lard Made from refined pork fat and used in the production of short pastry.

Loading The organisation of oven space to maximise efficiency and economic use.

Malted meal Used to make fruit malt loaves.

Margarine Produced from hydrogenated oil.

Marking To make an incision with a sharp blade to indicate portions or to decorate the top of goods.

Medium flour Made from a combination of strong flour and weak flour.

Pastry margarine A specially prepared margarine that is tougher than ordinary margarine and is suitable for making puff pastry.

Raisins There are two types: seedless and larger ones with stones (muscatel).

Recovery time The time needed by ovens between batches of food when cooking to return to the correct temperature.

Ribbon stage The stage at which a raw sponge mixture has doubled in bulk and is light and creamy.

Rub in method To incorporate fat into flour by rubbing between the fingers and thumbs to make a sandy texture.

Sago Produced from the pith of the sago palm. Used to garnish soups and in milk puddings.

Self-raising flour Produced by combining medium strength flour with baking powder – 10 g of baking powder to 500 g of flour. Sieve together at least three times.

Shortening A specially prepared fat, used in short pastry production.

Soft flour Sometimes known as weak flour, it is milled from predominantly English wheat. This flour is low in protein (gluten) – 8 per cent – and is ideally suited to rich cakes, sponges and short pastry. This flour may be labelled 'biscuit' or 'cake' flour.

Strong flour Milled from Canadian and American wheats and is high in gluten (13 per cent) which enables dough to be made which will hold its shape and become aerated with the gas of fermenting yeast, making it best suited to bread and puff pastry making.

Suet Prepared from the kidney fat of beef, used for suet pastry, dumplings, puddings and mincemeat.

Sugar Obtained from sugar beef or cane, sugar is available refined as granulated, castor, cube, or icing and unrefined as brown or demerara. It is used in most sweet preparations.

Sultanas A dried grape.

Tapioca Obtained from the roots of the cassava plant, it is available flaked or in seed form. Used for garnishing soups and in milk puddings.

Wash A liquid of egg, milk and/or water used to coat and give a glazed finish to baked items.

Well, to make a To part a dry mixture in a circular fashion on a table in order to mix in a liquid.

Wheatmeal flour A brown flour containing between 85–95 per cent of the whole grain, produced by blending a certain proportion of the brown skins of the wheat grain bran with white flour. Used for making scones and bread rolls.

White flour A general purpose flour made from milling the white floury endosperm of the wheat grain. The husk or bran and embryo germ being removed.

Wholemeal Contains 100 per cent of the whole grain.

Yeast Available fresh/pressed or dry/granules. It is a living organism, a minute fungus.

Chefs associated with bakery
The **Chef Pâtissier** bakes all doughs, pastry bases and sweet soufflés.
The **Chef Entremettier** bakes vegetables, potato dishes and savoury soufflés.
The **Chef Poisonnier** bakes all fish dishes.
The **Chef Saucier** will bake all savoury pastry goods.

SAFETY

Baking ovens can reach temperatures of 260°C and can give a nasty burn if due care and attention is not taken.

- Always use thick, dry, oven cloths/mittens when handling hot trays.
- Always take care when balancing and handling full baking trays in and out of ovens.
- Never overload trays or ovens.

FOODS SUITABLE FOR BAKING

Because of the dryness of the method, not all foods are suited to cooking by baking.

Meats, poultry and game

Joints of meats, poultry and game are not baked, but roasted in ovens. Meat, poultry and game preparations, usually in individual portions, can be coated with pastry, breadcrumbs or in a batter and be baked.

En papillotte is cooking in a sealed bag in an oven and is another way of baking meats, poultry, game and fish. Usually the food has been pre-cooked by another process. The specially prepared bag does not allow steam or cooking juices to escape, thus retaining a more natural flavour and nutritive value. The bag is usually served too and opened in front of the customer.

Cooked sausages are covered with batter and finished in the oven, as in toad in the hole.

Fish

Fish is baked either coated in breadcrumbs or pastry. Oily fish like herrings and mackerel need not be breadcrumbed and can be baked brushed with a little butter or fat to prevent the surface from drying out.

Rice

Rice always needs to be cooked in a liquid and when cooked in an oven the process is usually called braising. In sweet preparations rice is combined with milk, started off on top of the stove and finished in the oven to give a baked rice pudding.

Vegetables and fruits

There are few vegetables that can be cooked by this process. Potatoes and apples need their skins slitting to allow steam to escape and to prevent the potatoes from bursting during cooking.

Pastries, cakes and doughs

These foods are ideally suited to this method of cookery. The main ingredients of these foods are flour, milk and eggs and all contain protein. When the protein is baked it sets and this setting gives the food its final appearance. Flour also contains starch. Starch mixed with the liquid becomes thicker and this helps to hold the structure of the mixture in place until the proteins have set.

Doughs

A dough is made from strong flour, a little sugar, salt and a warm water (42°C) and yeast solution. Yeast is a living organism and can be killed by bad handling. It is not only used for its raising properties but also the flavour it produces. It needs to be mixed well into the dough so that the pockets of gas produced are the right size and are evenly distributed throughout.

Yeast needs four conditions for growth: moisture, warmth, food and time.

(a) The moisture is water, though milk is sometimes used. Milk, however, has the effect of retarding growth.

(b) Too high a temperature (60°C+) and it is killed, below 20°C and its growth is retarded, and at 0°C it is dormant. The ideal working temperature for yeast is between 25°–29°C. This

13

temperature and the moist conditions can be achieved by using a prover oven. Some doughs (brioche, danish and croissant) need to be fermented at a low temperature 15°–20°C.

(c) The food is sugar and the yeast converts it into dextrose to produce carbon dioxide, which in turn inflates the dough.

NOTES: Adding yeast directly to sugar will kill it and fermentation will not take place. Also, never add salt directly to yeast as this too will kill the yeast. It should also be noted that there are basic sugars present in wheat flour and so little or no sugar need be added to a basic bread dough.

(d) Yeast needs time to work and produce the required amount of carbon dioxide to give optimum size. Too much time and the yeast will over prove the item causing it to deflate. It might also mean that the dough has a sour taste and smell.

```
Terms associated with dough making

Baking Placing in a hot oven at a temperature
between 200°C–245°C for ordinary products and
175°C–195°C for sweetened doughs as the lower
temperature prevents the surface from browning
before the centre of the dough is cooked.
Bulk fermentation time (BFT) This is the period of
time from when the dough is made to the time
when it has doubled in size and is ready to be
knocked back.
Moulding Shaping the dough into an appropriate
shape.
Proving Allowing the shaped pieces of dough to
grow to size before being baked. This is carried
out in a prover with the aid of steam. The steam
not only helps growth, but also prevents the
dough from forming a dry skin.
Scaling Dividing the dough into pieces by weight.
```

CAKES

There are three types of cakes: plain, rich and sponge. They are classified according to the proportions of fat, sugar and eggs that they contain and the method by which they are made. The higher the proportion of fat and eggs in the mixture the richer the cake will be.

In general the rub-in method is used for plain cakes in which the proportion of fat to flour is half or less and the creaming method is used for richer cakes which contain more than half the amount of fat to flour. Before starting to prepare cakes it is useful to choose the correct size of cake tin and have the oven pre-heated.

```
Terms associated with doughs and cake
making

Pouring A mixture that is the consistency of
double cream and spreads slowly when dropped
from a spoon. Suitable for sponges.
Soft A mixture with as much liquid as possible
without the mixture becoming so soft that it
cannot be rolled. Suitable for yeast and scone
doughs.
Soft, dropping A mixture which is of a
consistency that will drop off a spoon easily but is
too thick to pour. Suitable for most cakes.
Stiff A mixture made with as little liquid as
possible. Suitable for biscuits and pastry.
Stiff consistency A mixture with enough liquid to
make a mixture that is too sticky to handle, but
will keep its shape when dropping from a spoon.
Suitable for rich fruit cakes.
```

EQUIPMENT USED IN BAKING

Bain-marie

A container part filled with water and used to cook delicate items in.

Baking sheets

Usually made from aluminium or steel. They should be wiped clean, not washed, as washing removes the non-stick surface.

Cutters

Shaped cutters used to cut out pieces of pastry.

Docker

A wooden disk with protruding points used to make small holes in pastry to prevent the pastry from rising.

Dredger

A container with small holes used to dust items with flour or icing.

Moulds

Used for making items such as Easter eggs. Never use a knife or scraper to clean moulds as this will damage them.

Oven trays

Usually made from black wrought steel. They are never washed, but scraped and wiped clean as washing removes their non-stick surface. New trays are made non-stick by heating in a very hot oven, removing and coating with a thin layer of oil. All oven trays are lightly greased before use.

Ovens, deck

Special ovens used for bread making. They have top and bottom and front heat regulators.

Pastry tins (moulds)

Used for baking small savoury and sweet preparations, these include tartlet tins, barquette (boat shaped) and patty tins.

Provers

Steam cabinets used to ferment yeast goods in.

Savoy bags and tubes

Traditionally made from cloth, but because of the new health regulations they must be disposable.

Sieves

Available in many sizes and degrees of fineness.

NOTE: Baking tins should always be prepared well in advance by lightly greasing and, in the case of sponges, lightly flouring before beginning to prepare the mixture. Swiss roll tins are lined with silicon or greased greaseproof paper before adding the mixture.

13

Doughs and dough products

Bread rolls

Step	Commodity	1 portion	10 portions				
				2 hr	20 min		240°C
1	Strong flour	30 g	300 g	Place into bowl.			
	Salt	½ g	5 g	Add.			
	Milk powder	½ g	5 g	Add and sieve together onto a clean working surface.			
	Butter or fat*	1 g	10 g	Add and rub in. Make a well.			
2	Yeast	1½ g	15 g	Place in a small jug.			
	Water	5 ml	50 ml	Heat to 27°C. Add to the yeast and stir until it has dissolved. Pour into the centre of the well and begin to mix in. Reshape into a well.			
	Water	10 ml	100 ml	Pour in and draw the flour from inside the bay to form the dough, ensuring that no liquid escapes. Mix well and knead for approximately 10 minutes to form a smooth dough. Cover with a clean cloth and leave to prove (B.F.T.) for 45 minutes. Knead (knock back) the dough to expel most of the air. Allow to rest for 15 minutes. Divide into appropriately sized pieces and mould into the required shapes. Arrange on a baking tray and place in a prover until they have doubled in size (30 minutes approximately). Brush with egg wash and sprinkle with poppy seeds/sesame seeds or leave plain. Place in a pre-heated oven and bake for the required time. Remove and allow to cool on a wire rack.			

* Fat = Margarine or compound fat

☐   ☐   ☐

Wholemeal bread rolls

Step	Commodity	1 portion	10 portions	
				⏺ 2 hr ☲ 20 min ≋ 240°C
1	Strong flour	30 g	300 g	Place into a bowl.
	Salt	½ g	5 g	Add.
	Milk powder	½ g	5 g	Add and sieve together onto a clean working surface.
	Butter or fat*	1 g	10 g	Add and rub in. Make a well.
2	Yeast	1½ g	15 g	Place in a small jug.
	Water	5 ml	50 ml	Heat to 27°C. Add to the yeast and stir until it has dissolved. Pour into the centre of the well and begin to mix in. Reshape into a well.
	Water	10 ml	100 ml	Pour into the centre of the well and draw the flour from the inside of the bay to form the dough, ensuring that no liquid escapes. Mix well and knead for approximately 10 minutes to form a smooth dough. Cover with a clean cloth and leave to prove (B.F.T.) for 45 minutes. Knead (knock back) the dough, expelling most of the air. Allow to rest for 15 minutes. Divide into appropriate pieces and mould into the required shapes. Arrange on a baking tray and place in a prover until they have doubled in size (45 minutes approximately). Brush with egg wash and sprinkle with poppy seeds/sesame seeds or leave plain. Place in a pre-heated oven and bake for the required time. Remove and allow to cool on a wire rack.

* Fat = Margarine or compound fat

☐   ☐   ☐

13

Basic sweet buns

Step	Commodity	1 portion	10 portions	
				⏺ 2 hr ☲ 20 min ≋ 230°C
1	Strong flour	30 g	300 g	Place into a bowl.
	Salt	½ g	5 g	Add.
	Milk powder	½ g	5 g	Add and sieve together onto a clean working surface.
	Castor sugar	3 g	30 g	Add.
	Butter or margarine	1 g	10 g	Add and rub in. Make a well.
2	Yeast	2 g	20 g	Place in a small jug.
	Water	10 ml	100 ml	Heat to 27°C. Add to the yeast and stir until it has dissolved. Pour into the centre of the well and draw the flour from inside to form the dough.

Step	Commodity	1 portion	10 portions	
3	Egg	¼	2½	Break into a jug and whisk together. Add to the dough and mix well. Knead for approximately 10 minutes to form a smooth dough. Cover with a clean cloth and leave to prove (B.F.T.) for 50 minutes. Knead (knock back) the dough, expelling most of the air. Allow to rest for 10 minutes. Divide into appropriately sized pieces and mould into the required shapes. Arrange on a baking tray and place in a prover until they have doubled in size (30 minutes approximately). Place in a pre-heated oven for the required time. Remove, brush with a bun wash and allow to cool on a wire rack.

NOTES: When cold they may be split at an angle, filled with 25 ml of whipped cream (per portion) and dredged with icing sugar to make cream buns.

This dough is used to make deep fried doughnuts. Cook at 175°C for approximately 15 minutes.

☐   ☐   ☐

Swiss buns

🥣 2 hr   ♨ 20 min   〰 230°C

Step	Commodity	1 portion	10 portions	
1	Strong flour	30 g	300 g	Place into a bowl.
	Salt	½ g	5 g	Add.
	Milk powder	½ g	5 g	Add and sieve together onto a clean working surface.
	Castor sugar	3 g	30 g	Add.
	Butter or margarine	1 g	10 g	Add and rub in. Make a well.
2	Yeast	2 g	20 g	Place in a small jug.
	Water	10 ml	100 ml	Heat to 27°C. Add to the yeast and stir until it has dissolved. Pour into the centre of the well and draw the flour from the inside of the bay to form the dough.
3	Egg	¼	2½	Break into a jug and whisk together. Add to the dough and mix well. Knead for approximately 10 minutes to form a smooth dough. Cover with a clean cloth and leave to prove (B.F.T.) for 50 minutes. Knead (knock back) the dough, expelling most of the air. Allow to rest for 10 minutes. Divide into appropriate pieces and mould into finger shapes. Arrange on a baking tray and place in a prover until they have doubled in size (30 minutes approximately). Place in a pre-heated oven for the required time and remove. Allow to go cold on a wire rack.
	Fondant	5 g	50 g	Heat and correct to a pouring consistency. Brush over the buns.

☐   ☐   ☐

Bun wash

Step	Commodity	1 portion	10 portions		🥄 30 min
1	Sugar	5 g	50 g	Place in a saucepan.	
	Water	5 ml	50 ml	Add and boil together to a thick syrup. Cool and use.	

☐　　☐　　☐

Jayzee

Step	Commodity	1 portion	10 portions		🥄 5 min
1	Plain flour	2 g	20 g	Place in a bowl.	
	Water	2.5 ml	25 ml	Add and whisk to a smooth paste. Use as required.	

☐　　☐　　☐

Extensions of bun dough
Fruit buns

Step	Commodity	1 portion	10 portions		🥄 2 hr　♨ 20 min　≋ 230°C
1	Strong flour	30 g	300 g	Place into a bowl.	
	Mixed spice		pinch	Add.	
	Salt	½ g	5 g	Add.	
	Milk powder	½ g	5 g	Add and sieve together onto a clean working surface.	
	Castor sugar	3 g	30 g	Add.	
	Butter or fat*	1 g	10 g	Add and rub in. Make a well.	
2	Yeast	2 g	20 g	Place in a small jug.	
	Water	10 ml	100 ml	Heat to 27°C. Add to the yeast and stir until it has dissolved. Pour into the centre of the well and draw the flour from the inside of the bay to form the dough.	
3	Egg	¼	2½	Break into a jug and whisk together. Add to the dough and mix well. Knead for approximately 10 minutes to form a smooth dough. Cover with a clean cloth and leave to prove (B.F.T.) for 50 minutes. Knead (knock back) the dough to expel most of the air.	
4	Dried fruit†	7 g	70 g	Wash, dry and add to the dough. Mix in well. Allow to rest for 10 minutes. Divide into appropriate pieces and mould into the required shapes. Arrange on a baking tray and place in a prover until they have doubled in size (30 minutes approximately). Place in a pre-heated oven for the required time. Remove, brush with a bun wash and allow to cool on a wire rack.	

* Fat = margarine or compound fat
† Dried fruit = sultanas and currants

☐　　☐　　☐

Bath buns

Step	Commodity	1 portion	10 portions	🥄 2 hr 🍲 20 min ≋ 230°C
1	Strong flour	30 g	300 g	Place into a bowl.
	Mixed spice		pinch	Add.
	Salt	½ g	5 g	Add.
	Milk powder	½ g	5 g	Add and sieve together onto a clean working surface.
	Nibbed sugar	5 g	50 g	Add.
	Butter or fat*	1 g	10 g	Add and rub in. Make a well.
2	Yeast	2 g	20 g	Place in a small jug.
	Water	10 ml	100 ml	Heat to 27°C. Add to the yeast and stir until it has dissolved. Pour into the centre of the well and draw the flour from inside of the bay to form the dough.
3	Egg	¼	2½	Break into a jug and whisk together. Add to the dough and mix well. Knead for approximately 10 minutes to form a smooth dough. Cover with a clean cloth and leave to prove (B.F.T.) for 50 minutes. Knead (knock back) the dough to expel most of the air.
	Dried fruit†	7 g	70 g	Wash, dry and add to the dough. Mix in well. Allow to rest for 10 minutes. Divide into appropriate pieces and mould into the required shapes. Arrange on a baking tray and place in a prover until they have doubled in size (30 minutes approximately).
4	Nibbed sugar	3 g	30 g	Sprinkle over the top. Place in a pre-heated oven for the required time, remove and allow to cool on a wire rack.

* Fat = Margarine or compound fat
† Dried fruit = sultanas, currants, mixed peel

Hot cross buns

Step	Commodity	1 portion	10 portions			
				⌣ 2 hr	🔥 20 min	≋ 230°C
1	Strong flour	30 g	300 g	Place into a bowl.		
	Mixed spice	pinch	½ tsp	Add.		
	Salt	½ g	5 g	Add.		
	Milk powder	½ g	5 g	Add and sieve together onto a clean working surface.		
	Castor sugar	3 g	30 g	Add.		
	Butter or fat*	1 g	10 g	Add and rub in. Make a well.		
2	Yeast	2 g	20 g	Place in a small jug.		
	Water	10 ml	100 ml	Heat to 27°C. Add to the yeast and stir until it has dissolved. Pour into the well and draw the flour from inside of the bay to form the dough.		
3	Egg	¼	2½	Break into a jug and whisk together. Add to the dough and mix well. Knead for approximately 10 minutes to form a smooth dough. Cover with a clean cloth and leave to prove (B.F.T.) for 50 minutes. Knead (knock back) the dough to expel most of the air.		
2	Dried fruit	7 g	70 g	Wash, dry and add to the dough. Mix in well. Allow to rest for 10 minutes. Divide into appropriate pieces and mould into the required shapes. Arrange on a baking tray and place in a prover until they have doubled in size.		
5	Jayzee	5 ml	50 ml	Place in a paper piping bag. Cut a small whole in the end. Pipe a cross shape over the bun. Place in a pre-heated oven for the required time. Remove, brush with a bun wash and allow to cool on a wire rack.		

* Fat = margarine or compound fat

☐   ☐   ☐

Chelsea buns

Step	Commodity	1 portion	10 portions			
				⌣ 2 hr	🔥 20 min	≋ 230°C
1	Strong flour	30 g	300 g	Place into a bowl.		
	Mixed spice	pinch	pinch	Add.		
	Salt	½ g	5 g	Add.		
	Milk powder	½ g	5 g	Add and sieve together onto a clean working surface.		
	Castor sugar	3 g	30 g	Add.		
	Butter or fat*	1 g	10 g	Add and rub in. Make a well.		
2	Yeast	2 g	20 g	Place in a small jug.		
	Water	10 ml	100 ml	Heat to 27°C. Add to the yeast and stir until it has dissolved. Pour into the well and draw the flour from inside of the bay to form the dough.		

13

Step	Commodity	1 portion	10 portions	
3	Egg	¼	2½	Break into a jug and whisk together. Add to the dough and mix well. Knead for approximately 10 minutes to form a smooth dough. Cover with a clean cloth and leave to prove (B.F.T.) for 50 minutes. Knead (knock back) the dough to expel most of the air. Roll into an oblong 1 cm thick.
4	Butter or margarine	3 g	30 g	Melt and brush over the dough.
	Castor sugar	2 g	20 g	Sprinkle over the top.
	Dried fruit†	7 g	70 g	Wash, dry and sprinkle over the sugar. Roll up and cut into 3 cm thick slices. Arrange on a baking tray and place in a prover until they have doubled in size (30 minutes approximately). Brush with butter or margarine. Place in a pre-heated oven for the required time. Remove, brush with a bun wash and allow to cool on a wire rack.

NOTE: * Fat = margarine or compound fat
† Dried fruit = mixed peel, sultanas and currants.

☐   ☐   ☐

Brioche

Step	Commodity	2 portions	20 portions	🥄 2½ hr ♨ 12–15 min ≋ 240°C
1	Strong flour	50 g	500 g	Sieve into a bowl.
	Eggs	¾	6	Break into a jug and whisk together. Add to the flour and mix in well.
2	Milk	10 ml	100 ml	Heat to 27°C
	Yeast	3 g	30 g	Add and dissolve.
	Castor sugar	2.5 g	25 g	Add and dissolve. Pour into the flour to form a dough. Knead to form a smooth dough. Prepare the brioche moulds (fluted patty tins), brushing with compound fat.
3	Butter, unsalted	25 g	250 g	Soften and beat in the butter until the dough is smooth and elastic. Cover and leave to prove for 1 hour. Fill the fluted patty tins by moulding first into a round and then into a pear shape with a small end about half the size of the other. Drop the longer bulbous end in the mould, keeping hold of the small end. Make a hole in the centre of the large bulb with the finger and allow the small bulb to rest in the impression so that the shape resembles a cottage loaf. Make a hole with a finger. Prove until they double in size (30–40 minutes). Brush with egg wash and place in a pre-heated oven for the required time. Turn out and allow to cool on a wire rack.

☐   ☐   ☐

Savarin syrup

Step	Commodity	1 portion	10 portions		🥣 15 min 🍲 15 min
1	Castor sugar	10 g	100 g	Place in a saucepan.	
	Water	25 ml	250 ml	Add.	
	Lemon	⅛	1	Grate the zest into the water and add the juice.	
	Coriander seeds	½–1	2–3	Add.	
	Bay leaf	¼ equiv	1 equiv	Add and boil. Simmer for 15 minutes and strain. The syrup is now ready for use.	

NOTE: For rum baba syrup add 5 ml of rum per portion.

☐   ☐   ☐

Savarin   Pâté à savarin

Step	Commodity	1 portion	10 portions		🥣 1½ hr 🍲 30 min ≈ 240°C
1	Strong flour	50 g	500 g	Sieve into a bowl.	
	Eggs	¾	7 equiv	Break into a jug and whisk together. Add to the flour and mix in well.	
2	Milk	10 ml	100 ml	Heat to 27°C.	
	Yeast	2 g	20 g	Add and dissolve.	
	Castor sugar	3 g	30 g	Add and dissolve. Pour into the flour to form a dough. Knead for approximately 10 minutes to form a smooth dough.	
	Butter	25 g	250 g	Soften and place on top of the dough. Cover with a clean cloth and leave to prove until it has doubled in size (30 minutes). Beat in the butter until the dough is smooth and elastic. Allow to rest for 15 minutes. Half fill a prepared savarin mould and prove for 30–40 minutes. Place in a pre-heated oven for the required time. Turn out and allow to cool on a wire rack. Soak in a savarin syrup.	
	Apricot glace	10 ml	100 ml	Brush over the savarin.	
3	Whipping cream	25 ml	250 ml	Whisk to a piping consistency and pipe a large rosette for each portion. The remaining cream should be piped into a sauceboat and served with the savarin.	
	Glacé cherries	½	5	Place on top of the cream.	
	Angelica	2 g	20 g	Cut into thin diamonds. Arrange either side of the cherry.	

NOTES: Savarin with fruit (savarin aux fruits) is a savarin with the centre filled with fresh fruit salad.
   Marignans are made from savarins cooked in barquette moulds, cut in half widthways when cold and decorated with 25 ml crème chantilly per portion.

☐   ☐   ☐

13

Rum baba

Baba au rhum

Step	Commodity	2 portions	20 portions			
				⏱ 3½ hr	🍲 20 min	≈ 240°C
1	Strong flour	50 g	500 g	Sieve into a bowl.		
	Eggs	¾	7½ equiv	Break into a jug and whisk together. Add to the flour and mix in well.		
	Currants	7.5 g	75 g	Wash, dry and add.		
2	Milk	10 ml	100 ml	Heat to 27°C.		
	Yeast	3 g	30 g	Add and dissolve.		
	Castor sugar	3 g	30 g	Add and dissolve. Pour into the flour to form a dough. Knead for approximately 10 minutes to form a smooth dough.		
	Butter	25 g	250 g	Soften and place on top of the dough. Cover with a clean cloth and leave to prove until it has doubled in size (30 minutes). Beat in the butter until the dough is smooth and elastic. Allow to rest for 15 minutes. Third fill the prepared dariole moulds and prove for 30 minutes or until the mixture reaches the top of the mould. Place in a pre-heated oven for the required time. Turn out and allow to go cold on a wire rack for 2 hours. Soak in a rum baba syrup for 2–3 minutes. Make a slanted incision on one side.		
	Apricot glace	10 ml	100 ml	Brush over the babas.		
3	Whipping cream	25 ml	250 ml	Whisk to a piping consistency and pipe the appropriate amount into the slit.		
	Glacé cherries	½	5	Place on top of the cream.		
	Angelica	2 g	20 g	Cut into thin diamonds and arrange either side of the cherry.		

☐   ☐   ☐

Pizzas

Pizza are made from a basic bread dough circle base, a basic filling and a variety of toppings of your choice; parma ham, mushrooms, anchovy fillets, olives, shellfish, sausage, etc. They can be any size, but usually start at 20 cm.

Pizza basic

Pizza Romana

⌣ 2 hr   ⌣ 20 min   ≋ 205°C

Step	Commodity	1 portion	10 portions	
1	Bread dough	100 g	1 kg	Knock back and roll out into the appropriate rounds and dock (i.e. prick with fork or baker's docker).
	Tomato concassé	50 g	500 g	Place on top of the dough.
	Chopped basil	pinch	1 tsp	Sprinkle over the top.
	Chopped marjoram	pinch	1 tsp	As above.
	Chopped oregano	pinch	1 tsp	As for marjoram. Season with salt and pepper.
	Mozzarella cheese	50 g	500 g	Grate or slice thinly over the top of the concassé.
	Parmesan cheese	10 g	100 g	Sprinkle over the top. Prove for 30 minutes before placing in a pre-heated oven for the appropriate time. Remove and serve immediately.

Extensions of basic pizza recipe

Dish	Additional ingredients per portion	Action
Capricciosa	25 g sliced cooked ham	Cut into 1 cm squares and place on top of the concassé. Cover with cheese.
	10 g cooked sliced mushrooms	Sprinkle over the cheese.
	10 g chopped cooked artichoke bottom.	Sprinkle over the top.
	2 olives	Arrange on top.
Funghi	50 g cooked sliced mushrooms	Sprinkle over the top of the cheese.
Napolitana	2 anchovy fillets	Cut in half lengthways and arrange on top of the cheese.
	2 black olives	Place in between the anchovies.
Mare	15 g cooked scampi	Place on top of the concassé.
	15 g prawns	As above.
	15 g cooked mussels	As for scampi. Cover with cheese.
Margherita	50 g pecorino cheese	Slice and use in place of the mozzarella cheese.
Prosciutto	50 g Parma ham	Slice thinly and place on top of the concassé. Cover with cheese.
Siciliana	50 g tuna fish	Chop finely and place on top of the concassé. Cover with cheese.
	2 olives	Cut into slices and arrange over the cheese.
Würstel	50 g sliced German sausage	Arrange on top of the concassé and cover with the cheese.

13

☐   ☐   ☐

Basic shortcrust pastry recipes

Shortcrust pastry

Pâte à foncer/pâté à brisée

⏲ 30 min   ≋ 200°–220°C

Step	Commodity	1 portion	10 portions	
1	Flour	40 g	400 g	Add a pinch of salt and sieve together.
	Lard	10 g	100 g	Cut into small pieces and place on top of the flour.
	Butter	10 g	100 g	Cut into small pieces and add to the flour. Rub in to a sandy texture. Make a well in the mixture.
2	Water	½ tbsp	5 tbsp	Add sufficient water to form a firm paste. Place in a bowl and cover. Allow the paste to rest for 20 minutes before using.

NOTE: This paste may be made with 50 per cent wholemeal and 50 per cent white flour. When covering pies with pastry, do not stretch the paste otherwise it will shrink during the cooking process and spoil the look of the finished item.

☐   ☐   ☐

Baked jam roll

⏲ 35 min   ♨ 30–40 min   ≋ 200°C

Step	Commodity	1 portion	10 portions	
1	Self-raising flour	40 g	400 g	Add a pinch of salt and sieve together.
	Lard	10 g	100 g	Cut into small pieces and place on top of the flour.
	Butter	10 g	100 g	Cut into small pieces and add to the flour. Rub in to form a sandy texture. Make a well in the mixture.
2	Water	½ tbsp	5 tbsp	Add sufficient water to form a firm paste. Place in a bowl and cover. Allow the paste to rest for 20 minutes before using. Roll out 3 mm thick.
	Jam	20 g	200 g	Spread over the pastry. Dampen the edges and fold over the short edges. Roll the pastry up and seal. Place on a baking tray and brush with water or milk.
3	Castor sugar	5 g	50 g	Sprinkle over the top and place in a pre-heated oven for the appropriate time. Remove and serve hot. Serve with a sauceboat of raspberry or custard sauce.

☐   ☐   ☐

Jam tarts

⏲ 30 min   ♨ 20 min   ≋ 235°C

Step	Commodity	1 portion	10 portions	
1	Shortcrust pastry	25 g	250 g	Roll out 3 mm thick. Place on a greased plate. Cut off any surplus pastry. Retain the excess. Dock the bottom.
2	Jam	20 g	200 g	Spread over the pastry. Dampen the edges with water. Roll out the left over pastry. Cut into ½ cm strips and arrange decoratively over the top. Place in the oven for the appropriate time, remove and serve.

NOTES: Lemon curd tart may be made using this recipe.
Tartlets are individual jam tarts made in tartlet tins.

☐   ☐   ☐

Treacle/syrup tarts

Step | Commodity | 1 portion | 10 portions | 🥄 30 min · 🍲 20 min · 〰 235°C

Step	Commodity	1 portion	10 portions	
1	Shortcrust pastry	25 g	250 g	Roll out 3 mm thick. Place on a greased plate. Cut off any surplus pastry. Retain the excess. Dock the bottom.
2	Treacle/syrup	25 g	250 g	Heat gently.
	Lemon juice		Few drops	Add and spread over the pastry.
3	Cake crumb	5 g	50 g	Sprinkle over the top. Place in the oven for the appropriate time, remove and serve.

☐   ☐   ☐

Baked apples dumplings

Step | Commodity | 1 portion | 10 portions | 🥄 30 min · 🍲 35 min · 〰 200°C

Step	Commodity	1 portion	10 portions	
1	Shortcrust pastry	25 g	250 g	Roll out 3 mm thick into squares of sufficient size to envelop an apple. Dampen the edges.
2	Cooking apple	1 small	10 small	Wash well, remove the core and make a 2 mm incision around the width of the apple. Place an apple on each piece of pastry.
	Brown sugar	15 g	150 g	Sprinkle down the centre of the apple.
	Clove	1	10	Place on the top of the sugar. Fold over the pastry to completely seal the apple. Arrange on a baking sheet. Brush the pastry with a milk wash. Place in a pre-heated oven and bake for the required time. Remove and serve hot.

NOTE: Serve with custard sauce or cream.

☐   ☐   ☐

SHORTCRUST PASTRY PRODUCTS

Cheese and bacon flan

Quiche lorraine

Step | Commodity | 1 portion | 10 portions | 🥄 45 min · 🍲 25 min · 〰 180°C

Step	Commodity	1 portion	10 portions	
1	Shortcrust pastry	100 g	1 g	Roll out 3 m thick. Grease the appropriate amount of suitably sized flan rings on a baking tray. Line the rings with the pastry, making sure not to break the pastry. Allow to rest for 20 minutes.
2	Eggs	1	10	Break into a bowl. Season with salt and pepper.
	Milk	40 ml	400 ml	Add and whisk together well. Strain through a fine sieve and pour into the pastry cases.
	Sliced bacon	50 g	500 g	Remove the rind and cut into lardons. Place the appropriate amount in the pastry cases.
	Cheddar cheese	50 g	500 g	Grate and sprinkle over the top.
	Chopped parsley	pinch	1 sp	Sprinkle over the top. Place in a pre-heated oven for the appropriate time. Remove and cool slightly to allow the egg mixture to set. Place on a serving flat and remove the ring. Serve cold or re-heated.

☐   ☐   ☐

13

Cheese and onion flan

⌣ 45 min ⌥ 25 min ≋ 180°C

Step	Commodity	1 portion	10 portions	
1	Shortcrust pastry	100 g	1 g	Roll out 3 m thick. Grease the appropriate amount of suitably sized flan rings on a baking tray. Line the rings with the pastry, making sure not to break the pastry. Allow to rest for 20 minutes.
2	Eggs	1	10	Break into a bowl. Season with salt and pepper.
	Milk	40 ml	400 ml	Add and whisk together well. Strain through a fine sieve and pour into the pastry cases.
	Sweated sliced onions	50 g	500 g	Sprinkle over the mixture
	Cheddar cheese	50 g	500 g	Grate and sprinkle over the top.
	Chopped parsley	pinch	1 tsp	Sprinkle over the top. Place in a pre-heated oven for the appropriate time. Remove and cool slightly to allow the egg mixture to set. Place on a serving flat and remove the ring. Serve cold or re-heated.

NOTE: This flan may be made without the cheese when it is just called onion flan (quiche aux oignons).

☐   ☐   ☐

Seafood flan

⌣ 45 min ⌥ 25 min ≋ 180°C

Step	Commodity	1 portion	10 portions	
1	Shortcrust pastry	100 g	1 g	Roll out 3 m thick. Grease the appropriate amount of suitably sized flan rings on a baking tray. Line the rings with the pastry, making sure not to break the pastry. Allow to rest for 20 minutes.
2	Eggs	1	10	Break into a bowl. Season with salt and pepper.
	Milk	40 ml	400 ml	Add and whisk together well. Strain through a fine sieve and pour into the pastry cases.
	Prawns	50 g	500 g	Chop finely and sprinkle over the top.
	Mussels	50 g	500 g	Chop and sprinkle over the top.
	Chopped parsley	pinch	1 tsp	Sprinkle over the top. Place in a pre-heated oven for the appropriate time. Remove and cool slightly to allow egg mixture to set. Place on a serving flat and remove the ring. Serve cold or re-heated.

☐   ☐   ☐

Cornish pasties

Step	Commodity	1 portion	10 portions	
				⤵ 45 min 🍲 30 min ≋ 180°C
1	Minced lamb	50 g	500 g	Place in a clean bowl.
	Potatoes	25 g	250 g	Peel, wash and cut into small dice. Add to the meat.
	Onions	25 g	250 g	Peel, cut into brunoise and add to the meat. Season with salt and pepper.
	Chopped parsley	pinch	2 tsp	Add and mix in well.
2	Shortcrust pastry	75 g	750 g	Roll out 3 mm thick and cut into 6 cm rounds with a cutter. Place the appropriate amount of filling in the centre. Moisten the edges with water and draw the opposite edges together. Seal well by crimping. Place on a baking tray and egg wash. Cut a small hole on the top to allow excess steam escape. Place in the oven and bake for the appropriate time. Remove and serve hot or cold.

NOTE: Cornish pasties may also be made with puff pastry.

☐   ☐   ☐

Puff pastry

Puff pastry (à l'anglaise)

Feuilletage

Step	Commodity	1 portion	10 portions	
				⤵ 3 hr ≋ 230°–250°C
1	Flour	40 g	400 g	Add a pinch of salt and sieve together into a clean bowl.
	Butter* or fat	10 g	100 g	Cut into small pieces and rub in. Make a well in the mixture.
	Lemon juice	Drop	Few drops	Squeeze into a jug.
	Water	25 ml	250 ml	Add to the lemon juice and pour into the well. Knead to a smooth dough. Place in a bowl and cover. Allow to rest for 20 minutes before going on to the next stage. Roll out into a 30 cm × 15 cm rectangle.
2	Butter* or fat	30 g	300 g	Plasticise the butter and place over two-thirds of the dough. Fold the remaining third of the dough over the portion spread with fat and fold the other end over the top of that so that there are two layers of fat and three layers of dough. Roll out into a 30 cm × 15 cm rectangle and fold in three as before. Cover, place somewhere cool and allow to rest for 20 minutes. Fold a further 5 times allowing the appropriate resting times in between. The pastry is now ready for use.

* A special pastry fat is advised when first making this pastry, though this does spoil the quality.

13

The star (French) method

An alternative method of rolling the pastry is to use what is known as either the star or French method of preparation.

The dough is made in the usual manner and allowed to rest. A cross is cut half way through the dough and the corners pulled out with a rolling pin to form a star shape, leaving the centre thick. The remaining fat is placed in the centre and the star flaps folded over the top. It is then rolled out to 30 cm × 15 m, covered, placed somewhere cool and allowed to rest for 20 minutes. It is then rolled out again to a 30 cm × 15 cm rectangle and the long ends are folded into the centre and folded in again to form a square. It is then rested for a further 20 minutes. This process is repeated a further 3 times with the appropriate rests in between. The pastry is now ready to use.

☐　☐　☐

Rough puff pastry (Scotch)

Step	Commodity	1 portion	10 portions		🥄 3 hr ≋ 230°–250°C
1	Flour	40 g	400 g	Add a pinch of salt and sieve together into a clean bowl.	
	Butter*	30 g	300 g	Cut into small pieces and rub in. Make a well in the mixture.	
	Lemon juice	Drop	few drops	Pour into a jug.	
	Water	25 ml	250 ml	Add to the lemon juice and pour into the well. Knead to a smooth dough. Roll out into a 30 cm × 15 cm oblong. The long ends are folded into the centre and folded in again to form a square. It is then rested for 20 minutes. This process is repeated a further 3 times with the appropriate rests in between. The pastry is now ready to use.	

* A special pastry fat is advised with first making this pastry, though this does spoil the quality.
NOTE: 50 per cent wholemeal and 50 per cent white flour may be used.

☐　☐　☐

PUFF PASTRY PRODUCTS

Meat pie

Step	Commodity	1 portion	10 portions	☞ 45 min 🍲 ¾–1 hr ≋ 160°C
1	Lean tender steak	125 g	1.25 kg	Trim, season with salt and pepper and pass through seasoned flour. Pat off excess flour. Place in a bowl.
	Onions	25 g	250 g	Peel, cut into brunoise and add to the meat. mix in well and place in the pie dishes.
	Chopped parsley	pinch	2 tsp	Add. Mix in well and place into the pie dishes.
	Brown stock	100 ml	1 litre	Pour over the meat, just covering.
2	Puff pastry	75 g	750 g	Roll into the required shape 5 mm thick. Remove the trimmings and roll into a square. Moisten the edge of the dish. Cut the trimmings into ¼ cm strips and line the edge of the dish. Moisten the pastry edge and cover the pie with the rolled out pastry, taking care not to stretch the paste as it will shrink during cooking. Seal well, trim and decorate the top. Egg wash and allow to rest for 15 minutes before baking. Egg wash once more before placing in the pre-heated oven for the appropriate time or until the pastry is a golden brown. Remove from the oven and clean the dish with a clean damp cloth. Place on a serving tray and surround with a pie collar.

NOTE: A pie flute is sometimes used when making large pies as this holds up the centre and allows excess steam to escape.

Extensions of steak pie

NOTE: Stewing steak may be used in these dishes, but it must be precooked by boiling before baking to ensure that it is tender.

Dish	Additional Ingredients per portion
Steak and mushroom pie	Allow 15 g of sliced mushrooms, added with the onions.
Steak and kidney pie	Allow 25 g of prepared ox or lambs' kidney and add with the onions.
Steak, mushroom and kidney pie	Allow 15 g of sliced mushrooms and 25 g of ox or lambs' kidney, added with the onions.
Steak, mushroom and oyster pie	Allow 15 g of mushrooms added with the onion. One clean oyster is placed on top of the steak in the pie dish before covering with pastry.
Steak, Guinness and oyster pie	Substitute Guinness for half of the stock and allow 1 oyster placed on top of the steak before covering with pastry.

□   □   □

Chicken pies

Step	Commodity	1 portion	10 portions		
				🥄 1 hr 🍲 ¾–1 hr ≋ 160°C	
1	Lean tender chicken	125 g	1.25 kg	Trim and season with salt and pepper.	
	Streaky bacon	2 slices	20 slices	Remove the rind and trim off any bones or excess fat. Wrap around the meat and lay in the prepared pie dishes.	
	Onions	25 g	250 g	Peel, cut into brunoise and sprinkle over the meat.	
	Chopped parsley	pinch	2 tsp	Add.	
	Button mushrooms	25 g	250 g	Wash, trim and slice. Sprinkle over the other ingredients.	
	White stock	100 ml	1 litre	Pour over the meat, just covering.	
2	Puff pastry	75 g	750 g	Roll into the required shape 5 mm thick. Remove the trimmings and roll into a square. Moisten the edge of the dish. Cut the trimmings into ¼ cm strips and line the edge of the dish. Moisten the pastry edge and cover the pie with the rolled out pastry, taking care not to stretch the paste as it will shrink during cooking. Seal well, trim and decorate the top. Egg wash and allow to rest for 15 minutes before baking. Egg wash once more before placing in the pre-heated oven for the appropriate time or until the pastry is golden brown. Remove from the oven and clean the dish with a clean damp cloth. Place on a serving tray and surround with a pie collar.	

NOTE: A pie flute is sometimes used when making large pies as this holds up the centre and allows excess steam to escape. This dish may be made with pigeon or rabbit.

☐   ☐   ☐

Hot veal and ham pie

Step	Commodity	1 portion	10 portions	⏱ 45 min 🍲 ¾–1 hr ≋ 160°C
1	Lean tender veal	100 g	1 kg	Trim and place in a bowl.
	Gammon	25 g	250 g	Trim the fat, cut into 2 cm dice and add to the veal. Pass through seasoned flour and place in the pie dishes.
	Onions	25 g	250 g	Peel, cut into brunoise and add to the meat.
	Button mushrooms	15 g	150 g	Wash, trim and slice. Sprinkle over the other ingredients.
	Chopped parsley	pinch	2 tsp	Add. Mix in well and place into the pie dishes.
	White stock	100 ml	1 litre	Place in a jug.
	Lemon juice	5 ml	50 ml	Add and pour over the meat, just covering it.
2	Puff pastry	75 g	750 g	Roll into the required shape 5 mm thick. Remove the trimmings and roll into a square. Moisten the edge of the dish. Cut the trimmings into ¼ strips and line the edge of the dish. Moisten the edge of the pastry and cover with the pie lid, taking care not to stretch the paste as it will shrink during cooking. Seal well, trim and decorate the top. Egg wash and allow to rest for 15 minutes before baking. Egg wash once more before placing in the pre-heated oven for the appropriate time or until the pastry is golden brown. Remove from the oven and clean the dish with a clean damp cloth. Place on a serving tray and surround with a pie collar.

NOTE: A pie flute is sometimes used when making large pies as this holds up the centre and allows excess steam to escape.

☐   ☐   ☐

Fillet of beef in pastry

Filet de boeuf Wellington (en croûte)

Step	Commodity	1 portion	10 portions	⏱ 1 hr 🍲 30 min ≋ 200°C
1	Fillet of beef	125 g	1.25 kg	Trim, lightly season with salt and pepper and seal in hot fat on all sides. Remove and allow to cool.
	Duxelle	25 g	250 g	Place in a bowl.
	Pâté de foie gras	15 g	150 g	Add and mix with the duxelle. Spread over the top of the fillet steak.
2	Puff pastry	75 g	750 g	Roll into an oblong wide enough to cover the steak and allow 5 cm either end longer than the fillet. Wrap the steak neatly in the pastry and seal well with egg wash underneath the steak. Use the trimmings to decorate the top. Brush with egg wash and allow to rest for 15 minutes before baking. Egg wash once more before placing in the pre-heated oven for the appropriate time or until the pastry is golden brown. Remove from the oven and place on a serving tray. Serve with a Madeira sauce.

NOTE: This dish is carved in front of the customer at the table.

☐   ☐   ☐

Vol au vents

Step	Commodity	1 portion	10 portions
1	Puff pastry	20 g	200 g

👐 1 hr 🍲 20 min ≋ 230°C

Roll out ¼ cm thick. Egg wash half and fold the other half on top. Cut out the vol au vents with a 5 cm fluted or plain cutter. Using a smaller plain cutter (3 cm) cut quarterway through the centre to create the lid. Brush with egg wash. Allow to stand for 30 minutes. Brush again and place in a pre-heated oven for the appropriate time. Remove when cooked. Place on a cooling rack. When cool, lift off the lids and remove the raw/damp pastry. Fill accordingly.

NOTE: Bouchées are small, mouth-sized vol au vents and are made the same way.

☐ ☐ ☐

Sausage rolls

Step	Commodity	1 portion	10 portions
1	Puff pastry	20 g	200 g
	Sausagemeat	40 g	400 g

👐 30 min 🍲 20 min ≋ 230°C

Roll out the pastry 3 mm thick into 10 cm wide.

Roll into lengths 2 cm in diameter. Place over the pastry. Brush the edges with egg wash. Fold over the other edges and crimp decoratively. Cut into 7 cm lengths and brush with egg wash. Allow to rest for 30 minutes. Brush again with egg wash. Arrange on baking trays and place in a pre-heated oven for the appropriate time or until golden brown. Remove and cool on a cooling rack.

☐ ☐ ☐

Palmiers

Step	Commodity	1 portion	10 portions
1	Puff pastry	10 g	100 g
	Castor sugar	5 g	50
2	Fresh cream	25 ml	250 ml
	Castor sugar	5 g	50 g

👐 15 min 🍲 10 min ≋ 230°C

Roll out to 2 mm thick in a rectangle. Brush with a little water.

Sprinkle half of the sugar over the top. Turn over and repeat the process. Lightly roll in the sugar with a rolling pin. Fold both ends in three times to give six folds, so they meet in the centre. Fold in two. Cut into 1 cm strips and arrange neatly on a well greased baking tray. Allow to rest for 30 minutes. Place in a pre-heated oven for half of the required time. Remove from the oven, turn over and replace in the oven. Finish cooking until they are golden brown. Remove and place straight on a cooling rack and allow to go cold.

Whip to a piping consistency.

Add and mix in. Place in a savoy bag with a small star nozzle and pipe the appropriate amount onto a cold palmier. Place another palmier on top to form a sandwich.

☐ ☐ ☐

Cream slices
Mille-feuilles

⤵ 1 hr   🍲 20 min   ≋ 230°C

Step	Commodity	1 portion	10 portions	
1	Puff pastry	30 g	300 g	Roll out (2 mm thick). Allow 3 × 30 cm × 8 cm for 10 portions. Dock the surface. Arrange on a baking tray. Allow to rest for 30 minutes. Place in a pre-heated oven for half of the appropriate time. Turn over each piece and return to the oven. Complete the cooking process. Remove and allow to cool on a rack. Select the best slice.
	Fondant	20 g	200 g	Warm and correct the consistency with sugar syrup. Keep 1 tbsp back. Spread the rest evenly over the best slice. Colour the remaining fondant with a little red colouring. Place in a small piping bag and pipe very thin lines lengthways 1 cm apart. With the back of the knife pass through the fondant widthways 1 cm apart, alternating the direction with each stroke. Wipe after each stroke. Allow to set.
	Raspberry jam*	10 g	100 g	Spread on one of the slices (the bottom piece). Place the second slice on top.
	Fresh cream	25 ml	250 ml	Whip to a piping consistency. Place in a savoy bag with a star nozzle and pipe onto the second slice. Carefully lift the top with a palette knife and lay on top. Using a clean knife, cut into the appropriate portions, wiping the knife after each slice.

* Seedless jam or boiled and strained jam.

□   □   □

Cream puffs

⤵ 1 hr   🍲 15 min   ≋ 215°–230°C

Step	Commodity	1 portion	10 portions	
1	Puff pastry	20 g	200 g	Roll out (2 mm thick) and allow 10 cm × 6 cm for each portion (30 cm × 20 cm for 10 portions). Dock the surface. Cut into 8 cm rounds of 10 cm × 6 cm rectangles. Dust accordingly. Arrange on a baking tray. Allow to rest for 30 minutes. Place in a pre-heated oven for the appropriate time. Remove and allow to cool on a rack. Split into two halves, laying the top piece facing up so as not to ruin the presentation side.
2	Raspberry jam*	10 g	100 g	Place in a small piping bag and pipe a line down the centre of the bottom piece.
3	Fresh cream	25 ml	250 ml	Whip to a piping consistency. Place in a savoy bag with a star nozzle and pipe the appropriate amount over the jam in each one. Replace the top carefully. Dust with icing sugar if required (see 'dusting' below).

* Seedless jam or boiled and strained.
NOTE: There are four ways of dusting.

(a) Puff royal, to spread with royal icing and pipe a thin line in the shape of a cross with raspberry jam*. Bake at 215°C.
(b) Sugar dressed, a wash of egg whites dipped in castor sugar. Bake at 215°C.
(c) Egg wash, brush twice with egg wash for a deep gloss. This item needs no additional egg wash after baking. Bake at 230°C.
(d) Dusted, with a dredging of icing sugar. This item is not dusted after baking. Bake at 230°C.

□   □   □

Jam turnovers

Step	Commodity	1 portion	10 portions	⏲ 30 min ♨ 15 min ≋ 230°C
1	Puff pastry	20 g	200 g	Roll out (2 mm thick) and allow 10 cm × 6 cm for each portion (30 cm × 20 cm for 10 portions). Dock the surface. Cut into 8 cm rounds. Using a rolling pin, elongate the circles to give a slightly oval shape. Moisten the edges.
2	Jam*	15 g	150 g	Place in the centre of the circle. Fold over the wide edges to meet and seal by crimping.
3	Egg white	½	4	Beat until smooth. Brush over the top of the turnover.
	Castor sugar	5 g	50 g	Sprinkle over the top. Arrange the turnovers on a baking tray. Allow to rest for 30 minutes. Place in a pre-heated oven for the appropriate time. Remove and allow to cool on a rack.

* Jam of your choice.
NOTE: This dish may be made with an apple purée.

☐   ☐   ☐

Mince pies

Step	Commodity	1 portion	10 portions	⏲ 30 min ♨ 20 min ≋ 230°C
1	Puff pastry	15 g	150 g	Roll the pastry out (3 mm thick) and cut with a 8 cm fluted cutter. Place in the prepared tins. Moisten the edges.
	Mincemeat	15 g	150 g	Place in the centre of the pastry.
2	Sugar pastry	10 g	100 g	Roll out 3 mm thick and cut with a 6 cm fluted cutter. Place on top of the mincemeat and seal the edges. Brush with egg wash. Place in a pre-heated oven for the appropriate time. Remove and allow to cool on a rack.
3	Icing sugar	2 g	20 g	Dredge over the top. Serve accompanied by brandy/rum butter, brandy cream, brandy/rum sauce or custard.

☐   ☐   ☐

Eccles cakes

Step	Commodity	1 portion	10 portions	

⌣ 30 min   🍲 15 min   ≋ 215°–230°C

Step	Commodity	1 portion	10 portions	
1	Puff pastry	20 g	200 g	Roll out (2 mm thick) and allow 10 cm × 6 cm for each portion (30 cm × 20 cm for 10 portions). Dock the surface. Cut into 8 cm rounds. Moisten the edges.
2	Filling (see below)	15 g	150 g	Place in the centre of the circle. Fold over the edges to meet and seal. Roll out to the original shape with a rolling pin.
3	Egg white	½	4	Beat until smooth. Brush over the top.
	Castor sugar	5 g	50 g	Sprinkle over the top. Arrange the Eccles cakes on a baking tray. Allow to rest for 30 minutes. Place in a pre-heated oven for the appropriate time. Remove and allow to cool on a rack.

NOTE: Banbury cakes are made in the same way as Eccles cakes but are oval in shape.

Fillings

(a)

Step	Commodity	1 portion	10 portions	
1	Sweet mincemeat	10 g	100 g	Place in a bowl.
	Breadcrumbs	5 g	50 g	Add and mix well together.

(b)

Step	Commodity	1 portion	10 portions	
1	Currants	15 g	150 g	Wash, dry and place in a bowl.
	Brown sugar	5 g	50 g	Add.
	Mixed spice	small pinch	pinch	Add.
	Golden syrup	½ tsp	5 tsp	Add.
	Cake crumbs	5 g	50 g	Add and mix well together.

□   □   □

13

Cream horns

👐 1 hr   🍲 20 min   ≋ 230°C

Step	Commodity	1 portion	10 portions	
1	Puff pastry	15 g	150 g	Roll out (2 mm thick) and allow 30 cm × 1½ cm for each portion (30 cm × 15 cm for 10 portions). Cut into 30 cm × 1½ cm lengths. Moisten one side of each strip. Wind each strip carefully around a greased cream horn mould, starting at the point and working to the open end, overlapping slightly. The finish should be on the bottom to keep it in place. Brush the top with egg wash.
	Castor sugar	5 g	50 g	Sprinkle over the top. Arrange on a baking tray. Leave to rest for 30 minutes. Place in a pre-heated oven for the required time or until golden brown. Remove from the oven and give each one a slight twist. Allow to cool and carefully remove the cream horns from the moulds. Allow to go cold.
2	Jam*	15 g	150 g	Place in a piping bag and pipe a little into the bottom of each horn.
	Fresh cream	25 ml	250 ml	Whip to a piping consistency. Place in a savoy bag with a small star nozzle and pipe the appropriate amount into each horn in a rosette.
	Glacé cherries	½	5	Wash, dry and place on top of the cream.

* Seedless or boiled and strained jam.

☐   ☐   ☐

Jalousie

👐 1 hr   🍲 30 min   ≋ 230°C

Step	Commodity	1 portion	10 portions	
1	Puff pastry	20 g	200 g	Roll out a third of the pastry (2 mm thick) and allow 6 cm × 2 cm for each portion (60 cm × 20 cm for 10 portions). Dock the surface. Cut into rectangles as suggested.
2	Frangipane	15 g	150 g	Place in a piping bag with a plain nozzle. Pipe two lengths down the centre of the pastry leaving a 2 cm border on all sides. Brush the edges with egg wash.
3	Raspberry jam*	5 g	50 g	Place in a small piping bag and pipe down the centre of the frangipane. Roll out the other two-thirds of the pastry a little wider and longer than the bottom pieces. Fold in half lengthways. Make an incision 2 cm long every 2 cm at a 45° angle. Open the pastry up and carefully place over the frangipane. Crimp the edges decoratively. Brush with egg wash and allow to rest for 30 minutes. Brush again with eggwash. Place in a pre-heated oven for the appropriate time.
4	Apricot jam	10 g	100 g	Place in a saucepan with a little water. Bring to the boil, reduce to a syrup and strain. Brush over the jalousie.
	Icing sugar	5 g	50 g	Sieve and add a little water to make a spreadable mixture. Carefully brush over the top of jalousie.

* Seedless or boiled and strained jam.

☐   ☐   ☐

Pithivier

Step	Commodity	1 portion	10 portions				
				☋ 1 hr	⏱ 30 min	≋ 230°C	
1	Puff pastry	20 g	200 g	Roll out a third of the pastry (2 mm thick). Allow 25 cm diameter round for 10 portions. Dock the surface. Arrange on a baking tray.			
2	Apricot jam	10 g	100 g	Spread over the pastry leaving a 2 cm border on all sides.			
3	Frangipane	15 g	150 g	Place in a piping bag with a plain nozzle. Pipe over the jam leaving a 2 cm border on all sides. Brush the edges with egg wash. Roll out the other two-thirds of the pastry a little wider than the bottom piece. Carefully place over the frangipane. Crimp the edges decoratively. Make 3 cm curved slits on the top at equal intervals. Brush with egg wash and allow to rest for 30 minutes. Brush again with eggwash. Place in a pre-heated oven for the appropriate time. Remove from the oven.			
4	Icing sugar	5 g	50 g	Dust the top of the pithivier and place back in the oven for 3–4 minutes until the sugar has melted and glazed the top. Remove and place on a cooking rack.			

☐   ☐   ☐

Roularde

Step	Commodity	1 portion	10 portions				
				☋ 15 min	⏱ 10 min	≋ 230°C	
1	Puff pastry	10 g	100 g	Roll out 2 mm thick into a rectangle. Brush with a little water.			
2	Filling*	2 g	20 g	Spread over the pastry. Fold both ends in three times to give six folds, so they meet in the centre. Fold in two. Cut into 1 cm strips and arrange neatly on a well greased baking tray. Allow to rest for 30 minutes. Place in a pre-heated oven for half of the required time. Remove from the oven, turn over and replace in the oven. Finish cooking until they are golden brown. Remove and place straight onto a cooling rack and allow to go cold. Serve as part of a buffet.			

* Filling can be creamed spinach, meat or fish paste or anchovy fillets chopped finely.

☐   ☐   ☐

Choux pastry

Choux pastry

Pâte á choux

🥄 30 min

Step	Commodity	1 portion	10 portions	
1	Water	25 ml	250 ml	Place in a saucepan and bring to the boil gently.
	Castor sugar	small pinch	large pinch	Add.
	Salt	small pinch	large pinch	Add.
	Butter*	10 g	100 g	Add and melt.
2	Strong flour	12.5 g	125 g	Sieve, add to the liquid and mix well with a spoon. Cook at a moderate heat, stirring continuously until the mixture leaves the sides of the pan. Remove and allow to cool.
3	Eggs	½ approx	4	Break into a jug and beat. Gradually add to the flour mixture until a dropping consistency is achieved.

* Margarine can be used in place of butter.

USED: To make choux buns, eclairs, profiteroles, cream buns.

☐   ☐   ☐

CHOUX PASTRY GOODS

Chocolate éclairs

🥄 1 hr   🍳 30 min   ≋ 210°C

Step	Commodity	1 portion	10 portions	
1	Choux pastry	10 ml	100 ml	Place in a piping bag with a 1 cm plain nozzle. Pipe 8 cm lengths onto a greased baking tray. Place in a pre-heated oven for the appropriate time. Remove and allow to cool. Make a small hole in one end, underneath.
	Whipping cream	15 ml	150 ml	Place in a bowl.
	Vanilla essence	1 drop	2–3 drops	Add.
	Icing sugar	5 g	50 g	Add and whisk to piping consistency. Place in a savoy bag with a 1 cm plain tube. Fill the eclair with the appropriate amount of cream.
2	Fondant	5 g	50 g	Heat in a bain-marie.
	Chocolate couverture	5 g	50 g	Chop finely and add to the fondant. Melt and mix in well. Dip each eclair in the chocolate fondant. Allow to cool on a cooling rack.

NOTE: Coffee flavoured éclairs (éclairs au café) may be made by the same process, replacing the chocolate couverture with coffee essence.

☐   ☐   . ☐

Cream buns

Choux à la crème

🥄 1 hr   🍲 30 min   ≋ 210°C

Step	Commodity	1 portion	10 portions	
1	Choux pastry	50 g	500 g	Place in a piping bag with a 1 cm plain nozzle. Pipe out onto a greased baking tray into circles the size of a walnut.
	Chopped almonds	2 g	20 g	Sprinkle over the top. Place in a pre-heated oven for the appropriate time. Remove and allow to go cold. Make a small hole on the underneath.
2	Whipping cream	15 ml	150 ml	Place in a bowl.
	Vanilla essence	1 drop	2–3 drops	Add.
	Icing sugar	5 g	50 g	Add and whisk to piping consistency. Place in a savoy bag with a 1 cm plain tube. Fill the bun with the appropriate amount of cream.
3	Icing sugar	5 g	50 g	Dust over the top of the buns and serve.

☐   ☐   ☐

Chocolate profiteroles

Profiteroles au chocolat

🥄 1 hr   🍲 20 min   ≋ 210°C

Step	Commodity	1 portion	10 portions	
1	Choux pastry	50 g	500 g	Place in a piping bag with a ½ cm plain nozzle. Pipe out onto a greased baking tray into circles ½ cm in diameter. Place in a pre-heated oven for the appropriate time. Remove and allow to go cold. Make a small cut in the underneath.
2	Whipping cream	15 ml	150 ml	Place in a bowl.
	Vanilla essence	1 drop	2–3 drops	Add.
	Icing sugar	5 g	50 g	Add and whisk to piping consistency. Place in a savoy bag with a 1 cm plain tube. Fill each profiterole with the appropriate amount of cream.
3	Icing sugar	5 g	50 g	Dust the profiteroles with the sugar. Serve with a sauceboat of chocolate sauce.

☐   ☐   ☐

13

Choux pastry fritters

⏲ 1 hr   ♨ 15 min   ≋ 170°C

Step	Commodity	1 portion	10 portions	
1	Choux pastry	50 g	500 g	Using two spoons dipped in oil, shape into walnut-sized pieces and dip into the pre-heated fat for the appropriate time. Remove and place on absorbent paper.
	Icing sugar	5 g	50 g	Dust over the top of the fritters and serve with apricot sauce or jam sauce.

☐   ☐   ☐

Sugar pastry

Method 1
Sugar pastry

Pâte à sucrée

⏲ 40 min

Step	Commodity	1 portion	10 portions	
1	Butter*	25 g	250 g	Place in a clean bowl.
	Castor sugar	10 g	100 g	Add to the butter and cream the ingredients together.
2	Eggs	¼ equiv	2½	Break into a jug and beat together. Add and mix in well.
3	Plain flour	45 g	450 g	Sieve with a pinch of salt. Gradually add to the wet ingredients and mix until light and smooth. Place in a clean bowl and rest in a cool place for 20 minutes before using.

* Margarine may be used in place of butter.

Method 2
Sugar pastry

Pâte à sucrée

⏲ 40 min

Step	Commodity	1 portion	10 portions	
1	Plain flour	45 g	450 g	Add a pinch of salt and sieve together into a clean bowl.
	Butter*	25 g	250 g	Cut into small pieces and add to the flour. Rub in to a sandy texture. Make a well in the mixture.
2	Egg	¼ equiv	2½	Break into a jug and beat together.
	Castor sugar	10 g	100 g	Add to the eggs and dissolve together. Pour into the well and incorporate into the dry mixture. Lightly work until a smooth paste is achieved. Place in a clean bowl and rest in a cool place for 20 minutes before using.

* Margarine may be used in place of butter.

☐   ☐   ☐

SUGAR PASTRY PRODUCTS

Apple pie

Step	Commodity	1 portion	10 portions		
				🥄 1½ hr	🔥 45 min ≋ 230°C
1	Apples	100 g	1 kg	Peel, remove the core and slice thinly. Place in a suitably sized pie dish.	
	Water	1 tsp	3 tbsp	Add.	
	Castor sugar	25 g	250 g	Sprinkle over the top of the fruit.	
	Cloves (optional)	¼	2	Add.	
2	Sugar pastry	75 g	750 g	Roll out ½ cm thick. Cut a strip ½ cm in width. Dampen the edge of the pie dish and lay the strip all the way around the edge. Dampen the top. Cut a piece to fit the top of the pie dish and carefully place over the top. Trim any excess pastry and crimp decoratively. Brush with milk. Place in an oven for the appropriate time. Remove and sprinkle with castor sugar. Clean the pie dish and decorate with a pie frill. Serve with a sauceboat of custard sauce.	

NOTE: If the pie browns too quickly, cover with greaseproof paper.

☐   ☐   ☐

Rhubarb pie

Step	Commodity	1 portion	10 portions		
				🥄 1½ hr	🔥 45 min ≋ 230°C
1	Rhubarb	100 g	1 kg	Remove the leaves, root and tough strings of the rhubarb. Wash, cut into 2 cm pieces and place in a suitably sized pie dish.	
	Water	1 tsp	3 tbsp	Add.	
	Castor sugar	25 g	250 g	Sprinkle over the top of the fruit.	
2	Sugar pastry	75 g	750 g	Roll out ½ cm thick. Cut a strip ½ cm in width. Dampen the edge of the pie dish and lay the strip all the way around the edge. Dampen the top. Cut a piece to fit the top of the pie dish and carefully place over the top. Trim any excess pastry and crimp decoratively. Brush with milk. Place in an oven for the appropriate time. Remove and sprinkle with castor sugar. Clean the pie dish and decorate with a pie frill. Serve with a sauceboat of custard sauce.	

NOTE: If the pie browns too quickly, cover with greaseproof paper.

☐   ☐   ☐

Cherry pie

🥄 1½ hr   ♨ 45 min   ≋ 230°C

Step	Commodity	1 portion	10 portions	
1	Cherries	100 g	1 kg	Wash, remove the stalk and rewash. Place in a suitably sized pie dish.
	Water	1 tsp	3 tbsp	Add.
	Castor sugar	25 g	250 g	Sprinkle over the top of the fruit.
2	Sugar pastry	75 g	750 g	Roll out ½ cm thick. Cut a strip ½ cm in width. Dampen the edge of the pie dish and lay the strip all the way around the edge. Dampen the top. Cut a piece to fit the top of the pie dish and carefully place over the top. Trim any excess pastry and crimp decoratively. Brush with milk. Place in an oven for the appropriate time. Remove and sprinkle with castor sugar. Clean the pie dish and decorate with a pie frill. Serve with a sauceboat of custard sauce.

NOTES: If the pie browns too quickly, cover with greaseproof paper.
Blackberry, damson, raspberry, redcurrant and gooseberry pies can be made using this method.

☐   ☐   ☐

Apple flan

Flan aux pommes

🥄 1½ hr   ♨ 45 min   ≋ 220°C

Step	Commodity	1 portion	10 portions	
1	Cooking apples	75 g	750 g	Peel, remove the core and cut into slices. Retain approximately a third of the best slices for the top. Place the remaining apple in a saucepan.
	Water	1 tsp	3 tbsp	Add.
	Castor sugar	25 g	250 g	Sprinkle over the top of the fruit and cook for 5 minutes to soften. Remove and pass through a fine chinois.
2	Sugar pastry	75 g	750 g	Roll out 3 mm thick. Carefully place in a greased flan ring on a baking sheet. Ensure that it fits into the edges properly. Trim any excess pastry. Line with greaseproof paper, allowing 2 cm above the top. Fill with baking beans and place in a pre-heated oven for 30 minutes. Remove from the oven. Remove the baking beans and greaseproof paper. Add the apple purée. Lay the good slices of apple decoratively on top. Place in a pre-heated oven for 15 minutes or until the apple is lightly browned.
3	Apricot glaze	5 ml	50 ml	Heat, strain and carefully brush over the top of the apples. Serve hot or cold.

☐   ☐   ☐

Strawberry flan

Flan aux fraises

Step	Commodity	1 portion	10 portions

🥣 1½ hr   🍲 45 min   ≋ 220°C

Step	Commodity	1 portion	10 portions	
1	Sugar pastry	75 g	750 g	Roll out 3 mm thick. Carefully place in a greased flan ring on a baking sheet. Ensure that it fits into the edges properly. Trim any excess pastry. Line with greaseproof paper allowing 2 cm above the top. Fill with baking beans and place in a pre-heated oven for 30 minutes.
2	Pastry cream	50 g	500 g	Spread over the bottom of the pastry case.
3	Strawberries	50 g	500 g	Trim the stalks. Cut in half and place decoratively on top of the pastry cream.
4	Fruit juice	10 ml	100 ml	Place in a saucepan and boil. Dilute with a little water and add to the boiling liquid. Simmer until the liquid goes clear. Brush the glaze over the top of the fruit and allow to go cold.

NOTE: Raspberry and banana flans can be made using this process.
Fruit tartlets and barquettes are small pastry cases and can be filled with a fruit filling or a savoury filling.

☐   ☐   ☐

Rhubarb flan

Flan au rhubarbe

🥣 1½ hr   🍲 30 min   ≋ 220°C

Step	Commodity	1 portion	10 portions	
1	Sugar pastry	75 g	750 g	Roll out 3 mm thick. Carefully place in a greased flan ring on a baking sheet. Ensure that it fits into the edges properly. Dock the bottom.
2	Rhubarb	75 g	750 g	Trim the root. Remove the leaves and stringly pieces. Cut into 2 cm pieces. Arrange neatly on the bottom of the flan case.
	Castor sugar	10 g	100 g	Sprinkle over the top. Place in a pre-heated oven for the appropriate time. Remove and place on a cooling rack.
3	Apricot glaze	5 ml	50 ml	Heat, strain and carefully brush over the top of the rhubarb. Serve hot or cold.

☐   ☐   ☐

Bakewell tart

Step	Commodity	1 portion	10 portions	
				⏲ 1½ hr 🍲 35 min ≋ 210°C
1	Sugar pastry	75 g	750 g	Roll out 3 mm thick. Carefully place in a greased flan ring on a baking sheet. Ensure that it fits into the edges properly. Trim any excess pastry. Brush with milk. Retain the trimmings.
2	Raspberry jam	5 g	50 g	Spread over the bottom of the flan.
	Frangipane	40 g	400 g	Place in a piping bag with a plain nozzle and pipe over the jam. Roll out the remaining pastry into long strips. Cut into ½ cm length and arrange neatly in a criss cross fashion over the top of the frangipane. Press down on the edges to keep in place. Trim off the excess pastry. Brush with milk wash and place in a pre-heated oven for the appropriate time. Remove from the oven.
3	Apricot glaze	5 ml	50 ml	Heat, strain and brush over the top of the Bakewell tart.
4	Icing sugar	10 g	100 g	Sieve and add a little water to make it spread. Brush over the Bakewell tart and allow to cool.

☐   ☐   ☐

Apple pie

Step	Commodity	1 portion	10 portions	
				⏲ 1½ hr 🍲 45 min ≋ 230°C
1	Cooking apples	100 g	1 kg	Peel, remove the cores and cut into slices. Place in a suitably sized pie dish.
	Water	1 tsp	3 tbsp	Add.
	Castor sugar	25 g	250 g	Sprinkle over the top of the fruit.
2	Sugar pastry	75 g	750 g	Roll out ½ cm thick. Cut a strip ½ cm in width. Dampen the edge of the pie dish and lay the strip all the way around the edge. Dampen the top. Cut a piece to fit the top of the pie dish and carefully place over the top. Trim any excess pastry and crimp decoratively. Brush with milk. Place in a pre-heated oven for the appropriate time. Remove and sprinkle with castor sugar. Clean the pie dish and decorate with a pie frill. Serve with a sauceboat of custard sauce.

NOTE: If the pie browns too quickly, cover with greaseproof paper.

☐   ☐   ☐

Lemon meringue pie

Flan aux citrons meringuées

🥄 1½ hr　🍲 45 min　≋ 220°C

Step	Commodity	1 portion	10 portions	
1	Sugar pastry	75 g	750 g	Roll out 3 mm thick. Carefully place in a greased flan ring on a baking sheet. Ensure that it fits into the edges properly. Trim any excess pastry. Line with greaseproof paper allowing 2 cm above the top. Fill with baking beans and place in a pre-heated oven for 30 minutes. Remove from the oven. Remove the baking beans and greaseproof paper. Reset the oven to 250°C.
2	Lemon curd	50 g	500 g	Spread over the bottom of the flan case.
3	Meringue	20 g	200 g	Place in a savoy bag with a medium-sized star nozzle. Pipe over the lemon curd. Flash in the oven until the meringue is golden brown.

☐　　☐　　☐

Baked fish dishes

Baked fish steak

Darne de poisson (cuire au four)

🥄 45 min　🍲 10 min　≋ 175°C

Step	Commodity	1 portion	10 portions	
1	Cod steak	1 × 150 g	10 × 150 g	Trim and place in an earthenware dish.
	Lemon juice	5 ml	50 ml	Sprinkle over the fish.
	Butter	15 g	150 g	Melt and brush over the top of the fish. Season with salt and pepper. Cover tightly with a buttered cartouche and place in the pre-heated oven for the appropriate time. Remove, clean the dish and serve.
	Lemon wedges	1	10	Use to garnish the fish.
	Parsley sprigs	1	10	Wash, trim and serve with the fish.

NOTE: This dish may be made with whole herrings, haddock, or hake and served with béchamel-based sauce.

☐　　☐　　☐

13

Baked stuffed trout

Truite farcie au four

🍽 1 hr   ⏲ 20 min   ≋ 175°C

Step	Commodity	1 portion	10 portions	
1	Whole trout	1 × 200 g	10 × 200 g	Trim, prepare and wash thoroughly.
	Lemon, parsley and thyme stuffing	50 g	500 g	Place in the stomach area.
2	Butter	15 g	150 g	Melt and brush the earthenware dish. Place the fish in the dish.
	Lemon juice	5 ml	50 ml	Sprinkle over the fish. Brush more butter over the top of the fish. Season with salt and pepper. Cover tightly with a buttered cartouche and place in the pre-heated oven for the appropriate time. Remove, clean the dish and serve.
3	Lemon wedges	1	10	Use to garnish and fish.
	Parsley sprigs	1	10	Wash, trim and place with the lemon. Serve with parsley butter.

NOTE: This dish may be made with whole herrings, mackerel or red mullet.

☐   ☐   ☐

Baked vegetables and potatoes

Baked potatoes

Pommes au four

🍽 15 min   ⏲ 1½ hr   ≋ 180°C

Step	Commodity	1 portion	10 portions	
1	Baking potatoes	1 × 175 g	10 × 175 g	Place under cold running water and scrub thoroughly. Dry and with a sharp knife make a thin incision around the length of the potatoes to prevent them from splitting. Place on a bed of rock or all purpose salt in a baking tray. Place in a pre-heated oven and bake for the appropriate time or until the potatoes are cooked. Remove from the oven. Make a cross incision ½ cm deep in the top and squeeze the potato open.
2	Butter	25 g	250 g	Place in the centre of the opening.
	Parsley sprigs	1	10	Wash, dry and place in the butter. Place in a rosette shaped serviette and present.

☐   ☐   ☐

Macaire potatoes

Pommes Macaire

🥄 15 min   ♨ 1½ hr   ≋ 180°C

Step	Commodity	1 portion	10 portions	
1	Baking potatoes	1 × 175 g	10 × 175 g	Place under cold running water and scrub thoroughly. Dry and with a sharp knife make a thin incision around the length of the potatoes to prevent them from splitting. Place on a bed of rock or all purpose salt in a baking tray. Place in a pre-heated oven and bake for the appropriate time or until the potatoes are cooked. Remove from the oven. Scoop the potato out into a clean bowl. Discard the skins.
2	Butter	25 g	250 g	Add to the potato and season with salt and pepper. Mash with a fork and mix together well.
3	Butter	5 g	50 g	Melt and brush the bottom and sides of an omelette pan. Place on the stove top and heat. Remove and fill with the potato mix. Press down lightly. Place back in the oven for 15 minutes so that the sides are golden brown. Turn out onto a chopping board and cut into the appropriate portions. Brush with butter and serve.

NOTE: A buttered anna mould may be used instead of an omelette pan. Pommes Macaire may also be shaped like individual fish cakes, lightly floured and fried in a pan.

Extensions of Macaire potatoes

Dish	Additional ingredients per 1 portion	Action
Pommes Robert	¼ egg yolk equiv	Add to the mashed potato and mix in well.
	pinch chives	Wash, dry and cut into small dice. Add to the other ingredients and mix in well. Shape as Macaire potatoes.
Pommes Byron		Shape potatoes like fish cakes and place on a baking tray. Make a hollow in the centre of each
	15 g cheddar cheese	Grate and place in the hollow.
	15 ml cream	Pour into the hollow and finish off under a pre-heated salamander.

☐   ☐   ☐

13

Anna potatoes

Pommes Anna

🥄 1 hr   ♨ 40 min   ≋ 210°C

Step	Commodity	1 portion	10 portions	
1	Potatoes	150 g	600 g	Peel, wash, dry and trim into cylindrical shape. Slice the potatoes into 1 mm pieces. Do not store in water.
2	Butter	30 g	300 g	Melt and butter the anna mould well. Heat the mould on the stove. Remove to the side and place the sliced potatoes in the mould, overlapping to form the bottom layer. Season with salt and pepper and repeat the process until the mould is full. Return the mould to the stove and heat until the potatoes become loose at the base. Press down lightly, cover with a lid and place in the pre-heated oven for the appropriate time. Press the potatoes down lightly occasionally during cooking. Remove from the oven and turn out for service.

Extensions of Anna potatoes

Dish	Additional ingredients per portion	
Pommes voisin/ Pommes ambassadeur	40 g Cheddar cheese	Grate the cheese and sprinkle between between each layer.
Pommes Dauphin		As for pommes Anna. Cut the potatoes into julienne.
Pommes Nana		As for pommes dauphin cook in individual copper dariole moulds.

☐　　☐　　☐

Gratin potatoes   Pommes Gratinées

⌣ 15 min　　♨ 1½ hr　　≋ 180°C

Step	Commodity	1 portion	10 portions	
1	Baking potatoes	1 × 175 g	10 × 175 g	Place under cold running water and scrub thoroughly. Dry and with a sharp knife make a thin incision around the length of the potatoes to prevent them from splitting. Place on a bed of rock or all purpose salt in a baking tray. Place in a pre-heated oven and bake for the appropriate time or until the potatoes are cooked. Remove from the oven. Cut through the centre lengthways and scoop out the centre. Retain the skins. Mash with a fork.
2	Chedder cheese	20 g	200 g	Grate and add to the potato.
	Butter	25 g	250 g	Add and mix well together. Refill the potato skins.
	Cheddar cheese	5 g	50 g	Grate and sprinkle over the top. Place in the oven for 10 minutes until the cheese has turned golden brown.
	Parsley sprigs	1	10	Wash, dry and place on the potatoes. Place in a rosette shaped serviette and present.

Extensions of gratin potatoes

Dish	Additional ingredients per portion	
Pommes ménagère	25 g cooked ham	Cut into small dice and add to the potato mixture.
Pommes Arlie	15 ml cream	Add to the potato mixture.
	pinch chives	Wash, dry and cut into small dice. Add to the other ingredients and mix in well.

☐　　☐　　☐

Baked stuffed courgettes

Courgettes farcies au four

⌣ 45 min   ▥ 20 min   ≋ 210°C

Step	Commodity	1 portion	10 portions	
1	Courgettes	1 × 100 g	10 × 100 g	Wash, remove the top and tail. Place in a saucepan of boiling salted water for 5 minutes. Refresh and drain. Cut in half lengthways. Remove the pulp and chop. Retain the skins. Sweat in a little butter and season with salt and pepper.
2	Mushroom duxelle	50 g	500 g	Add to the courgette mixture and refill the skins. Arrange on a baking tray. Brush lightly with melted butter. Place in a pre-heated oven for the appropriate time. Serve hot.

NOTE: This dish may be made with cucumber cut into 8 cm lengths.

☐   ☐   ☐

Baked stuffed mushrooms

Champignons farcis au four

⌣ 45 min   ▥ 4–5 min   ≋ 210°C

Step	Commodity	1 portion	10 portions	
1	Open cap mushrooms	3	30	Wash, remove the stalks, peel and rewash.
	Mushroom duxelle	50 g	500 g	Place in the upturned mushroom and season with salt and pepper. Arrange on a tray and place in a pre-heated oven for the appropriate time. Remove and serve hot.

☐   ☐   ☐

Baked tomatoes

Tomates au four

⌣ 15 min   ▥ 4–5 min   ≋ 210°C

Step	Commodity	1 portion	10 portions	
1	Medium tomatoes	2	20	Remove the eyes and score the other end. Arrange on a baking tray, eye down.
	Butter	5 g	50 g	Melt and brush over the tomatoes. Season with salt and pepper and place in a pre-heated oven for the appropriate time. Remove and serve immediately garnished with picked parsley.

☐   ☐   ☐

Tomatoes Provençale style

Tomates Provençale

⌣ 15 min   ▥ 5–7 min   ≋ 210°C

Step	Commodity	1 portion	10 portions	
1	Medium tomatoes	2	20	Remove the eye and cut the tomatoes in half. Scoop out the seeds and place in a bowl.
	Butter	5 g	25 g	Place in a frying pan and heat gently. Add the tomato seeds and sweat.
	Chopped parsley	pinch	2 tsp	Add.
	Dry white wine	10 ml	100 ml	Add and reduce.
	Breadcrumbs	10 g	100 g	Add and season with salt and pepper. Refill the tomatoes with the mixture. Place in a pre-heated oven for the appropriate time. Remove and serve.

☐   ☐   ☐

Cakes and biscuits

Plain scones

Step	Commodity	1 portion	10 portions			
				⌣ 30 min	🥧 15–20 min	≋ 200°C
1	Self raising flour	20 g	200 g	Sieve into a clean bowl.		
	Butter	5 g	50 g	Add to the flour and rub in to a sandy texture. Make a well.		
2	Milk/water 50%/50%	8 ml	80 ml	Measure into a jug.		
	Castor sugar	5 g	50 g	Add to the liquid and dissolve. Pour 75 per cent into the centre of the well and lightly incorporate into the flour. Pour in the remaining liquid and mix to a smooth dough.* Roll out into a round shape 1 cm thick. Using a sharp knife mark out the appropriate portions by making an incision ½ cm thick.		
3	Milk	5 ml	25 ml	Brush over the top. Place in a pre-heated oven for the appropriate time. Remove and place on a wire rack to cool.		

* The mixture might need more or less liquid to achieve this result.

☐   ☐   ☐

Fruit scones

Step	Commodity	1 portion	10 portions			
				⌣ 30 min	🥧 15–20 min	≋ 200°C
1	Self raising flour	20 g	200 g	Sieve into a clean bowl.		
	Butter	5 g	50 g	Add to the flour and rub in to a sandy texture.		
	Sualtanas	5 g	50 g	Wash thoroughly, dry and add to mixture. Make a well.		
2	Milk/water 50%/50%	8 ml	80 ml	Measure into a jug.		
	Castor sugar	5 g	50 g	Add to the liquid and dissolve. Pour 75 per cent into the centre of the well and lightly incorporate into the flour. Pour in the remaining liquid and mix to a smooth dough.* Roll out into a round shape 1 cm thick. Using a sharp knife mark out the appropriate portions by making an incision ½ cm thick.		
3	Milk	5 ml	25 ml	Brush over the top. Place in a pre-heated oven for the appropriate time. Remove and place on a wire rack to cool.		

* The mixture might need more or less liquid to achieve this result.

☐   ☐   ☐

Genoese sponge

Génoise

Step	Commodity	1 portion	10 portions				
				45 min	30 min	200°–220°C	
1	Eggs	1	10	Place in a clean warm, grease free bowl.			
	Castor sugar	25 g	250 g	Add and whisk with a balloon whisk over a bain-marie of warm water until the mixture has doubled and is light and creamy. This stage is called the ribbon stage.			
2	Cake flour	25 g	250 g	Sieve and carefully fold into the mixture. Ensure that all the flour has been incorporated into the egg mixture.			
3	Butter	10 g	100 g	Melt gently and fold in. Place the mixture into prepared tins. Place in the pre-heated oven and bake for the appropriate time. Remove and turn out onto a cooling rack. Allow to cool before using.			

NOTE: Margarine of a good quality oil may be used instead of butter.

□   □   □

Chocolate Genoese sponge

Génoise au chocolat

Step	Commodity	1 portion	10 portions				
				45 min	30 min	200°–220°C	
1	Eggs	1	10	Place in a clean warm, grease free bowl.			
	Castor sugar	25 g	250 g	Add and whisk with a balloon whisk over a bain-marie of warm water until the mixture has doubled and is light and creamy. This stage is called the ribbon stage.			
2	Cake flour	20 g	200 g	Place in a bowl.			
	Cocoa powder	5 g	50 g	Add and sieve well together three times and then fold into the mixture. Ensure that all the flour has been incorporated into the egg mixture.			
3	Butter	10 g	100 g	Melt gently and fold in. Place the mixture into prepared tins. Place in the pre-heated oven and bake for the appropriate time. Remove and turn out onto a cooling rack. Allow to cool before using.			

NOTE: Margarine or a good quality oil may be used instead of butter.

□   □   □

13

Victoria sponge sandwich

Step	Commodity	1 portion	10 portions	30 min · 12 min · 220°–230°C
1	Butter	25 g	250 g	Place in a clean bowl.
	Castor sugar	25 g	250 g	Add and cream together until the mixture is soft and fluffy.
2	Egg	½	5	Break into a jug and whisk together. Gradually add to the mixture.
3	Self raising flour	25 g	250 g	Sieve and carefully fold into the mixture. Ensure that all the flour has been incorporated completely. Divide into the appropriate number of tins, filling no more than half way. Place in a pre-heated oven and bake for the appropriate time. Remove and turn out onto a cooling rack. Allow to cool before using.
4	Raspberry jam	10 g	100 g	Spread one half of the sponges with the jam and place the other half on top.
5	Icing sugar	5 g	50 g	Place in a fine sieve and use to dust the top of the sponge.

NOTE: Some establishments add 1 g per portion of glycerine to improve the keeping quality by absorbing moisture.

□ □ □

Swiss roll (fatless sponge)

Step	Commodity	1 portion	10 portions	30 min · 5–6 min · 230°–250°C
1	Eggs	1	10	Place in a clean warm, grease free bowl.
	Castor sugar	25 g	250 g	Add and whisk with a balloon whisk over a bain-marie of warm water until the mixture has doubled and is light and creamy. This stage is called the ribbon stage.
2	Cake flour	25 g	250 g	Sieve and carefully fold into the mixture. Ensure that all the flour has been incorporated into the egg mixture. Pour into the prepared Swiss roll tins. Place in a pre-heated oven for the appropriate time.
3	Castor sugar	10 g	100 g	Sprinkle over a large sheet of greaseproof paper and lay on the work table. Remove the sponge from the oven and turn out onto the sugared paper. Remove the silicon/greaseproof paper from the other side.
4	Jam	10 g	100 g	Spread over the sponge quickly. Using the sugared paper for evenness, roll the sponge up towards yourself into a fairly tight roll. Leave the paper on the outside for a few minutes until the sponge has cooled slightly. Place on a cooling rack to go cold.

* Jam of your choice – raspberry, strawberry, blackcurrant etc.

□ □ □

Sponge fingers

Biscuits à la cuillère

Step	Commodity	1 portion	10 portions

☺ 45 min   🍲 8–10 min   ≋ 200°–220°C

Step	Commodity	1 portion	10 portions	
1	Eggs	1	10	Separate the whites from the yolks, cover and store the whites somewhere cool for the moment. Place the yolks in a clean, grease-free bowl.
	Castor sugar	25 g	250 g	Add and whisk with a balloon whisk until the mixture is light and creamy.
2	Cake flour	25 g	250 g	Sieve and carefully fold into the mixture. Ensure that all the flour has been incorporated into the egg yolk mixture. Place the egg whites into a bowl and whisk until the mixture peaks. Carefully fold the whites into the mixture. Place in a piping bag with a 1 cm plain nozzle and pipe 6 cm lengths on prepared silicon or greaseproof paper on an oven tray.
3	Icing sugar	5 g	50 g	Sprinkle liberally over the sponge fingers. Place in a pre-heated oven for the appropriate time. Remove from the oven and lift the sponges off on the paper and place face down on a clean surface; normally the biscuits should fall off. If using greaseproof paper, dampen the top of the paper lightly, this has the effect of loosening the biscuits on the other side. Place on a cooling rack to go cold.

☐   ☐   ☐

Large fruit cake

☺ 1 hr   🍲 2½ hr   ≋ 140°–170°C

Step	Commodity	1 portion	10 portions	
1	Butter*	25 g	250 g	Place in a suitably sized clean bowl.
	Castor sugar	25 g	250 g	Add to the butter and cream together until the mixture is soft and fluffy.
2	Eggs	½	5	Break into a jug and beat. Gradually add to the creamed mixture. Ensure that the egg is mixed in well.
	Mixed spice	pinch	1 tsp	Place in a bowl.
	Self raising flour	40 g	400 g	Add to the spice, sieve and carefully fold into the mixture. Ensure that all the flour has been completely incorporated.
	Glacé cherries	10 g	100 g	Chop small and add.
	Chopped peel	20 g	200 g	Add.
3	Mixed fruits†	40 g	400 g	Prepare, wash thoroughly, dry and add to the mixture. Place in the prepared cake tins‡ lined with greased greaseproof paper.
4	Almonds	10 g	100 g	Arrange on top of the mixture. Place in a pre-heated oven. Bake at 170°C for approximately 1 hour. Reduce the heat to 150°C for 30 minutes and reduce to 140°C for a further 45 minutes. Test to see if the cake is cooked by inserting a thin needle or skewer into the centre. If the cake is cooked the needle will come out clean, if it comes out sticky and damp it is not cooked. When ready, remove and cool on a wire rack.

*†‡ See notes following Christmas cake recipe.

☐   ☐   ☐

13

Christmas cake

Step	Commodity	1 portion	10 portions				
				🍽 1 hr	♨ 2½ hr	≋ 140°–170°C	
1	Butter*	20 g	200 g	Place in a suitably sized clean bowl.			
	Demerara sugar	20 g	200 g	Add to the butter and cream together until the mixture is soft and fluffy.			
	Eggs	½	5	Break into a jug and beat. Gradually add to the creamed mixture. Ensure that the egg is mixed in well.			
2	Mixed spice	pinch	1 tsp	Place in a bowl.			
	Glacé cherries	10 g	100 g	Chop small and add.			
	Chopped peel	20 g	200 g	Add.			
	Mixed fruits†	40 g	400 g	Prepare, wash thoroughly, dry and add to the mixture.			
	Ground almond	15 g	150 g	Add.			
	Brandy	15 ml	150 ml	Add.			
	Self raising flour	30 g	300 g	Add to the spice, sieve and carefully fold into the mixture. Ensure that all the flour has been completely incorporated. Place in the prepared cake tins‡ lined with greased greaseproof paper. Place in a pre-heated oven. Bake at 170°C for approximately 1 hour. Reduce the heat to 150°C for 30 minutes and reduce to 140° for a further 45 minutes. Test to see if the cake is cooked by inserting a thin needle or skewer into the centre. If the case is cooked the needle will come out clean, if it comes out sticky and damp it is not cooked. Remove and cool on a wire rack when ready.			

NOTE: When baking avoid slamming the oven door as moving or shaking may cause the cooking mixture to sink. Also the inrush of cold air may cause the mixture to rise unevenly.

* Margarine can be substituted.
† A combination of raisins, sultanas and currants.
‡ For 10 portions use 2 × 14 cm cake tins.

Cherry cakes

Step	Commodity	1 bun	10 buns	⌣ 30 min 🍲 15–20 min ≋ 220°C
1	Butter	12.5 g	125 g	Place in a suitably sized bowl.
	Castor sugar	12.5 g	125 g	Add to the butter and cream together until the mixture is soft and fluffy.
	Eggs	¼	2½	Break into a jug and beat together.
	Vanilla essence	1 drop	few drops	Sprinkle over the eggs and mix in. Gradually add the eggs to the mixture. Ensure that the egg is mixed in well.
2	Self raising flour	20 g	200 g	Sieve and fold into the creamed mixture.*
	Glacé cherries	5 g	50 g	Cut into small pieces, add and mix in well. Divide into the appropriate portions in paper cases or greased cake tins. Place in a pre-heated oven for the appropriate time. Remove and cool on a wire rack.

*NOTE: The mixture should be of a dropping consistency. It may be necessary to add a little milk to achieve the correct consistency.

☐   ☐   ☐

Coconut cakes

Step	Commodity	1 bun	10 buns	⌣ 30 min 🍲 15–20 min ≋ 220°C
1	Butter	12.5 g	125 g	Place in a suitably sized bowl.
	Castor sugar	12.5 g	125 g	Add to the butter and cream together until the mixture is soft and fluffy.
	Eggs	¼	2½	Break into a jug and beat together.
	Vanilla essence	1 drop	few drops	Sprinkle over the eggs and mix in. Gradually add the eggs to the mixture. Ensure that the egg is mixed in well.
2	Self raising flour	15 g	150 g	Sieve and fold into the creamed mixture.
	Desiccated coconut	5 g	50 g	Sprinkle over and mix in well.* Divide into the appropriate portions in paper cases or greased cake tins. Place in a pre-heated oven for the appropriate time. Remove and cool on a wire rack.

*NOTE: The mixture should be of a dropping consistency. It may be necessary to add a little milk to achieve the correct consistency.

☐   ☐   ☐

13

Queen cakes

Step	Commodity	1 bun	10 buns			
				🥄 30 min	🍲 15–20 min	≋ 220°C
1	Butter	12.5 g	125 g	Place in a suitably sized bowl.		
	Castor sugar	12.5 g	125 g	Add to the butter and cream together until the mixture is soft and fluffy.		
	Eggs	¼	2½	Break into a jug and beat together.		
	Vanilla essence	1 drop	few drops	Sprinkle over the eggs and mix in. Gradually add the eggs to the mixture. Ensure that the egg is mixed in well.		
2	Self raising flour	20 g	200 g	Sieve and fold into the creamed mixture.		
	Mixed fruit	10 g	100 g	Wash thoroughly, dry and add to the creamed mixture.		
	Glacé cherries	5 g	50 g	Cut into small pieces, add and mix in well.* Divide into the appropriate portions in paper cases or greased cake tins. Place in a pre-heated oven for the appropriate time. Remove and cool on a wire rack.		

*NOTE: The mixture should be of a dropping consistency. It may be necessary to add a little milk to achieve the correct consistency.

☐   ☐   ☐

PETIT FOURS

Petit fours are an assortment of small biscuits, cakes, sweets and glazed fruits (see also sugar boiling) served after special meals.

Cats' tongues   Langues du chat

Step	Commodity	2 portions	20 portions			
				🥄 30 min	🍲 3–4 min	≋ 230°C
1	Icing sugar	25 g	250 g	Place in a bowl.		
	Butter	20 g	200 g	Add and cream lightly.		
	Vanilla essence	1 drop	few drops	Add and mix in well.		
	Egg whites	½–¾	5–6	Add slowly taking care not to curdle the mixture.		
	Plain flour	20 g	200 g	Sieve and fold in gently. Place in a piping bag with a 3 mm plain nozzle and pipe 5 cm long 'tongues' onto a lightly greased baking sheet. Place in a pre-heated oven and bake until the edges are light brown and the centre yellow. Remove from the oven and, using a palette knife, place each on a cooling rack.		

NOTE: Cornets are made using the same mixture but are piped into 2½ cm diameter rounds. Using a palette knife, remove from the tray while hot and fold over a cream horn mould to create the horn shape. Allow to cool and set. Fill with cream and use as petit fours or use to decorate gateaux.

☐   ☐   ☐

Almond biscuits

🥄 30 min   🍲 10–15 min   ≋ 185°C

Step	Commodity	2 portions	20 portions	
1	Egg whites	¾	3	Place in a clean bowl and whisk until stiff.
	Ground almonds	20 g	200 g	Carefully stir into the egg whites.
	Castor sugar	10 g	100 g	Add carefully.
	Almond essence	1 drop	few drops	Add and mix in gently. Place in a piping bag with a medium star nozzle.
2	Rice paper sheets	¼	2	Lay carefully on a clean baking sheet. Pipe the mixture in a variety of shapes on top. Decorate with small pieces of glacé cherries and angelica. Place on a pre-heated baking tray and cook for the required time. Remove from the oven and place on a cooling tray with the aid of a palette knife. Cut off the excess rice paper with scissors or a sharp knife.

☐   ☐   ☐

Piped biscuits   Sablés à la poche

🥄 30 min   🍲 8–10 min   ≋ 190°C

Step	Commodity	2 portions	20 portions	
1	Castor sugar	15 g	150 g	Place in a bowl.
	Butter	30 g	300 g	Add and cream until light and creamy.
	Vanilla essence*	1 drop	few drops	Add and mix in well.
2	Eggs	¼ equiv	2	Add slowly, taking care not to curdle the mixture.
	Ground almonds	7 g	70 g	Carefully add to the mixture.
3	Plain flour	40 g	400 g	Sieve and fold in gently. Place in a piping bag with a small star nozzle or plain and pipe into a variety of shapes onto a lightly greased sheet. Decorate the top if required with halved glacé cherries, angelica, almonds or leave plain. Place in a pre-heated oven and bake until the biscuits are light brown. Remove from the oven and, using a palette knife, place on a cooling rack.

* Lemon zest may be used instead of vanilla.

☐   ☐   ☐

13

Shortbread biscuits

Step	Commodity	2 portions	10 portions					
				⌣ 30 min	🍲 12–15 min	≋ 190°C		
1	Flour	20 g	200 g	Place in a bowl.				
	Rice flour	20 g	200 g	Add and sieve together.				
	Butter	20 g	200 g	Cut into small pieces and rub in, to the texture of breadcrumbs.				
	Castor sugar	20 g	200 g	Add and mix in.				
2	Eggs	¼ equiv	2	Break into a jug and beat until smooth. Add to the mixture to mix to a stiff paste. Roll out 3 mm thick and cut into fancy shapes. Using a palette knife arrange on a baking tray and place in a pre-heated oven for the appropriate time or until golden brown. Remove and place on a cooling rack with the aid of a palette knife and allow to cool.				

☐ ☐ ☐

Baked fruit dishes

Baked apples

Pomme bonne femme

Step	Commodity	1 portion	10 portions					
				⌣ 30 min	🍲 35 min	≋ 200°C		
1	Cooking apples	1 medium	10 medium	Wash well, remove the core and make a 2 mm incision around the width of the apple. Place on a baking tray.				
2	Brown sugar	15 g	150 g	Sprinkle down the centre of the apple.				
	Cloves	1	10	Place on top of the sugar.				
3	Water	10 ml	100 ml	Pour over the sugar. Place in a pre-heated oven and bake for 15–20 minutes. Remove and turn over carefully. Return to the oven and complete the cooking process for the appropriate time. Serve on a flat with a little of the cooking liquor.				

NOTE: Serve with custard sauce or cream.

☐ ☐ ☐

Baked pears in pastry

Step	Commodity	1 portion	10 portions	⤵ 30 min 🍲 35 min ≋ 200°C
1	Pears	1 medium	10 medium	Wash well, remove the stalk and peel. Carefully remove the core from the bottom. Place in a bowl of water.
2	Sugar pastry	50 g	500 g	Roll out 3 mm thick and cut into the appropriate number of triangles with 20 cm sides. Brush with water.
3	Castor sugar	15 g	150 g	Sprinkle over the pastry. Remove the pears from the water and dry. Place a pear in the centre of a triangle. Dampen the edges with water and draw them up to enclose the pear. Crimp to seal. Arrange on a baking tray.
4	Egg wash	5 ml	50 ml	Brush over the pastry and place in a pre-heated oven for the appropriate time. Remove and serve hot.

NOTE: Serve with custard sauce or fresh cream.

☐   ☐   ☐

Basic pastry preparations

Butter cream

Step	Commodity	1 portion	10 portions	⤵ 30 min
1	Unsalted butter	50 g	500 g	Place in a suitably sized bowl and beat until light and creamy.
2	Icing sugar	35 g	350 g	Sieve over the butter and mix. Flavour accordingly.

☐   ☐   ☐

Boiled butter cream

Step	Commodity	1 portion	10 portions	⤵ 45 min
1	Boiled sugar	50 ml	500 ml	Cook to the soft ball stage and arrest immediately.
2	Eggs	1	10	Break into a mixing bowl.
	Icing sugar	10 g	100 g	Add and whisk to the ribbon stage. Gradually add the boiled sugar to the egg mixture and whisk continuously until the mixture begins to cool.
3	Unsalted butter	75 g	750 g	Cut into small pieces and add to the mixture. Whisk until a smooth cream is achieved.

☐   ☐   ☐

Crème chantilly

Crème chantilly

Step	Commodity	1 portion	10 portions	⤵ 15 min
1	Whipping cream	25 ml	250 ml	Place in a bowl and whisk to a piping consistency.
	Castor sugar	5 g	50 g	Add.
	Vanilla essence	1 drop	few drops	Add and mix well together. Place in the fridge for use when required.

☐   ☐   ☐

13

343

Pastry cream

Crème Pâtissière

⌣ 15 min   ♨ 30 min

Step	Commodity	1 portion	10 portions	
1	Eggs	½	5	Place in a bowl.
	Castor sugar	20 g	200 g	Add and whisk together until almost white.
	Flour	10 g	100 g	Add.
	Custard powder	5 g	50 g	Add and mix in well.
2	Milk	125 ml	1¼ litres	Place in a clean saucepan and boil. Pour over the ingredients in the bowl and mix well together. Strain into a clean saucepan.
3	Vanilla essence	1 drop	few drops	Add and stir to the boil, making sure that the mixture does not burn. Remove and place in a clean bowl.
4	Icing sugar	5 g	50 g	Sprinkle over the top to prevent a skin from forming. The cream is now ready for use.

NOTE: Chocolate pastry cream may be made by adding 20 g of chocolate couverture of 15 g of cocoa powder per portion. Coffee pastry cream may be made by adding 7 ml of coffee essence per portion.

☐   ☐   ☐

Frangipane filling

⌣ 30 min

Step	Commodity	1 portion	10 portions	
1	Butter	12.5 g	125 g	Place in a clean bowl and soften.
	Castor sugar	12.5 g	125 g	Add and cream until smooth and fluffy.
	Eggs	¼	2	Gradually beat in the eggs.
	Ground almonds	12.5 g	125 g	Add.
	Plain flour	1 g	10 g	Add and mix lightly.

☐   ☐   ☐

Lemon curd (A)

⌣ 30 min   ♨ 30 min

Step	Commodity	1 portion	10 portions	
1	Egg yolks	½	5	Place in a clean bowl.
	Castor sugar	25 g	250 g	Add and cream together.
	Butter	25 g	250 g	Soften and add to the other ingredients.
	Lemon	¼	2½	Remove the zest and add to the butter. Squeeze the juice into the mixture. Place in a bain-marie and whisk continuously until the mixture thickens. Do not allow the mixture to get too hot as it will curdle the egg.

☐   ☐   ☐

Lemon curd (B)

Step	Commodity	1 portion	10 portions			
					🥄 30 min	♨ 30 min
1	Water	25 ml	250 ml	Place in a saucepan and boil.		
	Castor sugar	10 g	100 g	Add.		
	Lemon	¼	2½	Remove the zest and add to the water. Squeeze the juice into the water and simmer gently for 5 minutes.		
2	Cornflour	1.5 g	15 g	Dilute in a little water and add to the liquid. Stir in thoroughly.		
	Egg yolks	½	5	Place in a clean bowl and whisk. Add the thickened liquid and mix in well.		
	Butter	2.5 g	25 g	Add and mix into the curd. Allow to cool, refrigerate and use as required.		

☐   ☐   ☐

Fondant

Step	Commodity	1 portion	10 portions			
					🥄 5 min	♨ 30 min
1	Cube sugar	60 g	600 g	Place in a suitably sized copper saucepan.		
	Confectioners' glucose	25 ml	250 ml	Add.		
2	Water	25 ml	250 ml	Add and cook to the feather degree (115°C). Pour onto an oiled slab. Use a palette knife to keep turning. Allow to cool to 100°C. Agitate with a metal spatula and the mass will become creamy and, as the agitation continues, thicker and whiter in colour. When it becomes too thick to work with a spatula use your hands until it is a smooth pliable glossy mass. Store in a clean container with an tight-fitting lid. Use as required. Fondant may be thinned down with stock syrup. The fondant is ready for use.		

13

☐   ☐   ☐

Praline

Step	Commodity	2 portions	20 portions			
					🥄 30 min	♨ 30 min
1	Chopped almonds	10 g	100 g	Place on a baking tray.		
	Chopped hazelnuts	10 g	100 g	Mix with the almonds and place under a pre-heated salamander. Cook until golden brown. Remove and allow to cool.		
2	Boiled sugar	25 ml	250 ml	Cook to the caramel stage. Arrest immediately and add the nuts. Mix together thoroughly. Turn out onto a lightly oiled marble slab to cool. Shape as required.		

NOTE: Praline may be cooled and crushed and used to decorate gateaux.

☐   ☐   ☐

Sugar boiling

Sugar boiling is considered to be an art and needs to be carried out under expert supervision as not only is it difficult, but also dangerous as the boiling sugar can reach temperatures in excess of 177°C.

Boiled sugar is used to make spun sugar for decorating gateaux, for caramel for crème caramels, in the production of Italian meringue, pulled sugar for making flower and leaf shapes, and to make fondant. Fondant is made by boiling sugar in three parts sugar to one part water. This solution is called 'super-saturated'. When agitated a super-saturated solution will crystallise. In fondant production, the technique is to control the crystal formation to produce minute light-reflecting crystals. In pulled sugar, care must be taken not to induce crystallisation by over agitating. To prevent crystalisation in sugar syrups 'confectioners' glucose' is added, approximately 1 part glucose to 3 parts sugar.

The best type of sugar to use for boiling is lump cane sugar or preserving sugar as this is sugar in its purest state. Beet sugar has a tendency to crystallise and become unusable.

What happens

If a solution of sugar undergoes prolonged boiling certain chemical changes take place. The sucrose is broken down into two simpler sugars, dextrose and laevulose. Combined they form invert sugar. The rate of boiling has an effect upon the amount of inversion that takes place; the slower the boil, the more invert sugar is produced.

The change from sucrose to invert sugar by boiling is increased by the presence of catalyst in the form of an acid. The simplest acid to use would be lemon juice or tartaric acid.

If the boiling sugar becomes contaminated by dirt it may crystallise.

Degree of cooking	Temperature	Test for degree
Boiling	104°–105°C	Effervescence on the liquid.
Thread	107°C	If the liquid is touched with a clean, dry finger and joined with the thumb, a thread of sugar should stretch between the two.
Pearl	110°C	If the liquid is touched with a clean, dry finger and joined with the thumb, a thread of sugar with pearl like beads should form between the two.
Blow	113°C	A loop of wire is inserted into the boiling syrup and a thin film of syrup is produced. It can be blown.
Feather	115°C	As before, but this time when blown it produces feather like shapes.

After this stage the sugar becomes too hot to test without first dipping the fingers into a bowl of ice cold water, plunging them into the syrup and immediately back into the water

Soft ball	118°C	Test as instructed. The sugar should act like plastic and can be manipulated between the fingers.
Hard ball	121°C	Test as before, this time it is much firmer.
Soft crack	132°C–138°C	Test as before. The ball of sugar formed has a thin skin that will crack easily.
Hard crack	138°C–154°C	As before, but this time it sets with a much thicker skin and it takes a lot of pressure to break it. After this the syrup takes on an amber colour and eventually emits an acrid smell.
Caramel	154°C–177°C	The syrup has a dark amber colour and will eventually turn black.

Boiled sugar for general use

$\smile$ 5 min   ♨ 30 min

Step	Commodity	1 portion	10 portions	
1	Cube sugar	60 g	600 g	Place in a suitably sized copper saucepan.
	Confectioners' glucose	25 ml	250 ml	Add.
	Water	25 ml	250 ml	Add and cook to the hard crack stage and arrest immediately. The sugar is ready for use.

☐   ☐   ☐

Boiled sugar for glazed fruits

$\smile$ 30 min   ♨ 30 min

Step	Commodity	1 portion	10 portions	
1	Cube sugar	60 g	600 g	Place in a suitably sized copper saucepan.
	Confectioners' glucose	25 ml	250 ml	Add.
	Water	25 ml	250 ml	Add and cook to the hard crack stage and arrest immediately. The sugar is ready for use.
2	Prepared fruits*	10 g	100 g	Allow the surface to dry. Using a fondue fork or similar, dip into the sugar and place onto a lightly oiled marble slab to set.

* Prepared fruits = Satsuma segments, grapes, cape gooseberries.
NOTE: Marzipan can be coloured, moulded into fruit shapes and dipped in the same way as prepared fruits.

Hot soufflés (savoury and sweet) and pudding soufflés

NOTE: Always have the soufflé mould prepared and the oven correctly adjusted before beginning to prepare the mixture.

Cheese soufflé

Soufflé au fromage

Prepare the mould by brushing liberally with melted butter.

$\smile$ 45 min   ♨ 45 min   ≋ 180°C

Step	Commodity	2 portions	10 portions	
1	Butter	25 g	250 g	Melt gently in a suitably sized saucepan.
	Flour	12.5 g	62.5 g	Add and cook to a first stage roux (blanch roux).
	Milk	100 ml	500 ml	Add and cook to a thick béchamel.
2	Gruyère cheese	50 g	250 ml	Grate and add to the sauce. Stir over the heat to blend. Remove and allow to cool slightly.
	Egg yolks	4	20	Add and blend in well. Season with salt and cayenne pepper.
3	Egg whites	4	20	Place in a clean bowl and beat until stiff. And a quarter of the egg whites to the mixture and mix in well. Gently fold in the remaining whites until they are evenly distributed throughout. Three-quarters fill the soufflé moulds, arrange on a baking sheet and place in a pre-heated oven for the appropriate time, until they have risen and are golden brown. Serve immediately.

☐   ☐   ☐

Chicken soufflé

Prepare the mould by brushing liberally with melted butter.

Step	Commodity	2 portions	10 portions	
				⏲ 45 min ♨ 45 min ≋ 180°C
1	Béchamel	75 ml	375 ml	Heat and keep warm in a bain-marie.
2	Cooked chicken	100 g	½ kg	Pass through a mincer. Moisten with a little béchamel and pass through a sieve or liquidise to form a purée. Heat the mixture in a suitably sized saucepan.
	Butter	25 g	125 g	Add and melt through. Season with salt and nutmeg.
	Lemon juice	5 ml	25 ml	Add, mix in well and allow to cool.
	Egg yolks	4	20	Add and blend in well.
3	Egg whites	4	20	Place in a clean bowl and beat until stiff. Add a quarter of the whites to the mixture and mix in well. Gently fold in the remaining whites until they are evenly distributed throughout. Three-quarters fill the soufflé moulds, arrange on a baking sheet and place in a pre-heated oven for the appropriate time, until they have risen and are golden brown. Serve immediately.

☐   ☐   ☐

Fish soufflé

Prepare the mould by brushing liberally with melted butter.

Step	Commodity	2 portions	10 portions	
				⏲ 45 min ♨ 45 min ≋ 180°C
1	Béchamel	75 ml	375 ml	Heat and keep warm in a bain-marie.
2	Cooked fish*	100 g	½ kg	Pass through a mincer. Moisten with a little béchamel and pass through a sieve or liquidise to form a purée. Heat the mixture in a suitably sized saucepan.
	Butter	25 g	125 g	Add and melt through. Season with salt and pepper.
	Lemon juice	5 ml	25 ml	Add, mix in well and allow to cool.
	Egg yolks	4	20	Add and blend in well.
3	Egg whites	4	20	Place in a clean bowl and beat until stiff. Add a quarter of the whites to the mixture and mix in well. Gently fold in the remaining whites until they are evenly distributed throughout. Three-quarters fill the soufflé moulds, arrange on a baking sheet and place in a pre-heated oven for the appropriate time, until they have risen and are golden brown. Serve immediately.

* The fish is usually cooked by poaching.
NOTE: Smoked fish may also be used in soufflés.

☐   ☐   ☐

Vanilla pudding soufflé   Pouding soufflé à la vanille/Pouding soufflé saxone

Prepare the mould by brushing liberally with melted butter.

Step	Commodity	1 portion	10 portions	� 45 min 🍲 30 min ≋ 180°C
1	Butter	10 g	100 g	Place in a bowl.
	Castor sugar	10 g	100 g	Add.
	Plain flour	10 g	100 g	Add and mix to a paste.
2	Milk	30 ml	300 ml	Place in a saucepan.
	Vanilla pod	¼	1	Add and bring to the boil. Pour the strained milk over the flour mixture and whisk in well. Place in a clean saucepan and stir until the mixture thickens. Remove from the heat and allow to cool slightly.
3	Egg yolks	½	5	Add to the cooled mixture and mix thoroughly.
4	Egg whites	½	5	Place in a clean bowl and whisk until stiff. Add a quarter of the egg whites to the mixture and mix in well. Fold in the remainder of the egg whites and divide the mixture into the appropriate portions and place in the moulds. Arrange in a bain-marie and place in a pre-heated oven for the appropriate time. Turn out onto hot plates and serve with a sauceboat of sauce anglaise.

☐   ☐   ☐

Lemon pudding soufflé   Pouding soufflé au citron

Prepare the mould by brushing liberally with melted butter.

Step	Commodity	1 portion	10 portions	� 45 min 🍲 30 min ≋ 180°C
1	Butter	10 g	100 g	Place in a bowl.
	Castor sugar	10 g	100 g	Add.
	Plain flour	10 g	100 g	Add and mix to a paste.
2	Milk	25 ml	250 ml	Place in a saucepan.
	Lemons	¼	2	Grate the zest into the milk and bring to the boil. Pour the strained milk over the flour mixture and whisk in well. Place in a clean saucepan and stir until the mixture thickens. Remove from the heat and allow to cool slightly.
3	Egg yolks	½	5	Add to the cooled mixture and mix thoroughly. Add the lemon juice.
4	Egg whites	½	5	Place in a clean bowl and whisk until stiff. Add a quarter of the egg whites to the mixture and mix in well. Fold in the remainder of the egg whites and divide the mixture into the appropriate portions and place in the moulds. Arrange in a pre-heated oven for the appropriate time. Turn out onto hot plates and serve with a sauceboat of sauce citron.

☐   ☐   ☐

13

Baked alaska

Omelette soufflée surprise

⏲ 1½ hr   🍲 7–10 min   ≋ 250°C

Step	Commodity	1 portion	10 portions	
1	Genoese sponge	50 g	500 g	Arrange on the bottom of a flat ovenproof dish. Brush with fruit syrup.
	Vanilla ice cream	50 ml	500 ml	Place on top of the sponge.
	Meringue	50 ml	500 ml	Spoon into a piping bag with a medium star nozzle and pipe all around the sponge and ice cream. Store in a freezer until ready to bake. Place in a pre-heated oven for the required time or until the meringue is golden brown. Serve immediately.

Extensions of baked alaska

Dish	Additional ingredients per portion	
With peaches (Omelette soufflée milady)	½ poached peach	Place on the sponge. Use raspberry ice cream instead of vanilla.
With pears (Omelette soufflée milord)	½ poached pear	Place on the sponge. Use raspberry ice cream instead of vanilla.

☐   ☐   ☐

Hot sweet sauces

Fresh egg custard sauce (English sauce)

Sauce à l'anglaise

⏲ 30 min   🍲 30 min

Step	Commodity	1 portion	10 portions	
1	Egg yolks	½	5	Place in a bowl.
	Vanilla essence	drop	few drops	Add.
	Castor sugar	5 g	50 g	Add and whisk together.
2	Milk	60 ml	600 ml	Place in a saucepan and boil. Pour over the other ingredients and whisk well together. Strain into a clean, thick-bottomed saucepan and return to a low heat. Stir with a spoon until the mixture coats the back of the spoon. Remove and strain into a container. Keep warm in a bain-marie

NOTE: Do not allow to boil as this will scramble the eggs.

☐   ☐   ☐

Chocolate sauce

⏱ 10 min   ♨ 30 min

Step	Commodity	1 portion	10 portions	
1	Milk	50 ml	500 ml	Place in a saucepan and boil, simmer.
	Cornflour	2 g	20 g	Dilute with a little cold milk.
	Cocoa powder	2 g	20 g	Add and pour into the simmering milk. Stir to the boil.
2	Castor sugar	10 g	100 g	Add.
	Butter	1 g	10 g	Add and stir in. Place in a bain-marie. Cover with a cartouche or cling film.

NOTE: This sauce may be made with chocolate block shredded in place of the cocoa.

☐   ☐   ☐

Apricot sauce
Sauce abricot

⏱ 5 min   ♨ 20 min

Step	Commodity	1 portion	10 portions	
1	Apricot jam	20 g	200 g	Place in a saucepan.
	Water	10 ml	100 ml	Add.
	Lemon juice	few drops		Add and bring to the boil. Simmer for 10 minutes.
	Arrowroot	1 g	10 g	Dilute with a little water and add to the simmering liquid. Reboil until the liquid goes clear. Pass through a conical strainer. The sauce is ready for service.

NOTE: Raspberry or strawberry sauce can be made using the same quantities of jam and this method.

☐   ☐   ☐

13

Melba sauce
Sauce melba

⏱ 5 min   ♨ 20 min

Step	Commodity	1 portion	10 portions	
1	Raspberry jam	20 g	200 g	Place in a saucepan.
	Water	10 ml	100 ml	Add and bring to the boil. Simmer for 10 minutes. Pass through a conical strainer and the sauce is ready for use.

☐   ☐   ☐

Orange sauce
Sauce à l'orange

⏱ 5 min   ♨ 20 min

Step	Commodity	1 portion	10 portions	
1	Orange juice	15 ml	150 ml	Place in a saucepan. Retain the zest.
	Water	50 ml	500 ml	Add and bring to the boil.
	Arrowroot	1 g	10 g	Dilute with a little water and add to the simmering liquid. Reboil until the liquid goes clear. Pass through a conical strainer. The sauce is ready for service.
2	Orange zest	2 g	20 g	Cut into julienne and place in boiling water for 1 minute. Remove and refresh. Drain and place the zest into the sauce.

NOTE: Lemon (sauce citron) or lime sauce can be made using the same quantities and this method.

☐   ☐   ☐

Sabayon sauce

👐 10 min   🍲 30 min

Step	Commodity	1 portion	10 portions	
1	Egg yolks	½	5	Place in a bowl.
	Castor sugar	10 g	1000 g	Add and whisk together until the mixture is white.
2	Dry white wine	15 ml	150 ml	Add and fold into the mixture. Place over a bain-marie and whisk continuously until the mixture is creamy and frothy and has increased 4 times in bulk. Flavour according to the dish it is being served with. Serve with a pudding soufflé.

☐   ☐   ☐

Sabayon with marsala wine

Zabaglione alla marsala

👐 10 min   🍲 30 min

Step	Commodity	1 portion	10 portions	
1	Egg yolks	1	10	Place in a bowl.
	Castor sugar	25 g	250 g	Add and whisk together until the mixture is white.
2	Marsala wine	20 ml	200 ml	Add and fold into the mixture. Place over a bain-marie and whisk continuously until the mixture is creamy and frothy and has increased 4 times in bulk. Pour into prepared glasses. Serve accompanied with biscuits à la cuillère.

NOTE: Zabaglione alla marsala may be served as a sauce with pudding soufflés. Flavour according to the dish it is being served with.

☐   ☐   ☐

Custard sauce

👐 10 min   🍲 20 min

Step	Commodity	1 portion	10 portions	
1	Milk	50 ml	500 ml	Place in a clean saucepan and boil.
	Custard powder	2 g	20 g	Dilute with a little milk and add to the boiling milk. Return to a simmer.
2	Castor sugar	5 g	50 g	Sprinkle over the top to prevent a skin from forming. Place in a bain-marie and cover to keep warm. Stir the sugar into the sauce before serving.

NOTE: Chocolate sauce may be made by replacing the custard with cornflour and adding 20 g of chocolate couverture or 15 g of cocoa powder per portion to the custard.
Almond sauce can be made by replacing the custard powder with cornflour and adding a few drops of almond essence.

☐   ☐   ☐

Sweet preparations

Crème caramels

Crème caramels

Step	Commodity	1 portion	10 portions	
				🥄 2½ hr 🍲 40 min ≋ 190°C
1	Boiled sugar	25 ml	250 ml	Cook to the caramel stage 160°C and arrest immediately. Pour into the prepared dariole mould.
2	Milk	125 ml	1.25 litres	Place in a clean saucepan and bring to the boil.
3	Eggs	1	10	Break into à bowl.
	Sugar	10 g	100 g	Add.
	Vanilla essence	drop	few drops	Add and whisk together. Pour over the hot milk and whisk. Strain through a fine sieve. Pour into the moulds over the caramel. Place in a bain-marie and put the bain-marie into the oven. Cook for the appropriate time. Allow the crème caramels to cool and then place in the fridge to set. To serve, loosen the edges and gently squeeze the rim of the mould to free the custard at the sides. Turn out onto a serving dish and pour the remaining caramel over the top.

☐   ☐   ☐

Meringue (for general use)

Step	Commodity	1 portion	10 portions	
				🥄 2 min
1	Egg whites	1	10	Whisk to a stiff mixture.
	Castor sugar	10 g	100 g	Sprinkle over the top and carefully mix in. The meringue is now ready to use.

☐   ☐   ☐

Meringue chantilly

Step	Commodity	1 portion	10 portions	
				🥄 25 min 🍲 2 hr ≋ 90°C
1	Egg whites	1	10	Whisk to a stiff mixture.
	Castor sugar	10 g	100 g	Sprinkle over the top and carefully mix in. Place in a piping bag with a large plain nozzle. Pipe onto silicon paper on a baking tray. Bake in an oven until they are dry. Allow to go cold.
2	Cream	15 ml	150 ml	Whip to a piping consistency and pipe the appropriate amount between 2 meringue shells.

☐   ☐   ☐

13

Blancmange

Step	Commodity	1 portion	10 portions			
				⤴ 30 min	♨ 45 min	
1	Milk	100 ml	1 litre	Place in a saucepan, boil and simmer.		
	Lemon	⅛	1	Julienne the zest, add to the milk along with the lemon juice.		
2	Cornflour	10 g	100 g	Dilute with a little cold milk. Add to the simmering milk and thicken. Pour into the prepared jelly moulds and allow to set. Dip the moulds into hot water for 2–3 seconds to help release the blancmange. Turn out on to a serving flat. Clean the flat and decorate with crème chantilly.		

NOTE: Lime or orange flavoured blancmange may be made by this method. Strawberry and raspberry blancmange can be made by adding 15 g of fruit purée to the simmering milk.

☐ ☐ ☐

Fruit fool

Step	Commodity	1 portion	10 portions			
				⤴ 45 min	♨ 40 min	
1	Fruit	100 g	1 kg	Prepare and place in a saucepan.		
	Water	15 ml	150 ml	Add.		
	Castor sugar	25 g	250 g	Add, bring to the boil and cook for 10 minutes. Remove from the heat. Pass through a fine sieve and allow to go cold.		
2	Milk	60 ml	600 ml	Place in a saucepan and boil.		
	Cornflour	6 g	60 g	Dilute with a little cold milk and add to the simmering milk. Cook for 5 minutes.		
	Castor sugar	60 g	600 g	Add and stir in well. Add the fruit purée and mix together thoroughly. Pour into the serving coupes and allow to set.		
3	Crème chantilly	10 ml	100 ml	Pipe a rosette over the top and serve.		

NOTE: This dish may be made with apples, gooseberries, rhubarb, raspberries or strawberries.

An alternative to using a milk and cornflour mixture is to add the fruit purée to 50 ml per portion of crème chantilly and fold together.

☐ ☐ ☐

Junket

Step	Commodity	1 portion	10 portions			
				⤴ 30 min	♨ 35 min	≋ 200°C
1	Milk	125 ml	1¼ litres	Warm to blood temperature and pour into a clean bowl.		
	Castor sugar	5 g	50 g	Add.		
	Rennet	¼ tsp	2½ tsp	Add and stir in thoroughly. Pass through a strainer into a serving bowl or individual glass serving dishes. Chill and allow to set.		
2	Whipping cream	15 ml	150 ml	Whisk to piping consistency and pipe a rosette per portion on top. Sprinkle with nutmeg and serve.		

☐ ☐ ☐

Vanilla bavarois

The moulds are prepared with a heavy brushing of almond oil before commencing preparation.

Step	Commodity	1 portion	10 portions		🥣 3 hr ♨ 45 min
1	Leaf gelatine	2.5 g	25 g	Place in a bowl of cold water.	
	Milk	50 ml	500 ml	Place in a saucepan.	
	Vanilla essence	drop	few drops	Add and boil	
	Egg yolks	½	5	Place in a suitably sized bowl.	
	Castor sugar	15 g	150 g	Add and whisk well together. Pour over the hot milk and whisk thoroughly. Return to the heat in a clean saucepan and cook gently, stirring with a spoon until the mixture has thickened and coats the back of the spoon.* Add the leaf gelatine and dissolve completely. Pass through a conical strainer.	
2	Cream	50 ml	500 ml	Place in a suitably sized bowl and lightly whip. Fold in the egg mixture and stir until it just sets. Pour into the prepared moulds. Place in the fridge and allow to set. Remove from the fridge and turn out onto a serving flat. Decorate and serve with créme chantilly.	

* Do not allow to boil as the eggs will curdle.

Extensions of vanilla bavarois (omit the vanilla)

Dish	Additional ingredients (per portion)	Action
Lemon bavarois (Bavarois au citron)	¼ lemon	Julienne the zest and add along with the lemon juice.
Orange bavarois (Bavarois à l'orange)	¼ orange	Julienne the zest and add along with the orange juice.
Lime bavarois (Bavarois au limon)	¼ lime	Julienne the zest and add along with the lime juice.
Coffee bavarois (Bavarois au café)	1 tsp coffee essence	Add to the milk.
Chocolate bavarois (Bavarois au chocolat)	15 chocolate couverture	Break into small pieces and add to the milk.

□   □   □

13

Strawberry bavarois

Bavarois aux fraises

The moulds are prepared with a heavy brushing of almond oil before commencing preparation.

Step	Commodity	1 portion	10 portions		
				⏲ 3 hr	♨ 45 min
1	Leaf gelatine	2.5 g	25 g	Place in a bowl of cold water.	
	Milk	50 ml	500 ml	Place in a saucepan.	
	Vanilla essence	drop	few drops	Add and boil.	
	Egg yolks	½	5	Place in a suitably sized bowl.	
	Castor sugar	15 g	150 g	Add and whisk well together. Pour over the hot milk and whisk thoroughly. Return to the heat in a clean saucepan and cook gently, stirring with a spoon until the mixture has thickened and coats the back of the spoon.* Add the leaf gelatine and dissolve completely. Pass through a conical strainer.	
2	Strawberries	50 g	500 g	Wash and prepare.	
	Water	5 ml	50 ml	Place in a saucepan and add the strawberries.	
	Castor sugar	15 g	150 g	Add and cook the fruit to a purée. Cool, pass through a fine sieve and allow to go cold. Add to the custard.	
3	Cream	50 ml	500 ml	Place in a suitably sized bowl and lightly whip. Fold in the egg mixture and stir until it just sets. Pour into the prepared moulds. Place in the fridge and allow to set. Remove from the fridge and turn out onto a serving flat. Decorate and serve with crème chantilly.	

* Do not allow to boil as the eggs will curdle.

☐　☐　☐

Russian charlotte

Charlotte russe

Step	Commodity	1 portion	10 portions		
				⏲ 3 hr	
1	Biscuits à la cuillère	1	10	Trim and cut one end to a point. Place on the bottom of the charlotte mould and fit tightly.	
	Biscuits à la cuillère	3	30	Trim and line the walls of the charlotte moulds tightly.	
2	Vanilla bavarois	100 g*	1 kg	Pour into the prepared mould and allow to set for 2 hours. Trim off the ends of the biscuits so that the bottom is flat. Turn out onto a serving flat.	

* Approximately.

☐　☐　☐

Royal charlotte

Charlotte royale

🥄 3 hr

Step	Commodity	1 portion	10 portions	
1	Raspberry jelly	15 ml	150 ml	Place a layer on the bottom of the charlotte mould.
	Swiss roll	50 g	500 g	Cut into 1 cm slices. Arrange on the bottom of the charlotte mould on top of the jelly and around the walls to fit tightly.
2	Vanilla bavarois	100 g*	1 kg	Pour into the prepared mould and allow to set for 2 hours. Trim off the ends of the Swiss roll so that the bottom is flat. Turn out the charlotte onto a serving flat.

* Approximately.

☐ ☐ ☐

Banana chartreuse

Chartreuse de bananes

🥄 3 hr

Step	Commodity	1 portion	10 portions	
1	Lemon jelly	25 ml	250 ml	Pour into the bottom of the charlotte moulds.
	Bananas	½ small	5	Cut into thin slices and add to the jelly. Allow to set.
2	Banana bavarois	100 g*	1 kg	Pour into the prepared mould and allow to set for 2 hours in a refrigerator. Remove, dip into hot water for 2–3 seconds to help loosen. Turn out on to a serving flat.

☐ ☐ ☐

Apple charlotte

Charlotte aux pommes

🥄 1 hr   🍲 35 min   ≋ 220°C

Step	Commodity	1 portion	10 portions	
1	Butter	25 g	250 g	Melt.
	Stale bread	100 g	1 kg	Cut into 3 mm slices, retain 2–3 slices for use later. Remove the crusts and cut into finger shapes. Brush with the melted butter. Arrange tightly, butter side down, in the prepared dariole moulds.
2	Apple purée	100 g	1 kg	Heat gently.
	Castor sugar	10 g	100 g	Add and mix in well.
	Breadcrumbs	10 g	100 g	Add and mix in well. Pour into the lined moulds. Cut the retained bread to fit over the top of the mould. Remove the crusts, brush with melted butter and seal in the apple. Place in a pre-heated oven for the required time. Remove, allow to cool slightly and turn out on to a serving flat.

NOTE: Serve with custard sauce or cream.

☐ ☐ ☐

13

Eve's pudding

Step	Commodity	1 portion	10 portions			
				🥄 30 min	♨ 45 min	≋ 210°C
1	Cooking apple	75 g	750 g	Peel, remove the core and cut into slices. Place in a saucepan.		
	Water	1 tsp	3 tbsp	Add.		
	Castor sugar	25 g	250 g	Sprinkle over the top of the fruit and cook for 5 minutes to soften. Pass through a fine chinois. Pour into the appropriate pie dishes and allow to cool.		
2	Butter	25 g	250 g	Place in a clean bowl.		
	Castor sugar	25 g	250 g	Add and cream together until the mixture is soft and fluffy.		
	Eggs	½	5	Break into a jug and whisk together. Gradually add to the mixture.		
	Self raising flour	25 g	250 g	Sieve and carefully fold into the mixture. Ensure that all the flour has been incorporated completely. Spread over the cold apple purée and place in a pre-heated oven for the appropriate time. Remove and serve hot with a sauceboat of custard sauce.		

☐ ☐ ☐

Baked rice pudding   Pouding de riz

Step	Commodity	1 portion	10 portions			
				🥄 20 min	♨ 1½–2 hr	≋ 180°C
1	Short grain rice	15 g	150 g	Wash in a conical strainer and place in a pie dish.		
	Castor sugar	10 g	100 g	Add.		
	Milk	125 ml	1¼ litres	Pour over the rice and mix in well.		
	Butter	2.5 g	25 g	Cut into small pieces and place on top of the milk.		
	Nutmeg	small pinch	large pinch	Sprinkle over the top. Arrange on a baking tray and place in a pre-heated oven until the rice is tender. Remove, clean the rim and surround with a pie frill. Serve hot.		

☐ ☐ ☐

Baked semolina pudding

Step	Commodity	1 portion	10 portions			
				🥄 20 min	♨ 1 hr	≋ 180°C
1	Short grain rice	15 g	150 g	Wash in a conical strainer and place in a pie dish.		
	Castor sugar	7.5 g	75 g	Add.		
	Milk	125 ml	1¼ litres	Pour over the semolina and mix in well.		
	Nutmeg	small pinch	large pinch	Sprinkle over the top. Arrange on a baking tray and place in a pre-heated oven until the rice is tender. Remove, clean the rim and surround with a pie frill. Serve hot.		

NOTE: Sago, tapioca and ground rice pudding may be made by this process.

☐ ☐ ☐

358

Pear Condé

Poire Condé

Step	Commodity	1 portion	10 portions		
				⏲ 1 hr	🍲 30 min
1	Short grain rice	15 g	150 g	Wash in a conical strainer and place in a suitably sized saucepan.	
	Castor sugar	10 g	100 g	Add.	
	Milk	125 ml	1¼ litres	Pour over the rice.	
	Vanilla essence	drop	few drops	Add and bring to the boil. Cook for 1 hour or until the rice is tender. Place in a serving bowl and allow to cool.	
2	Poached pears	½	5	Cut in half and arrange on top of the rice.	
	Apricot glaze	25 ml	250 ml	Strain and brush over the pears.	
	Angelica	2 g	20 g	Cut into thin strips.	
	Glacé cherries	1	10	Cut in half and use with the angelica to decorate the condé.	

NOTE: Other fruits such as pineapple, peaches and banana may be used instead of pears.

☐ ☐ ☐

Pineapple créole

Ananas créole

Step	Commodity	1 portion	10 portions		
				⏲ 1 hr	🍲 30 min
1	Short grain rice	15 g	150 g	Wash in a conical strainer and place in a suitably sized saucepan.	
	Castor sugar	10 g	100 g	Add.	
	Milk	125 ml	1¼ litres	Pour over the rice.	
	Vanilla essence	drop	few drops	Add and bring to the boil. Cook for 1 hour or until the rice is tender. Allow to cool slightly. Dress the cooked rice in the shape of a pineapple on a serving tray. Allow to go cold. Mark the rice with a knife in small diamonds.	
2	Currants	5 g	50 g	Wash well and dry. Place a currant in the centre of each diamond.	
3	Pineapple rings	1 small	10 small	Drain away the juice and arrange the pineapple around the outside of the dish.	
4	Apricot glaze	25 ml	250 ml	Strain and brush over the rice and pineapples.	
	Angelica	2 g	20 g	Cut into thin strips and use to decorate the créole, to represent the stalk.	

☐ ☐ ☐

Cabinet pudding

Pouding Cabinet

Step	Commodity	1 portion	10 portions	
				⏲ 1½ hr ♨ 40 min ≋ 190°C
1	Milk	125 ml	1¼ litres	Place in a clean saucepan and bring to the boil.
	Eggs	1	10	Break into a bowl.
	Sugar	10 g	100 g	Add.
	Vanilla essence	drop	few drops	Add and whisk together. Pour over the hot milk and whisk. Strain through a fine sieve into a clean bowl.
	Butter	5 g	50 g	Melt and brush the inside of the dariole moulds.
	Castor sugar	5 g	50 g	Place in the mould and swirl around so that there is sugar on all sides and the bottom.
	Glacé cherries	5 g	50 g	Dice and place on the bottom of the mould.
	Sultanas/currants	5 g	50 g	Wash, dry, chop finely and add.
2	Sponge cake/fingers	40 g	400 g	Cut into dice and place on top of the fruit. Pour over the prepared custard and allow to stand for 30 minutes. Arrange in a bain-marie and place into the oven. Cook for the appropriate time. Remove and loosen the edges and gently squeeze the rim of the mould to free the pudding at the sides. Turn out on to a serving dish. Serve with a custard sauce.

NOTE: Diplomat pudding is a cabinet pudding which is served cold.

☐ ☐ ☐

Bread and butter pudding

Step	Commodity	1 portion	10 portions	
				⏲ 30 min ♨ 40 min ≋ 190°C
1	Milk	125 ml	1¼ litres	Place in a clean saucepan and bring to the boil.
	Eggs	1	10	Break into a bowl.
	Sugar	10 g	100 g	Add.
	Vanilla essence	drop	few drops	Add and whisk together. Pour over the hot milk and whisk. Strain through a fine sieve into a clean bowl.
2	Sultanas	10 g	100 g	Wash, dry and place on the bottom of the dish.
	Bread	1 slice	10 slices	Remove the crusts.
	Butter	5 g	50 g	Butter the bread and cut into triangles. Arrange in the pie dish. Pour over half of the custard mixture and allow to stand for 30 minutes to prevent the bread from floating to the surface. Pour over the rest of the custard. Rearrange if necessary.
3	Castor sugar	10 g	100 g	Sprinkle over the top.
	Nutmeg	pinch	pinch	Sprinkle over the top. Arrange in a bain-marie and place into the oven. Cook for the appropriate time. Remove and serve hot.

☐ ☐ ☐

Baked egg custard

Step	Commodity	1 portion	10 portions	☞ 30 min ♨ 50 min ≋ 165°C
1	Milk	125 ml	1¼ litres	Place in a clean saucepan and bring to the boil.
	Eggs	1	10	Break into a bowl.
	Castor sugar	15 g	150 g	Add.
	Vanilla essence	drop	few drops	Add and whisk together. Pour over the hot milk and whisk. Strain through a fine sieve into a pie dish.
2	Nutmeg	pinch	pinch	Sprinkle over the top. Arrange in a bain-marie and place into the oven. Cook for the appropriate time. Remove and serve hot.

☐   ☐   ☐

Queen of puddings

Step	Commodity	1 portion	10 portions	☞ 1½ hr ♨ 40 min ≋ 190°–232°C
1	Milk	60 ml	600 ml	Place in a clean saucepan and bring to the boil.
	Butter	5 g	50 g	Add and allow to melt.
2	Egg yolks	1	10	Break into a bowl.
	Sugar	10 g	100 g	Add and beat to a creamy consistency. Pour in the milk and whisk well.
	Vanilla essence	drop	few drops	Add and strain through a fine sieve into a clean bowl.
	Butter	5 g	50 g	Melt and brush the inside of the pudding dish.
	Cake crumbs	20 g	200 g	Place on the bottom of the pudding dish. Pour over the strained custard and allow to stand for 30 minutes for the liquid to soak through. Arrange in a bain-marie and place in a pre-heated oven for 30 minutes. Remove and allow to cool. Turn the oven up to 232°C.
3	Raspberry jam	15 g	150 g	Spread over the cooled pudding.
	Egg whites	1	10	Whisk until stiff.
	Castor sugar	10 g	100 g	Fold into the egg white. Place in a piping bag with a star tube. Pipe over the top of the jam. Place in the pre-heated oven until it has a light brown tinge. Remove and serve on a flat.

13

☐   ☐   ☐

WHAT WENT WRONG

Problem	Caused by	To rectify
Cake has an open/ coarse texture.	(1) Too much raising agent.	Cannot be rectified.
	(2) Cooking at too high a temperature.	Cannot be rectified.
	(3) Insufficient mixing.	Cannot be rectified.
Cake has a close texture.	(1) Underbeating	Cannot be rectified.
	(2) Adding too much flour.	Cannot be rectified.
	(3) Baking at too high an oven temperature or in an oven that is not high enough	Cannot be rectified.

Problem	Caused by	To rectify
Cake had a cracked crust.	Baking at too high a temperature.	Cannot be rectified.
The produce has sunk in the middle.	(1) Baking at too high a temperature.	Cannot be rectified.
	(2) Opening the oven too often during cooking, or removing the item from the oven before it is cooked.	Cannot be rectified.
Cake has large holes and an uneven texture.	(1) Too much raising agent or insufficient mixing.	Cannot be rectified.
	(2) Oven temperature was too high.	Cannot be rectified.
Cake crust is too thick.	(1) Too much sugar or cooked for too long.	Cannot be rectified.
	(2) Oven temperature is too low.	Cannot be rectified.
Cooked choux pastry is greasy and heavy.	Pastry is over-cooked.	Cannot be rectified.
Cooked choux pastry has sunk.	(1) Insufficient baking.	Cannot be rectified.
	(2) Oven temperature too low.	Cannot be rectified.
	(3) Flour insufficiently cooked.	Cannot be rectified.
Cooked choux pastry is not aerated.	Eggs were insufficiently beaten into the mixture.	Cannot be rectified.
Pastry is hard.	(1) Adding too much water or too little fat.	Cannot be rectified.
	(2) Fat was not rubbed in sufficiently.	Cannot be rectified.
	(3) Over-handling or over-baking.	Cannot be rectified.
Pastry is crumbly.	Too little water or too much fat.	Cannot be rectified.
Pastry has blistered.	Adding too much water or not rubbing fat in evenly.	Cannot be rectified.
Pastry is soggy.	(1) Adding too much water.	Cannot be rectified.
	(2) Using too cool an oven or not enough baking time.	Cannot be rectified.
Pastry has shrunk	Over-handling or stretching while handling.	Cannot be rectified.
Puff pastry is not flaky.	Excessively heavy use of the rolling pin.	Cannot be rectified.
Fat oozes out of puff pastry.	(1) Dough or fat too soft.	Cannot be rectified.
	(2) Edges not sealed.	Cannot be rectified.
	(3) Uneven folding and rolling.	Cannot be rectified.
Puff pastry has an uneven rise.	(1) Uneven distribution of the fat.	Cannot be rectified.
	(2) Uneven folding and rolling.	Cannot be rectified.
Dough product has an under-developed crust.	(1) Too low an oven temperature.	Cannot be rectified.
	(2) Too dry an oven.	Cannot be rectified.
Dough product has cracked surface.	(1) Too little sugar used.	Cannot be rectified.
	(2) Not mixing the dough sufficiently.	Cannot be rectified.
	(3) Baking at too high a temperature.	Cannot be rectified.

COLD PREPARATIONS

Cold preparation involves the execution of any tasks from making sandwiches to decorating items for a buffet. There is usually no method of cookery involved as the foods for cold preparation are already cooked. Some items for cold preparation are cooked by other parties or are eaten raw or cured. Cold preparation also involves the production of sweet mousses and ice cream.

Terms associated with cold preparations

Aspic A clear jelly made from meat stock, gelatine and egg whites.

Bard, to To cover the surface of meat, poultry or game with thin slices of pork or bacon fat. This is done to protect the meat during cooking and prevent the flesh from drying out during the cooking process.

Brine Solution of salt and water used for curing meat.

Concassé Roughly chopped tomato flesh.

Cure To preserve items of food by smoking, pickling or salting.

Emulsion A suspension of one liquid in another.

Gelatine A preparation obtained from the bones,

connective tissue, and collagen of calves and other animals. Available in powder or leaf form. Used to set jelly, bavarois and mousse.

Lard, to Using a special larding needle, to insert thin strips of fat in meats, poultry or game to prevent the flesh from drying out during the cooking process.

Matignon A bed of large cut root vegetables used as a base in roasting.

Napper To coat with sauce or aspic.

Quenelles Small cigar shapes of minced meat, fish or vegetables.

Score To make light incisions on the surface of flesh prior to roasting or pot roasting.

BUFFETS

Traditionally buffets were decorated with sculptured fats and carved ice images and the foods given height and prominence by using socles made from rice or semolina.

Buffets should consist of a variety of different meats (roast ribs of beef, legs of lamb, suckling pig, boiled hams, gammons, pressed beef, ox tongues); fish (poached salmon, smoked trout, smoked salmon, mousses); poultry (roast turkey breast, mousses, pâtés, galantines, spring chicken, suprêmes of chicken); game (venison, pheasant); a variety of salads; eggs; and cold sweets. Some meats and fish can be coated with a chaudfroid sauce, decorated with thin cut vegetables, truffles and egg

Staff associated with cold preparation

Larder chef (chef garde-manger) for hors d'oeuvre, cold sauces (savoury), dressings and buffets.

Pastry chef (chef pâtissier) for cold sweet preparations and cold (sweet) sauces.

In large establishments the **cold buffet chef** (chef froitier) would be in charge of preparing items for a cold buffet though in most establishments it is the duty of the larder chef.

white and glazed with aspic jelly. The buffet items should be arranged in an attractive manner. They should be displayed in a refrigerated cabinet in the restaurant for the customers to choose from.

Sandwiches

Traditionally sandwiches were two slices of bread and butter with a filling of some sort but nowadays, with specialised packaging, improved refrigeration techniques, public awareness, many types of breads (local and continental), flavoured butters and a variety of fillings, both hot and cold, sandwiches have radically changed their role and image. Sandwiches are always garnished with suitable salad items appropriate to the colour and texture of the filling and may consist of a selection of the following: lettuce, tomatoes, cucumber, watercress, parsley, mustard and cress, spring onions, radishes and pickled gherkins.

Conventional sandwiches

These are also called closed or lunch box sandwiches. They can be served for any occasion and consist of two slices of bread (white or brown) spread with a flavoured butter and filled with slices of seasoned meat, cheese, eggs, poultry, game, fish or shellfish. Certain meats like cooked ham may be coated with a pickle or chutney while other meats and fish may be flavoured with a thin spreading of plain or flavoured (tomato, tartare or anchovy) mayonnaise and/or mustard. Conventional sandwiches are cut into triangles and served with a suitable garnish.

Buffet sandwiches

These are also known as reception sandwiches and are served on buffets and receptions. They consist of two slices of white or brown bread spread with a flavoured butter and filled with potted meats or fish, slices of seasoned meat, cheese, eggs, poultry, game, fish or shellfish. Certain meats, like cooked ham, may be coated with a pickle or chutney while other meats and fish may be flavoured with a thin spreading of plain or flavoured (tomato, tartare or anchovy) mayonnaise and/or mustard. Buffet and reception sandwiches have the crusts removed and are cut into a variety of shapes – squares, triangles or round, fluted or plain – using pastry cutters.

Tea sandwiches

These are served for afternoon tea and consist of two thin slices of white or brown bread, a plain butter, a light filling of thinly sliced cucumber, creamed and dry cheeses, pickles, sliced hard boiled eggs, meat or fish pastes, meat or fish spreads, tomatoes or fresh tomato purée, jams or thinly sliced fruit. Tea sandwiches have the crusts removed, are cut into a variety of shapes like buffet sandwiches and are garnished accordingly.

Pinwheel or roularde sandwiches

These sandwiches are made from loaves of brown or white bread sliced thinly lengthways which are spread with butter and filling. The fillings should be thin slices or pastes of meat, fish, vegetables or cheese. The sandwich roll is then sliced into individual 'wheels'.

Open sandwiches

Also known as Smörrebrod, these sandwiches are served as lunch-time snacks or on buffets. They may be made with slices of French stick (baguette), pumpernickel, rye or Vienna loaf. Ordinary bread may also be used. A flavoured bread may be used and filled with slices of seasoned meat, cheese, eggs, poultry, game, fish, shellfish, fruits, pickles, chutney, plain or flavoured (tomato, tartare or anchovy) mayonnaise and/or mustard. The items of food are arranged on the slices of bread in a decorative manner and are served, on a suitably sized serving flat or straight on to a plate, without covering.

Continental sandwiches

Also known as the French sandwich, these are usually served as a lunch-time snack. They are made with French stick (baguette) cut in half lengthways or slices of cottage loaf which are spread with a flavoured butter. They are filled with either a single filling or a combination of fillings including slices of seasoned meat, cheese, eggs, poultry, game, fish or shellfish. Certain meats, like cooked ham, may be coated with a pickle or chutney while other meats and fish may be flavoured with a thin spreading of plain or flavoured (tomato, tartare or anchovy) mayonnaise and/or mustard. They are garnished with prepared sprigs of parsley, watercress or mustard and cress.

Canapés

Canapés are served on buffets and receptions. They are not really sandwiches, but are made with a variety of thin sliced toast, crackers, water and/or cheese biscuits and puff pastry shapes. The fillings can be arranged by hand or piped on top and these include meat, cheese, eggs, poultry, game, fish or shellfish. They are flavoured with piped plain or flavoured (tomato, tartare or anchovy) mayonnaise or flavoured and coloured butter.

NOTE: Traditionally canapés were glazed with an aspic to enhance the colour and prevent the filling from drying out. This practice has diminished over the years:

(a) For health and hygiene reasons. The temperature fluctuation involved in putting warm aspic onto chilled food provides excellent growth conditions for bacteria.

(b) Because the flavour of aspic jelly, which is made from gelatine and clarified stock, is considered to detract from the true flavour of the sandwich.

HOT SANDWICHES

Hot sandwiches consist of a single or variety of fillings placed between two or more slices of toasted brown or white bread, spread lightly with butter, margarine or mayonnaise. The crusts are usually removed and the sandwich cut into four triangles.

Toasted sandwiches are served in most catering establishments and fillings can vary from scrambled egg, bacon and fried egg, cooked ham and cheese to the more traditional fillings of chicken breast and minute steak.

Hot sandwiches are served on a lined salver or plate. Traditionally cocktail sticks are placed in the corner of each triangle to keep the bread and filling in position for service.

14

Bookmaker sandwich

🥣 15 min   ♨ 2 min

Step	Commodity	1 portion	10 portions	
1	Sliced bread	2	20	Toast and butter.
	Minute steak*	1 × 100 g	10 × 100 g	Grill or sauté for 1 minute either side. Place each steak on a slice of toast. Spread lightly with English mustard. Cover with the other slice of toast. Remove the crusts and cut into triangles. Serve immediately.

* Prepared

365

Club sandwich

20 min

Step	Commodity	1 portion	10 portions	
1	Sliced bread	2	20	Toast and butter lightly. Spread with a thin layer of mayonnaise.
2	Lettuce leaves	1	10	Wash, trim and chiffonade. Place half on one of the slices of toast.
	Hard boiled eggs	½	5	Shell, slice and lay on top of the lettuce.
	Tomatoes	½	5	Remove and discard the stalks and eyes. Blanch in boiling water for 10 seconds and refresh immediately. Remove the skins. Cut into thin slices on top of the hard boiled egg slices.
	Cooked chicken breast	100 g	1 kg	Cut into slices and place the appropriate amount on each sandwich.
3	Slice of back bacon	2	20	Place under a pre-heated salamander and cook for 2–3 minutes on either side. Arrange on top of the chicken. Place the remaining lettuce on top and cover with the other slice of bread. Remove the crusts and cut into four triangles. Serve immediately.

☐   ☐   ☐

Hors d'oeuvre and salads

HORS D'OEUVRE

The general translation of hors d'oeuvre is appetiser. An hors d'oeuvre is traditionally served as the first course, usually at luncheon. Hors d'oeuvre may be an individual portion of, or a selection of: hard boiled eggs napped with a cold sauce, usually mayonnaise; pasta, pulse or rice salad; raw fruit bound in a dressing or cold sauce; cooked or raw vegetable salad; cooked, pickled, raw or smoked fish; cooked or smoked meats; poultry or game; mousses, pâtés or terrines. Some non-vegetable type hors d'oeuvre such as cantaloupe melon, caviar, smoked salmon and oysters are also served at dinner. There are two different types of hors d'oeuvre:

(a) Single hors d'oeuvre, (hors d'oeuvre singulier). A single side dish usually served at dinner.
(b) Selection of hors d'oeuvre (hors d'oeuvre variés). A selection of side dishes usually served at luncheon. Most salads can be served as part of hors d'oeuvre variés.

There is a third classification of hors d'oeuvre, hot hors d'oeurvre (hors d'oeuvre chaud). These are usually seen on buffet menus though they could be served for lunch or dinner. They are usually referred to as a hot savoury in Britain (see Chapter 21: British regional cookery) and are served as a separate course after the sweet. However, hors d'oeuvre are generally intended to be an appetiser, stimulating the appetite.

Traditionally hors d'oeuvre were served in glass raviers or in square or oblong dishes called 'plats russes'. The dishes were arranged on a large trolley or tray that was wheeled out to the customers' table from which they were able to inspect before choosing. These days such practices are considered a food hygiene risk and hors d'oeuvre variés are now displayed in a static refrigerated cabinet.

366

MEAT AND MEAT PRODUCT HORS D'OEUVRE

Pâté

Pâté is a highly seasoned preparation of lean pork, streaky bacon, fat pork and liver. The type of liver used (pigs, lambs or chicken liver) will depend on the type of pâté being made. Pâté is served accompanied with hot melba toast.

Liver pâté (any liver)   Pâté de foie

🥣 6 hr   ♨ 2½ hr   〰 125°C

Step	Commodity	1 portion	10 portions	
1	Liver	100 g	1 kg	Trim, remove the gallbladder, wash and place in a bowl.
	Lean pork	40 g	400 g	Trim, remove the sinew, dice and add to the liver.
	Fat bacon	40 g	400 g	Trim, dice and add.
	Spiced salt	pinch	5 g	Add.
	Larder spice	pinch	5 g	Add.
	Brandy	12 ml	125 ml	Pour over the meat.
	Dry sherry	12 ml	125 ml	Add and mix well together. Add to marinade for 4–5 hours. Pass through a mincer, first through a medium plate then through a fine plate.
2	Streaky bacon	25 g	250 g	Remove the rind and any bones. Line a suitably sized terrine mould or oven proof earthenware dish. Pour in the pâté mixture. Cover with a cartouche and/or lid. Place in a deep tray with hot water and cook in a pre-heated oven for the required time. To judge whether the pâté is cooked, pierce with a trussing needle; if it is cooked the juice and fat should be clear. Remove when cooked. Place the terrine in a press and weigh down. If using an earthenware dish, press down with a plate or flat dish and weigh down with a 1–2 kg weight. Allow to cool completely. Remove the weight.
3	Lard	5 g	50 g	Melt and pour a thin layer of lard over the pâté. Allow to go cold. Portion and serve garnished with a side salad. Serve accompanied with melba toast.

□   □   □

14

Liver pâté, house style

Pâté maison

Step	Commodity	2 portion	20 portions	⌣ 1½ hr ♨ 2½ hr ≋ 125°C
1	Liver	100 g	1 kg	Trim, remove the gallbladder, wash and place in a bowl.
	Lean pork	40 g	400 g	Trim, remove the sinew, dice and add to the liver.
	Fat bacon	40 g	400 g	Trim, dice and add.
2	Lard	5 g	50 g	Heat in a suitably sized frying pan. Add the meat mixture in batches and fry quickly. Remove immediately and place in clean bowl. Retain the fat.
	Onions	10 g	100 g	Peel, roughly chop and add to the fat. Cook without colouring for 2–3 minutes.
	Garlic	¼ clove	2½ cloves	Peel, crush with a little salt and add to the onions.
	Spiced salt	pinch	5 g	Add.
	Larder spice	pinch	5 g	Add.
	Brandy	12 ml	125 ml	Add and mix together well. Pass through a fine mincer and then through a fine sieve.
2	Streaky bacon	25 g	250 g	Remove the rind and any bones. Line a suitably sized terrine mould or oven proof earthenware dish. Pour in the pâté mixture. Cover with a cartouche and/or lid.
Place in a deep tray with hot water and cook in a pre-heated oven for the required time. To judge whether the pâté is cooked, pierce with a trussing needle; if it is cooked the juice and fat should be clear. Remove when cooked.
Place the terrine in a press and weigh down. If using an earthenware dish, press down with a plate or flat dish and weigh down with a 1–2 kg weight. Allow to cool completely. Remove the weight.
3	Lard	5 g	50 g	Melt and pour a thin layer of lard over the pâté. Portion and serve garnished with a side salad. Serve accompanied with melba toast.

Goose liver pâté

Pâté de foie gras

Pâté de foie gras is a delicacy made with goose liver. Originally from Alsace, France, the geese are force-fed to enlarge their livers.

Step	Commodity	1 portion	10 portions	⌛ 6 hr ♨ 2–2½ hr ≋ 150°C
1	Pork fillet	40 g	400 g	Cut into small pieces.
	Pork fat	45 g	450 g	Cut into small pieces and add to the pork. Mince twice, pass through a fine sieve.
	Raw truffles	10 g	100 g	Cut into quarters.
	Spiced salt	2 g	20 g	Sprinkle over the truffles.
2	Goose liver	75 g	750 g(1)	Stud with the spiced truffle and place in a bowl.
	Brandy	5 ml	50 ml	Pour over the liver and marinade for 3–4 hours.
3	Hot water paste	50 g	500 g	Line a suitably sized terrine mould (retain ¼ for the top) and allow to rest for 30 minutes. Add half of the minced forcemeat. Lay the livers on top and cover with the remaining forcemeat.
	Salt pork fat	10 g	100 g	Place on top of the forcemeat. Season with spiced salt.
	Bay leaves	½	5	Place on top of the salt pork. Dampen the sides of the pastry. Roll out the rest of the pastry and cover the top. Make 3–4 holes in the top. Place in a bain-marie and bake in a pre-heated oven for the required time. Allow to cool and go cold.
4	Gelantine*	15 ml	150 ml	Warm to melt.
	Madeira	2.5 ml	25 ml	Add and mix in well. Pour into the holes in the pastry using a funnel. Allow to go cold in a refrigerator for 2–3 hours. Remove the pastry lid and remove the pâté using two spoons. Serve either in the pastry surrounded by a folded serviette or sliced thinly on a bed of chopped aspic jelly with a small side salad. Serve accompanied with melba toast.

* Prepared

□   □   □

Ham pâté

Pâté de jambon

Step	Commodity	1 portion	10 portions	⌛ 2 hr ♨ 2 hr ≋ 125°C
1	Lean cooked ham	150 g	1½ kg	Trim any fat, cut into small pieces and mince finely. Place in a bowl.
	Cold béchamel	50 ml	500 ml	Add and mix together well. Season with salt and pepper.
	Paprika	pinch	1 tsp	Add.
	Cream, double	35 ml	350 ml	Add and pass through a blender then a fine sieve. Pour into a suitably sized terrine dish or earthenware bowl. Allow to go cold. Portion and serve garnished with a side salad. Serve accompanied with melba toast.

□   □   □

Salami, cooked and smoked sausage

Salami and cooked and smoked sausages are sliced thinly and served cold either separately or as an assortment. Salami comes from Italy and Hungary, cooked and smoked sausages usually come from France, Germany and Italy and are bought in.

Mortadella (Italy)   Large oval shaped sausage, made from pork and veal with large pieces of pork fat.

Salami (Italy/Hungary)   Made from bacon, pork and beef, salami is highly seasoned and coloured with red wine. It is dried and cured.

Frankfurt   There are many varieties of frankfurters which are made from pork or ham. They are first dried, then smoked before boiling.

Liver sausage   Made from a mixture of highly seasoned pigs' or calves' liver and minced pork.

Parma ham

Parma ham (jambon de parme) is bought in ready prepared either on the bone or boneless. The ham is cut very thinly with a sharp knife or on a slicing machine. Parma ham can be served with melon.

Smoked or cured raw ham

Jambon de bayonne/jambon de westphalie is similar to, and treated as for parma ham.

☐   ☐   ☐

Chicken galantine

Galantine de volaille

🥄 2 hr   ♨ 1½–2 hr

Step	Commodity	1 portion	10 portions	
1	Chicken	200 g	2.5 kg	Carefully remove the skin in one piece and place in cold water to remove dirt and blood spots. Bone the chicken. Retain one suprême for use later. Mince the rest.
	Minced veal	15 g	150 g	Add to the minced chicken.
	Lean minced pork	15 g	150 g	Add.
2	Breadcrumbs	10 g	100 g	Place in a bowl.
	Milk	10 ml	100 ml	Add and allow to soak. Squeeze dry and add to the minced meats. Mix well together.
	Eggs	¼	2	Add and pass the mixture through a sieve or a food processor. Season with salt, pepper and nutmeg. Place over a bowl of iced water.
	Double cream	25 ml	250 ml	Add slowly, mix together well. Place clean muslin cloth on the table. Place the skin on top. Spread one-third of the mixture onto the skin.
	Ham	5 g	50 g	Cut into jardinière
	Tongue	5 g	50 g	Cut into jardinière
	Bacon	5 g	50 g	Cut into jardinière

Step	Commodity	1 portion	10 portions	
3	Pistachio nuts (shelled)	5	50	Rinse and dry. Use the tongue, ham, bacon and nuts in alternative strips through the centre. Cover with another third of the mixture and repeat. Cover with the remaining mixture. Wrap the skin around the forcemeat and roll up to form a large sausage-like shape. Cover with the muslin cloth, secure and tie both ends. Poach in simmering stock for the required time. Allow to cool and go cold. Remove the cloth. Napper with velouté-based chaudfroid sauce. Decorate and finish with aspic jelly. Cut into slices and serve garnished with salad.

☐　　☐　　☐

Ham mousse   Mousse de jambon

☝ 1 hr

Step	Commodity	1 portion	10 portions	
1	Lean cooked ham	60 g	600 g	Pass through a fine mincer and then through a sieve. Place in a saucepan.
	Veal velouté	20 ml	200 ml	Add to ham and heat gently.
	Aspic jelly, melted	20 ml	200 ml	Add and mix together well. Place over a bowl of iced water and stir until just set. Remove and place to the side.
2	Whipped cream	30 ml	300 ml	Fold into the mixture. Season with salt and pepper. Pour into the serving dishes.
	Aspic jelly	10 ml	100 ml	Melt and pour over the mousse. Allow to set before serving.

NOTE: Lobster mousse (mousse de homard) and chicken mousse (mousse de volaille) may be made using this method.

☐　　☐　　☐

EGGS, PASTA AND RICE

Gulls' eggs   Oeufs de mouettes

Usually bought in already hard boiled. Serve two per portion on a bed of mustard and cress. Accompanied with brown bread and butter.

Quails' eggs   Oeufs de caille

Can be bought hard boiled. Usually served in aspic.

14

Egg mayonnaise

Oeuf mayonnaise

Oeuf mayonnaise

⤵ 20 min   🍲 10 min

Step	Commodity	1 portion	10 portions	
1	Eggs	½–1	5–10	Place in boiling water, return to the boil and simmer for the required time. Refresh and allow to go cold. Remove the shell. Cut in half and place on a salad of lettuce, sliced cucumber and sliced or wedged tomato.
2	Mayonnaise	20 ml	200 ml	Place in a jug.
	Cream	5 ml	50 ml	Add to jug and whisk together. Carefully napper over the eggs. Sprinkle with finely chopped parsley and/or paprika pepper.

☐   ☐   ☐

Stuffed eggs

Oeufs dur farci

⤵ 20 min   🍲 10 min

Step	Commodity	1 portion	10 portions	
1	Eggs	½–1	5–10	Place in boiling water, return to the boil and simmer for the required time. Refresh and allow to go cold. Remove the shell. Cut in half and remove the yolk. Pass the yolk through a sieve.
2	Butter	10 g	100 g	Melt and add to the yolks.
	Mayonnaise	15 ml	150 ml	Add and mix together thoroughly. Season with salt and pepper. Place in a piping bag with a star nozzle and pipe back into the egg whites. Dress on a salad of lettuce, sliced cucumber and sliced or wedged tomato. Sprinkle with finely chopped parsley and/or paprika pepper.

☐   ☐   ☐

Fruits of the sea salad

Salade de fruits de mer

⤵ 45 min

Step	Commodity	1 portion	10 portions	
1	Cooked pasta	25 g	250 g	Place in a large bowl.
	Shelled prawns	10 g	100 g	Add to bowl.
	Cooked mussels	15 g	150 g	Add.
	Scallops	10 g	100 g	Cut into macedoine and add.
	Cooked cod	15 g	150 g	Remove the skin and bones. Flake and add.
	Raw tomato concassé	15 g	150 g	Add. Season with salt and milled pepper. Bind with garlic flavoured vinaigrette. Sprinkle with finely chopped parsley.

NOTE: Other sea foods may be used.

☐   ☐   ☐

Rice salad

Salade de riz

⏲ 30 min

Step	Commodity	1 portion	10 portions	
1	Cooked rice	25 g	250 g	Place in a large bowl.
	Cooked tomato concassé	25 g	250 g	Add.
	Cooked garden peas	15 g	150 g	Add. Season with salt and pepper and bind with vinaigrette. Sprinkle with finely chopped parsley.

☐ ☐ ☐

Spanish style rice salad

Salade de riz espagnole

⏲ 1 hr

Step	Commodity	1 portion	10 portions	
1	Cooked patna rice	25 g	250 g	Place in a large bowl.
	Raw tomato concassé	10 g	100 g	Add to rice.
	Red peppers	10 g	100 g	Cut into brunoise and add to the other ingredients.
2	Stoned olives	1	10	Chop finely and add. Bind with garlic flavoured vinaigrette and season with salt, cayenne pepper and finely chopped parsley.

☐ ☐ ☐

FRUIT OR VEGETABLE HORS D'OEUVRE

Vegetable hors d'oeuvre

Most vegetable salads can be used as hors d'oeuvre varies (see vegetable salad section later in this chapter). Certain vegetables can be blanched in water then cooked to 'al dente' in a à la grecque or portugaise marinade.

Vegetables à la Grecque

à la grecque

Vegetables, Portuguese style

à la portugaise

Wash and prepare the vegetables. Cut into bâtons or florets to cook.

Suitable vegetables

Artichokes	Artichauts
Button onions	Oignons
Cauliflower	Choufleur
Celery	Celeri
Leeks	Poireaux
Mushrooms	Champignons

Fruit hors d'oeuvre

Fruits can be served as juices, with typical examples including tomato, pineapple, grapefruit, orange and grape juices.

14

Grapefruit, half

Demi pamplemousse

🥄 30 min

Step	Commodity	1 portion	10 portions	
1	Grapefruits	½	5	Cut in half. Remove the centre core and the pips using a grapefruit or small sharp knife. Loosen each segment from the dividing skin. Chill before serving.
2	Maraschino cherries	1	10	Place on top. Serve in a grapefruit holder, accompanied with castor sugar.

NOTE: Grapefruit can be sprinkled with demerara sugar, grilled (grillé) and served hot.

☐   ☐   ☐

Grapefruit cocktail

Cocktail de pamplemousse

🥄 45 min

Step	Commodity	1 portion	10 portions	
1	Grapefruits	1	10	Cut the top and bottom to expose the fruit. Remove the skin and pith. Cut each segment from the dividing skin. Squeeze the juice over the segments. Arrange neatly in a coupe dish. Pour over the strained juice.
2	Maraschino cherries	1	10	Place on top of the grapefruit. Serve cold, accompanied with castor sugar.

☐   ☐   ☐

Grapefruit and orange cocktail

Cocktail Florida

🥄 45 min

Step	Commodity	1 portion	10 portions	
1	Grapefruits	½	5	Cut the top and bottom to expose the fruit. Remove the skin and pith. Cut each segment from the dividing skin. Place in a bowl. Squeeze the juice over the segments.
2	Oranges	½	5	Cut the top and bottom to expose the fruit. Remove the skin and pith. Cut each segment from the dividing skin. Place in a separate bowl. Squeeze the juice over the segments. Arrange alternative slices of orange and grapefruit neatly in a coupe dish. Pour over the strained juice.
3	Maraschino cherries	1	10	Place on top of the cocktail. Serve cold, accompanied with castor sugar.

☐   ☐   ☐

Melon

There are three types of melon usually served as an hors d'oeuvre:

Cantaloupe This melon has a ribbed skin, mottled green and yellow in colour. It is round with a flattened top and bottom and pink flesh. Depending on the size (½–1 per portion), cut the top off or cut in half. Remove the pips.

Charentais Similar in appearance to cantaloupe, these melons are served 1 per portion. Cut the top off and remove the pips.

Honeydew These are large and oval shaped with hard green or smooth yellow skin. Cut into slices (¼ per portion). Cut a thin slice off the skin so that it stands up.

Step	Commodity	1 portion	10 portions	🥄 30 min
1	Melon	¼–½	3–5	Cut into the required size. Remove the pips and chill before service.

NOTE: Melon cocktail (Cocktail de melon) may be made with any type of melon. The flesh is scooped out with a parisienne spoon and dressed in a cocktail glass.

Extensions of melon

Melon with port (Charentais or Cantaloupe) Melon au porto
As for the basic recipe with a measure of port in the centre of each.

Melon with raspberries (Charentais or Cantaloupe) Melon aux framboises
As for the basic recipe with 50 g picked and washed raspberries in the centre of each portion.

Melon with strawberries (Charentais or Cantaloupe) Melon aux fraises
As for the basic recipe with 50 g picked and washed strawberries in the centre of each portion.

☐   ☐   ☐

Avocado pear   Poire d'avocat

Step	Commodity	1 portion	10 portions	🥄 20 min
1	Avocado pears	1	5	Cut in half lengthways. Remove the stone. Serve with a side salad and accompanied by vinaigrette.

NOTE: Avocados can be served with prawns or shrimps and shellfish sauce.

☐   ☐   ☐

FISH, SHELLFISH OR FISH PRODUCT HORS D'OEUVRE

Smoked eel   Anguille fumée

Smoked eels are skinned, filleted and cut into 6 cm lengths. They are served accompanied by prepared lemon wedges, brown bread and butter and horseradish sauce.

Caviar   Caviar

Prepared from the roe of the various types of sturgeon, caviar originates from Russia, Iran or Romania. The best known and most expensive types are Beluga, Ocietrova and Sevruga. Caviar should be stored at between 0–1°C.

It is served in a timbale or the original jar on a bed of ice, and accompanied by melba toast, butter, sieved egg yolks and egg whites, finely chopped onions and prepared lemon wedges.

Smoked salmon

Saumon fumé

Smoked salmon is purchased ready prepared either as sides of smoked salmon or thinly sliced. Sides are trimmed, cut into thin slices on a slant across the side. It is served accompanied by prepared lemon wedges, brown bread and butter.

Smoked trout

Truite fumée

Purchased ready prepared, smoked trout are skinned, the heads removed and filleted. They are served accompanied by prepared lemon wedges, brown bread and butter and horseradish sauce.

NOTE: Buckling (whole smoked herring) can be served as for smoked trout.

☐ ☐ ☐

Oysters

Les huîtres

Step	Commodity	1 portion	10 portions	
1	Oysters	6*	60	↻ 30 min

Oysters should be bought live and a clear indication of this is that the shells should be tightly shut. Open carefully with an oyster knife and release flesh where joined to shell. They should not be washed unless they are gritty. Serve with the natural juices. Accompany with prepared lemon wedges and brown bread and butter.

* 6–12 per portion

Types of oysters

British:	Royal Natives, Royal Whitstable, Colchester, Purfleet, Whitstable, Poole, Falmouth, Helford.
Irish:	Shannon.

Continental

French:	Marennes Vertes, Marennes Blanches, Belons, Cancale, Brittany.
Dutch:	Natives.
Belgian:	Victorias.
Portuguese:	Blue points (Gryphas).

☐ ☐ ☐

Anchovies

Anchois

Remove from the tin, drain away the excess oil. Place on a chiffonade of lettuce. Garnish with capers, sieved egg whites and sieved egg yolks.

Sardines in oil

Sardines a l'huile

Remove from the tin, drain away the excess oil. Dress on a chiffonade of lettuce and decorate with prepared lemon wedges and picked parsley.

NOTE: Fresh sardines may be grilled, allowed to go cold and used as an hors d'oeuvre.

☐ ☐ ☐

Soused herrings

Step	Commodity	1 portion	10 portions		⏲ 30 min · 🍲 20 min
1	Herrings	½	5	Clean, scale and fillet. Season with salt and pepper. Roll up with the skin on the outside. Place in an earthenware dish.	
2	Sousing marinade	25 ml	250 ml	Pour over the fish. Cover with greaseproof paper and place in a pre-heated oven for the required time. Allow to cool, serve in the dish and garnish with picked parsley.	

NOTE: This dish may also be made with fillets of mackerel.

☐   ☐   ☐

Dressed crab

Step	Commodity	1 portion	10 portions		⏲ 1 hr · 🍲 30 min
1	Crab meat	250 g	2½ kg	Drive a trussing needle 5 cm in between the eyes to kill the crab. Place the crabs in boiling water with a little vinegar for the required time. Allow to cool in the cooking liquor. When cold remove the large claws and sever the joints. Remove the pincers from the claw and carefully crack open to remove the flesh. Remove the flesh from the other joints in a similar manner using the handle of a teaspoon. Shred. For the body, carefully remove the soft undershell to expose the gills (also known as dead men's fingers) and the sac behind the eyes and discard. Scrape out the inside and pass through a sieve.	
2				Season with salt and pepper. Bind with a little mayonnaise flavoured with Worcester sauce. If the mixture is too thin thicken with fine breadcrumbs. Trim the shell and wash thoroughly. Allow to dry. Dress the brown meat down the centre of the shell and the shredded white meat on either side. Decorate with sieved egg yolk, sieved egg white, finely chopped parsley, olives and capers. Serve with a side salad, accompanied by a sauce boat of vinaigrette.	

14

☐   ☐   ☐

Fish mousse

Step	Commodity	1 portion	10 portions		⏲ 1 hr
1	Smoked/ plain* fish	35 g	350 g	Remove any bone or skin. Place in a blender. Season with salt and pepper, finely chopped parsley and chervil.	
2	Tomato purée	½ tsp	5 tsp	Add and liquidise.	
	Double cream	15 ml	150 ml	Whisk lightly to form peaks. Fold into the fish mixture. Correct the seasonings and place in serving dishes. Accompany with hot toast.	

* Cooked

NOTE: This dish may be made with smoked salmon, trout, mackerel or kippers.

☐   ☐   ☐

Potted prawns/shrimps

Crevettes roses/crevettes au beurre

🥄 45 min

Step	Commodity	1 portion	10 portions	
1	Butter	50 g	500 g	Place in a suitably sized saucepan and melt.
	Dry white wine	5 ml	50 ml	Add and season with salt, pepper and nutmeg.
2	Prawns or shrimps*	50 g	500 g	Wash and add to the butter. Bring to the boil. Place into potted moulds and allow to set. Refrigerate and allow to set until ready to use. Remove from the mould and place on a plate or serving dish with a small salad, and prepared wedges of lemon and picked parsley.

* Shelled

☐   ☐   ☐

Cold sauces, dressings, seasonings and basic preparations

Seasonings are prepared mixtures used to flavour dishes, dressings and sauces. Dressings and sauces are used to bind the ingredients together, add flavour, retain a fresh look to the dish and make the dish look attractive.

Stock syrup

🥄 5 min   ♨ 30 min

Step	Commodity	100 ml	1 litre	
1	Sugar	40 g	400 g	Place in a saucepan.
	Water	100 ml	1 litre	Add to the sugar.
	Lemon juice	5 ml	50 ml	Add, bring to the boil and simmer for 30 minutes. Allow to cool before using.

NOTE: Stock syrup may be flavoured with a spirit or liquor as required.

☐   ☐   ☐

Aspic jelly

🥄 20 min   ♨ 3 hr

Step	Commodity	1 litre	5 litres	
1	Egg whites	1	5	Place in a saucepan.
	Water	100 ml	500 ml	Add and whisk thoroughly together.
	Minced shin beef	250 g	1¼ kg	Add to saucepan.
	Salt	4 g	20 g	Add and mix well together.
2	Onions	30 g	150 g	Peel, cut into mirepoix and add.
	Carrots	30 g	150 g	Peel, cut into mirepoix and add.
	Leeks	20 g	100 g	Peel, cut into mirepoix and add.
	Celery	20 g	100 g	Peel, cut into mirepoix and add.
	Bay leaf	½	2	Add.
	Peppercorns	2	10	Add.
	Leaf gelatine	50 g	250 g	Place in a bowl with a little water and soak.
	Stock	1 litre	5 litres	Add to the vegetables and the soaked gelantine. Bring to the boil quickly, taking care not to disturb the mixture. Simmer for the required time or until the liquid is crystal clear. Strain carefully through a muslin cloth. Remove any fat. The aspic is ready to use.

☐   ☐   ☐

Chaudfroid sauce

This is made with 2 parts béchamel or velouté enriched with cream, or demi glace to 1 part aspic jelly. The two are mixed together thoroughly and are used to coat items for cold buffets.

NOTE: Mayonnaise colée (2 parts mayonnaise/1 part aspic jelly (according to use)) may also be used for this purpose.

☐   ☐   ☐

14

Rice socle

🥄 15 min   ♨ 3 hr   ≋ 130°C

Step	Commodity	1 portion	10 portions	
1	Patna rice	200 g	2 kg	Wash and place in a suitably sized saucepan. Cover with twice as much water, bring to the boil and cook for 5 minutes. Refresh and drain well.
	Powdered alum	1 g	10 g	Add and mix in well.
2	Sliced pork fat	50 g	500 g	Line a terrine mould with clean muslin cloth and then line the cloth with the pork fat. Add the rice.
	Lard	20 g	200 g	Cut into small pieces and place over the rice. Cover with the sliced pork fat and then completely cover with the cloth. Cover terrine with a lid. Place in a pre-heated oven for the required time. Remove and place in a bone chopper until the mixture is smooth. Carefully place the socle in the required greased moulds and allow to set. Glaze with aspic jelly and use as required.

NOTE: Semolina can be used instead of rice.

☐   ☐   ☐

Tomato concassé (cru = raw)

Step	Commodity	1 portion	10 portions	🥄 15 min
1	Tomatoes	50 g	500 g	Remove the eye of each tomato and make a light cross incision in the other end. Place in a saucepan of boiling water for 10 seconds. Remove and refresh. Peel the skin, cut in half and discard the seeds. Cut the flesh into small dice.

☐   ☐   ☐

Tomato concassé (cuit = cooked)

Step	Commodity	1 portion	10 portions	🥄 15 min
1	Tomatoes	50 g	500 g	Remove the eye of each tomato and make a light cross incision in the other end. Place in a saucepan of boiling water for 10 seconds. Remove and refresh. Peel the skin, cut in half and discard the seeds. Cut the flesh into small dice.
2	Butter	5 g	50 g	Melt in a suitably sized saucepan.
	Onions	10 g	100 g	Peel, dice finely and add to the butter. Cook without colouring for 2–3 minutes.
	Garlic cloves	½	5	Peel, crush with a little salt and add. Add the diced tomatoes. Season with salt and pepper and cook gently until all the moisture has evaporated.

☐   ☐   ☐

SEASONINGS

Fine spices
les épices fines

Step	Commodity	Quantity required	
1	White pepper	70 g	Place in a bowl.
	Paprika	30 g	Add.
	Mace	10 g	Add.
	Nutmeg	5 g	Add.
	Cloves	5 g	Add.
	Marjoram	5 g	Add.
	Rosemary	5 g	Add.
	Cinnamon	5 g	Add.
	Bay leaves	5 g	Add.
	Sage	5 g	Add and pound together in a mortar until fine. Alternatively ground in a blender. Pass through a fine sieve and store in an airtight container.

☐   ☐   ☐

Spiced salt
Le sel d'épice

Step	Commodity	Quantity required	
1	Table salt	100 g	Place in a bowl.
	White pepper	20 g	Add to salt.
	Fine spices	20 g	Add and mix together well. Store in an airtight container.

Larder seasoning
Épice de Charcutière

Step	Commodity	Quantity required	
1	Thyme	50 g	Place in a bowl.
	Bay leaves	50 g	Add.
	Cloves	25 g	Add.
	Mace	10 g	Add.
	Black peppercorns	35 g	Add.
	Allspice	25 g	Add.
	Nutmeg	15 g	Add.
	Marjoram	10 g	Add.
	Ginger	10 g	Add and pound together in a mortar until fine. Pass through a fine sieve and store in an airtight container.

14

Marinades

Marinades are liquors that are used to preserve (pickle), tenderise and give flavour to meat, game and vegetables. The item for marinading is soaked for a period of time varying between 2 and 24 hours before cooking.

NOTE: Always make sure that the item being marinaded is completely covered with the marinade. If this is not possible, the item must be regularly turned to ensure an even marinading.

Plain marinade

Marinade ordinaire

30 min

Step	*Commodity*	*1 litre*	*5 litres*	
1	Onions	150 g	750 g	Peel, cut into mirepoix and place in a bowl.
	Carrots	150 g	750 g	Peel, cut into mirepoix and add to the onions.
	Celery	100 g	500 g	Wash, trim, cut into mirepoix and add.
	Garlic (optional)	1 clove	5 cloves	Peel, crush and add.
	Peppercorns	10	50	Add.
	Bay leaves	1	5	Add.
	Thyme, sprig	1 small	1 large	Add.
	Cloves	2	10	Add.
	Parsley stalks	2–3	12	Wash and add.
	Red wine	1 litre	5 litres	Pour over the vegetables and herbs.
	Oil	100 ml	500 ml	Add and mix together. The marinade is now ready to use.

NOTE: Use for meats, poultry and game.

□ □ □

Fish sousing marinade

30 min

Step	*Commodity*	*1 litre*	*5 litres*	
1	Button onions	150 g	750 g	Peel, cut into thin rings and place in a bowl.
	Carrots	150 g	750 g	Peel, cut into thin slices and add to the onions.
	Vinegar	500 ml	2½ litres	Add.
	Water	500 ml	2½ litres	Add.
	Chillis	3	10	Add.
	Bay leaves	1	5	Add.
	Thyme, sprig	1 small	1 large	Add.
	Cloves	2	10	Add.
	Parsley stalks	2–3	12	Wash and add.
	Sugar	10 g	50 g	Add.
	Peppercorns	10	30	Add.
	Salt	10 g	50 g	Add.

NOTE: Use for herrings, mackerel, smelts and sardines.

□ □ □

Lemon marinade

Marinade au citron

Marinade au citron

⌣ 15 min

Step	Commodity	1 portion	10 portions	
1	Shallots	15 g	150 g	Peel, chop finely and place in a bowl.
	Lemon juice	10 ml	100 ml	Add to bowl.
	Chopped parsley	pinch	1 tbsp	Add.
	Oil	5 ml	50 ml	Add and mix together. The marinade is now ready to use.

NOTE: Use for fish and poultry.

☐   ☐   ☐

Greek style marinade

Marinade à la Grecque

⌣ 20 min

Step	Commodity	1 portion	10 portions	
1	Peppercorns	2	20	Place in a saucepan.
	Bay leaf	½	3	Add to peppercorns.
	Coriander seeds	1	5	Add.
	Lemon juice	10 ml	100 ml	Add.
	Water	25 ml	250 ml	Add.
	Oil	5 ml	50 ml	Add and bring to the boil. The marinade is now ready to use.

NOTE: Use for vegetables á la Grecque. The vegetables are first blanched and then refreshed. They are then placed in the boiling marinade for 2–3 minutes. The vegetables and marinade are allowed to cool together. Serve cold.

☐   ☐   ☐

14

Portuguese style marinade

Marinade à la Portugaise

⌣ 45 min

Step	Commodity	1 portion	10 portions	
1	Peppercorns	2	20	Crush and place in a saucepan.
	Shallots	5 g	50 g	Peel, chop finely and add to saucepan.
	Garlic	¼	2–3	Peel, crush with a little salt and add.
	Bay leaf	½	3	Add.
	Tomato concassé	50 g	500 g	Add.
	Tomato purée	5 g	50 g	Add and mix in well.
	Water	25 ml	250 ml	Add.
	Oil	5 ml	50 ml	Add and bring to the boil. The marinade is now ready to use.

NOTE: Use for vegetables á la Portugaise. The vegetables are first blanched and then refreshed. They are then placed in the boiling marinade for 2–3 minutes. The vegetables are marinade are allowed to cool. Serve cold.

☐   ☐   ☐

Melba toast

Step	Commodity	1 portion	10 portions	
1	Sliced bread*	1	10	Toast on either side. Remove the crusts and slice through the centre creating two slices from the one. Cut in triangles. Toast the uncooked sides. Serve warm.

⤸ 15 min

* Brown or white bread

☐   ☐   ☐

Dressings

Vinaigrette dressing

Vinaigrette

Step	Commodity	1 litre	
1	Malt vinegar	1 part (250 ml)	Place in a clean bowl. Season with salt and milled pepper.
	Olive/salad oil	3 parts (750 ml)	Slowly whisk into the vinegar until it forms an emulsion. Store in a refrigerator until required.

⤸ 5 min

Extensions of vinaigrette

Lemon dressing As for vinaigrette using lemon juice in place of vinegar.

English mustard dressing As for vinaigrette using 1 tsp of diluted English mustard per litre.

Placa dressing As for English dressing with the addition of chilli sauce and chutney to taste.

St Regis dressing As for English dressing with the addition of 50 ml Worcester sauce and 15 g paprika per litre.

French mustard dressing As for vinaigrette using 1 tsp of diluted French mustard per litre.

Fine herb dressing As for vinaigrette with the addition of 2 tbsp of fine herbs per 1 litre.

Marseillaise dressing As for vinaigrette with the addition of 1 clove of garlic, crushed to a paste with salt.

Paprika dressing As for vinaigrette with the addition of 100 g finely chopped shallots and 2 tsp of paprika per litre.

Tomato dressing As for vinaigrette with the addition of 350 g of tomato purée per litre.

Anchovy dressing As for vinaigrette with the addition of 50 g of sieved anchovy fillets per litre.

Chiffonade dressing As for vinaigrette with the addition of 2 sieved hard boiled eggs, 2 tsp finely chopped parsley and 50 g brunoise of cooked beetroot per litre.

Roquefort dressing As for vinaigrette with the addition of 100 g of sieved roquefort cheese per litre.

☐   ☐   ☐

Miscellaneous sauces

Shallot sauce
Sauce echalote

Step	Commodity	1 litre	5 litres		🥣 10 min
1	Shallots	1 kg	5 kg	Peel, cut into fine dice and place in a bowl.	
	Vinegar	1 litre	5 litres	Add, season with salt and ground black pepper. Whisk thoroughly together.	

NOTE: Serve with oysters.

☐   ☐   ☐

Sauce Gribiche

Step	Commodity	1 litre	5 litres		🥣 30 min
1	French mustard	1 tsp	5 tsp	Place in a bowl.	
	Vinegar	200 ml	1 litre	Add.	
	Salad/olive oil	700 ml	3½ litres	Add and mix together thoroughly.	
2	Gherkins	50 g	250 g	Chop finely. Add to the vinegar mix.	
	Capers	50 g	250 g	Chop finely and add.	
	Fine herbs	25 g	125 g	Chop finely and add. Season with salt and milled pepper. Mix thoroughly together.	

NOTE: Serve with cold fish and calf's head.

☐   ☐   ☐

Ravigote sauce

Step	Commodity	1 litre	5 litres		🥣 10 min
1	Vinegar	200 ml	1 litre	Place in a bowl.	
	Salad/olive oil	700 ml	3½ litres	Add.	
	Shallots	75 g	375 g	Peel, chop finely and add.	
	Capers	50 g	250 g	Chop finely and add.	
	Fine herbs	10 g	50 g	Add and mix together well.	

NOTE: Serve with calf's head and calf's feet.

☐   ☐   ☐

14

Escoffier sauce

Step	Commodity	1 litre	5 litres	
1	Mayonnaise	800 ml	4 litres	Place in a bowl.
	Lemon juice	100 ml	500 ml	Add to mayonnaise.
	Worcester sauce	50 ml	250 ml	Add.
	Chilli sauce	50 ml	250 ml	Add.
	Chives	50 g	250 g	Wash, dry and chop finely. Add to the other ingredients and mix well together.

☐ ☐ ☐

Thousand Island sauce

⌣ 10 min

Step	Commodity	1 litre	5 litres	
1	Mayonnaise	900 ml	4½ litres	Place in a bowl.
	Lemon juice	50 ml	250 ml	Add to mayonnaise.
	Red pepper	100 g	500 g	Remove the stalk and seeds. Dice finely and add.
	Green pepper	100 g	500 g	Remove the stalk and seeds. Dice finely and add.
	Chilli sauce	50 ml	250 ml	Add.
	Paprika	15 g	75 g	Add and mix well together.

NOTE: Serve with fish and shellfish salads and cocktails.

☐ ☐ ☐

Mint sauce

Sauce menthe

⌣ 40 min

Step	Commodity	1 portion	10 portions	
1	Mint	10 g	100 g	Pick the leaves, wash and dry.
	Castor sugar	5 g	50 g	Add to the leaves and chop finely (the sugar works as an abrasive to aid chopping). Place in a bowl.
	Water	10 ml	100 ml	Boil and pour over the mint.

NOTE: Serve with roast lamb.

Niçoise sauce

⌣ 40 min

Step	Commodity	1 litre	5 litres	
1	French dressing	1 litre	5 litres	Place in a bowl.
	Olives	50 g	250 g	Chop finely and add.
	Capers	50 g	250 g	Chop finely and add.
	Anchovy fillets	50 g	250 g	Chop finely and add.
	Parsley	50 g	250 g	Wash, dry, chop finely and add. Whisk together thoroughly.

NOTE: Serve with meat salads.

☐ ☐ ☐

Sour cream sauce

Crème acidule

⌣ 10 min

Step	Commodity	1 portion	10 portions	
1	Fresh cream	75 ml	750 ml	Place in a bowl.
	Lemon juice	25 ml	250 ml	Add and season with salt, milled pepper and paprika. Whisk until a light texture is achieved.

NOTE: Serve with salads containing fruit.

☐ ☐ ☐

Horseradish sauce (1)

Sauce raifort

⌣ 15 min

Step	Commodity	1 portion	10 portions	
1	Cream	35 ml	350 ml	Place in a clean bowl and whisk lightly.
	Horseradish	8 g	80 g	Grate finely and add to cream. Season with salt, milled pepper and cayenne pepper.

NOTE: Serve with smoked fish and roast beef.

☐ ☐ ☐

Horseradish sauce (2)

Sauce raifort

⌣ 30 min

Step	Commodity	1 portion	10 portions	
1	Breadcrumbs, white	8 g	80 g	Place in a bowl.
	Milk	15 ml	150 ml	Add to breadcrumbs and allow to soak.
2	Cream	35 ml	350 ml	Place in a clean bowl and whisk lightly.
	Horseradish	8 g	80 g	Grate finely and add to the cream. Squeeze the breadcrumbs and add to the horseradish. Season with salt and pepper.
	White wine vinegar	2 ml	20 ml	Add and mix together well.

NOTE: Serve with smoked fish and roast beef.

☐ ☐ ☐

14

Cumberland sauce

Step	Commodity	1 portion	10 portions	
1	Redcurrant jelly	50 g	500 g	Place in a saucepan and heat gently to dissolve. Allow to cool.
	English mustard, dry	pinch	½ tsp	Place in a small jug.
	Ground ginger	pinch	tsp	Add to jug.
	Port	15 ml	150 ml	Add and dilute the mustard. Add to the jelly. Mix well together.
	Shallots	1 g	10 g	Peel and dice finely.
	Lemons	1/10 equiv	1	Cut in half. Squeeze the juice into a jug.
	Oranges	2/10 equiv	2	Remove the zest and cut into julienne. Retain the fruit for use later. Place the orange zest along with the finely chopped shallots into boiling water for 3–4 minutes. Remove, drain well, dry and add to the jelly. Squeeze the juice of the oranges and lemon into the jelly. Whisk thoroughly.

NOTE: Serve with cold ham and game.

Extension of Cumberland sauce

Oxford sauce is made in a similar way to Cumberland sauce with the addition of lemon zest.

□   □   □

MAYONNAISE

Mayonnaise is an emulsion of oil and egg yolks, that is, the egg yolk is suspended in the oil. If the oil is added too fast or if the mixture is not beaten sufficiently, the egg and oil will separate. Avoid using metal bowls as the whisking action may cause the mayonnaise to discolour.

Mayonnaise

30 min

Step	Commodity	1 litre	5 litres	
1	Dry English mustard	1 tsp	5 tsp	Place into a clean bowl.
	Vinegar	25 ml	125 ml	Add and mix well together.
	Egg yolks	7	35	Break carefully into the bowl and whisk thoroughly until the mixture is creamy and light.
2	Olive/salad oil*	1 litre	5 litres	Add slowly and a little at a time, whisking briskly and continuously until all the oil is incorporated. Season with salt and white pepper.
3	Water	50 ml	250 ml	Add and mix in well to stabilise the mixture. Place in a clean airtight container and refrigerate.

* The oil should be left out in the kitchen and be allowed to reach a temperature of 20°C before using otherwise it may cause the mayonnaise to curdle.

NOTE: If the mayonnaise curdles:

(a) begin again by placing an egg yolk into a clean bowl and slowly adding the curdled mixture; or
(b) place a teaspoon into a clean bowl and add the curdled mixture a little at a time.

Extensions of mayonnaise

Mayonnaise Colée

Step	Commodity	1 litre	5 litres		45 min
1	Mayonnaise	750 ml	3¾ litres	Place in a clean bowl.	
	Cooled aspic jelly	250 ml	1¼ litres	Add and whisk well together.	

Use for coating and decorating cold fish for buffets and salads.

☐ ☐ ☐

Tartare sauce

Step	Commodity	1 litre	5 litres		45 min
1	Mayonnaise	800 ml	4 litres	Place in a clean bowl.	
	Gherkins	200 g	1 kg	Chop finely and add.	
	Capers	100 g	500 g	Chop finely and add.	
	Parsley	50 g	250 g	Wash, dry, chop finely and add. Correct the seasoning and store in an air tight container.	

Serve with deep fried fish.
NOTE: Sauce rémoulade is made by the addition of 2 tbsp of anchovy essence and 1 tbsp of fine herbs per litre.

☐ ☐ ☐

Sauce andalouse

Step	Commodity	1 litre	5 litres	
1	Tomato concassé	600 g	3 kg	Cook until fairly dry, pass through a fine sieve. Allow to cool and go cold.
	Mayonnaise	800 ml	4 litres	Add and mix well together.
2	Cooked red pimentoes	70 g	350 g	Cut into fine dice and add to the sauce.

Serve with cold meats, fish and salads.

☐ ☐ ☐

Mock mayonnaise

Step	Commodity	1 litre	5 litres		2 hr
1	Hot béchamel	700 ml	3½ litres	Pass through a fine sieve.	
	Vinegar	120 ml	600 ml	Add and mix in well.	
	English mustard	15 g	75 g	Dilute in a little water and add to the béchamel. Pass through a fine sieve into a clean bowl. Allow to go cold.	
	Whipping cream	100 ml	500 ml	Add and whisk together.	
	Cool aspic jelly	150 ml	750 ml	Mix in well. Correct the seasoning. Store in an airtight container.	

☐ ☐ ☐

14

Green sauce

⤵ 40 min

Step	Commodity	1 litre	5 litres	
1	Tarragon	15 g	75 g	Pick and wash the leaves.
	Chervil	15 g	75 g	Pick and wash the leaves. Add to the tarragon.
	Chives	15 g	75 g	Pick and wash the leaves. Place with the other herbs.
	Watercress	50 g	250 g	Pick and wash the leaves. Add.
	Spinach	150 g	750 g	Pick and wash the leaves. Add to the other herbs and blanch in boiling salted water for 4–5 minutes. Refresh, drain and squeeze to remove water. Pass through a fine sieve into a suitably sized bowl.
	Mayonnaise	700 g	3½ litres	Add to herbs and mix well together.

Serve with cold poached fish and shellfish (salmon, salmon trout and lobster).

☐ ☐ ☐

Cocktail sauce

⤵ 5 min

Step	Commodity	1 litre	5 litres	
1	Mayonnaise	700 ml	3½ litres	Place in a clean bowl.
	Tomato ketchup	200 ml	1 litre	Add.
	Worcester sauce	10 ml	100 ml	Add, season with salt and cayenne pepper. Mix together well.

Serve with fish and shellfish cocktails and salads.
NOTE: Tomato juice may be used in place of ketchup.

☐ ☐ ☐

Tyrolienne sauce

⤵ 1 hr

Step	Commodity	1 litre	5 litres	
1	Salad/olive oil	30 ml	150 ml	Place in a suitably sized saucepan and heat gently.
	Shallots	30 g	150 g	Peel, finely dice and add to the oil. Cook for 3–4 minutes without colouring.
	Bay leaf	½	2	Add to saucepan.
	Thyme	½ sprig	2 sprigs	Wash and add.
	Tomato concassé	400 g	2 kg	Add and cook until the mixture is soft. Pass through a fine sieve and allow to cool and go cold.
	Mayonnaise	900 ml	4½ litres	Add.
	Fine herbs	1 tbsp	5 tbsp	Add and mix together well.

Serve with fried fish and cold meats.

☐ ☐ ☐

Hard butter sauces/compound butter

Compound or hard butter sauces are usually served with grilled meats or fish, as a liaison of sauces or soups, as a garnish for certain sweet items and as an accompaniment for hors d'oeuvre.

Parsley butter

Beurre maitre d'hotel

🥣 30 min

Step	Commodity	1 portion	10 portions	
1	Butter	25 g	250 g	Place in a bowl and soften (not melt).
	Parsley	pinch	25 g	Wash, chop finely and add.
	Lemon juice	few drops	½ tsp	Add. Season with salt and pepper. Place on a sheet of damp greaseproof paper and roll into a cylinder 3 cm in diameter. Refrigerate and allow to harden before using. To use, cut into ½ cm slices and place in a bowl of iced water.

Serve with grilled meats and fish.

☐ ☐ ☐

Colbert butter

Beurre colbert

🥣 30 min

Step	Commodity	1 portion	10 portions	
1	Butter	25 g	250 g	Place in a bowl and soften (not melt).
	Parsley	pinch	25 g	Wash, chop finely and add.
	Chopped tarragon	pinch	1 tbsp	Add.
	Meat glaze	pinch	1 tsp	Add.
	Lemon juice	few drops	½ tsp	Add. Season with salt and pepper. Place on a sheet of damp greaseproof paper and roll into a cylinder 3 cm in diameter. Refrigerate and allow to harden before using. To use, cut into ½ cm slices and place in a bowl of iced water.

Serve with roast fillet of beef.
NOTE: For fish, Colbert style (à la Colbert) use fish glaze.

☐ ☐ ☐

Anchovy butter

Beurre d'anchois

🥣 30 min

Step	Commodity	1 portion	10 portions	
1	Butter	25 g	250 g	Place in a bowl and soften (do not melt).
	Anchovy essence	5 g	50 g	Pass through a sieve and add to the butter.
	Lemon juice	few drops	½ tsp	Add. Season with salt and pepper. Place on a sheet of damp greaseproof paper and roll into a cylinder 3 cm in diameter. Refrigerate and allow to harden before using. To use, cut into ½ cm slices and place in a bowl of iced water.

Serve with grilled meats and fish.

☐ ☐ ☐

14

Red wine butter

Beurre vin rouge

⏱ 30 min

Step	Commodity	1 portion	10 portions	
1	Butter	25 g	250 g	Place in a bowl and soften (do not melt).
	Shallots	10 g	100 g	Peel, chop finely and add to the butter.
	Red wine	10 ml	120 ml	Add. Season with salt and pepper. Place on a sheet of damp greaseproof paper and roll into a cylinder 3 cm in diameter. Refrigerate and allow to harden before using. To use, cut into ½ cm slices and place in a bowl of iced water.

Serve with roast fillet of beef and steaks.

☐ ☐ ☐

Wine merchant butter

Beurre marchand de vin

⏱ 30 min

Step	Commodity	1 portion	10 portions	
1	Butter	25 g	250 g	Place in a bowl and soften (do not melt).
	Chopped parsley	pinch	1 tbsp	Add to butter.
	Shallots	10 g	100 g	Peel, chop finely and add to the butter.
	Red wine	10 ml	120 ml	Add. Season with salt and pepper. Place on a sheet of damp greaseproof paper and roll into a cylinder 3 cm in diameter. Refrigerate and allow to harden before using. To use, cut into ½ cm slices and place in a bowl of iced water.

Serve with roast fillet of beef and steaks.

☐ ☐ ☐

English mustard butter

Beurre moutarde à l'anglaise

⏱ 30 min

Step	Commodity	1 portion	10 portions	
1	Butter	25 g	250 g	Place in a bowl and soften (do not melt).
	English mustard	5 g	50 g	Dilute with a little water and add to the butter.
	Lemon juice	few drops	½ tsp	Add. Season with salt and pepper. Place on a sheet of damp greaseproof paper and roll into a cylinder 3 cm in diameter. Refrigerate and allow to harden before using. To use, cut into ½ cm slices and place in a bowl of iced water.

Serve with grilled meats and fish.

NOTE: This butter may be made with French mustard in place of English mustard to make French mustard butter (Beurre moutarde à la francaise).

☐ ☐ ☐

Lobster butter

Beurre d'homard

⤵ 30 min

Step	Commodity	1 portion	10 portions	
1	Butter	25 g	250 g	Place in a bowl and soften (do not melt).
	Lobster*	10 g	100 g	Pound and pass through a fine sieve. Add to the softened butter.
	Lemon juice	few drops	½ tsp	Add. Season with salt and pepper. Place on a sheet of damp greaseproof paper and roll into a cylinder 3 cm in diameter. Refrigerate and allow to harden before using. To use, cut into ½ cm slices and place in a bowl of iced water.

* Lobster coral, eggs and creamy flesh cooked. Serve with grilled fish.
NOTE: This butter is sometimes known as red butter. Shrimp butter (Beurre de cervettes) is also made using this method.

☐   ☐   ☐

Caviar butter

Beurre de caviar

⤵ 30 min

Step	Commodity	1 portion	10 portions	
1	Butter	25 g	250 g	Place in a bowl and soften (do not melt).
	Caviar	5 g	50 g	Carefully add to the softened butter.
	Lemon juice	few drops	½ tsp	Add. Season with salt and pepper. Place on a sheet of damp greaseproof paper and roll into a cylinder 3 cm in diameter. Refrigerate and allow to harden before using. To use, cut into ½ cm slices and place in a bowl of iced water.

Serve with grilled fish.

☐   ☐   ☐

14

Garlic butter

Beurre d'ail

⤵ 30 min

Step	Commodity	1 portion	10 portions	
1	Butter	25 g	250 g	Place in a bowl and soften (do not melt).
	Garlic	½ clove	5 cloves	Crush with a little salt and pass through a sieve to purée.
	Lemon juice	few drops	½ tsp	Add. Season with salt and pepper. Place on a sheet of damp greaseproof paper and roll into a cylinder 3 cm in diameter. Refrigerate and allow to harden before using. To use, cut into ½ cm slices and place in a bowl of iced water.

Serve with grilled meats.

☐   ☐   ☐

Butter for snails

Beurre à la bourguignonne

⌣ 45 min

Step	Commodity	1 portion	10 portions	
1	Butter	25 g	250 g	Place in a bowl and soften (do not melt).
	Shallots	3 g	30 g	Peel, chop finely and add to the butter.
	Garlic	½ clove	5 cloves	Crush with a little salt and pass through a sieve to purée.
	Parsley	pinch	15 g	Wash, chop finely and add to the butter.
	Lemon juice	few drops	½ tsp	Add. Season with salt and pepper. Place on a sheet of damp greaseproof paper and roll into a cylinder 3 cm in diameter. Refrigerate and allow to harden before using. To use, cut into ½ cm slices and place in a bowl of iced water.

Serve with snails.

☐   ☐   ☐

SWEET BUTTERS

Butter cream

⌣ 30 min

Step	Commodity	1 portion	10 portions	
1	Butter	25 g	250 g	Place in a bowl and soften (do not melt).
	Icing sugar	25 g	250 g	Add to the butter and cream together.

Uses: Coloured and flavoured with vanilla, chocolate, coffee, orange or liquor and used for filling cakes and pastries.

NOTE: Flavoured butter cream can also be placed on a sheet of damp greaseproof paper, rolled into a cylinder 3 cm in diameter and refrigerated. It is then served as a sweet butter in ½ cm slices on Christmas pudding, mince pies and crêpes.

Extensions of sweet butter

Sherry butter – As for sweet butter with the addition of 5 ml (approximately) sherry per portion.

Brandy butter – As for sweet butter with the addition of 5 ml (approximately) brandy per portion.

Liquor butter – As for sweet butter with the addition of 5 ml (approximately) chosen liquor per portion.

☐   ☐   ☐

Salads

A salad is an agreeable combination of vegetables and/or fruit and/or meat, poultry, game or fish served as a first course (hors d'oeuvre), a main course, an accompaniment to a main course or as a sweet course – as in fruit salad.

Care must be taken to have a good variety of colour, texture, nutrients and flavours when offering a salad as a main course or accompaniment to a main course. If the main dish is fish, a fish salad or even a meat salad would not be appropriate to serve as an accompaniment.

There are two basic types of salads, broadly known as:

(a) simple or plain salads, which consist of one main item. i.e. beetroot, tomato or cucumber bound with a dressing or sauce, and
(b) compound or mixed salads which consist of several items marinaded and bound in a dressing or a sauce.

There is a conflict of opinion as to which salads go into what category. Some chefs class coleslaw as a simple salad because traditionally it has a main vegetable – cabbage with a little shredded carrot – similar to potato salad, but other chefs argue that it consists of more than one item and is bound with mayonnaise so it should be considered a compound salad. For the purpose of this book such salads are classed as compound or mixed salads.

All salads may be served as an hors d'oeuvre variés.

General rules for the preparation of salad stuffs

Care should be taken when preparing salad vegetables as rough treatment will most likely bruising and spoil the appearance of the finished dish. Leaves should be separated by hand, fruits and vegetables should be checked for bruising. Fruit and vegetables should be placed in a sink of cold water and rinsed to remove any dirt or flies.

Cooked vegetables used in salads are lightly cooked and refreshed to preserve nutrients, flavour and colour.

14

SINGLE OR SIMPLE SALADS

Beetroot salad

Salade de betterave

⌣ 30 min

Step	Commodity	1 portion	10 portions	
1	Cooked beetroot*	50 g	500 g	Peel, cut into macedoine, julienne of jardinière.
	Onions	2½ g	25 g	Peel, cut into brunoise and add to the beetroot. Season with salt and pepper. Bind with vinaigrette, mayonnaise or soured cream. Dress on a suitable serving dish.
2	Chopped parsley	pinch	½ tbsp	Sprinkle over the top.

* Beetroot is normally cooked by steaming.

☐ ☐ ☐

Raw cabbage salad

Salade de choux crus

⌣ 20 min

Step	Commodity	1 portion	10 portions	
1	White cabbage	50 g	500 g	Trim the outside leaves. Remove the stalk, wash thoroughly, dry and chiffonade. Toss in a little vinaigrette and dress on a suitable serving dish.

This salad is also known as German cabbage salad (Salade de choux allemands).

Swiss cabbage salad

Salade de choux suisses

🥄 30 min

Step	Commodity	1 portion	10 portions	
1	White cabbage	40 g	400 g	Trim the outside leaves. Remove the stalk, wash thoroughly, dry and chiffonade.
	Cooked streaky bacon	10 g	100 g	Remove any bones and rind. Cut into thin lardons and add to the cabbage.
	Vinegar	10 ml	100 ml	Add, season with salt and pepper. Dress on a suitable serving dish.

NOTE: Cabbage salads can be made more interesting by varying the dressing and by the addition of grated apple, pineapple pieces and sultanas.

☐   ☐   ☐

Red cabbage salad

Salade de choux rouges

🥄 30 min

Step	Commodity	1 portion	10 portions	
1	White cabbage	50 g	500 g	Trim the outside leaves. Remove the stalk, wash thoroughly, dry and chiffonade. Blanch in boiling water for 3–4 minutes. Refresh and drain thoroughly. Marinade in vinaigrette for 1 hour before service.
2	Dessert apples	15 g	150 g	Peel, remove the core, cut into dice and add to the cabbage. Dress on a suitable serving dish.

NOTE: Red cabbage salad can also be made as for Swiss cabbage salad.

☐   ☐   ☐

Tomato salad

Salade de tomate

🥄 15 min

Step	Commodity	1 portion	10 portions	
1	Tomatoes	1 medium	10 medium	Wash, remove the stalk and eye with a small knife. Make a slight cross incision in the other end. Blanch in boiling water for 10 seconds to remove the skins. Refresh immediately. Peel the skins. Cut the tomatoes into thin slices. Dress on a suitable serving dish. Sprinkle with finely chopped parsley.

NOTE: Tomato salad may be served with 10 g thinly sliced rings/brunoise of onion or chopped shallots.

☐   ☐   ☐

Cucumber salad

Salade de concombres

🥄 15 min

Step	Commodity	1 portion	10 portions	
1	Cucumber	50 g	500 g	Peel and cut into thin even slices. Dress on a suitable serving dish.
	Shallots (optional)	10 g	100 g	Peel, cut into brunoise and sprinkle over the cucumber. Napper with vinaigrette and sprinkle with finely chopped parsley.

NOTE: Russian cucumber salad (Salade de concombres à la russe) is made with the addition of a sour cream dressing.

☐   ☐   ☐

Celeriac salad (raw)

⏱ 30 min

Step	Commodity	1 portion	10 portions	
1	Celeriac	50 g	500 g	Wash thoroughly, peel and cut into fine julienne. Place in a suitably sized bowl. Season with salt and pepper.
	English mustard sauce	10 ml	100 ml	Bind with the celeriac. Dress on a suitable serving dish. Sprinkle with a little finely chopped parsley.

☐   ☐   ☐

Celeriac salad (cooked)

⏱ 30 min   ♨ 35 min approx.

Step	Commodity	1 portion	10 portions	
1	Celeriac	50 g	500 g	Select medium sized celeriac and wash thoroughly. Place in a suitably sized saucepan of boiling salted water and cook for the required time. Refresh, drain and peel. Cut into julienne or macedoine. Place in a bowl. Season with salt and pepper.
	Shallots	15 g	150 g	Peel, cut into brunoise and sprinkle over celeriac. Toss in vinaigrette. Dress on a suitable serving dish and sprinkle with a little finely chopped parsley.

☐   ☐   ☐

French bean salad

⏱ 20 min   ♨ 5 min

Step	Commodity	1 portion	10 portions	
1	French beans	50 g	500 g	Trim the tops and tails. Wash and place in a saucepan of boiling salted water for the required time. Refresh immediately and drain. Place in a bowl. Season with salt and pepper. Toss in a little vinaigrette. Dress on a suitable serving dish.

☐   ☐   ☐

Haricot bean salad

⏱ 10 min

Step	Commodity	1 portion	10 portions	
1	Haricot beans*	50 g	500 g	Place in a bowl. Season with salt and pepper.
	Shallots/ chives	10 g	100 g	Peel, cut into brunoise and add to the beans. Toss in vinaigrette. Dress on a suitable serving dish. Sprinkle with a little finely chopped parsley.

* Cooked

☐   ☐   ☐

14

Flageolets salad

👐 10 min

Step	Commodity	1 portion	10 portions	
1	Flageolet beans*	50 g	500 g	Place in a bowl. Season with salt and pepper.
	Fresh mixed herbs	pinch	2 tsp	Wash and chop finely. Add to the beans.
	Shallots (optional)	10 g	100 g	Peel, cut into brunoise and add to the beans. Toss in mayonnaise or vinaigrette. Dress on a suitable serving dish. Sprinkle with a little finely chopped parsley.

* Cooked

NOTE: A mixed bean salad may be made using a combination of haricot, red kidney, French and flageolet beans.

☐ ☐ ☐

Potato salad

Salade de pommes de terre

👐 20 min ♨ 20 min approx.

Step	Commodity	1 portion	10 portions	
1	Jacket potatoes	50 g	500 g	Scrub thoroughly and steam for the required time. Remove and allow to cool. Peel, cut into macedoine (½ cm dice) and place in a bowl.
2	Onions	10 g	100 g	Peel, cut into brunoise and add to the potato.
	Chives	5 g	50 g	Wash, chop into fine dice and add. Toss in vinaigrette or mayonnaise. Dress on a suitable serving dish and sprinkle with a little finely chopped parsley.

NOTE: Potato salad can be varied by using different dressings, adding additional vegetables or fruit (e.g., apple, sultanas) and adding herbs or spices.

☐ ☐ ☐

Hot potato salad

Salade de pommes de terre chaudes

👐 20 min ♨ 20 min approx.

Step	Commodity	1 portion	10 portions	
1	Jacket potatoes	50 g	500 g	Scrub thoroughly and steam for the required time. Remove and cut into ½ cm slices while hot. Place in a bowl. Pour over the vinaigrette.
	Onions	10 g	100 g	Peel, cut into brunoise and add to the potato. Mix well together. Season with salt and pepper. Dress on a suitable serving dish. Sprinkle with a little finely chopped parsley.

Extensions of hot potato salad

German potato salad

Salade de pommes de terre allemande

Add 15 g of thinly sliced dessert apples per portion.

Parisienne potato salad

Salade de pommes de terre à la Parisienne

As for German potato salad using half white wine and half vinaigrette. Finish with chopped chervil and chopped parsley.

Dutch potato salad

Salade de pommes de terre à la hollandaise

As for German potato salad with the addition of 15 g cooked lardons of bacon and 10 g julienne of smoked herring per portion.

☐ ☐ ☐

Rice salad

Salade de riz

🥣 20 min ♨ 12–16 min approx.

Step	Commodity	1 portion	10 portions	
1	Long grain rice	15 g	150 g	Place in a saucepan of boiling salted water and cook for the required time. Refresh immediately and drain well. Place in a bowl.
2	Tomato concassé*	10 g	100 g	Add to the rice. Season with salt and pepper. Add a little vinaigrette and toss lightly. Dress on a suitable serving dish. Sprinkle with a little finely chopped parsley.

* Cru

NOTE: Rice salad may also be made using cooked peas in place of the chopped parsley. Spanish style rice salad (Salade de riz espagnole) is made as per the basic recipe with the addition of 10 g brunoise of red peppers and 5 g chopped olives per portion.

☐   ☐   ☐

COMPOUND OR MIXED SALADS

VEGETABLE BASED COMPOUND SALADS

Coleslaw

🥣 30 min

Step	Commodity	1 portion	10 portions	
1	White cabbage	50 g	500 g	Trim the outside leaves. Remove the stalk, wash thoroughly, dry and chiffonade.
	Carrot	10 g	100 g	Peel, wash, finely shred and add to the cabbage. Bind with a little mayonnaise. Dress on a suitable serving dish.

NOTE: Some establishments add a little finely shredded onion to the coleslaw for extra flavour.

☐   ☐   ☐

Potato and watercress salad

Salade cressonnière

🥣 30 min

Step	Commodity	1 portion	10 portions	
1	Steamed potatoes	50 g	500 g	Peel and slice the potatoes. Place in a bowl.
	Cress	1 sprig	1 bunch	Pick and wash the leaves. Mix with the potatoes. Toss in vinaigrette or mayonnaise. Arrange neatly in a serving dish.
2	Hard boiled eggs	½	5	Sieve finely and sprinkle over the salad together with finely chopped parsley.

☐   ☐   ☐

American salad

⌣ 45 min

Step	Commodity	1 portion	10 portions	
1	Tomatoes	1 medium	10 medium	Remove the eye and make a cross incision in the other end of each tomato. Blanch in boiling water for 10 seconds, remove and refresh immediately. Discard the skins and cut into ½ cm slices. Place in a bowl.
	Celery	15 g	150 g	Wash, trim and cut into julienne. Add to the tomatoes.
	Boiled potatoes	1 small	10 small	Peel and cut into ½ cm slices.
2	Onions, small	50 g	500 g	Peel, remove the root and blanch in boiling salted water for 10 minutes. Remove, refresh and slice thinly into rings. Mix with the other ingredients. Toss in vinaigrette.
3	Lettuce leaves	1	10	Wash, trim and place on a serving dish. Carefully arrange the salad on top.
	Hard boiled eggs	½	5	Chop finely and sprinkle over the salad along with finely chopped parsley.

☐   ☐   ☐

French salad

⌣ 30 min

Step	Commodity	1 portion	10 portions	
1	Tomatoes	1 medium	10 medium	Remove the eye and make a cross incision in the other end of each tomato. Blanch in boiling water for 10 seconds, remove and refresh immediately. Discard the skins and cut into ½ cm slices.
	Cucumber	25 g	250 g	Peel and slice thinly.
	Cooked beetroot	25 g	250 g	Wash and drain well. Cut into thin slices.
2	Lettuce leaves	1	10	Wash, trim and arrange on a serving dish. Carefully arrange the tomato, beetroot and cucumber on top.
	Mustard cress	¹⁄₁₀ punnet	1 punnet	Trim, wash and arrange or sprinkle on the salad. Napper with a little vinaigrette.
	Hard boiled eggs	½	5	Cut into quarters and arrange with the salad.

NOTE: French salad may be flavoured with finely chopped herbs, i.e. tarragon or parsley.

☐   ☐   ☐

Italian salad

Step	Commodity	1 portion	10 portions		45 min
1	Cooked celeriac	15 g	150 g	Cut into ½ cm dice and place in a bowl.	
	Cooked carrots	15 g	150 g	Cut into ½ cm dice and add to the celeriac.	
	Cooked peas	5 g	50 g	Add.	
	Salami	10 g	100 g	Cut into ½ cm dice and add. Season with salt and pepper. Bind with mayonnaise.	
	Salami	1 slice	10 slices	Cut in half. Arrange around the outside of the serving dish. Place the salad in the centre.	
	Anchovy fillets	1	10	Cut in half lengthways and arrange in a criss cross pattern over the salad.	

☐   ☐   ☐

Bagatalle salad

Step	Commodity	1 portion	10 portions		30 min
1	Carrots	25 g	250 g	Peel, cut into julienne and place in a clean bowl.	
	Button mushrooms	15 g	150 g	Wash, trim and cut into thin slices. Add to the carrots. Marinade in vinaigrette.	
	Lettuce leaves	1	10	Wash, trim and place on a serving dish. Arrange the vegetables on top.	
2	Cooked asparagus tips	4	40	Arrange on the salad.	
	Fine herbs	pinch	1 tbsp	Sprinkle over the salad.	

☐   ☐   ☐

Andalouse salad

Step	Commodity	1 portion	10 portions		45 min
1	Tomatoes	1 medium	10 medium	Remove the eye and make a cross incision in the other end of each tomato. Blanch in boiling water for 10 seconds, remove and refresh immediately. Discard the skins and cut into quarters.	
	Red peppers	25 g	250 g	Wash, remove the stalk and seeds. Cut into julienne and mix with the tomatoes.	
	Plain boiled rice	15 g	150 g	Add to the other ingredients.	
	Onions	25 g	250 g	Cut into thinly sliced rings and add to the salad.	
	Parsley	pinch	½ tbsp	Add, along with garlic flavoured vinaigrette.	
2	Lettuce leaves	1	10	Wash, trim and place on a serving dish. Carefully arrange the salad on top.	

☐   ☐   ☐

14

Green salad

Salade verte

🥣 30 min

Step	Commodity	1 portion	10 portions	
1	Lettuce*	3 × 1	3 × 10	Wash, trim and place in iced water.
	Chicory leaves	2	20	Wash, trim and add to the lettuce until ready to use. Arrange on a serving dish.
	Spring onions	1	10	Wash, trim the root and top. Arrange on the lettuce.
	Chives	¹⁄₁₀	1 bunch	Wash, trim, chop finely and sprinkle over the salad.

* A variety of types, e.g. cos, round, iceberg, lamb's, oak leaf, etc.

☐ ☐ ☐

Niçoise salad

Salade niçoise

🥣 1 hr

Step	Commodity	1 portion	10 portions	
1	Tomatoes	1 medium	10 medium	Remove the eye and make a cross incision in the other end of each tomato. Blanch in boiling water for 10 seconds, remove and refresh immediately. Discard the skins, cut in half and discard the seeds. Cut the flesh into ½ cm dice or julienne. Place in a bowl.
	Cooked potato	25 g	250 g	Cut into ½ cm dice and add to the tomato.
	Cooked French beans	25 g	250 g	Trim and add to the other ingredients. Season with salt and pepper. Bind with a little vinaigrette.
2	Lettuce leaves	1	10	Wash, trim and place on a serving dish. Arrange the salad on top.
	Stoned olives	2	20	Cut into thin slices and arrange on top.
	Anchovy fillets	1	10	Cut in half lengthways and arrange on top of the salad.
	Capers	2 g equiv	20 g	Arrange on top of the anchovy fillets.

NOTE: Cooked tuna is sometimes added to this salad.

☐ ☐ ☐

Russian salad   Salade russe

Step	Commodity	1 portion	10 portions	
1	Cooked carrots	25 g	250 g	Cut into ½ cm dice and place in a clean bowl.
	Cooked turnip	25 g	250 g	Cut into ½ cm dice and add to the carrots.
	Cooked French beans	15 g	150 g	Trim, cut into small diamond shapes and add.
	Cooked garden peas	10 g	100 g	Add. season with salt and pepper and bind with mayonnaise. Dress in a serving dish.

⌣ 45 min

NOTE: Classical Russian salad includes 15 g diced cooked mushrooms, 5 g diced gherkin, 10 g diced cooked ham, 10 g diced cooked tongue, 10 g diced cooked lobster and one diced anchovy fillet (per portion) mixed in with the vegetables. The salad is arranged in a pyramid shape on a serving dish. It is garnished with small balls made from 5 g cavier and a few capers, and a border of alternative slices of beetroot (10 g) and sliced hard boiled eggs (½) per portion.

NOTE: All vegetable based salads can be served as a side salad to accompany a main meal or as an hors d'oeuvre varié.

☐   ☐   ☐

FRUIT BASED SALADS

Alice salad   Salade Alice

Step	Commodity	1 portion	10 portions	
1	Dessert apples	1	4	Peel, remove the core. Place in a bowl of water.
	Lemon juice	10 ml	100 ml	Add.
2	Dessert apples	¼ equiv	2½	Peel, core and dice. Place in a clean bowl and sprinkle with a little lemon juice.
	Redcurrants	15 g	150 g	Add and bind with acidulated cream. Remove the applies from the water. Neatly fill the centre of each with the appropriate amount of mixture.
	Lettuce hearts	1	10	Wash and trim. Place on the serving dish and carefully arrange the apples on top.
	Split almonds	5 g	50 g	Sprinkle over the top.

⌣ 45 min

14

☐   ☐   ☐

403

Eve's salad

Step	Commodity	1 portion	10 portions	
1	Dessert apple	1	10	Wash, remove the lid and cut out the core. Place in a bowl of water.
	Lemon juice	10 ml	100 ml	Add.
2	Dessert apples	¼	2½	Peel, core and dice. Place in a clean bowl and sprinkle with a little lemon juice.
	Banana	¼	2½	Peel, cut into dice and add to the diced apple.
	Pineapple	10 g	100 g	Cut into dice and add. Bind with acidulated cream. Remove the apples from the water. Neatly fill the centre with the appropriate amount of mixture and replace the lid.
3	Lettuce hearts	1	10	Wash and trim. Place on the serving dish and carefully arrange the apples on top.

☐ ☐ ☐

Apple salad

Salade de pommes

Step	Commodity	1 portion	10 portions	
1	Dessert apples	1	4	Peel, remove the core, cut into thin slices and place in a clean bowl.
	Lemon juice	10 ml	100 ml	Add.
	Blanched onions	15 g	150 g	Cut into thinly sliced rings and place with the apples. Bind with mayonnaise.
2	Lettuce hearts	1	10	Wash and trim. Place on the serving dish and carefully arrange the salad on top. Sprinkle with finely chopped parsley.

☐ ☐ ☐

Fresh fruit salad

Step	Commodity	1 portion	10 portions	
1	Stock syrup	10 ml	100 ml	Place in a bowl.
2	Oranges	½	5	Remove the top and bottom to reveal the fruit. Remove the skin and pith. Cut each segment from the dividing skin and place in the bowl. Squeeze the juice over the segments.
	Dessert apples	½	5	Skin, remove the core, cut into thin slices and add to the orange.
	Dessert pears	½	5	Skin, remove the core, cut into thin slices and add to the other fruit.
	Grapes	10 g	100 g	Wash, cut in half and remove the pips. Add to the fruit.
	Bananas	½	5	Peel, cut into thin slices and add to the other fruit.

NOTE: A fruit salad may consist of the above fruit combinations or other fruits, including pineapple, melon, strawberries, peaches, pears, apricots and cherries. A more exotic fruit salad may be made using kiwi fruit, passion fruit, mangoes, pawpaws, lychees, etc. In fruit salads the fruit can be cut into slices or diced as macedoine.

☐ ☐ ☐

Japanese salad

Salade Japonaise

⌣ 45 min

Step	Commodity	1 portion	10 portions	
1	Tomatoes	1 medium	10 medium	Remove the eye and make a cross incision in the other end of each tomato. Blanch in boiling water for 10 seconds, remove and refresh immediately. Discard the skins, cut in half and discard the seeds. Cut the flesh into ½ cm dice or julienne. Place in a bowl.
2	Oranges	½	5	Remove the skin and pith. Cut into segments discarding the pips. Place the orange segments with the tomatoes. Squeeze the juice over the top.
3	Pineapple	50 g	500 g	Cut into dice and add to the tomatoes. Season with salt and pepper.
4	Castor sugar	1 tsp	20 g	Add and mix together well. Bind with acidulated cream dressing.
5	Lettuce hearts	1	10	Wash and trim. Place on the serving dish and carefully arrange the salad on top.

☐   ☐   ☐

Mimosa salad

Salade mimosa

⌣ 30 min

Step	Commodity	1 portion	10 portions	
1	Oranges	½	5	Remove the skin and pith. Cut into segments discarding the pips. Place the orange segments in a bowl and squeeze over the orange juice.
	Grapes	15 g	150 g	Wash, cut in half and remove the pips. Add to the orange.
	Banana	½	5	Remove the skin and slice thinly. Add to the other fruit. Bind with acidulated cream dressing.
2	Lettuce hearts	1	10	Wash and trim. Place on the serving dish and carefully arrange the salad on top.

14

☐   ☐   ☐

Waldorf salad

Salade Waldorf

⌣ 30 min

Step	Commodity	1 portion	10 portions	
1	Celeriac* or celery	50 g	500 g	Cut into ½ cm dice and place in a clean bowl.
	Lemon juice	10 ml	100 ml	Add.
	Russet apples	½	5	Peel, core and cut into thin slices or ½ cm dice. Place in the bowl and mix in. Bind with mayonnaise. Place on a serving dish.
	Peeled walnut halves	2	20	Arrange on top of the salad.

* Cooked

NOTE: An alternative method of presentation would be to remove the top of the apple, scoop out the fruit and serve the salad in the apple.

NOTE: All fruit based salads can be served as a side salad to accompany a main meal or as an hors d'oeuvre varié.

☐   ☐   ☐

MEAT BASED SALADS

Beatrice salad

Salade Beatrice

⌣ 30 min

Step	Commodity	1 portion	10 portions	
1	Cooked chicken breast	50 g	500 g	Cut into julienne and place in a bowl.
	Cooked potatoes	35 g	350 g	Peel, cut into macedoine and place with the chicken.
	Truffles	5 g	50 g	Cut into julienne and add to the other ingredients. Season with salt and pepper. Bind with English mustard mayonnaise.
2	Lettuce hearts	1	10	Wash, trim and carefully arrange on a serving dish. Arrange salad mixture on the serving dish in a pyramid shape.
	Asparagus tips	3	30	Arrange on the salad.

☐　　☐　　☐

Carmen salad

Salade Carmen

⌣ 45 min

Step	Commodity	1 portion	10 portions	
1	Cooked chicken breast	50 g	500 g	Cut into macedoine and place in a bowl.
	Cooked red peppers	50 g	50 g	Cut into fine dice and add to the chicken.
	Cooked garden peas	10 g	100 g	Add and marinade with French flavoured vinaigrette.
	Cooked patna rice	15 g	150 g	Add, season with salt and pepper and mix together well.
2	Lettuce hearts	1	10	Wash, trim and carefully arrange on a serving dish. Neatly place the salad in the centre.
	Chopped tarragon	pinch	2 tsp	Sprinkle over the top.

☐　　☐　　☐

Egyptian salad

Salade egyptienne

⟍ 45 min

Step	Commodity	1 portion	10 portions	
1	Cooked chicken livers	15 g	150 g	Chop finely and place in a bowl.
	Boiled ham	15 g	150 g	Cut into brunoise and place with the livers.
	Cooked mushrooms	10 g	100 g	Dice and add.
	Artichoke bottoms	10 g	100 g	Dice and add.
	Cooked garden peas	10 g	100 g	Add.
2	Tomatoes	½ medium	5 medium	Remove the eye and make a cross incision in the other end of each tomato. Blanch in boiling water for 10 seconds, remove and refresh immediately. Discard the skins, cut in half and discard the seeds. Cut the flesh into ½ cm dice and add to the other ingredients.
	Cooked red peppers	10 g	100 g	Dice and add. Marinade in vinaigrette.
3	Lettuce leaves	1	10	Wash, trim and arrange on the serving dish. Neatly arrange the salad in the centre. Sprinkle with finely chopped parsley.

☐   ☐   ☐

Opera salad

Salade à l'opera

⟍ 30 min

Step	Commodity	1 portion	10 portions	
1	Cooked chicken breast	50 g	500 g	Cut into julienne and place in a bowl.
	Cooked tongue	15 g	150 g	Cut into julienne and add.
	Truffles	5 g	50 g	Cut into julienne and add to the other ingredients.
	Celery	15 g	150 g	Wash, trim, cut into julienne and add. Bind with mayonnaise.
2	Lettuce leaves	1	10	Wash, trim and arrange on a serving dish. Neatly arrange the salad in the centre.
	Asparagus	2	20	Place in a criss-cross fashion on top of the salad.
	Gherkins	1	10	Cut into fan shapes and dress on top of the asparagus.

☐   ☐   ☐

14

Meet salad

Salade de viande

🥣 45 min

Step	Commodity	1 portion	10 portions	
1	Cooked lean beef*	50 g	500 g	Cut into ½ cm dice and place in a bowl.
	Gherkins	5 g	50 g	Cut into thin slices and add to the beef.
	Cooked French beans	15 g	150 g	Trim, cut into ½ cm dice and add to the other ingredients.
	Tomatoes	15 g	150 g	Remove the eye and make a cross incision in the other end of each tomato. Blanch in boiling water for 10 seconds, remove and refresh immediately. Discard the skins, cut in half and discard the seeds. Cut the flesh into ½ cm dice and add.
	Onions	5 g	50 g	Peel, cut into brunoise and add to the salad. Bind with vinaigrette, season with salt and pepper and mix well.
2	Lettuce leaves	1	10	Wash and trim. Place on the serving dish. Arrange the salad in the centre.
	Gherkins	1	10	Cut into fan shapes and dress on top of the salad. Sprinkle with finely chopped parsley.

* Boiled or roast beef.

NOTE: Other meats can be used in place of beef. All meat salads can be served as a single hors d'oeuvre or an hors d'oeuvre varié.

☐   ☐   ☐

FISH BASED SALADS

Dutch salad

Salade hollandaise

🥣 50 min

Step	Commodity	1 portion	10 portions	
1	Smoked salmon	50 g	500 g	Cut into ½ cm dice and place in a bowl.
	Cooked potatoes	50 g	500 g	Peel, cut into ½ cm dice and add to the salmon.
	Onions	10 g	100 g	Cut into brunoise and add to the other ingredients. Marinade with lemon vinaigrette.
2	Lettuce leaves	1	10	Wash and trim. Place on the serving dish. Arrange the salad in the centre.
	Dutch caviar	15 g	150 g	Shape the caviar between two teaspoons and dress on top of the salad.
	Chives	pinch	2 tsp	Sprinkle over the top.

☐   ☐   ☐

Beauty of the night salad

Salade belle de nuit

45 min

Step	Commodity	1 portion	10 portions	
1	Crayfish tails	2	20	Remove the shell and discard. Cut the tail into ½ cm slices and place in a bowl.
	Truffles	5 g	50 g	Cut into slices and add. Marinade with white wine vinaigrette.
2	Lettuce hearts	1	10	Wash and trim. Place on the serving dish. Arrange the fish on top.
	Cooked egg whites	½	5	Chop finely and sprinkle over the top. Season with milled black pepper.

☐   ☐   ☐

Fish salad

20 min

Step	Commodity	1 portion	10 portions	
1	Cooked cod fillet	25 g	250 g	Remove any bones and skin and discard. Flake the fish into a bowl.
	Hard boiled eggs	½	5	Cut into ½ cm dice and add to the fish.
	Cucumber	15 g	150 g	Peel, cut into ½ cm dice and add. Add a little vinaigrette and season with salt and pepper.
2	Lettuce leaves	1	10	Wash and trim. Cut into chiffonade and place on the serving dish. Arrange the fish salad on top.
	Tomatoes	15 g	150 g	Remove the eye and make a cross incision in the other end of each tomato. Blanch in boiling water for 10 seconds, remove and refresh immediately. Discard the skins, cut in half and discard the seeds. Cut the flesh into julienne, dress over the salad.
	Anchovy fillets	1	10	Cut lengthways and arrange in a criss-cross fashion over the tomato julienne.
	Gherkins	½	5	Cut and fan out. Place on top.

NOTE: This dish may be served as a main course.

NOTE: Shellfish salad can be made using this method by omitting the fish and replacing it with the desired cooked shellfish.

☐   ☐   ☐

Shellfish mayonnaise

30 min

Step	Commodity	1 portion	10 portions	
1	Cooked shellfish*	50 g	500 g	Cut into ½ cm dice and season with salt and pepper.
	Lettuce leaves	1	10	Wash and trim. Cut into chiffonade and place on a serving dish. Arrange the shellfish on top.
	Mayonnaise	50 ml	500 ml	Napper over the shellfish. Sprinkle with paprika pepper and finely chopped parsley.

* Prawns, lobster, crab, crayfish or shrimps can be used. Fish mayonnaise may be made using this recipe, substituting cooked fish for the shellfish.

NOTE: This dish may be served as a main course.

☐   ☐   ☐

14

Salmon mayonnaise

Step	Commodity	1 portion	10 portions	
1	Cooked salmon	50 g	500 g	Remove any skin and bones and discard.
	Lettuce leaves	1	10	Wash and trim. Cut into chiffonade and place on a serving dish. Arrange the salmon on top.
2	Mayonnaise	50 ml	500 ml	Napper over the salmon.
	Cucumber	10 g	100 g	Peel and cut into thin slices.
	Peeled tomatoes	25 g	250 g	Cut into thin slices and arrange alternatively with the cucumber around the salmon.
	Hard boiled eggs	½	5	Cut into quarters and dress on top of the tomato and cucumber.
	Capers	2 g	20 g	Chop and sprinkle over the top along with finely chopped parsley and paprika.

⌣ 30 min

NOTE: This dish may be served as a main course.

☐   ☐   ☐

Monte Cristo salad

Salade Monte Cristo

⌣ 45 min

Step	Commodity	1 portion	10 portions	
1	Peeled shrimps*	50 g	500 g	Place in a bowl.
	Artichoke bottoms	1	10	Cut into julienne and add.
	Shallots	10 g	100 g	Peel, finely dice and add to the other ingredients. Season with salt and cayenne pepper. Bind with mayonnaise. Place on a serving dish.
2	Lettuce hearts	½	5	Wash and trim. Cut in half and arrange around the salad.
	Slices of truffle	2	20	Dress on the salad.

* Prawns may be used in place of shrimps.
NOTE: All fish salads can be served as a single hors d'oeuvre or an hors d'oeuvre varié.

☐   ☐   ☐

410

Ice cream

It is thought that ice cream probably originated in China and was brought to Europe in the Thirteenth Century by Marco Polo. Others claim that an iced dish made from honey, fruit juices and milk has been here since the time of Alexander the Great. Ice cream can be made in kitchens using the correct machinery and following strict legislation, though it is expensive and is usually bought in from a commercial manufacturer. Sorbets are lightly frozen water ices flavoured with a liquor or champagne and are served before the roast course/main course in a classic dinner menu. Commercially made ice cream is normally produced in five phases:

1. *Blending the ingredients*. The ingredients are blended in a giant vat and heated to a temperature of 70°C.
2. *Homogenising*. Homogenising involves forcing the mixture under high pressure through a specially designed valve to ensure that the fat remains evenly distributed throughout the mixture.
3. *Pasteurising*. Pasteurising is carried out to kill any harmful bacteria that may be present and is done by raising the temperature to a minimum of 79°C for 15 seconds, then rapidly cooling to below 4°C.
4. *Agitating and freezing*. After pasteurising the mixture is passed through a continuous freezer where air is incorporated. Within seconds the temperature of the mixture drops and it becomes semi-frozen. Microscopic air bubbles and the quick freezing prevent all but the smallest ice crystals from forming.
5. *Final hardening*. The semi-frozen ice cream is poured into appropriate containers and passed through a hardening tunnel to lower the temperature and freeze completely.

Vanilla ice cream

Glacé à la vanille

🥄 4 hr   ♨ 1½ hr

Step	Commodity	1 portion	10 portions	
1	Milk	100 ml	1 litre	Place in a suitably sized, thick-bottomed saucepan and bring to the boil. Remove from the heat.
	Vanilla essence	Drop	few drops	Add.
2	Egg yolks	1	10	Place in a clean bowl.
	Castor sugar	30 g	300 g	Add and whisk together until smooth and creamy. Pour over the milk and whisk together thoroughly. Place in a clean saucepan and return to the heat. Stir continuously and thoroughly until the mixture thickens and coats the back of the spoon. Do not allow to re-boil. Pass through a fine sieve into a clean bowl and allow to cool.
3	Whipping cream	30 ml	300 ml	Whisk lightly and add to the cool mixture. Mix in well. Pour into ice cream machine and freeze. Serve with wafer/pompadour biscuits.

Extensions of basic ice cream

Chocolate ice cream
Glacé au chocolat
As for basic recipe, omitting the vanilla essence and including 15 g of grated chocolate per portion.

Coffee ice cream
Glacé au café
As for basic recipe, omitting the vanilla essence and including coffee flavouring or concentrate (camp coffee) instead to taste.

Pistachio ice cream
Glacé à la pistache
As for basic recipe, omitting the vanilla essence and including a little pale green colouring and 5 g of pistachio nuts passed through a blender per portion.

Praline ice cream
Glacé au praliné
As for basic recipe, omitting the vanilla essence and including 15 g of praline per portion.

Strawberry ice cream

⏲ 4 hr ♨ 1½ hr

Step	Commodity	1 portion	10 portions	
1	Milk	30 ml	300 ml	Place in a suitably sized, thick-bottomed saucepan and bring to the boil. Remove from the heat.
2	Egg yolks	1	10	Place in a clean bowl.
	Castor sugar	15 g	150 g	Add and whisk together until smooth and creamy. Pour over the milk and whisk together thoroughly. Place in a clean saucepan and return to the heat. Stir continuously and thoroughly until the mixture thickens and coats the back of the spoon. Do not allow to re-boil. Pass through a fine sieve into a clean bowl and allow to cool.
3	Strawberries	35 g	350 g	Wash, trim and pass through a fine sieve. Add to the mixture and mix in well.
4	Whipping cream	30 ml	300 ml	Whisk lightly and add to the cool mixture. Mix in well. Pour into ice cream machine and freeze. Serve with wafer/pompadour biscuits.

NOTE: Raspberry ice cream (glacé aux framboises) may be made using raspberries in place of the strawberries.

□   □   □

ICE CREAM SWEETS

Fraise cardinal

Washed and prepared strawberries, two balls of vanilla ice cream, piped crème chantilly, coated with melba sauce and sprinkled with toasted flaked almonds. Served with wafer/pompadour biscuits.

NOTE: Peach, raspberry or apricot cardinal may be made in the same way.

Peach melba

Two halves of peaches with one large ball of vanilla ice cream, piped crème chantilly, coated with melba sauce. Serve with wafer/pompadour biscuits.

NOTE: Strawberry or raspberry melba may be made in the same way.

Meringue glacée

Chosen ice cream sandwiched between two meringue shells, chosen fruit (i.e. strawberries, raspberries), piped crème chantilly.

Pear Belle Hélène

Poached pear half, 2 balls of vanilla ice cream, piped crème chantilly and hot chocolate sauce. Serve with wafer/pompadour biscuits.

□   □   □

COUPES

Coupes are ice cream sweet preparations served in special silver or glass dishes. Usually finished off with crème chantilly and served with wafer/pompadour biscuits.

Coupe Alexandra

Kirsch flavoured fresh fruit salad with 2 balls of strawberry ice cream, piped crème chantilly and a washed and prepared strawberry on top. Served with wafer/pompadour biscuits.

Coupe Jacques

Kirsch flavoured fresh fruit salad, one ball of strawberry ice cream and one of lemon ice water, piped crème chantilly and a washed and prepared grape on top. Served with wafer/pompadour biscuits.

Coupe Jamaique

Rum flavoured pineapple pieces with two balls of coffee flavoured ice cream, piped crème chantilly. Served with wafer/pompadour biscuits.

☐   ☐   ☐

BOMBES

Bombes are ice cream sweets made in special elongated, dome shaped bombe moulds that are lined with an ice cream and filled with a flavoured bombe mixture. The bombe is covered and frozen.

Bombe mixture

Pâte à bombe

🥣 4 hr   ♨ 1 hr

Step	Commodity	1 litre	5 litres	
1	Egg yolks	10	50	Place in a clean bowl.
	Water	25 ml	125 ml	Add to egg yolks.
	Castor sugar	250 g	1¼ kg	Add and whisk together. Place in a bain-marie and whisk vigorously until the mixture becomes thick and creamy and forms peaks. Remove from the heat and allow to go cold.
2	Double cream	35 ml	175 ml	Whisk lightly and add to the cold mixture and fold in. Freeze.

NOTE: Bombe mixture can be flavoured with liquors, spirits, glacé fruits and praline.

Extensions of basic bombe

Bombe Archiduc
Line a bombe mould with strawberry ice cream and fill the centre with praline flavoured bombe mixture. Freeze and use as required. Serve with crème chantilly and glacé fruits, nuts or violets.

Bombe Ceylan
Line a bombe mould with coffee ice cream and fill the centre with rum flavoured bombe mixture. Freeze and use as required. Serve with crème chantilly and glacé fruits, nuts or violets.

Bombe reine
Line a bombe mould with vanilla ice cream and fill the centre with diced marrons glacé flavoured bombe mixture. Freeze and use as required. Serve with crème chantilly and glacé fruits, nuts or violets.

☐   ☐   ☐

Water ices and sorbets

Lemon sorbet

Sorbet au citron

⏱ 2 hr 🍲 1 hr

Step	Commodity	1 portion	10 portions	
1	Water	50 ml	500 ml	Place in a suitably sized saucepan.
	Sugar	25 g	250 g	Add and bring to the boil.
	Lemon	¼	2½	Remove the zest and add. Squeeze and retain the juice. Reduce the syrup until it registers 18°–20° Baume on a saccharometer. Strain the lemon juice and add. Place in the ice cream machine and begin to freeze.
2	Egg whites*	25 g	250 g	Add to the lemon ice as it begins to thicken and freeze. Continue to freeze until the sorbet is light and fluffy. Serve in coupes or goblets.

* Italian meringue
NOTE: Orange sorbet (sorbet à l'orange) may be made in a similar way.

☐   ☐   ☐

Champagne sorbet

Sorbet champagne

⏱ 1 hr 🍲 1 hr

Step	Commodity	1 portion	10 portions	
1	Water	100 ml	1 litre	Place in a saucepan.
	Sugar	50 g	500 g	Add and bring to the boil. Reduce until the syrup registers 22° Baume on the saccharometer. Allow to cool completely.
2	Champagne	35 ml	350 ml	Add to the cool syrup which should register 15°–16° Baume on the saccharometer. Pour into the ice cream machine and begin to freeze.
	Egg whites*	25 g	250 g	Add to the champagne ice as it begins to thicken and freeze. Continue to freeze until the sorbet is light and fluffy. Serve in coupes or goblets.

* Italian meringue

☐   ☐   ☐

Lemon water ice

Glacé au citron

⏱ 1 hr 🍲 1 hr

Step	Commodity	1 portion	10 portions	
1	Water	100 ml	1 litre	Place in a saucepan.
	Sugar	50 g	500 g	Add and bring to the boil. Reduce until the syrup registers 22° Baume on the saccharometer. Allow to cool completely.
2	Lemons	½	5	Remove the zest and add half to the water. Squeeze the juice into a jug and strain onto the water. Mix together well. Pour into the ice cream machine and freeze.

NOTE: Orange water ice (Glacé à l'orange) may be made in the same manner, omitting the lemons and substituting oranges.

☐   ☐   ☐

Peach water ice

Glace aux pêches

⏱ 1 hr   ♨ 1 hr

Step	Commodity	1 portion	10 portions	
1	Water	100 ml	1 litre	Place in a saucepan.
	Sugar	50 g	500 g	Add and bring to the boil. Reduce until the syrup registers 30° Baume on the saccharometer. Allow to cool completely.
2	Peaches	75 g	750 g	Wash, remove the stones and pass through a sieve. Add to the water. Mix together well. Pour into the ice cream machine and freeze.

NOTE: Apricot water ice (Glacé à l'abricots) may be made in the same manner, omitting the peaches and substituting apricots.

☐   ☐   ☐

14

⓮ MICROWAVE COOKERY

Microwave cookery takes place in a specially designed electrical oven. Microwaves are transferred to the food by electro-magnetic radiation. These waves travel through the air and, because food is a poor conductor of energy, the waves pass into the food causing the water molecules in the food to oscillate (vibrate) and heat up very quickly.

Microwave energy is generated by a magnetron. These microwaves operate at a high frequency (2,450 MHz) and are part of the radiation spectrum which includes X-rays, ultra violet light, infra-red light and radio waves. Microwave power is measured in watts; watts equal the amount of microwave energy generated. Domestic microwave ovens have an output of between 400 and 800 watts while commercial microwaves have outputs of 1000 watts (1 kW) to 2000 watts (2 kW). The greater the wattage, the less time required for cooking.

Certain foods need to be removed when underdone for them to finish cooking during 'standing time'. Standing time is important since during this time food continues to cook without further addition of energy: fish turns from opaque to white, flaky and tender and scrambled eggs turn creamy.

NOTE: No heat is generated in the oven cavity, only in the food itself.

Terms associated with microwave cookery

Carry over cooking Also known as standing time, this is the cooking that occurs in the food after it has been removed from the oven.

Combination ovens Microwave ovens that have an addition of an infra-red grill, and/or electric elements or gas burners.

Covering Covering food with absorbent kitchen paper or clingfilm speeds cooking time, helps to retain moisture, ensures a more even cooking and prevents spattering.

Input wattage The amount of electricity used in creating the microwave energy and operating the moving parts such as the fan and the turntable (optional).

Output wattage The energy measurement of an oven.

Piercing To pierce the skin of certain foods to prevent a build up of pressure and eventual explosion.

Spacing When possible, foods should be arranged in a circular pattern with a centimetre distance between each item.

Standing time This is time allowed during which the food continues to cook after it has been removed from the oven.

Stirring To move the food from the outside to the centre of the dish during cooking to equalise heat and speed microwaving.

Thermoplastic dishes Special plastics that can withstand extreme temperatures.

USES OF A MICROWAVE OVEN

1 As a quick method of cooking raw foods.
2 To re-heat par-cooked, pre-cooked or pre-assembled foods.
3 To accelerate the defrosting cycle of frozen foods.
4 As a quick method of heating liquids.

THE HISTORY OF MICROWAVE COOKERY

Microwave cookery was developed in the 1940s and microwave ovens have been with us commercially since the 1960s. Since their inception various techniques have been developed whereby the normal microwave oven has become linked to the dual facility of conventional forced air cooking and microwave combined. Most recent models in the 1990s include one or more of the following features: dual cooking (combination of conventional and microwave); a grill; two level cooking; automatic timing; and touch control.

SAFETY IN MICROWAVE COOKERY

A microwave oven must comply to strict standards because of the danger of the leak of microwave energy. Poorly maintained ovens that leak can cause burns and there is a possibility that being exposed to such a leakage over a long period of time can contribute to the development of eye cataracts. The seal around the door of the oven must be intact and free from dirt. Do not use the oven if the seal is damaged in any way.

Microwave ovens are manufactured and designed to international standard IEC335 which covers the maximum amount of microwave leakage allowed. All commercially available microwave ovens comply with British Standard 5175 which requires that the power density should be less than 5 milliwatts per square centimetre (5 mW/cm) at points 5 cm or more from the external surfaces of the appliance.

Microwave ovens must be cleaned immediately after use. Wash the interior, the door and the seals with hot detergent water. Rinse with hot water and dry thoroughly. Air filters should be removed regularly and cleaned thoroughly.

MICROWAVE OVENS, COOKING VESSELS AND EQUIPMENT

Microwave ovens come in different sizes with varying levels of power. Additions to standard models include browning elements, stay hot controls, combination cookers (microwave plus forced air convection). Combination ovens overcome the limitations of simple microwave ovens by being able to cook in a conventional mode at the same time. This allows the food to be browned and the surface to have a crisp finish – something an ordinary microwave cannot do. Combination ovens can have gas burners, electric elements and/or an infra-red grill.

Microwave oven doors are made with a perforated metal screen that allows light to pass through so that the food may be viewed while cooking, but does not allow the microwaves to leak.

Using metal cooking vessels will damage the magnetron in certain types of microwave ovens. Cooking vessels should always be made from glass, ceramics, thermoplastic or paper. Only use metal or foil vessels in an appliance if recommended in the manufacturer's instructions. Never use plastic or paper cooking vessels in combination ovens. There are specialised utensils such as plastic rings to stack plates of food in the microwave.

FACTORS INFLUENCING THE COOKING OF FOOD BY MICROWAVE

(a) The *density* of the food. The more dense (closely compacted in substance), the more difficult the food will be to microwave. For example, microwaves will not penetrate easily or uniformally a joint of meat, but will do so in liquids, fish and white meat.

(b) The *thickness* of the food. Microwave penetration is only effective up to 4 cms. If the food is thicker the centre will be cooked by conduction of heat from the outer layer. When reheating, the food should be arranged evenly on the plate to ensure even cooking.

(c) The *quantity* of food. With microwave cookery the heating/cooking time is directly proportional to the quantity of food in the oven. The more foods placed in the oven the longer the cooking time.

(d) Whether the oven has a turntable or not.

15

Because most foods are uneven in shape there is a need to turn the items regularly to ensure even cooking.

The advantages of microwave cookery

Because microwave ovens do not generate heat or steam they are safer than conventional ovens. They are also cleaner as steam and heat are the main causes of dirt. When the door of the oven closes the latch activates the oven and when the door is opened the oven shuts off automatically.

Microwave ovens are simple to use and are economical in terms of energy conservation and time saved (saving between 50–70 per cent on conventional cooking time). Speed of cooking encourages flavour and nutritional retention of food.

The disadvantages of microwave cookery

The limited space in the oven cavity restricts the amount of food that can be cooked. Not all foods can be cooked successfully by the microwave method, depending on the water content of the food and its thickness. Certain foods that have a skin such as baked apples and baked potatoes must have their skin pierced to release any pressure built up and to prevent them from bursting. For this reason eggs must be removed from their shells to microwave.

Microwaves have very little effect on food frozen to − 18°C and below. This is because the waves pass straight through ice with little effect on the water molecules.

Microwave ovens are fitted with a defrost button. This setting has the effect of turning the microwave on and off in short bursts. The 'on' periods thaw the ice near the surface. The 'off' periods give the heat generated by defrosting water molecules time to thaw the still frozen molecules. The more ice that turns to water, the more microwaves the food absorbs.

COOKING TIMES AND SETTINGS

Cooking times and oven settings will depend on the power output of the microwave oven. All recipes in this chapter are based on a microwave oven with a power output of 1400 watts. Below is a chart to help you calculate the correct times and settings for your oven.

Power output	Time	Setting
500–600 watts	Double the time required.	High
600–700 watts	Increase the time by half again	High
900 watts	As per recipe	High
1.4 kW	As per recipe	Medium
2 kW	Decrease time by one third to a half	Low–medium

Standard cooking settings		
Defrost	1	Warm
	2	Simmer
	3	Stew
	4	Defrost
Medium	5	Bake
	6	Roast
High	7	Full

Cooking meat and poultry by microwave

Microwave is most effective with small pieces or individual portions of tender cuts of meat and poultry because the microwaves can penetrate the food successfully and, therefore, cook it rapidly.

Larger joints of meat and poultry can be cooked, but must either be turned regularly or placed on a rotating turntable to ensure a more even cooking. Special temperature probes can be used to ensure that the internal temperature of the joint is sufficient to cook the food correctly and also to kill any bacteria. For exact times and settings refer to the manufacturer's handbook.

NOTE: Though basic microwave ovens are not capable of browning there are special dishes and roasting bags available that encourage the browning process.

	Cooking times	Special notes
Roast beef (boeuf rôti)	(minutes per kilo) Rare – 10 Medium – 12–14 Well done – 14–16	Place in a microwave roasting bag. Allow to stand for 15–20 minutes before carving.
Minced beef (hachis de boeuf)	(minutes per kilo) 10 (40 ml *Liquid per 10 portions*)	Stir throughout the cooking process.
Beef steaks (bifteck)	(minutes per 250 g) Rare – 2 Medium – 2–4 Well done – 4	Steaks must be browned on a pre-heated browning dish.
Roast Chicken (Poulet rôti)	(minutes per kilo) 12–15	Protect the wing tips and drumsticks with greaseproof paper. Place in a microwave roasting bag with a little stock to keep moist. Allow to stand for 15–20 minutes before carving.
Chicken portions	(minutes per 120 g portion) 3–5	Place the narrowest part to the centre of the dish. Brush with a little melted butter and season lightly. Cover with a buttered cartouche.
Roast lamb (D'agneau rôti)	(minutes per kilo) Pink – 12 Medium – 14–16	Place in a microwave roasting bag. Allow to stand for 15–20 minutes before carving.
Lamb chops (Chop d'agneau)	(minutes per 2 × 100 g portion) 1 portion 7–8 minutes 2 portions 8–10 minutes 3 portions 15–18 minutes	Chops must be browned on a pre-heated browning dish.

NOTE: This also applies to lamb cutlets.

Roast duck (Canard rôti)	(minutes per kilo) 12–15	Protect the wing tips and drumsticks with greaseproof paper. Dock the skin thoroughly to aid the release of fat. Place in a microwave roasting bag with a little stock to keep moist. Turn occasionally through the cooking process. Allow to stand for 15–20 minutes before carving.
Roast pork (Porc rôti)	(minutes per kilo) Well done 20–25 min	Score fat with sharp knife and sprinkle with salt to get a crisp crackling. Place in a microwave roasting bag. Allow to stand for 15–20 minutes before carving.
Pork chops (Chop de porc)	(minutes per 1 × 250 g portion) 12–15 minutes	Chops must be browned on a pre-heated browning dish.

Cooking fish and shellfish by microwave

Fish and shellfish are ideal for cooking by microwave because of their high water content, though care must be taken not to over-cook.

	Cooking times	Special notes
Cod, haddock and salmon fillets and steaks	(minutes per 120 g portion) 3–4	Make 2–3 light incisions on the skin side before cooking. Place the narrow end to the centre of the dish. Brush with melted butter and season lightly. Cover with a greased cartouche.
Whole salmon trout and salmon	(minutes per kilo) 12–14	Make 2–3 light incisions on both sides of the skin before cooking. Cover the tail and the head with clingfilm to protect them. Brush with melted butter and season lightly. Cover with a greased cartouche.
Whole rainbow trout	(minutes per ½ kilo) 5–7	Make 2–3 light incisions on both sides of the skin before cooking. Cover the tail and the head with clingfilm to protect them. Brush with melted butter and season lightly. Cover with a greased cartouche.

Cooking eggs by microwave

Because of the high protein content of eggs and cheese special care must be taken not to over-cook them as they become rubbery.

Scrambled eggs

Oeufs brouillés

3 min   3 min

Step	Commodity	per portion	
1	Eggs	2	Break into a suitably sized bowl. Season lightly with salt and pepper. Whisk thoroughly.
2	Butter	10 g	Melt and mix thoroughly with the eggs. Place in the microwave for 3 minutes on medium. Remove and stir after every minute. Cook until the correct consistency is achieved.

□   □   □

Omelette

Omelette

3 min   2½ min

Step	Commodity	per portion	
1	Eggs	3	Break into a suitably sized bowl. Season lightly with salt and pepper. Whisk thoroughly.
2	Butter	10 g	Melt and coat onto a shallow flan or pie plate. Pour over the eggs and place in the microwave on high setting for 30 seconds. Remove and stir the outside towards the centre. Return to the oven and cook on a medium setting for 2 minutes, stirring at least twice in that time to ensure even cooking. Remove when the correct consistency is achieved. Fold and serve.

420

Cooking potatoes and vegetables by microwave

The advantages of cooking vegetables by microwave is that the speed of cooking and minimal liquid used means that vegetables retain more vitamins, minerals and natural than those cooked by conventional methods.

Though potatoes can be cooked successfully by microwave other fibrous vegetables like cabbage and cauliflower are not really suited to this method of cookery. To cook vegetables by microwave use a medium setting and cover during cooking unless stated otherwise. Follow the recipes and quantities for cooking vegetables given in other chapters, but alter the cooking times and cooking liquid as follows.

	Cooking time from fresh	Cooking time from frozen	Liquid per 10 portions	Special notes
Asparagus (D'asperge)	13–15 mins	8–10 mins	50 ml water	Arrange the asparagus on a dish with the thicker stems on the outside.
Aubergine (sliced) (Aubergine)	8–10 mins	9–11 mins	15 ml water	Lay the slices neatly on the dish.
Beans, French (Haricots verts)	10–15 mins	8–10 mins	75 ml water	Cover with the water. Stir regularly to ensure even cooking.
Broccoli (Brocolis)	15–17 mins	8–10 mins	75 ml water	Place in a dish, arranging the stalks to the outside. Rearrange halfway through the cooking process.
Brussel sprouts (Choux de Bruxelles)	12–15 mins	8–10 mins	50 ml water	Use even-sized sprouts. Stir occasionally.
Cabbage (shredded)* (Chou)	10–12 mins	5–7 mins	75 ml water	Use a large dish ensuring that the cabbage fits loosely. Stir occasionally.
Carrots (whole) (Carottes)	15–20 mins	8–10 mins	75 ml water	Stir occasionally throughout the cooking process.
Cauliflower (whole)* (Choufleur)	12–15 mins	N/A	75 ml water	
Cauliflower (florets)	10–12 mins	8–10 mins	75 ml water	Turn the whole cauliflower or stir the florets halfway through the cooking process. Allow to stand for 2–3 minutes before serving.
Celery (whole) (Celeri)	15–17 mins	N/A	45 ml water	Stir halfway through the cooking process.

15

	Cooking time from fresh	Cooking time from frozen	Liquid per 10 portions	Special notes
Courgette (whole) (Courgette)	6–8 mins	N/A	25 g butter	Melt the butter. Pour over the courgettes and cook. Stir halfway through the cooking process.
Leeks (sliced) Poireaux	12–14 mins	8–10 mins	45 ml water	Stir halfway through the cooking process.
Mushrooms (whole or sliced) (Champignons)	5–7 mins	8–10 mins	25 g butter 15 ml water	Melt the butter. Pour over the mushrooms and cook. Stir halfway through the cooking process.
Parsnips (Panais)	10–12 mins	8–10 mins	75 ml	Stir halfway through the cooking process.
Garden peas (Petits pois)	10–12 mins	7–8 mins	25 g butter 75 ml	Stir halfway through the cooking process. Melt the butter and add after draining.
Potatoes (Pommes de terre)	12–15 mins	N/A	75 ml	Stir occasionally throughout the cooking process.
Spinach (Épinards)	7–8 mins	8–9 mins	None	Wash, but do not dry as the retained moisture will be sufficient to cook the spinach. Cook in a microwave roasting bag.
Tomatoes (Tomates)	1–1½ mins	N/A	10 g butter	Brush with melted butter.

*NOTE: Extra care must be taken when microwaving cabbage and cauliflower to ensure even cooking.

COOKING VARIOUS OTHER FOODS BY MICROWAVE

Pasta and rice

Pasta and rice has a low moisture content and absorbs plenty of liquid during the cooking process. It is best to pre-cook pasta and rice in the conventional way and use the microwave to complete the dish.

Pastry

Pastry goods tend to become soggy when cooked by microwave so this technique is not recommended for pastry cooking.

Shortbread

Using the basic 10 portion recipe, cook for approximately 25 minutes on medium power.

Victoria sponge

Using the 100 g of flour recipe, place in a microwave sponge dish and cook for 4 minutes on full power. Remove and stand for 10 minutes before lifting from the dish.

WHAT WENT WRONG?

Problem	Caused by	To rectify
Liquid starts to spill over.	Container too small.	Wipe clean and transfer to a larger container.
Foods such as apples and potatoes explode.	Surface of the food has not been pierced.	Cannot be rectified.
Food has dried up.	(1) Over-cooking.	Cannot be rectified.
	(2) Too high a power setting.	Cannot be rectified.
	(3) Insufficient protection of delicate foods during cooking.	Cannot be rectified.
	(4) Salt added to food before cooking.	Cannot be rectified.
Sauces, soups or gravies have gone lumpy.	Insufficient stirring during cooking.	Strain, correct the consistency and continue cooking.
Condensation forms in the oven.	Too high a moisture level in the oven.	Open the door of the oven and allow the condensation to disperse.

16

COOK-CHILL

Under normal temperature conditions the actions of micro-organisms and enzymic and chemical reactions on food causes rapid deterioration. The purpose of cook-chill is to prolong the storage life of food by inhibiting the multiplication of bacteria and other micro-organisms and slowing down the chemical and enzymic reactions. Though food poisoning bacteria cannot be killed by chilling, the low temperature (below 5°C) ensures that they cannot grow/reproduce.

The Department of Health have specified a number of requirements for cook-chilled foods and their production and storage in a leaflet called *Guidelines on Pre-cooked Chilled Foods*.

Cook-chill is based on the central preparation and cooking of food in bulk and the use of rapid chilling techniques and refrigeration to store the food. The chilled food is then transported in refrigerated containers to satellite kitchens to be regenerated before consumption.

USES OF COOK-CHILL

Cook-chill foods are used extensively in shipping and aircraft catering operations, leisure centres, welfare catering, school meals, industrial catering for multi-sited operations, night service and weekends, conference centres and, in some hotels, for banqueting, room service and staff catering.

The advantages of cook-chill

Prolonged storage life means that a greater range of dishes can be produced without excessive wastage. While 0°–3°C does not give a storage life comparable to frozen foods, it can ensure the preservation of cooked products for up to five days. This allows food to be cooked in batches and, therefore, production can be scheduled to maximise use of equipment, staff, space and time. In addition, bulk or quantity buying of commodities for batch cooking greatly reduces food costs without lowering quality.

Cook-chill operations are less costly as fewer staff are needed. Production times are not geared to services so straight shifts for skilled staff at more economic times can be operated. This in turn reduces energy costs as equipment is on only when it is being used – and being used to its full capacity.

Conditions are also improved for staff; unlike conventional kitchens, with peaks of activity leading up to and during service times, cook-chill operations

---

Terms associated with cook-chill

Batch cooking Splitting large quantities of particular commodities into batches to cook when either the cooking equipment are not large enough to process the entire quantity at once.

Blast chilling The rapid chilling of food in special chillers.

CPU The abbreviation used for the Central Production Unit where the food is initially prepared and chilled.

Regeneration The final stage in the cook-chill process when the chilled food is quickly heated to a safe temperature for consumption.

Satellite kitchen The term given to the unit(s) where the final stage of the cook-chill process is carried out and the food is served to the customer.

Time buffer The term used for the extra time between preparation and service that the cook-chill systems can provide.

allow the staff to prepare the food in a more orderly and relaxed atmosphere.

Finally, because equipment and operations are rationalised, less space is needed cutting down capital costs.

The disadvantages of cook-chill

Specialised cook-chill equipment is very expensive to install. The cook-chill process can effect the flavour and appearance of some foods:

(a) Dishes containing starch can taste stale.
(b) In general, fresh vegetables discolour and have a strong taste.
(c) The flavour of delicate meats such as veal and poultry deteriorates after 2–3 days.
(d) Meat dishes without sauces can develop acidic tastes.
(e) Sauced meat dishes nearing the end of their storage life tend to develop a 'flat taste' and if spiced the flavour overwhelms the flavour of the meat.
(f) Oil oxidisation causes fatty meat and fish to develop 'off' flavours.

THE COOK-CHILL PROCESS

Cook chill is split into four processes:

1 Basic preparation
2 Initial cooking and portioning
3 Chilling and storage
4 Re-heating/regenerating.

NOTE: To avoid cross-contamination, each area in the process must be separate from the others. The staff and equipment must also be assigned to a particular area and not touch food or equipment in any other area. Staff should be checked regularly to ensure that they are not carriers of any contagious disease.

1 Basic preparation

Always ensure only top quality raw ingredients are used and that they are stored at the correct temperature under the strict conditions of hygiene. The food preparation area should be separate from the other areas to avoid the possibility of cross-contamination.

Although all food items are suitable for cook-chill, some combinations can withstand the changes in temperature better than others and look and taste better after re-heating.

2 Initial cooking and portioning

To ensure foods are kept only for a minimum length of storage, careful planning must go into a cook-chill operation.

Maximum nutritional value must be preserved and the method of cookery chosen must produce the most acceptable flavour and textures of the final product. Certain nutrients, especially vitamins from the B group and vitamin C, are easily lost in prolonged cooking.

Care must be taken that the core/centre temperature of the cooking food reaches a minimum temperature of *at least* 70°, though most all experts in this field recommend 75°C as a safer minimum.

Portioning should be carried out quickly and hygienically in an area separate from the cooking area. The area temperature should be no more than 10°C.

As well as portioning for individuals' requirements, the size and the shape of the container should be selected for fast chilling. The depth of the container should be no more than 5 cm. The containers must be clearly labelled with the contents, net weight, the date of cooking, number of portions, information on storage and re-heating instructions. The majority of this information may be put on using a bar code system and read by a light pen.

3 Chilling and storage

The DoH guidelines recommend that cooked foods must be chilled within 30 minutes of cooking and reduced to a temperature of between 0°–3°C within a further period of 90 minutes. Temperatures are monitored regularly and immediately adjusted accordingly to meet requirements.

Food must always be left uncovered while chilling otherwise it may not reach its optimum chilling temperature and will have to be discarded.

The chilled foods must be stored in a special refrigeration area, apart from and never next to conventionally prepared foods.

Portioning after chilling

Portioning after chilling must be carried out within 30 minutes of the food leaving chilled storage at a

16

temperature below 10°C and before re-heating starts.

To avoid any possibility of cross-contamination, the food preparation area should be separate from the cooking area, as should the portioning/packaging area. Equipment and utensils for raw foods and cooked foods should be kept separate and identified by colour code. Staff dealing with cook-chill must be suitably trained and able to uphold strict standards of professional practice.

4 Re-heating/regenerating

Cook-chill foods must be heated as quickly as possible to a *minimum* temperature of 70°C but, as with initial cooking, a more ideal temperature would be 75°C.

EQUIPMENT USED IN COOK-CHILL OPERATIONS

To facilitate the passage from cooking to chilling, the equipment used to cook the food should match the capacity of the chilling equipment.

Initial cooking and portioning equipment

(a) Atmospheric and high pressure steamers for steaming.
(b) Bratt pans for boiling, stewing, shallow frying and poaching.
(c) Combination ovens using more than one source of heat, usually convection and microwave or convection and infra-red grill.
(d) Convection steamers using convected super-heated steam to reduce baking, roasting, steaming and braising times.
(e) Re-usable containers to store and protect the cooked, portioned item.
(f) Conveyor belts to help with portioning and speed up production cycles.
(g) Forced-air convection ovens for baking, roasting and braising.
(h) Pressure and automatic fryers with integral oil filters, basket lifting mechanisms and programmable controls for high performance in deep frying.
(i) Steamed jacket kettles or boilers for boiling.
(j) Temperature probes should be used to ensure that the centre/core of the food reaches a temperature of at least 70°C.
(k) Tilting kettles are similar to steamed jacket kettles, with a tilting action from the vertical to the pouring position. Ideal for continued batch cooking.

Chilling and storage equipment

(a) Blast chillers, sometimes known as air blast chillers, are capable of taking large trolley loads of cooked foods. Low temperature air is passed along the trolleys shelves to chill cooked foods evenly and rapidly.
(b) Cryogenic batch chilling tunnels use carbon dioxide or liquid nitrogen at a temperature of $-196°C$ which are sprayed into a chilling cabinet containing the warmed foods. The heat is quickly absorbed by the cold liquid or gas.

NOTE: CO_2 chilling tunnels were originally designed for the chilling of fresh poultry. The disadvantage of using carbon dioxide (CO_2) is that it is expensive.

(c) Insulated boxes, purpose built, are used to transport and hold chilled food between the central kitchen and a satellite unit. With increased insulation the boxes are capable of holding the temperature for up to 3 hours, though this figure will depend on ambient temperature, traffic conditions and the initial temperature of the food.
(d) Labels – important for ensuring that different dishes can be identified for date of production and use-by date.
(e) Refrigerators and cold storerooms maintained at a temperature of below 3°C. These should be capable of taking complete trolley loads of food straight from the blast chiller. They are usually fitted with special alarms to indicate any rise in temperature.
(f) Refrigerated vans are used to distribute the chilled foods between the central kitchen and the satellite units.
(g) Tunnel chillers/roll through chillers use a conveyor belt system to move the warm foods through rapidly-moving cold air.
(h) Water chilling baths are used to cool foods that are sealed in special plastic bags.

Re-heating/reconstituting/regenerating equipment

(a) Combi-ovens which incorporate steam.
(b) Infra-red ovens are specifically designed for regenerating foods and use high intensity infra-red heat radiating from elements at the top and bottom of the oven. They are suitable for re-heating individual or small quantities of chilled foods.
(c) Microwave ovens are suitable for re-heating individual or small quantities of chilled foods rapidly.
(d) Régéthermic ovens are specially manufactured for the reconstitution/regeneration of cook-chilled foods.
(e) Steamers are ideal for re-heating large quantities of chilled foods.

WHAT WENT WRONG?

Problem	Caused by	To rectify
Food has not been put into the chiller within 30 minutes of being cooked.	A hold up in portioning because of staff shortage on the shift.	Cannot be rectified. Discard the food.
Food has not reached the required temperature within the given time.	(1) A lid being left on the foods while chilling or the food being packed too deep in the container.	Cannot be rectified. Discard the food.
	(2) Possibly a malfunction in the chilling equipment.	Have the equipment checked.
Food that has passed its sell-by date is still in stock.	A disorganised food control system.	Foods will have to be discarded.
The temperature of the foods rises above 10°C during transport	(1) Too long a journey, using a refrigerated unit that is not working properly.	Cannot be rectified. Discard the food.
	(2) If insulated boxes were used, the boxes were not pre-cooled before use or the lid was not fitted properly.	Cannot be rectified. Discard the food.
Regenerated food is over-cooked.	Re-heating temperature was too high or the food was heated for too long.	Cannot be rectified. Discard the food.
Food does not reach 70°C within the 30 minutes allowed for re-heating.	If the lids are not fitted properly, the food will not re-heat properly. Possibly the re-heating instructions were mis-read or the foods were labelled with incorrect information for regenerating.	Cannot be rectified. Discard the food.

16

17

COOK-FREEZE

The cook-freeze system is based on the central preparation, production and freezing of cooked foods. Recipes need to be re-formulated to allow for changes in freezing. Cooking equipment is not greatly different than that of a conventional kitchen. Once cooked the food needs to be portioned quickly. Guidelines published by the Department of Health state that once cooked the food should take no longer than 15 minutes (with the

---

Terms associated with cook-freeze

Batch cooking Splitting large quantities of particular commodities into batches to cook because either the cooking equipment or the freezing equipment are not large enough to process them all at once.

Blast freezing The rapid freezing of food using high speed cold air to reduce the temperature quickly.

CPU The abbreviation used for the Central Production Unit where the food is initially prepared and frozen.

Defrosting Raising the temperature of the food slowly until it has reached its pre-frozen state.

Instability Some foods have a tendency to separate during the cook-freeze process and are deemed as 'unstable'.

Recrystallisation This is where smaller, thawing ice crystals attach themselves to larger ice crystals and refreeze damaging the food.

Regenerating The final stage in the cook-freeze process when the thawed food is quickly heated to a safe temperature for consumption.

Satellite kitchen The term given to the unit(s) where the final stage of the cook-freeze process is carried out and the food is served to the customer.

---

exception of meat which needs to 'set' for 15 minutes before carving or being sliced) to be portioned. Portioned and packaged foods are loaded onto trolleys which are wheeled into a freezer.

Blast freezing is the most widely-used method of freezing. A blast freezer is an insulated refrigerated tunnel in which refrigerated air is 'blasted' over the food at a velocity of approximately 5.0 m/s (metres per second). The food is then frozen in special fast freezers. As with chilled foods, the foods must be frozen to at least -5°C immediately and never take longer than 90 minutes to reach this temperature. The temperature should then drop again to -20°C.

Another method of freezing is to spray liquid nitrogen at -196°C over the food while it is being conveyed through a freezing tunnel. This is especially useful for freezing soft fruits as this process has the effect of almost instantaneous freezing.

Once the food is frozen it is stored in a cold store at a temperature of between -18°C and -20°C from where it is distributed to satellite kitchens for regeneration and consumption.

THE EFFECTS OF FREEZING ON FOODS

Not all foods respond well to freezing. It demands care and understanding to ensure that the benefits of the process outweigh the potential damage that can be caused. Some foods change in flavour, texture and colour. Meat will eventually turn a brownish grey if stored too long. The structure of the food can be quite badly damaged during the critical period when the ice crystals are forming. Freezing must be rapid since the slower the freezing, the more damage is likely to happen.

The processes that cause food to spoil or deteriorate are linked to temperature, exposure to air (which can result in oxidisation) or exposure to moisture which is often present in the air surrounding food. Freezing makes food last longer by stopping or at least slowing down the processes, and the lower the temperature, the more effective this is. To ensure that frozen foods are kept at their peak and lessen the chance of spoilage the storage temperature should be at a constant minimum of $-18^\circ C$ and preferably as low as $-30^\circ C$.

The food must always be properly covered to prevent ice building up on the surface of the cooked food and to protect from freezer burn which is caused by excessive moisture evaporation.

EQUIPMENT USED IN COOK-FREEZE

As in conventional catering, the menu and the way it is to be presented needs to be 'tailor-made' for the customer, which in turn affects the equipment requirements in both the production and finishing kitchens.

Initial cooking and portioning equipment

(a) Atmospheric and high pressure steamers for steaming.
(b) Bratt pans for boiling, stewing, shallow frying and poaching.
(c) Combi-ovens or convection steamers using convected super-heated steam to reduce baking, roasting, steaming and braising times.
(d) Re-usable containers to store and protect the cooked, portioned item.
(e) Continuous cookers, where food is stacked on specially designed trolleys is fed through the pre-heated 'cook zone' of the continuous cooker at a controlled rate on a conveyor belt.
(f) Conveyor belts to help with the portioning and to speed up production cycles.
(g) Forced-air convection ovens for baking, roasting and braising.
(h) Pressure and automatic fryers with integral oil filters, basket lifting mechanisms and programmable controls for high performance in deep frying.
(i) Steamed jacket kettles or boilers for boiling.
(j) Temperature probes should be used to ensure that the centre/core of the food reaches at temperature of *at least* $70^\circ C$.
(k) Tilting kettles are similar to steamed jacket kettles with a tilting action from the vertical to the pouring position. Ideal for continued batch cooking.

Packaging equipment

Containers used to store frozen foods can be made from special plastic compounds, tin, aluminium or cardboard plastic laminates and come in single portion packs, complete meal packs and bulk packs. They must protect the food against oxidisation.

Freezing and storage equipment

(a) Blast freezers, sometimes known as air blast freezers are capable of taking large trolley loads of cooked foods. Low temperature air (between $-32^\circ C$ and $-40^\circ C$) is passed along the trolleys' shelves, freezing foods evenly and rapidly within 90 minutes.
(b) Cryogenic batch freezing tunnels use carbon dioxide or liquid nitrogen (at a temperature of $-196^\circ C$) which is sprayed into a freezing cabinet containing the warmed foods and quickly absorbs the heat.

NOTE: CO_2 freezing tunnels were originally designed for the freezing of fresh poultry. The disadvantage of using carbon dioxide (CO_2) is that it is expensive.

(c) Deep freezers or freezer rooms capable of storing foods at temperatures of between $-20^\circ C$ and $-30C$.
(d) Insulated boxes, purpose built, used to transport and hold frozen food between the central kitchen and a satellite unit. With increased insulation the boxes are capable of holding the temperature for up to 3 hours, though this figure will depend on ambient temperature, traffic conditions and the initial temperature of the food.
(e) Labels – important for ensuring that different dishes can be identified for date of production and use-by date.
(f) Plate freezers are used to freeze meat, fish and fragile vegetables such as asparagus and spinach.

17

(g) Refrigerated vans are used to distribute frozen foods between the central kitchen and the satellite units.

(h) Tunnel freezers/roll through freezers use a conveyor belt system to move foods such as peas and sliced vegetables through rapidly-moving cold air.

Re-heating/reconstituting/regenerating equipment

(a) Combination ovens incorporate a second heat source useful for regenerating or thawing frozen foods. The second heat source is usually from an infra-red grill or a microwave oven.

(b) Infra-red ovens are specifically designed for regenerating foods and use high intensity infra-red heat radiating from elements at the top and bottom of the oven. They are suitable for re-heating individual portions or small quantities of frozen foods.

(c) Microwave ovens are suitable for re-heating individual/small quantities of frozen foods rapidly.

(d) Régéthermic ovens are specially manufactured for the reconstitution/generation of frozen foods.

(e) Rapid-thawing cabinets are used to defrost containers of frozen meals to a temperature of 3°C before regenerating.

(f) Steamers are ideal for re-heating large quantities of frozen foods.

(g) Thawing cabinets operate at a temperature of 10°C and are used to speed up the thawing of frozen delicate foods before regenerating.

The advantages of cook-freeze

The nutritional content of foods is more likely to be retained as food is not kept hot for long periods of time before being frozen.

Food production planning is easier and food wastage should be cut down or eliminated. Production can be scheduled to optimise the use of equipment, reduce staff and maximise space and time. In addition, bulk or quantity buying of commodities for each batch cooking greatly reduces food costs without lowering quality.

Production times are not geared to services so straight shifts for skilled staff at more economic times can be operated. Conditions are also improved for staff; unlike conventional kitchens, with peaks of activity leading up to and during service times, cook-freeze operations allow the staff to prepare the food in a more orderly and relaxed atmosphere.

The disadvantages of cook-freeze

Specialised cook-freeze equipment is very expensive to install and to run.

Some dishes containing starch can taste stale.

FREEZING MEATS AND POULTRY

Freezing does not give an infinite life to foods, it merely extends the life. Even frozen, the enzymes present in the fat of meat and some poultry oxidise and deteriorate. Chicken fat on the other hand contains a natural antioxidant and does not spoil as quickly.

Covering the cooked food with a sauce or gravy can help to prolong the beneficial effects of freezing by excluding air but, in general, cooked meats and poultry should never be kept frozen for more than 3 months.

Sauce recipes have to be modified as wheat flour has a tendency to split when frozen. A specially manufactured starch can be obtained commercially or a waxy starch made from rice, maize or tapioca may be used. Egg yolks can also be used to thicken sauces, but care must be taken when regenerating not to use too high a temperature otherwise they will curdle.

FREEZING FISH

Fish has a delicate flavour and in freezing is prone to flavour loss while oily types of fish are likely to spoil due to fat oxidisation. The best way to preserve the delicate flavour of fish is to cover it with a sauce or a coating such as breadcrumbs or batter. Batter recipes also have to be modified by adding a waxy starch.

Protecting cooked fish dishes as recommended will give an expected freezer life of 8 weeks. After that time the fats in the sauces and coatings become rancid.

FREEZING VEGETABLES

Not all vegetables are suitable for freezing. The cellular structures of cucumber, tomatoes, lettuce and other salad vegetables disintegrate. Vegetables are only suitable for cook-freeze if they have been purchased and processed within 3–4 hours of harvesting.

The vegetables are blanched in a high pressure steamer sufficiently to arrest the actions of enzymes and prevent them from creating an acidic flavour at a later stage. Blanching for too long will destroy the structure of the vegetables and make them appear limp; the colour in green vegetables fades and cauliflower goes yellow. Over-blanching will also destroy the vitamin content of the vegetables.

Cooked potato dishes are ideal for freezing. French fries and roast potatoes need to be blanched in a deep fryer before freezing. Duchesse potato extensions such as croquettes freeze particularly well.

FREEZING FRUIT

Freezing has the effect of softening the texture of fruits. Fruits such as grapes or strawberries have a tendency to collapse when defrosted and lose their appeal. Sliced apples and peaches go brown unless they have been frozen in an acidulate liquid or syrup.

FREEZING EGGS, PASTA AND RICE

Though frozen pasturised scrambled eggs and hard boiled eggs are commercially available, soft boiled egg yolk changes into a stiff paste when frozen.

Pasta and rice should be frozen undercooked so that they do not overcook during regenerating.

WHAT WENT WRONG?

Problem	Caused by	To rectify
Meat or fish tastes rancid.	Bad preparation or storing for too long.	Cannot be rectified. Discard the food.
Pastry or dough products are soggy.	The food has been covered when regenerating.	If caught in time, the lid can be removed and the food allowed to 'dry out'.
Food has dried up.	Over-regenerating.	Cannot be rectified.
Prepared food did not begin the freezing process within the time allowed after cooking.	Bad production planning.	Cannot be rectified. The food cannot be frozen.

VACUUM COOKERY

Vacuum or sous vide (second life) cookery is the process of placing prepared food – raw, blanched or seared – in special plastic pouches, extracting all the air, sealing the bag and then cooking it in a combination oven.

The raw foods are prepared as for cooking. Some foods which need browning such as cutlets and steaks are first seared then laid on a special wide spatula, seasoned lightly (because the foods cook in their own juices they do not need much seasoning), placed in the plastic pouch and the bag is then sealed. The food is then cooked ensuring that the core (centre) temperature reaches at least 70°C for a specified time to kill off food poisoning bacteria. The length of time this core temperature needs to be maintained depends on the type of food and the portion size.

Air causes many changes in foods: dehydration, weight loss, colour loss and aroma changes. By excluding oxygen from foodstuffs, preventing oxidisation, the foods retain their properties longer and one set of spoilage bacteria are stopped. Most vacuum chambers are fitted with an inert gas carbon dioxide and nitrogen flushing system. Carbon dioxide (CO_2) inhibits the growth of bacteria and mould, and nitrogen (N_2) acts as a pressure equaliser, ensuring that the foods stay in their original shape.

There are different shaped bags for different foods. Each bag is made up on numerous layers. The outer and inner layers are called 'scuff layers' and are made of reinforced plastic to avoid tears from sharp bones, etc. The other layers are treated with special chemicals that counteract any toxins that might be produced from the plastics during cooking.

There are three variations of the pouches used in vacuum cookery. One is non-heat treatable and is used solely for vacuuming foods for storage. The other two differ in thickness, their use depending on the firmness of the food being vacuumed. Thick bags are used for vacuuming fragile foods such as fish, vegetables, stews, sauces and soups. They are suitable because they do not lose their shape so the foods do not lose their shape either. The thinner bags are used for large joints of meat, steaks, chops, cutlets and escalopes and, like the storage bags, are pre-stretched.

Once filled, the bags are placed into the vacuum machine and the air is gradually removed. It is essential to extract the air slowly otherwise the contents will be discharged from the bag. Once sealed, the pre-stretched bags are plunged into hot water at 90°C for just 1 second and they shrink back to their original size to form a second skin around the food, helping to retain most of the 'cooked out' juices in the 'body' of the meat.

Terms associated with vacuum cookery

Batch cooking Splitting large quantities of particular commodities into batches to cook either the cooking equipment or the chilling equipment are not large enough to process.

Blast chilling The rapid chilling of vacuumed food in special chillers.

CPU The abbreviation used for the Central Production Unit where the food is initially prepared, vacuumed and chilled.

Regenerating The final stage in vacuum cookery when the food is quickly heated to a safe temperature to consumption.

Satellite Kitchen The term given to the unit(s) where the final stage of vacuum cookery is carried out and the food is served to the customer.

In every batch one pouch must contain a thermocouple to record the core/internal temperature. The pouches are then labelled with details of their contents, the production date, use-by/consumption date and details for cooking and re-heating.

Foods can either be cooked immediately or packed on trays so that the air can freely circulate around them and chilled to a temperature of between 0°–3°C within 90 minutes, at which temperature they can be kept for up to 3 days.

If the foods are to be cooked the steamer oven is pre-heated and the time selected to cook the food and ensure that the core temperature reaches at least 70°C in order to make the food safe.

Time and temperature are also important to ensure that the best flavour and texture are achieved from the food being cooked.

CHILLING

Chilling after cooking is necessary:

(a) to arrest the cooking process, and
(b) to lower the temperature to a 'hygienically safe' temperature of 3°C within 90 minutes, to prevent the growth of micro-organisms which are either present in the food or have been introduced into it during handling.

Strict hygiene rules must be adhered to so as not to cause cross-contamination on a grand scale. The more the food is handled and the longer it is stored, the greater the risk of spoilage and food poisoning. To minimise the risks involved the DoH have published *Guidelines on pre-cooked chilled foods*, 1980.

FOODS SUITABLE FOR VACUUM COOKERY

Meats, poultry and game

All meats, poultry and game can be cooked by vacuum cookery, though the effects associated with roasting such as the crust formation and the crisp surfaces achieved in shallow frying cannot be recreated in this method. When vacuum cooking foods like these, they first have to be seared or browned beforehand.

Fish

Fish is very fragile and is not vacuum cooked very successfully as it tends to become distorted and crushed in the process. Usually fish is placed in bags and the air is removed and replaced by a mixture of carbon dioxide and nitrogen, which are both sterile gases, which cushion the food as well as inhibiting the growth of harmful bacteria.

NOTE: It has been discovered that raw mousses do not have to be aerated before cooking as the gas mixture does so during vacuuming.

Vegetables and fruit

Most vegetables can be cooked by vacuum cookery though green vegetables will turn yellow if they are not blanched before vacuuming. Other vegetables with strong smells must be blanched otherwise the smell becomes pungent and spoils the food. Soft fruits are not vacuumed successfully, though hard fruits such as apples and pears can be.

Pasta, rice and pulses

Pasta, rice and pulses cannot be vacuum cooked from raw and must first be cooked by conventional means.

The advantage of vacuum cookery

As with cook-chill and cook-freeze, vacuum cookery offers the ability to give a wider choice of interesting dishes. Vacuum cookery maximises the potential of the workforce because production schedules are organised to ensure maximisation of equipment, energy and staff time. Computer controlled cooking ensures that the food is cooked to as near perfection as possible every time.

Because cooking temperatures are lower than normal there are less cooked out juices, ensuring higher portion yields. It should be noted that with conventional cooking yield loss is around 25–30 per cent, but with vacuum cookery it is more likely to be between 2–8 per cent. There is minimal change in the texture of the food after cooking. There is little colour deterioration and no drying out of the food.

One phenomenon experienced with vacuum cookery is that some foods expand when vacuumed. This is explained by the fact that all foods contain dissolved air and have internal pressures which push

18

433

outwards and help to retain the shape and the structure of the food. During the vacuuming process the pressure in the bag drops below normal atmospheric pressure. This has the effect of forcing the inner gases outwards, expanding the product. In some circumstances this can be used to the chef's advantage as with such products as pâtés and mousses.

The disadvantages of vacuum cookery

The major disadvantage of vacuum cookery is the cost of specialised equipment and the training of staff to operate the equipment.

In some cases the quality of vacuumed foods can be inferior when compared to that of fresh or conventionally cooked dishes.

Certain fruits, such as strawberries, raspberries, cherries, damsons, apricots and peaches, break up during the process because of their delicate cellular structures.

Short-crust pastry does not brown in vacuum bags as it needs to dry out and the sealed bags prevent this. Puff pastry does not rise because the sealed bags restrict the lamination process.

EQUIPMENT USED IN VACUUM COOKERY OPERATIONS

(a) Dual purpose cooking/chilling equipment is used to first steam the vacuumed food and then, when the process is complete, to expel the steam and replace it with iced water.

(b) Thermocouples are used in the same way as temperature probes and are inserted into the vacuumed foods to measure the core temperature of the food and ensure that it reaches a temperature of at least 70°C.

(c) Blast chiller, sometimes known as air blast chillers, are capable of taking large trolley loads of cooked foods. Low temperature air is passed along the trolleys' shelves, chilling cooked foods evenly and rapidly.

(d) Cryogenic batch chilling tunnels use carbon dioxide or liquid nitrogen (at a temperature of -196°C) which is sprayed into a chilling cabinet containing the warmed foods and quickly absorbs the heat.

NOTE: CO_2 chilling tunnels were originally designed for the chilling of fresh poultry. The disadvantage of using carbon dioxide (CO_2) is that it is expensive

(e) Insulated boxes, purpose built, are used to transport and hold chilled food between a central kitchen and the satellite units. With increased insulation the boxes are capable of holding the temperature for up to 3 hours, though this figure will depend on ambient temperature, traffic conditions and the initial temperature of the food.

(f) Labels – important for ensuring that different dishes can be identified for date of production and use-by date.

(g) Refrigerators and cold storerooms maintained at a temperature of below 3°C, capable of taking complete trolley loads of food straight from the blast chiller. These are usually fitted with special alarms to indicate any rise in temperature.

(h) Refrigerated vans used to distribute the vacuumed foods from the central kitchen to the satellite units.

(i) Vacuum pouches are made from special plastics and are used to hygienically store and cook foods in.

(j) Water chilling baths are used to cool foods that are sealed in pouches.

(k) Combi-ovens which incorporate steam are used for re-heating vacuumed foods.

(l) Microwave ovens are suitable for re-heating individual portions or small quantities of vacuumed foods rapidly.

(m) Steamers, ideal for re-heating vacuumed foods.

WHAT WENT WRONG?

Problem	Caused by	To rectify
The vacuumed food is distorted.	Vacuuming too quickly.	Cannot be rectified. Once the food is distorted there is no way the food can regain its original shape. Care must be taken to vacuum slowly so the plastic gradually nestles around the food.
The food has disintegrated in the bag.	Using commodities unsuitable for.	Cannot be rectified. Ensure that no water is added to the vegetables. Instead of vacuuming fish and soft fruits, a special mixture of sterile gases can be used to replace the air which effectively steams the food in the bag.
The food was not cooked properly.	(1) Not cooking for long enough or the oven temperature was not high enough.	Place the food in another pouch for vacuuming.
	(2) The bags did not contain equal amounts of food or were not evenly spaced in the oven.	Re-distribute the food in the bags and, spreading evenly, return to the oven.
Vegetables have an over-powering flavour.	Not blanching the vegetables before vacuuming.	Cannot be rectified.
Green vegetables have turned yellow.	Not pre-blanching the vegetables before vacuuming.	Cannot be rectified.
The pouch tears after sealing.	Setting the sealing temperature too high for the thickness of the pouch used or a sharp edge of a bone has pierced the pouch.	Remove the food and place in another bag for vacuuming.

18

PART THREE

SPECIALIST COOKERY

FARINACEOUS COOKERY

The word 'farinaceous' is derived from the Latin *farina* meaning flour. The word farinaceous, encompasses the range of Italian pasta dishes made from a milled wheat base, i.e. noodles, gnocchi, spaghetti and macaroni, but also includes hot savoury rice dishes, i.e. pilaff and risotto (*see* Chapter 4: Boiling and Simmering, and Chapter 7: Braising), spatzle and gnocchi.

Gnocchi are small-shaped savoury dumplings or cakes made from poached semolina or polenta, mashed potato or choux paste. They are served plain with melted butter and grated cheese or with a variety of sauces. They may be served as a course on their own or as a traditional Italian accompaniment to grilled meats or roast chicken.

Pasta products are normally made from a high gluten wheat. The wheat is milled to produce a fine semolina-type flour and mixed with salt, oil and water. The dough can also be coloured and flavoured with either eggs, tomato purée, cooked spinach or beetroot juice. There are over 600 shapes and sizes of Italian pasta. Pasta on its own has little taste and it is for this reason it is always served with butter and garlic and grated cheese or a sauce.

It can be cooked and used in a variety of ways. Traditionally it is served on a luncheon menu, coming after the soup or instead of an hors d'euvre item. Pasta may be used as a garnish for soup, to accompany a meat, poultry or fish dish or as a sweet pudding such as macaroni pudding. Some establishments serve pasta as a main course. When it is served as a starter cause it is usually referred to as an antipasto.

THE HISTORY OF PASTA

The origin of pasta is not certain. It appears to have been influenced by many nationalities. The ancient Romans baked a floury soup mixture which was cut into strips and eaten as an accompaniment to meat. The Etruscans developed a dish from a Greek recipe called laganon thought to be the origin of lasagne. One of the first words for pasta was tri from the Arabic *itriyah*, meaning string which is a description of spaghetti.

By the Middle Ages special shapes were beginning to be developed. Ribbons, cords and tubes were all originally developed for a specific characteristic, either their ability to retain heat, absorb liquid or to hold sauces. By the 13th century stuffed pastas and ravioli were becoming popular, but was too expensive to be part of the average family's diet.

By the 15th century pasta known as vermicelli (little worms) appeared. In Sicily a pasta known as maccheroni, thought to be the original macaroni, appeared. Once it was soon discovered that pasta could be dried by direct sunlight pasta became more widely used.

Italians began to cook and eat pasta and tomato dishes from the 17th century. Soon the popularity of pasta spread to America and eventually to Britain, although initially it was not popular with the British palette. Today the average Italian's yearly consumption of pasta per year is 35 kg.

Staff responsible for farinaceous dishes

Chef Entremettier (Vegetable chef) Responsible for cooking and distribution of pasta for garnishes, salads, side dishes and main course.

Chef Pâtissier (Pastry chef) Responsible for cooking puddings, condés and Creole cookery.

THE PRODUCTION OF PASTA

Pasta production began as a cottage industry. Long-cut products such as spaghetti were spread evenly by hand on wooden dowels ½ cm thick by 1 m long. The filled sticks were placed on racks for sun-drying. Short cut products such as macaroni were scattered onto wire mesh trays and left to dry in the sun.

In early factories a batch of semolina and water was kneaded to form a smooth dough paste. The kneaded dough was then extruded through presses containing dies. These dies were perforated plates which determined the shape of the finished product. In modern production, however, the bulk of the alimentary paste is made by continuous processing. In commercial processing the semolina used is the granular product obtained from the endosperm of a special what called 'durum wheat'. The resulting durum flour is purified to remove bran specks that are found in normal semolina. The regularity in the size of semolina granules is important for water absorption which should be approximately 13–15 per cent. A pasta dough should have an overall moisture content of 30 per cent.

Durum wheat has a high gluten content which enables it to be rolled thinly enough to obtain the different types of pasta. Hollow tubes such as macaroni are made when the perforation in the dies are small and contain steel pins. Spaghetti is formed through smaller holes without any pins. Small fancy shapes are produced by the action of a rotary knife slicing through the dough as it emerges from the die.

Once formed, the products are dried by a process which reduces the overall moisture content from 31 to 12 per cent. The drying process is carefully regulated as rapid drying can cause the pasta to crack to too slow a drying can cause stretching, produce souring in the product and encourage the growth of mould.

Pastas can be divided into four main classifications according to its size and shape:

(a) **Long pasta**. This group includes **smooth** rods such as spaghetti; vermicelli; **tubular** forms of which the outer surface may be smooth or corrugated, e.g. long macaroni, mizzoni; and **flat** forms such as noodles and lasagne.

(b) **Short pasta** This group contains cut macaroni, ziti, tubetti lunghi, ditali.

(c) **Pasta suitable for filling**. In this group there are two main types,

   (i) Those that are filled while the pasta is raw, e.g. ravioli, tortellini, and then cooked.

   (ii) Those that are partly cooked before filling, e.g. cannelloni, and then finished off in the oven.

(d) **Small fancy pasta**. This group consists of a large variety of small pastas which are used mainly for garnishing, e.g. alfabeto (alphabets), numeri (numbers) and stellette (small stars).

Pasta also falls into two main types: (a) factory-made; or (b) home-made. Home-made include ravioli, tortellini, lasagne, cannelloni, tagliatelle and noodles. All others are factory-made, though home-made pastas can also be factory-made.

POPULAR TYPES OF PASTA

Anelli	Ring-shaped pasta pieces.
Bozzoli	Cocoon-like shapes.
Bucatini	Small whole wheat pieces of macaroni cut at a slant.
Cannelloni	Large hollow pipe shapes.
Cappelletti	Small hat-shaped pasta.
Capellini d'angelo	The finest type of ribbon pasta. Capelli d'angelo means angel's hair.
Casareccia	Twisted pasta lengths 4 cm long.
Cavatappi	Twisted ridged pasta pieces.
Conchiglie piccole rigate	Small sea shell shapes.
Conchiglie rigate	Large sea shell shapes.
Creste di gallo	Elbow-shaped, ridged mane, cut macaroni pieces.
Diamanti	Elongated diamond shapes.
Ditali	Finger or thimble shape.
Ditalini	Smaller version of ditali.
Elicoidali	Small hollow lengths with spiral line pattern.
Farfalle	Butterfly-shaped pieces.
Farfalline	Small butterfly-shaped pieces.
Fedelini	A very fine cylindrical pasta similar to vermicelli.
Festonati	Garland or festoon shapes.
Fusilli	Corkscrew-shaped pasta.
Fusilli bucati	Spring-shaped pieces.

Gnocchi	Small dumpling shapes also available made from potato.
Gnoccchetti sardi	A smaller-sized version of gnocchi.
Gramigna	Small grass or weed-like shapes.
Lasagne	Broad 8 cm approx flat ribbon-shaped.
Lasagnette	A flat ribbon pasta with ruffled edges. A smaller version of lasagne.
Lumache	Snail shell-shaped pasta.
Macaroni	A hollow-shaped version of spaghetti.
Orecchiette	Ear-shaped pasta pieces.
Pastina	General term used for a variety of different shapes, e.g. alphabets, etc.
Pipe rigate	Ridged pipe-shaped pasta.
Ravioli	Small square-shaped envelope. Stuffed.
Riccini	Ridged shell-like pasta.
Rigatoni	Large hollow lengths with spiral line pattern.
Ruotine	Wheel-shaped pasta.
Spaghetti	Available in plain, whole and buck wheat. Known as vermicelli in southern Italy. The word spaghetti means 'little strings'.
Spirali	Pasta lengths twisted together to form a spiral.
Tagliarini	A flat 3 mm ribbon noodle.
Tagliatelle	Flat 6 mm ribbon noodles.
Tortellini	Small stuffed pasta dumplings.
Tubetti lunghi	Elbow-shaped macaroni shapes.
Ziti	A large macoroni shape cut into pieces.

THE COOKING OF PASTA

Pasta should be cooked by immersing in plenty of boiling salted water, with a little olive oil to prevent sticking and simmering for between 10–20 minutes. Pasta should be cooked to the stage known as 'al dente' (to the tooth), which means that there should be a slight firmness in the cooked dough.

Pasta should, if possible, be cooked to order or cooked in batches.

Cooking times

Vermicelli	5 minutes
Noodles	10 minutes
Spaghetti	10 minutes
Lasagne	12 minutes
Macaroni	20 minutes

19

Terms associated with farinaceous dishes

Al dente To cook 'to the tooth', i.e. with a little bite.

Buckwheat An annual grain plant native to China.

Gratinate To brown the surface of a cooked dish either under a pre-heated salamander or a hot oven.

Pilaff Sometimes known as a pilau, it is a braised rice dish made from long grain rice and cooked with the minimum amount of stock 2 parts stock to 1 part rice.

Polenta A type of meal ground from Indian corn.

Risotto An Italian rice dish cooked on top of the stove. It was made from a special Italian rice but can be made from caroline rice with 1 part rice to 3 parts stock.

Pasta dishes

Basic noodle paste
Pâte à nouilles

⏲ 1 hr   ♨ 13 min

Step	Commodity	1 portion	10 portions	
1	Flour	60 g	600 g	Sieve into a suitably sized bowl, add a pinch of salt and make a well.
	Egg	1	10	Break into a jug and whisk together. Pour into the well.
	Water	50 ml	500 ml	Add and mix thoroughly (more or less water may be required) to achieve the correct consistency.
	Olive oil	few drops	2 tsp	Add and knead to a smooth dough. Cover with a dampened cloth and leave to rest for 30 minutes before using.

NOTE: For green noodles reduce the water by 7.5 ml per portion and add 15 g of well cook and puréed spinach. For red noodles add ½ tsp of tomato purée per portion.
   Use a pasta rolling machine for speed and to achieve the correct thickness.

☐   ☐   ☐

Ravioli paste
Pâte ravioli

⏲ 1½ hr   ♨ 12 min

Step	Commodity	1 portion	10 portions	
1	Flour	50 g	500 g	Sieve into a suitably sized bowl and add a pinch of salt.
	Olive oil	10 ml	100 ml	Add.
	Water	25 ml	250 ml	Add and mix thoroughly (more or less water may be required) to achieve the correct consistency. Cover with a damp cloth and leave to rest for 30 minutes.

☐   ☐   ☐

Ravioli filling

⏲ 1 hr   ♨ 1 hr

Step	Commodity	1 portion	10 portions	
1	Lean veal	50 g	500 g	Pass twice through a fine mincer.
	Oil	1 ml	10 ml	Place in a suitably sized saucepan and heat.
	Onion	5 g	50 g	Peel, finely dice and add to the hot fat. Cook with colouring for 2–3 minutes.
	Garlic	¼ clove	2 cloves	Peel, crush with a little salt and add. Add the minced veal and cook for 15 minutes.
	Cooked spinach	25 g	250 g	Drain well and add to the minced meat. Season with salt and pepper.
2	Demi glace	25 ml	250 ml	Add to bind (not all the demi glace will be required) and keep the mixture firm. To use allow to cool, but not go cold.

☐   ☐   ☐

Napolitaine sauce

Sauce Napolitaine

⏳ 30 min 🍲 30 min

Step	Commodity	1 portion	10 portions	
1	Butter	5 g	50 g	Place in a suitably sized sauteuse and heat.
	Tomato concassé (see Chapter 14: Cold preparations)	25 g	250 g	Add and cook for 4–5 minutes without colouring.
	Tomato sauce (see Chapter 4: Boiling and simmering)	60 ml	600 ml	Add, correct the seasoning and bring to the boil. Reduce to a simmer and use accordingly.

☐ ☐ ☐

Milanaise sauce

Sauce Milanaise

⏳ 45 min 🍲 30 min

Step	Commodity	1 portion	10 portions	
1	Butter	5 g	50 g	Place in a suitably sized sauteuse and heat.
	Tomato sauce (see Chapter 4: Boiling and simmering)	60 ml	600 ml	Add, correct the seasoning and bring to the boil. Reduce to a simmer and strain.
2	Cooked ham	15 g	150 g	Cut into julienne and add.
	Cooked tongue	10 g	100 g	Cut into julienne and add.
	Cooked mushrooms	5 g	50 g	Cut into julienne and add. Correct the seasoning and use accordingly.

☐ ☐ ☐

Bolognaise sauce

Sauce Bolognaise

⏳ 1 hr 🍲 1 hr

Step	Commodity	1 portion	10 portions	
1	Lean beef	35 g	250 g	Pass twice through a fine mincer.
	Oil	1 ml	10 ml	Place in a suitably sized saucepan and heat.
	Mushrooms	25 g	250 g	Wash, trim and stalk and finely dice. Add to the fat and cook for 2–3 minutes without colouring.
	Onion	5 g	50 g	Peel, finely dice and add to the hot fat. Cook without colouring for 2–3 minutes.
	Garlic	¼ clove	2 cloves	Peel, crush with a little salt and add. Add the minced beef and cook for 15 minutes.
	Marjoram	pinch	¼ tsp	Add.
	Oregano	pinch	¼ tsp	Add.
	Tomato purée	25 g	250 g	Add and mix well. Season with salt and pepper.
2	Demi glace	25 ml	250 ml	Add, bring to the boil and simmer gently for 30 minutes.

☐ ☐ ☐

Niçoise sauce

Sauce Niçoise

🥄 1 hr   🍲 25 min

Step	Commodity	1 portion	10 portions	
1	Olive oil	50 ml	500 ml	Place in a suitably sized sauteuse and heat.
	Garlic	¼ clove	2 cloves	Peel, crush, with a little salt, chop finely and add to the oil. Cook gently.
	Onion	20 g	200 g	Peel, finely dice and add to the oil. Cook gently.
	Tomato concassé	50 g	500 g	Add and cook for a further 5 minutes.
	Dry white wine	15 ml	150 ml	Add.
	Chopped basil	pinch	¼ tsp	Add and simmer for 10 minutes. Serve as required.

☐   ☐   ☐

Cannelloni au jus

🥄 1 hr   🍲 1 hr   ≋ 175°C

Step	Commodity	1 portion	10 portions	
1	Noodle paste	100 g	1 kg	Dust with flour and roll into an oblong 2 mm thick. Cut into 8 cm × 8 cm squares.
	Semolina	5 g	50 g	Spread onto a tray and lay the squares on top. Leave to rest and dry for 20 minutes. Place in a saucepan of boiling salted water with a little oil and simmer for 10 minutes. Remove and refresh. Drain and lay out singly onto a cloth.
2	Ravioli filling	50 g	500 g	Place in a piping bag with a 1 cm plain nozzle and pipe a length along one side of each square and roll up.
3	Thickened veal gravy	25 ml	350 ml	Pour half of the gravy on the bottom of an earthenware dish(es) and arrange the cannelloni on top. Cover with the remaining gravy.
4	Butter	5 g	50 g	Melt and pour over the cannelloni.
	Grated Parmesan	5 g	50 g	Sprinkle over the top and gratinate in a preheated oven for 10–15 minutes or until the cheese browns. Serve immediately.

☐   ☐   ☐

Gnocchi Parisienne

Step	Commodity	1 portion	10 portions		30 min	30 min
1	Water	50 ml	500 ml	Place in a suitably sized saucepan and bring to the boil. Add a pinch of salt and reduce to a simmer.		
	Butter	10 g	100 kg	Add, melt and remove from the heat.		
	Flour	35 g	350 g	Add and mix in well. Return to the stove and continue mixing until the paste becomes smooth and leaves the sides of the saucepan.		
	Eggs	¾ equiv	8	Add one at a time and mix thoroughly.		
	Grated parmesan	5 g	50 g	Add and mix in well. Allow to cool slightly and place in a piping bag with a 1 cm nozzle.		
2	Water	200 ml	2 litres	Place in a sauteuse, add a little salt, bring to the boil and reduce to a simmer. Pipe 2 cm lengths of the mixture into the simmering water. Cook for approximately 10 minutes or until the gnocchi floats and becomes pale. Remove and drain well. Place in a serving dish(es) and keep warm.		
3	Crème sauce	50 ml	500 ml	Warm and napper over the gnocchi.		
	Grated parmesan	5 g	50 g	Sprinkle over the top and brown lightly until a pre-heated salamander. Serve immediately.		

☐   ☐   ☐

Spatzle

Step	Commodity	1 portion	10 portions		45 min	15 min
1	Flour	50 g	500 g	Sieve into a bowl and add a pinch of salt.		
	Eggs	¼ equiv	2½	Add and season with salt, pepper and a pinch of nutmeg.		
	Milk	40 ml	400 ml	Add and mix to thick paste (more or less milk may be required). Allow to rest for 30 minutes. Fill a saucepan with cold water. Season with salt and pepper. Bring to the boil and reduce to a simmer. Place a colander above the simmering liquid and pour the mixture into it so as to let the paste run out through the small holes. Simmer gently for 6–7 minutes. Refresh and drain well.		
2	Butter	10 g	100 g	Place in a suitably sized sauteuse and heat gently. Place in a pre-heated serving dish(es) and keep warm.		
	Butter	5 g	50 g	Place in a sauteuse and heat until brown.		
	Lemon juice	Few drops	1 tsp	Add and pour over the spatzle. Serve immediately.		

☐   ☐   ☐

19

Macaroni cheese

🍲 1 hr   ♨ 45 min

Step	Commodity	1 portion	10 portions	
1	Water	50 ml	500 ml	Place in a suitably sized saucepan and bring to the boil. Add a pinch of salt and reduce to a simmer.
	Macaroni	25 g	250 g	Add and simmer for 15 minutes. Refresh and drain well.
	Butter	10 g	100 g	Place in a sauteuse, melt and heat. Add the macaroni and reheat.
	Thin béchamel	100 ml	1 litre	Add, mix well and bring to the boil.
	Diluted mustard	⅛ tsp	1½ tsp	Add and season with salt and milled pepper.
	Grated cheese	25 g	250 g	Add two-thirds of the cheese and mix in. Place in an oven-proof dish(es). Sprinkle with the remaining cheese and place in a pre-heated oven or under a salamander until the surface is golden brown. Remove and serve.

☐   ☐   ☐

Lasagne (garnished with a Bolognaise, Milanaise or Niçoise sauce)

🍲 1 hr   ♨ 45 min   ≋ 180°C

Step	Commodity	1 portion	10 portions	
1	Noodle paste	50 g	500 g	Roll out 2 mm thick and cut into oblongs 6 cm × 4 cm wide. Dust with a little flour, cover with a cloth and allow to rest for 15 minutes. Simmering for 10 minutes in boiling salted water with a little olive oil. Refresh in running cold water and drain. Butter a suitably sized oven-proof dish and place a layer of lasagne on the bottom. Season with salt and pepper.
2	Suitable sauce	100 ml	1 litre	Ladle one third of the sauce over the pasta. Repeat the process finishing with a layer of pasta.
3	Thin bèchamel	50 ml	500 ml	Ladle a layer of the bèchamel over the lasagne.
	Grated Parmesan cheese	5 g	50 g	Sprinkle over the top and place in a preheated oven for 30 minutes or until the surface is golden brown. Remove, clean the dish and serve.

☐   ☐   ☐

Spaghetti Italienne

Step	Commodity	1 portion	10 portions		
				⏲ 15 min	🍲 30 min
1	Spaghetti	50 g	500 g	Place in a suitably sized saucepan of boiling salted water with salt, pepper and a little olive oil. Simmer for between 12–15 minutes. Remove and refresh. Drain well.	
2	Butter	15 g	150 g	Melt in a suitably sized sauteuse and heat. Add the spaghetti, season with salt and milled black pepper and stir gently to prevent sticking. Place in a pre-heated serving dish(es).	
	Grated Parmesan cheese	15 g	150 g	Sprinkle over the top and serve.	

NOTE: Spaghetti au gratin is made by placing the prepared dish under a pre-heated salamander and gratinate. This dish may be made with any long, short-cut pasta or fancy pasta.

☐   ☐   ☐

Spaghetti Bolognaise

Step	Commodity	1 portion	10 portions		
				⏲ 15 min	🍲 30 min
1	Spaghetti	50 g	500 g	Place in a suitably sized saucepan or boiling salted water with salt, pepper and a little olive oil. Simmer for between 12–15 minutes. Remove and refresh. Drain well.	
2	Butter	15 g	150 g	Melt in a suitably sized sauteuse and heat. Add the spaghetti, season with salt and milled black pepper and stir gently to prevent sticking. Place in pre-heated serving dish(es) and make a well.	
3	Bolognaise sauce	100 ml	1 litre	Ladle into well.	
	Grated Parmesan cheese	15 g	150 g	Sprinkle over the top and serve.	

NOTE: For traditional silver service the sauce and spaghetti are served separately and accompanied with grated Parmesan cheese.
This dish may be made with any long, short-cut pasta or fancy pasta.

☐   ☐   ☐

19

Spaghetti Milanaise

Step	Commodity	1 portion	10 portions	
				👌 15 min 🍲 30 min
1	Spaghetti	50 g	500 g	Place in a suitably sized saucepan of boiling salted water with salt, pepper and a little olive oil. Simmer for between 12–15 minutes. Remove and refresh. Drain well.
2	Butter	15 g	150 g	Melt in a suitably sized sauteuse and heat. Add the spaghetti, season with salt and milled black pepper and stir gently to prevent sticking. Place in a pre-heated serving dish(es) and make a well.
3	Milanaise sauce	100 ml	1 litre	Ladle into the well.
	Grated parmesan cheese	15 g	150 g	Sprinkle over the top and serve.

NOTE: This dish may be made with any long, short cut pasta or fancy pasta.

□   □   □

Spaghetti Napolitaine

Step	Commodity	1 portion	10 portions	
				👌 15 min 🍲 30 min
1	Spaghetti	50 g	500 g	Place in a suitably sized saucepan of boiling salted water with salt, pepper and a little olive oil. Simmer for between 12–15 minutes. Remove and refresh. Drain well.
2	Butter	15 g	150 g	Melt in a suitably sized sauteuse and heat. Add the spaghetti, season with salt and milled black pepper and stir gently to prevent sticking. Place in a pre-heated serving dish(es) and make a well.
3	Napolitaine sauce	100 ml	1 litre	Ladle into the well.
	Grated Parmesan cheese	15 g	150 g	Sprinkle over the top and serve.

NOTE: This dish may be made with any long, short-cut pasta or fancy pasta.

□   □   □

Spaghetti Niçoise

Step	Commodity	1 portion	10 portions		
				🥄 15 min	♨ 30 min
1	Spaghetti	50 g	500 g	Place in a suitably sized saucepan of boiling salted water with salt, pepper and a little olive oil. Simmer for between 12–15 minutes. remove and refresh. Drain well.	
2	Butter	15 g	150 g	Melt in a suitably sized sauteuse and heat. Add the spaghetti, season with salt and milled black pepper and stir gently to prevent sticking. Place in a pre-heated serving dish(es) and make a well.	
3	Niçoise sauce	100 ml	1 litre	Ladle into the well.	
	Grated Parmesan cheese	15 g	150 g	Sprinkle over the top and serve.	

NOTE: This dish may be made with any long, short-cut pasta or fancy pasta.

☐   ☐   ☐

Rice dishes

Braised rice

Riz pilaff

Step	Commodity	1 portion	10 portions	⌣ 15 min ♨ 20–25 min ≋ 200°C (400°F)
1	Butter/ margarine	5 g	50 g	Melt in a suitably sized sauteuse.
2	Onions	10 g	100 g	Peel, cut in half and finely dice. Add to the butter and sweat without colour.
3	Long grain rice	50	500 g	Wash, drain and add to the onions. Cook until the rice becomes a light brown in colour.
4	Bayleaves	¼	2	Add.
5	White stock	100 ml equiv	1 litre	Bring to the boil and pour over the rice. Season with salt and pepper. Cover with a buttered cartouche and tight-fitting lid. Place in the preheated oven until the rice is cooked and all the stock absorbed. Stir occasionally with a fork to keep the rice grains separated.
6	Butter/ margarine	10 g	100 g	Remove the rice from the oven. Cut the butter into knobs and stir into the rice.
7	Chopped parsley	1 tsp	1 tbsp	Sprinkle over the cooked rice.

NOTE: If all the stock is absorbed before the rice is cooked, just add more.

Extensions of braised rice

Preparation: as for braised rice, with the addition of:

Braised rice with chicken
(Riz pilaff à volaille)

50 g cooked chicken per portion.

Braised rice with ham
(Riz pilaff au jambon)

50 g diced cooked ham per portion.

Braised rice with chicken liver
(Riz pilaff au foie de volaille)

50 g diced sautéed chicken livers per portion.

Braised rice with mushrooms
(Riz pilaff aux champignons)

50 g sliced sautéed mushrooms per portion.

Braised rice with prawns
(Riz pilaff aux crevettes roses)

50 g cooked prawns per portion.

Braised rice Creole style
(Riz Pilaff creole)

25 g of sliced sautéed mushrooms, 10 g cooked pimento and 10 g tomato concassé per portion.

Braised rice Piemontaise style
(Riz pilaff Piemontaise)

25 g sliced sautéed mushrooms, 10 g cooked piemento, 10 g tomato concessé (as above), and 15 g of grated parmesan cheese and 5 g diced truffle per portion.

Braised rice Italian style
(Riz pilaff Italienne)

15 g grated parmesan cheese per portion.

Braised rice Milan style
(Riz pilaff Milanaise)

Two-thirds of a strand of saffron in the stock to flavour and colour, 25 g sliced sautéed mushrooms, 15 g tomato concassé and 15 g of grated parmesan cheese.

Braised rice Greek style
(Riz à la Grèque)

1 grilled pork chipolata cut into 3. 15 g cooked garden peas and 10 g cooked diced red pimento per portion mixed with the rice.

Preparation: as for braised rice, with the addition of:

Braised rice with saffron
(Riz pilaff safranne)

1–2 strands of saffron per portion added to the rice as it is fried.

Braised rice Turkish style
(Riz à la Turque)

1–2 strands of saffron per portion added to the rice as it is fried (as above), and a garnish of 25 g tomato concassé per portion placed on top.

☐ ☐ ☐

Risotto

⌓ 10 min ♨ 30–40 min

Step	Commodity	1 portion	10 portions	
1	Butter/margarine	10 g	100 g	Melt in a suitably sized sauteuse.
2	Onions	10 g	100 g	Peel, cut in half and finely dice. Add to the butter, and sweat without colour.
3	Italian rice	50 g	500 g	Wash, drain and add to the onions. Cook until the rice is golden brown.
4	Bayleaves	¼	2	Add.
5	White stock	150 ml equiv	1½ litres	Bring to the boil and pour over the rice. Season with salt and pepper. Bring to the boil. Cover with a buttered cartouche and a lid. Cook on the side of the stove, stirring occasionally to prevent the bottom from burning. Continuing cooking the rice until all the stock is absorbed. Stir occasionally with a fork to keep the rice grains separated.
	Grated Parmesan cheese	10 g	100 g	Add half to the rice and mix in. Sprinkle the remaining over the top and serve.

NOTE: If all the stock is absorbed before the rice is cooked just add more.

For extensions of risotto, use the same as for pilaff.

☐ ☐ ☐

19

20
VEGETARIAN COOKERY

Vegetarian cookery is based on fresh vegetables, pulses, grains, nuts, fruits and, in some cases, dairy products.

People are or become vegetarians for many reasons, such as moral, religious or health. Basically there are two main types of vegetarians: lacto-vegetarians, who abstain from meats and animal products such as gelatine, aspic, lard and suet and vegans, who abstain from meat, animal products, all dairy products such as milk, cheese, yoghurt, eggs and, in extremes cases, honey.

Many traditional recipes can be adapted for vegetarians. Normally vegetarian dishes are based on wholefoods. Wholefoods are foods that have had nothing added to or taken from them. Diets must be well planned and varied to ensure the necessary vitamins, minerals, carbohydrates, fats and protein essential to good health are absorbed.

Terms and ingredients associated with vegetarian cookery

Carob Produced from the carob bean and is naturally sweet. Carob contains vitamins A and D, some B vitamins, magnesium, protein and a small amount of fibre. Carob bars are available in health food shops.

Polenta flour Made from cornmeal.

Smetana Cultured milk product similar to yoghurt, but thick and creamy in texture and about half the calorific value. It is used like sour cream.

Tahini paste A sesame seed paste widely used in the Middle East. Strong and nutty, it can be used as a dip on its own or to flavour other dips and sauces, such as houmous.

Tofu Also known as bean curd. Made from heavily pressed bean curd. Tofu is high in protein and is a good source of calcium, iron, B vitamins, thiamin and riboflavin.

Some people, especially children, may have problems eating the large amounts of foods necessary to give the required nutrients, so careful consideration must be given to their needs.

NOTE: Forward planning is necessary when cooking vegetarian dishes as pulses should always be soaked for at least 3–4 hours and usually overnight before cooking.

NUTRIENTS IN FOODS

Protein	Milk, cheese, yoghurt, eggs, fish, beans, lentils, nuts, seeds, cereals (rice, wheat, etc.) and vegetables.
Vitamin C	Bananas, blackcurrants, brussel sprouts, grapefruit, kiwi fruit, oranges, potatoes, strawberries, tomatoes.
Vitamin B	Wholegrain cereals, bread, green vegetables, lentils and yeast extract.
Vitamins B12	Milk, eggs, cheese, yoghurt, fish, soya milk and breakfast cereals.
Vitamin A	Carrots, milk, cheese, fish (herring), spinach, watercress, tomatoes, apricots.
Vitamin D	Oily fish, eggs, butter, margarine, dried milk, breakfast cereals and yoghurt.
Iron	Eggs, beans, lentils, wholegrain bread and cereals, nuts, dried fruits, green vegetables and cocoa.
Calcium	Milk and dairy products, seeds (sesame seeds, etc.), nuts, leaf vegetables, wholegrain cereals, beans, modified soya milk and lentils.

GENERAL POINTS ABOUT VEGETARIAN DIETS

It is unlikely that protein will be short in a vegetarian diet, but it is important to have a good balance of protein foods at each meal to ensure a good quality of protein.

Do not over-cook vegetables as this destroys the vitamins. Vitamin B12 is only found naturally in animal foods and fish so it will need to be introduced to the diet by other means in a vegan diet. Never overdose on vitamin supplements.

Iron from vegetables is not absorbed very well and is supplemented by drinks enriched with vitamin C such as citrus juices (orange, lemon, etc.).

Stocks

Vegetable stock

Step	Commodity	1 litre	10 litres		⌣ 30 min	♨ 1½ hr
1	Water	1 litre	10 litres	Place in a suitable saucepan.		
	Carrots	100 g	1 kg	Peel, cut into mirepoix and add to the water.		
	Onions	100 g	1 kg	Peel, cut in half and then into mirepoix and add.		
	Celery	100 g	1 kg	Wash, cut into mirepoix and add.		
	Leeks	100 g	1 kg	Cut lengthways and wash. Cut into mirepoix and add. Bring to the boil, lower to a simmer and cook for 1½ hours. Skim and strain to use.		

☐   ☐   ☐

Brown vegetable stock

Step	Commodity	1 litre	10 litres		⌣ 45 min	♨ 1½ hr
1	Carrots	100 g	1 kg	Peel, cut into mirepoix.		
	Onions	100 g	1 kg	Peel, cut in half and then into mirepoix.		
	Celery	100 g	1 kg	Wash, cut into mirepoix.		
	Leeks	100 g	1 kg	Cut lengthways and wash. Cut into mirepoix.		
	Vegetable oil	50 ml	250 ml	Place in a suitably sized frying pan and heat. Add the vegetables and fry until golden brown.		
	Black peppercorns	6	12	Add.		
2	Water	1 litre	10 litres	Place in a saucepan and add the browned vegetables.		
	Tomatoes	50 g	500 g	Remove the stalk and add.		
	Mushroom trimmings	50 g	500 g	Wash and trim the stalk. Add to the other vegetables. Bring to the boil and simmer for 1½ hours.		
	Yeast extract	5 g	50 g	Add and mix in well. Skim and strain to use.		

☐   ☐   ☐

20

Soups

Any traditionally made vegetable or pulse soup may be made suitable for a vegetarian diet by replacing the meat stock with vegetable stock and the butter with sunflower/soya margarine or vegetable ghee. Cream for enriching may be replaced by soya milk. Cheese croûtons may be made with soya cheese. Broths may be made using meat substitutes/protein extenders such as T.V.P. or quorn.

Tofustroni soup

Step	Commodity	1 portion	10 portions		🥄 1 hr ♨ 1 hr
1	Vegetable oil	5 ml	50 ml	Place in a suitably sized saucepan and heat gently.
	Onions	15 g	150 g	Peel, cut in half and finely dice. Add to the oil and sweat gently for 2–3 minutes.
	Garlic	½ clove	5 cloves	Peel, crush with a salt and add. Continue cooking for 2–3 minutes.
	Carrot	50 g	500 g	Wash, peel, cut into paysanne and add.
	Celery	75 g	750 g	Wash, cut in paysanne and add.
	Tomatoes	15 g	150 g	Remove the stalk and eye from each tomato. Place in a saucepan of boiling water for 10 seconds. Refresh immediately. Remove the skin, cut in half and discard the seeds. Dice and add the flesh to the other ingredients. Cover with a lid and sweat for 5 minutes.
	Bay leaves	½ small	3	Add.
	Chives	pinch	½ bunch	Wash, trim and add.
	Tofu	25 g	250 g	Cut into ½ cm dice and add.
	Soya sauce	1 tsp	10 tsp	Add.
	White stock	200 ml	2 litre	Add and bring to the boil.
	Mini pasta shells	15 g	150 g	Add and simmer for 45 minutes, correct the seasoning and serve.

☐   ☐   ☐

Iced sweet pepper soup

Step	Commodity	1 portion	10 portions		🥄 40 min ♨ 40 min
1	Water	25 ml	250 ml	Place in a jug.
	Coriander leaves	15 g	150 g	Wash and remove any damaged leaves or stalks. Dry, and chop finely and add to the water. Pour into an ice cube mould and freeze.
2	Red peppers	75 g	750 g	Discard and stalk and seeds. Cut the flesh into thin slices.
	Onions	25 g	250 g	Peel, cut in half and slice thinly.
	Tomatoes	50 g	500 g	Remove the eye and make a thin incision in the other end of each tomato. Place in a pan of boiling salted water for 10 seconds and refresh immediately in cold water. Discard the skin and cut in half. Remove the seeds and cut the flesh into thin slices. Add to the other ingredients.
3	White stock	200 ml	2 litres	Place in a suitably sized saucepan and add the onions, tomatoes and peppers. Bring to the boil, then simmer for 30 minutes. Purée in a liquidiser and place in a tureen. Allow to go cold and garnish with the coriander ice cubes.

Haricot bean soup

Step	Commodity	1 portion	10 portions	
1	Haricot beans	50 g	500 g	Place in a bowl and cover with water. Allow to soak overnight. Drain and rinse.
	Vegetable oil	5 ml	50 ml	Place in a saucepan and heat.
	Garlic cloves	½	5	Peel, crush with a little salt and add to the oil. Cook gently for 2–3 minutes. Remove from the heat and add the beans.
2	White stock	400 ml	4 litres	Pour over the beans and place on the heat. Bring to the boil and simmer for 2½ hours or until the beans are tender. Purée and season with salt and pepper. Correct the consistency. Pour into a serving tureen.
3	Chopped parsley	pinch	1 tsp	Sprinkle over the top.

☐   ☐   ☐

Chilled cucumber soup

Step	Commodity	1 portion	10 portions	
1	Cucumber	100 g	1 kg	Peel and grate finely into a bowl.
	Yoghurt	100 ml	1 litre	Add and mix together well.
	Garlic cloves	½	5	Peel, crush finely with a little salt and add to the mixture.
	White wine vinegar	5 ml	50 ml	Add.
	Mint	5 g	50 g	Wash thoroughly and chop finely. Add to the other ingredients. Season with salt and black pepper.
	Soya milk	100 ml	1 litre	Add, mix together well and allow to chill for 1 hour. Pour into a serving tureen.
	Mint sprigs	1	10	Wash thoroughly and use to garnish the soup.

NOTE: This soup may be made using chives instead of the mint.

☐   ☐   ☐

20

Hungarian cherry soup

⌣ 1½ hr   ♨ 45 min

Step	Commodity	1 portion	10 portions	
1	Red cherries	100 g	1 kg	Wash, remove the stones and retain. Keep 1 cherry per portion back for garnishing.
	Water	150 ml	1½ litres	Place in a suitably sized saucepan.
	Sugar	5 g	50 g	Add along with the cherries. Bring to the boil and simmer for 15 minutes.
2	Red wine	50 ml	500 ml	Pour into a saucepan. Place the cherry stones in a clean tea towel. Break open with a rolling pin and add to the wine.
	Cinnamon stick	½ small	1	Add.
	Lemon juice	10 ml	100 ml	Add to the wine, bring to the boil and simmer for 10 minutes. Strain the resulting liquid into the cherry liquid. Retain the whole cherries. Pass the liquid through a sieve or purée in a liquidiser. Re-heat and correct the consistency. Allow to cool for 1 hour. Pour into a serving tureen.
3	Yoghurt/ soya milk	25 ml	250 ml	Add and swirl in. Garnish with the whole cherries. Serve chilled.

☐   ☐   ☐

Cream of lemon soup

⌣ 1 hr   ♨ 1 hr

Step	Commodity	1 portion	10 portions	
1	Margarine	5 g	50 g	Place in a suitably sized saucepan and heat gently.
	Onions	25 g	250 g	Peel, cut in half and slice finely. Add to the margarine.
	Carrots	15 g	150 g	Wash, peel, chop finely and add.
	Bay leaf	1 small	2 large	Add.
	Celery	25 g	250 g	Wash, chop finely and add. Cover and sweat for 10 minutes
2	Lemons	½	5	Remove the rind and blanch in boiling water for 2 minutes. Remove and allow to cool. Cut into julienne. Squeeze the lemon juice into a bowl. Add the rind and the strained lemon juice to the vegetables.
	White stock	200 ml	2 litres	Add, bring to the boil and simmer for 45 minutes. Season with salt and pepper. Remove the bay leaf and pass the soup through a sieve or purée in a liquidiser. Re-heat and correct the consistency.
3	Soya milk/ smetana	50 ml	500 ml	Pour into the soup and stir in well. Do not re-boil.
	Lemon slice	1	10	Place on the soup as garnish.
	Chopped parsley	pinch	1 tsp	Sprinkle over the top.

NOTE: This soup may be served hot or cold.

☐   ☐   ☐

Cauliflower and almond soup

Step	Commodity	1 portion	10 portions		45 min 1 hr
1	Margarine	5 g	50 g	Place in a suitably sized saucepan and heat gently.	
	Onions	15 g	150 g	Peel, cut in half and add to the margarine.	
	Cauliflower	100 g	1 kg	Wash, cut into small florets and add to the onions. Cover and sweat for 10 minutes.	
	Flaked almonds	25 g	250 g	Place on a tray and toast under a pre-heated salamander until golden brown on all sides. Retain 3 almonds per portion. Add to the cauliflower and continue cooking for a further 10 minutes.	
	Nutmeg	Small pinch	pinch	Add	
2	White stock	200 ml	2 litres	Add, bring to the boil and simmer gently for 45 minutes. Pass through a sieve or purée in a liquidiser. Re-heat, season with salt and pepper and correct the consistency. Pour into a serving tureen.	
	Soya milk	25 ml	250 ml	Swirl into the soup. Sprinkle the toasted almonds over the soup.	

☐   ☐   ☐

Iced sorrel soup

Step	Commodity	1 portion	10 portions		30 min 50 min
1	Sorrel leaves	25 mg	250 g	Wash the leaves thoroughly and shred.	
	Margarine	5 g	50 g	Melt and heat gently in a suitably sized saucepan.	
	Onions	15 g	150 g	Peel, cut in half and dice finely. Add to the margarine, cover with a lid and sweat for 5 minutes without colouring. Add the sorrel leaves and continue cooking.	
	Potatoes	50 g	500 g	Peel, wash, chop finely and add to the other ingredients. Sweat for a further 5 minutes.	
2	White stock	200 ml	2 litres	Add, bring to the boil and simmer for 30 minutes. Pass through a sieve or purée in a liquidiser. Re-heat, season with salt and pepper and correct the consistency. Pour into a serving tureen.	
	Soya milk	10 ml	100 ml	Swirl into the soup.	
	Chopped parsley	pinch	1 tsp	Sprinkle over the soup. Serve with croûtons.	

☐   ☐   ☐

20

Carrot and cardamom soup

⏲ 45 min   ♨ 1¼ hr

Step	Commodity	1 portion	10 portions	
1	Carrots	75 g	750 g	Peel, wash and cut into julienne.
	Onions	25 g	250 g	Peel and slice into thin rings.
	Margarine	5 g	50 g	Place in a suitably sized saucepan and heat gently. Add the onions and carrots, cover with a lid and sweat without colouring for 5 minutes.
2	Cardamom pods	2	20	Split and remove the black seeds. Crush the seeds and add to the carrots.
	Lentils	15 g	150 g	Add and cook for a further 2 minutes.
	White stock	200 ml	2 litres	Add, bring to the boil, reduce to a simmer and cook for 1 hour. Season with salt and pepper.
	Parsley sprigs	1 small	10 small	Wash and use to garnish the soup.

☐ ☐ ☐

Vegetable and oatmeal broth

⏲ 1 hr   ♨ 1 hr

Step	Commodity	1 portion	10 portions	
1	Onions	25 g	250 g	Peel, cut in half and dice finely.
	Leeks	25 g	250 g	Discard the root and outer leaves and wash. Dice finely and add to the onions.
	Carrots	50 g	500 g	Peel, wash and dice finely. Add to the leeks.
	Turnip	35 g	250 g	Peel, wash and dice finely. Add.
	Margarine	5 g	50 g	Melt in a suitably sized saucepan and add the vegetables. Cover with a lid and sweat gently for 10 minutes without colouring.
	Oatmeal	5 g	50 g	Add and mix in well.
2	White stock	200 ml	2 litres	Add, bring to the boil and simmer for 45 minutes. Season with salt and pepper. Skim and pour into a soup tureen.
	Soya milk (optional)	15 ml	150 ml	Swirl into the soup before serving.
	Chopped parsley	pinch	1 tsp	Sprinkle over the top.

☐ ☐ ☐

Starter dishes

Nutty Camembert pâté

Step	Commodity	1 portion	10 portions			
					⏲ 30 min	♨ 45 min
1	Ripe Camembert	50 g	500 g	Remove the rind and discard. Place the cheese into a liquidiser and purée until smooth. Remove and place in a bowl.		
	Full fat cheese	50 g	500 g	Add to the Camembert.		
	Paprika	pinch	½ tsp	Add.		
	Blanched almonds	20 g	200 g	Chop finely and add to the cheese. Mix together thoroughly. Place in a prepared mould and refrigerate for 3 hours. Dip the mould in hot water to aid the removal of the pâté. Place on a serving flat.		
	Flaked almonds	5 g	50 g	Sprinkle over the top.		
	Paprika	pinch	½ tsp	Sprinkle over the almonds and serve accompanied by toasted wholemeal bread.		

☐   ☐   ☐

Butter bean pâté

Step	Commodity	1 portion	10 portions			
					⏲ Overnight	♨ 2½ hr
1	Dried butter beans	50 g	500 g	Place in a clean bowl and cover with 3 times as much water. Leave to soak overnight. Drain and rinse thoroughly. Replenish with clean water. Place on the stove, bring to the boil and simmer for 2 hours or until the beans are tender. Refresh and drain. Place the beans in a liquidiser.		
2	Olive oil	10 ml	100 ml	Add.		
	Lemon or lime juice	15 ml	150 ml	Add.		
	Tomato purée	1 tsp	10 tsp	Add.		
	Garlic	½ clove	5 cloves	Peel, crush to a purée with salt and add.		
	Fresh coriander	pinch	½ bunch	Wash, dry, remove the stalk, chop finely and add. Purée to a smooth paste. Season with a little salt and black pepper. Place in a serving bowl and refrigerate.		
	Black olives	4	40	Use to decorate the pâté.		
	Chopped parsley	pinch	2 tsp	Sprinkle over the top. Serve cold.		

NOTE: This dish may be done with brown lentils.

☐   ☐   ☐

Houmous

Step	Commodity	1 portion	10 portions		⏱ 30 min	🍲 2½ hr
1	Dried chick peas	25 g	250 g	Place in a saucepan and add three times the amount of water. Bring to the boil and simmer gently for 2 hours or until the peas are tender. Drain, leaving a little of the cooking liquor. Place in a liquidiser.		
	Garlic	½ clove	5 Cloves	Peel, crush to a purée with salt and add.		
	Lemon juice	15 ml	150 ml	Pour over the peas and purée to a smooth paste. Season with black pepper.		
	Tahini paste	15 g	150 g	Add and mix well. Pour into a serving dish.		
2	Black olives	4	40	Arrange on the top.		
	Chopped parsley	pinch	2 tsp	Sprinkle over the houmous. Serve with pitta bread.		

☐ ☐ ☐

Falafel

Chick pea patties

Step	Commodity	1 portion	10 portions		⏱ Overnight	🍲 2 hr
1	Chick peas	50 g	500 g	Place in a clean bowl and cover completely with water. Leave to soak overnight. Drain away the water and rinse well in cold running water. Place in a suitably sized saucepan and cover with 3 times as much water. Bring to the boil, simmer for 1½ hours or until tender. Skim as required. Drain and place peas in a liquidiser.		
2	Onion	15 g	150 g	Peel, remove the root, cut in half and add to the chick peas.		
	Garlic	½ clove	5 cloves	Peel, crush with salt and add.		
	Cumin seed	½ tsp	5 tsp	Add.		
	Fresh coriander	pinch	½ bunch	Wash, dry, discard stalk, chop leaves finely and add. Purée to a smooth paste. Season with a little salt and chilli pepper. Place in a bowl and allow to go cold. Portion and shape into small fishcake shapes.		
	Flour	15 g	150 g	Place in a tray.		
	Soya milk	15 ml	150 ml	Pour into a deep tray. Pass the cakes through the flour, then the milk and the flour again. Deep fry (180°C) for 2–3 minutes. Drain and serve.		

☐ ☐ ☐

Main course dishes

Chick pea and tomato stew

Step	Commodity	1 portion	10 portions	
				⌣ Overnight 2½ hr
1	Chick peas	50 g	500 g	Place in a clean bowl and cover completely with water. Leave to soak overnight. Drain away the water and rinse well in cold running water. Place in a suitably sized saucepan and cover with 3 times as much water. Bring to the boil, simmer for 1½ hours or until tender. Drain and place to one side for use later.
2	Soya oil	5 ml	50 ml	Place in a suitably sized saucepan and heat.
	Onion	50 g	500 g	Peel, remove the root, cut in half and add.
	Garlic	½ clove	5 cloves	Peel, crush with salt and add. Cook for 3–4 minutes without colouring.
	Paprika	½ tsp	5 tsp	Add.
	Ground cumin	½ tsp	6 tsp	Add.
	Garam masala	½ tsp	5 tsp	Add.
	Coriander leaves	4	½ bunch	Wash, dry, chop finely and add.
	Tomatoes	100 g	1 kg	Remove and discard the stalk and eye of each tomato. Slice thinly and add. Cook gently for 5 minutes. Add the cooked chick peas and simmer for a further 10 minutes. Season with salt and pepper. Place in a serving dish.
	Mint leaves	2	20	Wash and use to garnish.

☐ ☐ ☐

20

461

Kidney bean and ginger stew

Step	Commodity	1 portion	10 portions			
				�′ Overnight	♨ 45 min	
1	Kidney beans	50 g	500 g	Place in a clean bowl and cover completely with water. Leave to soak overnight. Drain away the water and rinse well in cold running water. Place in a suitably sized saucepan and cover with 3 times as much water. Bring to the boil, simmer for 1 hour or until tender. Drain and allow to cool.		
2	Soya oil	5 ml	50 ml	Place in a suitably sized saucepan and heat gently.		
	Green chillies	¼ equ	2	Discard the stalk and seeds. Cut into thin slices and add to the oil.		
	Onion	15 g	150 g	Peel, remove root, cut in half, dice finely and add to the oil.		
	Garlic	½ clove	5 cloves	Peel, crush with salt and add.		
	Root ginger	5 g	50 g	Peel, grate and add, along with the cooked beans.		
	Tomato purée	5 g	50 g	Add and mix in well. Simmer for 10 minutes. Season with salt and ground pepper.		
	Soya milk	15 ml	150 ml	Add and place in a serving dish.		
	Chopped parsley	pinch	2 tsp	Sprinkle over the top and serve.		

☐   ☐   ☐

Pepperonata

Sweet pepper and tomato stew

Step	Commodity	1 portion	10 portions			
				�′ 3 hr	♨ 4–5 min	
1	Tomatoes	150 g	1½ kg	Discard the stalk and the eye and make an incision in the other end with a knife. Place in a pan of boiling salted water for 10 seconds and refresh immediately. Discard the skins, cut in half and remove the seeds. Cut the flesh into julienne.		
2	Vegetable oil	10 ml	100 ml	Place in a suitably sized saucepan and heat gently.		
	Garlic	½ clove	5 cloves	Peel, crush with a little salt and add to the hot oil. Cook for 2–3 minutes without colouring.		
	Onion	25 g	250 g	Peel, cut in half and dice finely. Add to the garlic.		
	Red peppers	150 g	1½ kg	Discard the stalk and seeds. Cut the flesh into julienne and add to the oil. Cover with a lid and cook for 5 minutes. Add the tomatoes and simmer for 40 minutes or until the vegetables are tender. Serve either hot or cold.		
	Chopped parsley	pinch	2 tsp	Sprinkle over the top.		

☐   ☐   ☐

Vegetable hotpot

Step	Commodity	1 portion	10 portions	
				⏲ 1 hr 🍲 1½ hr
1	Leeks	100 g	1 kg	Cut in half lengthways, wash thoroughly. Cut into 1 cm lengths.
	Swede	50 g	500 g	Peel, wash and cut into thin slices.
	Turnip	50 g	500 g	Peel, wash and cut into thin slices.
	Carrots	50 g	500 g	Peel, wash and cut into thin slices.
	Mushrooms	50 g	500 g	Wash, trim the stalks and cut into thin slices.
	Celery	50 g	500 g	Wash and cut into thin slices. Layer the vegetables in a casserole dish. Seasoning each layer with salt and pepper.
2	Brown stock	100 ml	1 litre	Pour over the vegetables just covering the top layer.
	Potatoes	100 g	1 kg	Peel, wash, slice thinly and layer over the vegetables.
	Soya margarine	5 g	50	Melt and brush over the top of the potatoes. Season, place in a pre-heated oven (180°C) for 1½ hours. Flatten the potatoes during cooking. Brush occasionally with margarine.
	Soya cheese	25 g	250 g	Grate and sprinkle over the top.
	Breadcrumbs	15 g	150 g	Sprinkle over the top and bake for a further 10 minutes. Serve hot.

☐ ☐ ☐

Stuffed courgettes with walnuts and sage

Step	Commodity	1 portion	10 portions	
				⏲ 1 hr 🍲 40 min ≋ 190°C
1	Courgettes	1 × 150 g	10 × 150 g	Wash, trim both ends of the courgette and cut in half lengthways. Using a teaspoon, hollow out the centre of each courgette. Retain the pulp and chop finely. Blanch the courgette in boiling salted water for 5 minutes. Refresh under cold water until cold.
2	Soya margarine	5 g	50 g	Place in a suitably sized frying pan and heat.
	Onions	15 g	150 g	Peel, cut in half, finely dice and cook gently in a frying pan.
	Chopped sage	pinch	½ tsp	Add along with the pulp.
	Chopped parsley	pinch	1 tsp	Add.
	Walnuts	15 g	150 g	Wash, chop finely and add.
	Tomato purée	½ tsp	5 tsp	Add and mix thoroughly with the other ingredients.
	Breadcrumbs	10 g	100 g	Add, mix well and season with salt and pepper. Divide the filling into the appropriate portions and spread into each courgette. Place on a tray in a pre-heated oven for the required time. Remove and garnish with washed parsley and sage sprigs.

☐ ☐ ☐

20

Imam Bayildi

Stuffed baked aubergine

⏱ 30 min 🔥 1½ hr

Step	Commodity	1 portion	10 portions	
1	Tomatoes	150 g	1½ kg	Discard the stalk and the eye of each tomato and make an incision in the other end with a knife. Place in a pan of boiling salted water for 10 seconds and refresh immediately. Discard the skins, cut in half and remove the seeds. Dice the flesh.
	Aubergines	1 medium	10 medium	Wash, remove the stalk and cut in half lengthways. Scoop out the flesh, cut into large dice and place to the side for use later. Sprinkle the inside of the skins with a little salt and lemon juice to remove the bitter taste. Place upside down on a tray and refrigerate.
2	Vegetable oil	10 ml	100 ml	Place in a suitably sized saucepan and heat.
	Onions	25 g	250 g	Peel, cut in half and dice. Add to the oil and sweat for 2–3 minutes.
	Garlic	½ clove	5 cloves	Peel, crush with a little salt and add to the onions. Cook for a further minute. Add the aubergines and the tomatoes and cook for a 3–4 minutes.
	Allspice	pinch	1 tsp	Add.
	Sugar	pinch	2 tsp	Add, season with salt and ground black pepper. Divide the mixture into the appropriate portions and fill the skins. Place in a pre-heated oven (150°) for 1 hour or until the vegetable are tender. Serve either hot or cold.
	Chopped parsley	pinch	2 tsp	Sprinkle over the dish before serving.

☐   ☐   ☐

Okra and courgette in spiced lentil sauce

⏱ 30 min 🔥 1½ hr

Step	Commodity	1 portion	10 portions	
1	Red lentils	50 g	500 g	Wash, drain and place in a suitably sized saucepan. Cover with cold water, bring to the boil and reduce to a simmer.
	Onions	25 g	250 g	Peel, cut in ½ cm dice and add.
	Carrots	25 g	250 g	Peel, wash, cut into ½ cm dice and add.
	Root ginger	5 g	50 g	Peel, grate and add.
	Turmeric	pinch	20 g	Add.
	Ground coriander	pinch	10 g	Add and simmer until the lentils are tender. Liquidise to a smooth consistency. Keep warm.
2	Okra	100 g	1 kg	Wash and trim both ends. Place in a saucepan of boiling water for 5 minutes. Remove, refresh and drain.
	Courgettes	100 g	1 kg	Wash, peel and slice. Place in a saucepan of boiling water and blanch for 3 minutes. Remove, refresh and drain. Add to the okra.
	French beans	50 g	500 g	Wash, top and tail and place in a saucepan of boiling water for 2–3 minutes to blanch. Remove, refresh and drain. Place with the other vegetables.
4	Margarine	5 g	50 g	Place in a suitably sized saucepan and heat. Add the vegetables and season with salt and pepper. Pour over the sauce and serve.

☐   ☐   ☐

Cauliflower and courgette bake

Step	Commodity	1 portion	10 portions		⏲ 1 hr 🍲 1 hr
1	Cauliflower	150 g	1½ kg		Wash, trim and discard the leaves and root. Cut into small florets. Place in a pan of boiling salted water. Return to the boil and simmer for 15 minutes. Remove, refresh and drain.
2	Soya margarine	5 g	50 g		Place in a suitably sized saucepan and heat gently.
	Courgettes	50 g	500 g		Wash, peel and cut into thin slices. Add to the margarine and cook for 2–3 minutes until the courgettes are softened. Remove and drain on absorbent paper.
3	Soya margarine	5 g	50 g		Melt in a saucepan.
	Flour	5 g	50 g		Add and cook to a blanc (first stage) roux. Allow to cool.
	Soya milk	50 ml	500 ml		Warm. Add a quarter to the roux and mix in well. Add another quarter, mix and bring to the boil. Add the remaining milk, bring to the boil and return to a simmer. Cook gently for 15 minutes in a bain-marie. Add the cauliflower and place in a liquidiser. Purée to a smooth paste. Season with salt and pepper.
4	Egg yolks	1	10		Place in a clean bowl and whisk. Add the puréed mixture. Mix well.
	Egg whites	1	10		Place in a clean bowl and whisk to a firm meringue. Fold in the cauliflower mixture. Spoon the mixture into the prepared souffle dishes (halfway up). Arrange the courgettes on the top. Place in a pre-heated oven 195°C) for 30–40 minutes or until it is golden brown. Serve immediately.

☐   ☐   ☐

Spiced lentils with aubergines and mushrooms

Step	Commodity	1 portion	10 portions		⏲ 1 hr 🍲 1½ hr
1	Lentils	50 g	500 g		Wash, rinse and drain. Place in a suitably sized saucepan and cover with 3 times as much water.
	Garlic	½ clove	5 cloves		Peel, crush to a purée with salt and add. Bring to the boil and simmer for 30 minutes.
	Sugar	pinch	1 tsp		Add and season with a little salt and black pepper.
	Fennel seeds	pinch	1 tsp		Add.
	Garam masala	pinch	1 tsp		Add.
2	Aubergines	150 g	1½ kg		Wash, remove and discard the stalk and skin. Cut the flesh into ½ cm dice. Add to the lentils.
	Mushrooms	75 g	750 g		Wash, trim the stalk and slice thinly. Add to the lentils. Stirring continuously to prevent burning, continue cooking for 20 minutes or until the vegetables and lentils are tender. Remove from the heat, turn into an ovenproof baking dish. Cover with a lid and place in a pre-heated oven (185°C) for 20 minutes. Remove from the oven.
	Coriander leaves	2	20		Wash and use to garnish.

☐   ☐   ☐

465

Vegetable kebabs with tofu sauce

Step	Commodity	1 portion	10 portions		⌣ 2 hr ♨ 15 min per portion
1	Button mushrooms	8	80	Wash and trim. Leave whole.	
	Courgettes	2	20	Wash, trim both ends and cut into 2 cm pieces.	
	Baby sweetcorn	4	40	Wash, trim and cut in half.	
	Bay leaves	2	20	Wash.	
	Cherry tomatoes	6	60	Wash and remove the stalks. Allowing two kebabs per portion. Alternate the vegetables and bay leaves on skewers. Brush with sesame seed oil.	
	Sesame seeds	pinch	2 tsp	Sprinkle over the kebabs. Place on a pre-heated salamander and grill for 7–8 minutes on both sides. Serve on a bed of braised rice.	
2	Tofu	150 g	1½ kg	Place in a liquidiser.	
	Olive oil	10 ml	100 ml	Add.	
	Soy sauce	5 ml	50 ml	Add.	
	Garlic	½ clove	5 cloves	Peel, crush with a little salt and add.	
	Lemon juice	10 ml	100 ml	Add and purée to a smooth paste. Season to taste and chill for use. Pour over the kebabs.	

☐ ☐ ☐

Almond and polenta roast

Step	Commodity	1 portion	10 portions		⌣ 30 min ♨ 15 min
1	Olive oil	5 ml	50 ml	Place in a suitably sized saucepan and heat.	
	Onions	25 g	250 g	Peel, cut in half and finely dice. Add to the oil and brown lightly.	
	Polenta	20 g	200 g	Add.	
	Water	35 ml	350 ml	Add, bring to the boil, stir continuously and simmer for 6–7 minutes. Remove and allow to cool slightly.	
2	Ground almonds	35 g	350 g	Add.	
	Yeast extract	1 g equiv	10 g	Add.	
	Egg	¼ equiv	2½	Add.	
	Dried sage	pinch	¼ tsp	Add and mix together thoroughly.	
4	Margarine	5 g	50 g	Melt and use to liberally grease an ovenproof dish. Spoon in the mixture and bake in a pre-heated oven (190°C) for 45 minutes.	

NOTE: This dish may be served with a tomato sauce (see Chapter 4: Boiling) or broccoli sauce

☐ ☐ ☐

466

Gratin of nuts

Step	Commodity	1 portion	10 portions	⏲ 30 min ♨ 1½ hr ≋ 190°C
1	Margarine	5 g	50 g	Place in a saucepan and heat.
	Onion	10 g	100 g	Peel, cut in half and finely dice. Add to the margarine.
	Garlic	½ clove	5 cloves	Peel, finely crush with a little salt and add to the onions.
	Green pepper	15 g	150 g	Remove, discard the stalk and seeds, finely dice the flesh and add.
	Red pepper	15 g	150 g	As for green pepper.
	Celery	10 g	100 g	Wash, trim and dice. Add to the other vegetables and sweat gently for 2–3 minutes.
2	Cooked chestnuts	20 g	200 g	Finely chop and add.
	Cashew nuts	50 g	500 g	Finely chop and add.
	Cheese	25 g	250 g	Grate and add. Mix well together. Remove from the heat.
3	Red wine*	15 ml	150 ml	Add.
	Thyme	pinch	1 tsp	Add.
	Chopped parsley	pinch	2 tsp	Add.
	Egg	¼ equiv	2	Add and bind the ingredients together. Select a suitably sized baking tin and line with silicon paper.
4	Margarine	5 g	50 g	Melt and brush onto the paper liberally. Add the mixture and place in a pre-heated oven (190°C) for 1 hour.
5	Tomatoes	25 g	250 g	Remove the stalk and eye of each tomato and make an incision in the other end. Place in a saucepan of boiling water for 10 seconds. Remove and refresh. Discard the skin. Cut in half and remove the seeds. Cut the flesh into fine tomato concassé. Remove the nut gratin from the oven. Portion and garnish with the tomato concassé. Serve with a tomato coulis.

* Grape juice may be used instead.

☐   ☐   ☐

467

Spinach roulade

⏱ 1 hr   ♨ 45 min

Step	Commodity	1 portion	10 portions	
1	Spinach	250 g	2½ kg	Wash, remove and discard the outer leaves and any damaged leaves. Rewash and drain. Place in a saucepan of boiling salted water, bring to the boil and simmer for 5 minutes. Refresh immediately, drain thoroughly and chop finely. Select a suitable sized baking tray. Lay a sheet of silicon paper on top and grease lightly.
2	Egg yolks	1	10	Place in a clean bowl. Season with salt, ground black pepper and nutmeg. Add to the spinach and beat together well.
	Egg whites	1	10	Place in another clean bowl and whisk to a stiff meringue. Fold into the spinach mixture. Place on the prepared baking tray and bake in a pre-heated oven (200°C) for 15–20 minutes or until the mixture is firm. Remove from the oven.
3	Margarine	5 g	50 g	Place in a saucepan and heat.
	Onions	15 g	150 g	Peel, cut in half and dice finely. Add to the fat and sweat without colouring for 3–4 minutes. Remove from the heat.
	Curd cheese	25 g	250 g	Add.
	Soya cheese	15 g	150 g	Add.
	Soured cream	10 ml	100 ml	Add, season with salt and ground black pepper, mix together thoroughly. Spread over the top of the cooked spinach and roll up into a cylinder. Serve hot or cold in slices.

☐   ☐   ☐

Broccoli fritters

⏱ 45 min   ♨ 2–3 min

Step	Commodity	1 portion	10 portions	
1	Broccoli	200 g	2 kg	Trim, discard the root and any damaged broccoli and cut into florets. Place in a saucepan of boiling salted water, return to the boil and simmer for 10 minutes. Refresh immediately and drain. Cover and place in the fridge.
2	Flour	25 g	250 g	Place in a clean bowl.
	Vegetable oil	5 ml	50 ml	Add.
	Water	30 ml	300 ml	Add and mix together well.
	Egg white*	½	5	Place in a clean bowl and whisk to a stiff meringue. Fold into the batter. Use immediately.
3	Plain flour	15 g	150 g	Place on a tray and season with salt and ground pepper. Mix together well. Give the broccoli a light coating of flour and then pass through the batter. Deep fry at 180°C for 2–3 minutes approximately. Drain onto absorbent paper, then onto a serving dish.

*The egg whites are only whisked up just before use as the longer the batter lays about the more likely the meringue will collapse and ruin the batter.

NOTE: Serve with a tomato sauce.

☐   ☐   ☐

Alternative batter

Step	Commodity	1 portion	10 portions		⌣ 15 min
1	Self-raising flour	20 g	200 g	Sift into a clean bowl and add a pinch of salt.	
2	Water/ soya milk	25 ml	250 ml	Add to the flour and whisk to a smooth paste. Cover and leave for 10 minutes before using.	

☐   ☐   ☐

Tagliatelle with cheese and nuts

Step	Commodity	1 portion	10 portions		⌣ 30 min ♨ 30 min
1	Tagliatelle	100 g	1 kg	Plunge into a saucepan of boiling salted water with a teaspoon of oil. Return to the boil and simmer for 10–12 minutes or until the pasta is *al dente*. Refresh and drain.	
2	Soya cheese	25 g	250 g	Grate into a bowl.	
	Walnuts	25 g	250 g	Chop finely and add.	
	Chopped sage	pinch	2 tsp	Add and mix together.	
3	Vegetable oil	5 ml	50 ml	Place in a suitably sized frying pan and heat. Add the tagliatelle and nut mixture, allowing the cheese to melt. Season with salt and black pepper. Serve hot.	
	Walnuts	5 g	50 g	Wash, chop and sprinkle over the pasta.	
	Chopped parsley	pinch	2 tsp	Sprinkle over the top.	

☐   ☐   ☐

20

Fried cornmeal cakes

Step	Commodity	1 portion	10 portions		⌣ 30 min ♨ 45 min
1	Water	250 ml	2½ litre	Place in a saucepan, season with salt and boil.	
	Cornmeal flour	65 g	650 g	Gradually add and mix thoroughly with a wooden spoon. Simmer gently for 20–30 minutes or until the mixture leaves the side fo the saucepan.	
	Cheese	75 g	750 g	Grate and add to the mixture. Turn out onto a clean surface to cool. Shape like fishcakes.	
2	Olive oil	5 ml	50 ml	Place in a frying pan and heat. Add the cornmeal cakes in 'batches' and cook for 2–3 minutes on each side. Serve with tomato sauce.	

☐   ☐   ☐

Accompaniments

Hot potatoes with dill

Step	Commodity	1 portion	10 portions				
					⏲ 30 min		♨ 20 min
1	Potatoes	150 g	1½ kg	Peel, wash, cut into 1 cm dice. Place in a saucepan and cover with water. Bring to the boil and simmer for 10 minutes. Drain away the water.			
	Spring onions	10 g	100 g	Wash, trim and discard the root and other leaves. Cut into thin slices and add to the potatoes.			
	Chopped dill	pinch	1 tbsp	Add.			
	Sour cream	15 ml	150 ml	Add and mix together well. Place in a pre-heated service dish and serve immediately.			

☐ ☐ ☐

Fried masala potatoes

Step	Commodity	1 portion	10 portions				
					⏲ 30 min		♨ 20 min
1	New potatoes	150 g	1½ kg	Wash thoroughly and cut into 2 cm pieces.			
	Vegetable ghee	10 g	100 g	Place in a suitably sized saucepan and heat. Add the potatoes and cook gently for 7 minutes, stirring from time to time to prevent burning.			
2	Cumin seeds	½ tsp	5 tsp	Place in a liquidiser.			
	Coriander seeds	½ tsp	5 tsp	Add.			
	Garam masala	pinch	2 tsp	Add.			
	Root ginger	5 g	50 g	Peel and add.			
	Garlic	½ clove	5 cloves	Peel and add.			
	Onions	15 g	150 g	Peel, remove the root and cut in half. Add, along with 1 tbsp of water and purée to a smooth paste. Pour over the potatoes, mix in well and continue cooking for 6–7 minutes.			
	Chilli powder	pinch	1 tsp	Add.			
	Turmeric	pinch	2 tsp	Add.			
	Yoghurt	50 ml	500 ml	Pour over the potatoes and mix together well. cook for a further 5 minutes. Place in a pre-heated serving dish.			
	Chopped parsley	pinch	2 tsp	Sprinkle over the top and serve.			

☐ ☐ ☐

Cucumber with rosemary

Step	Commodity	1 portion	10 portions		30 min	15 min
1	Cucumber	100 g	1 kg	Wash, peel, cut in half lengthways. Cut in quarters and then into 5 cm lengths. Place on a dish, sprinkle with salt and leave for 30 minutes.		
2	Soya margarine	5 g	50 g	Place in a frying pan and heat.		
	Onions	15 g	150 g	Peel, cut in half and finely dice. Add and sweat for 2–3 minutes without cooking. Add the cucumber pieces.		
	Chopped rosemary	½ tsp	5 tsp	Add.		
	Sugar	pinch	1 tsp	Add and continue cooking gently for 5 minutes.		
	Soured cream	15 ml	150 ml	Pour over the cucumber and place in a pre-heated serving dish. Garnish with chopped rosemary.		

☐ ☐ ☐

Fried okra with green chillies

Step	Commodity	1 portion	10 portions		30 min	25 min
1	Okra	100 g	1 kg	Wash and trim both ends.		
	Vegetable ghee	5 g	50 g	Place in a suitably sized frying pan and heat.		
	Onion	15 g	150 g	Peel, cut in half and finely dice. Add to hot fat and fry for 1 minute		
	Green chillies	½	5	Remove and discard the stalk and seeds. Cut into thin slices and add to the frying pan along with the okra. Cook for 15 minutes stirring constantly. Place in a pre-heated serving dish.		

☐ ☐ ☐

Baked fennel

Step	Commodity	1 portion	10 portions		30 min	15 min
1	Fennel	150 g	1½ kg	Trim the base and the top stems. Retain the feathery green tops. Cut the fennel into quarters. Place in boiling salted water for 5 minutes. Refresh and drain.		
2	Soya margarine	10 g	100 g	Melt and pour into an ovenproof dish.		
	Lemon	½	5	Grate the rind and sprinkle over the margarine. Cut the lemon in half and pour the strained lemon juice over the grated rind. Arrange the fennel on top. Season with salt and pepper. Cover with a tight-fitting lid and place in a pre-heated oven (160°C) for 1 hour or until the fennel is tender. Serve in the ovenproof dish. Garnish with the fennel tops.		

☐ ☐ ☐

20

Broccoli sauce

Step	Commodity	1 portion	10 portions	
1	Broccoli	50 g	500 g	Wash, trim and remove the stalk and damaged leaves. Place in a saucepan of boiling salted water. Bring to the boil and simmer for 12 minutes. Remove, refresh and drain. Place in a liquidiser.
	Sunflower seeds	10 g	100 g	Add.
	Sementa	35 ml	350 ml	Add.
	Lemon juice	5 ml	50 ml	Add and blend to a smooth texture. Season with salt and pepper. Strain and heat gently for use.

⌣ 1 hr   ♨ 15 min

☐   ☐   ☐

Barbecued kidney beans

Step	Commodity	1 portion	10 portions	
1	Kidney beans	75 g	750 g	Place in a clean bowl and cover completely with water. Leave to soak overnight. Drain away the water and rinse beans well in cold running water. Place in a suitably sized saucepan and cover with 3 times as much water. Fast boil for 10 minutes to kill the toxins, then simmer for 30 minutes. Drain and place in an ovenproof dish.
2	Tomato juice	250 ml	2½ litres	Pour over the beans.
	Soy sauce	5 ml	50 ml	Add.
	Onion	15 g	150 g	Peel, remove root, cut in half, dice finely and add.
	Honey	1 tsp	10 tsp	Add.
	Tomato purée	5 g	50 g	Add.
	Chilli pepper	pinch	1 tsp	Add.
	Mustard	¼ tsp	2½ tsp	Add.
	Yeast extract	¼ tsp	2½ tsp	Add and mix together well. Bring to the boil and cover with a lid. Place in a pre-heated oven (160°C) for 2½ hours or until the beans are tender. Season with salt and ground pepper.
3	Chopped parsley	pinch	2 tsp	Sprinkle over the top and serve.

⌣ Overnight   ♨ 3 hr

☐   ☐   ☐

Marinaded mushrooms

8 hr

Step	Commodity	1 portion	10 portions	
1	Button mushrooms	100 g	1 kg	Wash, trim the stalks and place in a suitably sized bowl.
2	White wine vinegar	10 ml	100 ml	Pour into a jug.
	Dry English mustard	pinch	½ tsp	Add to vinegar.
	Sugar	pinch	1 tsp	Add to jug.
	Salad oil	25 ml	250ml	Add and season with salt and pepper. Whisk well and pour over the mushrooms. Cover and place in the refrigerator for 8 hours. Drain into a serving dish.
	Chopped parsley	pinch	1 tsp	Sprinkle over the top.

☐   ☐   ☐

Grated raw vegetables with garlic dressing

1 hr

Step	Commodity	1 portion	10 portions	
1	Carrot	50 g	500 g	Peel, grate and place in a bowl.
	Courgettes	50 g	500 g	Peel, grate and add to the carrots and mix.
	Celeriac	50 g	500 g	Peel, grate and add to the other ingredients.
	Lemon juice	5 ml	50 ml	Pour over to prevent the celeriac from discolouring.
	Raw beetroot	50 g	500 g	Peel, grate and add. Mix well together.
2	Olive oil	25 ml	250 ml	Pour into a clean bowl.
	White wine vinegar	10 ml	100 ml	Add.
	Mustard	pinch	1 tsp	Add.
	Garlic	½ clove	5 cloves	Peel, crush to a purée with salt and add.
	Sugar	pinch	1 tsp	Add and whisk thoroughly. Pour over the vegetables and leave to marinade for 30 minutes before serving.
	Chopped parsley	pinch	2 tsp	Sprinkle over the top.

☐   ☐   ☐

20

Desserts

Fruit flambé

Step	Commodity	1 portion	10 portions		🍳 1 hr	♨ 30 min
1	Pineapple	100 g	1 kg	Prepare the pineapple by removing and discarding the stalk, skin and core. Cut the flesh into 1 cm cubes.		
	Dried figs	25 g	250 g	Cut into coarse shreds and scatter into the pineapple cubes.		
	Lemon juice	5 ml	50 ml	Pour over the fruits.		
	Demerara sugar	25 g	250 g	Add.		
	Mixed spices	pinch	1 tsp	Sprinkle over the top.		
	Rum (optional)	10 ml	100 ml	Add.		
	Soya margarine	10 g	100 g	Melt and pour over the other ingredients. Mix together well. Spoon into an ovenproof dish, cover and place in a pre-heated oven (200°C) for 30 minutes or until the fruit is tender. Serve hot.		

☐ ☐ ☐

Cinnamon pears with wine and honey

Step	Commodity	1 portion	10 portions		🍳 45 min	♨ 40 min
1	White wine*	20 ml	200 ml	Pour into a bowl.		
	Honey	10 ml	100 ml	Add to wine.		
	Cinnamon	pinch	1 tsp	Add and mix together.		
2	Margarine	10 g	100 g	Place in a suitably sized pan and heat gently.		
	Breadcrumbs	25 g	250 g	Add and remove from the heat.		
	Demerara sugar	10 g	100 g	Add.		
	Cinnamon	pinch	1 tsp	Add and mix well together.		
3	Dessert pears	1	10	Remove the stalks and cut down the centre longways. Remove the core.		
	Margarine	5 g	50 g	Melt and brush into an ovenproof dish. Arrange the pears on top, flat side down. Pour over the wine and honey mixture. Sprinkle the breadcrumbs over the dish and place in a pre-heated oven (185°C) for 30–40 minutes. Serve hot.		

* Sherry or vermouth may be used instead.

☐ ☐ ☐

Cakes

Carob and nut cake

Use 2 × 20 cm tins for 10 portions

Step	Commodity	1 portion	10 portions	⏲ 1½ hr 🍲 30 min ≋ 180°C
1	Wholemeal flour	15 g	150 g	Place in a bowl.
	Carob powder	5 g	50 g	Add, along with a pinch of salt, and sieve together twice. Mix the bran back into the flour.
	Orange rind	½	5	Remove the pith and cut into julienne. Add to the flour.
2	Margarine	25 g	250 g	Place in a bowl.
	Sugar	20 g	200 g	Add and beat until creamy in texture and pale in colour.
	Egg yolks	1	10	Whisk and gradually add to the creamed mixture. Gradually add the flour mixture.
	Orange juice	5 ml	50 ml	Add and mix in well.
3	Egg whites	1	10	Whisk to a stiff meringue, carefully fold into the cake mixture. Place in the prepared cake tin(s), two-thirds fill and bake in a pre-heated oven (180°C) for 25–30 minutes. Test for dampness in the centre of the cake(s). Remove when cooked, turn out on to a wire rack and allow to cool completely.
4	Carob bars	25 g	150 g	Break into a saucepan.
	Orange juice	5 ml	50 ml	Add and heat gently to melt. Remove and allow to cold.
	Margarine	10 g	100 g	Place in a bowl and soften. Add the carob and orange mix and blend together. Spread over the top of the cake with a palette knife.
	Shelled walnuts	15 g	150 g	Chop finely and use to decorate the cake.

□   □   □

20

475

Carrot cake

Use 1 x 20 cm tin per 10 portions

Step	Commodity	1 portion	10 portions		⌣ 1½ hr	♨ 1½ hr	≋ 180°C
1	S R wholemeal flour	30 g	300 g	Place in a bowl.			
	Sugar	30 g	300 g	Add to flour			
	Vegetable oil	25 ml	250 ml	Add.			
	Eggs	½	5	Whisk together and add.			
	Carrots	50 g	500 g	Peel, wash, grate and add.			
	Lemon juice	5 ml	50 ml	Add.			
	Lemon rind	¼	1	Finely grad and add to the mixture.			
	Shelled walnuts	15 g	150 g	Chop finely and add. Beat the ingredients together well.*			
3	Honey	1 tbsp	10 tbsp	Incorporate into the mix here.			
	Demerara sugar	10 g	100 g	Sprinkle over the top. Place in the baking tin and bake in a pre-heated oven (180°C) for 1½ hours. Remove and turn out onto a wire rack. Allow to go cold.			
3	Quark	15 g	150 g	Place in a bowl.			
	Honey	1 tbsp	10tbsp	Add to the quark and mix well together. Spread over the top of the cake.			
	Shelled walnuts	1	10	Use to garnish.			

* If the mixture is too thick add a little water or milk to take it to dropping consistency (where it easily drops off the spoon).

☐   ☐   ☐

Drinks

Yoghurt drink

Step	Commodity	1 portion	10 portions		⌣ 10 min
1	Bananas	1	10	Peel and place in a liquidiser.	
	Wheatgerm	10 g	100 g	Add to bananas.	
	Orange juice	50 ml	500 ml	Add.	
	Egg yolks	1	10	Add.	
	Yoghurt	100 ml	1½ litres	Add and purée until it is smooth. Chill for 1 hour before serving.	

NOTE: This drink may be made using pineapples, oranges, peaches or apricots.

☐   ☐   ☐

Citric drink

Step	Commodity	1 portion	10 portions		20 min
1	Fruit juice*	100 ml	1 litre	Place in a liquidiser.	
	Eggs	1	10	Add.	
	Honey	15 ml	150 ml	Add.	
	Wheatgerm	5 g	50 g	Add and purée until it is smooth. Chill for 1 hour before serving.	

* Citrus fruit juice: Lemon, orange, grapefruit.

☐   ☐   ☐

Tomato and yoghurt drink

Step	Commodity	1 portion	10 portions		20 min
1	Tomatoes	2	20	Remove and discard the stalks and eyes. Make a narrow incision in the bottoms. Place in boiling water for 10 seconds. Remove, refresh and discard the skins and seeds. Place in a liquidiser.	
	Yoghurt	75 ml	750 ml	Add to liquidiser.	
	Lemon juice	½ tsp	5 tsp	Add.	
	Tabasco sauce	few drops	1 tsp	Add.	
	Paprika	pinch	1 tsp	Add and purée until the mixture is smooth. Chill for 1 hour before serving.	
	Mint leaves	1	10	Use to garnish the drink.	

☐   ☐   ☐

Carrot and orange drink

Step	Commodity	1 portion	10 portions		20 min
1	Carrots	100 g	1 kg	Peel, wash, slice and place in a saucepan.	
	Orange juice	150 ml	1½ litres	Pour over the carrots, bring to the boil and simmer for 20 minutes or until the carrots are cooked. Place the carrots and orange juice in a liquidiser. Purée until the mixture is smooth. Allow to chill for 1 hour before serving. Half fill a glass with the mixture and fill up with an equal amount of soda water.	

☐   ☐   ☐

21

TRADITIONAL BRITISH AND IRISH COOKERY

Virtually every corner of the United Kingdom and Ireland yields fine products and produce. There are cheeses from Stilton, Cheshire, Cheddar, Lancashire, Leicester, Wensleydale, Gloucester, Caerphilly and Derby; beef and salmon from Scotland and Ireland; lamb from Wales; game from Hampshire and the Scottish Highlands; cured hams from York, Cookstown and Cumberland; smoked fish from the Isle of Man and Arbroath, Scotland; and fruit and vegetables from Kent, the garden of England.

This chapter only includes dishes peculiar to the regions and does not include general dishes that may use produce from a particular region, for example, Aberdeen Angus fillet steak, Welsh lamb, roast rib of Irish beef, and Scottish salmon etc.

English regional cookery

RECIPES FROM NORTHERN ENGLAND

Tripe and onions

🥄 15 min ♨ 2 hr

Step	Commodity	1 portion	10 portions	
1	Dressed tripe	150 g	1½ kg	Wash and cut into 5 cm squares. Place in a suitably sized saucepan.
	Cold water	2 ml	2 litres	Pour over the tripe (ensure that the tripe is covered with water). Bring to the boil and simmer for 10 minutes. Drain and discard the water. Return the tripe to the saucepan.
2	Onions	75 g	750 g	Peel, cut into thin slices and place with the tripe. Season with salt, pepper and a pinch of nutmeg.
	Milk	150 ml	1½ litres	Pour over the tripe. Return to the heat, bring to the boil and simmer for 1½ hours, or until the tripe is tender.
3	Butter	25 g	250 g	Add and allow to melt. Correct the seasoning and serve.

NOTE: The tripe cooking liquor may be drained and lightly thickened with a white roux (see Chapter 4: Boiling and simmering).

☐   ☐   ☐

Potted char

Step	Commodity	1 portion	10 portions		30 min	45 min
1	Medium char	1	10	Clean, prepare and wash. Dry with a clean cloth or kitchen paper. Season inside and outside with salt and pepper.		
	Ground mace	pinch	1 tsp	Sprinkle inside and over the top of the fish.		
	Ground nutmeg	pinch	1 tsp	Sprinkle inside and over the top of the fish.		
	Ground cloves	pinch	1 tsp	Sprinkle inside and over the top of the fish. Wrap in buttered greaseproof paper and secure. Place in a suitably sized oven-proof dish. Cover with water and simmer for 35 minutes. Remove and allow to cool. Remove the skin and bones and discard. Flake the fish into a bowl and correct the seasoning. Divide and portion into pots.		
	Butter	30 g	300 g	Melt and clarify. Pour over the fish and allow to set. Chill before use. Serve with lemon wedge, brown bread and butter.		

NOTE: Char is a rare fish caught only in the deepest water of the Lake District. Trout may be used if char is not available. Peeled Morecambe Bay shrimps (100 g per portion) or cooked salmon may also be potted in this manner.

☐   ☐   ☐

Fish cakes

Step	Commodity	1 portion	10 portions		30 min	45 min
1	Cooked fish*	50 g	500 g	Flake into a bowl.		
	Potatoes	35 g	350 g	Peel, wash, cut into small pieces and place in a saucepan of cold water. Season with salt and pepper, bring to the boil and cook for 20 minutes. Remove, drain, dry and sieve. Add to the flaked fish and season with salt and pepper.		
	Egg yolk	¼ equiv	2½	Add and mix thoroughly.		
	Chopped parsley	½ tsp	5 tsp	Add.		
	Butter	10 g	100 g	Melt, add and mix well. Shape into 1 cm thick × 4 cm rounds and allow to cool.		
2	Flour	5 g	50 g	Season with salt and pepper and place on a tray.		
	Egg whites	¼ equiv	2½	Whisk and place in a bowl.		
	Breadcrumbs	25 g	250 g	Place on a tray. Pass the fish cakes through the flour, egg white and breadcrumbs.		
3	Cooking oil	2.5 ml	25 ml	Place in a thick-bottomed frying pan and heat. Add the fishcakes and fry on both sides for 5 minutes or until golden brown. Remove and serve hot. Serve with parsley or anchovy sauce. Accompany with buttered bread.		

* Free from skin and bones.

☐   ☐   ☐

Fish and chips

Step	Commodity	1 portion	10 portions	⏲ 1 hr 20 min ≋ Blanching 170°C Frying 180°C
1	Plain flour	40 g	400 g	Place in a bowl.
	Bicarbonate of soda	¼ tsp	2½ tsp	Add, along with a pinch of salt. Sieve three times into the bowl. Make a well.
	Egg	¼	2½	Break into the well.
	Water	60 ml	600 ml	Add and whisk to a smooth batter. Cover and allow to stand for 1 hour.
2	Large potatoes	200 g	2 kg	Peel and cut into chips 6 cm long and 1 cm thick. Wash to remove the starch. Dry in a clean cloth or kitchen paper. Blanch in deep fat for 10 minutes to soften. Remove, drain well and arrange on a tray. Turn the temperature of the oil up to the frying temperature.
3	Cod/ haddock fillet	1 × 150 g	10 × 150 g	Skin, wash and dry. Pass through seasoned flour and then through the batter. Deep fry in the pre-heated fat for 10 minutes or until the fish is cooked and golden brown. Cook the blanched chips in a basket alongside the fish. Remove the chips when they are golden brown. Serve with mushy peas (*see* below). Add salt and vinegar to taste.

☐   ☐   ☐

Mushy peas

Step	Commodity	1 portion	10 portions	⏲ overnight 2½ hr
1	Dried marrowfat peas	100 g	1 kg	Wash, drain and place in a bowl. Cover with water and leave to soak overnight. Drain and rewash. Place in a suitably sized saucepan. Cover with water (sufficient to cover the peas by 4 cm).
	Bicarbonate of soda	⅒ tsp	1 tsp	Add, bring to the boil and simmer for the appropriate time or until the peas are tender and mushy. Place in a bain-marie to prevent the bottom from burning. Serve with fried fish and chips and roast meats.

☐   ☐   ☐

Peas pudding

Step	Commodity	1 portion	10 portions		Overnight	2½ hr
1	Dried split yellow peas	100 g	1 kg	Wash, drain and place in a bowl. Cover with water and leave to soak overnight. Drain and rewash. Place in a suitably sized saucepan. Cover with water (sufficient to cover the peas by 4 cm). Add, bring to the boil and simmer for 1 hour. Remove and pass through a sieve or a liquidiser into a clean bowl.		
2	Egg	¼	2½	Break into a bowl and add to the sieved peas. Mix thoroughly together.		
	Butter	15 g	150 g	Add and mix in. Season with salt and pepper. Place the peas pudding into an oven-proof dish. Cover and bake for another hour or until the peas are tender.		

NOTE: Serve with boiled beef or boiled gammon ham.

☐   ☐   ☐

Pan haggerty

Step	Commodity	1 portion	10 portions		45 min	45 min
1	Lard/bacon fat	15 g	150 g	Melt and heat gently in a thick-bottomed frying pan.		
	Potatoes	150 g	1½ kg	Peel, cut into thin slices and layer half of the potatoes on the bottom of the frying pan. Season with salt and pepper.		
	Onions	50 g	500 g	Peel, slice thinly and layer on top of the potatoes.		
	Cheese	25 g	250 g	Grate and sprinkle over the top. Layer the remaining potatoes on top. Brush with melted lard/bacon fat and place in a pre-heated oven for the required time or until the potatoes are cooked and golden brown. Turn out onto a suitably sized plate and cut into portions. Serve hot.		

NOTE: Serve with boiled gammon ham or roast meats.

☐   ☐   ☐

Barnsley chop

Step	Commodity	1 portion	10 portions		30 min	20 min
1	Barnsley cut chop	1 × 250 g	10 × 250 g	Trim and season with salt and pepper.		
	Lard or dripping	15 g	150 g	Melt and heat in a thick-bottomed frying pan. Add the chops and cook for the required time. Serve hot with jacket potato and salad.		

NOTE: A Barnsley cut chop is a 2 cm chop cut across the whole of the loin.

☐   ☐   ☐

Lancashire hotpot

Step	Commodity	1 portion	10 portions	
				🍳 45 min 🍲 2½ hr ≋ 160°C
1	Lamb/ mutton shoulder chops	2 × 125 g	20 × 125 g	Trim, remove the gristle and season with salt and pepper.
	Dripping	15 g	150 g	Place in a thick-bottomed frying pan and heat. Add the chops and seal on both sides. Place in a deep-sided oven-proof dish.
2	Onions	100 g	1 kg	Peel, cut into thin slices and lay one third on top of the chops.
3	Potatoes	200 g	2 kg	Peel, cut into thin slices and wash. Lay one third on top of onions. Brush with a little melted butter and season with salt and pepper. Repeat the process with the onions and the potatoes ending with a layer of potatoes.
4	Brown mutton stock	150 ml	1½ litres	Pour over the hotpot two-thirds of the way up. Cover with a lid and place in a pre-heated oven for 2 hours. Remove the lid and return to the oven for 30 minutes to brown. Serve in the earthenware dish. Accompany with pickled red cabbage.

NOTE: Traditionally Lancashire hotpot was served with the addition of 2 oysters per portion.

☐ ☐ ☐

Toad in the hole (traditional)

Step	Commodity	1 portion	10 portions	
				🍳 20 min 🍲 30 min ≋ 200°C
1	Rump steak	75 g	750 g	Remove the fat and gristle. Cut into 2 cm dice, place in a bowl.
	Lambs' kidneys	½	5	Skin, core and trim. Wash, dry and cut into quarters. Add to the steak.
	Onions	25 g	250 g	Peel, finely dice and add.
2	Plain flour	20 g	200 g	Sieve into a suitably sized bowl.
	Egg	⅓	3	Break and add.
	Milk	80 ml	800 ml	Add gradually and whisk to a smooth batter (a little more milk may be required). Cover and place to the side.
3	Dripping	5 g	50 g	Place in the bottom of a large roasting tray or large Yorkshire pudding dish(es). Place in a pre-heated oven or on top of the stove and heat until it begins to smoke. Add the appropriate portion of meat. Pour in the appropriate amount of batter and return to the oven. Bake for the required time or until the pudding is golden brown and well risen (do not open the oven door as this will cause the pudding to deflate).

NOTE: In London, toad in the hole is made with lamb chop and kidneys.

☐ ☐· ☐

Shepherd's pie

Step	Commodity	1 portion	10 portions					
					🍲 1 hr	♨ 45 min	〜 160°C	
1	Potatoes	150 g	1½ kg	Peel, wash and cut into small pieces. Place in a saucepan of cold water. Season with salt and pepper, bring to the boil and simmer for 20 minutes. Remove, drain and dry out. Mash with a fork and correct the seasoning.				
	Butter	10 g	100 g	Add and mix thoroughly. Allow to cool.				
2	Butter	5 g	50 g	Melt in a thick-bottomed saucepan.				
	Onions	15 g	150 g	Peel, dice finely and add. Cook until light brown.				
	Minced lamb	150 g	1½ kg	Add, season with salt and pepper and fry until the meat is golden brown.				
	Plain flour	2½ kg	25 g	Sprinkle over the mince and mix in well.				
	Brown mutton stock	50 ml	500 ml	Add and mix to form a smooth sauce. Pour into a suitably sized oven-proof dish and allow to cool. Spread or pipe over the mashed potatoes. Place in a pre-heated oven for 30 minutes or until the potato is well browned on top. Serve hot.				

NOTE: Shepherd's pie may be made with left over cooked meat.

☐   ☐   ☐

Pot roast meat (veal, lamb, venison, whole pheasant, chicken and duck)

Pot roast is a traditional English method of cookery which is similar to French 'poêle'. Only tender joints of meat, poultry or game may be pot roasted. Traditionally carried out in a cauldron over an open fire, the meat, which was regularly turned, was rested on a trivet of bones with roughly cut root vegetables and herbs for flavour. Some stock may have been used to prevent the item from burning and a lid was used to aid the cooking process. *See* Pot Roasting.

☐   ☐   ☐

Beef cobbler

Step	Commodity	1 portion	10 portions				
					🍲 30 min	♨ 45 min	
1	Butter	5 g	50 g	Melt in a thick-bottomed saucepan.			
	Onions	15 g	150 g	Peel, dice finely and add. Cook until light brown.			
	Minced beef	150 g	1½ kg	Add, season with salt and pepper and fry until the meat is golden brown.			
	Plain flour	2½ kg	25 g	Sprinkle over the mince and mix in well.			
	Brown mutton stock	50 ml	500 ml	Add and mix to form a smooth sauce. Pour into a suitably sized ovenproof dish and allow to cool.			
2	Self-raising flour	50 g	500 g	Sieve into a clean bowl.			
	Butter	15 g	150 g	Add and rub into a sandy texture.			
	Egg	¼ equiv	2½	Add and mix in.			
	Milk	20 ml	200 ml	Add and form a smooth dough (more or less milk may be required). Roll out 1 cm thick and cut into 3 cm scone shapes. Place the scones in overlapping circles on top of the cooked mince. Brush with milk and place in a pre-heated oven for 20 minutes or until the scones are well risen and browned. Serve hot or cold.			

Lobscouse, 'Scouse' (Liverpool stew)

Step	Commodity	1 portion	10 portions	⤵ Overnight ♨ 2½–3 hr
1	Marrowfat peas	50 g	500 g	Wash, place into a clean bowl and cover with water. Soak overnight.
2	Dripping	10 g	100 g	Melt in a suitably sized saucepan and heat.
	Diced stewing meat	100 g	1 kg	Add to the hot dripping and brown on all sides. Reduce the heat.
	Potatoes	100 g	1 kg	Peel, wash, slice and add.
	Onion	25 g	250 g	Peel, cut into medium sized dice and add.
	Carrot	25 g	250 g	Peel, slice thinly and add. Seal the vegetables. Drain the peas and add.
	Dried thyme	pinch	1 tsp	Add.
	Pearl barley	5 g	50 g	Wash and add. Season with salt and pepper.
	Water	200 ml	2 litres	Add, bring to the boil and simmer for the required time or until the meat is tender (ensure that the water covers the meat during cooking). Skim as required. Correct the seasoning and serve.

☐   ☐   ☐

Yorkshire pudding

Step	Commodity	1 portion	10 portions	⤵ 30 min ♨ 40 min ≋ 220°C
1	Plain flour	20 g	200 g	Sieve into a suitably-sized bowl.
	Egg	⅓	3	Break and add.
	Milk	80 ml	800 ml	Add gradually and whisk to a smooth batter (a little more milk may be required). Cover and place to the side.
2	Dripping	5 g	50 g	Place in the bottom of a Yorkshire(s) pudding dish. Place in a pre-heated oven or on top of the stove and heat until it begins to smoke. Pour in the appropriate amount of batter and return to the oven. Bake for the required time or until the pudding is golden brown and well risen (do not open the oven door as this will cause the pudding to deflate).
3	Thickened gravy	150 ml	1½ litres	Heat and pour over the pudding.

NOTES: Yorkshire puddings are also used to accompany roast beef.

Traditionally Yorkshire puddings were served with a thickened roast gravy and served as a separate course before the main course.

☐   ☐   ☐

Witherslack damson cobbler

Step	Commodity	1 portion	10 portions				
				⏱ 30 min	🍲 1 hr	≋ 220°C	
1	Damsons	150 g	1½ kg	Wash and place in a suitably-sized saucepan.			
	Caster sugar	25 g	250 g	Add.			
	Water	½ tsp	5 tsp	Add, cover with a lid, bring to the boil and simmer gently for 30 minutes. Remove and place to the side to cool. Remove the stones. Place in a suitably sized oven-proof dish.			
2	Self-raising flour	50 g	500 g	Sieve into a clean bowl.			
	Butter	15 g	150 g	Add and rub into a sandy texture.			
	Egg	¼ equiv	2½	Add and mix in.			
	Milk	20 ml	200 ml	Add and form a smooth dough (more or less milk may be required). Roll out 1 cm thick and cut into 3 cm scone shapes. Place the scones in overlapping circles on top of the damsons. Brush with milk and place in a pre-heated oven for 20 minutes or until the scones are well risen and browned. Serve hot or cold.			

NOTE: Serve with double cream or custard.

☐   ☐   ☐

Yorkshire curd tarts

Step	Commodity	1 portion	10 portions				
				⏱ 1 hr	🍲 35 min	≋ 180°C	
1	Shortcrust pastry	25 g	250 g	Roll out ¼ cm thick and line the appropriate tartlet/patty tins, allowing 2 per portion. Flute the edges or use a fork.			
2	Butter	7.5 g	75 g	Place in a bowl and soften.			
	Caster sugar	5 g	50 g	Add and cream together.			
	Curd cheese	20 g	200 g	Add.			
	Currants	10 g	100 g	Add.			
	Eggs	¼	2½	Break into a bowl and beat. Add to the mixture.			
	Nutmeg	pinch	¼ tsp	Add and mix thoroughly. Pour into the pastry case and place in a pre-heated oven for the required time or until the filling is firm and has a golden brown surface.			

☐   ☐   ☐

Angels on horseback

Step	Commodity	1 portion	10 portions	
				🥣 1 hr 🍲 6 min
1	Lemon juice	10 ml	100 ml	Place in a bowl.
	Tabasco sauce	few drops	½ tsp	Add.
	Oysters	4	40	Remove from the shells and pass through the lemon juice.
2	Sliced bacon	2	20	Remove the rind and cut in half. Roll each oyster in a piece of bacon and secure with a cocktail stick. Place under a preheated salamander for 5–6 minutes. Do not overcook as the oysters will toughen. Garnish with watercress and serve.

NOTE: It is common practice to serve Angels on Horseback on sliced buttered toast (with crusts removed) as a savoury.

☐   ☐   ☐

Baked Cromer crab

Step	Commodity	1 portion	10 portions	
				🥣 2 hr 🍲 30 min ≋ 220°C
1	Cooked crabs	1	10	Remove the claws and legs and break open. Remove the white meat and place in a bowl. Discard the dead man's fingers and any green matter. Remove the brown meat and place with the other meat. Retain the shells and wash thoroughly.
	Breadcrumbs	10 g	100 g	Add to the meat.
	Lemon juice	½ tbsp	5 tbsp	Add to the meat.
	Vinegar	½ tbsp	5 tbsp	Add, season with salt, pepper and cayenne pepper and mix thoroughly. Arrange in the clean shell.
	Cheese	15 g	150 g	Grate and sprinkle over the top of the crab.
	Breadcrumbs	5 g	50 g	Sprinkle over the cheese and place in a pre-heated oven for 15–20 minutes or until the cheese is brown.

☐   ☐   ☐

Norfolk salt beef and floaters (dumplings)

Step	Commodity	1 portion	10 portions	
1	Water	½ litre	5 litres	Place in a suitably sized bowl.
	Saltpetre	7.5 g	75 g	Add.
	Sea salt	75 g	750 g	Add.
	Brown sugar	40 g	400 g	Add and mix thoroughly together.
2	Silverside of beef*	300 g	3 kg	Secure with string, place in the brine mixture and cover completely. Pickle for 5 days. Remove and wash. Place in a suitably sized saucepan.
	Carrots	50 g	500 g	Peel, turn with knife and add.
	Button onions	3	30	Peel, trim the root and add.
	Bayleaves	½	1	Add.
	Black peppercorns	2	20	Add.
	Bouquet garni		1	Add, cover with cold water, bring to the boil and simmer for 2½ hours.
3	Plain flour	150 g	1½ kg	Sieve into a bowl and add to pinch of salt.
	Milk	100 ml	1 litre	Warm slightly.
	Butter	10 g	100 g	Melt and add.
	Dried yeast	4 g	40 g	Add.
	Castor sugar	½ tsp	5 tsp	Add and mix thoroughly until the sugar and yeast have dissolved. Allow to stand for 15 minutes. Add to the flour and mix to a firm dough. Knead for 10 minutes. Place in a bowl and allow to ferment for 1 hour. Divide into the appropriate portions and roll into small balls. Allow to double in size. Place into a saucepan of boiling salted water, cover with a lid and cook for 15 minutes. Remove the meat from the saucepan and discard the string. Cut the meat into slices and arrange on a warm serving dish. Arrange the vegetables around the mat and place the cooked dumpling on the side. Strain the cooking liquor into a sauceboat and serve. Accompany with English mustard.

* Prepared.

□   □   □

Huntington fidget pie

Step	Commodity	1 portion	10 portions				
				⏲ 1½ hr	♨ 30 min	≋ 180°C	
1	Sliced bacon	175 g	1.75 kg	Remove the rind.			
	Onions	50 g	500 g	Peel and cut into thin slices.			
	Cooking apples	100 g	1 kg	Peel, remove the core and cut into thin slices. Place in a bowl of water and lemon juice. Lay alternate layers of the bacon, onion and apple in a buttered pie dish. Season each layer with salt and pepper and sprinkle with 1 tsp of castor sugar. Finish with a layer of bacon.			
	Thyme	pinch	1 sprig	Wash and sprinkle over the top.			
	White chicken stock	40 ml	400 ml	Pour over enough to cover the filling by two-thirds.			
2	Shortcrust pastry	60 g	600 g	Roll out ½ cm thick and place on top of the pie. Crimp the edges between two fingers and brush the surface with egg wash. Place in a pre-heated oven for the required time or until the pastry is golden brown.			

☐   ☐   ☐

Marlborough's Ipswich almond pudding

Step	Commodity	1 portion	10 portions				
				⏲ 1 hr	♨ 45 min	≋ 150°C	
1	Milk	100 ml	1 litre	Place in a suitably sized saucepan.			
	Double cream	50 ml	500 ml	Add to the milk and heat.			
	Breadcrumbs	15 g	150 g	Add to warm milk and cream and stir.			
	Castor sugar	15 g	150 g	Add.			
	Ground almonds	50 g	500 g	Add and stir into the other ingredients. Leave aside for 20 minutes.			
2	Eggs	1	10	Break into a bowl and whisk until the mixture forms peaks. Pour into the breadcrumb mixture and mix well. Place in a buttered oven-proof dish or dishes.			
	Butter	5 g	50 g	Cut into small pieces and place on top of the pudding. Arrange in a bain-marie and place in a pre-heated oven for 30 minutes. Serve with compote of fruit.			

☐   ☐   ☐

Syllabub

Step	Commodity	1 portion	10 portions		⤵ Overnight
1	White wine	40 ml	400 ml	Pour into a suitably sized bowl.	
	Orange	¼	2½	Remove the zest and blanch in boiling water for 1 minute. Refresh, dry and add to the wine. Squeeze the juice and pass through a strainer and add to the wine.	
	Sugar	10 g	100 g	Add and stir in. Cover and allow to marinade overnight.	
2	Double cream	75 ml	750 ml	Pour slowly into the wine mixture whisking continuously. Whisk until the mixture forms peaks. Pour into a serving glass and refrigerate for 1 hour. Sprinkle with a little nutmeg and serve.	

NOTE: Syllabub can also be made with cider, beer, brandy or sherry.

☐   ☐   ☐

Samphire

Samphire is an edible marsh plant. It is harvested in July and August. Sometimes known as the poor man's asparagus.

Step	Commodity	1 portion	10 portions		⤵ 30 min 🍲 20 min
1	Samphire	100 g	1 kg	Prepare and wash thoroughly. Place in a saucepan of slightly salted water with ground black pepper. Cook for 15 minutes. Drain well and serve.	

NOTE: Samphire may also be pickled raw in vinegar.

☐   ☐   ☐

21

Brown Windsor soup

Step	Commodity	1 portion	10 portions		⤵ 30 min 🍲 2 hr
1	Butter	10 g	100 g	Melt in a thick bottomed saucepan.	
	Onion	10 g	100 g	Peel, dice finely and add.	
	Carrot	10 g	100 g	Peel, dice finely and add.	
	Green of leek	10 g	100 g	Wash, trim, dice and add.	
	Coarsely minced beef	100 g	1 kg	Add and brown well.	
	Plain flour	15 g	150 g	Add and cook to a brown roux.	
	Brown beef stock	250 ml	2½ litres	Add a quarter and thicken. Add another quarter and bring to the boil. Add the remaining stock, bring to the boil and reduce to a simmer.	
	Bouquet garni	1 small	1 large	Tie on a piece of string and place in the soup. Simmer for 1½ hours. Remove the bouquet garni. Place in a blender and liquidise. Pass through a strainer and return to the heat in a clean saucepan.	
2	Cream sherry	½ tbsp	5 tbsp	Add to the soup just before serving.	

☐   ☐   ☐

Bedfordshire clanger

Step	Commodity	1 portion	10 portions	
				⏲ 1½ hr ♨ 2 hr
1	Butter	7½ g	75 g	Melt in a thick-bottomed frying pan and heat.
	Onions	25 g	250 g	Peel, dice finely and add. Cook until golden brown.
	Diced beef steak	100 g	1 kg	Add.
	Diced ox kidney	25 g	250 g	Add, season with salt and pepper and seal. Remove from the heat and allow to cool.
2	Suet pastry	150 g	1½ kg	Roll out into a rectangle ½ cm thick. Cut a thin strip off from the shorter end and place in the middle to divide the pastry in two. Spread the cold meat mixture on one half.
3	Cooking apples	100 g	1 kg	Peel, remove the core and cut into thin slices. Place in a bowl.
	Raisins	20 g	200 g	Add.
	Castor sugar	5 g	50 g	Add and mix well together. Place on the other half of the pastry. Roll up gently like a Swiss roll. One end being the meat and the other the sweet. Moisten and seal each end. Wrap loosely in buttered foil. Secure each end and place in a pre-heated steamer for 1½ hours. Serve the savoury end first with suitable vegetables and gravy and the other end for 'afters' with custard.

☐   ☐   ☐

Oxford John

Step	Commodity	1 portion	10 portions	
				⏲ 1 hr ♨ 20 min
1	Leg of lamb steaks	1 × 150 g	10 × 150 g	Trim excess fat, season with salt, pepper and nutmeg.
2	Chopped parsley	½ tbsp	5 tbsp	Place on a tray.
	Chopped parsley	½ tbsp	5 tbsp	Add.
	Shallots	10 g	100 g	Peel, finely dice and add. Mix well together.
	Butter	10 g	100 g	Melt and place on another tray. Pass the steaks through the melted butter and then coat the steaks with the herb and onion mixture.
3	Cooking oil	5 ml	50 ml	Place in a thick-bottomed frying pan and heat. Add the steaks and cook for 6 minutes on both sides. Place in a dish and keep warm. Retain the cooking fat.
4	Plain flour	5 g	50 g	Add and cook to a brown roux.
	Brown mutton stock	50 ml	500 ml	Add a quarter and mix well, add another quarter and bring to the boil. Add the remaining stock, bring to the boil and simmer.
	Lemon juice	5 ml	50 ml	Add.
	Port	5 ml	50 ml	Add, mix well with the other ingredients. Season with salt and pepper. Return the steaks to the frying pan and simmer the steaks in the sauce for 10 minutes. Place the steaks in a serving dish and pour over the strained sauce. Sprinkle with finely chopped parsley.

☐   ☐   ☐

490

Poor Knights of Windsor

Step	Commodity	1 portion	10 portions		45 min	30 min
1	Slices of white bread	2	20	Remove the crusts and cut in half.		
	Castor sugar	15 g	150 g	Place in a bowl.		
	Milk	75 ml	750 ml	Add.		
	Cream sherry	½ tbsp	5 tbsp	Add, mix well together until the sugar has dissolved. Pour into a shallow dish.		
	Eggs	1	10	Break into a bowl and whisk. Dip the bread into the milk and sherry mixture and then into the egg mixture.		
2	Clarified butter	40 g	400 g	Melt and heat in a thick-bottomed frying pan. Add the bread in 'batches' and cook on both sides until golden brown. Drain well.		
3	Castor sugar	10 g	100 g	Place on a tray.		
	Cinnamon	pinch	2 tsp	Mix well with the sugar. Pass the fried bread through the flavoured sugar. Serve hot with strawberry or raspberry jam.		

☐ ☐ ☐

Richmond maids of honour

Step	Commodity	1 portion	10 portions		1 hr	20 min	200°C
1	Curd cheese	22.5 g	225 g	Place in a bowl.			
	Butter	7.5 g	75 g	Soften, add to the curd cheese and mix well together.			
2	Eggs	⅟₁₀	1	Break into a clean bowl.			
	Sugar	2 g	20 g	Add.			
	Ground almonds	½ tbsp	5 tbsp	Add.			
	Grated lemon rind	2 g	20 g	Add.			
	Nutmeg	pinch	½ tsp	Add.			
	Brandy	few drops	1 tsp	Add and beat thoroughly. Mix well with the butter and curd cheese.			
3	Puff pastry	22.5 g	225 g	Roll out ¼ cm thick and line the appropriate, greased pastry tins. Dock well with a fork. Half fill each with the curd mixture. Place in a pre-heated oven for the required time or until golden brown. Remove and allow to cool and set.			

☐ ☐ ☐

21

Hollygog pudding

Step	Commodity	1 portion	10 portions	⌣ 30 min ♨ 45 min ≋ 200°C
1	Plain flour	45 g	450 g	Sieve into a suitably sized bowl and add a pinch of salt.
	Lard	20 g	200 g	Cut into small pieces and add. Rub into form a coarse sandy texture.
	Milk	50 ml	500 ml	Add and mix to a smooth dough (more or less milk might be needed). Roll out into a 1 cm thick, rectangle on a floured surface.
	Golden syrup	1 tbsp	10 tbsp	Spread over the surface and roll up like a Swiss roll. Place in a greased baking tin and bake for 45 minutes or until golden brown. Remove, serve hot or cold with custard.

☐   ☐   ☐

RECIPES FROM THE WEST COUNTRY

Cornish crab soup

Step	Commodity	1 portion	10 portions	⌣ 45 min ♨ 1 hr
1	Butter	5 g	50 g	Place in a thick-bottomed saucepan and heat gently.
	Patna rice	10 g	100 g	Add and stir.
	Stock	10 ml	1½ litres	Add, bring to the boil and simmer for 15 minutes.
2	Milk	100 ml	1 litre	Add.
	Nutmeg	pinch	½ tsp	Add, season with salt and milled black pepper and return to the boil. Simmer for a further 10 minutes.
	Cooked and prepared crab	100 g	1 kg	Dice finely and add. Bring to the boil and simmer for a further 5 minutes. Place in a blender and liquidise. Return to the stove in a clean saucepan.
	Crab clawmeat	25 g	250 g	Chop finely and add. Return to the boil, reduce to a simmer. Correct the seasoning.
3	Cream	10 ml	100 ml	Pour into the soup, sprinkle with finely chopped parsley and serve. Do not reboil.

☐   ☐   ☐

Star gazey pie

Step	Commodity	1 portion	10 portions				
				⏲ 1 hr	🍲 55 min	≋ 200°C	
1	Eggs	1	10	Place in a saucepan of boiling water and boil for 10 minutes. Refresh and cool. Remove the shell, slice and place on the bottom of a buttered pie dish.			
	Herring	1	10	Clean the fish and fillet. Remove any tail or fin and wash. Season with salt and pepper. Place on top of the egg.			
	Onion	25 g	250 g	Peel, slice into thin rings and lay on top.			
	Bacon	25 g	250 g	Remove any rind and bone and discard. Cut into thin slices and sprinkle over the onion.			
2	Egg	½	5	Break into a bowl.			
	Cream	10 ml	100 ml	Add.			
	Chopped parsley	pinch	2 tsp	Add and whisk thoroughly. Pour over the fish.			
3	Puff pastry	50 g	500 g	Roll out ½ cm thick and place over the top of the dish. Pinch the edges of the pastry between two fingers. Brush with egg wash and place in a pre-heated oven for 45 minutes. Remove and serve.			

NOTE: Traditionally, the cleaned fish heads were set in the pastry and baked.

☐   ☐   ☐

Devonshire squab pie

Step	Commodity	1 portion	10 portions				
				⏲ 1 hr	🍲 50 min	≋ 200°C/150°C	
1	Cooking apples	100 g	1 kg	Peel, core and slice thinly. Place in a bowl of water and lemon juice.			
	Onion	50 g	500 g	Peel, slice into thin rings.			
	Boneless shoulder lamb	150 g	1½ kg	Remove excess fat and any gristle. Butter a suitably sized pie dish. Place layers of apple, onion and lamb. Season each layer with salt and pepper and a pinch of allspice. Finish with a layer of apples.			
	Castor sugar	5 g	50 g	Sprinkle over the top.			
	Cider	35 ml	350 ml	Pour over the other ingredients.			
2	Puff pastry	50 g	500 g	Roll out ½ cm thick and place over the top of the pie dish. Pinch the edges of the pastry between two fingers. Brush with egg wash and place in a pre-heated oven for 35 minutes at the high temperature. Reduce to the lower temperature and cook for 15 minutes. Remove and serve.			

☐   ☐   ☐

21

Glazed Wiltshire gammon

Step	Commodity	1 portion	10 portions			
				🥣 Overnight	♨ 3½ hr	🌫 220°C
1	Wiltshire gammon	200 g	2 kg	Soak in cold water overnight to remove the saltiness. Rinse and place in a suitably sized saucepan. Cover with cold water and boil for 3 hours. Remove and score the skin.		
2	Urchfont mustard	½ tbsp	5 tbsp	Place in a bowl.		
	Brown sugar	½ tbsp	5 tbsp	Add.		
	Cream	1 tbsp	10 tbsp	Add and mix thoroughly together. Spread over the gammon. Stud with whole cloves. Place in a pre-heated oven for 30 minutes. Baste regularly with the cooking juices. Remove and allow to cool. Serve hot or cold.		

☐   ·   ☐   ☐

Cornish pasties

Traditionally Cornish pasties contain turnips, potatoes and meat, and were made as a portable meal in one that was cooked the night before and taken to work in the pockets of tin miners of Pendeen, Boscaswell and St Agnes.

Step	Commodity	1 portion	10 portions			
				🥣 1½ hr	♨ 40 min	🌫 180°C
1	Swede	100 g	1 kg	Peel, wash, cut into ½ cm dice and place in a bowl.		
	Potatoes	100 g	1 kg	Peel, wash, cut into ½ cm dice and add to the swede.		
	Coarse minced beef	100 g	1 kg	Add.		
	Onion	25 g	250 g	Peel, finely dice and add.		
	Butter	5 g	50 g	Cut into small pieces and add. Season with salt and pepper and mix thoroughly together.		
2	Shortcrust pastry	75 g	750 g	Roll out into ¼ cm thick × 20 cm circles. Brush with water. Divide the meat mixture into portions and place the appropriate amount in the centre of the pastry. Fold the edges up to the centre so that the seam is halfway between the top and the side edges. Pinch the seams together to seal. Prick the surface with a fork to allow the cooking steam to escape. Brush with eggwash and arrange on greased baking trays. Place in a pre-heated oven for the required time. Serve hot or cold.		

☐   ☐   ☐

Somerset pork and apples in cider

Step	Commodity	1 portion	10 portions		⏱ 45 min 🍲 2 hr
1	Butter	5 g	50 g	Place in a thick-bottomed saucepan.
	Cooking oil	5 ml	50 ml	Add and heat.
	Onions	25 g	250 g	Peel, finely dice and add.
	Diced pork	150 g	1½ kg	Add and brown, reduce the heat.
	Cooking apples	50 g	500 g	Peel, remove the core and slice thinly. Add to the meat.
	Sage	pinch	½ tsp	Add and season with salt and pepper.
	Bayleaves	½	1	Add.
	Dry cider	100 ml	1 litre	Add, bring to the boil and simmer for 1½ hours, replenishing the cooking liquor if it evaporates too much.
	Clotted cream	1 tbsp	10 tbsp	Place in a bowl and add a little of the cooking liquor. Pour into the casserole and stir well. Do not reboil. Serve in a casserole dish. Sprinkle with finely chopped parsley.

☐   ☐   ☐

Wiltshire lardy cake

Step	Commodity	1 portion	10 portions		⏱ 2½ hr 🍲 40 min ≋ 200°C
1	Plain flour	50 g	500 g	Sieve into a suitably sized bowl and add a pinch of salt.
	Butter	5 g	50 g	Add and rub in.
	Milk	35 ml	350 ml	Warm gently. Remove from the heat.
	Castor sugar	2 g	20 g	Add.
	Dried yeast	2.5 g	25 g	Add and mix thoroughly. Place to the side for 15 minutes. Pour into the flour and mix to a smooth dough. Knead for 10 minutes. Place in a bowl, cover with a lid and leave to double in size. Roll out onto a floured table ½ cm thick.
2	Lard	12.5 g	125 g	Cut into small pea-size pieces. Place a third of the lard on the dough. Fold over both sides and roll out to the original size. Add another third and repeat the process. Place the remaining lard on top.
	Castor sugar	12.5 g	125 g	Sprinkle over the lard.
	Mixed fruit	15 g	150 g	Add.
	Mixed spice	pinch	2 tsp	Add, fold the sides of the pastry over and roll out. Place in a greased baking tin and bake for the required time. Remove from baking tin.
3	Golden syrup	2 ml	25 ml	Brush over the top. Serve hot or cold.

☐   ☐   ☐

21

Cornish fairings

Step	Commodity	1 portion	10 portions	
				🥄 30 min ♨ 20 min ≋ 190°C
1	Self-raising flour	10 g	100 g	Sieve into a bowl and add a pinch of salt.
	Ground ginger	pinch	1 tsp	Add.
	Allspice	pinch	1 tsp	Add.
	Cinnamon	pinch	1 tsp	Add.
	Castor sugar	½ tsp	5 tsp	Add.
	Butter	5 g	50 g	Add and rub in to form a sandy texture.
	Lemon rind	10 g	100 g	Add.
	Golden syrup	1 tsp	10 tsp	Warm and add. Shape into balls the size of walnuts and arrange 2 cm apart on a greased baking tray. Place in a pre-heated oven for the required time or until they are golden brown. Remove and allow to cool on a rack.

☐   ☐   ☐

Saffron cake

Step	Commodity	1 portion	10 portions	
				🥄 2½ hr ♨ 50 min ≋ 180°C
1	Saffron threads	2	20	Place in a bowl, barely cover with boiling water and leave to soak for 30 minutes.
	Plain flour	90 g	900 g	Sieve into a bowl and add a pinch of salt.
	Allspice	pinch	1 tsp	Add.
	Castor sugar	10 g	100 g	Add.
	Butter	20 g	200 g	Cut into small pieces and add.
	Lard	15 g	150 g	Cut into small pieces and add. Rub in to form a coarse sandy texture.
2	Milk	10 ml	100 ml	Warm gently and remove from the heat.
	Castor sugar	pinch	1 tsp	Add.
	Dried yeast	2 g	20 g	Add and mix thoroughly. Place to the side for 15 minutes. Pour into the flour mixture. Add the saffron and liquid and mix to a smooth dough. Knead for 15 minutes. Place in a bowl, cover and allow to ferment for 1 hour. Roll out onto a floured surface 1 cm thick.
	Dried mixed fruit	45 g	450 g	Sprinkle over the top.
	Mixed peel	5 g	50 g	Sprinkle over the top. Work the fruit into the dough and knead well. Place in greased baking tins. Allow to double in size. Place in a pre-heated oven and bake for 50 minutes.

☐   ☐   ☐

London Particular (Green pea soup)

Step	Commodity	1 portion	10 portions			
				☕ (Overnight)	🍲 2½ hr	
1	Split green peas	100 g	1 kg	Wash, rinse and cover with water. Allow to soak overnight.		
2	Margarine/ butter	5 g	50 g	Place in a suitably sized saucepan and heat gently.		
	Streaky bacon	15 g	150 g	Cut into lardons and add.		
	Onion	10 g	100 g	Peel, roughly cut and add.		
	Carrot	10 g	100 g	Peel, roughly cut and add.		
	Celery	10 g	100 g	Wash, trim, roughly cut and add. Sweat for 15 minutes until soft. Drain the liquid off the peas and rinse. Pour the drained peas over the sweated vegetables.		
3	Chicken/ ham stock	500 ml	5 litres	Pour over the ingredients, bring to the boil and simmer for 2 hours approximately or until the peas are tender. Place in a blender and liquidise until smooth. Return to a clean saucepan. Bring to the boil, correct the seasoning and consistency.		
4	Sliced bread	1	10	Remove the crusts. Cut into ½ cm cubes. Shallow fry until golden brown. Remove and place on absorbent paper. Place in a sauceboat and use to accompany the soup.		
	Sliced streaky bacon	15 g	150 g	Remove the rind and bone. Arrange on a tray and grill on both sides. Allow to cool. Chop finely and sprinkle over the soup as a garnish.		

☐   ☐   ☐

Palestine soup

Step	Commodity	1 portion	10 portions			
				☕ 1 hr	🍲 1½ hr	
1	Butter	10 g	100 g	Melt and heat gently in a thick-bottomed saucepan.		
	Jerusalem artichokes	75 g	750 g	Peel, dice and add to the butter.		
	Onions	15 g	150 g	Peel, finely dice and add.		
	Celery	20 g	200 g	Wash, trim, cut into fine dice and add.		
	Garlic	¼ clove	2 cloves	Peel, crush with a little salt and add. Sweat for 10 minutes without colouring.		
2	White chicken stock	300 ml	3 litres	Add, bring to the boil, season with salt and pepper and simmer for 45 minutes. Pass through a sieve or liquidise. Pour into a clean saucepan and re-boil. Return to a simmer.		
3	Milk	30 ml	300 ml	Add and stir in. Correct the seasoning.		
	Toasted cobnuts	2	20	Chop finely and add. Sprinkle with finely chopped parsley and serve.		

NOTE: Palestine soup is sometimes made with 10 g of chopped bacon per portion added at the same time as the garlic.

☐   ☐   ☐

21

Jellied eels

Step	Commodity	1 portion	10 portions	
				🥄 4 hr ♨ 30 min
1	Eels	200 g	2 kg	Skin and clean the eel. Cut into 2 cm pieces. Wash under cold running water. Place in a suitably sized saucepan.
	Water	200 ml	2 litres	Add.
	Malt vinegar	1 tbsp	10 tbsp	Add.
	Peppercorns	2	20	Add.
	Onion	10 g	100 g	Peel, dice finely and add.
	Carrot	15 g	150 g	Peel, slice thinly and add. Season with a pinch of salt.
	Chopped parsley	pinch	2 tsp	Add, cover with a lid, bring to the boil and simmer for 25 minutes. Remove and place in a bowl. Pour over the strained cooking liquor. Allow to cool, place in the refrigerator until the liquor has jellified. Serve cold from the bowl with malt vinegar.

□ □ □

Pie mash and liquor

Step	Commodity	1 portion	10 portions	
				🥄 1 hr ♨ 1 hr ≋ 190°C
1	Butter	5 g	50 g	Melt in a thick-bottomed saucepan.
	Onions	15 g	150 g	Peel, dice finely and add. Cook until light brown.
	Minced beef	150 g	1½ kg	Add, season with salt and pepper and fry until the meat is golden brown.
	Plain flour	2½ g	25 g	Sprinkle over the mince and mix in well.
	Brown mutton stock	50 ml	500 ml	Add and mix to form a smooth sauce. Pour into a suitably sized pie dish(es) and allow to cool.
2	Puff pastry	50 g	500 g	Roll out ½ cm thick. Allow to rest for 20 minutes. Cover the pie and crimp the edges with two fingers or a fork. Brush with eggwash and bake for 30 minutes. Remove and keep warm.
3	Potatoes	150 g	1½ kg	Peel, wash cut into small pieces. Place in a saucepan of cold water. Season with salt and pepper, bring to the boil and simmer for 20 minutes. Remove, drain and dry out. Mash with a fork and correct the seasoning. Serve with the pie. A sauce made from strained eel liquor, chopped parsley, thickened with diluted cornflour is poured over the meal.

□ □ □

Bubble and Squeak

Step	Commodity	1 portion	10 portions	
				🥣 30 min ♨ 30 min
1	Dripping	10 g	100 g	Melt and heat in a thick-bottomed frying pan.
	Onions	15 g	150 g	Peel, cut into fine dice and add to the hot fat.
	Cooked roast beef	70 g	700 g	Cut into ¼ cm dice and add. Brown well on all sides.
	Cooked mashed potato	90 g	900 g	Add and mix in.
	Cooked cabbage	35 g	350 g	Cut into small pieces and add. Season well with pepper and a little salt. Cook to a golden brown. Serve accompanied with Worcester sauce.

NOTE: Sprouts and peas may also be added.

☐   ☐   ☐

Steak and kidney pudding

Step	Commodity	1 portion	10 portions	
				🥣 2½ hr ♨ 2½ hr
1	Rump steak	150 g	1½ kg	Trim and cut into 1 cm cubes. Place in a bowl.
	Lamb's kidney	25 g	250 g	Wash, peel, remove the core and dice. Add to the steak. Season with salt and pepper.
	Onions	10 g	100 g	Peel, cut into fine dice and add.
	Worcester sauce	few drops	2 tsp	Add and mix well. Allow to marinade for 2 hours.
2	Suet pastry	75 g	750 g	Roll out ¼ cm thick and line a pudding dish. Add the appropriate amount of filling. Dampen the edges and cover with a pastry lid. Secure. Cover with greaseproof paper and tin foil. Place in a pre-heated steamer for the required time. Serve hot.

☐   ☐   ☐

RECIPES FROM THE SOUTH AND SOUTH-EAST

Whitstable dredgerman's breakfast

Step	Commodity	1 portion	10 portions	
				🥣 15 min ♨ 20 min
1	Sliced streaky bacon	2	20	Remove the rind and bones. Place in a pre-heated frying pan with a little oil. Cook for 3 minutes on each side.
	Oysters	2	20	Remove from the shells and rinse. Add to the bacon and cook for 3–4 minutes. Serve on hot buttered toast.

☐   ☐   ☐

Kentish chicken pudding

Step	Commodity	1 portion	10 portions		👐 1 hr 🍲 2½ hr
1	Suet pastry	75 g	750 g	Roll out ½ cm thick and line the appropriate individual pudding dishes.
	Chicken cut for sauté	200 g	2 kg	Wash, season with salt and pepper and place in the centre of the lined pudding dish.
	Belly pork	75 g	750 g	Cut into 1 cm pieces and place on top of the chicken.
	Onion	25 g	250 g	Peel, finely dice and add.
	Cider	60 ml	600 ml	Add. Dampen the edges with a little water or cider. Cover with a pastry lid, greaseproof paper and tin foil. Steam for the required time. Serve with parsley sauce.

☐   ☐   ☐

Beachy Head prawns

Step	Commodity	1 portion	10 portions		👐 1 hr 🍲 1 hr
1	Patna rice	10 g	100 g	Wash thoroughly. Place in a saucepan and cover with 1½ times as much water. Season with salt and ground pepper. Bring to the boil, simmer for 15 minutes and refresh. Drain well.
	Cucumber	15 g	150 g	Wash, peel and cut into ½ cm dice. Add to the rice.
	Red pepper	10 g	100 g	Remove the stalk and seeds. Cut the flesh into ½ cm dice and add to the other ingredients. Season with salt and pepper, bind with a little vinaigrette and arrange in a ring shape on a serving flat. Refrigerate.
2	Peeled prawns	50 g	500 g	Wash, dice and place in a bowl.
	Cooked chicken breast	50 g	500 g	Remove any skin and fat. Dice and place with the prawns.
	Dessert apples	25 g	250 g	Remove the stalk, cut into quarters and discard the seeds. Cut into ½ cm dice and add to the chicken. Carefully mix all the ingredients together and refrigerate.
3	Mayonnaise	50 ml	500 ml	Place in a blender.
	Chutney	½ tsp	5 tsp	Add.
	Tomato purée	½ tsp	5 tsp	Add.
	Dried apricots	½	5	Add.
	Curry powder	½ tsp	5 tsp	Add and liquidise. Bind with the chicken mixture. Place the mixture in the centre of the rice ring.
4	Whole prawns	2	20	Arrange on top.
	Toasted flaked almonds	5 g	50 g	Sprinkle over the top.

☐   ☐   ☐

Venison stew

Step	Commodity	1 portion	10 portions			
				🥣 Overnight	♨ 2½ hr	≋ 180°C
1	Shoulder of venison*	150 g	1½ kg	Trim and cut into 1 cm dice. Place in a bowl.		
	Juniper berries	1	10	Crush and add.		
	Bayleaves	½	5	Add.		
	Ground nutmeg	pinch	1 tsp	Add.		
	Cinnamon	pinch	½ tsp	Add.		
	Celery	25 g	250 g	Wash, trim the root, finely dice and add.		
	Carrots	50 g	500 g	Peel, dice finely and add.		
	Onion	25 g	250 g	Peel, dice finely and add.		
	Thyme	pinch	½ sprig	Add, season with salt and milled black pepper.		
	Red wine	100 ml	1 litre	Pour over the top ensuring that the meat and vegetables are covered. Cover with cling film and refrigerate overnight.		
2	Butter	5 g	50 g	Place in a thick-bottomed saucepan and heat. Drain and pat dry the venison, retaining the marinade. Add the meat to the hot butter and seal on all sides.		
	Bacon	15 g	150 g	Remove any rind and bone. Cut into thin strips 1½ cm long and add to the venison and fry. Drain the vegetables. Add to the meat.		
	Plain flour	5 g	50 g	Add, mix well with the other ingredients and brown. Add a quarter of the marinade and mix thoroughly. Add another quarter and bring to the boil. Add the remaining marinade and return to the boil. Correct the seasoning and simmer gently for the required time. Serve with quince jelly.		

* Boneless

NOTE: Venison stew may be cooked in a casserole dish in the oven.

□   □   □

Quince jelly

Step	Commodity	1 portion	10 portions		
				🥣 30 min	♨ 1½ hr
1	Quince	100 g	1 kg	Wash and roughly chop. Place in a suitably sized saucepan and cover with water.	
	Lemon	2½ ml	25 ml	Add, bring to the boil and simmer for 30 minutes. Carefully strain through a muslin cloth without squeezing as this makes the jelly cloudy. Place in a clean saucepan and heat.	
2	Castor sugar	45 g	450 g	Add and stir until the sugar has completely dissolved. Bring to the boil and simmer for 45 minutes or until the jelly reaches setting point. Allow to cool and bottle.	

□   □   □

21

Sussex casserole

Step	Commodity	1 portion	10 portions	
				⏱ 45 min ♨ 2½ hr ≋ 180°C
1	Onions	25 g	250 g	Peel, finely dice and place in a buttered oven-proof dish.
	Lentils	5 g	50 g	Sprinkle over the top.
	Brown sugar	10 g	100 g	Add and season with salt and pepper.
2	Lamb chops	2	20	Trim and arrange on top of the lentils.
	Curry powder	pinch	2 tsp	Add.
	Brown stock	100 ml	1 litre	Pour over the chops and barely cover.
	Potatoes	100 g	1 kg	Peel, wash, slice thinly and arrange on top of the chops. Brush with butter, cover with a lid and place in a pre-heated oven for the appropriate time. Remove the lid 15 minutes before the meat is cooked to brown the potatoes. Serve hot.

☐　☐　☐

Hampshire haslet

Step	Commodity	1 portion	10 portions	
				⏱ 30 min ♨ 1½ hr ≋ 190°C
1	Unsliced bread	50 g equiv	500 g	Remove the crusts, cut into ¼ cm dice and place in a suitably sized bowl.
	Milk	50 ml	500 ml	Add and allow to soak for 10 minutes, then squeeze and drain excess milk.
2	Minced pork	250 g	2½ kg	Add.
	Onion	50 g	500 g	Peel, finely dice and add.
	Chopped sage	pinch	1 tsp	Add, season with salt and milled black pepper. Mix all the ingredients together. Place in a suitably sized, greased loaf tin and bake in a pre-heated oven for the required time. Remove, allow to cool. Serve cold with salad or hot with mashed potatoes, marrowfat peas and a thickened gravy.

☐　☐　☐

Buttered hops

Step	Commodity	1 portion	10 portions	
				⏱ 30 min ♨ 10 min
1	Hop shoots	100 g	1 kg	Wash thoroughly. Place in a saucepan of boiling water. Return to the boil and simmer for 2–3 minutes. Remove and drain. Keep warm.
2	Butter	15 g	150 g	Melt and pour into a serving dish. Add the hops and completely cover with the melted butter. Serve with chicken or fish dishes.

☐　☐　☐

Oast cakes

Step	Commodity	1 portion	10 portions		🥣 45 min
1	Self-raising flour	40 g	400 g	Sieve into a bowl and add a pinch of salt.	
	Lard	10 g	100 g	Add and rub into a sandy texture.	
	Castor sugar	5 g	50 g	Add.	
	Currants	7.5 g	75 g	Add.	
	Lemon juice	few drops	1 tsp	Add, along with sufficient water to form a smooth dough. Divide into the appropriate portions allowing 2 pieces per portion. Roll out into 1 cm thick circles.	
2	Cooking oil/lard	5 g	50 g	Melt and heat in a thick-bottomed frying pan. Add the cakes and cook on both sides until golden brown. Remove and drain the excess fat on kitchen paper. Serve hot.	

☐ * ☐ ☐

Kentish huffkins

Step	Commodity	1 portion	10 portions		🥣 2½ hr	♨ 20 min	≋ 220°C
1	Plain flour	100 g	1 kg	Sieve into a bowl and add a pinch of salt.			
	Lard	10 g	100 g	Cut into small pieces, add and rub in to a sandy texture.			
	Milk	70 ml	700 ml	Place in a suitably sized saucepan and heat gently. Remove from the stove.			
	Dried yeast	2 g	20 g	Add, dissolve and set aside for 15 minutes until it begins to froth. Pour into the flour mixture, mix well and knead to a smooth dough. Place in a bowl, cover and allow to ferment for 1 hour. Knock back and divide into the appropriate portions. Roll out 1 cm thick into oval shaped cakes. Place to the side until they double in size. Place in a pre-heated oven and bake for the required time. Serve hot with butter and jam.			

☐ ☐ ☐

Sussex pond pudding

Step	Commodity	1 portion	10 portions		🥣 30 min	♨ 2½ hr
1	Suet pastry	75 g	750 g	Roll out ½ cm thick and line the appropriate individual pudding dishes.		
	Lemon	1	10	Wash, trim the top and tail. Prick all over with a fork and place into the lined pudding dish.		
	Butter	25 g	250 g	Cut into small pieces and add.		
	Demerara sugar	25 g	250 g	Add, dampen the edges with water, cover with a pastry lid, greaseproof paper and tin foil. Place in a pre-heated steamer and cook for the required time. Turn out onto a serving dish. Serve with custard sauce.		

☐ ☐ ☐

Guernsey apple cake

Use 1 × 20 cm tin per 10 portions

Step	Commodity	1 portion	10 portions		☺ 1 hr	♨ 1½ hr	≋ 180°C
1	Self-raising wholemeal flour	30 g	300 g	Place in a bowl.			
	Grated nutmeg	¼ tsp	2½ tsp	Add.			
	Cinnamon	pinch	1 tsp	Add and sieve together twice.			
	Apples	30 g	300 g	Peel, remove and discard the core. Slice and add to the flour.			
2	Margarine	15 g	150 g	Place in a clean bowl.			
	Demerara sugar	25 g	250 g	Add and beat until creamy in texture and pale in colour.			
	Eggs	¼ equiv	2	Whisk and gradually add to the flour. Beat well together. Gradually add the flour mixture. Place in the baking tin and bake in a pre-heated oven for 1½ hours. Remove and turn out onto a wire rack. Allow to cool.			
3	Honey	1 tbsp	10 tbsp	Spread over the top of the cake.			
	Demerara sugar	10 g	100 g	Sprinkle over the top and allow to go cold.			

NOTE: If the mixture is too thick, add a little water or milk to bring it to dropping consistency (i.e. so it easily drops off the spoon).

☐   ☐   ☐

Recipes from Scotland

Highland game soup

Step	Commodity	1 portion	10 portions		
				⟍ 1 hr	♨ 2½ hr
1	Butter	5 g	50 g	Melt in a thick-bottomed saucepan.	
	Lean bacon	25 g	250 g	Cut into lardons and add.	
	Game bones	200 g	2 kg	Wash, chop finely and add.	
	Carrots	25 g	250 g	Peel, dice finely and add.	
	Onions	20 g	200 g	Peel, dice finely and add.	
	Celery	15 g	150 g	Wash, trim, dice finely and add.	
	Parsnips	15 g	150 g	Peel, dice finely and add.	
	Leeks	15 g	150 g	Wash, remove the root, trim and dice finely. Add to the other ingredients. Brown the vegetables and bones.	
	Brown game stock	350 ml	3½ litres	Add, bring to the boil.	
	Bouquet garni		1	Add.	
	Peppercorns	2	20	Add, season with salt and simmer for 2 hours. Remove the bones and skim.	
2	Left over game	100 g	1 kg	Dice finely and add. Simmer for a further 20 minutes. Correct the seasoning.	
3	Port	10 ml	100 ml	Add, sprinkle with finely chopped parsley and serve.	

☐   ☐   ☐

Highland brose

Step	Commodity	1 portion	10 portions		
				⟍ 20 min	♨ 10 min
1	Medium oatmeal	40 g	400 g	Place in a serving dish.	
	Boiling water	100 ml	1 litre	Pour over the oatmeal to make a soupy porridge. Add a pinch of salt. Make a well in the centre.	
	Double cream	2 tbsp	20 tbsp	Pour into the centre.	
	Honey	1 tbsp	10 tbsp	Add.	
	Whisky	25 ml	250 ml	Pour over the cream and honey.	

Highland brose is eaten for breakfast.

☐   ☐   ☐

Kail brose

Step	Commodity	1 portion	10 portions	
1	Minced shin of beef	25 g	250 g	Place in a suitably sized saucepan.
	Cooked ox cheek	15 g	150 g	Mince and add.
	Beef skirt*	25 g	250 g	Mince and add. Season with salt and pepper.
	Marrow/ cow heel†	25 g	250 g	Cut into small pieces and add.
	Water/stock	250 ml	2½ litres	Add, bring to the boil and simmer for 2 hours.
2	Curly kale	50 g	500 g	Wash, rinse, remove the stalk and cut into chiffonade. Add to the soup. Return to the boil and simmer for 15–20 minutes. Correct the seasoning and skim.
3	Toasted oatmeal	15 g	150 g	Place in the bottom of the serving dish. Pour over the soup and serve.

NOTE: This soup may be made using mussels in place of meat and nettles and/or leeks in place of curly kale.
* Beef skirt: Celtic name for thin flank of beef.
† Cooked.

☐   ☐   ☐

Cockie leekie

Step	Commodity	1 portion	10 portions	
1	Boiling fowl	200 g equiv	2 kg equiv	Wash, prepare and place in a saucepan.
	Water	400 ml	4 litres	Add, bring to the boil and skim.
	Bouquet garni	1 small	1 large	Add and boil for 3 hours or until the chicken is tender. Remove the chicken and allow to cool, retain the cooking liquor. Discard the skin and bones and chop the flesh into small dice.
2	Leeks	100 g	1 kg	Wash, remove the root and trim. Cut into 1 cm × 1 cm slices and rewash. Add to the cooking liquor along with the diced chicken. Reboil and simmer for 15 minutes.
	Soaked Prunes	1	10	Carefully remove the stone and cut the fruit into thin slices. Add to the soup. Reheat, sprinkle with finely chopped parsley. Serve.

☐   ☐   ☐

Lentil brö

Step	Commodity	1 portion	10 portions		
				🥄 1 hr	🍲 2½ hr
1	Butter	5 g	50 g	Place in a large, thick-bottomed saucepan and heat gently.	
	Lentils	40 g	400 g	Wash and add.	
	Carrots	25 g	250 g	Peel, cut into fine dice and add.	
	Onions	25 g	250 g	Peel, cut into fine dice and add.	
	Celery	15 g	150 g	Wash, trim and dice finely. Add to the other vegetables. Sweat the vegetables for 5 minutes without colouring.	
	Cabbage	15 g	150 g	Wash, trim, remove the stalk and cut into ½ cm × ½ cm slices.	
2	Ham stock	300 ml	3 litres	Add, bring to the boil and simmer for 2 hours. Season with a little salt and pepper.	
	Boiled ham	50 g	500 g	Cut into fine dice and add. Re-boil, correct the consistency and seasoning. Sprinkle with finely chopped parsley. Serve.	

☐　　☐　　☐

Barley broth (Scotch broth)

Step	Commodity	1 portion	10 portions		
				🥄 1 hr	🍲 1½ hr
1	Barley	10 g	100 g	Wash and place in a saucepan.	
	White mutton stock	400 ml	4 litres	Pour over the barley. Bring to the boil and simmer for 1 hour.	
2	Turnips	25 g	250 g	Peel, cut into 1 cm × 1 cm thin slices.	
	Carrots	50 g	500 g	Peel, cut into 1 cm × 1 cm thin slices. Cook for 10 minutes.	
	Leeks	25 g	250 g	Remove the root, trim and wash. Cut into 1 cm × 1 cm thin slices.	
	Cabbage	25 g	250 g	Wash, discard the stalk and cut into 1 cm × 1 cm thin slices. Cook for 5 minutes.	
	Garden peas	15 g	150 g	Add.	
	Cooked lamb scrag	100 g	1 kg	Mince or chop finely and add. Season with salt and pepper. Cook for a further 10 minutes. Correct the seasoning and skim. Sprinkle with finely chopped parsley. Serve hot with oatcakes.	

☐　　☐　　☐

Cullen skink

Step	Commodity	1 portion	10 portions	
1	Finnan haddock	100 g	1 kg	Place in a suitable saucepan.
	Water	175 ml	1.75 litres	Place in a saucepan, cover and boil. Pour over the haddock and bring to the boil gently.
	Onion	15 g	150 g	Peel, cut in half and add. Simmer for 15 minutes until the haddock is tender. Remove and allow to cool. Retain the cooking liquor and onion.
	Milk	125 ml	1.25 litres	Add to the cooking liquor, bring to the boil and return to a simmer. Remove and discard the bones. Flake the haddock with a fork, place in a suitably sized saucepan and set aside.
2	Potatoes	150 g	1½ kg	Wash, peel and rewash. Place in a saucepan of cold water, bring to the boil, season with salt and pepper and cook for 20 minutes. Remove and allow to dry. Purée with a potato masher (or moulie). Place with the haddock. Pour over the strained cooking liquor and milk. Bring to the boil, correct the consistency and seasoning. Sprinkle with chopped parsley.

☐   ☐   ☐

Mussel pot

Step	Commodity	1 portion	10 portions	
1	Fresh mussels	12	120	Clean and scrape the mussels. Place in a saucepan of boiling water, return to the boil and simmer for 2–3 minutes. Refresh immediately. Remove the mussels from their shells and place in a deep sided, oven-proof dish.
	Butter	5 g	50 g	Place in a suitably sized, thick-bottomed saucepan.
	Shallots	15 g	150 g	Peel, finely dice and add. Cook without colouring for 2–3 minutes.
	Lemon	⅒	1	Pour the strained juice over the shallots.
	Dry white wine	50 ml	500 ml	Add.
	Shellfish stock	50 ml	500 ml	Add and reduce by half.
	Double cream	50 ml	500 ml	Add and simmer for another 2–3 minutes. Season with salt and cayenne pepper. Pour over the mussels and allow to cool.
3	Scotch puff*	75 g	750 g	Roll out ½ cm thick and place over the oven-proof dish. Pinch the edges between two fingers or with a fork. Eggwash the surface. Using the back of a knife, score the pastry in a criss-cross fashion. Bake for the appropriate time or until the pastry has become golden brown.

NOTE: This dish may be done in individual portions.
* See Chapter 13: Baking and sweet preparations.

☐   ☐   ☐

Herring in oatmeal

Step	Commodity	1 portion	10 portions	
				🍲 1 hr 🍳 10 min
1	Herring	1	10	Clean, scale and wash. Remove the backbone and score the skin. Season with salt and pepper.
	Milk	25 ml	250 ml	Place in a bowl.
	Oatmeal	25 g	250 g	Place on a tray. Pass the herring through the milk and then the oatmeal. Press firmly to stay on.
2	Dripping	25 g	250 g	Place in a thick-bottomed frying pan and heat. Add the herring and cook on each side for 5 minutes or until golden brown. Drain and arrange on a serving dish.
	Lemon wedge	1	10	Place with the fish. Garnish with washed, picked parsley. Serve with oatcakes.

☐ ☐ ☐

Tweed kettle

Step	Commodity	1 portion	10 portions	
				🍲 1 hr 🍳 45 min
1	Fresh salmon	15 g	150 g	Clean, scale and wash. Place in a large pan or fish kettle and barely cover with water. Slowly bring to the boil and simmer for 5 minutes. Remove and allow to cool. Retain the cooking liquor. Skin, remove the bones and retain. Flake the fish into a bowl. Place the bones and skin back into the cooking liquor. Boil and simmer for 15 minutes. Strain and place two-thirds in a clean saucepan. Add the fish. Season with salt and ground black pepper.
	Shallots	15 g	150 g	Peel, dice and add.
	Mace	small pinch	large pinch	Add.
	White wine	25 ml	250 ml	Add, cover with a lid and simmer for 15 minutes.
2	Butter	5 g	50 g	Place in a clean saucepan and melt.
	Mushrooms	10 g	100 g	Wash, chop finely and add. Cook gently for 2–3 minutes without colouring. Drain and add to the salmon. Cook for a further 5 minutes. Sprinkle with finely chopped parsley. Serve with swede and/or potatoes.

☐ ☐ ☐

☐

21

Haggis

Step	Commodity	1 portion	10 portions			
				🥄 2 hr	♨ 3 hr	
1	Lamb's liver	25 g	250 g	Wash and prepare. Cut into 1 cm cubes and place in a saucepan.		
	Lamb's heart	25 g	250 g	Wash and prepare. Cut into 1 cm cubes and place with the liver.		
	Onions	15 g	150 g	Peel, dice and add. Cover with water, bring to the boil and simmer for 45 minutes. Drain into a colander. Retain the cooking liquor. Pass the meat and onions through a medium mincer twice into a bowl.		
2	Coarse oatmeal	25 g	250 g	Place in a pre-heated, thick-bottomed frying pan. Stir continually until it has toasted all over. Add to the meat. Allow to cool.		
	Minced suet	15 g	150 g	Add and mix in. Season with salt and pepper. Place in a haggis casing/sleeve* and secure. Place in a pre-heated steamer for 1½–2 hours.		

* Traditionally the haggis sleeve/casing was made from sheep's bladder, but is no longer considered hygienic enough.

NOTE: Haggis is traditionally served on Robbie Burns night and Hogmanay with mashed potatoes and mashed turnips (Haggis, tatties and neeps).

Most establishments south of the Scottish border prefer to buy ready prepared haggis from reputable butchers.

☐   ☐   ☐

Forfar bridies

Step	Commodity	1 portion	10 portions			
				🥄 30 min	♨ 45 min	≋ 200°C
1	Rump steak	1 × 125 g	10 × 125 g	Trim excess fat. Cut into ½ cm strips and place in a bowl.		
	Minced suet	15 g	150 g	Add.		
	Onions	20 g	200 g	Peel, cut into fine dice and add. Season with salt and pepper.		
2	Shortcrust pastry	150 g	1½ kg	Roll out in 12 cm ovals, ½ cm thick. Divide the meat in the appropriate portions and place on one side of the pastry. Brush the edge with water or egg. Fold the other side over and pinch between two fingers or with a fork. Make a hole in the top of each bridie and arrange on a lightly greased baking tray. Place in a pre-heated oven for the required time or until they are golden brown.		

☐   ☐   ☐

Skirlie

Step	Commodity	1 portion	10 portions		⏲ 30 min	♨ 10–15 min
1	Beef suet	15 g	500 g	Place in a thick-bottomed pan and heat.		
	Onions	50 g	500 g	Peel, mince finely and add. Cook until golden brown.		
	Oatmeal	25 g	250 g	Add, season with salt and pepper.		
	Ground mace	pinch	1 tsp	Add.		
	Ground coriander	pinch	1 tsp	Add.		
	Ground nutmeg	pinch	1 tsp	Add and mix well together. Fry until the oatmeal is brown and crunchy. Serve as a side dish or a stuffing.		

☐　　☐　　☐

Howtowdie

Step	Commodity	1 portion	10 portions		⏲ 1 hr	♨ 1½ hr	≋ 180°C
1	Roasting chicken	200 g equiv	2 kg equiv	Prepare for roasting and wash the insides. Retain the liver.			
	Skirlie	50 g	500 g	Stuff inside the cavity of the bird and secure.			
2	Butter	15 g	150 g	Melt in a casserole dish.			
	Button onions	2	20	Peel, trim and add. Cook gently until soft. Add the chicken.			
	Whole cloves	½ equiv	5	Add.			
	Ground nutmeg	pinch	1 tsp	Sprinkle over the top of the chicken. Season with salt and ground black pepper.			
	Brown chicken stock	125 ml	1.25 litre	Pour over the top. Bring to the boil. Cover with a tight-fitting lid and place in a pre-heated oven 40 minutes per kilo, plus 20 minutes. Remove the chicken from the cooking liquor and keep warm. Strain the cooking liquor into a suitably sized saucepan.			
	Chicken liver	¼	2½	Wash and prepare. Chop finely and add to the stock. Bring to the boil. Skim if required. Season lightly with salt and pepper and reduce the cooking liquor by half. Place the chicken on a serving tray. Garnish with watercress.			

NOTE: Traditionally served with cooked spinach and poached egg.

☐　　☐　　☐

21

511

Highland beef balls

Step	Commodity	1 portion	10 portions		1 hr — 7–8 min — 170°C
1	Minced beef	100 g	1 kg	Place in a bowl.	
	Minced suet	10 g	100 g	Add.	
	Ground ginger	pinch	1 tsp	Add.	
	Ground mace	pinch	1 tsp	Add.	
	Ground coriander	pinch	1 tsp	Add.	
	Ground cloves	pinch	½ tsp	Add.	
	Brown sugar	pinch	1 tsp	Add.	
	Egg	¼	2½	Add, season with salt and black pepper. Mix well together. Divide into the appropriate portions and shape into balls (1–2 per portion).	
2	Medium oatmeal	30 g	300 g	Place on a tray and roll the meatballs through to coat. Place in pre-heated oil for the required time or until golden brown. Serve hot.	

☐   ☐   ☐

Rumbledethumps

Step	Commodity	1 portion	10 portions		45 min — 1½ hr — 190°C
1	Potatoes	100 g	1 kg	Peel, wash place in a saucepan of cold salted water. Bring to the boil and simmer for 20 minutes. Drain thoroughly and mash.	
	Cabbage	100 g	1 kg	Wash, remove damaged leaves and stalks. Shred and place in a saucepan of boiling salted water. Cook for 15 minutes. Drain thoroughly.	
2	Butter	15 g	150 g	Melt in a thick-bottomed frying pan.	
	Onions	25 g	250 g	Peel, cut into fine dice and add. Cook gently without colouring for 2–3 minutes. Add the mashed potatoes and cabbage and mix well. Season with salt and pepper. Place in an oven-proof dish.	
	Dunlop cheese	15 g	150 g	Grate and sprinkle over the top of the potato and cabbage. Place in a pre-heated oven for the required time or until the top is golden brown. Serve hot as an accompaniment for stews or for supper.	

☐   ☐   ☐

Stovies

Step	Commodity	1 portion	10 portions		
				⌣ 1 hr	♨ 1½ hr
1	Dripping	10 g	100 g	Melt in a thick-bottomed frying pan.	
	Onions	25 g	250	Peel, cut into fine dice and add. Cook gently without colouring for 3–4 minutes.	
	Potatoes	150 g	1½ kg	Peel, wash, slice thinly and add to the onions. Season with salt and pepper.	
	Brown meat stock	50 ml	500 ml	Pour over the potatoes. Bring to the boil, cover with a tight-fitting lid and simmer for 1 hour. Stir occasionally to prevent sticking.	
2	Cooked chicken beef or lamb	50 g	500 g	Chop finely and add. Simmer for a further 10 minutes. Serve hot.	

NOTE: Stovie is made to use up left over cooked meat.

☐　　☐　　☐

Fruity pudding

Step	Commodity	1 portion	10 portions		
				⌣ 2 hr	≋ 2 hr
1	Dried breadcrumbs	30 g	300 g	Place in a bowl.	
	Plain flour	15 g	150 g	Add.	
	Sugar	6 g	60 g	Add.	
	Currants	7.5 g	75 g	Add.	
	Sultanas	7.5 g	75 g	Add.	
	Raisins	7.5 g	75 g	Add.	
	Ground ginger	pinch	1 tsp	Add.	
	Ground cinnamon	pinch	1 tsp	Add.	
	Milk	17.5 ml	175 ml	Add and mix thoroughly together. Place to the side for 1 hour to swell. Place in a sleeve or casing and secure. Steam for 2 hours. Allow to cool and set. Remove from the casting, cut into slices and fry. Serve for breakfast.	

NOTE: A baking tin may be used in place of casings or a sleeve.

☐　　☐　　☐

Scotch pies

Step	Commodity	1 portion	10 portions				
				⌣ 1½ hr	♨ 40 min	≋ 190°C	
1	Mutton/ lamb	60 g	600 g	Trim excess fat and discard. Mince the meat and place in a bowl.			
	Onions	40 g	400 g	Peel, finely dice and add to the mince. Season with salt and pepper.			
2	Water	17.5 ml	175 ml	Place in a saucepan and bring to the boil. Reduce to a simmer.			
	Lard	30 g	300 g	Add and melt.			
	Flour	50 g	500 g	Sieve into a bowl. Add a pinch of salt and add to the liquid. Mix thoroughly together. Remove from the heat. Cover and allow to cool. Divide the meat and pastry into the appropriate portions. Retain one quarter of the paste for lids. Roll each portion of pastry out ½ cm thick and place into greased moulds. Add the appropriate amount of meat. Brush the edge with water. Roll out sufficient pastry to cover the top. Place over the meat and seal. Brush with water. Make a hole in the top. Place in a pre-heated oven for the required time or until golden brown. Serve hot or cold.			

☐　　☐　　☐

Oatcakes

Step	Commodity	1 portion	10 portions			
				⌣ 30 min	♨ 15 min	
1	Medium oatmeal	25 g	250 g	Place in a bowl.		
	Bicarbonate of soda	pinch	½ tsp	Add.		
	Salt	pinch	1 tsp	Add and mix well together.		
2	Bacon fat	½ tsp	5 tsp	Melt and add. Stir into the mixture.		
	Hot water	1 tbsp	10 tbsp	Add and stir in well. Make a stiff dough. Turn out onto a clean table dusted with oatmeal. Roll out into ½ cm thick rounds and cut into quarters.		
3	Bacon fat	5 g	50 g	Place on a pre-heated griddle plate or a thick-bottomed frying pan. Cook on both sides for 7–8 minutes. Allow to cool on a wire rack. Served warmed or cold.		

☐　　☐　　☐

Pitcaithly bannock

Step	Commodity	1 portion	10 portions	
				🥄 1 hr 🍲 1–1½ hr 〰 150°C
1	Butter	25 g	250 g	Place in a bowl.
	Icing sugar	10 g	100 g	Add.
	Castor sugar	10 g	100 g	Cream well together.
2	Plain flour	25 g	250 g	Place in a clean bowl.
	Rice flour	20 g	200 g	Add and sieve together 3 times. Add to the creamed butter and mix in well.
	Flaked almonds	10 g	100 g	Add and mix together. Roll out on into 1 cm thick rounds. Pinch the edges between two fingers or with a fork.
	Flaked almonds	5 g	50 g	Press onto the surface in a decorative manner.
	Lemon and orange zest	2 g	20 g	Sprinkle over the top. Arrange on a baking tray and place in a pre-heated oven for the required time or until golden brown. Remove, place on a cooling rack and dust with castor sugar. Serve hot.

☐   ☐   ☐

Cranachan crowdie

Step	Commodity	1 portion	10 portions	
				🥄 2 hr 〰 200°C
1	Pinhead oatmeal	15 g	150 g	Toast in a pre-heated oven until golden brown.
	Double cream	75 ml	750 ml	Whisk until fairly stiff.
	Malt whisky	10 ml	100 ml	Add and fold in.
	Honey	½ tbsp	5 tbsp	Add and fold in.
	Raspberries	25 g	250 g	Wash and discard any bad fruit. Add to the cream along with most of the toasted oatmeal. Spoon in serving glasses. Sprinkle with the remaining oatmeal and chill for 1 hour before serving.

NOTE: This dish is also called Cream crowdie.

☐   ☐   ☐

21

Edinburgh fog

Step	Commodity	1 portion	10 portions			
				2 hr		200°C
1	Double cream	100 ml	1 litre	Whisk until fairly stiff.		
	Castor sugar	½ tbsp	5 tbsp	Add.		
	Vanilla essence	drop	few drops	Add.		
	Whisky	1 tbsp	10 tbsp	Add.		
	Flaked almonds	15 g	150 g	Toast in a pre-heated oven, allow to cool. Add most to the cream mixture and spoon into serving glasses. Sprinkle with the remaining almonds. Chill for 1 hour before serving.		

NOTE: This dish got its name from the thick fog that once plagued Edinburgh.

☐ ☐ ☐

Scotch pancakes (some chefs refer to these as Welsh drop scones)

Step	Commodity	1 portion	10 portions			
				30 min		8 min
1	Self-raising flour	12.5 g	125 g	Sieve into a bowl. Add a pinch of salt.		
	Egg	1/10	1	Add.		
	Cooking oil	¼ tbsp	2½ tbsp	Add.		
	Milk	12½ ml	125 ml	Add and mix well together to a smooth batter (more or less milk may be needed).		
2	Cooking oil	2 ml	20 ml	Spread on a preheated griddle plate or a thick bottomed frying pan. Pour in a measured amount of batter (25 ml). Cook until the raw side is full of bubbles. Turn over and cook on the other side until golden brown. Serve hot with butter.		

☐ ☐ ☐

Recipes from Wales

Mecryll mewn saws

Caveach of mackerel

Step	Commodity	1 portion	10 portions			
				1 day		15 min
1	Mackerel	½ equiv	5	Clean, prepare and fillet. Season with salt and pepper.		
	Olive oil	5 ml	50 ml	Heat in a suitably sized frying pan and add the mackerel. Fry briskly on both sides for 3–4 minutes. Remove, place in an earthenware dish. Retain the oil.		
2	Onions	75 g	750 g	Peel, cut into thin rings. Add to the hot oil.		
	Garlic	1/10 clove	1 clove	Peel, crush with a little salt and add. Fry until golden brown. Remove and spoon over the fish.		
	White spirit vinegar	½ tbsp	5 tbsp	Pour over the fish. Cover with clingfilm and place in a fridge. Leave to marinade for 24 hours. Serve cold.		

☐ ☐ ☐

Herring supper

Step	Commodity	1 portion	10 portions			
				⌣ 1 hr	♨ 1 hr	≋ 180°C
1	Herring	2	20	Clean and prepare. Remove the head and backbone.		
	Mustard	1 tsp	10 tsp	Spread over the inside of the fish. Season with salt and pepper and roll each fish up lengthways. Butter a suitably sized oven-proof dish.		
2	Potatoes	100 g	1 kg	Peel, wash and cut into thin slices. Arrange neatly in the dish.		
	Onions	25 g	250 g	Peel, slice in thin rings and arrange on top of the potato.		
	Cooking apples	100 g	1 kg	Peel, remove the core, cut into thin slices and arrange neatly on top of the onion. Lay the fish on top. Season with salt and pepper.		
	Chopped sage	pinch	1 tsp	Sprinkle over the top.		
	Potatoes	100 g	1 kg	Peel, wash and cut into thin slices. Arrange neatly on top of the fish. Pour in enough water to come half way up the dish. Brush with melted butter. Cover with cooking foil and place in a pre-heated oven for 45 minutes. Remove the foil and cook for a further 15 minutes. Remove and serve.		

☐   ☐   ☐

Anglesey eggs

Step	Commodity	1 portion	10 portions			
				⌣ 1½ hr	♨ 1 hr	≋ 200°C
1	Potatoes	100 g	1 kg	Peel, wash and cut into small pieces. Place in a saucepan of cold water, bring to the boil and simmer for 20 minutes. Drain, mash and keep warm.		
	Leeks	150 g	1½ kg	Wash, remove the root and trim the leaves. Cut in half lengthways and slice thinly. Place in a saucepan of boiling salted water, bring to the boil. Simmer for 10 minutes. Drain and add to the potatoes. Season with salt and pepper.		
	Butter	5 g	50 g	Melt and add. Mix thoroughly with the other ingredients. Place in an oven-proof dish(s).		
2	Hard boiled eggs	1	10	Peel, cut into thin slices and arrange over the potatoes and leeks.		
	Nutmeg	pinch	½ tsp	Sprinkle over the eggs.		
	Mornay sauce	25 ml	250 ml	Pour over the top. Place in a pre-heated oven for the 20 minutes or until golden brown.		

21

☐   ☐   ☐

Faggots

Step	Commodity	1 portion	10 portions	
				👐 1 hr 🍲 1 hr ≋ 180°C
1	Minced pig's liver	100 g	1 kg	Place in a bowl.
	Minced belly pork	50 g	500 g	Add.
	Garlic	¼ clove	2 cloves	Peel, crush with a little salt and add.
	Onions	25 g	250 g	Peel, finely dice and add.
	Breadcrumbs	25 g	250 g	Peel, finely dice and add.
	Mace	pinch	1 tsp	Add.
	Chopped sage	pinch	2 tsp	Add, season with salt and pepper and mix well together. Divide into the appropriate portions and divide each portion into two. Roll each piece into a ball shape.
2	Caul fat	20 g	200 g	Place into a bowl of warm water and soak for 15 minutes. Remove and stretch to its maximum. Cut into pieces big enough to envelope the individual balls and cover. Place close together on a buttered gratin dish.
3	Brown stock	50 ml	500 ml	Pour over enough stock to cover the faggots by 1 cm. Place in an oven and cook for the required time. Add stock if required. Serve hot with boiled marrowfat peas.

☐ ☐ ☐

Cawl

Step	Commodity	1 portion	10 portions	
				👐 1 hr 🍲 2½–3 hr
1	Lard	5 g	50 g	Place in a large thick-bottomed saucepan and heat.
	Onions	15 g	150 g	Peel, roughly chop and add.
	Parsnips	35 g	250 g	Peel, roughly chop and add.
	Carrots	50 g	500 g	Peel, roughly chop and add.
	Swede	25 g	250 g	Peel, roughly chop and add. Cook quickly until golden brown. Remove with a perforated spoon and place to the side. Retain the fat on the side of the stove.
2	Neck of lamb*	75 g	750 g	Trim, cut into 1 cm pieces and add to fat and brown quickly. Return the vegetables to the pan.
	Smoked bacon	100 g	1 kg	Cut into 1 cm pieces and add. Cover with water† and bring to the boil.
	Thyme	pinch	1 sprig	Wash and add.
3	Bouquet garni	1 small	1 large	Add. Skim and simmer for 2–2½ hours.
4	Potatoes	100 g	1 kg	Peel, cut into small pieces and add. Cook for a further 20 minutes, or until the potatoes are cooked.
5	Leeks	50 g	500 g	Wash, trim and root and discard outer and damaged leaves. Cut into thin rings. Divide the meat into the appropriate portions and place in bowls. Pour over the cooking liquor and garnish with raw leeks. Serve with bread and cheese.

* Trimmed brisket of beef may be used in place of neck of lamb.
† or lamb stock.
NOTE: It is traditional to cook cawl the day before and leave overnight for the flavour to improve.

☐ ☐ ☐

Poached sewin (sea trout) steaks with cucumber sauce

🥄 1 hr ♨ 20 min

Step	Commodity	1 portion	10 portions	
1	Sea trout steaks	150 g	1.5 kg	Clean, remove the scales and wash. Cut into the correct size portions. Place in a saucepan of simmering water. Season with a little salt.
	Black peppercorns	2	20	Add.
	Onions	50 g	500 g	Peel, cut into thin rings and add.
	Carrot	25 g	250 g	Peel, slice thinly and add.
	Bay leaf	¼	2	Add.
	Vinegar	½ tsp	5 tsp	Add. Poach for 15 minutes. Remove the fish, reserve the liquor. Discard the bones and skin from the fish. Place on a serving dish.
2	Cucumber sauce	100 ml	1 litre	Pour over the fish, sprinkle with finely chopped parsley and serve.

☐ ☐ ☐

Cucumber sauce

🥄 30 min ♨ 30 min

Step	Commodity	1 portion	10 portions	
1	Butter	25 g	250 g	Place in a suitably sized saucepan and melt.
	Onions	5 g	50 g	Peel, dice finely and add. Cook for 2–3 minutes without colouring.
	Lettuce	50 g	500 g	Wash, discard withered leaves and stalk. Cut into chiffonade and add to the butter and onions.
	Cucumber	50 g	500 g	Peel, discard the skin and cut the flesh into fine dice. Add to the lettuce.
	Water	1 tsp	10 tsp	Add and simmer gently for 15 minutes. Season with salt and pepper. Serve as required.

☐ ☐ ☐

21

Welsh onion cake

Teisen nionod

🥄 1 hr ♨ 1½ hr ≋ 200°C

Step	Commodity	1 portion	10 portions	
1	Potatoes	150 g	1½ kg	Peel, wash and slice thin. Place in a bowl of water to remove the starch. Remove and dry.
	Onions	75 g	750 g	Peel, slice into thin rings.
	Butter	25 g	250 g	Melt and use to liberally brush a suitably sized cake tin. Place a layer of potatoes and then onions. Brush with melted butter and season with salt and pepper. Repeat the process to the top finishing with a layer of potato. Cover with cooking foil and place in a pre-heated oven and bake for 1 hour, pressing the potatoes with a palette knife to form the cake. Remember to replace the foil. Discard the foil after the hour and allow the potatoes to brown. Remove from the oven and turn out of the cake tin. Serve hot with a little cream or stock over the top.

☐ ☐ ☐

Glamorgan sausage

Step	Commodity	1 portion	10 portions		⏲ 1 hr	🍲 10 min	〰 175°C
1	Cheese	10 g	100 g	Grated and place into a bowl.			
	White breadcrumbs	10 g	100 g	Add.			
	Onion	5 g	50 g	Peel, dice finely and add.			
	Dry mustard	pinch	1 tsp	Sprinkle over the top.			
	Finely chopped parsley	pinch	2 tsp	Add.			
	Thyme	pinch	½ tsp	Add and season with salt and milled black pepper.			
	Egg yolk	¼ equiv	2½	Add and mix thoroughly together. Divide into the appropriate portions and shape into sausage shapes.			
	Egg whites	¼	2½	Place in a clean bowl and whisk.			
	Breadcrumbs	20 g	200 g	Place on a tray. Pass the 'sausage' through the egg white and breadcrumbs.			
2	Cooking oil	5 ml	50 ml	Place in a thick-bottomed frying pan and heat. Add the sausages and cook all around for the required time. Serve at tea-time.			

NOTE: Glamorgan sausages may be deep fried.

☐   ☐   ☐

Laver bread
Bara lawr

Step	Commodity	1 portion	10 portions		⏲ 30 min	🍲 6 hr
1	Laver	200 g	2 kg	Wash thoroughly to remove all grit and sand. Place in a suitably sized saucepan. Add a little water and bring to the boil. Simmer for 6 hours, stirring regularly to prevent it from sticking. Allow the excess liquid to evaporate. Remove and divide into the appropriate portions.		

NOTE: Laver is a fine edible seaweed. It may be served with fried bacon for breakfast.

☐   ☐   ☐

Welsh rarebit

Caws pobi

🥣 30 min   ♨ 15 min

Step	Commodity	1 portion	10 portions	
1	Thick sliced bread	1	10	Remove the crusts and toast on both sides. Spread with butter cut into triangles and keep warm.
	Cheese	50 g	500 g	Cut into thin slivers.
	Butter	40 g	400 g	Place in a thick-bottomed frying pan and heat. Add the cheese and melt slowly.
	Double cream	1 tsp	10 tsp	Add and stir in until the mixture is smooth. Remove from the heat.
2	Egg	½	5	Break into a bowl. Whisk thoroughly and slowly add to the cheese mixture stir all the time.
	Ale (optional)	1 tsp	10 tsp	Add and mix in well. Pour into individual portioned dishes and brown under a pre-heated salamander. Place on the centre of a serving dish. Surround with toast and serve.

NOTE: This traditional way of making Welsh rarebit is nothing like the modern day version. Most establishments prepare a rich cheese sauce flavoured with ale which is spread on the toast and browned under a salamander. Buck rarebit is made by placing a poached egg on the toast for service.

☐   ☐   ☐

Cinnamon cake

Teisen sinamon

🥣 30 min   ♨ 50 min   ≋ 150°C

Step	Commodity	1 portion	10 portions	
1	Self-raising flour	50 g	500 g	Sieve into a bowl and add a pinch of salt.
	Cinnamon	pinch	2 tsp	Add.
	Butter	20 g	200 g	Add and rub in to form a sandy texture.
	Sugar	20 g	200 g	Add.
	Egg yolks	½	6	Add and mix well to form a stiff dough.
	Milk	1 tsp	10 tsp	Add to the mixture (more or less may be required). Place into a greased shallow tin and bake in a pre-heated oven for 25–30 minutes or until cooked. Allow to cool.
2	Raspberry jam	30 g	300 g	Spread over the top of the sponge.
3	Egg whites	½	6	Place in a clean bowl and whisk to a stiff meringue.
	Castor sugar	4 g	40 g	Add and fold in. Spread over jam. Return to the oven and bake for a further 20 minutes or until the meringue is set and a pale gold in colour. Remove and serve immediately.

☐   ☐   ☐

21

Welsh cakes

Step	Commodity	1 portion	10 portions			
				🥄 30 min	🍲 6–8 min	
1	Self-raising flour	45 g	450 g	Sieve into a bowl and add a pinch of salt.		
	Allspice	small pinch	large pinch	Add and mix in.		
	Butter	10 g	100 g	Cut into small pieces and place on top of the flour.		
	Lard	10 g	100 g	Cut into small pieces and place on top of the flour. Rub in to form a sandy texture.		
	Raisins	10 g	100 g	Add.		
	Castor sugar	20 g	200 g	Add.		
	Eggs	¼ equiv	2	Add.		
	Milk	10 ml	100 ml	Add and mix to a stiff dough (less milk may be required). Roll out 1 cm thick and cut into rounds using a pastry cutter.		
3	Lard	2 g	20 g	Place in a thick-bottomed frying pan or on a pre-heated griddle. Add the Welsh cakes and cook on both sides until they are cooked through to the centre and golden brown on the outside. Remove and sprinkle with castor sugar.		

□   □   □

Recipes from Ireland

Nettle soup

Step	Commodity	1 portion	10 portions			
				🥄 30 min	🍲 1 hr	
1	Mutton stock	150 ml	1½ litres	Place in a suitably sized saucepan and bring to the boil.		
	Butter	5 g	50	Add.		
	Rolled oats	15 g	150 g	Add and mix in. Return to the boil.		
	Young nettle leaves	75 g	750 g	Wash and cut into chiffonade and add. Season with salt and pepper. Simmer for 1 hour. Correct the seasoning. Sprinkle with finely chopped parsley. Add cream to enrich (optional).		

□   □   □

Potato soup

Step	Commodity	1 portion	10 portions	
1	Potatoes	160 g	1½ kg	Peel, wash and cut into small pieces. Place in a suitably sized saucepan.
	Onions	50 g	500 g	Peel, slice and add to the potatoes.
	Milk	150 ml	1½ litres	Add.
	White meat or vegetable stock	15 ml	150 ml	Add and bring to the boil. Season lightly with salt and ground pepper.
	Mixed herbs	pinch	1 tbsp	Chop finely and add. Simmer for the required time. Pass through a sieve or liquidise. Place in a clean saucepan and reboil, return to a simmer.
2	Single cream	25 ml	250 ml	Swirl into the soup. Sprinkle with finely chopped parsley and serve.

☐   ☐   ☐

Fish chowder

Step	Commodity	1 portion	10 portions	
1	Butter	15 g	150 g	Melt in a suitably sized thick-bottomed saucepan and heat gently.
	Onion	50 g	500 g	Peel, finely dice and add.
	Carrot	25 g	250 g	Peel, finely dice and add.
	Celery	25 g	250 g	Wash, trim, finely dice and add. Cook without colouring until the vegetables are soft.
2	Haddock, cod or hake	100 g	1 kg	Remove the skin and bones, cut into small pieces and add. Cook for 4–5 minutes without colouring.
	Milk	125 ml	1¼ litres	Add.
	Water	125 ml	1¼ litres	Add, bring to the boil.
	Thyme	pinch	¼ bunch	Tie together and add. Simmer for 45 minutes.
3	Potatoes	125 g	1.25 kg	Wash, trim, cut into thin slices and add to the soup. Return to the boil, reduce to a simmer and cook until the potatoes disintegrate. Remove the thyme.
	Cream	10 ml	100 ml	Pour in and swirl.
	Fine chopped parsley	pinch	2 tsp	Sprinkle over the top and serve.

☐   ☐   ☐

Oysters with Guinness

Step	Commodity	1 portion	10 portions	
1	Oysters	8–12	80–120	Prepare in the usual manner (see Chapter 14: Cold preparations). Serve with tabasco sauce, salt and pepper, lemon wedges, buttered soda bread and Guinness.

☐   ☐   ☐

21

Sweet pickled herrings

Step	Commodity	1 portion	10 portions				
				⏲ 1 hr	🍲 15 min	🔥 180°C	
1	Malt vinegar	100 ml	1 litre	Place in a suitably sized saucepan.			
	Brown sugar	½ tbsp	5 tbsp	Add.			
	Thyme	pinch	1 sprig	Wash, dry and add.			
	Bay leaves	1 small	10 small	Add.			
	Onions	50 g	500 g	Peel, cut into thin rings and add.			
	Peppercorns	2	20	Add, season with salt and mixed spice. Mix well together. Bring to the boil and allow to cool.			
	Herrings	1 × 250 g	10 × 250 g	Prepare and fillet the herrings. Wash thoroughly to remove any blood. Place on their backs on a chopping board. Remove the onions and bayleaves from the marinade. Place the appropriate amount of onions and one bayleaf on each fillet. Roll up and secure. Place in a suitably sized earthenware dish. Pour over the marinade. Cover with buttered greaseproof paper and place in a pre-heated oven for the appropriate time. Remove, allow to go cold and serve either as a starter or main course.			

☐   ☐   ☐

Champ

Step	Commodity	1 portion	10 portions				
				⏲ 30 min	🍲 40 min	🔥 200°C	
1	Potatoes	150 g	1½ kg	Wash, peel and rewash. Place in a saucepan of cold water, season, bring to the boil and simmer for 20 minutes. Drain well, place in a bowl and mash roughly.			
	Butter	15 g	150 g	Cut into small pieces and mix in. Season with salt and pepper.			
2	Scallions	1 large	10 large	Wash, trim and cut into ½ cm rings.			
	Milk	50 ml	500 ml	Place in a suitably sized saucepan and add the scallions. Season with salt and pepper. Place on the stove, bring to the boil and simmer for 15 minutes. Pour half of the liquor over the potatoes and mix in. Place in a heat-resistant serving dish or dishes. Mould into mounds with a well in the centre. Place in a pre-heated oven for 8 minutes to reheat. Remove and divide the remaining liquor into the appropriate portions and place in the well. Serve immediately.			

☐   ☐   ☐

Colcannon

Step	Commodity	1 portion	10 portions			
				🥄 30 min	♨ 35 min	
1	Potatoes	100 g	1 kg	Peel, wash and cut into even pieces. Place in a saucepan of salted water and bring to the boil. Simmer for 20 minutes then drain.		
	Curly kale	100	1 kg	Wash thoroughly. Remove and discard the stalk and damaged leaves. Shred and place in a saucepan of boiling salted water for 15 minutes then drain.		
2	Butter	10 g	100 g	Melt in a suitably sized saucepan.		
	Onion	15 g	150 g	Peel, cut in half, slice thinly and add. Cook for 2–3 minutes without colouring. Add the potato and re-heat. Add the curly kale and mix together. Season with salt and pepper.		
	Milk/cream	15 ml	150 ml	Pour over the vegetables and mix thoroughly. Place in a pre-heated serving dish.		

☐   ☐   ☐

Irish stew

Step	Commodity	1 portion	10 portions			
				🥄 45 min	♨ 2½ hr	≋ 160°C
1	Mutton chops	250 g	2½ kg	Wash, trim excess fat and season with salt and pepper.		
	Dripping	20 g	200 g	Place in a suitably sized frying pan and heat. Add the chops and fry lightly on both sides. Place in a deep oven-proof dish.		
	Onions	100 g	1 kg	Peel, cut into large dice and sprinkle over the meat.		
	Carrots	75 g	750 g	Peel, cut into thin slices and add to the onions.		
	Mutton stock/water	125 ml	1¼ litres	Pour over the other ingredients and bring to the boil on top of the stove.		
	Potatoes	100 g	1 kg	Peel, cut into thin slices and add to the stew.		
	Thyme	pinch	1 sprig	Wash and add.		
	Chopped parsley	pinch	1 tbsp	Sprinkle over the other ingredients and mix in well. Correct the seasoning. Place in a pre-heated oven for the required time. Remove and serve.		

☐   ☐   ☐

21

Coddle (Saturday night stew)

Step	Commodity	1 portion	10 portions	
				⏱ 30 min 🍲 2½ hr
1	Lean bacon pieces	100 g	1 kg	Cut into 1 cm cubes and place in a suitably sized saucepan.
	Pork sausage	30 g	300 g	Cut into 1 cm pieces and add to the bacon.
	Pork/lamb kidney	25 g	250 g	Remove the skin, core and trim. Cut into small pieces and add.
	Onions	50 g	500 g	Peel, cut into medium dice and add.
	Thyme	pinch	1 sprig	Wash and add.
	Mutton/chicken stock	100 ml	1 litre	Pour over the other ingredients, bring to the boil and simmer.
2	Potatoes	75 g	750 g	Peel, cut into 2 cm pieces and add. Season with salt and white pepper. Simmer for the required time. Correct the seasoning.
3	Milk	25 ml	250 ml	Add and mix in. Sprinkle with finely chopped parsley. Serve immediately.

☐   ☐   ☐

Pig's cheek and cabbage

Step	Commodity	1 portion	10 portions	
				⏱ overnight 🍲 4 hr
1	Prepared pork cheek	150 g	1½ kg	Place in a saucepan of cold water. Bring to the boil and simmer for 4 hours. Lift out of the liquid and remove the meat from the cheek. Place the meat in a deep-sided dish. Cover with a plate, weigh the plate down to press the meat. Refrigerate overnight.
2	Potatoes	150 g	1½ kg	Peel, wash, cut into small pieces and place in a saucepan of cold water. Bring to the boil, season with salt and pepper. Simmer for 25 minutes and drain away the water.
	Butter	25 g	250 g	Add.
	Milk	15 ml	150 ml	Add, mix well, correct the seasoning.
	Cabbage	150 g	1½ kg	Wash, trim, discard the stalk and place in a saucepan of boiling salted water. Simmer for 20 minutes. Drain and add to the potato. Place in an oven-proof dish and re-heat. Cut the meat into the appropriate portions. Serve hot or cold with the cabbage and potatoes.

☐   ☐   ☐

Cruibins

Step	Commodity	1 portion	10 portions				🍲 overnight ♨ 3 hr
1	Pickled pig's trotters	2	20	Wash and soak overnight. Place in a suitably sized saucepan.
	Onions	50 g	500 g	Peel, cut into large dice and add.
	Carrots	50 g	500 g	Peel, slice thinly and add.
	Bayleaf	¼	2	Add.
	Thyme	pinch	1 sprig	Wash and add. Season with salt and pepper. Cover with cold water, bring to the boil and simmer for the required time. Remove, strain the cooking liquor and use for soup. Serve the trotters hot or cold with buttered soda bread.

☐   ☐   ☐

Guinness beef stew

Step	Commodity	1 portion	10 portions		🍲 overnight ♨ 2½ hr
1	Stewing beef	150 g	1½ kg	Cut into 2 cm cubes and place in a suitably sized bowl.
	Carrots	50 g	500 g	Peel, slice thinly and sprinkle over the beef.
	Onions	50 g	500 g	Peel, slice thinly and add.
	Brown sugar	½ tbsp	5 tbsp	Sprinkle over the other ingredients.
	Thyme	pinch	1 sprig	Wash and add.
	Parsley	pinch	1 sprig	Wash, trim and add. Season with salt and pepper.
	Guinness	100 ml	1 litre	Add and leave to marinade overnight. Place all the ingredients in a suitably sized saucepan.
2	Beef stock	100 ml	1 litre	Add, bring to the boil and simmer for 2 hours.
3	Cornflour	5 g	50 g	Dilute in a little water. Pour a sufficient amount into the stew to thicken so the sauce coats the back of the spoon. Correct the seasoning. Serve with colcannon or champ.

NOTE: This stew may be made with the addition of oysters or prunes.

☐   ☐   ☐

21

527

Spiced beef

Step	Commodity	1 portion	10 portions	
1	Brisket of beef	200 g	2 kg	Trim excess fat and lay on a clean meat tray.
	Sea salt	35 g	350 g	Sprinkle over the surface.
	Ground cloves	pinch	1 tsp	Sprinkle over the meat.
	Ground mace	pinch	1 tsp	Sprinkle over the meat.
	Ground cinnamon	pinch	1 tsp	Sprinkle over the meat.
	Ground nutmeg	pinch	1 tsp	Sprinkle over the meat.
	Ground juniperberries	pinch	1 tsp	Sprinkle over the meat.
	Ground allspice	pinch	1 tsp	Sprinkle over the meat.
	Milled black pepper	pinch	1 tsp	Sprinkle over the meat.
	Saltpetre	pinch	1 tsp	Sprinkle over the meat
	Bayleaves	¼	2	Crush and sprinkle over the meat.
	Brown sugar	25 g	250 g	Sprinkle over the meat. Cover with clingfilm and marinade in a refrigerator for four days, rubbing the seasonings into the meat. Roll and tie securely. Place in a suitably sized saucepan.
2	Carrots	50 g	500 g	Peel, slice thinly and add.
	Onions	50 g	500g	Peel, slice thinly and add.
	Celery	50 g	500 g	Wash, trim, cut into thin slices and add to the other ingredients.
	Thyme	pinch	1 sprig	Wash and add. Cover completely with cold water, bring to the boil and simmer for the required time. Remove and press with weights. Serve cold.

☐   ☐   ☐

Shanagarry porter steak

Step	Commodity	1 portion	10 portions	☝ 1 hr ♨ 45 min ≋ 190°C
1	Rump steak	1 × 200 g	10 × 200 g	Trim excess fat. Season with salt and milled black pepper.
	Butter	15 g	150 g	Place in a frying pan and heat. Add the steaks and fry on each side for 5 minutes. Remove and place in a pre-heated oven-proof dish. Keep warm.
2	Butter	10 g	100 g	Place in the same frying pan and heat.
	Onions	50 g	500 g	Peel, slice into rings and add.
	Brown sugar	½ tsp	5 tsp	Add and stir in. Cook until it has caramelised.
	Guinness	15 ml	150 ml	Add.
	Beef stock	15 ml	150 ml	Add.
	Mixed herbs	pinch	2 tbsp	Sprinkle over the liquid and mix in. Correct the seasoning. Pour over the steak and place in a pre-heated oven for 15 minutes. Sprinkle with finely chopped parsley.

☐ ☐ ☐

Carragheen moss pudding

Step	Commodity	1 portion	10 portions	☝ 2 hr ♨ 30 min
1	Carragheen	1 g	10 g	Place in a bowl. Cover with warm water and soak for 15 minutes. Drain and place in a saucepan.
	Milk	125 ml	1¼ litres	Add.
	Vanilla pod	¹⁄₁₀ stick	1 stick	Add, bring to the boil and simmer for 20 minutes. Strain into a clean bowl. Discard the vanilla pod. Sieve the jelly from swollen carragheen into the milk. Whisk thoroughly until smooth.
	Castor sugar	½ tbsp	5 tbsp	Add.
	Egg yolk	¼ equiv	2½	Place in a bowl and beat until white. Add the flavoured milk.
	Egg whites	¼ equiv	2½	Place in a clean bowl. Whisk until stiff peaks are formed. Fold into the mixture. Pour into the serving glasses. Refrigerate for 1½ hours.

NOTE: Carragheen moss pudding can be flavoured with fruit purée or Irish coffee sauce. (Carragheen is a type of seaweed.)

☐ ☐ ☐

21

Irish coffee sauce

Step	Commodity	1 portion	10 portions		🥄 30 min
1	Castor sugar	50 g	500 g	Place in a suitably sized saucepan.	
	Water	1 tbsp	10 tbsp	Add and dissolve. Bring to the boil, reduce to a simmer and cook to the caramel stage. Arrest immediately.	
	Water	½ tbsp	5 tbsp	Add and allow the effervescence to subside. Return to the heat and cook gently.	
	Coffee essence	1 tsp	10 tsp	Add and stir in.	
	Whiskey	½ tsp	5 tsp	Add and mix with the other ingredients. Allow to cool. The sauce is now ready to use.	

☐　　☐　　☐

Barm brack

Step	Commodity	1 portion	10 portions		🥄 1½ hr　♨ 1 hr　≋ 200°C
1	Plain flour	100 g	1 kg	Place in a suitably sized bowl.	
	Salt	small pinch	large pinch	Add.	
	Nutmeg	pinch	1 tsp	Add.	
	Cinnamon	pinch	1 tsp	Add, sieve into another bowl.	
	Butter	10 g	100 g	Add and rub in.	
2	Fresh yeast	3 g	30 g	Place in a jug.	
	Tepid water	35 ml	350 ml	Add and cream with the water.	
	Castor sugar	pinch	2 tbsp	Add, dissolve with the other ingredients and place somewhere warm for 15 minutes. Add to the flour and mix in.	
	Tepid milk	35 ml	350 ml	Place in a jug.	
	Egg	¼ equiv	2	Add and whisk thoroughly.	
	Castor sugar	pinch	3 tbsp	Add and dissolve. Add and knead for 10 minutes until a soft dough is achieved. Allow to prove for 30 minutes. Knock back and roll out on a floured surface.	
3	Currants	45 g	450 g	Wash and rinse. Add to the dough.	
	Mixed candied peel	20 g	200 g	Add to the dough and knead until the fruit is evenly spread throughout. Place into the appropriately sized greased bread tins and allow the dough to double in size. Brush with eggwash and place in a pre-heated oven for the appropriate time. Turn out onto a wire rack. Serve with butter.	

☐　　☐　　☐

Traditional Irish Christmas pudding

Step	Commodity	1 portion	10 portions	⌣ overnight ♨ 7 hr
1	Fresh breadcrumbs	50 g	500 g	Place in a suitably sized bowl.
	Brown sugar	30 g	300 g	Add.
	Currants	30 g	300 g	Add.
	Seedless raisins	50 g	500 g	Add.
	Sultanas	30 g	300 g	Add.
	Chopped mixed peel	7½ g	75 g	Add.
	Prepared suet	30 g	300 g	Add.
	Mixed spice	pinch	2 tsp	Add.
	Lemon	⅛	1½	Remove the rind and add. Cut the lemon in half. Squeeze the juice through a strainer and into the fruit.
	Eggs	¼	2½	Add.
	Milk	20 ml	200 ml	Add.
	Guinness	35 ml	350 ml	Add and mix well together. Cover with a cloth and leave overnight in a cool area. Divide into the appropriate steaming bowls. Cover and steam for 6–7 hours. Serve with custard or rum sauce.

NOTE: Allow 2–2½ hours for reheating.

□   □   □

21

531

Soda farls

Step	Commodity	1 portion	10 portions	
1	Self-raising flour	25 g	250 g	Place in a bowl.
	Bicarbonate of soda	1/10 tsp	1 tsp	Add and sieve together 3 times.
	Salt	1/10 tsp	1 tsp	Add.
	Sugar	1/10 tsp	1 tsp	Add.
	Sour or butter milk	30 ml	300 ml	Add and mix to a soft dough (more or less milk might be needed). Roll out into 8 cm rounds, 1 cm thick. Either cook on a hot, dry griddle or in a little pre-heated bacon fat in a frying pan. Serve with butter and jam.

☐ ☐ ☐

Soda bread loaf

Step	Commodity	1 portion	10 portions	
1	Self-raising wholewheat flour	10 g	100 g	Place in a bowl.
	Self-raising flour	10 g	100 g	Sieve over the wholemeal flour and mix in. Add a pinch of salt.
	Egg	1/10	1	Add.
	Sour or butter milk	25 ml	250 ml	Add and mix to a soft dough (more or less milk might be needed). Roll out into a circle on a floured surface. Make a deep cross shape on the top. Leave to rest for 10 minutes. Place in a pre-heated oven for 15–20 minutes. Remove and cool on a wire rack. Slice and serve with butter. Serve with breakfast or any other meal.

☐ ☐ ☐

EASTERN COOKERY

Asia contains over half the world's population and its cookery encompasses the diversity in culture and religion of the peoples and countries of India, Pakistan, Bangladesh, Malaysia, Singapore, Indonesia, Burma, Thailand, Kampuchea, Laos, Vietnam, China, Japan, the Philippines and Korea.

Terminology and ingredients associated with Eastern cookery

Aburage Fried soybean cake.

Agar-agar Known as kanten in Japan. A kind of seaweed available in long white strands or powdered form. To be used in very small quantities, as a little will quickly set a large volume of liquid. It has almost no taste or colour. Powdered gelatine may be substituted, allowing 4 tablespoons gelatine to 25 g/1 oz agar-agar.

Akamiso Soybean paste, reddish brown in colour.

Ata A type of wholemeal (wholewheat) flour used in the preparation of breads. Sometimes sold in the West as chappati flour.

Azuki Red beans. Sweetened azuki beans are available in cans.

Bagoong See fish paste.

Balachan See terasi.

Bamboo shoots, dried Not a substitute for fresh or canned bamboo shoots. Dried bamboo shoots have their own special flavour and texture. Soak in hot water for at least 2 hours before using.

Bean curd Known as tahu or taukwa in Indonesia/Malaysia. Made of puréed and pressed soya beans, its texture is like soft cheese. Sold in cakes, 7.5 cm/3 inches square and 2.5 cm/1 inch thick. It will keep fresh for several days if stored in water in the refrigerator. Dried bean curd skin is also available, in packets of sheets or sticks; soak in cold water overnight or in warm water for 1 hour before using.

Beans, salted Known as tao chiew in Thailand and tauco in Indonesia/Malaysia. Black soya beans which have been steamed, spiced and preserved in salt. Sold in cans and packets. Should be transferred to an airtight jar and stored in the refrigerator; will then keep for up to 1 year.

Bean sauce Also known as yellow bean sauce and brown or black bean sauce. Crushed yellow soya beans, mixed to a paste with flour, vinegar, spices and salt; sold in jars and cans.

Bean threads See mung bean threads.

Belimbing wuluh A sour kind of fresh fruit. Common in South-East Asia, but unobtainable in Europe and USA. Lemon, lime or rhubarb may be used as a substitute.

Bengi-shoga Red salt preserved ginger.

Besan See terasi.

Biryanis Biryanis are festive casseroles in which partially cooked rice is layered over cooked meat. Biryanis are perfumed with the scent of saffron.

Boo A long white radish resembling a parsnip in appearance. It has a mild flavour and English radishes should not be used as a substitute. If unobtainable, use tender white turnips as a substitute.

Buah keras See kemiri.

Bumbu A general term for any mixture of ingredients that gives a strong flavour to a dish. It can refer to the dry ingredients, or to the sauces that are made from them.

Bun tau See mung bean threads.

Cabe rawit Small, very hot chillis – red, green or sometimes white in colour.

Candlenut See kermiri.

Cardamom (elaichi) Black, green and white varieties used in both savoury and sweet dishes.

Cellophane noodles *See* mung bean threads.

Chatties Round bottomed earthenware cooking dishes. Can be substituted by a wok or skillet.

Chillies (hari mirch) Strong peppers, should be used sparingly.

Chinese parsley *See* cilantro, see coriander.

Cinnamon (dalchini) Available in stick form (quills) and ground.

Citronella *See* lemon grass.

Cloud ear *See* wood ear.

Clove (lavang) Available whole or ground, used in both sweet and savoury dishes.

Coconut milk Best made from fresh coconuts: grate the flesh of 1 coconut into a bowl, pour on 600 ml/1 pint/2½ cups boiling water, then leave to stand for about 30 minutes. Squeeze the flesh, then strain before using. This quantity will make a thick coconut milk, add more or less water as required. Desiccated (shredded) coconut can be used instead of fresh coconut. Use 350 g/12 oz/4 cups to 600 ml/1 pint/2½ cups boiling water. Use freshly made coconut milk within 24 hours. Canned coconut milk is also available.

Coconut sugar Also known as palm sugar. Brown sugar may be substituted.

Coriander Also known as pak chee, dhania, ngo, Chinese parsley and cilantro. Widely used in South-East Asian cooking in the form of leaves, roots, stems, seeds and powder. In Vietnam, Laos and Kampuchea only the fresh leaves and stems are used and are indispensable to these cuisines. The fresh leaves are usually chopped, the roots will keep in an airtight jar. Can easily be grown outdoors in summer. Parsley is often substituted for fresh coriander although it does not impart the same flavour.

Creamed coconut Sold in slabs and cakes. More concentrated than coconut milk. Cut up roughly before using, then heat gently with water, stirring frequently, until melted. Use as coconut milk.

Culantro Also known as ngo tay. A member of the coriander family. Each stem has 1 elongated leaf which grows in a dark green cluster.

Cumin (zeera) White cumin seeds are sweet and aromatic, black are more aromatic.

Curry leaves (kariapath) Curry leaves are aromatic and have an earthy flavour.

Daikon A long white radish. Sometimes referred to as the 'workhorse' of the Japanese diet, it is a basic vegetable in Japanese cooking. Use both raw and cooked.

Daun Jeruk purut The leaf of a fruit similar to a lime.

Dhal The general name given to a variety of pulses grown in the Indian sub-continent. Along with rice, these pulses form the stable diet of millions of peasants. There are several varieties – moong, urhad, chenna and the dhal, which most people in the West are familiar with and know as the lentil. They are all interchangeable, and the cooking method is the same for each.

Dhania *See* coriander.

Dried mushrooms *See* mushrooms, dried.

Ebi Tiny uncooked dried shrimps.

Fiddlehead ferns *See* paku.

Fish paste Known as bagoong in the Philippines. It is a thick paste made from fermented fish or shrimps and salt. Used in small quantities as a relish. Kampuchean fish paste is made from whole preserved anchovies which are strained when required.

Fish sauce Known as patis in the Philippines, nam pla in Thailand, nuoc cham or nuoc mam in Kampuchea, Laos and Vietnam. Prepared from fresh anchovies and salt which are layered in wooden barrels and left to ferment. The liquid that is drained off initially is light and clear and considered to be the best quality; the two subsequent extractions are darker and of a poorer quality.

Five spice powder A reddish-brown aromatic powder made from a combination of ground spices – anise, cloves, cinnamon, fennel and Szechuan pepper. These spices are sold as 'five spices', ready mixed but whole. Will keep indefinitely in an airtight container.

Galingale Known as laos in Malaysia, kha in Thailand. It is the root of a plant resembling ginger, with a delicate flavour. Used fresh, but only dried galingale is obtainable in the West. Soak in hot water for 1 hour before using in cooking, then remove before serving. Galingale powder is also available.

Garam masala Made from a mixture of cinnamon stick, green cardamom pods, whole cloves, cumin seeds, coriander seeds and black pepper. A must to create that Indian flavour to food.

Garbanzo beans Chick peas.

Ghee Clarified butter. To make pure ghee: heat 1.5 kg/3 lb unsalted (sweet) butter over a low heat in a heavy pan. Skim off any floating impurities, then maintain the heat at just below simmering point for 1 hour. Strain through several layers of cheescloth (muslin), then store in a cool place. It will keep for several months. Many Indian cooks use a ghee substitute derived from vegetable oil; this is available from Asian stores.

Ginger Fresh root ginger, sometimes referred to as 'green ginger'. Peel before using, then slice, crush or chop finely. To keep fresh: peel, then wash and place in a jar, cover with pale dry sherry, seal and store in the refrigerator. Ground ginger is not an acceptable substitute, but fried root ginger may be used, in which case the quantity should be decreased as it is sharper in taste.

Glutinous (sweet) rice Known as mochigome in Japan. Also sometimes referred to as 'sticky rice'. Short grain rice that becomes very sticky when cooked. Used in stuffings, cakes and puddings. In Laos it is used in place of long grain rice and served with all meals.

Glutinous (sweet) rice flour Known as mochiko in Japan. Made from ground glutinous (sweet) rice. There is no substitute.

Gobo Edible burdock roots.

Goma *See* sesame seeds.

Goma jio Salted sesame seeds. Dry fry 1 tablespoon black sesame seeds in a hot frying pan (skillet) until they 'jump', shaking the pan constantly. Transfer to a bowl and then sprinkle with 2 teaspoons of salt.

Gula jawa Also known as gula malaka. Brown palm sugar, sold in thin blocks. Demerara or Muscovado sugar may be used as a substitute.

Gyoza skins Round in shape. Wun tun (wonton) skins may be used as a substitute.

Hakusai *See* napa.

Harusame Soya bean noodles. Can be used instead of mung bean threads if these are unobtainable.

Hijiki Brown algae seaweed.

Hoi sin (hosin) sauce Also known as Chinese barbecue sauce. Made from soya beans, flour, sugar, spices and red food colouring.

Horapa A member of the ocimum family, like sweet basil. Use fresh rather than dried. Sweet basil may be used as a substitute.

Jelly mushrooms *See* wood ear.

Kamaboko Japanese fish cake.

Kapi *See* terasi.

Karhai An Indian karhai is used to cook deep-fried items.

Kasu Rice wine lees.

Katsuobshi Dried bonito fish.

Kecap Indonesian soy sauce. Darker and sweeter than Chinese light soy sauce which is very salty.

Kemiri Pale yellow nuts, roughly the same size as chestnuts.

Kha *See* galingale.

Kochujang Hot bean mash paprika paste. The nearest equivalent is mashed onions and chilli powder fried in oil.

Kombu Tangle or kelp seaweed. Used in making dashi.

Konnyaku Tuber root cake.

Laksa *See* rice vermicelli.

Laos *See* galingale.

Lemon grass The lower third of the stalk, the bulb-like portion, is the part to use when a recipe specifies 'chopped or sliced lemon grass'. Alternatively, the whole stalk may be bruised and added during cooking, but removed before serving. Dry lemon grass is a good substitute – soak for 2 hours before serving. Powdered lemon grass is also available.

Lime leaves Fresh lime leaves are preferred, but they are virtually unobtainable in the West. Dry lime leaves are available from Oriental stores.

Lombok Chilli – red (lombok merah) green (lombok hijau). Lombok rawit are the hottest and are available in dried form in the West.

Makrut An ugly-looking citrus fruit which has a very strongly flavoured peel and leaves. The peel is ground with other ingredients in curry pastes and the leaves used in soups. Lemon leaves may be used as a substitute.

Matcha Powdered green tea used for the traditional Japanese tea ceremony. The tea is made from the most tender tea leaves of the first spring picking, and is processed by a very expensive and tedious method.

Mint *See* saranae.

Mirin Sweetened sake (rice wine) used in cooking and for seasoning. If unavailable, dry sherry and sugar may be substituted.

Miso *See* soy bean paste.

Miti Wide egg noodles can be used as a substitute.

Mochigome *See* glutinous (sweet) rice.

Mochiko *See* glutinous (sweet) rice flour.

Monosodium glutamate A chemical compound sometimes known as 'taste essence'. Used for bringing out the natural flavours of food, it is entirely optional in all recipes.

22

Mung beans Dried mung beans are very small and green in colour. Dried split peas may be used as a substitute. Mung beans are usually available in good health and food stores. When their green husks have been removed, dry mung beans are yellow in colour.

Mung bean threads These are very fine dried noodles made from mung bean flour. Sold in packets. Soak in water for approximately 10 minutes before using.

Mushrooms, dried Chinese and Japanese dried mushrooms (lentinus edoces) are sold in Oriental stores, are very fragrant, and will keep almost indefinitely in an airtight jar. Ordinary mushrooms do not make a good substitute.

Mushrooms, dried jelly See wood ear.

Nam pla See fish sauce.

Napa Chinese cabbage occasionally referred to as celery cabbage. Napa has very delicate leaves and is used both raw and cooked. Bok choy can be used as a substitute.

Ngapi See terasi.

Ngo See coriander.

Ngo tay See culantro.

Nori Dried seaweed. Ofted toasted, then shredded and used as a garnish.

Nuoc cham/Nuoc mam See fish sauce.

Oyster sauce A thickish brown sauce with a rich flavour. Made from oysters and soy sauce. It will keep indefinitely in the refrigerator.

Pak chee See coriander.

Paku Young edible fern shoots. Young curly kale may be used as a substitute.

Panko Coarse breadcrumbs.

Patis See fish sauce.

Prawns, dried Sold in packets in Chinese supermarkets. The best kind are bright pink in colour as they are the freshest. Rinse before use to remove dirt and excess salt.

Puris Puris are a deep fried bread made from a mixture of plain and wheatmeal flour and resemble puffed up balloons. They are served hot as an accompaniment to any meal.

Radish, white Chinese See boo.

Rice flour Made from ground rice. Can be made at home using an electric blender, coffee mill or pestle and mortar.

Rice papers, dried Thin, brittle, disc-like pancakes (crêpe) used in many ways: to make spring rolls and as a wrapper for a variety of foods. Moisten with water or egg to make them flexible before using.

Rice powder Extremely fine powdered rice. When specified in a recipe, it must be assumed that rice flour may not be used.

Rice vermicelli Rice sticks or rice noodles in North America. Noodles made from rice flour which come in a variety of sizes. In soups, the very thin string-like variety called bun are used. The different sizes may be interchanged in recipes if it is difficult to obtain the exact type specified.

Rice wine See sake.

Rijsttafel Rice table. The name given by the Dutch to a variety of Indonesian dishes that are all served together.

Rock sugar Crystallised sugar, amber in colour. It is used to give a glaze to certain dishes.

Saifun See mung bean threads.

Sake Rice wine. Dry sherry makes an acceptable substitute.

Salam The leaves of this plant are used extensively in Malaysian cooking. Bay leaves can be used as a substitute.

Salt fish, dried Sword fish is the commonest fish used. Rinse well to remove excess salt before serving. Available at Oriental stores.

Sambal ulek Used as an accompaniment and in cooking. It is made by crushing fresh red chillies with a little salt. Also available ready-prepared in small jars from Oriental stores and delicatessens.

Sansho The fresh leaves of this bush are used for fragrance and garnish. Powdered sansho, a fragrant pepper, is also available.

Santen See coconut milk.

Saranae Mint. Always use spearmint in preference to other types of mint for Thai recipes.

Saté A general name for any kind of meat, poultry or fish that is grilled (broiled) on a skewer.

Serai/Sereh See lemon grass.

Sesame seeds There are two types of sesame seeds, white and black and they may be used raw or toasted. To toast sesame seeds, dry fry in a hot frying pan (skillet) until they 'jump', shaking the pan constantly.

Sesame seed oil A strongly-flavoured seasoning oil made from roasted sesame seeds. Used for its fragrance and the flavour it imparts to other foods. Sold in bottles.

Shio Shio is a mixture of 7 spices, ground to a spicy hot powder. Not to be confused with Five spice powder. Used in noodles and other cooked dishes.

Shiitake, dried *See* mushrooms, dried.

Shiitake, fresh Japanese mushrooms, which have an entirely different, more delicate flavour than their dried counterparts. Vitamin-packed and exalted as 'the elixir of life' in many Asian countries. Ordinary mushrooms do not make a good substitute.

Shirataki Yam noodles. Sold in cans. Mung bean threads may be substituted.

Shiromiso White soy bean paste.

Shoyu Light soy sauce prepared from fermented cooked soya beans, wheat malt and salt. Do not substitute Chinese or other soy sauces; their flavour is completely different and will spoil Japanese dishes.

Shrimps, dried Available whole, pounded or powdered, from Oriental stores.

Shrimp-flavoured soy sauce It gives a fishy taste to dishes. Ordinary soy sauce can be used as a substitute. Available from Chinese stores.

Shrimp paste Made from salted dried shrimps. Greyish pink in colour. Anchovies mixed with a little vinegar may be used as a substitute, but is not really satisfactory. Available in jars from Chinese stores.

Silver leaf *See* verak.

Somen Very thin, thread-like wheat vermicelli.

Soy bean paste A basic seasoning made from cooked soya beans, malt and salt. Sold in plastic packs at Oriental stores.

Split pea flour Made from ground or pounded split peas. Can be made at home using an electric blender or a pestle and mortar.

Su Rice vinegar, distilled from white rice. It has a very sweet aromatic quality and is much milder than cider vinegar. If unobtainable, substitute distilled white vinegar and mix with water. Seasoned rice vinegars, with sugar and monsodium glutamate added, are also available.

Szechuan preserved vegetable A root vegetable pickled in salt and chilli, which is therefore very hot and salty to the taste. Sold in cans, it should be transferred to an airtight jar once opened, then it will keep for several months in the refrigerator.

Tahu/taukwa *See* bean curd.

Takrai *See* lemon grass.

Tamarind An acid-flavoured fruit resembling a bean pod. It is sold as dried tamarind pulp in blocks and is dark brown in colour. The dried tamarind pulp must be made into tamarind water before using. The longer the tamarind is left to soak, the stronger the flavour. The amount of tamarind pulp and water can be adjusted according to the thickness required; the thicker the water, the more sour it tastes. Lemon, lime or mango juice or vinegar may be used as substitutes but the flavour of the finished dish will not be the same. Tamarind paste is also available, packaged in plastic bags. Once opened, it should be refrigerated and it will then keep indefinitely. Available from Oriental stores.

Tao chiew *See* beans, salted.

Tauco *See* beans, salted.

Tawa A convex griddle used to cook unleavened bread. An upturned cast iron skillet may be used in its place.

Tepung beras *See* rice powder.

Terasi A kind of pungent shrimp paste. It is used in very small quantities. Depending on the recipe in which it is used, it may be crushed with spices to make a paste which is then sautéed in oil. Alternatively, it may be grilled (broiled) or fried first, then added to other ingredients.

Tiger lily A dried bud, golden-yellow in colour and crunchy in texture. Soak in water before using. It keeps indefinitely.

Tofu Soy bean curd 'cake'.

Tonkatsu sauce A commercially-prepared thick brown sauce made from fruit and vegetables combined with spices and seasonings. Soy sauce or ketchup may be used as substitutes.

Transparent noodles *See* mung bean threads.

Tree ear *See* wood ear.

Tung chai Tiensin-preserved vegetables. Obtainable from Chinese supermarkets.

Udon A thick, broad noodle made from flour and water (without eggs).

Verak Used solely for decorative purposes, although it is said to aid the digestion. Available from most Indian food suppliers.

Wakame Lobe leaf seaweed. Traditionally, the heavy vein is removed; the vein can be eaten, but it is rather chewy.

Wasabi A green horseradish grated from the root of the Eutrema Wasabi. Use green horseradish powder, which is very pungent and hot, for convenience as fresh wasabi is both difficult to obtain and very expensive. Dry mustard mixed to a

22

paste with a little water may be used as a substitute.

Water chestnut A walnut-sized bulb with brown skin; the inside flesh is white and crisp. Canned water chestnuts are ready peeled and will keep for approximately 1 month in the refrigerator.

Wood ear A dried tree fungus. To be used in small quantities. Soak in water for approximately 20 minutes before using, until they become glutinous and crinkly. The dried fungus will keep indefinitely. Available at Chinese supermarkets.

Wun sen See mung bean threads.

Wun tun skins Paper-thin squares or circles of dough. Can be made at home, or bought ready-rolled and trimmed at Chinese supermarkets. Store in the refrigerator or freezer.

Indian, Pakistani and Bangladeshi cookery

Indian cookery is greatly influenced by the various cultures of the many immigrants who have settled there, none more so than the Persians who, among other dishes, introduced pilaffs (pilau, pilow). Pilau is rice-based and is cooked in ghee. It is heavily spiced and sometimes contains sultanas, raisins and almonds.

It seems to be a rule that the hotter the temperature the hotter the food. Vindaloo, the hottest of all curries, hails from Madras. Madras cooking is very much more pungent than anything in Hindustan, and Madrassi curries tend to be thin and watery.

In the North, particularly northern Pakistan, tandoori cooking has dominated for centuries. A tandoor is a clay oven, conically shaped like a bee-hive. Tandoori recipes depend on quick cooking. Meat is cut into portions and marinaded, then cooked in the searing temperatures reached inside the oven.

Mogul style cookery extends down towards central India and lays great emphasis on presentation. From Mogul cooking a new and differing style developed around Delhi. Bombay, being a major port, has developed a very cosmopolitan style including various multi-cultural additions to traditional cookery such as sweet and sour dishes learned from the Chinese.

The west coast Christian Indians have developed their own styles, particularly in Goa. Further south on the Keralanese coast the use of fenugreek has been developed into a fine art, mainly to absorb odours in fish dishes.

The Tamils make use of the plentiful supplies of coconut and hardly a main dish is prepared without the use of coconut in one form or another. Biryanis are a form of pilau and most people think of them as Indian foods. Bengalis specialise in fish and bamboo curries, cooked in mustard oil, and in rice. In the Punjab the flat, unlevened, wholewheat bread called parathaas often replaces rice and lentils, of which a great variety are eaten. Kaleja kari (curried calf's liver) and Cobbi ki sabzi (curried cauliflower) also originate from the area. Baingan ka raita (aubergine in yoghurt) and Kheema biryani (minced lamb rice) are from Northern India, while the south supplies us with dishes such as Baingan pakora (deep fried aubergine) and chapatis (wholemeal bread).

Hindus' main celebrations are Holi, the end of winter, and Janam Ashtami, the birth of Krishna. Dishes are usually vegetarian and Hindu cookery specialises in cakes of wheat and rice dishes prepared in a multitude of ways. Muslims celebrate the birth of Mohammed in late February or early March. Only meat prepared by a halal butcher (by Muslim law) is permitted. Ramadan is one month of fasting when strict Muslims do not eat or drink anything between the hours of sunrise and sunset. The end of Ramadan is celebrated by the feast of Idd-ul-Fitar. Muslims will eat dishes containing game, fish, fowl, mutton and beef but pork is taboo. Muslim cooking tends to be drier in texture than Hindu. Sikhs do not have any rules regarding diet.

Indian food is made to be eaten by hand. Generally speaking the food is offered like a buffet and people help themselves to how much and the variety they require. In parts of India foods are served prearranged on large individual metal platters (thalis), with the more 'wet' dishes being served in smaller bowls called katoris. These platters contain everything, from salty snacks such as samosas to sweets.

CURRY INGREDIENTS

Curry powder is not just one spice; it is made up of a mixture of the following spices. The more chilli used the stronger or more 'hot' the curry powder will be.

English	Indian	English	Indian	English	Indian	English	Indian
Aniseed	Souf	Coriander	Dhummia	Black	Kala	Turmeric	Huldie
Allspice	Setul		or	pepper	mirchi	Fenugreek	Mayti
Cardamom	Elaichi		Kotimear	Mustard	Rai	Garlic	Lassoon
Mace	Jawatrie	Cloves	Laoong	seeds		Ginger	Udruck
Nutmeg	Jauphul	Cumin	Zeera	Chillies	Lal mirchi	Poppy	Khush-
Cinnamon	Kulmie darchini	seeds				seeds	khush

Deep fried puffy bread   Puris

👋 5 min   ♨ 10 min

Step	Commodity	1 portion	10 portions	
1	Wheatmeal flour	25 g	250 g	Sieve into a bowl. Add a pinch of salt.
	Plain flour	25 g	250 g	Add to the wheatmeal flour.
	Vegetable oil	½ tbsp	5 tbsp	Pour over the flour and rub in until the mixture resembles coarse breadcrumbs.
	Water	25 ml	250 ml	Slowly add the water to form a stiff ball of dough. Knead the dough for 10 minutes or until it is smooth. Cover and allow the dough to rest for 30 minutes. Knead again and divide into the appropriate pieces, allowing three per portion. Flatten each ball out into a 13 cm round. Deep fry each round for about 20–30 seconds on each side at 190°C until they 'blister and puff up'.

☐   ☐   ☐

Crisp rice pancakes   Hoppers

👋 10 min   ♨ 1 min each

Step	Commodity	1 portion	10 portions	
1	Creamed coconut	10 g	100 g	Place in a saucepan.
	Water	15 ml	150 ml	Pour over the coconut, place on the heat and boil. Stir until all the creamed coconut is dissolved. Allow to cool.
2	Rice flour	25 g	250 g	Place in a bowl.
	Baking powder	pinch	½ tsp	Add to the rice flour and sieve together a couple of times. Whisk in the liquid to form the batter. Lightly grease a hot frying pan with a little ghee. Pour in a little of the batter, tilting the pan so the batter spreads. Cook for the required time or until the centre is solid. Do not turn over. Serve hot.

☐   ☐   ☐

22

Naan bread

Traditionally baked in the clay tandoor oven, naan bread is served with tandoori dishes.

Step	Commodity	1 portion	10 portions		⏱ 1 hr 35 min	♨ 10–12 min
1	Plain flour	50 g	500 g	Place in a bowl.		
	Baking powder	¼ tsp	2 tsp	Add to the flour and sieve thoroughly.		
	Plain yoghurt	50 ml	500 ml	Add and mix well to a dough. Allow to rest for 20 minutes. Divide into the correct number of portions and roll out to 1 cm thickness. Cover with a damp cloth. Place in a warm place and allow to rest for 1½ hours or until they have doubled in size.		
	Poppy seeds	pinch	2 tsp	Sprinkle over the breads. Bake for 10–12 minutes. If a tandoor is not available, cook under the grill or on top of a stove until they puff up and are light brown in colour.		

☐ ☐ ☐

Chapatis

Unleavened bread, cooked on a convex griddle known as a 'tawa'.

Step	Commodity	1 portion	10 portions		⏱ 35 min	♨ 20 min
1	Wholewheat flour (ata)	50 g	500 g	Place in a bowl.		
	Salt	pinch	1 tsp	Add to the flour and sieve thoroughly.		
	Tepid water	40 ml	400 ml	Add and mix well to form a dough. Turn out onto a lightly floured surface and knead for 5 minutes. Allow to rest for 20 minutes. Divide into the correct number of portions and roll out to 1 cm thickness. Dust an upturned frying skillet lightly and place over the heat. Allow to get very hot. Place the chapati over the top and cook for 3–4 minutes. Turn over and cook the other side for the same time. Remove the chapati with tongs. To achieve the blistered effect characteristic of chapatis they must be placed immediately onto direct heat for a few seconds until they swell up. Keep hot to serve.		

☐ ☐ ☐

Fresh mango chutney

Step	Commodity	1 portion	10 portions	�̮ 35 min Marinading time: Overnight
1	Mangoes	½	5	Peel and remove the stones. Cut the flesh into thin slices and place in a bowl.
	Green chillies	¼	2	Remove the seeds and the stalk. Finely chop and add to the mangoes.
	Ginger	5 g	50 g	Peel, chop finely and add.
	Onion	10 g	100 g	Peel, cut in half, dice finely and add.
	Garlic	¼ clove	1 clove	Peel, crush and add.
	Cumin powder	pinch	1 tsp	Add.
2	Vinegar	1 tsp	1 tbsp	Pour over the ingredients.
	Lemon	1 tsp	1 tbsp	Pour over the ingredients. Add a pinch of salt and a pinch of sugar. Stir well and cover. Place in the fridge and allow to marinade overnight.

☐   ☐   ☐

Lime pickle

Step	Commodity	1 portion	10 portions	⏝ 48 hr Marinading time: 20 min
1	Limes	1	10	Wash and cut the limes into thin wedges. Remove the pips and pith. Place in a bowl and sprinkle with salt. Cover with a clean cloth and allow to stand for 48 hours. Stir occasionally. Place the limes and the juice into a saucepan.
2	Seedless raisins	40 g	400 g	Wash and place in a blender.
	Chilli powder	pinch	2 tsp	Add.
	Garlic	½	5	Peel and add.
	Ginger	5 g	50 g	Peel and add.
	Cider vinegar	30 ml	300 ml	Pour over the other ingredients and liquidise. Add to the limes.
3	Brown sugar	40 g	400 g	Add.
	Grated horseradish	½ tsp	4 tbsp	Add, bring to the boil and simmer until thick. When cold, pour into an appropriate container.

NOTE: In India, cooling yoghurt dishes are served with all meals.

☐   ☐   ☐

541

Lassi

Step	Commodity	1 portion	10 portions	
1	Natural yoghurt	150 ml	1½ litres	Place in a suitably sized bowl.
	Iced water	50 ml	500 ml	Add to the yoghurt.
	Fresh chopped mint	1 tsp	10 tsp	Add and whisk until smooth and creamy. Season with salt to taste. Serve chilled in glasses, garnish with sprigs of fresh mint and ground cardamom.

☐   ☐   ☐

Yoghurt with cucumber and mint

Kheere ka raita

Step	Commodity	1 portion	10 portions	
1	Natural yoghurt	150 ml	1½ litres	Place in a suitably sized bowl.
	Cucumber	50 g	500 g	Peel, grate and add to the yoghurt.
	Fresh chopped mint	1 tsp	10 tsp	Add.
	Roast cumin seeds	pinch	2 tsp	Add.
	Cayenne pepper	pinch	½ tsp	Add and season mixture with salt and black pepper. Whisk until smooth and creamy. Serve chilled.

☐   ☐   ☐

Chicken korma

Kookarh korma

Step	Commodity	1 portion	10 portions	Marinading time: Overnight 1 hr approximately
1	Yoghurt	50 ml	500 ml	Place in a suitably sized bowl. Season with salt and crushed black pepper.
	Onion	25 g	250 g	Peel, dice and add.
	Garlic	¼ clove	2 cloves	Peel, crush and add to the yoghurt. Add a pinch of chilli powder and whisk the ingredients together.
	Prepared chicken	1 × 250 g	10 × 250 g	Remove the skin and place chicken in the yoghurt mixture. Allow to marinade overnight.
2	Ghee	20 g	200 g	Place in a suitably sized wok and heat.
	Ginger	5 g	50 g	Peel and place in a blender.
	Garlic	½ clove	5 cloves	Peel and add to the ginger and blend. Fry in the hot fat.
	Coriander seed	¼ tsp	2 tsp	Add to the hot fat.
	Cinnamon stick	1 cm	10 cm	Add.
	Cardamom pods	1	10	Add.
	Cinnamon	½ cm piece	2 cm piece	Add.
	Cumin seed	pinch	2 tsp	Add and cook for 1 minute. Reduce the heat. Add the chicken and the marinade.
	Desiccated coconut	¼ tsp	2 tsp	Add and cook for 50 minutes or until the chicken is tender. Serve hot.

☐   ☐   ☐

Chicken palak

Spiced chicken with spinach

⏲ 30 min 🍲 45 min ≋ 180°C

Step	Commodity	1 portion	10 portions	
1	Ghee	15 g	150 g	Place in a suitable frying pan, melt and heat.
	Garlic	½ clove	2 cloves	Peel, crush and add to the ghee.
	Chicken	350 g equiv	3½ kg	Clean and prepare as for sautéing. Place in the pre-heated ghee and cook.
	Onions	15 g	150 g	Peel and cut into slices. When the chicken is nearly brown, add the onions to the chicken and continue cooking until golden brown. Lower the heat.
	Fresh ginger	10 g	75 g	Peel, chop and add.
	Chilli powder	¼ tsp	2 tsp	Add to the ginger.
	Ground cumin	¼ tsp	2 tsp	Add.
	Garam masala	¼ tsp	2 tsp	Add.
	Coriander	¼ tsp	2 tsp	Add and sweat for 2–3 minutes.
	Spinach	60 g	600 g	Wash, remove the stalk, chop finely and add to the chicken.
2	Chicken stock	60 ml	600 ml	Pour over the ingredients, bring to the boil, cover with a lid and place in a pre-heated oven for 30 minutes. Serve with rice, chapatis and dhal.

□ □ □

Chicken tikka

Marinaded chicken with yoghurt

⏲ 4 hr 🍲 30 min ≋ 180°C

Step	Commodity	1 portion	10 portions	
1	Chicken pieces	250 g	10 × 250 g	Place in a suitably sized bowl.
	Yoghurt	30 ml	300 ml	Pour over the chicken. Season with salt and black pepper.
2	Ginger	5 g	50 g	Peel, chop finely and add to the chicken mixture.
	Onions	15 g	150 g	Peel, cut in half and dice finely. Add to the chicken.
	Cumin seeds	¼ tsp	2 tsp	Add.
	Coriander	¼ tsp	2 tsp	Add.
	Cayenne pepper	¼ tsp	2 tsp	Add.
	Garlic	½ clove	2 cloves	Peel, crush and add.
	Tomato purée	15 g	150 g	Add.
	Lemon juice	10 ml	100 ml	Pour over the other ingredients and mix together well. Allow the chicken to marinade in this mixture for a minimum of 4 hours, preferably overnight. Remove the chicken from the marinade and arrange on an oiled tray. Place under a pre-heated salamander for the required time, turning regularly to ensure even cooking. Serve garnished with lettuce and lemon wedges.

NOTE: The chicken may be cooked in a pre-heated oven.

□ □ □

22

Chhote kofte

Spiced meatballs with sauce

🥄 30 min   ♨ 40 min

Step	Commodity	1 portion	10 portions	
1	Minced lamb	125 g	1¼ kg	Place in a bowl. Season with salt, black pepper and cayenne pepper.
	Cumin seed	¼ tsp	2 tsp	Add to the lamb.
	Coriander seed	¼ tsp	2 tsp	Add.
	Garam masala	pinch	1 tsp	Add and mix thoroughly.
	Yoghurt	1 tbsp	5 tbsp	Pour into the mixture and combine all the ingredients. Shape into the appropriate portions allowing four meatballs per portion.

Sauce

Step	Commodity	1 portion	10 portions	
1	Ghee	10 g	100 g	Melt in a wok and heat gently.
	Cinnamon stick	1 small	1 large	Place in the ghee.
	Cardamom pods	2	10	Add.
	Cloves	2	10	Add.
	Garlic	1 clove	5 cloves	Peel, crush and add to the ghee.
	Fresh ginger	5 g	50 g	Peel, chop finely and add. Stir and cook for 2–3 minutes.
	Onions	25 g	250 g	Peel, dice finely and add. Cook until the onions are reddish brown in colour.
	Tomatoes	1 medium	10 medium	Blanch to remove the skins. Discard the seeds. Dice the flesh and add to the sauce.
	Cayenne pepper	pinch	1 tsp	Add.
	Paprika pepper	¼ tsp	2 tsp	Add.
	Yoghurt	1 tbsp	10 tbsp	Add and mix in thoroughly. Add the same amount of water. Bring to the boil then allow to simmer. Add the meat balls and cook for 30 minutes. Stir carefully every 5 minutes or so, making sure not to damage the meatballs. Serve accordingly.

☐   ☐   ☐

Lamb pasandeh

Spiced lamb with yoghurt

🥣 4½ hr ♨ 1 hr

Step	Commodity	1 portion	10 portions	
1	Lean diced lamb	100 g	1 kg	Place in a large bowl. Season with salt, black pepper and cayenne pepper.
	Ginger	5 g	50 g	Peel, dice and add.
	Garlic	½ clove	5 cloves	Peel, crush and add.
	Turmeric	pinch	2 tsp	Add.
	Garam masala	½ tsp	5 tsp	Add.
	Cardamom pods	½	5	Add.
	Black cumin seeds	¼ tsp	2 tsp	Add.
	Yoghurt	30 ml	300 ml	Pour over the ingredients and mix in well. Allow to marinade for 3–4 hours.
2	Sliced almonds	10 g	100 g	Place on a suitably sized tray.
	Desiccated coconut	5 g	50 g	Sprinkle over the almonds.
	Poppy seeds	5 g	50 g	Add.
	Sesame seeds	5 g	50 g	Add and spread out. Place in a pre-heated oven and dry roast until they are all golden brown. Remove and allow to cool. Chop finely with a large knife. Add to the marinade.
3	Ghee	5 g	50 g	Place in a suitably sized wok and heat.
	Onions	25 g	250 g	Peel, cut into thin slices, add to the hot fat and cook for a few minutes. Remove and place to the side.
4	Ghee	25 g	250 g	Place in a suitably sized wok and heat. When the fat is very hot add the lamb and seal quickly. NOTE: If there is a large amount to cook it must be batch cooked. Add the onions and some of the marinade.
5	White lamb stock	50 ml	500 ml	Add, bring to the boil and simmer.
	Green chillies	¼	2	Remove the stalk, chop very finely and add to the stock.
	Coriander leaves	½ tsp	2 tsp	Wash and add. Simmer for 50 minutes. Serve with chapatis.

22

☐   ☐   ☐

Roghan gosht

Spiced lamb with yoghurt

🥣 6–8 hr (overnight) ♨ 1 hr

Step	Commodity	1 portion	10 portions	
1	Lean leg of lamb	125 g	1½ kg	Cut into 3 cm cubes. Season with salt and crushed black pepper.
	Lemon juice	10 ml	100 ml	Pour over the lamb.
	Yoghurt	25 ml	250 ml	Add and mix in well. Cover and leave to marinade overnight.

Step	Commodity	1 portion	10 portions	
2	Ghee	10 g	100 g	Melt in a suitably sized sauté pan and gently heat.
	Garlic	½ clove	2 cloves	Peel, crush and add to the hot fat.
	Onion	10 g	100 g	Peel, dice, add and cook gently.
	Garam masala	½ tsp	5 tsp	Place in a bowl.
	Coriander powder	pinch	1 tsp	Add.
	Cumin powder	pinch	1 tsp	Add.
	Chilli powder	pinch	1 tsp	Add.
	Ginger	5 g	50 g	Peel, cut into small dice and add. Stir the spices into the lamb. Cook for 2 minutes. Add the meat and marinade and cook for a further 10 minutes.
	Tomato purée	25 g	250 g	Add and mix in well.
	Water	50 ml	500 ml	Add, bring to the boil and cover with a tight fitting lid. Simmer for 45 minutes or until the meat is tender and the sauce is fairly thick.

☐   ☐   ☐

Shikar vindaloo

Vinegared pork curry

🍲 20 min   ♨ 1½ hr

Step	Commodity	1 portion	10 portions	
1	Turmeric	pinch	1 tsp	Place in a mixing bowl.
	Ground coriander	pinch	1 tsp	Add.
	Curry powder	pinch	2 tsp	Add.
	Garam masala	½ tsp	5 tsp	Add.
	Cardamom seeds	2	20	Crush and add.
	Cumin seeds	¼ tsp	2 tsp	Add.
	Ginger	5 g	50 g	Peel, cut into small dice and add to the spices.
	Chilli powder	½ tsp	5 tsp	Add.
	Vinegar	5 ml	50 ml	Pour over the spices and mix to a paste.
2	Lean pork	125 g	1¼ kg	Cut into 3 cm cubes, season with salt and crushed black pepper and add to the spices.
3	Ghee	10 g	100 g	Melt in a suitably sized wok.
	Garlic	1 clove	10 cloves	Peel, crush and add to the hot fat. Add the pork and fry quickly.
	Vinegar	45 ml	450 ml	Pour over the pork. Bring to the boil, simmer and cook for the required time or until the meat is tender. Serve with chapatis and plain yoghurt.

☐   ☐   ☐

Pork with chick peas

Chhole wala gosht

Step	Commodity	1 portion	10 portions	⌣ Overnight ♨ 2½ hr approximately
1	Chick peas (soaked overnight)	50 g	½ kg	Place in a suitably sized saucepan and season with salt and black pepper. Cover with twice the amount of water, bring to the boil and simmer for 1¼ hours with the lid on.
	Potatoes	50 g	500 g	Peel, wash, place in cold water, bring to the boil and cook for 10 minutes. Refresh under cold water, drain, cut into small dice and place to the side for use later.
	Tomatoes	50 g	500 g	Remove the eyes, score the bottoms and blanch in a pan of boiling water for 10 seconds. Refresh in cold water. Discard the skins and the seeds. Chop the flesh into small dice. Place to the side for use later.
2	Ginger	5 g	50 g	Peel and place in a blender.
	Garlic	1 clove	10 cloves	Peel and add to the ginger.
	Water	2 tsp	5 tsp	Add and liquidise to a paste.
3	Ghee	20 g	200 g	Place in a suitably sized wok and heat.
	Lean diced pork	125 g	1¼ kg	Add to the hot fat in batches and seal. Remove and place to the side for use later.
4	Cardamom pods	2	20	Add to the hot fat.
	Cinnamon	½ cm piece	2 cm piece	Add.
	Bay leaves	½	5	Add.
	Cumin seeds	pinch	2tsp	Add and cook for 1 minute. Reduce the heat.
	Onions	25 g	250 g	Peel, cut into small dice and add to the fat. Cook for a further minute. Add the liquidised paste.
	Turmeric	½ tsp	5 tsp	Add.
	Ground cumin seeds	½ tsp	5 tsp	Add and stir together. Add the potatoes, tomatoes, pork, chick peas and the cooking liquor. Simmer for 45 minutes.
5	Button mushrooms	50 g	500 g	Wash and add to the other ingredients. Simmer for a further 15 minutes. Adjust the consistency accordingly and serve.

☐   ☐   ☐

22

Tandoori (prawn or chicken)

🥣 35 min   Marinading time 6–8 hr or overnight   ♨ 20 min

Step	Commodity	1 portion	10 portions	
1	Yoghurt	50 ml	500 ml	Place in a suitably sized bowl. Season with salt and crushed black pepper.
	Cinnamon	¼ tsp	1 tsp	Add to the yoghurt.
	Ginger	10 g	100 g	Peel, cut in small dice and add.
	Garam masala	10 g	100 g	Sprinkle over the other ingredients.
	Paprika	1 tsp	75 g	Sprinkle over the other ingredients.
	Garlic	½ clove	2 cloves	Peel, crush and add to the yoghurt.
	Cumin seeds	¼ tsp	2 tsp	Place in a pre-heated oven (200°C) for 15 minutes to roast. Remove, crush and add.
	Coriander seed	¼ tsp	2 tsp	Add.
	Lemon juice	15 ml	150 ml	Add and stir all the ingredients together. A dash of red food colouring can be added to improve the colour if so required.
2	Chicken/ prawns	1 × 200 g 1 × 150 g	10 × 200 g 10 × 150 g	The prepared meat or prawns are then placed in the marinade which permeates the flesh, tenderising and flavouring it. Once marinaded, the prepared meat is removed from the mixture and any excess marinade shaken off. Place in the tandoor if available or under a pre-heated grill and cook for 10–15 minutes on each side. In the case of prawns or shrimps 5–6 minutes. Serve with naan bread.

NOTE: In the North Indian district of the Punjab, tandoori is cooked in a clay oven. To ensure that the marinade coats the food thoroughly, the skin of chicken is removed.

☐　　☐　　☐

Baked spiced fish (sole, plaice or haddock)

Masala dum machchi

🥣 35 min   Marinading time 6–8 hr or overnight   ♨ 30 min   ≋ 180°C

Step	Commodity	1 portion	10 portions	
1	Yoghurt	50 ml	500 ml	Place in a suitably sized bowl. Season with salt and crushed black pepper.
	Onion	25 g	250 g	Peel, dice and add.
	Garlic	½ clove	2 cloves	Peel, crush and add to the yoghurt. Add a pinch of chilli powder and whisk the ingredients together.
	Cumin seeds	¼ tsp	2 tsp	Place in a pre-heated oven (200°C) for 15 minutes to roast. Remove, crush and add.
	Coriander seeds	¼ tsp	2 tsp	Add.
2	Prepared fish	1 × 200 g	10 × 200 g	The prepared fish is scored with a knife and placed in an ovenproof dish.
	Lemon juice	15 ml	150 ml	Sprinkle over the fish. Pour over the marinade which permeates the flesh, tenderising and flavouring it. Once marinaded the fish is cooked in the marinade in a pre-heated oven for 30 minutes.
	Lemon	¼	2	Cut into wedges and use to garnish the fish. Serve with picked coriander leaves and naan bread.

☐　　☐　　☐

Quick fried prawns

Tali hui jhinga

⏳ 45 min   🍲 5 min

Step	Commodity	1 portion	10 portions	
1	Rice flour	15 g	150 g	Place in a bowl.
	Turmeric	½ tsp	5 tsp	Add.
	Cayenne pepper	¼ tbsp	2 tbsp	Add.
	Ground cumin seed	½ tbsp	5 tbsp	Add, season with salt and black pepper and mix well.
	Peeled prawns	100 g	1 kg	Pat dry, dip into the mixture and coat well. Place on a clean dry tray.
2	Ghee	10 g	100 g	Place in a suitably sized wok and heat. When the fat is hot add the prawns and fry until the prawns are crisp, turning over as often as is required to ensure even cooking.

NOTE: If you are cooking large amounts there will be a need to batch cook. Remove and place on absorbent paper. Serve with lemon wedges.

☐   ☐   ☐

Spiced prawns in coconut milk

Jhinga pathia

⏳ 30 min   🍲 7 min

Step	Commodity	1 portion	10 portions	
1	Turmeric	½ tsp	5 tsp	Place in a bowl.
	Cayenne pepper	¼ tbsp	2 tbsp	Add.
	Chilli powder	pinch	2 tsp	Add.
	Ginger	5 g	50 g	Peel, dice finely and add to the other ingredients.
	Ground coriander	½ tbsp	5 tbsp	Add, season with salt and black pepper and mix well.
	Vinegar	1 tsp	2 tbsp	Mix in well to form a paste. Place to the side for use later.
2	Ghee	10 g	100 g	Place in a suitably sized wok and heat.
	Onions	10 g	100 g	Peel, cut into fine dice and add to the hot fat.
	Garlic	¼ clove	2 cloves	Peel, crush and add to the fat. Fry gently for 2–3 minutes. Add the spice paste and continue cooking, stirring continuously.
	Coconut milk	40 ml	400 ml	Pour over the other ingredients, bring to the boil and then simmer.
	Peeled prawns	100 g	1 kg	Add and continue cooking for 5 minutes.
	Tomato purée	1 tsp	2 tbsp	Add and mix in well. Cook for another 3 minutes or until the prawns are fully coated with the thickened sauce. Serve with lemon wedges.

NOTE: A similar dish can be made by replacing the prawns with duck and allowing ½ tsp of garam masala per portion – Meen molee (spiced duck in coconut milk).

☐   ☐   ☐

22

Deep fried vegetables and shrimps in batter

Pakora

⌣ 20 min   ♨ 10 min

Step	Commodity	1 portion	10 portions	
1	Bessan (chick pea flour)	25 g	250 g	Place in a large bowl. Season with salt, cayenne and black pepper.
	Turmeric	pinch	1 tsp	Add.
	Ground coriander	pinch	1 tsp	Add.
	Curry powder	pinch	2 tsp	Add.
	Water	75 ml	700 ml	Using a whisk, add carefully and make into a batter with the consistency of double cream.
2	Peeled shrimps	75 g	750 g	Pass through seasoned flour and dip into the batter. Deep fry in hot oil (190°C) until a golden brown in colour.
	Prepared vegetables*	100 g	1 kg	Pass through seasoned flour and dip in the batter. Deep fry in hot oil (190°C) until a golden brown in colour. Remove and place on absorbent paper to remove excess fat. Serve with mango chutney.

*NOTE: The vegetables can be any one or a variety of the following: sliced courgettes, potatoes or aubergines, bâtons of carrots, celery, parsnips, and small florets of cauliflower or broccoli.

☐   ☐   ☐

Vegetable biryani

Mughlai biryani

🍲 45 min   🔥 1 hr

Step	Commodity	1 portion	10 portions	
1	Brown rice	50 g	500 g	Place in a pan of boiling salted water and cook for 40 minutes. Refresh and drain.
2	Ghee	10 g	100 g	Melt in a suitably sized sauté pan and heat gently.
	Garam masala	½ tsp	5 tsp	Add to the ghee.
	Coriander seeds	pinch	1 tsp	Add.
	Cumin seeds	pinch	1 tsp	Add and cook over a low heat for 2–3 minutes. Add the drained rice and stir to ensure an all-round coating of the spices. Cover with a lid and place to the side of the stove. Do not allow to burn.
3	Red pepper	25 g	250 g	Dice and place in a bowl.
	Green pepper	25 g	250 g	Dice and add to the red peppers.
	Courgettes	50 g	500 g	Peel, dice and add to the other vegetables.
	Onion	10 g	100 g	Peel, dice and add.
	Cauliflower	50 g	500 g	Wash, trim, cut into small florets and add.
	French beans	25 g	250 g	Wash, trim and add.
	Mushrooms	25 g	250 g	Wash, cut into thin slices and add.
	Cooking oil	½ tbsp	50 ml	Place in a suitably sized wok and heat.
	Garlic	½ clove	2 cloves	Peel, crush and add to the hot fat.
	Ginger	5 g	50 g	Peel, cut into small dice and add to the oil. Add all the vegetables and cook quickly.
	Yoghurt	25 ml	250 ml	Stir into the vegetables slowly and bring to the boil. Simmer for 10 minutes. Layer the rice and vegetables into a serving dish. Serve with sultanas, quarters of hard boiled eggs and sprinkle with fried sliced almonds.

NOTE: Biryani can be made with lean minced lamb (Kheema biryani) instead of the peppers, courgettes, cauliflower and French beans. White rice replaces the brown rice and the meat is first sealed in hot fat before simmering for 1 hour.

□   □   □

22

Samosa

Deep fried, stuffed, savoury pastry. Generally eaten as a snack or an appetiser.

Step	Commodity	1 portion	10 portions		🥄 35 min 🍲 20 min

Dough

1	Plain flour	50 g	500 g	Sift the flour into a bowl and add a pinch of salt.
	Vegetable oil	1 tbsp	10 tbsp	Add and rub in well until the mixture resembles coarse breadcrumbs.
	Water	1 tbsp	10 tbsp	Add slowly and gather into a dough. Cover and allow to rest for 20 minutes.

Filling

1	Potatoes	50 g	500 g	Peel, wash and boil for 10 minutes. Refresh, drain and cut into small dice. Season with salt and a little cayenne pepper.
2	Ghee	5 g	50 g	Place in a wok and heat.
	Minced lamb	25 g	250 g	Add to the hot fat and cook for 6 minutes.
	Onions	10 g	100 g	Peel, cut into small dice and add.
	Cooked peas	5 g	50 g	Add and stir.
	Green chillies	¼	2	Remove the stalk, discard the seeds, dice the flesh finely and add. Drain off surplus fat. Remove from the heat and allow to cool.
	Ginger	5 g	50 g	Peel, dice finely and add to the cooled ingredients.
	Lemon juice	5 ml	50 ml	Pour over.
	Fresh coriander	1 tbsp	5 tsp	Chop finely and add.
	Cumin seed	½ tbsp	2 tbsp	Sprinkle over and add the potatoes.

Allowing 2 samosas per portion, divide the dough into the appropriate portions. Roll out into an 18 cm round. Cut in half. Pick up one half and form a cone making a 5 mm overlapping seam.

Brush the seam with a little water and fold over. Fill the cone with 2 tbsp of filling. Close the top of the cone by sticking the open edges together with a little water. Press the seams together with a fork, flute or fingers. Continue filling the pieces of pastry until all the mixture is used up. Pre-heat the deep fryer. In India they use a frying pan called a Karhai. Fry slowly, turning regularly, until the samosas are golden brown and crisp. Drain on kitchen paper and serve hot.

NOTE: A little fresh mint may be added to flavour the lamb. The lamb may be replaced by minced beef and vegetarian samosas can be made by omitting the meat and including vegetables of your choice. Samosas may be eaten with fresh coriander chutney.

□   □   □

Tala hua baingan

Fried aubergine slices

⤵ 35 min   ♨ 15 min

Step	Commodity	1 portion	10 portions	
1	Aubergines	100 g	1 kg	Peel, cut in quarters lengthways then slice thinly. Season with salt and crushed black pepper. Place into a suitably sized bowl.
	Turmeric	pinch	1 tsp	Sprinkle over the aubergines.
	Cayenne	pinch	1 tsp	Sprinkle over the aubergines.
2	Cooking oil	10 ml	100 ml	Place in a suitably sized wok and heat. When the oil is very hot add the aubergines and fry until they are reddish-golden on both sides. Remove and drain on kitchen paper. Serve accordingly.
3	Lemons	¼	2	Cut into wedges, remove the pith and pips. Serve with the aubergines.

NOTE: If you are attempting to cook large amounts, the aubergines should be cooked in batches.

☐   ☐   ☐

Aubergines in the pickling style

Baingan achari

⤵ 20 min   ♨ 30 min

Step	Commodity	1 portion	10 portions	
1	Ginger	5 g	50 g	Peel, dice finely. Place in a blender.
	Garlic	1 clove	10 cloves	Peel and add to the ginger. Season with salt and cayenne pepper.
	Water	10 ml	100 ml	Pour over the other ingredients and liquidise to a paste.
2	Aubergines	125 g	1¼ kg	Wash, remove the stalk and cut into 1½ cm slices.
	Ghee	15 g	150 g	Place in a suitably sized wok and heat. Fry the aubergines in batches until all are cooked to a reddish-brown colour. Place onto kitchen paper to remove excess fat.
3	Tomatoes	60 g	600 g	Remove the eyes and score the bottoms. Place in a pan of boiling water and blanch for 10 seconds. Refresh, skin and discard the seeds. Chop the flesh into small dice.
4	Ghee	10 g	100 g	Place in a clean wok.
	Fennel seeds	½ tsp	5 tsp	Add.
	Cumin seeds	½ tsp	5 tsp	Add and fry for a few seconds to release their flavour. Add the tomatoes and the liquidised paste.
	Coriander seeds	¼ tsp	2 tsp	Add.
	Turmeric	½ tsp	5 tsp	Sprinkle over the other ingredients and mix in well. Add the aubergines and cook for approximately 8 minutes. Skim off excess oil as required. Serve accordingly.

☐   ☐   ☐

22

Dhal

Lentil purée

Step	Commodity	1 portion	10 portions	
				⏱ 10 min 🍲 1 hr approximately
1	Garlic	¼ clove	2 cloves	Peel, chop finely and place to the side.
	Onions	15 g	150 g	Peel, cut into small dice and place with the garlic.
	Ghee	10 g	100 g	Place in a suitably sized wok and heat gently. Add the garlic and onions and sweat.
	Cumin seeds	pinch	2 tsp	Add and stir in.
2	Lentils	50 g	500 g	Add to the other ingredients and cover with water.
	Turmeric	pinch	2tsp	Add, bring to the boil and simmer. Cook until tender and fairly thick. Served hot as an accompaniment to other dishes.

☐   ☐   ☐

Pilau

Savoury rice

Step	Commodity	1 portion	10 portions	
				⏱ 2 hr 🍲 30 min approximately
1	Basmati rice	100 g	1 kg	Wash thoroughly and drain. Place in a bowl and leave to soak for 2 hours.
2	Ghee	40 g	400 g	Place in a suitably sized wok and melt.
	Sliced almonds	15 g	150 g	Add and fry until lightly browned. Remove from the pan, place on kitchen paper and leave to the side for use later.
3	Onions	25 g	250 g	Peel, dice and add to the hot fat.
	Garlic	½ clove	5 cloves	Peel, crush and add. Drain the rice of any excess liquid and add to the onions and garlic. Fry for 2–3 minutes, stirring constantly. Season with salt and crushed black pepper.
	Cardamom pods	2	20	Add.
	Cloves	2	20	Add.
	Water	300 ml	3 litres	Add, bring to the boil and then simmer. Cover with a lid and cook for 25–30 minutes or until the rice has absorbed all of the water. Serve hot sprinkled with the almonds.

NOTE: This dish may be prepared with the addition of saffron and called Kersari chawal (saffron rice).

☐   ☐   ☐

Sewaiian

🥄 10 min   🍲 30 min approximately

Step	Commodity	1 portion	10 portions	
1	Vermicelli	50 g	500 g	Place in a saucepan and cover with twice as much water. Bring to the boil, simmer and cook for 10 minutes or until the vermicelli softens and sinks to the bottom of the saucepan. Drain off enough water to leave the vermicelli just covered.
	Ghee	15 g	150 g	Add to the vermicelli, bring to the boil, then simmer for another 10 minutes.
2	Sultanas	5 g	50 g	Add to the vermicelli.
	Pistachio nuts	5 g	50 g	Add.
	Nibbed almonds	5 g	50 g	Add.
	Rose water	5 ml	50 ml	Add and stir in carefully. Transfer into a serving dish.
3	Whipping cream	50 ml	500 ml	Pour over the vermicelli.
	Desiccated coconut	pinch	2 tsp	Sprinkle over the top.
	Castor sugar	pinch	2 tsp	Sprinkle over the top. Serve hot or cold.

☐   ☐   ☐

Halva

🥄 10 min   🍲 1 hr approximately

Step	Commodity	1 portion	10 portions	
1	Semolina	50 g	500 g	Place in a thick-bottomed pan.
	Desiccated coconut	½ tbsp	5 tbsp	Add.
	Poppy seeds	½ tsp	2 tbsp	Add.
	Cardamon pods	1	10	Add and mix well.
	Water	125 ml	1¼ litres	Add, bring to the boil, then simmer for approximately 1 hour. Stir frequently to prevent the mixture from sticking.
2	Castor sugar	75 g	750 g	Add.
	Ghee	25 g	250 g	Add gradually and mix in well. Transfer the mixture into a shallow tray and spread evenly. Allow to cool, then cut into triangle shapes. Serve cold.

☐   ☐   ☐

22

Chaat

Step	Commodity	1 portion	10 portions	
1	Oranges	½	5	Peel, remove the pith and cut into segments. Place in a bowl. Squeeze the juice of the oranges over the segments.
	Lemon juice	25 ml	250 ml	Pour over the oranges.
	Pears	½	5	Wash, peel, remove the core and slice thinly. Add to the oranges.
	Red apples	½	5	Wash, cut into quarters, remove the core and cut into thin slices. Add to the other fruit.
	Guavas	½	5	Peel the guava and cut into dice.
	Bananas	½	5	Peel, cut into slices and add to the other fruit. Season with salt and ground black pepper.
2	Chilli powder	¼ tsp	3 tsp	Sprinkle over the fruit.
	Ground ginger	pinch	1 tsp	Sprinkle over the fruit.
	Garam masala	pinch	1 tsp	Sprinkle over the fruit and stir in carefully until all the spices are mixed thoroughly. Refrigerate and chill before serving.

☐   ☐   ☐

Kulfi

Step	Commodity	1 portion	10 portions	
1	Milk	200 ml	2 litres	Place in a saucepan and bring to the boil. Simmer and reduce by two-thirds.
	Rice flour	10 g	100 g	Stir into the milk and mix thoroughly.
	Single cream	60 ml	600 ml	Add carefully and mix well. Bring to the boil, then simmer for 15 minutes.
	Castor sugar	25 g	250 g	Add and dissolve completely. Allow to cool.
2	Pistachio nuts	10 g	100 g	Chop finely and add to the mixture.
	Nibbed almonds	5 g	50 g	Add and mix well. Transfer to an ice cream machine and freeze. Serve sprinkled with chopped pistachio nuts.

☐   ☐   ☐

Thai cookery

Rice is the staple diet of Thais; all main meals are based on rice and though noodles are served, they are usually eaten as a snack. The climate of Southern Thailand allows 2 or 3 rice harvests a year as well as producing a plentiful supply of many varieties of vegetables.

Traditionally the cooker is a simple charcoal stove and the food is cooked in a wok which is used to boil, fry and steam. For steaming, the food is placed in covered bamboo sieves which are suspended over a wok of boiling water.

The majority of Thai people are Buddhists, whose major festival is Veesak, the festival to celebrate the life of Buddha. Though there are no religious restrictions on their diet, the majority of Buddhists are vegetarian.

In Thailand curries are prepared with a spicy paste made from fresh ingredients rather than powdered dried spices because of the superior quality of their ingredients.

There are two main types of soups eaten: Kang Chud (similar to a consomme) and Tom Yum, which usually contains pieces of prawns, pork, beef, chicken or fish.

Fish is plentiful in Thailand and is usually included in every Thai meal. The most common fish is pla tu (mackerel family). Boiled pla muek (squid) is used in salads, and it is also stewed, grilled fried and added to other dishes.

Prawn and squid soup

Tom yum kung lae pla muk

⏳ 1 hr   🍲 30 min approximately

Step	Commodity	1 portion	10 portions	
1	Fish stock	250 ml	2½ litres	Place in a suitably sized saucepan and boil.
	Squid	50 g	500 g	Clean the squid, cut off the tentacles and cut them into rings. Wash thoroughly and add to the stock.
	Lemon grass	½ stalk	5 stalks	Add.
	Lime leaves	½	5	Add, bring to the boil and simmer for 10 minutes.
2	Cooked prawns	50 g	500 g	Dice and add to the simmering soup.
	Chinese cabbage or Chinese leaves	10 g	100 g	Dice and add.
	Garlic	½ clove	5 cloves	Peel, crush with a little salt and add.
	Green chillies	½	5	Remove the stalks and slice into rounds. Add.
	Lemon juice	5 ml	50 ml	Add and simmer for a further 10 minutes. Remove the scum and correct the seasoning.
3	Coriander leaves	few	½ bunch	Wash, chop and use to garnish the soup.

□   □   □

Fried mackerel and tamarind sauce

Pla prio wan

⏳ 30 min   🍲 1½ hr

Step	Commodity	1 portion	10 portions	
1	Mackerel	1	10	Clean the mackerel, fillet and remove the skin. Place on a buttered tray. Brush with butter. Season with salt and black pepper. Cover with cooking foil and place in a pre-heated oven (160°C) for 40 minutes. Remove and discard the foil. Allow the fish to cool. Cut into 1 cm pieces. Fill a wok with cooking oil and pre-heat to 185°C. Add the fish in 'batches' and cook until golden brown. Remove and place on absorbent paper to remove the excess fat, then place on a serving dish and keep warm. Pour the oil into another vessel. Return the wok to the heat.
2	Garlic	½ clove	5 cloves	Peel, crush with a little salt and place in the wok. Fry until lightly brown.
	Fresh ginger	5 g	50 g	Peel, grate and add. Cook for 1–2 minutes.
	Water	1 tbsp	10 tbsp	Add.
	Sugar	¼ tsp	2½ tsp	Add.
	Tamarind water	1 tbsp	10 tbsp	Add, mix all the ingredients together and boil. Simmer for 5 minutes. Pour over the fish.

Step	Commodity	1 portion	10 portions	
3	Cucumber, peeled	4 slices	40 slices	Place by the side of the fish.
	Spring onions	25 g	250 g	Wash, remove the stalk and cut into thin rings. Use to garnish the fish.

☐ ☐ ☐

Fried fish balls
Tod mun pla

🥄 45 min ♨ 5 min

Step	Commodity	1 portion	10 portions	
1	Garlic	½ clove	5 cloves	Peel, crush and place in a liquidiser.
	Peppercorns	4	40	Crush and add.
	Coriander root	½	5	Wash, dry, grate and add.
	Chillies	½	5	Remove the stalk discard the seeds and add the flesh.
	Sugar	pinch	2 tsp	Add.
	Cod fillet	150 g	1½ kg	Add and liquidise to a smooth paste.
	Flour	1 tsp	2 tbsp	Add.
	Soya sauce	1 tsp	2 tbsp	Add and mix together thoroughly. Shape into balls, 6 per portion.
2	Cooking oil	15 ml	150 ml	Place in a wok and heat. Add the fish balls in 'batches'. Cook until golden brown. Remove and place on absorbent paper. Place on a serving dish and keep warm.
3	Cucumber	⅛	1	Peel and cut into slices. Place in a bowl.
	Carrots	25 g	250 g	Peel, grate and add.
	Shallots	25 g	250 g	Remove the root and outer leaves. Slice thinly and add to the carrots.
	Vinegar	½ tsp	5 tsp	Add.
	Water	½ tsp	5 tsp	Add.
	Sugar	½ tsp	5 tsp	Add and mix together thoroughly. Place in bowls and serve with the fish balls.

NOTE: Chicken (Kai) and pork (Moo) balls may be made using this recipe.

☐ ☐ ☐

Masamam curry

Kang masaman

Step	Commodity	1 portion	10 portions			
				🥄 30 min	♨ 2 hr	
1	Stewing steak	100 g	1 kg	Cut into 2 cm cubes. Place in a wok and cover with water. Bring to the boil and simmer for 1½ hours or until the meat is tender. If necessary replenish with water as required.		
2	Chillies	2	20	Discard the stalks and seeds. Chop the chilli finely. Place in a liquidiser.		
	Ground black pepper	pinch	2 tsp	Add.		
	Coriander seeds	½ tbsp	5 tbsp	Crush and add.		
	Cumin seeds	½ tbsp	5 tbsp	Add.		
	Lemon grass	½ tbsp	2 tbsp	Wash, shred and add.		
	Cinnamon stick	¼	2	Add.		
	Cardamom seeds	1	10	Add.		
	Grated nutmeg	pinch	½	Add.		
	Shallots	2	20	Peel, remove the stalk and add.		
	Garlic	½ clove	5 cloves	Peel, crush with a little salt and add to the other ingredients.		
	Shrimp paste	¼ tsp	2 tsp	Add and liquidise to a paste. Add to the meat and continue cooking.		
	Creamed coconut	50 ml	500 ml	Chop finely, add and stir in well.		
	Peanuts	25 g	250 g	Add and cook until the meat is tender and the liquid is reduced by a third.		
3	Tamarind water	15 ml	150 ml	Add, re-boil and serve.		

22

Son-in-law eggs

Kai look koei

⏲ 30 min ♨ 20 min

Step	Commodity	1 portion	10 portions	
1	Cooking oil	15 ml	150 ml	Place in a wok and heat.
	Shallots	25 g	250 g	Remove the stalks and outer leaves. Cut into thin rings and add to the hot oil. Cook until golden brown. Remove and place on absorbent paper. Keep warm.
	Hard boiled eggs	1	10	Peel, cut into quarters and add to the oil until the egg blisters and goes crisp on the outside. Remove and place with the onions.
2	Tamarind water	15 ml	150 ml	Place in the wok.
	Water	5 ml	50 ml	Add.
	Brown sugar	10 g	100 g	Add and cook for 5 minutes. Return the eggs to the wok and heat gently for 2–3 minutes. Place in a serving dish and garnish with the fried shallots.

☐ ☐ ☐

Sweet mung beans with coconut

Maled khanum

⏲ Overnight ♨ 1 hr

Step	Commodity	1 portion	10 portions	
1	Mung beans	50 g	500 g	Soak overnight in water. Drain away the water and wash to remove the skins. Place in a liquidiser and blend to a paste. Place in a pan and cover with twice as much water. Bring to the boil and simmer for 20 minutes or until soft. Drain away the cooking liquid and place in a clean pan. Cook until the beans are dry.
	Creamed coconut	50 g	500 g	Cut into small pieces and add. Mix in well.
	Coconut milk	50 ml	500 ml	Add.
	Sugar	50 g	500 g	Add, stir in well and bring to the boil. Cook for 30 minutes, stirring frequently to avoid burning. Remove and allow to go cold. Shape into balls, 6 per portion.
	Egg yolks	1	8	Whisk in a bowl. Pass the balls through the egg.
2	Golden syrup	50 ml	500 ml	Place in a pan and heat. Add the balls and cook for a few seconds. Remove and arrange on a serving dish. Do not allow to touch each other. Chill for 3 hours before serving.

☐ ☐ ☐

Sticky rice and custard

Kow neo sang kaya

🥄 30 min   🍲 2 hr approximately

Step	Commodity	1 portion	10 portions	
1	Coconut milk	100 ml	1 litre	Place in a pan and heat.
	Rose water	½ tbsp	5 tbsp	Add.
	Brown sugar	15 g	150 g	Add, bring to the boil and then simmer.
	Egg yolks	1	10	Whisk briskly and add to the simmering milk. Mix thoroughly and simmer until it thickens and coats the back of a spoon. Strain into a clean saucepan and cook in a bain-marie in a pre-heated oven (180°C) for 1½ hours.
2	Pudding rice	50 g	500 g	Place in a clean saucepan.
	Coconut milk	100 ml	1 litre	Add.
	Sugar	10 g	100 g	Add.
	Creamed coconut	25 g	250 g	Chop finely and add to the rice. Bring to the boil and simmer on the side of the stove for 30 minutes or until the rice is cooked. Place in a serving dish. Pour the custard over the top.
	Lime	2 slices	20 slices	Use to decorate the finished dish. Serve hot or cold.

☐   ☐   ☐

Chinese cookery

Most Chinese foods are either stir fried or steamed. Chinese cooking is based on five flavours which affect different parts of the body: sweet, acid, sour, bitter and sharp. Diets are based on a subtle blend of positive foods (cooling foods), crab and duck (yin); negative foods (heating foods), beef, coffee and smoked fish (yang); and neutral foods, fruit, rice and vegetables (yin yang).

China is a vast country and its climate and food products are very varied, with each region having its own specialties and different methods of cookery. There are four broadly defined regional styles of cookery:

1 **Eastern** (Lower Jiangsi basin, Shanghai and the provinces of Jiagsi and Fujian.) Dishes are delicately seasoned. Known as the 'land of rice and fish', it is also known for it various dumplings and noodles.
2 **Western** (Sichuan.) Fruit, meat and fish are widely available. Dishes from this region are richly flavoured and have a very piquant quality. Hot spices predominate.

3 **Southern** (Guangshau, Canton.) Rice is the staple food. This region is known for its Dim sums (parcels) and sweet and sour dishes. Dishes are lightly cooked and lightly flavoured.
4 **Northern** (Beijing, Peking, Shandong and Henan.) Known as the land of corn and wheat, this region is famed for its dumplings, noodles and pancakes. Little meat is used. Most dishes include sesame seeds and usually have garlic, leeks, and onions.

Every dish in a Chinese meal should include two or more of the following textures: tenderness, crispness, crunchiness, smoothness and softness. The main flavours in Chinese cookery come from soy sauce, rice wine, sugar, vinegar, ginger and spring onions, garlic and peppers.

Most Chinese foods are cut into small pieces before cooking to accommodate the fast method of cookery employed. The slicing of food is an important technique; the ingredients are cut very thin and cut at a slant so the larger surface can absorb more flavours. Shredding involves the ingredients being cut into thin strips the size of matchsticks.

Normally meat is marinaded to flavour and to tenderise it. Salt, egg white and cornflour are used for chicken and fish, and soy sauce, sugar, rice wine and cornflour for meats.

It may be surprising to heat the the famous dish chop suey has never been heard of in China, nor has the soggy sweet and sour pork served in restaurants in Europe.

Cooking equipment

The wok is the most widely used cooking utensil. Normally made from beaten iron, it keeps an intense heat throughout cooking. The shape of the wok encourages ingredients to return to the centre, however vigorously you stir them.

Woks are used to boil, stir fry and steam.

Beef and egg flower soup

Niurou danhua tang

🥢 30 min   🍲 45 min approximately

Step	Commodity	1 portion	10 portions	
1	Beef stock	250 ml	2½ litres	Place in wok and boil.
	Topside of beef	25 g	250 g	Cut into thin strips and add.
	Celery	25 g	250 g	Cut thinly and add. Season with salt and ground black pepper. Simmer and cook for 30 minutes.
2	Eggs	½	5	Break into a clean bowl and whisk briskly. Bring the soup back to the boil and add the egg a little at a time, stirring vigorously to achieve the egg flower effect.
3	Spring onions	15 g	150 g	Wash, remove the root, peel and slice thinly. Sprinkle over the soup and serve.

☐   ☐   ☐

Duck and cabbage soup

Yagu baicai tang

🥢 10 min   🍲 50 min

Step	Commodity	1 portion	10 portions	
1	Duck stock	250 ml	2½ litres	Place in a wok.
	Cooked duck	50 g	500 g	Remove the fat and slice thinly. Add to the stock.
	Root ginger	5 g	50 g	Peel and add to the stock. Simmer for 30 minutes.
	Chinese cabbage	100 g	1 kg	Wash, slice thinly and add. Bring back to the boil and simmer for a further 20 minutes. Season with salt and ground black pepper. Remove the ginger. Serve accordingly.

☐   ☐   ☐

Shredded pork and noodle soup

Rousi tangmian

Step	Commodity	1 portion	10 portions	
				⟡ 1 hr ♨ 45 min
1	Dried mushrooms	1	10	Place in a bowl of warm water and soak for 30 minutes. Remove, squeeze dry and cut into thin strips. Retain the liquid.
	Lean pork	50 g	500 g	Cut into thin strips and place in a bowl.
	Soy sauce	¼ tbsp	3 tbsp	Add.
	Sugar	pinch	1 tbsp	Add.
	Rice wine	¼ tbsp	3 tbsp	Add.
	Cornflour	½ tsp	5 tsp	Add and marinade for 20 minutes.
2	Egg noodles	75 g	750 g	Place in a wok of boiling salted water and cook for 5 minutes. Remove, refresh and drain. Return the wok to the stove.
	Sesame oil	½ tbsp	5 tbsp	Add and heat. Add the pork mixture and stir fry until golden brown. Remove and place on absorbent kitchen paper. Retain the oil. Add the mushrooms.
3	Spring onions	25 g	250 g	Wash, remove the root and outer leaves. Cut into thin slices and add to the hot oil.
	Bamboo shoots	25 g	250 g	Cut into thin strips and add. Return the pork along with the liquor from the mushrooms and cook for 5 minutes.
4	Chicken stock	200 ml	2 litres	Add, bring to the boil and simmer for 30 minutes. Place the egg noodles in a serving bowl. Pour over the soup and serve.

☐   ☐   ☐

Cauliflower gruel

Caihua geng

Step	Commodity	1 portion	10 portions	
				⟡ 30 min ♨ 50 min
1	Cauliflower	150 g	1½ kg	Wash, remove the stalk and dice finely. Place in a wok.
	Chicken stock	200 g	2 litres	Add, bring to the boil and simmer for 30 minutes.
2	Eggs	½	5	Break into a clean bowl and whisk briskly. Season with salt and ground black pepper. Pour into the soup and mix in well.
	Cooked ham	25 g	250 g	Dice finely and add. Simmer for a further 15 minutes and serve.
3	Coriander leaves	4	40	Wash and sprinkle over the soup to garnish.

☐   ☐   ☐

22

Stir fried squid with mixed vegetables

Zajin chao xianyou

🥄 45 min   ♨ 20 min

Step	Commodity	1 portion	10 portions	
1	Jelly mushrooms	5 g	50 g	Place in a bowl and cover with warm water. Soak for 20 minutes.
	Squid	50 g	500 g	Clean the squid, cut off the tentacles and cut them into rings. Wash thoroughly and place in a bowl. Season with salt and crushed black pepper.
	Root ginger	5 g	50 g	Peel, grate and add to the squid.
	Rice wine	½ tsp	5 tsp	Add.
	Cornflour	½ tsp	5 tsp	Add, mix well and leave to marinade for 20 minutes.
2	Cooking oil	½ tbsp	5 tbsp	Place in a wok and heat.
	Spring onions	15 g	150 g	Wash, remove the root and outer leaves. Cut into rings and add to the hot oil.
	Cauliflower	50 g	500 g	Wash, remove the stalk, cut into small florets and add.
	Broccoli	50 g	500 g	Wash, remove the stalk, cut into florets and add.
	Carrots	50 g	50 g	Wash, peel and cut into thin slices. Add to the other vegetables along with the jelly mushroom. Stir fry for 5 minutes. Add a little water to aid cooking.
	Sugar	pinch	1 tbsp	Add, season with salt and ground black pepper. Remove and keep warm. Wipe the wok clean and place on the stove.
	Cooking oil	½ tbsp	5 tbsp	Add to the wok and heat. Add the squid mixture and stir fry for 2 minutes. Return the vegetables and continue cooking for a further 2 minutes.
3	Sesame seed oil	drop	1 tbsp	Pour over and serve.

☐   ☐   ☐

Bean curd and prawns

Xiaren shao doufu

🥄 15 min   ♨ 5 min

Step	Commodity	1 portion	10 portions	
1	Bean curd	75 g	750 g	Cut into ½ cm slices and then into ½ cm squares.
	Vegetable oil	½ tbsp	5 tbsp	Place in a wok and heat. Add the bean curd and fry until golden brown.
	Rice wine	10 ml	100 ml	Add.
	Soy sauce	½ tbsp	5 tbsp	Add.
	Sugar	pinch	1 tbsp	Add, season with salt and ground black pepper. Stir fry for 30 seconds.
2	Peeled prawns	25 g	250 g	Add and stir fry for 1–2 minutes. Place in a serving dish.
	Spring onions	15 g	150 g	Wash, remove the root and outer leaves. Cut into rings and sprinkle over the bean curd and prawns.

☐   ☐   ☐

Prawn balls with broccoli

Jielan chao xiaqiu

⌣ 30 min   ♨ 20 min

Step	Commodity	1 portion	10 portions	
1	Uncooked prawns*	75 g	750 g	Wash thoroughly and dry. Remove the shell. Use a sharp knife to make a shallow incision down the back and pull out the black intestinal vein. Wash the prawns and cut into ½ cm pieces. Place in a bowl.
	Root ginger	5 g	50 g	Peel, grate and add.
	Rice wine	½ tsp	5 tsp	Add.
	Egg white	¼ equiv	2½ equiv	Add.
	Cornflour	5 g	50 g	Add and mix to a paste. Marinade in the refrigerator for 20 minutes.
2	Broccoli	50 g	500 g	Wash, remove the stalks and cut into small florets. Place in a wok of boiling salted water and simmer for 10 minutes. Remove and refresh. Drain and place to the side.
3	Vegetable oil	20 ml	200 ml	Place in a clean wok and heat. Add the prawn pieces in 'batches' and cook until golden brown. Remove and place on absorbent paper and keep warm.
	Spring onions	15 g	150 g	Wash, remove the root and outer leaves. Cut into rings and add to the hot oil. Stir fry for 30 seconds. Add the broccoli and continue to stir.
	Sugar	5 g	50 g	Add and season with salt and ground black pepper. Add the prawn balls and mix together. Place in a dish and serve.

* Dublin Bay prawns or king prawns.

☐   ☐   ☐

22

Fish steaks in bean sauce

Jian doubian yu

⌣ 30 min   ♨ 10 min

Step	Commodity	1 portion	10 portions	
1	Fish steak	1 × 100 g	10 × 100 g	Wash the fish and remove the bone and skin. Place the fish in a bowl.
	Black bean sauce	1 tsp	10 tsp	Add to the fish.
	Soy sauce	5 ml	50 ml	Add.
	Rice wine	1 tsp	10 tsp	Add.
	Sugar	1 tsp	10 tsp	Add.
	Chilli sauce	few drops	½ tbsp	Add.
	Fish stock	10 ml	100 ml	Add and allow the mixture to marinade in the refrigerator for 20 minutes.
2	Vegetable oil	15 ml	150 ml	Place in a wok and heat. Remove the fish from the marinade and add to the hot oil. Stir fry until golden brown on all sides. Add the marinade, bring to the boil and simmer until most of the liquid has evaporated. Serve accordingly.

☐   ☐   ☐

Braised chicken wings

🕒 50 min ♨ 20 min

Step	Commodity	1 portion	10 portions	
1	Chinese mushrooms	5 g	50 g	Place in a bowl and cover with warm water. Soak for 30 minutes. Squeeze dry, discard the stalks and cut the mushrooms into small, thin slices.
	Chicken wings	4	40	Trim the knuckles off either end. Remove any excess skin and feathers.
	Vegetable oil	10 ml	100 ml	Place in a wok and heat fiercely.
	Spring onions	15 g	150 g	Wash, remove the root and outer leaves. Cut into rings and add to the hot oil.
	Root ginger	5 g	50 g	Peel, grate and add to the hot oil. Add the chicken wings and stir fry for 4–5 minutes.
2	Soy sauce	½ tbsp	5 tbsp	Add to the wok.
	Rice wine	½ tbsp	5 tbsp	Add.
	Sugar	5 g	50 g	Add.
	Five spice	pinch	1 tbsp	Add and stir in well. Cover with a lid and cook gently for a further 5 minutes until the liquor has reduced by half.
3	Bamboo shoots	50 g	500 g	Slice thinly and add to the chicken. Add the mushrooms.
	Cornflour	1 tsp	2 tbsp	Dilute in a little water and add to the chicken. Return to the boil and simmer. Serve accordingly.

☐   ☐   ☐

Soy chicken

🕒 45 min ♨ 50 min

Step	Commodity	1 portion	10 portions	
1	Chicken	300 g	3 kg	Cut as for sauté. Place in a pan of boiling salted water and cook for 5 minutes. Remove and refresh. Place in a bowl.
	Soy sauce	½ tbsp	5 tbsp	Add to the chicken.
	Rice wine	½ tbsp	5 tbsp	Add and allow to marinade in the refrigerator for 30 minutes.
2	Spring onions	15 g	150 g	Wash, remove the root and outer leaves, cut into dice and place in a skillet.
	Root ginger	5 g	50 g	Peel, grate and add.
	Garlic	¼ clove	2½ cloves	Peel, crush with a little salt and add.
	Sugar	5 g	50 g	Add.
	Vinegar	½ tbsp	5 tbsp	Add.
	Yellow bean sauce	1 tbsp	10 tbsp	Add and place on the heat. Bring to the boil and simmer gently.
3	Vegetable oil	10 ml	100 ml	Place in a wok and heat. Remove the chicken from the marinade and fry for 30 minutes until browned on all sides. Add the marinade to the sauce. Place the chicken in a serving dish and pour the sauce over.

NOTE: Traditionally the cleaned neck and head was cooked and served as well.

☐   ☐   ☐

566

Golden flower and jade tree chicken

Zinhua yushu ji

🥣 30 min ♨ 50 min

Step	Commodity	1 portion	10 portions	
1	Chicken	300 g	3 kg	Cut as for sauté. Season with salt and ground black pepper. Place in a bowl.
	Egg whites	¼ equiv	2½ equiv	Whisk and add.
	Cornflour	5 g	50 g	Add and mix to a paste. Marinade in the refrigerator for 20 minutes.
2	Vegetable oil	15 ml	150 ml	Place in a suitably sized wok and heat. Add the chicken and stir fry over a moderate heat for 5 minutes. Remove, place on a tray on absorbent paper and keep warm. Return the wok to the heat.
	Spring onions	15 g	150 g	Wash, remove the root and outer leaves, cut into rings and add to the hot oil.
	Root ginger	5 g	50 g	Peel, grate and add.
	Red peppers	25 g	250 g	Remove the stalks and the seeds. Cut into thin slices and add to the onions.
	Green peppers	25 g	250 g	Remove the stalks and the seeds. Cut into thin slices and add to the onions.
	Celery	25 g	250 g	Wash, slice thinly, add and stir fry for 5 minutes.
	Soy sauce	½ tbsp	5 tbsp	Add.
	Sugar	5 g	50 g	Add.
	Vinegar	¼ tsp	2½ tsp	Add.
	Chilli sauce	½ tsp	5 tsp	Add and mix all the ingredients well. Return the chicken to the wok and simmer for 10 minutes. Serve accordingly.

☐   ☐   ☐

Roast duck Peking style

Beijing kao ya

🥣 2 days ♨ 1½ hr

Step	Commodity	1 portion	10 portions	
1	Duck	500 g	5 kg	Clean thoroughly and hang up overnight in a well ventilated room to dry completely.
	Sugar	10 g	100 g	Place in a bowl.
	Salt	5 g	50 g	Add to the sugar and dissolve the two in a little water. Rub all over the duck. Leave to dry for several hours. Lay on a tray and place in a preheated oven (200°C) for approximately 1 hour.
2	Yellow bean sauce	1 tbsp	10 tbsp	Place in a skillet.
	Sugar	½ tbsp	5 tbsp	Add.
	Sesame seed oil	1 tsp	10 tsp	Add and bring to the boil, lower to a simmer and cook for 20 minutes. Place in a serving bowl. Carve the duck into 1 cm slices and arrange on a serving dish.
	Spring onions	15 g	150 g	Wash, remove the root and outer leaves, cut into rings and sprinkle over the duck and sauce. Serve with mandarin pancakes.

☐   ☐   ☐

22

Mandarin pancakes

⏱ 5 min ♨ 20 min

Step	Commodity	1 portion	10 portions	
1	Plain flour	100 g	1 kg	Sift into a bowl.
	Water	50 ml	500 ml	Add and whisk together.
	Vegetable oil	few drops	1 tsp	Add and mix in well. Knead the mixture into a firm dough and split into the appropriate number of pieces. Divide each piece into 6 portions. Roll each portion into a flat pancake 12 cm in diameter and brush each side with a little oil. Heat the wok and add the pancakes one at a time. Cook until air bubbles appear. Turn over and cook the other side. Remove and fold each pancake into four.

☐   ☐   ☐

Bean sprouts with shredded pork

Douya chao rousi

⏱ 1 hr ♨ 40 min

Step	Commodity	1 portion	10 portions	
1	Bean shoots	75 g	750 g	Rinse in a bowl of cold water. Discard the husks that float to the top. Drain the remaining shoots.
	Lean pork	100 g	1 kg	Cut into fine strips and place in a bowl.
	Soy sauce	½ tbsp	5 tbsp	Add.
	Rice wine	½ tsp	5 tsp	Add.
	Cornflour	5 g	50 g	Add and mix to a paste. Marinade in the refrigerator for 20 minutes.
2	Vegetable oil	10 ml	100 ml	Place in a wok and heat.
	Spring onions	15 g	150 g	Wash, remove the root and outer leaves, cut into rings and add to the hot oil.
	Root ginger	5 g	50 g	Peel, grate and add. Add the pork and stir fry for 3–4 minutes. Remove and drain. Place in a bowl and keep warm. Wipe the wok clean and return to the heat.
3	Sesame seed oil	5 ml	50 ml	Pour into the wok and heat. Add the drained bean shoots. Season with salt and ground black pepper.
	Leeks	25 g	250 g	Wash, remove the root and outer leaves, slice thinly and add. Stir fry for 1 minute. Return the pork to the pan and continue cooking for 3–4 minutes. Serve hot.

☐   ☐   ☐

Steamed spareribs in black bean sauce

Chizhi zheng paigu

🍲 1 hr   ♨ 50 min

Step	Commodity	1 portion	10 portions	
1	Spareribs	150 g	1½ kg	Place in a bowl.
	Root ginger	5 g	50 g	Peel, grate and add.
	Garlic	¼ clove	2½ cloves	Peel, crush with a little salt and add.
	Black bean sauce	1 tsp	10 tsp	Add.
	Soy sauce	½ tbsp	5 tbsp	Add.
	Sugar	½ tsp	5 tsp	Add.
	Rice wine	1 tbsp	10 tbsp	Add and mix together. Allow to marinade in the refrigerator for 1 hour. Lay on a wok rack over boiling water. Cover with a lid and steam for 45 minutes. Replenish the water as required. Place on a serving dish.
2	Sesame seed oil	5 ml	50 ml	Place in a wok and heat.
	Red peppers	25 g	250 g	Remove the stalks and the seeds, cut into thin slices and add to the oil.
	Green peppers	25 g	250 g	Remove the stalks and the seeds, cut into thin slices and add. Stir fry for 30 seconds. Pour over the ribs and serve accordingly.

☐   ☐   ☐

Stir fried pork with bamboo shoots

Dongsun chao rousi

🍲 1½ hr   ♨ 20 min

Step	Commodity	1 portion	10 portions	
1	Lean pork	75 g	750 g	Cut into thin slices and place in a bowl.
	Rice wine	½ tsp	5 tsp	Add to the pork.
	Soy sauce	½ tbsp	5 tbsp	Add and mix together well. Place in the refrigerator and marinade for 30 minutes.
2	Sesame seed oil	15 ml	150 ml	Place in a wok and heat.
	Garlic	¼ clove	2½ cloves	Peel, crush with a little salt, add to the oil and fry until golden brown. Remove from the pan. Add the pork and stir fry for 8 minutes or until light brown.
	Bamboo shoots	75 g	750 g	Cut into thin slices and add.
	Soy sauce	½ tbsp	5 tbsp	Add and stir fry for 30 seconds. Place in a serving dish.
3	Spring onions	15 g	150 g	Wash, remove the root and outer leaves, cut into rings and sprinkle over the pork.

☐   ☐   ☐

22

569

Stir fried liver with spinach

Bocai chao zhugan

🍲 20 min   ♨ 15 min

Step	Commodity	1 portion	10 portions	
1	Prepared pork liver	100 g	1 kg	Cut into thin slices, place in a wok of boiling salted water and blanch for 1 minute. Drain, refresh and dry.
	Cornflour	5 g	50 g	Place in a tray and pass the liver through it.
	Vegetable oil	5 ml	50 ml	Place in a clean wok and heat.
	Spinach leaves	100 g	1 kg	Wash thoroughly and dry. Add to the hot oil and stir fry for 2 minutes. Remove and arrange on the bottom of a serving dish. Keep warm.
2	Vegetable oil	5 ml	50 ml	Place in a clean wok and heat.
	Root ginger	5 g	50 g	Peel, grate and add, along with the liver.
	Soy sauce	½ tbsp	5 tbsp	Add.
	Rice wine	½ tsp	5 tsp	Add and stir fry for 4–5 minutes. Arrange on top of spinach.
	Spring onions	15 g	150 g	Wash, remove the root and outer leaves, cut into rings and sprinkle over the liver. Serve.

☐   ☐   ☐

Stir fried beef with green peppers

Quig jiao niurou pian

🍲 30 min   ♨ 20 min

Step	Commodity	1 portion	10 portions	
1	Topside of beef	100 g	1 kg	Remove any fat and gristle and slice thinly. Season with salt and ground black pepper.
	Sugar	1 tsp	10 tsp	Sprinkle over the beef.
	Chilli sauce	few drops	1 tsp	Add.
	Soy sauce	½ tbsp	5 tbsp	Add.
	Cornflour	5 g	50 g	Add and mix to a paste. Marinade in the refrigerator for 20 minutes.
	Vegetable oil	10 ml	100 ml	Place in a clean wok and heat.
2	Green peppers	50 g	500 g	Remove the stalks and seeds and discard. Cut into thin slices and add to the hot oil.
	Tomatoes	50 g	500 g	Cut into slices and add. Season with a little salt and ground black pepper and stir fry for a few seconds. Remove and keep warm. Clean the wok and return to the heat.
3	Vegetable oil	5 ml	50 ml	Place in the clean wok and heat.
	Spring onions	15 g	150 g	Wash, remove the root and outer leaves and cut into rings. Add to the oil.
	Root ginger	5 g	50 g	Peel, grate and add along with the meat. Stir fry for 3–4 minutes. Add the green pepper mixture and heat. Mix well and serve.

☐   ☐   ☐

Mongolian lamb hot pot/Chinese fondue

Shua yangrou

🥣 3 hr

Step	Commodity	1 portion	10 portions	
1	Shoulder of lamb, bone in	400 g	4 kg	Remove any fat, gristle and bone. Cut the meat into very thin slices and arrange in a serving bowl. Place the bones in a large wok and add three times as much water.
	Carrot	50 g	500 g	Peel, cut thinly and add.
	Onion	50 g	500 g	Peel, cut into quarters and add. Cook for 2 hours and strain.
	Mung bean threads	25 g	250 g	Place in a bowl and cover with cold water. Soak for 15 minutes. Drain and place in a serving dish.
	Spinach leaves	100 g	1 kg	Wash and remove and discard outer stalks and any withered leaves. Cut into large pieces and place in a serving dish.
	Chinese cabbage	100 g	1 kg	Wash and remove and discard stalks and any withered leaves. Cut into large pieces and place in a serving dish.
	Bean curd	100 g	1 kg	Cut into 1 cm cubes and place in a serving dish.
2	Hoi sin sauce	1 tbsp	10 tbsp	Place in a serving bowl.
	Chilli sauce	1 tbsp	10 tbsp	Place in a serving bowl.
	Soy sauce	1 tbsp	10 tbsp	Place in a serving bowl.
	Spring onions	15 g	150 g	Wash, remove the root and outer leaves, cut into rings and place in a bowl.
	Root ginger	5 g	50 g	Peel, grate and add. Place the stock in the fondue and boil. Pieces of meat and vegetables are placed into the simmering stock and cooked for 30 seconds, then dipped into the sauce of choice.

NOTE: **Fondues.**

Traditionally a fondue is made with gruyère and emmenthal cheese, wine and seasoning and is heated in a glazed earthenware dish that is kept warm over a small spirit lamp and served at the table. Cubes of crusty bread are speared with a serving skewer and dipped into the fondue.

Alternatively the glazed earthenware dish may be half filled with oil that is heated with the spirit lamp, and small pieces of prepared tender pieces of meat, poultry and fish are cooked in the hot fat. The cooked meat, poultry or fish is then dipped into a prepared sauce (cheese sauce, flavoured mayonnaise, mustard sauce).

□   □   □

22

Ten variety fried rice

Shijin chaofan

🥣 50 min   ♨ 30 min

Step	Commodity	1 portion	10 portions	
1	Chinese mushrooms	5 g	50 g	Place in a bowl and cover with warm water. Soak for 30 minutes. Squeeze dry, discard the stalks and cut the mushrooms into small, thin slices.
	Long grain rice	75 g	750 g	Place in a bowl and wash in cold running water. Place in a wok and cover with twice as much water. Bring to the boil and simmer for 15 minutes. Refresh and drain.
2	Vegetable oil	5 ml	5 ml	Place in a wok and heat.
	Eggs	1	10	Break into a bowl and whisk. Add to the hot oil and make an omelette. Remove and allow to go cold. Cut into thin slices.

Step	Commodity	1 portion	10 portions	
3	Vegetable oil	5 ml	50 ml	Place in a clean wok and heat.
	Spring onions	15 g	150 g	Wash, remove the root and outer leaves, cut into rings and add.
	Peeled prawns	50 g	500 g	Add.
	Cooked ham	25 g	250 g	Dice finely and add.
	Cooked chicken	25 g	250 g	Dice finely and add along with the mushrooms.
	Bamboo shoots	15 g	150 g	Cut into thin slices and add.
	Cooked peas	15 g	150 g	Add and stir fry for 1 minute. Add the rice and re-heat.
	Soy sauce	½ tbsp	5 tbsp	Add along with the omelette. Mix well together and serve hot.

NOTE: This dish may be made using noodles in place of rice.

☐   ☐   ☐

Bean sprout salad

Laingban douyar

🥄 30 min   ♨ 20 min

Step	Commodity	1 portion	10 portions	
1	Bean sprouts	100 g	1 kg	Place in a bowl of cold water and remove any damaged beans and husks. Drain and place in a wok of boiling salted water. Return to the boil and cook for 3 minutes. Refresh and drain. Place aside for use later.
2	Vegetable oil	5 ml	5 ml	Place in a clean wok and heat.
	Sliced cooked ham	25 g	250 g	Cut into thin strips and place in a bowl.
	Eggs	1	10	Break into a bowl and whisk. Add to the wok and cook gently to make a thin omelette. Remove, cool, cut into thin strips and add to the ham. Wipe the wok clean and return to the heat.
3	Soy sauce	¼ tbsp	5 tbsp	Add.
	Vinegar	½ tsp	5 tsp	Add.
	Sesame seed oil	5 ml	50 ml	Add and heat. Bring to the boil and add the bean sprouts. Stir fry for 2 minutes and arrange on a serving dish. Wipe the wok clean and return to the heat.
4	Sesame seed oil	5 ml	50 ml	Place in the wok and heat. Add the ham and egg and stir fry for 30 seconds. Arrange on top of the bean sprouts.
	Red peppers	25 g	250 g	Remove the stalks and seeds and cut into thin strips. Sprinkle over the dish and serve.

☐   ☐   ☐

Kidney flower salad

Liangban yaohua

🍵 45 min ♨ 50 min

Step	Commodity	1 portion	10 portions	
1	Pigs' kidneys	100 g	1 kg	Skin, split in half lengthways. Remove the core and any tubes. Cut into 4 cm pieces and score the surface in a criss-cross pattern to create the 'flower'. Place in a wok of boiling water and blanch for 10 minutes. Remove, refresh and drain. Place on a serving dish.
	Celery	100 g	1 kg	Wash and discard any damaged leaves. Cut into thin slices and arrange around the kidneys.
2	Soy sauce	½ tbsp	5 tbsp	Place in a bowl.
	Vinegar	½ tsp	5 tsp	Add.
	Sesame seed oil	15 ml	150 ml	Add.
	Chilli sauce	few drops	1 tsp	Add.
	Root ginger	5 g	50 g	Peel, grate and add.
	Sugar	½ tsp	5 tsp	Add.
	Pineapple pieces	25 g	250 g	Cut into small pieces and add.
	Spring onions	15 g	150 g	Wash, remove the root and outer leaves, cut into rings and add half of the onions to the other ingredients. Mix together well, pour over the kidneys and leave to marinade for 30 minutes before serving. Sprinkle with the remaining onions and serve.

☐   ☐   ☐

22

Steamed dumplings with sweet filling

Dousha bao

🍵 2½ hr ♨ 45 min

Step	Commodity	1 portion	10 portions	
1	Dried yeast	½ tbsp	5 tbsp	Place in a bowl and just cover with water.
	Sugar	½ tsp	5 tsp	Sprinkle over the water and mix in well. Place in a warm place for 15 minutes.
	Plain flour	150 g	1½ kg	Sift into a bowl. Add the yeast mixture.
	Lukewarm milk	100 ml	1 litre	Add the required amount and mix to a firm dough. Leave in a warm place for 1½ hours or until doubled in size. Knead the dough on a lightly floured surface. Roll into a long cylinder 5 cm in diameter. Cut into 2 cm pieces and roll each into a 10 cm round.
2	Filling	75 g	750 g	Divide into the appropriate portions and place in the centre of each round. Brush the edges together and gather up the dough around the filling. Twist the top to enclose the filling and leave to rest for 20 minutes. Part fill a wok with water and place a metal trivet in the centre. Place the steamer above. Place a damp cloth in the steamer and arrange the dumplings on the cloth leaving 2 cm between each. If necessary, place another steamer above and repeat the process. Steam for 45 minutes. Serve hot.

NOTE: The fillings can be yellow bean sauce, sweetened chestnut purée or any fruit purée.

☐   ☐   ☐

Plum blossom and snow competing for spring

Mexixue zhenghun

⏱ 1 hr   ♨ 30 min

Step	Commodity	1 portion	10 portions	
1	Dessert apples	1	10	Peel and remove the core. Cut into thin slices. Place in a bowl.
	Lemon juice	½ tsp	5 tsp	Pour over the apples.
	Bananas	1	10	Peel, slice and place with apples.
	Lemon juice	½ tsp	5 tsp	Pour over the bananas. Arrange the bananas and the apples in alternate slices in an ovenproof dish.
2	Milk	100 ml	1 litre	Place in a wok and boil.
	Cornflour	5 g	50 g	Dilute with a little milk and add to the boiled milk. Reduce the heat to a gentle simmer.
	Egg yolks	½	5	Place in a bowl.
	Sugar	25 g	250 g	Add and mix together well. Add to the simmering milk and whisk thoroughly to make a custard. Pour over the fruit and allow to cool.
3	Egg whites	½	5	Place in a bowl and whisk until firm and stiff. Place on top of the custard. Cook in a pre-heated oven (220°C) for about 5 minutes or until the surface is golden brown. Serve hot or cold.

☐   ☐   ☐

Japanese cookery

Japanese cookery is unique in that there are no foreign influences. Japanese cuisine is exquisite, aesthetic and sophisticated, cooking being considered an art. Visual feasting is a part of the traditional Japanese meal. Food is prepared artistically, arranged and garnished on beautiful ceramic plates and bowls. Japanese cooking is relatively simple with each food being prepared separately, even if served together. Knives are not used during eating

the food is cut into small pieces during preparation and is eaten with chop sticks.

Fish, a medium grained rice (served at all meals), noodles and vegetables are used extensively, and a speciality is raw fish (sushi). Japanese soy sauce (shoya), which is light coloured, is used to flavour Japanese foods and most dishes are served at room temperature.

Dashi

Japanese basic stock

⏱ 30 min   ♨ 1 hr

Step	Commodity	1 portion	10 portions	
1	Kombu	100 g	1 kg	Rinse and wipe with a damp cloth. Place in a pan.
	Water	500 ml	5 litres	Add and bring to the boil. Remove the kombu and retain for use.
2	Flaked katsuobushi	5 g	50 g	Add to the boiling liquid. Remove from the heat and allow to stand for 5 minutes.
	Shoyu	pinch	3 tsp	Add. Season with salt. Strain for use.

☐   ☐   ☐

Karashi

Mustard sauce

🥄 10 min

Step	Commodity	1 portion	10 portions	
1	Dry mustard	½ tsp	5 tsp	Place in a bowl.
	Warm water	½ tsp	5 tsp	Add to the mustard and dilute.
	Shoyu	1 tbsp	10 tbsp	Add.
	Sesame seed oil	¼ tsp	2½ tsp	Add and mix together well. Pour into individual serving dishes.

☐ ☐ ☐

Ponzu

Tart sauce

🥄 10 min

Step	Commodity	1 portion	10 portions	
1	Shoyu	50ml	500 ml	Pour into the bowl.
	Lime/lemon juice	50 ml	500 ml	Add.
	Mirin	1 tbsp	10 tbsp	Add and mix together well. Pour into individual serving dishes.

☐ ☐ ☐

Dumplings

🥄 20 min   🍲 1 hr approximately

Step	Commodity	1 portion	10 portions	
1	Dried yeast	½ tbsp	5 tbsp	Place in a bowl and just cover with water.
	Sugar	1 tsp	7 tsp	Sprinkle over the water and mix in well. Place in a warm place for 15 minutes.
	Plain flour	150 g	1½ kg	Sift into a bowl. Add the yeast mixture.
	Lukewarm milk	100 ml	1 litre	Add the required amount and mix to a firm dough. Leave in a warm place for 1½ hours or until doubled in size. Knead the dough on a lightly-floured surface. Roll into a long cylinder 5 cm in diameter. Cut into 2 cm pieces and roll each into a round ball.

☐ ☐ ☐

22

Harusame soup

Step	Commodity	1 portion	10 portions	
1	Mung bean threads	25 g	250 g	Place in a bowl, cover with boiling water and allow to soak for 30 minutes. Remove and drain. Cut into 5 cm pieces.
	Japanese mushrooms (dried) shiitake	5 g	50 g	Place in a bowl, cover with boiling water and soak for 20 minutes. Drain and reserve the mushroom liquid in a jug, ensuring any sediment is left at the bottom of the bowl.
	Dashi	250 ml	2½ litres	Place in a pan and add the mushroom liquid. Bring to the boil, then reduce to a simmer.
	Sake	1 tsp	10 tsp	Add. Season with salt.
2	Gobo	50 g	500 g	Peel, place in a pan of cold water. Bring to the boil and cook for 25 minutes. Remove, drain and allow to cool.
	Mangetout	25 g	250 g	Remove the tops and tails and place in a pan of boiling salted water for 2 minutes. Remove, drain and arrange on a serving dish. Cut the gobo into decorative shapes and place on the serving dish.
	Spring onions	15 g	150 g	Wash, remove the root and outer leaves and place on the serving dish.
	Peeled prawns	25 g	250 g	Arrange alongside the other ingredients on the serving dish.
	Carrots	25 g	250 g	Peel, cut decorative shapes and arrange with the other ingredients.
	Cucumber	3 slices	30 slices	Arrange on the dish.
	Napa	25 g	250 g	Wash, remove the large stalks and arrange on the dish.
	Daikon	½ tsp	5 tsp	Arrange on the plate.
	Spring onions	15 g	150 g	Wash, remove the root and outer leaves, cut into rings and sprinkle over the ingredients.
	Root ginger	5 g	50 g	Peel, grate and sprinkle over the top. Pour the soup into serving bowls. Serve with the vegetables.

Spring rain soup

🥄 2 hr   ♨ 30 min

☐   ☐   ☐

Hotate gai shoyu yaki

Step	Commodity	1 portion	10 portions	
1	Scallops	2	20	Wash well. Place on top of a hot stove to force open. Carefully remove the scallop from the shell. Retain the shell. Wash and trim the scallops. Place in a bowl.
	Soy sauce	10 ml	100 ml	Add to the scallops.
	Sake	10 ml	100 ml	Add and mix together. Clean the scallop shell. Place one scallop in each. Pour over the liquor. Place under a pre-heated salamander and cook for 2–3 minutes on each side.
2	Lemon wedge	1	10	Serve with the scallops.
	Parsley	sprig	10 sprigs	Wash, remove the stalk and place on the scallops. Serve immediately.

Grilled scallops with soy sauce

🥄 30 min   ♨ 30 min

☐   ☐   ☐

Tempura with tentsuyu sauce

Assorted fritters with dipping sauce

1½ hr 20 min

Step	Commodity	1 portion	10 portions	
1	Fresh prawns	150 g	1½ kg	Split down the centre and remove the black vein. Leave the last part of the shell and the tail on the meat. Dry the prawns with kitchen paper and place in the refrigerator.
	Sweet potatoes	100 g	1 kg	Peel and slice into ½ cm rounds.
	Aubergines	75 g	750 g	Cut in half lengthways and peel. Cut into ½ cm slices.
	Mangetout	15 g	150 g	Top and tail. Wash and dry on kitchen paper.
	Onions	25 g	250 g	Peel, cut into thin rings.
	French beans	15 g	150 g	Wash, top and tail, and dry. Place with the other ingredients.
	Mushrooms	3	30	Trim the stalks and dry. Place with the other vegetables. Keep cool.
2	Dashi	100 ml	1 litre	Place in a pan.
	Shoyu	½ tbsp	5 tbsp	Add to dashi.
	Mirin	½ tbsp	5 tbsp	Add. Season with salt and monosodium glutamate. Mix together well and bring to the boil. Place in individual serving bowls.
3	Plain flour	15 g	150 g	Place in a chilled bowl.
	Cornflour	15 g	150 g	Place in a chilled bowl.
	Monosodium glutamate	pinch	2 tsp	Add.
	Baking flour	½ tsp	5 tsp	Add and sieve together three times.
	Eggs	¼	3	Add.
	Iced water	65 ml	650 ml	Add and mix lightly together. Place in the refrigerator.
4	Vegetable oil	100 ml	1 litre	Heat in a deep fryer. Dip the prawns and the vegetables a few pieces at a time and fry until light golden brown. Drain onto absorbent paper. Serve immediately in a folded napkin with the sauce.

☐ ☐ ☐

22

Nuta negi

Step	Commodity	1 portion	10 portions	
1	Wakame	1 strip	10 strips	Place in a bowl of cold water and soak for 10 minutes. Drain and rinse under cold running water. Cut into thin strips.
	Spring onions	½ bunch	5 bunch	Wash and remove the root and outer leaves. Place in a pan of boiling salted water for 3 minutes. Refresh and drain. Cut into 5 cm pieces. Place aside for use later.
2	Shiromiso	1 tbsp	10 tbsp	Place in a suitably sized saucepan.
	Dashi	1 tbsp	10 tbsp	Add.
	Su	½ tbsp	5 tbsp	Add.
	Dry mustard	¼ tsp	2 tsp	Diluted in a little water and add. Bring the ingredients to the boil and simmer for 5 minutes, stirring constantly as the mixture thickens. Reduce to a simmer. Place the spring onions and the wakame in a serving bowl and pour the sauce over the top. Serve immediately.

☐   ☐   ☐

Kyuri to kani no sunomono

Crab and cucumber with vinegar sauce   ⏲ 40 min

Step	Commodity	1 portion	10 portions	
1	Cucumber	50 g	500 g	Peel the skin. Cut down the centre lengthways and slice thinly. Place in a bowl and sprinkle with salt. Place in the refrigerator for use later.
2	Su	1 tbsp	10 tbsp	Place in a bowl.
	Sugar	1 tbsp	10 tbsp	Add.
	Monosodium glutamate	pinch	½ tsp	Add, season with salt and mix together well to form the sauce. Discard any liquid from the cucumber and place the cucumber in a serving bowl.
3	Cooked crabmeat	50 g	500 g	Add, mix together well and pour the sauce over it.
	Toasted sesame seeds	1 tsp	10 tsp	Sprinkle over the crab and cucumber.
	Lemon	1 slice	10 slices	Use to garnish.

☐   ☐   ☐

Sashimi

Sliced raw fish

🥣 40 min

Step	Commodity	1 portion	10 portions	
1	Prepared fillets of fish*	175 g	1.75 kg	Remove any skin or bones. Wash to remove blood. Cut the fish into 2 cm × ½ cm diagonals. Place on a serving platter.
	Daikon	50 g	500 g	Arrange in a mound alongside the fish.
	Carrots	25 g	250 g	Wash, peel and shred. Arrange in a mound and place by the daikon.
	Spring onions	1	10	Wash and remove the root and outer leaves. Shred, arrange in a mound and place on the platter.
	Mangetout	2	20	Wash, trim the tops and bottoms and arrange on the platter.
	Cooked king prawns, shell on	2	20	Wash and arrange on the platter.
	Lemon wedges	2	20	Place on the platter.
	Root ginger	5 g	50 g	Peel, grate and arrange in a mound on the platter.
	Wasabi	1 tsp	10 tsp	Place on the platter.
2	Shoyu	10 ml	100 ml	Place in individual serving bowls. Customers add wasabi and ginger to the shoyu to taste and dip the fish and vegetables in the mixture.

* Herring, seabass, tuna or any other salt water fish may be used.

NOTE: Serve with boiled rice.

☐   ☐   ☐

22

Shake no kasuzuke

Salmon with sake lees

🥣 10 days   ♨ 15 min

Step	Commodity	1 portion	10 portions	
1	Salmon steak	1 × 120 g	10 × 120 g	Place in a bowl, season with salt and cover with cling film. Place in the refrigerator and allow to marinade for 4 days or until the flesh becomes firm. Drain away the liquid and dry the salmon with absorbent paper. Place in a clean bowl.
2	Kasu	100 ml	1 litre	Place in a jug.
	Sugar	50 g	500 g	Add and mix in well. Pour over the fish and re-cover with cling film. Refrigerate for a further 6 days. Remove and cook under a pre-heated salamander for 7 minutes on either side. Remove the skin and the bone and serve.
3	Lettuce	25 g	250 g	Wash, shred and place in a mound on the serving plate.
	Puréed daikon	10 g	100 g	Arrange alongside the lettuce. Place the fish on the plate and serve hot.

☐   ☐   ☐

Shio yaki

Salt grilled fish

Step	Commodity	1 portion	10 portions	
				👐 40 min ♨ 15 min
1	Red snapper	1 × 500 g	10 × 500 g	Wash and clean the fish by removing the guts and eyes and scales. Make 3 long thin incisions diagonally along each side of the flesh. Place in a bowl and sprinkle with salt. Cover and refrigerate for 1 hour. Place under a pre-heated salamander for 7 minutes on each side.
	Lemon wedges	2	20	Arrange alongside the fish. Serve with a light soya sauce (shoyu).

☐   ☐   ☐

Gomatare

Sesame seed sauce

Step	Commodity	1 portion	10 portions	
				👐 30 min ♨ 30 min
1	Shiromiso	1 tsp	10 tsp	Place in a pan.
	Toasted sesame seeds	1 tbsp	10 tbsp	Crush and add to the shiromiso.
	Mirin	½ tbsp	5 tbsp	Add.
	Sugar	1 tsp	10 tsp	Add.
	Shoyu	1 tsp	10 tsp	Add.
	Dashi	50 ml	500 ml	Add, bring to the boil and simmer for 20 minutes. Allow to go cold and pour into a serving bowl.

☐   ☐   ☐

Mizutaki

🍲 1½ hr　♨ 15 min

Step	Commodity	1 portion	10 portions	
1	Dried shiitake	2	20	Place in a bowl, cover with boiling water and allow to soak for 30 minutes. Drain, squeeze dry and discard the stems. Slice into thin strips.
2	Cooked chicken meat (no bone)	150 g	1½ kg	Cut into 2 cm pieces and arrange on the serving plate.
	Green peppers	25 g	250 g	Remove the stalks and seeds. Cut the flesh into thin strips and arrange alongside the chicken.
	Cucumber	25 g	250 g	Wash, cut in a decorative manner and arrange on the plate.
	Carrots	25 g	250 g	Peel, use a special cutter to create different shapes and arrange on the plate.
	Mangetout	4	40	Wash, trim the tops and tails and arrange on the plate.
	Tofu	25 g	250 g	Cut into 2 cm cubes and arrange on the plate.
	Napa	10 g	100 g	Wash, gather together and cut into 2 cm strips. Arrange on the plate.
	Spring onions	1	10	Wash, trim the root and discard the outer leaves. Cut in half lengthways and arrange on the plate.
3	Dashi	250 ml	2½ litres	Place in a pan and bring to the boil.
	Sake	1 tsp	10 tsp	Add and simmer for 10 minutes. Pour into individual serving bowls. Guests help themselves to vegetables and dip them into the stock. Serve with sesame sauce.

☐　　☐　　☐

Buta teriyaki

🍲 2½ hr　♨ 6 min

Step	Commodity	1 portion	10 portions	
1	Pork fillet	150 g	1½ kg	Remove any fat. Cut into 2 cm pieces. Place in a bowl.
	Spring onions	2	20	Wash, remove the root and cut into 2 cm pieces. Add.
	Root ginger	5 g	50 g	Peel, shred and sprinkle over the other ingredients.
2	Shoyu	50 ml	500 ml	Place in a bowl.
	Sugar	15 g	150 g	Add.
	Sake	50 ml	500 ml	Add, sprinkle with a little monosodium glutamate (optional) and whisk together. Pour over the meat and spring onions, cover and marinade in a refrigerator for 1½ hours. Alternate pieces of the pork and spring onions on a skewer. Place on a pre-heated barbecue or under a pre-heated salamander for 6 minutes. Turn regularly, basting with the marinade until cooked.

☐　　☐　　☐

22

Teppanyaki

Step	Commodity	1 portion	10 portions			
				⏱ 1½ hr	🔥 15 min	
1	Fillet of beef	50 g	500 g	Cut into 1 cm × 5 cm lengths. Arrange decoratively on a serving plate.		
	Chicken breast	50 g	500 g	Cut into 1 cm × 5 cm lengths. Arrange decoratively along side the beef.		
	Unshelled cooked prawns	2	20	Arrange alongside the meats.		
	Courgettes	50 g	500 g	Peel, cut into 1 cm × 5 cm lengths and arrange alongside the other ingredients.		
	Spring onions	1	10	Wash and discard the root and outer leaves. Cut into 5 cm lengths and arrange on the serving plate.		
	Bean sprouts	50 g	500 g	Wash and arrange.		
	Button mushrooms	25 g	250 g	Wash, remove the stalks and arrange. The decorated meats are placed on the table and a fondue set with heated oil is placed in the centre of the table. When the correct temperature (185°C) is reached the meat, prawns and/or vegetables are added and cooked. Once cooked the meat/prawns/vegetables are removed and dipped into Ponzu (tart sauce) and Karashi (mustard sauce).		

☐ ☐ ☐

Hijiki to aburage

Step	Commodity	1 portion	10 portions			
				⏱ 1½ hr	🔥 25 min	
1	Seaweed (hijiki)	1 tbsp	10 tbsp	Place in a bowl. Cover with twice as much water and allow to soak for 1 hour. Drain, rinse away any sediment and strain through a fine sieve.		
	Aburage	100 g	1 kg	Place in a pan of boiling water for 2 minutes. Refresh, drain and cut into ½ cm cubes.		
2	Vegetable oil	1 tsp	10 tsp	Place in a skillet and heat. Add the seaweed and fry gently for 2 minutes. Add the aburage and continue cooking for a further 3 minutes.		
	Dashi	50 ml	500 ml	Pour over the ingredients, bring to the boil and simmer for 5 minutes.		
	Mirin	½ tsp	5 tsp	Add.		
	Sugar	½ tsp	5 tsp	Add.		
	Shoyu	½ tbsp	5 tbsp	Add and simmer for a further 10 minutes. Pour into individual serving dishes.		

☐ ☐ ☐

Shiitake no amanie

Sweet black mushrooms

🥣 50 min　🍲 25 min

Step	Commodity	1 portion	10 portions	
1	Dried shiitake	4	40	Rinse, place in a bowl and cover with boiling water. Allow to soak for 30 minutes. Strain the mushroom liquor into a jug. Discard the mushroom stems and leave the mushroom cap whole. Pour the mushroom liquor into a pan. Add the mushrooms, bring to the boil and simmer for 5 minutes.
	Sugar	½ tsp	5 tsp	Add.
	Mirin	½ tbsp	5 tbsp	Add.
	Shoyu	½ tsp	5 tsp	Add, season with salt and a pinch of monosodium glutamate (optional) and simmer for 15 minutes. Arrange on a serving plate.
2	Spring onions	2	20	Wash, remove the root and outer leaves, cut into 2 cm lengths and use to garnish the mushrooms.

☐　☐　☐

Sukiyaki

Meat with vegetables

🥣 40 min

Step	Commodity	1 portion	10 portions	
1	Dried shiitake	25 g	250 g	Rinse, place in a bowl and cover with boiling water. Allow to soak for 30 minutes. Discard the mushroom stems. Cut into thin slices and arrange on a serving platter.
	Mung bean threads	25 g	250 g	Place in a bowl and cover with boiling water. Leave to soak for 30 minutes. Drain and cut into 5 cm lengths. Arrange on the platter.
	Fillet of beef	150 g	1½ kg	Cut into 1 cm × 5 cm lengths. Arrange on the platter.
	Onions	50 g	500 g	Peel, cut into thin rings and arrange on the platter.
	Spring onions	1	10	Wash, discard the root and outer leaves. Cut into 5 cm lengths and arrange on the platter.
	Carrots	50 g	500 g	Wash, peel and cut into thin 2 cm lengths.
	Bean sprouts	50 g	500 g	Wash and arrange on the platter.
	Water chestnuts	25 g	250 g	Cut into slices and arrange on the platter.
	Spinach leaves	3	30	Wash, remove the stalk and arrange on the platter.
	Tofu	50 g	500 g	Dice into 2 cm cubes and arrange on the platter.
2	Shoya	50 ml	500 ml	Place in a jug.
	Sugar	1 tbsp	10 tbsp	Add to the shoya.
	Dashi	50 ml	500 ml	Add.
	Mirin	50 ml	500 ml	Add and mix together well to form the sauce. The food is cooked at the table on a griddle. A little of the sauce is poured onto the hot griddle, a variety of the foods are added and cooked for a few minutes. As they cook they are turned and eventually pushed to the side of the griddle ready to eat. Continue to add more sauce and foods as required.

NOTE: Each person may be offered a bowl with a whisked raw egg flavoured with soy sauce. The cooked food is dipped into the mixture and the heat from the food is sufficient to cook the egg slightly.

☐　☐　☐

583

Shimeji

Step	Commodity	1 portion	10 portions	
1	Fresh shimeji	100 g	1 kg	Cut into 1 cm × 1 cm pieces.
	Butter	10 g	100 g	Place in a skillet and heat gently.
	Garlic	½ clove	5 cloves	Peel, crush with a little salt and add to the butter. Add the shimeji and cook for 2 minutes.
	Sake	½ tsp	5 tsp	Add.
	Dashi	1 tbsp	10 tbsp	Add, season with a little ground black pepper and monosodium glutamate (optional). Cook for a further 2 minutes and serve.

☐   ☐   ☐

Horenso tamago maki

Step	Commodity	1 portion	10 portions	
1	Spinach leaves	150 g	1½ kg	Wash, remove the stalk and place in a pan of boiling salted water for 1½ minutes. Drain, refresh and squeeze the leaves to remove excess water. Sprinkle with light soy sauce and shape into a cylinder 3 cm in diameter. Place to the side for use later.
2	Eggs	1	10	Break into a bowl and whisk together. Season with salt.
	Sugar	¼ tsp	2½ tsp	Add and mix well.
3	Cooking oil	1 tsp	10 tsp	Pour into a frying pan and heat. Add the eggs 2–3 portions at a time. Stir frequently and cook until set. Once cooked, remove and place on a clean cloth or bamboo mat. Place the appropriate amount of spinach on top and roll up the omelette firmly. Cut into 2 cm slices and arrange on a serving dish. Accompany with a bowl of shoyu.

☐   ☐   ☐

Nasu no karashi

Step	Commodity	1 portion	10 portions	
1	Aubergine*	150 g	1½ kg	Wash, remove the stalk and cut into thin slices. Place in a bowl, sprinkle with salt, cover with water and soak for 1 hour.
2	Dry mustard	¼ tsp	2½ tsp	Place in a bowl.
	Shoyu	1 tbsp	10 tbsp	Add to the mustard.
	Mirin	1 tbsp	10 tbsp	Add.
	Sugar	1 tbsp	10 tbsp	Add and mix all the ingredients together to form the marinade. Monosodium glutamate may be added if required. Drain the aubergines and dry with a cloth or kitchen paper. Arrange on a serving dish. Pour over the marinade, cover and refrigerate for a minimum of 4 hours before serving.

* Japanese eggplants are an elongated version of the more common aubergine.

☐   ☐   ☐

Gyoza

Fried dumplings

⤵ 40 min 🍲 1 hr

Step	Commodity	1 portion	10 portions	
1	Napa leaves	1	10	Wash, place in a pan of boiling salted water for 2 minutes. Refresh, drain and squeeze to remove excess water. Chop coarsely and place in a bowl.
	Minced lean pork	75 g	750 g	Add.
	Spring onions	½	5	Wash and discard the root and outer leaves. Chop the onions into fine dice and add to the other ingredients.
	Garlic	½ clove	5 cloves	Peel, crush with a little salt and add.
	Root ginger	5 g	50 g	Peel, shred and add.
	Shoyu	½ tbsp	5 tbsp	Add.
	Sesame seed oil	1 tsp	10 tsp	Add and mix together well.
2	Gyoza skins*	4	40	Divide the meat filling into the appropriate number of portions. Divide the portions into 4 and place each quarter portion in the centre of a gyoza skin. Brush the rim with water and fold in half, enclosing the filling. Pleat the sides.
3	Cooking oil	10 ml	100 ml	Place in a suitably sized frying pan and heat. Add the filled gyozas. Cover with a lid and cook for 5 minutes. Remove the lid and pour in sufficient water to cover the gyozas. Replace the lid and simmer gently until all the water has evaporated.
4	Su	½ tbsp	5 tbsp	Place in a bowl.
	Dry mustard	½ tbsp	5 tbsp	Sprinkle over the top.
	Shoya	½ tbsp	5 tbsp	Add and whisk together well to make the dipping sauce. Place in individual bowls and serve with the gyoza yaki.

* Gyoza skins are a product available in Oriental shops.

□ □ □

Gohan

Plain steamed rice

⤵ 10 min 🍲 35 min

Step	Commodity	1 portion	10 portions	
1	Short/ medium rice	100 g	1 kg	Wash thoroughly under cold running water. Leave the water running until the rinsing water becomes clear. Allow to drain in a colander for 30 minutes. Place in a suitably sized pan.
2	Water	150 ml	1½ litres	Pour over the rice, cover with a lid, bring to the boil and simmer gently for 20 minutes or until most of the water has been absorbed. Remove from the heat and allow to stand for 10 minutes before removing the lid. Fluff up the rice with a fork. Serve hot in individual bowls.

□ □ □

22

Sushi

Basic vinegared rice

🍲 1½ hr   🍳 25 min

Step	Commodity	1 portion	10 portions	
1	Medium rice	100 g	1 kg	Wash thoroughly under cold running water. Leave the water running until the rinsing water becomes clear then drain. Place in a suitably sized pan.
	Water	150 ml	1½ litres	Pour over the rice and leave to soak for 1 hour.
	Kombu, piece of	1 cm sq	5 cm sq	Add to the rice. Cover with a lid, bring to the boil and simmer gently for 3 minutes. Remove the kombu, replace the lid and cook for a further 12 minutes. Remove from the heat and allow to stand for 10 minutes before removing the lid. Fluff up the rice with a fork then place in individual serving bowls.
2	Su	25 ml	250 ml	Place in a saucepan.
	Sugar	1 tbsp	10 tbsp	Add.
	Salt	½ tsp	5 tsp	Add and bring to the boil. Simmer for 5 minutes. Remove from the heat and pour over the rice.
3	Toasted sesame seeds	½ tbsp	5 tbsp	Sprinkle over the rice. Serve hot.

NOTE: This dish may be garnished with beni-shoga or sansho.

☐   ☐   ☐

Nigiri zushi

Rice balls with toppings

🍲 2½ hr   🍳 25 min

Step	Commodity	1 portion	10 portions	
1	Sushi (as above)	100 g	1 kg	Using two tablespoons, scoop up an amount of sushi and make an oval shape 5 cms long. Place on a tray.
	Su	10 ml	100 ml	Brush over the sushi.
2	Wasabi	10 g	100 g	Place in a bowl.
	Water	10 ml	100 ml	Add and mix to a paste. Brush over the top of the sushi.
3	Prepared topping/s*	150 g	1½ kg	Cut into thin slices to fit on top of the sushi. Press down firmly. Arrange on an oval serving plate.
4	Parsley	5 g	50 g	Wash, discard the stalks and use the leaves to decorate.

* The topping can be any raw fish (herrings, seasbass, tuna) or shellfish. Slices of beni shoga may also be used to garnish.

☐   ☐   ☐

Tsukimi udon

Noodles with broth

🍜 1 hr   ♨ 40 min

Step	Commodity	1 portion	10 portions	
1	Large noodles	100 g	1 kg	Place in a pan of boiling salted water. Cook for 12 minutes until the noodles are *al dente*. Drain, refresh and drain again. Retain for use later.
2	Dashi	200 ml	2 litres	Place in a saucepan.
	Sugar	1 tsp	25 g	Add.
	Salt	¼ tsp	2½ tsp	Add and bring to the boil. Add the noodles, return to the boil and simmer for 5 minutes. Pour into individual serving bowls.
	Eggs	1	10	Break a whole egg into the centre of the broth. Cover with lids to allow the egg to cook.
3	Spring onions	5 g	50 g	Wash, discard the root and outer leaves, cut into thin rings and sprinkle over the broth.

☐　　☐　　☐

Kasutera

Sponge cake

🍜 40 min   ♨ 30 min

Step	Commodity	1 portion	10 portions	
1	Eggs	1	10	Break into a bowl.
	Sugar	30 g	300 g	Add to the eggs.
	Honey	1 tsp	10 tsp	Add and beat until thick and pale.
2	Self raising flour	15 g	150 g	Fold into the egg mixture gently. Pour into a prepared cake tin and place into a pre-heated oven (180°C) for the appropriate time. Remove from the oven and allow to cool before transferring to a wire rack. Allow to go cold.
3	Icing sugar	10 g	100 g	Sprinkle over the cake. Cut into squares to serve.

☐　　☐　　☐

Matcha ice cream

Green tea ice cream

🍜 4 hr approximately   ♨ 1 hr approximately

Step	Commodity	1 portion	10 portions	
1	Milk	200 ml	2 litres	Place in a saucepan and bring to the boil. Reduce to a simmer and reduce by two-thirds.
	Rice flour	10 g	100 g	Stir into the milk and mix thoroughly.
	Single cream	60 ml	600 ml	Add carefully and mix well. Bring to the boil, then simmer for 15 minutes.
	Castor sugar	25 g	250 g	Add and dissolve completely. Allow to cool.
	Matcha	½ tsp	5 tsp	Add and mix in well. Transfer to an ice cream machine and freeze. Scoop into serving bowls.
2	Sweetened azuki	50 g	500 g	Serve with the ice cream.

☐　　☐　　☐

Malaysia, Singapore and Indonesian cookery

The cuisine of South East Asia is very much influenced by Chinese and Indian cookery. Coconut flesh, rice, fish and vegetables are the staple diet. Cooking is usually done on an open fire in a wajan (a round bottomed frying pan similar to a wok).

Mie bakso

Origin: Indonesia

Noodle soup with meatballs

🥄 40 min   ♨ 1 hr

Step	Commodity	1 portion	10 portions	
1	Egg noodles	25 g	250 g	Place in a pan of boiling salted water and simmer for 5 minutes. Remove from the simmering water and refresh. Retain the water.
2	Lean minced beef	75 g	750 g	Place in a bowl.
	Cornflour	1 tbsp	10 tbsp	Add.
	Egg whites	¼ equiv	2½ equiv	Add, season with salt and pepper and mix well together. Shape into small balls. Drop them, one at a time, into the simmering water and cook for 10 minutes. Remove and place to the side.
3	Vegetable oil	½ tbsp	5 tbsp	Place in a frying pan and heat.
	Spring onions	1	10	Wash and discard the root and outer leaves. Cut into thin rings and add to the hot oil.
	Carrots	50 g	500 g	Peel, cut into thin rings and add.
	Garlic	½ clove	5 cloves	Pell, crush with a little salt and add.
	Shallots	25 g	250 g	Peel, dice finely and add. Stir fry for 2–3 minutes.
	Root ginger	5 g	50 g	Peel, grate and add.
	Soy sauce	1 tsp	10 tsp	Add.
	Meat stock	25 ml	250 ml	Add and simmer for 15 minutes.
	Mangetout	25 g	250 g	Top and tail and add.
	Chinese cabbage	25 g	250 g	Wash, remove the root, shred finely and add. Cook for another 5 minutes. Add the noodles and the meatballs. Cook for a further 5 minutes. Serve immediately.

☐   ☐   ☐

Soto madura

Origin: Indonesia

Spicy beef soup

Step	Commodity	1 portion	10 portions	🥄 45 min ♨ 1½ hr
1	Boned brisket of beef	125 g	1¼ kg	Place in a pan of boiling water. Season with salt and pepper. Simmer for 1 hour. Drain the cooking liquor into a saucepan. Place the meat to the side and cut into 2 cm dice.
2	Peeled prawns	25 g	250 g	Place in a blender.
	Kemiri	1	10	Add.
	Shallots	25 g	250 g	Peel and add.
	Garlic	½ clove	5 cloves	Peel, crush with a little salt and add. Blend to a paste.
3	Cooking oil	½ tbsp	5 tbsp	Place in a frying pan and heat. Add the blended mixture and cook for 1 minute.
	Root ginger	5 g	50 g	Peel, grate and add.
	Turmeric powder	¼ tsp	2½ tsp	Add along with half of the beef cooking liquor. Cover and simmer for 15 minutes.
4	Cooking oil	½ tbsp	5 tbsp	Place in a frying pan and heat. Add the diced beef.
	Chilli powder	pinch	1 tsp	Add and mix in well. Add the remaining beef cooking liquor. Bring to the boil and simmer for 5 minutes. Strain the prawn liquid into the beef. Return to the boil and simmer for a further hour. Season to taste.
5	Onions	25 g	250 g	Peel, dice finely and add raw to the soup as a garnish.
	Coriander leaves	2	20	Wash, chop finely and add.
	Lemon slices	1	10	Cut in half and add.

☐   ☐   ☐

22

Rempah-rempah

Origin: Malaysia

30 min   5 min

Step	Commodity	1 portion	10 portions	
1	Peeled prawns	25 g	250 g	Place in a bowl.
	Bean sprouts	50 g	500 g	Wash and place in the bowl.
	Spring onions	15 g	150 g	Wash, discard the stalk and outer leaves and cut into 2 cm lengths.
	Garlic	½ clove	5 cloves	Peel, crush with a little salt and add.
	Coriander leaves	2	20	Wash, chop finely and add.
	Desiccated coconut	5 g	50 g	Add.
	Self raising flour	15 g	150 g	Add.
	Coriander powder	pinch	1 tsp	Add.
	Ground ginger	pinch	1 tsp	Add.
	Chilli powder	pinch	1 tsp	Add.
	Water	1 tbsp	10 tbsp	Add.
	Eggs	¼ equiv	2½ equiv	Add and mix well together. Form small balls the size of walnuts. Deep fry a few at a time, in hot fat (190°C) for 3–4 minutes. Remove and drain on kitchen paper. Place on a serving dish.
2	Lemon slices	2	20	Garnish on top of the rempah-rempah.

□   □   □

Bola bola tahu

Fried prawns and bean curd balls

Origin: Malaysia

Step	Commodity	1 portion	10 portions			🥣 40 min ♨ 10 min
1	Tahu	100 g	1 kg	Place in a bowl and mash to a smooth paste.
	Peeled prawns	75 g	750 g	Place in an electric blender. Add the tahu.
	Garlic	½ clove	5 cloves	Peel, crush with a little salt and add.
	Cornflour	½ tbsp	5 tbsp	Add.
	Eggs	¼ equiv	2½ equiv	Add and mix together well. Remove from the blender and season with salt and black pepper. Cover and place in the refrigerator for 30 minutes.
2	Ripe tomatoes	50 g	500 g	Remove the stalks and eyes. Place in a saucepan.
	Shallots	25 g	250 g	Peel, dice finely and add.
	Garlic	½ clove	5 cloves	Peel, crush with a little salt and add.
	Water	50 ml	500 ml	Pour over the ingredients and bring to the boil. Simmer for 5 minutes. Strain the sauce into a clean saucepan.
3	Light soy sauce	1 tbsp	10 tbsp	Add.
	Lemon juice	½ tsp	5 tsp	Add.
	Sugar	½ tsp	5 tsp	Add.
	Mangetout	10 g	100 g	Top and tail and add. Season with salt and pepper and simmer for 10 minutes. Place the prawns, two to three at a time, into a deep frying pan (190°C). Cook until golden brown, add to the sauce and simmer for 1–2 minutes until the prawn balls have absorbed some sauce.
4	Onions	25 g	250 g	Peel, cut into rings and use to garnish.

22

591

Ayam goreng Jawa

Fried chicken Javanese-style

Origin: Indonesia

⏲ 45 min   🍲 1 hr 15 min

Step	Commodity	1 portion	10 portions	
1	Pieces of chicken	250 g	2½ kg	Remove excess skin and fat and wash well. Place in a suitably sized saucepan.
	Shallots	25 g	250 g	Peel, dice finely and add.
	Garlic	1 clove	10 cloves	Peel, crush with a little salt and add.
	Coriander powder	½ tsp	5 tsp	Add.
	Cumin powder	pinch	1 tsp	Add.
	Sereh	pinch	½ tsp	Add.
	Nutmeg	pinch	½ tsp	Add.
	Bay leaves	½ small	2	Add.
	Brown sugar	½ tsp	5 tsp	Add and cover completely with water. Cover and bring to the boil. Simmer for 1 hour or until the chicken is tender. Do not allow the water to evaporate; replenish as required. Remove the chicken and place on a tray.
2	Cooking oil	20 ml	200 ml	Heat in a suitably sized frying pan. Add the chicken in 'batches' and cook until golden brown. Remove and drain on kitchen paper. Serve hot.

☐ ☐ ☐

Kelia ayam

Indonesian chicken curry

Origin: Indonesia

⏲ 45 min   🍲 1½ hr

Step	Commodity	1 portion	10 portions	
1	Shallots	50 g	500 g	Peel, remove the roots and place in a blender.
	Garlic	½ clove	5 cloves	Peel, crush with a little salt and add.
	Kemiri	1	10	Chop finely and add.
	Water	½ tbsp	5 tbsp	Add and blend to a smooth paste. Place in a suitably sized wok.
2	Santen	150 ml	1½ litres	Add.
	Ground ginger	pinch	2 tsp	Add.
	Chilli pepper	pinch	2 tsp	Add.
	Turmeric	pinch	2 tsp	Add.
	Chicken pieces	250 g	2½ kg	Remove excess fat and skin. Wash well and add.
	Salam leaf	½	2	Add and mix together well. Simmer for 1½ hours until the chicken is cooked and the liquor thick. Season with salt and black pepper. Serve immediately.

☐ ☐ ☐

Sate babi

Origin: Singapore

Step	Commodity	1 portion	10 portions			☞ 4 hr ♨ 3 min
1	Pork fillet	150 g	1½ kg	Remove any fat and cut the pork fillet into thin slices. Place in a bowl.
	Light soy sauce	½ tbsp	5 tbsp	Add.
	Garlic	½ clove	5 cloves	Peel, crush with a little salt and add to the other ingredients.
	Shallots	15 g	150 g	Peel, cut in half and dice finely. Add.
	Five spice	½ tsp	5Ttsp	Add.
	Honey	1 tsp	10 tsp	Add and mix together well. Season with salt and black pepper and leave to marinade for 4 hours. Divide the pork into the appropriate number of portions. Place on skewers and bake in a pre-heated oven (180°C) for 20 minutes. Remove and finish under a pre-heated salamander for 5–8 minutes.

NOTE: Lamb sate (Sate kambing) may be made using this recipe, replacing the light soy sauce with dark and the pork with lamb.

☐   ☐   ☐

Saté

Origin: Indonesia/Thailand

Step	Commodity	1 portion	10 portions			☞ 40 min ♨ 1 hr
1	Vegetable oil	1 tbsp	10 tbsp	Place in a suitably sized frying pan and heat.
	Shelled peanuts	25 g	250 g	Add and cook for 5 minutes until golden brown. Allow to cool and place in a blender.
	Shallots	25 g	250 g	Peel, remove the root and add.
	Garlic	¼ clove	2 cloves	Peel, crush with a little salt and add.
	Terasi	½ tsp	5 tsp	Add, season and blend to a smooth paste.
2	Peanut oil	1 tsp	10 tsp	Place in a suitably sized frying pan and heat. Add the peanut paste.
	Water	75 ml	750 ml	Add.
	Tamarind water	1 tsp	10 tsp	Add.
	Brown sugar	¼ tsp	2 tsp	Add and mix together well. Bring to the boil and simmer until the sauce is thick. Place in a serving bowl.

☐   ☐   ☐

22

Kambling korma

Origin: Malaysia

⏱ 1½ hr   ♨ 1 hr

Step	Commodity	1 portion	10 portions	
1	Garlic	½ clove	5 cloves	Peel, crush with a little salt and place in a blender.
	Shallots	25 g	250 g	Peel, remove the stalks and add.
	Kemiri	1	10	Add, sprinkle with a little water and blend to a smooth paste. Transfer to a suitably sized bowl.
2	Boneless lamb	150 g	1½ kg	Remove the fat or gristle and cut into 2 cm cubes. Add to the paste and leave to marinade for 1 hour.
3	Cooking oil	15 ml	150 ml	Place in a suitably sized frying pan and heat.
	Onions	25 g	250 g	Peel, cut in half and cut into thin slices. Add to the lamb and fry gently for 10 minutes.
	Coriander powder	pinch	3 tsp	Add.
	Cumin seeds	pinch	1 tsp	Add.
	Ground ginger	pinch	2 tsp	Add.
	Laos powder	small pinch	large pinch	Add.
	Cinnamon stick	1 cm	4 cm	Add.
	Whole cardamoms	1	10	Add.
	Sereh leaf	¼ leaf	2 leaves	Add.
	Salam leaf	½ small	2	Add and stir fry for 5 minutes.
4	Tamarind water	1 tbsp	10 tbsp	Add, season with salt and black pepper.
	Santen	150 ml	1½ litres	Add, bring to the boil and simmer gently for 45 minutes or until the meat is cooked and the sauce is thick. Discard the salam leaf, sereh leaf, cardamoms and cinnamon stick before serving.

☐   ☐   ☐

Tumis buncis

Origin: Indonesia

⏱ 30 min   ♨ 15 min

Step	Commodity	1 portion	10 portions	
1	Cooking oil	15 ml	150 ml	Place in a suitably sized frying pan and heat.
	Garlic	½ clove	5 cloves	Peel, crush with a little salt and add.
	Shallots	25 g	250 g	Peel, remove the roots and add. Cook for 2 minutes.
	Ginger	¼ tsp	2 tsp	Add.
	Chilli powder	pinch	½ tsp	Add.
	Grated nutmeg	pinch	½ tsp	Add.
	French beans	100 g	1 kg	Remove the tops and tails, wash and add. Stir fry for 5 minutes. Season with salt and black pepper.
2	Chicken stock	25 ml	250 ml	Add, cover with a lid, re-boil and simmer for a further 2–3 minutes. Serve hot.

☐   ☐   ☐

Gado gado

Origin: Malaysia

Cooked mixed salad with peanut dressing

Step	Commodity	1 portion	10 portions	
				⏲ 45 min ♨ 40 min
1	Potato	50 g	500 g	Wash, peel, place in a saucepan of cold water, bring to the boil and cook for 20 minutes. Remove and allow to go cold. Cut into 1 cm dice. Place in a suitably sized bowl.
	Eggs	1	10	Place in a pan of cold water. Bring to the boil and cook for 10 minutes. Refresh in cold water and shell. Leave to the side for use later.
	Tomatoes	25 g	250 g	Remove the eyes and score the other ends. Place in a pan of boiling water for 20 seconds and refresh immediately. Remove the skins and seeds and discard. Cut the flesh into dice and add to the potatoes.
	Cabbage leaves	50 g	500 g	Wash, remove the stalks and shred finely. Add.
	Bean sprouts	25 g	250 g	Wash and add to the cabbage. Mix together well. Season with salt and pepper and place in individual serving dishes. Place in the refrigerator until used.
2	Vegetable oil	1 tbsp	10 tbsp	Place in a suitably sized frying pan and heat.
	Shelled peanuts	25 g	250 g	Add and cook for 5 minutes until golden brown. Allow to cool and place in a blender.
	Shallots	25 g	250 g	Peel, remove the root and add.
	Garlic	¼ clove	2 cloves	Peel, crush with a little salt and add.
	Terasi	½ tsp	5 tsp	Add, season and blend to a smooth paste.
	Peanut oil	1 tsp	10 tsp	Place in a suitably sized frying pan and heat. Add the peanut paste.
	Water	75 ml	750 ml	Add.
	Tamarind water	1 tsp	10 tsp	Add.
	Brown sugar	¼ tsp	2 tsp	Add and mix together well. Bring to the boil and simmer until the sauce is the consistency of double cream. Pour over the salads and serve.

☐   ☐   ☐

22

Kue dadar

Coconut pancakes

Origin: Singapore

🥄 40 min ♨ 1 hr

Step	Commodity	1 portion	10 portions	
1	Plain flour	25 g	250 g	Add a pinch fo salt and sieve into a bowl.
	Eggs	¼ equiv	2½ equiv	Add.
	Milk	75 ml	750 ml	Add and beat to a smooth paste. Cover and allow to rest for 10 minutes. Grease a pancake pan and place on a moderate heat. Pour in sufficient batter to thinly coat the base of the pan. Cook for approximately 1 minute and turn. Cook for another minute and remove. Repeat the process until all the mixture is used.
2	Gula jawa	50 g	500 g	Place in a saucepan.
	Water	75 ml	750 ml	Add and gently heat for 5 minutes.
	Creamed coconut	75 g	750 g	Add.
	Cinnamon	pinch	¼ tsp	Add.
	Grated nutmeg	pinch	¼ tsp	Add.
	Lemon juice	½ tsp	5 tsp	Add, mix together well and simmer until the coconut has absorbed all the liquid. Divide the filling into the appropriate number of portions. Place a portion in the centre of a pancake and roll up into a cylinder. Serve accordingly.

AFRICAN-CARIBBEAN COOKERY

African-Caribbean cookery encompasses the cuisine of the Caribbean Islands. Almost all the foods of this area are, by tradition, highly spiced. This is historically due to the climate and the lack of refrigeration. It was thought in the past that spicing foods helped to preserve them when, in fact, it did little except mask the flavour of emaciated (i.e. decaying, rancid) meat.

Before attempting Caribbean dishes, one must be aware of the various fishes, herbs, spices, vegetables, fruits and nuts which are used.

Not all foodstuffs are readily available in Britain, but there are speciality shops in most major cities. Outside these areas ingenuity must prevail and one is expected to use the nearest alternative.

African-Caribbean cookery is very much the product of the contributions of the various peoples who have settled in the Caribbean region. The following text is a reflection of the most popular methods of cookery and dishes.

HERBS, SPICES AND FLAVOURS COMMONLY USED IN AFRICAN-CARIBBEAN COOKERY

Agbono	The seeds of the mango fruit that are dried. They are used to flavour and thicken soups.	**Cassareep**	Made from cassava juice. Used for traditional stews and pepperpots.
Annatto	Native to the West Indies and tropical Americas, the seeds are an orangy-red in colour and are used to colour and flavour various soups, stews and fish dishes.	**Cinnamon**	The sticks and leaves of the cinnamon plant are used to flavour 'country chocolate', puddings, porridge and other sweets.
Bay	An evergreen with dark green leaves, used in soups and stews.	**Coconut**	Coconut is the seed of the coconut palm. Coconut meal is used as a snack. Coconut milk is used in baking, rice dishes and curries. Coconut oil is used as a cooking medium.
Black and white pepper	Both black and white pepper come from the berries of the pepper plant; black peppers are unripened berries and white peppers are ripe berries whose skins are removed.	**Curry powder**	Curry powder is made up of 4 parts coriander seeds, ground turmeric, ground ginger, ground black pepper to 1 part ground fenugreek, ground cardamon and ground cinnamon.
Bouquet garni	A combination of sprig of thyme, sprig of parsley, sprig of marjoram, bayleaf and chives or spring onion wrapped in muslin cloth.	**Egusi**	This is melon seeds. The outer shell of the seed can be removed

and the creamy inner part is ground raw or roasted and is used in soups and stews. The oil can be extracted and used for cooking. Alternatively, the whole seed can be fermented and made into a substance called oriri used in preparing soups.

Ginger	The rhizome of the ginger plant is dried to make powdered/ground ginger. Sometimes it is added to black pepper and salt to make a seasoning for steaks. Fresh green ginger is used to 'perfume' puddings, cakes and sweets.
Mace	Mace is the outer covering of the nutmeg. Mace oil is used to flavour porridge.
Marjoram	Used to flavour fish, meat, pork and meat marinades.
Nutmeg	Nutmeg is grated when required and used to flavour cakes and puddings.
Peppers	The Capsicum frutescens family includes both hot and sweet peppers. Hot peppers, when dried, are sold as cayenne or chilli pepper; dried sweet peppers are known as paprika.
Pimento (allspice)	This is a mixture of ground nutmeg, cinnamon and cloves.
Sapote	This brown fruit has a rich, sweet flavour and is used for preserves and sherbert.
Thyme	Used mainly in Caribbean cookery, there are two varieties used: the broad leaved French thyme and the small leaved thyme which is more fragrant.
Tonka bean	Sometimes used instead of vanilla.
Turmeric	Turmeric is a member of the ginger family and is mild in flavour. It is used in curry powder and as a cheap substitute for saffron.
Vanilla	This is the pod of the climbing orchid. It is used to flavour puddings, cakes, ice cream and sweet dishes.

TRADITIONAL AFRICAN-CARIBBEAN COOKING UTENSILS

Canarees	Earthenware pie dishes and casseroles.
Coalpots	Cooking pots made from clay or iron, used for cooking stews and pepperpots.
Pestles and mortars	Used for pounding herbs, spices and other foods.
Watercoolers	Made from glazed earthenware for general duties in the kitchen.
Yabbas	Glazed claypots used for cooking, mixing and storage.

FRUITS COMMONLY USED IN AFRICAN-CARIBBEAN COOKERY

Avocado	Green or purple skinned, with a soft waxy flesh.
Banana	Often called 'fig', especially the small variety. Fig bluggoes, which are rust skinned, are used for cooking.
Barbados cherry	Similar in looks to the European white cherry, but too sharp to eat raw. Used for preserves.
Custard apple	A brown fruit with a sweet, moist pulp flesh. Similar in colour to custard.
Ginep	Small green fruit with apricot coloured flesh.
Grenadilla	A fruit about the size of a melon which grows on a vine and is used to flavour soft drinks and desserts.

598

Guava	Guava is a small yellow skinned fruit with pink or yellow flesh. It is usually stewed or made into jelly or 'cheese' and cut into squares to eat.		seeds and skin are useful as a meat tenderiser.
Hog plum	Similar in size to a European plum, these are usually made into preserves.	**Sapodilla/ naseberry**	Fruit about the size of a large plum, brown skinned with a sweet, yellow flesh.
Mamee apple	An oval fruit with rough brown skin and apricot coloured and flavoured flesh. Used in stews or eaten raw.	**Sea or bay grapes**	These grow on vines and are suitable only for preserving and jellies.
		Shaddock	Pink fleshed grapefruit.
Mango	Very sweet-tasting, apricot coloured fruit with greenish yellow skin. Unripened they can be used for chutney. Small varieties are stringy in texture, larger varieties, such as Julies and Bombays, are smooth and delicate.	**Sorrel**	A plant whose sepals, left when the flower petals drop away, are red and fleshly. Used as to make a drink or for jelly or preserves.
		Soursop	A large green skinned fruit covered in soft spines. The centre is sieved and makes a creamy drink or ice cream.
Ortanique	Originating from Jamaica, this is a cross between an orange and a tangerine.	**Star apple**	A purple skinned fruit which is picked and then ripened off the tree. The white flesh is rather tasteless. Mixed with orange it makes a pleasant dessert.
Otaheite apple	Pear-shaped fruit with a polished bright red skin which has little taste. Used mainly in stews and preserves.	**Sugar apple/ sweetsop**	Rubbery scaled skin. The flesh is creamy, sweet and pleasant.
		Tamarind	A long brown pod which becomes sweet and brittle when ripe.
Pawpaw/ papaya	When unripened pawpaw can be used as a vegetable. Ripened it has a greenish yellow skin. The flesh is delicate in flavour. The	**Ugli fruit**	Large citrus fruit, with uneven and thick skin, which is not unlike grapefruit when peeled.

23

NUTS USED IN AFRICAN-CARIBBEAN COOKERY

Cashew	Kidney shaped, red or yellow in colour when ripe.		is used to make coconut milk and can also be grated or flaked.
Coconut	Green when unripe, brown when ripened. The white coloured flesh	**Peanuts (groundnuts)**	Puréed to make soups, sauces and dips. It is small and oblong shaped, with a brown husk.

FISH USED IN AFRICAN-CARIBBEAN COOKERY

Bonito	A game fish that can weigh up to 6 kg.	**Conch**	A large mollusc, up to a foot long, with a delicate pink flesh.
Butter fish	Inshore fish, 200 g in weight.	**Crayfish**	Small colourful crustacea, similar to lobster with no claws.
Calepeave	A river fish not unlike salmon.		

Cutlass A ribbon-like fish whose small bones must be removed with care.

Dolphin Up to 15 kg in weight, a delicacy in the Caribbean.

Flying fish 200 g in weight, these fish have wing-like fins.

Grouper A game fish that can weigh up to 4 kg, similar in flavour to bass.

Jack Several fish go by this name, varying in size from 200 g to 1½ kg. There are varieties such as goggle eye, horse eye and married woman.

Jonga A river fish

Kingfish Sometimes known as King mackerel, these fish can weigh up to 50 kg.

Mackerel Sometimes known as Kingfish, these fish are not as big in size, weighing only about ½–1½ kg.

Marlin A much sought after delicacy found in reefs and rocks, sometimes known as white fox or big daddy.

Mullet Offshore fish, weighs 750 g–1½ kg.

Oyster Found in mango swamps, it has a spiny shell that clings to trees.

Sailfish Deep sea fish with large dorsal fin that has the appearance of a sail, hence the name.

Shark A variety of sharks are used in African-Caribbean cookery.

Snapper or redfish A delicacy in the Caribbean, this fish feeds off crabs and small fish.

Tarpon The tarpon can weigh up to 30 kg and has a sail-like fin.

Titiri Tiny fish, smaller than whitebait.

Tuna A delicacy in the Caribbean. Tuna can weigh up to 60 kg.

Turtle Specially-bred for consumption.

Whelk Small shellfish.

VEGETABLES USED IN AFRICAN-CARIBBEAN COOKERY

Ackee This vegetable grows on trees and is also known as 'free food'. Ackee is the seeds of the ripened fruit. It is yellow in colour and looks like scrambled eggs. NOTE: Ackee is very poisonous when unripened.

Bhagi Comes from a weed and is not unlike spinach.

Breadfruit Large rough-skinned vegetable that grows on trees and can weigh up to 2 kg.

Callaloo or Calalu The leaves of the eddo. This vegetable is not unlike spinach.

Cassava A thin root containing prussic acid. It is grated, then boiled or roasted to extract the poison. It then becomes a coarse flour/tapioca.

Chocho See cristophene.

Coco See eddo.

Cristophene A pear shaped member of the melon family with pale green skin and flesh that tastes of marrow.

Cush cush This is thought to be the best variety of yam.

Dasheen See eddo.

Eddo A hairy root vegetable similar in size and taste to a large potato.

Escallion/ eschalot This is a bulb type plant that resembles a spring onion in appearance but is much stronger in flavour.

Okra/ochra A spear-shaped green pod filled with glutinous seeds. Eaten with rice, in soups and stews.

Pea What is called pea in the Caribbean is known in Britain as a red or kidney bean. There are various types of pea, including black eye, chick and gunga.

Plantain	Similar to a large banana.
Potato	In the Caribbean, potato means sweet potato. There are various types, both brown and red skinned. Unsweet potatoes are called English or Irish potatoes.
Pumpkin	Often called by its American name, squash.

Sorrel leaves	Green leaves that are chopped and used in soups and salads.
Tannia	Similar to an eddo.
Topi tampo	This vegetable looks like a small potato and tastes like a Jerusalem artichoke.
Yam	A root vegetable, yams are brown and hairy in appearance.

Hot soups

Peanut butter cream soup

Step	Commodity	1 portion	10 portions	⤵ 20 min approximately (per 10 portions)	♨ 20 min
1	Butter	10 g	100 g	Melt in a suitable saucepan.	
2	Flour	10 g	100 g	Add to the butter to form a roux and cook gently for 2 minutes.	
3	Peanut butter	60 g	600 g	Add to the cooked out roux.	
4	Chicken stock	350 ml	3½ litres	Add a quarter of the stock and thicken, add another quarter and bring to the boil. Add the remaining stock and cook for 10 minutes.	
5	Cooked chicken	15 g	150 g	Chop the chicken finely and add to the soup.	
6	Parsley	1 tsp	1 tbsp	Finely chop the parsley and sprinkle over the finished soup.	

NOTE: This soup can be served with Foo foo.

☐   ☐   ☐

Calypso cucumber cream soup

Step	Commodity	1 portion	10 portions	⤵ 15 min approximately (per 10 portions)	♨ 45 min
1	West Indian cucumbers	1	10 approx.	Peel the cucumbers and remove the seeds.	
2	Butter	10 g	100 g	Melt gently in a suitable saucepan and add the cucumber.	
3	Onions	25 g	250 g	Peel, slice thinly and add to the cucumber. Cook gently for 10 minutes without colouring.	
4	Plain flour	10 g	100 g	Add to the vegetables and butter to form a roux.	
5	Chicken stock	100 ml	1 litre	Add a quarter of the stock and thicken. Add another quarter and bring to the boil. Add the remaining stock, boil and simmer for 10 minutes. Pass through a chinois into a clean saucepan. Return to the boil and simmer gently. Season accordingly.	
6	Single cream	50 ml	500 ml	Add to the soup just before serving. Do not re-boil.	
7	Chives	10 g	100 g	Wash and chop finely. Sprinkle over the finished soup.	

NOTE: West Indian cucumbers differ from European cucumbers in that they are either dark green or yellow in colour, and are short and stubby.

☐   ☐   ☐

23

Callaloo soup

Step	Commodity	1 portion	10 portions	☟ 20 min approximately (per 10 portions) ♨ 1½ hr
1	Salt pork/ lean bacon	25 g	250 g	Cut the pork into ½ in (1 cm) pieces. If using bacon, remove the rind before cutting up. Place in a suitable saucepan with cold water and pepper. Bring to the boil.
2	Bouquet garni	1 small	1 large	Add to the boiling liquid and simmer for 45 minutes.
3	Cooked crabmeat/ fresh crabs	25 g	250 g	Add to the liquid. If using fresh crabs these must first be cooked in boiling water and cooled.
4	Callaloo leaves	125 g	1¼ kg	Remove the veins (stalks) and shred into a chiffonade. Add to the soup.
5	Okra	2	20	Wash, slice into rounds and add to the liquid.
6	Onions	25 g	250 g	Cut the onions in half and slice thinly. Add to the soup.
7	Garlic	½ clove	2 cloves	Peel, place on a chopping board and sprinkle with salt. Crush with the back of a knife and add to the liquid. Cook for a further 30 minutes.
8	Butter	10 g	100 g	Chop the butter into small pieces and stir into the soup until it has dissolved completely. The soup is usually garnished with crabs' claws.

NOTE: This soup can be served with dumplings.

☐   ☐   ☐

Red peas soup

Step	Commodity	1 portion	10 portions	☟ 15 min approximately (per 10 portions) ♨ 3 hr
1	Kidney beans	50 g	500 g	Soak the beans overnight in water before using.
2	Salt pork or bacon	25 g	250g	Cut the meat into small cubes and cook in a little water for about 5 minutes to remove the fat.
3	Onions	25 g	250 g	Peel, slice the onions thinly and add to the meat.
4	Carrots	25 g	250 g	Peel, cut roughly and add to the meat. Cook for a further 5 minutes. Drain the kidney beans and fast boil for 10 minutes to kill toxins. Stir the kidney beans into the meat and vegetables.
5	Water	350 ml	3½ litres	Add the water and bring to the boil and simmer.
6	Bay leaves	1	3	Place in the soup.
7	Peppercorns	2	10	Add to the liquid and simmer for 2½ hours. Remove the meat and sieve the remaining ingredients. Return the meat to the soup and serve.

☐   ☐   ☐

Cold soups, appetisers and salads

Grapefruit consommé

Step	Commodity	1 portion	10 portions	
				20 min (per 10 portions)
1	Grapefruit juice	100 ml	1 litre	Place in a suitable bowl.
2	Orange juice	20 ml	200 ml	Add to the grapefruit juice.
3	Lime juice	5 ml	50 ml	Add to the orange juice.
4	Angostura bitters	small dash	large dash	Blend with the fruit juice.
5	Packet lemon jelly	¼	2	Dissolve completely in ½ litre boiling water and allow to cool before adding to the fruit juices. Pour into individual dishes.
6	Grapefruit	½	2	Peel, remove the pith and pips and cut into segments. Portion the segments and place neatly in each bowl.
7	Chopped mint	1 tsp	1 tbsp	Sprinkle on top of each bowl of soup. Chill before serving.

☐   ☐   ☐

Jug-jug

Soaking time 12 hr

Step	Commodity	1 portion	10 portions	
				25 min (per 10 portions) 1½ hr
1	Salt pork	50 g	500 g	Place in large bowl.
2	Salt beef	50 g	500 g	Add to the beef. Cover with cold water and leave overnight. Remove from the water. Cut the pork into 1 cm cubes. Place in a suitable saucepan and add sufficient water to cover. Bring to the boil and simmer for 20 minutes. Cut the beef into 1 cm cubes and add to the pork.
3	Soaked pigeon peas	125 g	1¼ kg	Add to the meat and cook for 30 minutes or until the peas are soft. Strain the cooking liquid into another saucepan. Place the meat and the peas in a blender to produce a purée. Put to the side for use later.
4	Onions	50 g	500 g	Place in the saucepan containing the liquid.
5	Chopped parsley	1 tsp	1 tbsp	Add to the onions.
6	Chopped thyme	1 tsp	1 tbsp	Add to the onions.
7	Chopped chives	1 tsp	1 tbsp	Add to the onions, bring to the boil and simmer for 10 minutes.
8	Guinea corn	25 g	250 g	Add slowly and cook for 10 minutes, stirring briskly. Add the meat and peas, and cook for 20 minutes on a low heat.
9	Butter	10 g	100 g	Stir into the mixture until it is completely melted. Serve accordingly.

☐   ☐   ☐

Roti

Step	Commodity	1 portion	10 portions	
				🥣 20 min (per 10 portions) 🍲 15 min
1	S.R. flour	25 g	250 g	Sieve the flour into a bowl. Add a pinch of salt.
2	Milk	1 tbsp	5 tbsp	Add sufficient milk to make a stiff dough. Divide into the appropriate portions. Roll out into ½ cm egg-shaped pieces.
3	Ghee	10 g	100 g	Melt and spread over the flattened dough. Cook in a frying pan or on a grill plate, turning frequently and brushing with the ghee until cooked.

☐   ☐   ☐

Coo coo

Soaking time 12 hr

Step	Commodity	1 portion	10 portions	
				🥣 25 min (per 10 portions) 🍲 1¼ hr
1	Dried peas	50 g	500 g	Soak overnight with a pinch of bicarbonate of soda. Drain and place in a pan.
2	Water	½ litre	5 litres	Pour over the peas.
3	Salt beef	50 g	500 g	Cut into small dice and add to the peas. Bring to the boil and simmer for 40–50 minutes.
4	Cornflour	100 g	1 kg	Dilute with a little water and add to the peas, stirring vigorously until a smooth paste is formed. If any lumps are present, pass through a sieve. Season with salt and pepper.

☐   ☐   ☐

Foo foo

Step	Commodity	1 portion	10 portions	
				🥣 25 min (per 10 portions) 🍲 30 min
1	Plantains	1	10	Leave in their skins and place in a pan of boiling water for approximately 30 minutes. Allow to cool, peel and pound in a mortar until smooth. Season with salt and pepper. Shape into small balls. Re-heat and serve.

☐   ☐   ☐

Dal

Soaking time 12 hr

Step	Commodity	1 portion	10 portions	
				🥣 25 min (per 10 portions) 🍲 30 min
1	Dried peas	50 g	500 g	Soak overnight with a pinch of bicarbonate of soda. Drain and place in a pan.
2	Water	½ litre	5 litre	Pour over the peas. Season with salt and pepper.
3	Saffron	pinch	5 g	Add to the peas, bring to the boil and simmer for 25 minutes or until tender.
4	Coconut oil	1 tsp	2 tbsp	Place in a frying pan and heat.
5	Garlic	¼ clove	2 cloves	Peel, crush and add to the oil to extract the flavour. Pour over the peas and mix in. Cook for a further 5 minutes. Serve immediately.

NOTE: This dish is usually served with boiled rice.

☐   ☐   ☐

Piononos

Step	Commodity	1 portion	10 portions			
				🥄 20 min (per 10 portions)		♨ 30 min
1	Plantain	1	10	Peel and cut lengthways into four slices.		
2	Butter	10 g	100 g	Melt in a suitable frying pan and fry the plantain for 5 minutes or until they are tender. Remove from the frying pan and place to the side for use later. Leave the frying pan on the stove.		
3	Minced beef	75 g	750 g	Place in the frying pan.		
4	Minced ham	10 g	100 g	Add to the beef.		
5	Green peppers	10 g	100 g	Cut in half, remove the seeds and finely dice. Add to the meat.		
6	Onions	10 g	100 g	Add to the other ingredients.		
7	Tomatoes	50 g	500 g	Remove the eyes and made x-shaped incisions in the other ends. Place in a pan of boiling water for 10 seconds then transfer to cold water. Remove the skins and discard. Cut in half, remove the seeds and discard. Cut the flesh into dice and add to the other ingredients. Cook for 20 minutes. Season with salt and black pepper. Allow to cool. Portion and shape the mixture into fishcake shapes. Place a slice of the plantain around the mixture and skewer with a cocktail stick.		
8	Eggs	½	3	Place in a bowl and whisk. Brush each side of the piononos with the egg.		
9	Olive oil	5 ml	50 ml	Place in a clean frying pan and heat. Add the piononos and cook for a few minutes. Serve immediately.		

☐   ☐   ☐

23

Surim curried salad

Step	Commodity	1 portion	10 portions		
				🥄 40 min (per 10 portions)	
1	Water	250 ml	2½ litres	Place in a suitably sized saucepan, season with salt and pepper and boil.	
2	Long grain rice	15 g	150 g	Add to the boiling water and cook for 15 minutes. Refresh in cold water until cold. Drain and store for use later.	
3	Mayonnaise	2 tbsp	10 tbsp	Place in a clean bowl.	
4	Curry powder	½ tspn	5 tspn	Add to the mayonnaise. Mix in the cooked rice.	
5	White vinegar	5 ml	50 ml	Pour into the mixture. Arrange in a salad dish in a dome shape.	
6	Sliced cooked meat (beef, veal or chicken)	50 g	500 g	Lay around the rice.	
7	Tomatoes	1 small	10 small	Remove the eyes, slice and surround the meat.	
8	Hard boiled eggs	1	10	Cut into quarters and arrange on the tomatoes.	
9	Cooked cristophenes	¼	2	Peel and cut into 1 cm slices. Lay on top of the rice. Sprinkle with chopped parsley.	

☐   ☐   ☐

Port-au-prince salad

Step	Commodity	1 portion	10 portions		25 min (per 10 portions)
1	Lettuce	¼	2	Wash, drain and arrange on the serving dish.
2	Green peppers	¼	2	Cut in two lengthways, remove the seeds and slice into 1 cm pieces. Place in a clean bowl.
3	Celery	100 kg	1 kg	Wash, slice and add to the peppers.
4	Spring onions	¼ bunch	2 bunches	Remove the outer skins and roots. Slice into thin pieces and add to the celery.
5	Carrots	50 g	500 g	Peel and finely dice. Add to the other ingredients.
6	Cooked breadfruit	50 g	500 g	Peel and cut into 1 cm cubes.
7	Butter	10 g	100 g	Melt in a frying pan and add the breadfruit.
8	Garlic	¼ clove	2 cloves	Peel, crush and add to the breadfruit. Cook for 2 minutes. Add to the other ingredients and arrange on the lettuce.
9	Avocado pear	½	5	Peel, remove the stone and cut into 1 cm wedges. Arrange over the salad.
10	Lime juice	10 ml	100 ml	Pour over the top of the avocado pear. Sprinkle with chopped parsley.

☐   ☐   ☐

Breadfruit salad

Step	Commodity	1 portion	10 portions		25 min (per 10 portions)
1	Hard boiled eggs	1	10	Cut in half. Separate the egg yolks from the whites. Chop the egg whites up and place in a bowl in the refrigerator to use later. Place the egg yolks in another bowl. Season with salt and pepper.
2	Hot mustard	¼ tsp	2 tsp	Add to the egg yolks.
3	Butter	10 g	100 g	Melt, add to the egg yolks and mix thoroughly.
4	Cooked breadfruit	50 g	500g	Peel, core and cut into 1 cm slices. Arrange on a salad dish. Sprinkle with the egg whites.
5	Onions	10 g	100 g	Peel, slice and arrange on the egg whites. Spoon the egg yolks on top of the whites.
6	Worcester sauce	¼ tsp	2 tsp	Place in a jug.
7	Wine vinegar	1 tsp	8 tsp	Add to the sauce and mix. Pour over the salad and serve.

☐   ☐   ☐

Spiced island beetroot salad

25 min (per 10 portions)   1½ hr
Marinading time 12 h   190°C (375°F)

Step	Commodity	1 portion	10 portions	
1	Beetroot	1 medium	10 medium	Wash and scrape lightly, leaving the stems intact. Place on a baking tray and cook until tender. Cool, remove the stems, skin and slice thinly. Arrange with ground cloves.
2	Olive oil	1 tbsp	5 tbsp	Place in a bowl.
3	Garlic	¼ clove	2 cloves	Peel, crush and add to the oil.
4	Wine vinegar	½ tbsp	2 tbsp	Add to the mixture and whisk in. Pour over the beetroot and marinade for 12 hours. Serve accordingly.

☐   ☐   ☐

Fish dishes

Codfish creole style

Step	Commodity	1 portion	10 portions	
				🍲 20 min (per 10 portions)
				♨ 1 hr ≋ 190°C (375°F)
1	Saltfish	125 g	500 g	Soak the saltfish in cold water overnight. To cook, place the fish in cold water, bring to the boil and simmer for 15 minutes. Drain, discard the cooking liquor and allow the fish to cool before removing the skin and any bones. Using a fork, flake the fish. Place in the refrigerator to use later.
2	Onions	25 g	250 g	Peel and cut into thin slices.
3	Lard or bacon fat	10 g	100g	Place in a suitable frying pan, heat and add the onions and brown.
4	Tomatoes	20 g	200 g	Remove the eyes, blanch for 10 seconds in boiling water and then plunge into cold water. Remove the skins and discard. Cut the tomatoes into quarters and add to the onions.
5	Green peppers	20 g	200g	Cut in half, remove the seeds and discard. Cut the peppers into small dice. Add to the other ingredients. Season with salt and black pepper. Cook until soft and remove from the heat. Add the saltfish.
6	Yams or English potatoes	50 g	500g	Peel, slice and boil for 15 minutes. Butter a suitable ovenproof dish and arrange the yams/potatoes on the bottom and the sides. Fill the centre with the saltfish mixture.
7	Butter	25 g	250 g	Cut into small pieces and spread over the fish.
8	Milk	50 ml	500 ml	Pour over the fish and bake for 20 minutes.
9	Parsley	1 tsp	1 tbsp	Sprinkle over the finished item just before serving.

☐   ☐   ☐

23

Saltfish and ackee

Step	Commodity	1 portion	10 portions	
				🍲 20 min (per 10 portions) ♨ 45 min
1	Saltfish	125 g	500 g	Soak the saltfish in cold water overnight. To cook, place the fish in cold water, bring to the boil and simmer for 15 minutes. Drain, discard the cooking liquor and allow the fish to cool before removing the skin and any bones. Using a fork, flake the fish.
2	Streaky bacon	25 g	250 g	Remove the rind and any bones and cut into thin strips.
3	Onions	10 g	100 g	Peel and slice thinly.
4	Green peppers	10 g	100 g	Cut in half, de-seed and slice into thin strips.
5	Butter	10 g	100 g	Melt the butter in a suitable pan. Add the bacon and fry. Add the onions and sliced green peppers and continue cooking until they are soft. Remove the ingredients and keep warm. Place the saltfish in the pan and warm through.
6	Ackee	4	40	Add the ackee to the saltfish and continue cooking. Turn the saltfish and ackee onto a serving dish. Garnish with the bacon, green peppers and onions. Sprinkle with crushed black pepper.

☐   ☐   ☐

Stewed shark

⌣ 20 min (per 10 portions)
Marinading time 1 hr ⌣ 45 min

Step	Commodity	1 portion	10 portions	
1	Shark meat	200 g	2 kg	Clean and slice into steaks. Place in a suitable bowl.
2	Onions	25 g	250 g	Peel, cut in half and slice thinly. Add to the shark meat.
3	Chopped chives	1 tsp	1 tbsp	Sprinkle over the meat.
4	Chopped thyme	½ tsp	½ tbsp	Add to the other ingredients.
5	Dark rum	1 tsp	1 tbsp	Pour over the meat, mix thoroughly and marinade for 1 hour.
6	Vegetable oil	1 tsp	1 tbsp	Place in a thick-bottomed pan and heat gently.
7	Garlic	1 clove	3 cloves	Peel and place on a chopping board. Sprinkle with a little salt and, using the back of a knife, crush and chop. Add to the hot fat. Remove the fish from the marinade and add it to the pan. Fry the fish for 5 minutes on both sides.
8	Worcester sauce	1 tsp	1 tbsp	Sprinkle over the fish steaks.
9	Water	1 tbsp	5 tbsp	Add to the frying pan and simmer for 10 minutes. Season with salt and pepper, cover with a lid and cook gently for another 20 minutes. When cooked, arrange on a serving dish, pour the cooking liquor over the steaks and garnish with lime wedges.

☐   ☐   ☐

Stuffed crayfish anchorage style

⌣ 20 min (per 10 portions)
⌣ 15 min   ≋ 215°C (425°F)

Step	Commodity	1 portion	10 portions	
1	Fillet of grouper, snapper or plaice	100 g	1 kg	Skin the fillets. Cut the flesh up small, then pound with a pestle and mortar. Place in the refrigerator until required.
2	Crayfish	1 small	5 large	Place the live crayfish on a chopping board. Split the crayfish in half lengthways with a sharp knife. Extract the green meat, discarding the stomach and black thread. Leave the tails in their shells. Wash the empty part of the shell. Mix the green meat from the crayfish with the pounded fish fillets. Season with a little salt and nutmeg.
3	Chopped parsley	1 tsp	1 tbsp	Add to the mixture.
4	Chillies	¼	1½	Slice in two. Remove and discard the seeds and chop the chillies small.
5	Egg whites	½	2	Add to the fish.
6	Dark rum	25 ml	250 ml	Add to the mixture.
7	Breadcrumbs	25 g	250 g	Bind with the other ingredients to form a stuffing. Fill the gap between the crayfish head and tail with the mixture. Place on a baking tray or in an ovenproof dish in a pre-heated oven for 15 minutes. Serve immediately.

☐   ☐   ☐

Curried prawns in pineapple

Step	Commodity	1 portion	10 portions	
				⌣ 30 min (per 10 portions) ⌇ 35–45 min
1	Peeled prawns	100 g	1 kg	Wash and place in a large bowl.
2	Lime juice	10 ml	100 ml	Pour over the prawns and place in the refrigerator to use later.
3	Olive oil	25 ml	250 ml	Place in a suitable frying pan and heat. Add peeled prawns.
4	Onions	50 g	500 g	Peel, slice thinly, add to the oil and brown lightly.
5	Curry powder	½ tbsp	3 tbsp	Add to the onions and stir well.
6	Eschalots	25 g	250 g	Wash, peel, slice thinly and add to the curry powder.
7	Tomatoes	20 g	200 g	Remove the eyes and blanch for 10 seconds in boiling water, then plunge into cold water. Remove the skins and discard. Cut the tomatoes into quarters and add to the onions and curry powder.
8	Water	50 ml	500 ml	Add to the prawns and simmer on a low heat for 15 minutes.
9	Pineapples	1 small	5 medium	Plunge into a pan of boiling water for 3 minutes. Remove and cut in half lengthways, leaving the leaves on each piece. Hollow out the flesh and chop it into small pieces. Add the pulp to the prawns. Fill the pineapple with the pineapple and prawn mixture.
10	Chopped parsley	1 tsp	1 tbsp	Sprinkle over the pineapple and serve immediately.

□   □   □

23

Meat and poultry dishes

Caribbean pepperpot

Step	Commodity	1 portion	10 portions	
				⌣ 20 min (per 10 portions) ⌇ 2½–3 h
1	Salt pork	50 g	500 g	Wash and cut into small dice. Place in a thick-bottomed saucepan.
2	Chopped chives	1 tsp	1 tbsp	Add to the pork.
3	Chopped thyme	1 tsp	1 tbsp	Add to the pork.
4	Stewing beef	100 g	1 kg	Cut into small dice and add to the pork.
5	Salt beef	50 g	500 g	Wash and cut into small dice. Add to the beef. Cover with water, bring to the boil and simmer for 1½ hours. Remove any scum that may form on the surface. Add water to cover the meat as required.
6	Pigeon peas or split peas	125 g	1¼ kg	Place in a saucepan, cover with water and cook for 1 hour. Refresh and place aside for later use.

Step	Commodity	1 portion	10 portions	
7	Callaloo leaves or spinach	2	20	Wash and chop finely. Add to the meat.
8	Aubergines	1	10	Slice into thin roundels and add to the meat.
9	Onions	50 g	500 g	Peel, cut in half and slice thinly. Add to the other ingredients.
10	Pumpkin	125 g	1¼ kg	Peel, cut in half and dice. Add to the stew.
11	Tomatoes	20 g	200 g	Remove the eyes, blanch for 10 seconds in boiling water, then plunge in cold water. Remove the skins and discard. Cut the tomatoes into quarters and add to the other ingredients.
12	Okra	2	20	Slice into thin roundels and add to the stew. Cook for another hour, skimming as required. Stir in the cooked peas 10 minutes before service. Season with salt and black pepper.

☐   ☐   ☐

Curried goat

Step	Commodity	1 portion	10 portions	🥣 1½ hr (per 10 portions) ♨ 1 hr–1¼ hr
1	Goat or mutton	150 g	1½ kg	Trim and cut into 2 cm cubes. Place in a large bowl. Season with salt and black pepper.
2	Curry powder	10 g	100 g	Add to the meat. Set aside in the refrigerator for 1 hour to marinade.
3	Lard or dripping	10 g	100 g	Melt in a suitable frying pan. Add the marinaded meat and brown.
4	Onions	25 g	250 g	Peel, slice, add to the frying pan and continue to brown.
5	Chilli peppers	½	2	Cut in half, de-seed and chop finely. Add to the other ingredients.
6	Suitable stock or water	200 ml	2 litres	Add to the meat. Bring to the boil, cover with a lid and simmer for 1 hour.
7	English potatoes	25 g	250 g	Peel, slice and add to the curry. Continue to cook for a further 30 minutes until the sauce thickens.

NOTE: This dish is usually served with boiled rice.

☐   ☐   ☐

Devilled chicken parts

Step	Commodity	1 portion	10 portions	
				⏱ 10 min (per 10 portions) ♨ 40 min
1	Chicken	20 g	2 kg	Cut into quarters.
2	Plain flour	10 g	100 g	Place on a tray and season with salt and black pepper. Cover the chicken with the flour, dusting off any excess.
3	Butter	10 g	100 g	Melt the butter and place on a tray. Pass the chicken through it.
4	Breadcrumbs	30 g	300 g	Roll the chicken in the breadcrumbs.
5	Butter	15 g	150 g	Heat in a suitably sized frying pan.
6	Vinegar	½ tsp	4 tsp	Add to the hot butter. Cook the chicken for 30 minutes, turning frequently to ensure even cooking. As breadcrumbs tend to absorb it, there may be a need to add more butter during cooking. Remove from the frying pan and keep warm.
7	Butter	10 g	100 g	Melt in a clean frying pan.
8	Garlic	¼ clove	2 cloves	Peel, crush and add to the melted butter. Season with salt, a bay leaf and cayenne pepper.
9	Vinegar	½ tbsp	5 tbsp	Add to the garlic and reduce by half. Discard the bay leaf and garlic.
10	Tomato ketchup	½ tbsp	5 tbsp	Add to the vinegar mixture and season with a dash of tabasco sauce. Bring to the boil. Place the chicken on a serving dish. Cover with the sauce.

NOTE: This dish can be served with fried bananas and boiled rice.

☐   ☐   ☐

Cold crystal chicken

Step	Commodity	1 portion	10 portions	
				⏱ 20 min (per 10 portions) ♨ 15 min
1	Water	100 ml	1 litre	Place in a suitably sized pan and boil.
2	Onions	25 g	250 g	Peel, slice and place in the boiling water.
3	Green ginger	10 g	100 g	Chop finely and add.
4	Poussin	½	5	Wash and leave whole. When the water re-boils add the poussin. Return to the boil for 15 minutes. Cover the saucepan with a tight-fitting lid and turn the heat off. Allow to cool completely.
5	Butter	25 g	250 g	Melt the butter in a suitably sized frying pan.
6	Chopped chives	1 tsp	2 tbsp	Add and cook gently. A dash of soy sauce can be added. Remove the chicken from the cold cooking liquor, place on a serving dish and coat with the butter and chives. Chill before serving.

☐   ☐   ☐

23

Blue mountain pigeon

⤵ 20 min (per 10 portions)
Marinading time 2 hr ♨ 45 min

Step	Commodity	1 portion	10 portions	
1	Pigeon	½	5	Split in two, lenthways, through the back. Flatten with a chopper or broad knife. Refrigerate to be used later.
2	Oil	25ml	250 ml	Place in a bowl.
3	Chopped thyme	½ tsp	2 tbsp	Add to the oil.
4	Chopped parsley	½ tsp	2 tbsp	Add to the oil. Season with salt and black pepper. Marinade the pigeons for 2 hours. Pre-heat the grill and cook the pigeon, skin side down, for 20 minutes on each side. Baste frequently with the marinade. Place on a serving dish and keep warm.
5	Butter	25 g	250 g	Melt in a clean frying pan. Season with crushed black pepper and cook until golden brown. Pour over the pigeon.

NOTE: This dish is usually served with lime wedges and breadfruit chips.

☐   ☐   ☐

Condado duck

⤵ 30 min (per 10 portions) ♨ 1¾ hr

Step	Commodity	1 portion	10 portions	
1	Oil	½ tbsp	5 tbsp	Place in a frying pan.
2	Paprika	1 tsp	5 tsp	Add to the oil and heat.
3	Duck	500 g	5 kg	Cut into portions and fry in the oil until golden brown all over. Remove and allow to cool.
4	Onions	25 g	250 g	Peel, dice and add to the hot fat. Cook for 5 minutes.
5	Flour	10 g	100 g	Stir into the oil, cook to a blond roux and allow to cool.
6	Duck stock	100 ml	1 litre	Add a quarter of the stock and thicken. Add another quarter and bring to the boil. Add the remaining stock, bring to the boil and simmer.
7	Dark rum	10 ml	100 ml	Add and cook out. Place the chicken in the sauce.
8	Green peppers	¼	3	Cut in half, remove the seeds and dice. Add to the duck.
9	Tomatoes	20 g	200 g	Remove the eyes, blanch for 10 seconds in boiling water, then plunge into cold water. Remove the skins and discard. Cut the tomatoes into quarters and add to the other ingredients. Cover with a lid and cook for 1½ hours or until the duck is tender. Serve in a suitable dish. Sprinkle with parsley and paprika.

☐   ☐   ☐

Oiled down

Step	Commodity	1 portion	10 portions	
1	Salt meat	50 g	500 g	Place in a bowl. Cover with cold water and soak overnight.
2	Cooked saltfish	125 g	500g	Soak the raw saltfish in cold water overnight. To cook, place the fish in cold water, bring to the boil and simmer for 15 minutes. Drain the liquid and place the cooked fish aside to use later.
3	Breadfruit	½ small	2 large	Cut into sections 1 cm thick. Select a suitable saucepan and lay alternate layers of the meat, fish and breadfruit. Season each layer with salt and black pepper.
4	Celery	25 g	250 g	Wash and cut into thin slices. Place in the saucepan.
5	Chilli	1 small	1 large	Cut in two and remove the seeds.
6	Sprig of thyme	¼	2	Place on one half of chilli.
7	Chives	¼	2	Lay on top of the thyme. Place the other half of the chilli on top and tie together with string. Add to the saucepan.
8	Coconut milk	500 ml approx.	5 litres approx.	Pour over the meat and vegetables. Cover with a lid, bring to the boil and simmer for 50 minutes. Remove the chilli and herbs. The liquid should be absorbed and the stew oily. Serve accordingly.

☐   ☐   ☐

Fried mountain chicken

Step	Commodity	1 portion	10 portions	
1	Frogs' legs	2 pairs	20 pairs	Wash the frogs' legs and place in a large bowl.
2	Vinegar	50 ml	500 ml	Pour over the frogs' legs, making sure to keep covered. Season with salt and black pepper. Leave to marinade for the appropriate time. The liquid is then drained away and the frogs' legs re-seasoned.
3	Butter	25 g	250 g	Place in a suitable frying pan and heat. Add the frogs' legs and cook on both sides until golden brown.
4	Lime juice	10 ml	100 ml	Pour over the cooked legs and continue cooking until all the juice has evaporated. Place in a serving dish.
5	Chopped parsley	1 tsp	1 tbsp	Sprinkle over the frogs' legs.

☐   ☐   ☐

23

Caribbean kebabs

⤴ 20 min (per 10 portions)
Marinading time 12 hr   ♨ 10 min

Step	Commodity	1 portion	10 portions	
1	Butter	10 g	100 g	Melt in a suitable frying pan.
2	Onions	25 g	250 g	Peel, cut into rough pieces and add to the butter.
3	Garlic	½ clove	3 cloves	Peel, crush and add to the onions. Fry until golden brown. Place on a tray and allow to cool.
4	Vinegar	½ tbsp	5 tbsp	Pour over the onions.
5	Mangoes	½	3	Peel, remove the stone, chop the flesh up and add to the onions. Season with salt and cayenne pepper.
6	Curry powder	1 tsp	2 tbsp	Add to the other ingredients.
7	Demerara sugar	1 tsp	2 tbsp	Sprinkle over the mixture. Mix well and place to the side for use later.
8	Prepared grilling meat (lamb, beef, chicken or pork)	150 g	1½ kg	Cut into 4 cm cubes. Place in the marinade for the appropriate time.
9	Pineapple	100 g	1 kg	Prepare and cut into 4 cm cubes.
10	Pawpaw/ apricot	100 g	1 kg	Peel and cut into 4 cm cubes.
11	Bananas	½	5	Peel and slice into 4 cm pieces. Using the appropriate number of skewers, alternate pieces of meat, pineapple, pawpaw and banana. Discard the marinade and place the kebabs in the refrigerator. Pre-heat the grill. Cook the kebabs as required, turning regularly to ensure even cooking.

NOTE: This dish can be served with plain boiled rice.

614

Creole roast lamb

15 min (per 10 portions)
1 h–1¼ hr   200°C (400°F)

Step	Commodity	1 portion	10 portions	
1	Vinegar	2 tsp	2 tbsp	Place in a suitable saucepan.
2	Worcester sauce	1 tbsp	4 tbsp	Add to the vinegar.
3	Cassareep	¼ tsp	2 tsp	Mix with the other ingredients
4	Tabasco sauce	dash	dash	Add to the mixture.
5	Chopped thyme	pinch	1 tsp	Sprinkle over the liquid.
6	Bay leaves	1	2	Add to the other ingredients. Season with salt and pepper.
7	Onions	100 g	1 kg	Peel, slice and add to the other ingredients
8	Garlic	1 clove	4 cloves	Peel, place on a chopping board, sprinkle with salt and chop finely. Add to the onions. Cook for 5 minutes on the stove. Allow to cool. Place to the side for later use.
9	Prepared leg of lamb	350 g equiv.	3½ kg	Place on a roasting tray.
10	Olive oil	1 tbsp	4 tbsp	Pour over the lamb. Season with salt and black pepper and place in the pre-heated oven for 20 minutes. Remove and baste with the marinade. Return to the oven and repeat the process every 15 minutes until it is cooked. Allow to cool for 15 minutes to facilitate carving. The resulting cooking liquor is served as a gravy with the sliced meat.

☐   ☐   ☐

23

Stuffed festal suckling pig

Festal pig is, by tradition, served at New Year and it is often roasted on an open spit.

45 min (per 10 portions)
4 hours approximately   190°C (375°F)
(40 minutes per kilo plus 20 minutes over)

Step	Commodity	1 portion	10 portions	
1	Breadcrumbs	50 g	500 g	Place in a large bowl.
2	Dark rum	10 ml	100 ml	Add to the breadcrumbs.
3	Dripping or lard	10 g	100 g	Melt in a suitable pan.
4	Onions	50 g	500 g	Peel and dice finely. Add to the hot fat.
5	Garlic	½ clove	2 cloves	Peel, crush and add to the onions. Fry lightly for 3–4 minutes then add to the breadcrumbs. Season with salt and pepper.
6	Ground ginger	½ tsp	1 tbsp	Stir into the mixture.
7	Thyme	½ tsp	1 tbsp	Add to the ginger.
8	Grated nutmeg	pinch	1 tsp	Add to the other ingredients.
9	Rind of lime	5 g	50 g	Grate and add to the stuffing. Cook for about 5 minutes or until all the fat is absorbed. Remove from the heat.
10	Washed raisins	5 g	50 g	Add to the cooled mixture.

Step	Commodity	1 portion	10 portions	
11	Worcester sauce	½ tsp	1 tbsp	Add.
12	Egg yolks	½	2	Stir into the mixture to bind together. Cover and allow to stand. This mixture is used as the stuffing for the suckling pig.
13	Suckling pig	1/10	1	Wash in lightly salted water, inside and out. Wipe with vinegar. Loosely fill the inside with the stuffing and sew the stomach with string and a trussing needle.
14	Garlic	½ clove	½ bulb	Peel, crush and spread over the skin of the suckling pig. Prop open the mouth with a piece of wood. Tie the forelegs together and place in front. Tie the hind legs together under the belly. Place tin foil over the ears and on the tail to prevent scorching. Score in a criss-cross pattern with the tip of a sharp knife.
15	Dripping	25 g	250 g	Melt and brush the pig all over. Season with salt and black pepper.
16	Dark rum	1 tbsp	100 ml	Pour over the pig. Place in a pre-heated oven for the appropriate time. Baste frequently with the cooking juices. Remove from the oven, place on a serving dish and keep warm. Collect all the cooking juices in a suitably sized saucepan.
17	Green peppers	¼	2	Cut in half, remove the seeds, dice and add to the juices.
18	Onions	25 g	250 g	Peel, slice roughly and add to the other ingredients. Add 250 ml of water per portion and bring to the boil.
19	Flour	10 g	100 g	Dilute with a little water and add to the boiling liquid. Stir and thicken, season with salt and pepper and strain into a gravy boat. Remove the prop from the pig's mouth. Remove any string and tin foil. Place a red apple in the pig's mouth. Arrange fruits and flowers around the pig. Serve with the sauce.

☐   ☐   ☐

Vegetable and rice dishes

Baked aubergines in coconut cream

15 min (per 10 portions)
1 h   175°C (350°F)

Step	Commodity	1 portion	10 portions	
1	Aubergines	1 small	5 large	Wash, remove the stalk and slice into 2 cm pieces. Lay in a suitably sized baking dish.
2	Onions	25 g	250 g	Peel, cut into slices and lay on top of the aubergines. Season with salt and pepper.
3	Coconut cream	125 ml	1¼ litres	Pour over the vegetables.
4	Red chillies	¼	2	Cut in half, remove the seeds and slice thinly. Sprinkle evenly over the milk. Cover and bake for 1 hour.

☐   ☐   ☐

Creamed breadfruit

Step	Commodity	1 portion	10 portions	
1	Water	100 ml	1 litre	Place in a suitably sized saucepan, season with salt and pepper and bring to the boil.
2	Breadfruit	150 g equiv	1½ kg equiv	Prepare and cook for 30–40 minutes or until tender. Peel, core and mash.
3	Butter	10 g	100 g	Add to the warm breadfruit.
4	Milk	25 ml	250 ml	Blend into the mixture until it is creamy.
5	Egg yolks	½ equiv	3 equiv	Beat in a separate bowl and add to the other ingredients, stirring constantly. Season with salt and pepper. Place in the serving dish and return to the oven for 10–15 minutes or until golden brown on top.

NOTE: This mixture can also be shaped between two spoons and deep fried.

☐   ☐   ☐

Fried breadfruit

Step	Commodity	1 portion	10 portions	
1	Water	100 ml	1 litre	Place in a suitably sized saucepan, season with salt and pepper and bring to the boil.
2	Breadfruit	150 g equiv	1½ kg equiv	Par-boil for 15 minutes. Peel, core and slice into 2 cm pieces. Season with salt and pepper.
3	Cooking oil	25 ml	125 ml	Heat in a suitably sized frying pan. Quickly fry the slices of breadfruit until golden brown. Place in a warmed serving dish.
4	Chopped chives	1 tsp	1 tbsp	Sprinkle over the breadfruit just before serving.

15 min (per 10 portions)   30 min

☐   ☐   ☐

23

Stuffed breadfruit

🍲 15 min (per 10 portions)   ♨ 1 hr   〰 190°C (375°F)

Step	Commodity	1 portion	10 portions	
1	Water	100 ml	1 litre	Place in a suitably sized saucepan, season with salt and pepper and bring to the boil.
2	Breadfruit	150 g equiv	1½ kg equiv	Prepare and par-cook for 15 minutes. Remove the stem and retain. Scoop out the core and mash. Leave to the side for use later.
3	Butter	10 g equiv	100 g equiv	Melt in a frying pan.
4	Minced beef	25 g	250 g	Add to the melted butter.
5	Minced salt pork	25 g	250 g	Add and fry gently.
6	Tomatoes	20 g	200 g	Remove the eyes, blanch for 10 seconds in boiling water, and plunge into cold water. Remove the skin and discard. Cut the tomatoes into dice and add to the other ingredients.
7	Onions	25 g	250 g	Peel, slice and add. Season with salt and pepper and continue to cook gently for 10 minutes. Fill the cavity of the breadfruit with the mixture. Replace the stems, covering with tin foil to hold in place. Bake in a pre-heated oven for 45 minutes. Serve immediately.

☐   ☐   ☐

Young Barbados cabbage

🍲 15 min (per 10 portions)   ♨ 30 min

Step	Commodity	1 portion	10 portions	
1	Water	150 ml	1½ litres	Place in a suitably sized saucepan. Season with salt and pepper and bring to the boil.
2	Cabbage	150 g equiv	1½ kg equiv	Trim the stalk and outer leaves and leave whole. Place in the boiling water for 30 minutes or until tender. Remove and cut almost into quarters, cutting through nearly to the stalk.
3	Butter	20 g	200 g	Fill the centre with the butter. Season with salt and pepper. Serve immediately.

☐   ☐   ☐

Creamed callaloo

🥄 15 min (per 10 portions)
🍲 1 hr ≋ 215°C (425°F)

Step	Commodity	1 portion	10 portions	
1	Water	100 ml	1 litre	Place in a suitably sized saucepan, season with salt and pepper and bring to the boil.
2	Callaloo leaves	4	16	Wash the callaloo, remove the stem and veins from each leaf. Simmer in the boiling water for 30–40 minutes or until tender. Drain and pass through a sieve.
3	Butter	10 g	100 g	Warm in a frying pan.
4	Onion	25 g	250 g	Peel, dice finely and add to the butter. Cook until transparent. Add to the sieved callaloo.
5	Cream	15 ml	150 ml	Add to the other ingredients, stirring constantly. Season with salt and pepper.
6	Breadcrumbs	10 g	100 g	Mix into the callaloo.
7	Cheese	10 g	100 g	Sprinkle over the mixture and stir in. Season with salt, pepper and nutmeg. Place in the serving dish. Place in a pre-heated oven for 10 minutes to heat through.

NOTE: This mixture can also be made with breadfruit.

☐ ☐ ☐

Callaloo with crab

🥄 15 min (per 10 portions) 🍲 1 hr

Step	Commodity	1 portion	10 portions	
1	Callaloo	3 leaves	30 leaves	Wash, remove the veins and chop the stems. Place in a pan of boiling seasoned water.
2	Onions	15 g	150 g	Peel, cut into rings and add to the callaloo.
3	Okra	2	20	Remove the stalks, cut into slices and add to the saucepan.
4	Garlic	¼ clove	2 cloves	Peel, crush and add to the other vegetables.
5	Chopped thyme	¼ tsp	2 tsp	Add and cook for 40 minutes.
6	Cooked crabmeat	25 g	250 g	Chop, add to the vegetables and cook for a further 10 minutes. Season with salt, pepper and tabasco sauce.
7	Butter	10 g	100 g	Stir into the mixture and serve immediately.

☐ ☐ ☐

Eddo in cream sauce

🥄 30 min (per 10 portions) 🍲 30 min

Step	Commodity	1 portion	10 portions	
1	Water	125 ml equiv	1½ litres	Place in a suitably sized saucepan, season with salt and pepper and boil.
2	Eddoes	1	10	Wash the eddoes and cook for 30 minutes in the boiling water. Drain, cut off the tops and remove the pulp.
3	Butter	10 g	100 g	Place in a frying pan and heat.
4	Onions	15 g	150 g	Peel, dice and add to the butter. Cook without colouring.
5	Chillies	¼	2	Cut in half lengthways. Remove the seeds and finely dice. Add to the onions and continue to cook for 5 minutes.
6	Lime juice	10 ml	100 ml	Add and cook for a further 2 minutes. Add the eddo pulp. Season with salt and pepper. Add a dash of angostura bitters. Serve in a suitable dish.

☐ ☐ ☐

23

619

Baked cristophene

Step	Commodity	1 portion	10 portions	
1	Water	125 ml equiv	1½ litres	Place in a suitably sized saucepan, season with salt and pepper and boil.
2	Cristophenes	1 small	5 large	Place in the pan of boiling water and cook for 20 minutes or until they become soft. Cut in half lengthways, scoop out the flesh leaving the skin intact. Retain the shells. Chop the pulp and place to the side for use later.
3	Butter	10 g	100 g	Melt in a frying pan.
4	Minced beef	25 g	250 g	Add to the butter and cook slowly for 10 minutes.
5	Onions	10 g	100 g	Peel, chop finely, add to the meat and continue to cook for a further 5 minutes. Season with salt and pepper. Add the cristophene pulp and cook for 5 minutes.
6	Breadcrumbs	10 g quiv	100 g equiv	Add to the mixture to absorb the liquid. Fill the shells with the mixture, place on a baking tray and bake for 20 minutes. Serve immediately.

☐   ☐   ☐

Eddo pudding

Step	Commodity	1 portion	10 portions	
1	Water	125 ml equiv	1½ litres	Place in a suitably sized saucepan, season with salt and pepper and boil.
2	Eddoes	1	10	Wash the eddoes and cook for 30 minutes in the boiling water. Drain, cut off the tops and remove the pulp.
3	Butter	10 g	100 g	Add to the eddoes. Season with salt and pepper.
4	Egg yolks	½ equiv	4	Lightly beat and add.
5	Egg whites	½ equiv	4	Place in a clean bowl and whisk to a peak. Carefully fold into the mixture.
6	Butter	5 g	50 g	Melt and brush an earthenware dish. Pour in the eddo mixture, filling two-thirds of the dish. Bake for 25–30 minutes or until it has risen to the top of the dish. Serve immediately.

☐   ☐   ☐

Fried okra

Step	Commodity	1 portion	10 portions	
1	Okra	4	40	Wash and trim the stalks.
2	Flour	10 g	100 g	Place on a tray and season with salt and pepper.
3	Eggs	½	4	Beat and place on another tray.
4	Breadcrumbs	25 g	250 g	Place on another tray. Pass the okra through the flour, egg-wash and breadcrumbs.
5	Cooking oil	10 ml	100 ml	Heat in a suitably sized frying pan and fry the okra quickly. Drain and serve immediately.

☐   ☐   ☐

620

Stewed okra

Step	Commodity	1 portion	10 portions	
1	Tomatoes	20 g	200 g	Remove the eyes, blanch for 10 seconds in boiling water, then plunge into cold water. Remove the skins and discard. Cut the tomatoes into dice. Place to the side.
2	Okra	4	40	Wash and trim the stalks. Cut into 1 cm slices.
3	Butter	25 g	250 g	Melt in a frying pan and add the okra.
4	Onions	10 g	100 g	Peel, slice, add to the okra and brown. Add the prepared tomatoes and cook for a further 30 minutes on a low heat. Take care to stir regularly. Season with salt, pepper and tabasco sauce.

☐   ☐   ☐

Baked green pawpaw

Step	Commodity	1 portion	10 portions	
1	Water	125 ml equiv	1½ litres	Place in a suitably sized saucepan, season with salt and pepper and boil.
2	Green pawpaw	¼ medium	3 medium	Wash and cook in the boiling water for 30 minutes. Remove and cut in half lengthways. Remove the seeds and scoop out the flesh.
3	Butter	5 g	50 g	Melt in a frying pan.
4	Onions	10 g	100 g	Peel, dice and cook gently.
5	Chopped chives	¼ tsp	2 tsp	Add to the onions and cook for 2 minutes. Mix with the pawpaw and put back into the skins.
6	Breadcrumbs	5 g	50 g	Sprinkle over the top and bake for 25 minutes, until brown.

☐   ☐   ☐

Curried plantains

Step	Commodity	1 portion	10 portions	
1	Butter	15 g	150 g	Melt in a frying pan.
2	Curry powder	½ tsp	2 tbsp	Add and cook gently for 2 minutes.
3	Plantains	1	10	Peel, slice lengthways and brown lightly. Season with salt and pepper.
4	Coconut milk	75 ml	750 ml	Pour over the plantains, stirring continually. Simmer on a low heat for 30 minutes.
5	Eggs	½	4	Lightly beat and stir into the mixture. Do not re-boil. Serve immediately.

NOTE: Green bananas can be used in place of plantains. This dish is usually served with boiled rice.

☐   ☐   ☐

23

Mashed plantains

Step	Commodity	1 portion	10 portions	⤵ 15 min (per 10 portions) ♨ 35 min
1	Plantains	1	10	Peel, cut into 1 cm pieces. Place in a suitably sized saucepan.
2	Lime juice	25 ml	250 ml	Pour over the plantains.
3	White wine vinegar	25 ml	250 ml	Add to the other ingredients. Season with salt and pepper. Bring to the boil, cover with a lid and simmer for 30 minutes or until tender. Using a fork or potato masher, pound the plantains until smooth.
4	Butter	10 g	100 g	Place in a clean bowl and soften.
5	Flour	5 g	50 g	Blend into the flour. Add to the hot mixture and mix thoroughly.
6	Ground cinnamon	pinch	tsp	Add and mix thoroughly
7	Grated nutmeg	pinch	½ tsp	Add and mix thoroughly. Further season with salt and cayenne pepper. Return to the heat for 5 minutes. Serve immediately.

NOTE: Green bananas can be used in place of plantains.

☐   ☐   ☐

Baked candied sweet potatoes

Step	Commodity	1 portion	10 portions	⤵ 15 min (per 10 portions) ♨ 50 min ≋ 175°C (350°F)
1	Water	125 ml equiv	1½ litres	Place in a suitably sized saucepan, season with salt and pepper and boil.
2	Sweet potatoes	150 g	1½ kg	Scrub, place in the boiling water and boil for 20 minutes. Refresh in cold water until cold. Peel and cut into 1 cm slices. Arrange the potatoes in a buttered earthenware dish.
3	Butter	25 g	250 g	Melt in a saucepan and pour over the potatoes.
4	Demerara sugar	15 g	150 g	Sprinkle over the potatoes.
5	Oranges	¼	2	Remove the zest with a cutter. Cut the oranges in half and extract the juice. Pour the juice over the potatoes and sprinkle with zest. Pour enough water over the potatoes to just cover. Cook on top of the stove for 5 minutes, then transfer to the pre-heated oven for the remaining cooking time. Baste occasionally with the cooking liquor.

☐   ☐   ☐

Baked sweet potatoes in oranges

🥄 15 min (per 10 portions)
♨ 50 min   ≋ 175°C (350°F)

Step	Commodity	1 portion	10 portions	
1	Water	125 ml equiv	1½ litres	Place in a suitably sized saucepan, season with salt and pepper and boil.
2	Potatoes	150 g	1½ kg	Peel, wash, place in the water and boil for 30 minutes or until tender. Drain and mash.
3	Oranges	1	10	Remove the tops of the oranges and scoop out the flesh. Squeeze the juice from the flesh and retain. Add 10 ml per portion to the potato.
4	Cream	½ tsp	4 tbsp	Blend into the mixture.
5	Butter	25 g	250 g	Melt in a saucepan and add to the potatoes. Season with salt and pepper. Place the mixture in a piping bag and pipe into the oranges. Replace the top. Bake in the pre-heated oven for 20 minutes. Garnish with a sprig of parsley.

☐   ☐   ☐

Baked squash/pumpkin

🥄 15 min (per 10 portions)
♨ 50 min   ≋ 190°C (375°F)

Step	Commodity	1 portion	10 portions	
1	Squash	500 g equiv	5 kg equiv	Divide into wedges and remove the seeds.
2	Butter	25 g	250 g	Melt in a saucepan and brush over the squash. Season with salt and black pepper. Bake for the required time, basting frequently with the cooking liquor, or until the squash is tender.

☐   ☐   ☐

Stuffed pumpkin

🥄 25 min (per 10 portions)
♨ 1¼ hr   ≋ 215°C (425°F)

Step	Commodity	1 portion	10 portions	
1	Pumpkin	500 g	5 kg	Cook as for baked squash/pumpkin. Scoop the pumpkin flesh from the skin. Mash the pulp well.
2	Butter	10 g	100 g	Melt in a frying pan.
3	Minced beef	25 g	250 g	Add to the butter and cook slowly for 10 minutes.
4	Onions	10 g	100 g	Peel, chop finely and add to the meat and continue to cook for a further 5 minutes. Season with salt and pepper. Place to the side and allow to cool for use later.
5	Butter	10 g	100 g	Melt and add to the pumpkin.
6	Egg yolks	½	4	Beat lightly and blend with the other ingredients. Season with salt and black pepper.
7	Whipping cream	5 ml	50 ml	Stir into the mixture and divide between the shells. Make a hole in the centre of each piece and fill with the cooked mince mixture. Bake in a pre-heated oven for 15 minutes. Serve immediately.

☐   ☐   ☐

23

Baked tannia

🥄 20 min (per 10 portions)
🍲 1½ hr   ≋ 200°C (400°F)

Step	Commodity	1 portion	10 portions	
1	Tannias	1	10	Wash, place on a baking tray and cook for 1¼ hours in the pre-heated oven. Cut in half.
2	Chopped parsley	½ tsp	4 tsp	Sprinkle over the tannias.
3	Chopped chives	½ tsp	4 tsp	Sprinkle over the tannias.
4	Lime juice	5 ml	50 ml	Pour over the tannias. Season with salt and pepper.
5	Butter	10 g	100 g	Melt and pour over the tannias. Return to the oven for 10 minutes. Serve immediately.

☐   ☐   ☐

Tannia cakes

🥄 30 min (per 10 portions)   🍲 20 min

Step	Commodity	1 portion	10 portions	
1	Water	125 ml equiv	1 litres	Place in a suitably sized saucepan, season with salt and pepper and boil.
2	Tannias	1	10	Wash and place in the boiling water for 10 minutes. Cool, peel and grate into a bowl.
3	Chopped parsley	½ tsp	4 tsp	Add to the tannias.
4	Chopped chives	½ tsp	4 tsp	Add to the tannias.
5	Self-raising flour	5 g	50 g	Sprinkle over the tannias and mix well. Season with salt and pepper.
6	Eggs	½	4	Beat into the mixture. Shape between two spoons and deep fry until golden brown. Remove from the fat and place on absorbent paper. Serve immediately.

☐   ☐   ☐

Baked yams

🥄 25 min (per 10 portions)
🍲 1 hr 10 min   ≋ 200°C (400°F)

Step	Commodity	1 portion	10 portions	
1	Yams	200 g equiv	2 kg equiv	Peel and cut into quarters.
2	Plain flour	10 g	100 g	Place on a tray and season with salt and pepper.
3	Milk	10 ml	100 ml	Dip the yams in the milk then coat the yams in the flour. Place on a baking tray and cook in a pre-heated oven for 50 minutes or until tender. Remove and allow to cool sufficiently to handle. Scoop out the soft centre of the yams into a bowl and mash.
4	Milk	5 ml equiv	50 ml equiv	Add to the mashed yams. Season with salt and pepper.
5	Butter	10 g	100 g	Melt and add to the mixture. Fill the skins with the mashed yams. Return to the oven for 20 minutes and brown.

NOTE: This dish is usually served with fried bacon.

☐   ☐   ☐

TERMINOLOGY

à la In the style of.

à la crème Served in or napped with a cream sauce or fresh cream.

à la menthe Cooked with fresh mint leaves and garnished with whole or chopped blanched leaves.

Abats Offal (head, heart, liver, kidneys and feet).

Abbatir To batten out.

Aboyeur 'Shouter' — person who calls out the orders in the kitchen.

Abricot Apricot.

Accolade (en) Piece of meat arranged back to back on a dish.

Africaine (à l') Flat mushrooms, tomatoes, egg plants and chateau potatoes.

Agneau Lamb.

Aiglefin Haddock.

Aigre Sour.

Aigre-doux Sweet and sour.

Ail (gousse d'ail) Garlic (clove of garlic).

Aile Wing (poultry game birds).

Aileron Winglet.

Alaska Omelette soufflé (baked Alaska).

Alphabetiques Pasta shaped into letters and used to garnish soups.

Albufera Suprême sauce, meat glaze and pimento, foie gras.

Aloyau Beef sirloin (on the bone).

Alphonse XIII Egg plant, tomato sauce and pimento.

Algerienne Small peeled tomatoes, artichokes and croquette of sweet potatoes.

Allemande White sauce blended with egg yolks and cream.

Allumette (a) Potatoes cut to the size of matchsticks. (b) A sort of dry petit four.

Alsacienne (à l') Sauerkraut in small tartlets.

Amandes mondées Shelled almonds.

Amandine Garnished with sliced sautéed almonds and finely chopped parsley.

Ambassadeur (à l') Artichokes and duchess potatoes.

Amer (picon) Bitter.

Américaine (homard à l') Lobster cooked with

chopped onions, shallots, garlic, parsley, tarragon, tomatoes and brandy.

Ananas Pineapple.

Ancienne (à l') (a) Garnish consisting of sweated button mushrooms and button onions, velouté, liaison, heart-shaped croûtons and finely chopped parsley.
(b) Kidney beans, hard boiled eggs and braised lettuce.

Anchois Anchovy.

Andouillete Chitterling sausages with tripe.

Anges à Cheval A savoury made from oysters wrapped in bacon and served on a piece of toast (Canapé).

Anguille Eel.

Anis Aniseed flavour.

Anna, pommes Thinly sliced seasoned potatoes, layered in an Anna mould and cooked in an oven.

Appareil Culinary term indicating a basic mixture.

Arachide (l'huile d') Groundnut oil.

Archiduc (a) Brunoise of vegetables, Madeira wine, port, fish stock and truffle.
(b) Can be applied to dishes seasoned with paprika, red pepper and blended with fresh cream.

Archiduchesse Mixed nuts, ham, mushrooms and asparagus tips.

Ardennaise (à l') Small game birds cooked in a cocotte with juniper berries.

Arenberg (à l') Bavarois with pears, candied fruit and biscuit in kirsch.

Argenteuil (à l') Asparagus from the region of Argenteuil, France.

Arlequin Chocolate and vanilla soufflé.

Arlesienne (à l') Preparation of white wine, garlic, eggplant, onion and chopped tomatoes.

Armagnac French brandy from the district of Armagnac in France.

Arôme Aroma.

Aromates (aux) With herbs.

Artichaut Globe artichoke.

Asperge Asparagus.

Aspic A savoury jelly made from calves foot.

Assaisonnements Seasonings, condiments.

Assisette (charcutière) A selection of delicatessen sausages, garlic sausage, salami, mortadella.

Assorti Assorted.

Aubergine Egg plant.

Au beurre A light coating of butter.

Au gratin Coated with cheese sauce, sprinkled with grated cheese and breadcrumbs and browned under a salamander.

Aux fines herbes Finished with a sprinkling of fresh fine herbs.

Avocat Avocado pear.

Baba An enriched dough product, soaked in a light syrup and rum.

Ballotine Boned, stuffed and rolled chicken leg, braised. Can be served hot or cold.

Banane Banana.

Barbue Brill (fish).

Barbes de bouc Root vegetables.

Baron d'agneau Saddle and legs of lamb.

Baron de boeuf Double sirloin of beef.

Barquette Boat shaped pastry case.

Basse-côte Spare rib of pork.

Bataille Potatoes cut into 1 cm dice and deep fried.

Batch cooking The technique of cooking in small quantities as required.

Bavarois A cold sweet made from a fresh egg custard mixture, gelatine and cream.

Bavette Thin flank of beef.

Baveuse Term used to describe an underdone (soft) omelette.

Béarnaise An extension of hollandaise sauce.

Béchamel A basic sauce made with a blond roux, milk and onion pique.

Beurre fondu Accompanied by a sauceboat of melted butter.

Beurre manié A paste made from blending equal quantities of butter and flour which is used to thicken liquids.

Beurre noisette Butter cooked to a nut brown colour.

Blanc Cooking in a liquid consisting of water, lemon juice and flour used to protect the colour and texture of light coloured vegetables and meats.

Blanched (a) a method of partially cooking food for use at a later stage.
(b) a method used to remove impurities from meat by placing them in cold water, bringing to the boil, discarding the water and replacing with fresh water.

Bouquet garni Thyme, bayleaf, parsley stalks placed in a small piece of muslin cloth or wrapped in leek leaves and celery then tied with string.

Bouquetière A selection of cooked vegetables, usually carrots, cauliflower, French beans and turnips served au beurre.

Brunoise A cut of vegetable, 2 mm dice.

Bruxelloise (à la) Brussels sprouts in butter and olive-shaped potatoes cooked in butter.

Bucarde Cockle.

Buccin Whelk.

Buche de Noël Yuletide log (French Christmas cake).

Buffet froid Cold buffet.

Byron (pommes) Potatoes with a hollow top, sprinkled with cheese, covered with cream and glazed.

Cabernet (Sauvignon) Type of wine grapes.

Cabillaud Cod.

Cabillons Small type of cheese made from goats' milk.

Cacao Cocoa.

Coco (noix de) Coconut.

Caille Quail.

Caisses (en) Wrapped in paper cases.

Calon segur Wine from Medoc district of Bordeaux, France.

Calvados Apple brandy.

Camembert Ripe, mature soft cheese made in Normandy.

Camomille Camomile (herbal tea).

Campagne (de) Country (from the).

Campagne (pâté de) Country-style pâté.

Canapé (diane, ecossais, epicure) Hors d'oeuvre or savoury presented on a small slice of toasted bread sometimes covered in aspic jelly.

Canard (caneton) Duck (duckling).

Cannelle Cinnamon.

Cannelloni Rolls of pasta stuffed with beef, spinach and seasoning made in veal stock.

Cantaloup Melon originally grown at Cantalupo, near Rome.

Capitolade Chicken stew, demi glace, with white wine.

Câpres Capers.

Caprice Fish filleted and dipped in butter and breadcrumbs and garnished with half a banana cooked in butter and grilled with sauce Robert.

Capucine (café) Coffee with cream and sprinkled with powdered chocolate.

Carafe Glass decanter or carafe.

Caramel Sugar cooked until brown.

Carbonnade de boeuf Beef steak stewed in beer.

Cardinal (a) Béchamel sauce and fish stock, truffle essence, lobster butter, cayenne pepper.
(b) Lobster, truffles and cardinal sauce.

Cardon Cardoon, similar to an artichoke.

Carème (a) Name of famous chef of early 19th century and dishes called after him.
(b) Hard-boiled egg, artichoke bottoms, truffles and Nantua sauce.

Cari (currie or kari) Consommé clarified with tomato juice, capsicums garnished with chunks of tomatoes.

Carotte (rapée) Carrot (grated).

Carpe Carp.

Caroline Medium grain rice.

Carre d'agneau Best end of lamb.

Carry over cooking This is when whole poached fish prepared for cold buffets are usually allowed to cool in the cooking liquor to avoid damage and drying out while cooling. The carry over cooking time must be taken into account when calculating the cooking times.

Carte du jour Menu of the day.

Carte (à la) Dishes chosen from the menu card.

Cartouche A piece of greaseproof paper cut to the circumference of the cooking vessel. It is brushed with butter, seasoned and placed butter side down on the food being cooked. It has the effect of generating steam and aiding the complete cooking of the food in the shortest time. It also prevents the food from drying out.

Cassata Neopolitan ice-cream with glacé fruit.

Casse-croute Snack.

Casserole (en) Saucepan (cooked in a fireproof dish).

Cassis Blackcurrant or blackcurrant liqueur.

Cassoulet A stew dish originating from the Languedoc region of France, prepared from port, lamb, or goose with haricot beans.

Castillane (à la) Chopped tomatoes cooked in oil with small onion rings, croquette potatoes and pieces of meat.

Catalane (a) Garnish of aubergines sauteed in oil, served with pilaw of rice and large pieces of meat.
(b) Artichoke bottoms.

Caviare Caviar–roe of sturgeon fish.

Cavour (à la) Small pieces of veal escalopes and calves sweetbreads dressed on small circles of polenta garnished with spiced mushrooms and filled with pieces of chicken liver and slices of truffles.

Celeri (celeri rave) Celery (celeriac or celery roots).

Celestine Consommé thickened with tapioca garnished with julienne of savoury pancake.

Cendres Ashes.

Cepes Type of edible mushrooms.

Cereales Cereal plants, e.g. oats, wheat, barley.

Cerf Stag.

Cerfeuil Chervil.

Cerises (glacées, and ubilées au maraschino) Cherries (sugared, soaked in kirsch syrup, flamed, soaked in maraschino).

Cervelle Brain.

Cervelas Saveloy, type of sausage.

Chambéry Thin slice of potatoes, bacon and grated cheese.

Chambord (à la) Garnish for fish with mushrooms, fish quenelles, soft fish roe tossed in butter, crayfish tails, slices of truffles and fleurons.

Chambré (vin) Wine at room temperature.

Champeaux For chicken-sautéed, white wine and meat glaze, garnished with small onions and cocotte potatoes.

Champignons Mushrooms.

Champvallon Cutlets cooked in stock with boulangère potatoes without onions.

Chantilly (à la) Whipped cream and sugar.

Chapelure White breadcrumbs which have been kept for two or three days mainly used for coating dishes cooked 'au gratin'.

Capon Capon (chicken).

Charcuterie Meat delicatessen such as sausages and pâtés.

Chassagne Montrachet Wine from Burgundy.

Châtaigne Sweet chestnut.

Charentais Type of melon from Charentes (France).

Charlotte (a) russe Sweet made from Bavarian cream and served cold, lined with sponge fingers.
(b) de fruits Confection of fruit served in a mould lined with thin slices of bread. Served hot.

Charollaise Garnish of cauliflower and croustades filled with turnip purée for large joints.

Chartres (a) Garnish for tournedos and noisettes: fondantes potatoes and tarragon leaves.
(b) Stuffed mushrooms and braised lettuce.

Chartreuse Liqueur made by the monks of Chartres.

Chasseur (à la) Hunter-style: with mushrooms, shallots, white wine and demi glace.

Chateaubriand Thick slice taken from the middle of a fillet of beef.

Château (pommes) Barrel-shaped potatoes cooked in butter to a golden brown colour.

Châtelaine Artichoke bottoms, tomatoes, braised celery and château potatoes (garnish for large joints).

Chauchat Garnish for fish (border of cooked potato round fish).

Chaudfroid Cold béchamel sauce used as a basis for aspic decorating of poultry, game.

Chauffant Pan of boiling salted water used to re-heat foods.

Chauffe-plat Hot plate.

Chausson de pommes Apple turnover.

Chef (specialité du) Speciality of the chef.

Cheval Horse (horsemeat).

Cheveux d-Anges Name given to a very fine type of vermicelli.

Chèvre Goat (usually refers to cheese made from goats' milk).

Chevreuil Roebuck (venison).

Chicorée (a) Vegetable: Belgian endive or chicory. (b) Used as flavouring essence in coffee.

Chiffonade Thinly shred lettuce or sorrel.
(oeuf) Hard boiled egg yolk mixed with duxelles, chopped parsley, cream, seasoning, placed in hard boiled egg white and covered in Mornay sauce and glazed.

Chinois Conical strainer.

Chipolata (a) Small sausages.
(b) Garnish of braised chestnuts, glazed onions, diced breast of pork and chipolata sausages.

Chocolat (au) With chocolate.

Choix (au) At your choice (choice of).

Choron (a) Sauce Béarnaise with tomato purée.
(b) Garnish (garnish of artichoke bottoms, peas and noisette potatoes).

Chou (rouge, vert, frise) Cabbage (red, green, curly).

Choucroute Sauerkraut.

Choux de Bruxelles Brussels sprouts.

Chou de mer Sea kale.

Chou-fleur Cauliflower.

Ciboulettes Chives.

Cidre Cider.

Cisalaying Making shallow incisions on the skin side of the filleted fish to prevent it from curling during cooking.

Citron (au, pressé) Lemon (with lemon, lemon juice).

Citronnade Lemonade.

Civet de lièvre, de lapin Brown hare stew, rabbit (jugged hare).

Clair Light colour.

Clairet Bordeaux wine (English claret).

Clarmart Garnish of artichoke bottom with purée of pea and château potatoes.

Cleopatre (truite) Trout garnished with shrimps, capers, soft herring roe.

Clermont Garnish for tournedos: chestnuts, soubise sauce covered with egg yolk and onions.

Cloche (sous) Usually for chicken with a cream sauce. Refers to way of service (originally a cooking method) under a glass, airtight, bell-shaped lid.

Clou de girofle Clove.

Clouté Usually refers to an onion with a bay leaf placed on the surface and pierced with three cloves.

Cochenille Cochineal.

Cochon (de lait) Pig (suckling pig).

Cocotte (en) Cooked and served in small, round earthenware or porcelain dish (as for eggs).

Cocette minute Pressure cooker.

Coeur d'artichaut Artichoke heart (bottom).

Coeur de boeuf Ox heart.

Coeur de laitue Lettuce heart.

Coing Quince (for compotes and jelly).

Colbert (sole) Sole with the backbone broken, breadcrumbed and deep fried, decorated with maitre d'hotel butter.

Colin Hake.

Collation Light meal, snack.

Commis (de partie) Assistant chef.

Complet (café) Full, complete (coffee and continental breakfast).

Compote Poached fruit, fresh and dried.

Compris (service) Included (service included).

Concassé (tomate) Roughly chopped tomato flesh.

Concombre Cucumber.

Conde (poire) Pear on a bed of sweet rice covered with apricot glaze.

Confiserie Confectionery goods.

Confit Crystallised.

Confiture Jam.

Conserves (au vinaigre) Preserved foods (pickles).

Consommé (de boeuf, de volaille) en gelée Clarified stock (of beef, chicken) jellied consommé.

Contrefilet Boned out sirloin of beef.

Cooked out Usually describes flour that has been cooked to the stage when it loses its starchy taste.

Coq au vin Chicken cooked in wine, with pork, onion, mushrooms, brandy.

Coq de bruyère Wood grouse.

Coquille Saint Jacques Scallops.

Cou de veau Scrag of veal.

Corbeille (de fruits) Basket (of fruit).

Coriandre Coriander (spice).

Cornet de York Ham moulded in the shape of a cone.

Cornichon Gherkin (pickled cucumber).

Côte de boeuf Rib of beef.

Côte rotie Roasted rib.

Côtelette Cutlet.

Coulibiac Hot fish and chicken pie (Russian cookery).

Courge (courgette) Marrow (baby marrow) *see also* Zucchini.

Couronne (en) In a crown shape.

Coupe Jacques Fruit soaked in liqueurs and covered with various assorted ices.

Court bouillon A cooking liquor for fish consisting of water or stock, wine or vinegar and root vegetables.

Couscous North African speciality – meat and grain stew.

Couvert Cover, cover charge.

Crabe dressé Dressed crab.

Crapaudine Pigeon or chicken cut up and flattened in the shape of a toad, grilled and garnished with sliced gherkins.

Crécy (potage) Purée of carrot soup.

Crème acidulée Cream, soured.
　　　anglaise egg yolk custard.
　　　fouette whipped.
　　　patisseur pastry cream.

Crème caramel Caramel custard.

Creole (à la) Rice pilaf garnished with red peppers, tomatoes and mushrooms, cooked in oil, flavoured with pineapple or orange.

Crêpe (flambée fourrée, suzette or Grand Marnier, normande, à la confiture) Pancake (flamed, filled, flamed with Grand Marnier and brandy, with apple, with jam).

Crepinetta Little flat sausage.

Cresson de fontaine Watercress.

Crevette grise, rose Shrimp, prawn.

Croissant Crescent-shaped bread made of puff pastry.

Croquant (chocolat) Plain chocolate.

Croquembouche balls Crisp pastries, made of small chou paste.

Croque Monsieur Toasted ham and cheese sandwich.

Croquignolles Pastry: kind of fondant icing sugar.

Croquette (pommes) Cooked food in a cylindrical shape and deep fried (mashed potato cooked in this fashion).

Croustade Pastry case (puff pastry).

Croûte (en) In pastry.

Croûtons Shaped pieces of bread, shallow fried.

Cru (Cru) Growth, also wines of a similar standard (Raw).

Crudités Raw vegetables (assorted).

Crustaces Shellfish.

Cuisine (regionale, internationale) Kitchen or cooking (regional, international cooking).

Cuisse (de grenouille, de porc, de poulet Leg (frog, pork, chicken).

Cuissot de porc Leg of pork.

Cuit à point Medium cooked.
　　　bleu Very underdone.
　　　saignant Rare (bloody).
　　　bien cuit Well cooked.

Cuire To cook.

Culinaire Culinary.

Culotte de boeuf Rump of beef.

Cumin Dried seed used for flavouring.

Curaçao Orange liqueur.

Cutting and tying Cutting of foods into even pieces and tying them up to retain the shape and give ease of handling.

Cuvée Blending of wines.

Dame blanche (a) Type of chicken consommé with tapioca and almond milk.
(b) Ice cream with crushed fresh and bitter almonds, sometimes with peach.

Dariole Small cylindrical mould (for puddings).

Darnes A steak cut from a round fish.

Darphin Like 'pommes Anna' but cut in strips.

Dartois (a) Two puff pastry layers with almond or pastry cream in between.
(b) Garnish: turned carrot, turnip, celery and rissoled potatoes.

Datte Date.

Daube Method of braising meat (usually beef) in red wine and stock.

Dauphine (pommes) Chou paste mixed with potato, deep fried.

Dauphinoise (à la) Dauphine method of preparing vegetables with grated Gruyère.

Débarrasser To clear up tables.

Décanter To decant.

Déglacer Swilling out a pan or roasting tray in which food has been cooked with water, wine or stock in order to extract the flavourings from the sediment to make an accompanying sauce or gravy.

Dégraisser The process of skimming fat.

Dégustation Tasting (of wines, teas, food).

Déjeuner (à la fourchette) Lunch (knife and fork meal).

Délice A cut of fish with either ends folded underneath itself for cooking and presentation.

Delmonico (pommes) Cubes of potato coated in milk, covered in breadcrumbs and grilled.

Demi Half.

Demi-chef Assistant waiter.

Demi-deuil Food (poultry, fish, veal) covered with a sauce suprême with truffles.

Demidoff (consommé) Chicken consommé garnished with dices of vegetables, truffles, quenelles, mushrooms and chervil.

Demi-glace Refined Espagnole or brown sauce reduced by half.

Demi sel Type of cream cheese.

Derby (croûtes) Garnish: ham purée and pickled walnuts.

Dés Dice, e.g. of vegetables.

Désosser To bone out.

Diable (à la) Usually applied to poultry. Battered, seasoned, grilled, sprinkled with breadcrumbs browned and served with devilled sauce: shallots, pepper, white wine reduced and cayenne.

Diable à cheval (canapé) Prunes stuffed with chutney wrapped in bacon served on toast.

Diablotins (canapé) Small pieces of Welsh rarebit.

Diane (steak) Thin slices of entrecote steak cooked in wine, Worcester sauce and shallots flamed with brandy.

Dieppoise Garnish: shrimps' tails, mussels, mushrooms.

Digestif Digestive.

Dijonnaise (escargots à la) Snails with reduced wine and shallots mixed with marrow, salt, pepper, spices, garlic and truffles treated as Bourguignonne.

Dinde (dindonneau) Turkey (young turkey).

Dîner Dinner.

Diplomate Fish velouté with mushrooms, oysters cohered with yolk of egg, cream and lobster butter.

Dom Perignon Benedictine monk: reputed creator of 'methode champenoise'.

Doré Brushed with beated egg to brown.

Doria Garnish: Cucumber turned into 'clove of garlic shape' cooked slowly in butter.

Doucette Corn salad.

Dosage Syrup added to champagne before final bottling.

Dragée Almond covered with hard sugar.

Dubarry (crème) (a) Cauliflower (soup).
(b) Cauliflower with cheese sauce.

Duchesse (pommes) Purée of potatoes dried, mixed with egg yolks and butter, seasoned and piped.

Duglere Fish sauce made from tomatoes, parsley, onions, shallots, reduced stock.

Duxelles Chopped mushrooms and shallots cooked in butter.

Du jour (plat) Of the day (dish).

Draining Draining or drying off all the cooking liquor from the food before coating with sauce. Usually done by placing the poached food on to a clean cloth or absorbent paper. This is important as the undrained liquor mixing with the masking sauce will spoil both appearance and consistency.

Edbarbé Bearded.

Ecarlatte Shallot.

Echine de porc Collar of pork.

Éclair Chou pastry good filled with cream or pastry cream.

Ecossaise (à l) Scotch egg sauce, thin béchamel garnished with white and yolk of eggs.

Ecrémé (lait) Skimmed milk.

Ecrevisse Crayfish.

Egyptienne (à l) Purée egyptienne is prepared from yellow split peas.

Elizabeth (a) Coupe — cherries soaked in kirsch and cherry bandy covered in whipped cream with cinnamon.
(b) Escalope cooked with cream and cognac.

Emmenthal Cheese from Switzerland.

Emince (de volaille) Thin slice (of chicken).

En branche Whole (spinach) as opposed to purée.

En buissons Crayfish cooked in court bouillon, cooled in their juice, served hung by the tail on a stand, garnished with parsley.

En cascade Usually prawns arranged in a dish like a waterfall.

Endive Chicory.

En robe de chambre (pommes) In their jacket (potatoes): steamed.

Entier Whole.

Entrecôte (minute, double) Steak cut from the sirloin.

Entrée The first meat dish to figure on the menu.

Entrements (a) *sucres* Sweet course.
(b) *de legumes* Vegetables.

Entremettier Vegetable cook.

Epaule Shoulder.

Eperlan Smelt.

Epices Spices (the word 'condiments' is also used).

Epicure (canapé) Roquefort cheese, butter with chopped onions.

Epinards Spinach.

Esau Lentil juice with rice, butter and cream.

Escalope Thin slice usually of veal (scallop).

Escargot Snail.

Espagnole (a) Omelette (with onions, tomatoes, pimentos, potatoes) served flat on a plate not folded.
(b) Rich brown sauce which is the foundation of demi glace and many brown sauces. Made from fat and flour, cooked in the oven to a light brown colour and to which stock is added.

Essence d-amande (de citron) Almond essence (lemon essence).

Essence de vanille (d'anchois) Vanilla essence (Anchovy essence).

Estouffade (a) Food slowly stewed.
(b) Basic brown stock.

Estragon Tarragon.

Esturgeon Sturgeon (caviar-producing fish).

Etamine Sieve or butter muslin; familiarly known as a 'tammy cloth'.

Etuvée (à l') Method of cooking food in tightly covered container with little or no water.

Envoyez Kitchen order: 'send up'.

Excelsior Garnish for tournedos and noisettes. Fresh lettuce or dondantes potatoes.

Extrait Extract.

Faisan Pheasant.

Faites marcher Start preparation of.

Farce (farci) Stuffing (stuffed).

Farine Flour.

Faubonne Purée of green peas or haricot beans with julienne of vegetable, chervil, butter and cream.

Faux-filet (contrefilet) Boned sirloin of beef.

Favorite (salade) Crayfish tails with truffles, asparagus tips, seasoned with lemon juice, olive oil, salt, pepper, celery and parsley.

Fécule Thickening starch from potatoes.

Fenouil Fennel.

Fermierer (à la) With vegetables, i.e. carrots, turnips, onions and celery cut roughly. Usually applies to large joints of meat or poultry, also with soup and omelettes.

Feuilletage (pâte-feuilletée) Puff pastry.

Fève Broad bean.

Figue Fig.

Filet (d'Anvers) Fillet (of meat, fish or poultry) (cornets of York).

Filet mignon Thin end of fillet.

Financière (à la) (a) With quenelles, truffles, cocks' combs, kidneys, mushrooms, herbs and olives.
(b) Madeira sauce with truffle essence.

Fines herbes Mixed herbs (parsley, chervil, chives, rosemary).

Flageolet Small kidney bean.

Flamande (à la) (a) Carbonnade made of slices of beef cooked in beer with slices of onions.
(b) With the inclusion of Brussels sprouts.

Flambé Flamed.

Flan Flan.

Flétan Halibut.

Fleurons Quarter moon-shaped puff pastry used as a decoration for various dishes.

Fleuriste (garniture) Tournedos and noisettes: tomatoes stuffed with jardinière and château potatoes (garnish).

Florentine (à la) Garnish with spinach and cheese sauce.

Florian Garnish for large joints — braised lettuce, glazed onions, carrots and fondante potatoes.

Florida (Cocktail) Cocktail of orange and grapefruit segments.

Foie Liver.

Foie gras (de Strasbourg) Fatted liver of geese with truffles.

Fond d'artichaut Artichoke bottom.

Fondant Sugar, water and glucose used to coat sweet buns, éclairs.

Fondantes (pommes) Potatoes cooked in stock in oven.

Fonds de cuisine Basic stocks.

Fondue (au fromage) Melted cheese with wine and seasonings.

Fondue Bourguignonne Fillet steak dices cooked in oil at the table: eaten with many accompanying sauces.

Fontainebleau (garniture) Tournedos and noisettes: bouchées made with duchess potatoes filled with jardinière of vegetables (garnish).

Forestiére (a la) (a) Morels tossed in butter, dices of bacon and parmentière potatoes.
(b) Cepes tossed in butter, mushrooms and pommes cocottes.
(c) Crème forestière (cream of mushroom soup garnished with julienne of mushrooms).

Fouettée (crème) Whipped (cream).

Four (au) Cooked in the oven.

Fourré Filled or stuffed.

Fraise (des bois) Strawberry (wild strawberry).

Fraises (Romanoff) Strawberries with curaçao and fresh cream.

Framboise Raspberry.

Francillon Chicken consommé garnished with poached eggs and chicken quenelles.

Frangipane Pastry made of butter, sugar, eggs, almonds and flour.

Frappé Chilled.

Friandises Sweet delicacies (petits fours, crystallised fruit).

Fricadelles Chopped meat with onion and bread, fried.

Fricassée White ragoût (chicken, rabbit or veal) cooked in a sauce.

Frite (pommes frites) Fried (fried potatoes).

Frite à la française Covered with milk and flour, deep fried.

Frit à l'anglaise Covered in flour, egg, breadcrumbs, deep fried.

Frit à l'Orly Covered in batter and deep fried, served with tomato sauce.

Fritot de chou-fleur Cauliflower bouquet dipped in batter and deep fried.

Friture (a) Fried food (small fish).
(b) Vessel for deep frying.

Froid Cold.

Fromage (au) Cheese (with).

Fromage de tête de porc Pork brawn.

Frou frou Vanilla, rum and candied fruit.

Fruits Fruit.

Fruits confits Crystallised fruit.

Fruits de mer Sea food (assorted shellfish).

Fumé (anguille, saumon) Smoked (eel, salmon).

Fumet A concentrated fish stock used to give more flavour to the finished fish dishes.

Galantine Cold poultry or game that has been boned, stuffed, rolled and glazed.

Galette Round puff pastry cake.

Garbure Vegetable purée, butter and cream and fried croûtons.

Garçon Waiter.

Garde-manger Larder.

Garnir (garniture) To garnish (garnish).

Gasconne Tomato velouté, onions, garnished with dices of goose legs and butter.

Gazpacho Cold soup made of cucumber, pimentos, garlic, tomatoes, oil, onions, pepper and salt; a Spanish speciality.

Gastronome Consists of chestnuts, small truffles, morels and cocks' kidneys.

Gâteau Cake.

Gaufre Waffle.

Gaufrette (pomme) Like game chips with a lace effect.

Gauloise Chicken consommé thickened with yolk of eggs and garnished with cocks' combs and kidneys, roundels of ham.

Gelatine Gelatine (for setting jellies, aspics and sweets).

Gelée (en) (gelée d'aspic) Jelly (in) (savoury jelly for coating chaud-froid dishes and for decorating).

Gelinotte Hazel grouse.

Gendarme Type of pickled herring or sausage.

Genevoise (sauce) Chopped salmon head tossed in butter with pepper, thyme and bay leaves with red wine and finished with butter and anchovy essence.

Génoise (a) Sponge pastry: also entrements made with sponge pastry.
(b) Purée of herbs, pistachios, almonds cooked with yolk of eggs, lemon juice, salt and pepper and finished with oil.

George Sand Fish consommé with fish quenelles, blended with crayfish butter and quarter of cooked morels.

Gervais Cheese producer from France.

Gibier (à poils, à plume) Game (furred, feathered).

Gigot d'agneau mouton Leg of lamb or mutton.

Gingembre Ginger.

Girofle (clou de) Clove.

Girolle Type of mushroom.

Gîte à la noix Silverside of beef.

Glacé (a) Ice.
(b) Ice-cream.
(c) Sugar icing.

Glace Iced, glazed.

Glace de viandes Meat juices or meat glaze.

Glacier Man who makes ice cream.

Glaçon Ice cube.

Gnocchi (Romaine) Semolina with egg yolk, cheese and butter.

Gnocchi (Parisienne) Chou pastry and béchamel sprinkled with cheese and browned.

Godard Reduction of white wine with mirepoix of vegetable, chopped ham, half glaze and mushroom essence passed through a fine sieve.

Goujon de sole (goujonnette) Gudgeon (small strips of fish).

Goulache Kind of beef stew with diced onions and seasoned with garlic and paprika.

Gourmand Greedy.

Gourmandises Petit fours (fancy cakes).

Gourmet Connoisseur of food.

Gousse (d'ail) Pod (clove of garlic).

Gout Taste.

Grain (poulet de) Grain (small corn-fed chicken).

Grande Champagne One of the cognac districts.

Grand Duc Asparagus heads, slices of truffles for chicken.

Grand Marnier Orange liqueur from France.

Grand-mère Button onions, mushrooms and diced bacon.

Grand Veneur Poivrade sauce with venison flavour, redcurrant jelly and cream.

Grappe (de raisins) Bunch (of grapes).

Gras Fat.

Gratin (au) Food put under the grill until brown (sometimes covered with breadcrumbs or cheese).

Gratiner To cover with Mornay sauce, sprinkle with cheese and put under the grill until browned.

Grecque (a la) (a) Velouté of tomatoes with pumpkin and fried croûtons.
(b) Green pea purée with mutton stock and julienne of carrots, leeks, cabbages and butter.
(c) Type of hors d'oeuvre with rice.

Grenade Pomegranate.

Grenobloise (poisson meunière) Cooked 'meunière' with capers and peeled wedge of lemon.

Grenouille (cuisses de) Frog (legs).

Gribiche Oily sauce made of yolk of eggs and hard boiled eggs, oil and vinegar seasoned with mustard, capers, and chopped gherkins, parsley and tarragon and dices of white of hard boiled eggs.

Grillade Grilled meat, grills.

Grillé Grilled.

Groseille Redcurrant.

Groseille à maquereau Gooseberry.

Gruyère Waxy textured cheese from France and Switzerland: distinctive appearance on account of its large holes.

Haché Minced.

Hachis Mince (meat or poultry).

Haddock Smoked haddock.

Hareng Herring.

Harengs de Baltique Similar to Bismarck Herrings.

Haricots (verts, blancs) Beans (French, haricots).

Haut Brion Red wine from Medoc district of Bordeaux.

Haute cuisine Cooking at its best.

Havanaise Salad lettuces, shrimps, asparagus heads, mayonnaise thinned with cucumber purée.

Hélène Salad-green pimentos, truffles, asparagus heads, tangerines, vinaigrette with brandy.

Henri IV For tournedos and noisette-Pont-Neuf potatoes and water cress.

Herbes Herbs.

Hochepot Stewed meat.

Hollandaise Yolks of eggs and butter sauce.

Holstein Veal escalope with breadcrumbs served with fried egg, anchovies, and olives.

Homard Lobster.

Hongroise (a) For large joints: balls of cauliflower covered with Mornay sauce and paprika, mixed with ham and glazed.
(b) Sauce: chopped onions and parsley fried in butter.
(c) Sauce with chopped onions, parsley fried in butter, paprika, wine, faggots, reduced and mixed with suprême sauce.
(d) Consommé flavoured with tomato and paprika, rondelles of chicken, forcemeat and quenelles of calves' liver.

Hors d'oeuvre (au choix, variés) Hors d'oeuvre (choice of, variety of).

Huile (à l') With oil.

Huîtres (de Colchester) Oysters (Colchester oysters).

Huîtres natives Home-bred oysters.

Huîtres de Whitstable Whitstable oysters.

Hure de sanglier Boar's head.

Hussarde (*a*) Garnish for large joints: potatoes and eggplants stuffed with horseradish.
(*b*) Sauce: minced onions and shallots, fried in butter with wine.

Ile flottante Savoy biscuits with jam and fruit covered with whipped cream, surrounded by cold cream.

Imperator Lentil soup, pheasant flavoured with marsala.

Imperatrice (riz à l') Cooked rice with salpicon of mixed fruit soaked in liqueur, red jelly on top of dish.

Imperial (à l') Mushrooms, truffle and foie gras.

Indienne (à l') Indian style: can be potatoes cut in ribbons and steamed, usually refers to curry (for puddings: usually with ginger).

Infusion Infusion, steeping in liquid.

Italienne (à l') (*a*) Italian style, usually with cooked spaghetti, butter, cream and grated Parmesan cheese.
(*b*) Duxelles sauce, brunoise of ham and herbs.
(*c*) Mayonnaise with lemon juice, garnished minced brain and chopped parsley.

Ivanhoe (canapé) May be shaped like Ivanhoe shield; purée of haddock with cream and grilled mushrooms.

Ivoire (sauce) Ivory: a suprême sauce with a meat glaze to give it an ivory colour.

Jaffa Praline and curaçao-flavoured ice bombe.

Jalousie Flaky pastry slice filled with jam and baked in oven.

Jambon (de York, de Parme, de Bayonne) Ham (York ham, smoked Parma ham, smoked Bayonne ham) (last two are usually served as an hors d'oeuvre).

Jambonneau Part of pork at the end of the ham.

Japonaise (*a*) Garnish for meat: croustade filled with Japanese artichokes and croquette potatoes.
(*b*) Tomato and dice of pineapple served on lettuce leaves with an acidulated cream dressing (lemon juice, castor sugar and cream).

Jardinière Mixed vegetables cut into small sticks.

Jarret Knuckle.

Jaune d'oeuf Yolk of egg.

Javanaise (salade) Javanese style: orange segments, julienne rind of oranges, grated horseradish and acidulated cream.

Jeanette (*a*) Usually with forcemeat and foie gras.

(*b*) Cold chicken, decorated and covered with aspic jelly.

Joinville (Fish) Normande sauce with crayfish and shrimps garnished with truffles.

Josephine Poached pears with apples dressed round; Imperatrice rice, strawberry purée.

Jubilées (cerises) Poached and stoned cherries, flambéed with kirsch.

Julienne A cut of vegetable, 2 mm × 2 mm × 4 cm.

Julienne (consommé) Clear soup with julienne of vegetables cut into fine strips.

Jus de citron, tomate, orange, pamplemousse, ananas Lemon juice, tomato, orange, grapefruit, pineapple.

Jus de viande Natural meat juice.

Jus lié Gravy thickened with arrowroot.

Jus de rôti Roast gravy.

Kari Curry.

Kebab Lamb or mutton cut into small pieces/cubes and cooked on a skewer, served with rice, peas and onions.

Kefir Beverage made from cow's or camel's milk: of Caucasian origin.

Kilkis Type of fish preserved like anchovy.

Kirsch Liqueur made from cherries; also used for flavouring or flambés.

Kleber Braised turbot, truffles, mushrooms, crayfish tails, white wine sauce, and parsley.

Koumis Mare's milk originating from Turkey.

Kummel Liqueur flavoured with cumin.

Lait Milk.

Laitance Soft roe, usually served on toast (herring).

Laitue (pommée, romaine) Lettuce (cabbage lettuce, cos lettuce).

Langouste Crayfish.

Langoustine Dublin Bay prawn.

Langue (de chat) Tongue (pastry in the shape of a cat's tongue).

Languedocienne Garnish for entrées: fried eggplants, slices of cep mushrooms, garnished with tomatoes.

Lapin (domestique, de Garenne) Rabbit (tame, wild).

Lard (gras, maigre) Bacon (fat, lean).

Lardons Small dice of bacon.

Laurier (feuilles de) Bay leaves.

La vallière (*a*) Poached fish dressed in a crown, normande sauce, oysters, quenelles, soft roes, mushrooms, truffles.

(b) For poultry and sweetbread, truffles, trussed crayfish.

Lasagne verdi Green colour Italian pasta: usually served with alternate layers of cheese and minced meat.

Légumes (entremets de) Vegetables.

Lentilles Lentils.

Leopold Vanilla and wild strawberries with kirsch flavour and ice cream dessert.

Levure Yeast.

Liaison (a) A binding ingredient such as egg yolk or cream.
(b) A mixture of egg yolks and cream whisked together and used to enrich and thicken sauces.

Liègoise (à la) From Liège: offal cooked in a casserole with juniper flavouring and flavoured with gin.

Lier To bind.

Lièvre (levreau) Hare (young hare).

Limande Lemon sole.

Limonade Lemonade.

Limousine From the Limousin district of France: garnish of cooked chestnuts.

Longschamps (crème) Fresh pea soup garnished with vermicelli, sorrel and chervil.

Longe (de porc, d'agneau, de veau) Loin of pork, lamb, veal.

Lorette (a) pommes (b) salad (a) as 'dauphine': cigar shaped (potatoes).
(b) Corn salad with beetroot and celery.

Lorgnette (a) Fried onions in rings.
(b) Type of small biscuits.

Lotte (de mer) Angler: used mainly as an ingredient for bouillabaisse or fish soups.

Oup de mer Sea bass.

Louisiane (à la) Louisiana style: creamed sweet corn, rice, fried bananas cut in roundels.

Lucifer Poached oysters, rolled, in English mustard, egg and breadcrumbs, deep fried.

Lucine Clam (type of mollusc).

Lucullus (tournedos) On a fried croûton: truffle, mushrooms, cocks' combs, kidney, asparagus tips, half glaze sauce, truffle essence and Madeira wine.

Lyonnaise (pommes) (a) Sauté potatoes and shallow fried onions.
(b) Half glaze sauce with white wine and vinegar reduction and onions.

Macaire (pommes) Mashed baked potatoes, seasoned and moulded into 5 cm diameter rounds and shallow fried.

Macaron Macaroon.

Macaroni Type of farinaceous dish.

Macédoine (a) A cut of vegetables, ½ cm dice.
(b) Garnish of macédoine of vegetables.

Macère (Fruit) soaked in liqueur to give flavour.

Macis Mace, dried shell of nutmeg, used to flavour marinades, brines and sauces.

Madeleine Small light cake.

Madère (au) (a) Madeira wine from island of same name.
(b) Half glazed sauce with Madeira wine.

Madras From the city of Madras in India: garnish of rice, usually used with curry.

Madrilene (consommé) Clear soup flavoured with celery and tomatoes, garnished with roughly chopped tomatoes, sorrel, pimento and vermicelli.

Magnum Bottle twice the normal size.

Maintenon Suprême sauce, slices of truffle and chopped mushrooms.

Mais Sweetcorn.

Maison House speciality.

Maître d'hôtel (beurre) Head water. (butter softened to a cream with chopped parsley and lemon juice).

Malakoff (crème) Tomato and potato soup: garnished with julienne of spinach.

Maltaise Maltese style: hollandaise sauce with zest of blood oranges and their juice.

Mandarine Tangerine.

Mange-tout Variety of sweet peas of which the pod is also eaten.

Manié (beurre) Butter and flour kneaded and used as a thickening or binding agent.

Maquereau Mackerel.

Marbre Marbled: used in connection with certain sweet and pastry dishes.

Marcassin Very young wild boar.

Marechale (a) Asparagus tips and slices of truffle garnish.
(b) Quenelles, truffles, cocks' combs.

Marengo (poulet sauté) Sautéed chicken, half glazed with tomatoes, white wine, mushrooms, truffles, croûtons, fresh water crayfish.

Marie-Louise (a) Chicken velouté with barley flour, vegetables, macaroni and cream.
(b) Garnished artichoke fond with mushroom purée and noisette potatoes.

(c) Artichoke bottoms, half tomatoes, braised lettuce and château potatoes.

Marie Stuart Chicken velouté (barley flour) carrot and cream.

Marie Thérèse Tournedos or noisette, cooked in butter, half glazed, tomatoes, risotto and truffle.

Marignan Type of savarin pastry: small boat-shaped.

Marigny (a) Green pea soup garnished with peas, sorrel and chervil, butter and cream.
(b) Garnish for entrées: tartlets, filled with peas and lozenges of beans fondantes potatoes.

Marinade Liquor to tenderise meat: root vegetables, bouquet garni, white wine, vinegar and oil.

Mariner To keep meat in a marinade to make it more tender.

Marinière (a) Marine style (see Moules Marinières).
(b) White wine sauce with mussels.

Marivaux Oval nests of duchess potatoes.

Marjolaine Marjoram (aromatic herb).

Marmelade Purée of cooked fruit.

Marmite Stockpot.

Marquise (pommes) Duchess potatoes with roughly chopped tomatoes in the centre.

Marsals Fortified wine from Sicily (very sweet).

Marron (marron glacé) Chestnut (chestnut glazed in sugar).

Marseillaise (a) Fish stew speciality from Marseilles.
(b) Tomatoes, stuffed olives, garlic, anchovy, potatoes.

Massepain Marzipan: almond paste for decorating cakes made from ground almonds, sugar and white of egg.

Martel Name of cognac shippers and suppliers.

Maryland (suprême de volaille) Breadcrumbed chicken, shallow-fried, sweetcorn pancake, bacon and half-fried banana.

Mascotte Garnish for meat and poultry: artichoke bottoms, truffle slices, cocotte potatoes.

Matelote (a) Fish garnish: mushroom, onions, heart-shaped croûtons, crayfish slices.
(b) Fish stew made with white or red wine.

Mayonnaise Sauce made of egg yolk, oil vinegar and mustard.

Medaillon Medallion of meat and other round-shaped preparations.

Medicis Garnish for meat of artichoke bottoms, peas, carrots and turnips, noisette potatoes, sauce Choron: béarnaise sauce with tomato purée.

Mélange Mixture; assortment.

Melba (a) Peche Melba, poached peach, vanilla ice cream, whipped cream and Melba sauce (a raspberry purée). In honour of Nellie Melba, the famous opera singer.
(b) Toast Melba: thin toast.

Melon Melon.
(a) *Cantaloup* (a) From Cantalupo near Rome.
(b) *Charentais* (b) From Charente in France.

Menthe (crème de, frappé) Mint (mint liqueur, served with shaved ice).

Menu (gastronomique, touristique) Menu (gastronomic, touristic).

Mercedes Garnish of tomatoes, mushrooms, braised lettuce and croquette potatoes.

Meringue Meringue (made with beaten white of eggs and sugar).

Merian (en colère) Whiting (whole whiting: deep fried).

Methode Champenoise Method of producing champagne with a second fermentation in the bottle.

Meunière Miller's wife style: floured, shallow-fried, noisette butter, lemon slices, lemon juice and parsley.

Mexicaine (omelette) (a) Flat omelette with mushrooms, pimento and tomatoes.
(b) Meat garnished with mushrooms, roughly chopped tomatoes, grilled peppers, and grilled half egg plants.

Miel Honey.

Mignon (a) Thin end of fillet of beef.
(b) Poultry and sweetbread, artichoke bottoms, halved tomatoes, braised lettuce and château potatoes.

Mignonette (a) *poivre* (b) *pommes* (a) Roughly chopped peppercorns.
(b) Potatoes chopped in small bâtons.

Mijoter To simmer gently.

Milanaise (spaghetti) (a) Cooked spaghetti, butter, grated Parmesan cheese, julienne of tongue, ham, mushrooms, truffles and tomato sauce.
(b) Garnish for veal scallops.

Millefeuille (A thousand leaves) cream slice of puff pastry.

Mimosa (salade) (a) Lettuce heart sprinkled with hard white of egg and yolk with chopped parsley.
(b) Lettuce heart, orange quarters, grapes, bananas, cream and lemon juice dressing.

Minute (entrecôte) Thin sirloin steak taking one minute to cook.

Mirabeau Garnish of olives, anchovies, tarragon leaves. Optional: watercress and matchstick potatoes.

Mirepoix Carrots, onions, cut into dice, lardons used as a base for sauces.

Miroton A type of dish made of boiled slices of beef and covered with a sauce; usually re-heated.

Mise en place Basic preparation for the service of a meal.

Mode, à la In the fashion of.

Moderne Cauliflower and cheese sauce, stuffed tomatoes and duchess potatoes.

Moelle (de boeuf) Marrow (of beef).

Moka (gâteau) (a) Type of coffee.
(b) Coffee-flavoured gateau.

Monaco Poached fish, fine herb sauce with tomato flavouring, poached bearded oysters, truffle slices.

Mont Blanc (crème) Whipped cream mixed with chestnut purée.

Monter au beurre The process of incorporating chilled butter pieces into sauces to thicken and improve the glaze.

Monte Carlo (a) Poached haddock, cream sauce, poached egg and roughly chopped tomatoes.
(b) Mousse with chantilly and meringues.

Monter To whip up cream.

Montmorency (caneton) (a) Half glazed sauce and cherries.
(b) Garnish for noisette and tournedos; artichoke bottoms, carrots, noisette potatoes.

Montpellier A savoury herb butter.

Morelle Type of mushroom.

Mornay Béchamel sauce with grated Parmesan cheese.

Mortadelle Italian type of sausage served as an hors d'oeuvre.

Morue Salted cod.

Moussaka Mutton dish, demi glace, slices of eggplant, covered with tomato or cheese sauce cooked in the oven.

Moscovite (canapé) Moscow style: various appetisers on toast cut into different shapes and covered with aspic jelly.

Mouiller To wet or add a little liquid.

Moules (marinières) Mussels (cooked in stock with white wine, chopped shallots and parsley).

Moulin à poivre Peppermill.

Mousse Whipped white of egg with cream; various flavourings.

Mousseline (sauce) (a) Hollandaise sauce with whipped cream.
(b) Mashed potatoes with whipped cream.

Moutarde (anglaise) Mustard (English) blended with flour and a small amount of turmeric, diluted with water or white wine.

Mouton Mutton.

Mulligatawny Curry soup with rice and diced meat.

Mûre Mulberry.

Muscade (noix de) Nutmeg.

Muscadelle White grape wine from the Bordeaux region.

Nantais(e), salade From Nantes. Cucumber, watercress, tomatoes, French beans, tartare sauce.

Nantua (sauce) (a) Fish velouté, white wine, cognac, tomatoes and crayfish butter.
(b) Garnish for fish: crayfish tails, nantua sauce, truffles.

Napolitaine (a) (spaghetti) Cooked spaghetti as Italienne and cooked tomatoes, tomato sauce.
(b) Garnish for veal scallops.

Nappe Tablecloth.

Napper To coat or cover with a sauce.

Nature Plainly cooked. Also applies to wine to which nothing has been added.

Navarin Brown lamb stew.

Navarraise Chops or cutlets. Salpicon of ham, mushrooms, peppers, béchamel sauce, grated cheese, tomatoes.

Navet Turnip.

Neige (à la) Snow (white of egg beaten to a stiff consistency).

Newburg (homard) Cooked, sliced lobster, cream, madeira or sherry, crab served with rice.

Niçoise (a) Usually indicates presence of tomatoes, French beans, olives and peppers.
(b) Fish garnish, chopped tomatoes, garlic, capers, slices of lemon, anchovy butter.

Nids d'Hirondelles Literally 'swallows nests': garnish for chicken consommé.

Ninon (salade) Apple, pineapple, lettuce, shrimps, mayonnaise and horseradish.

Nivernaise Garnish of carrots, olive-shaped, small glazed onions.

Noisette (a) Hazelnut.
(b) (Potatoes) small hazelnut-size roasted in clarified butter.
(c) Hollandaise sauce with noisette butter.

Noisette d'agneau Boned out lamb chop or nut of loin.

Noix (de brésil, de coco) Walnut (Brazil nut, coconut).

Noix de veau Cushion of veal.

Normande (crêpes) (a) Pancakes filled with chopped cooked apples.
(b) Fish velouté, mushroom essence, liaison yolk of egg and cream.

Norvégienne (omelette) See Omelette surprise.

Nougat Nougat.

Nougatine (gâteau) Genoise cake with praline cream and chocolate fondant icing.

Nouilles Noodles.

Nuits St Georges Côtes de nuits: famous red Burgundy wine.

Nymphes (cuisse de) Frog legs. Also poached in white wine, served cold with chaudfroid and aspic jelly.

Oeufs brouillés Scrambled eggs.

Oeuf (dur, mollet) Egg (hard, soft boiled).

Oeuf à la coque Boiled egg.

Oeuf à la poêle (sur le plat) Fried egg (cooked in a special earthenware dish).

Oeuf Georgette Poached egg served on half-baked potato, American sauce, cheese sauce.

Oeuf poché Poached egg.

Office Still room.

Oie (Oison) Goose (Gosling).

Oignon Onion.

Oiseaux (sans têtes) Birds (stuffed fillets of various meats, specially beef, braised in beer — Belgian cookery).

Olive (huile d') Olive (olive oil).

Olivette (pommes) Roast potatoes the size of a small olive.

Omelette Omelet, omelette.

Omelette Norvégienne (see Alaska).

Opéra (crème) (a) Cream caramel cooked in a circular savarin mould, strawberry soaked in Kirsch, crème caprice (whipped cream mixed with small pieces of meringue) placed in centre.
(b) Noisette and tournedos garnish: tartlets filled with chicken liver, scallops, Madeira sauce, duchess potatoes, asparagus tips.

Orange sanguine Blood orange.

Orge (perle) Barley (pearl barley).

Orientale (meon à l') (a) Chilled melon, wild strawberries, flavoured with kirsch.
(b) Oriental meat garnish: halved tomatoes filled with Greek style rice, croquette potatoes.
(c) American sauce with curry powder, cream.

Orléans Consommé with tapioca and coloured quenelles of chicken, tomatoes and spinach.

Orloff (a) Scrambled egg garnished with crayfish tails and slice of truffle.
(b) Meat garnish: braised celery in Timbale, celery puree, tomatoes, braised lettuce, château potatoes.

Orly (à l') For fish: dipped in batter, deep fried, tomato sauce.

Ostendaise Fish dish with poached oysters, truffles, normande sauce, orange shaped croquette of fillet of sole.

Os Bone.

Oseille Sorrel.

Osso Buco Knuckle of veal served with rice.

Oursin Sea urchin.

Oxford (salade) (a) Dice of chicken, gherkins, hard white of egg, truffles, tomato slices on lettuce leaves, vinaigrette with chopped tarragon.
(b) Sauce: redcurrant jelly and port wine, shallots, zest of lemon and orange, orange and lemon juice, cayenne, mustard and ginger (cold).

Paille (pommes) Straw (potatoes cut into straw-like strips).

Paillettes de fromage Cheese straws.

Pain (bis, blanc, complet, frais, baguette de, de seigle, flute de) Bread (brown, white, wholemeal, fresh, stick of, rye bread, slightly larger than 'baguette').

Pain grillé Toasted bread, toast.

Palestine Soup made with Jerusalem artichoke, cream added.

Palmier (coeurs de) Palm hearts.

Pamplemousse Grapefruit.

Panache A selection of vegetables served au beurre.

Panachée (salade, glace) Mixed (mixed salad, assorted ice cream).

Panade A binding agent; may be flour, butter and water.

Panais Parsnip.

Pané Breadcrumbed.

Paprika Red and mild Hungarian pepper.

Parfait glace Coffee ice cream.

Parfum Perfume, scent, flavour.

Papillote (en) Meat cooked in heart-shaped oiled paper bag folded over the edges like a hem.

Parisienne (pommes) Round, ball-shaped potatoes.

Parme (jambon de) Parma ham (smoked).

Parmentier Diced potato. Named after Baron Parmentier who introduced potatoes into France.

Parmesan Italian hard goat cheese.

Passer To strain.

Passoir Strainer.

Pastèque Water melon.

Pâte Pastry.
   à beignets, à chou For fritters, chou pastry.
   brisée Made from flour, butter and water.
   à brioche, levée Brioche pastry, risen pastry.
   à foncer, à nouille Short pastry, noodle pastry.
   à frire Frying batter.

Pâtes alimentaires Pasta (macaroni, spaghetti, lasagne).

Pâté (*a*) Pie made of pastry with assorted fillings, such as meat, vegetables, fish, fruit.
(*b*) Liver pate.

Pâté de campagne Country pâté.

Patissier (Patissière) Pastry chef (Pastry cream).

Pauillac Red wine from the commune of Medoc in the Bordeaux district.

Paupiette Rolled fillet of fish or meat.

Pavé (pommes) Paving stone (large dice of potatoes, roasted).

Paysanne Cut of vegetable – small round or triangle shape.

Paysanne (à la) Peasant style.

Pêche Peach.

Peler To peel.

Perche Perch, bass.

Perdreau (perdrix) Partridge.

Perigord (perigourdine) Region of France renowned for its truffles and à la pâté de foie gras.

Pernod Aniseed-flavoured aperitif.

Perrier (Perrier Jouet) Sparkling mineral water (make of champagne).

Persil Parsley.

Péruvienne (*a*) For grilled steak, tomato sauce, stuffed oxalis.
(*b*) Meat dishes: oxalis filled with ham, chicken, oxalis salpicon, half glazed sauce.

Pessac Home of famous red Château Haut-Brion. First growth.

Petite Champagne Region of the Cognac district of France producing the brandy of that name.

Petit déjeuner Breakfast.

Petit duc (*a*) Snipe-flavoured velouté, snipe scallops, royale of game essence.
(*b*) Entrée garnish tartlet filled with creamed chicken, asparagus tips in bunches, truffles.

Petits fours Small cakes, crystallised fruit or sweets; sometimes called friandises.

Petite marmite Beef and chicken consommé garnished with vegetables, pieces of beef and chicken served in a small earthenware pot.

Petit pain Roll.

Petits pois Green peas.

Petit suisse Cream cheese.

Piece montée Elaborate and decorative culinary work.

Pieds (de port) Pig's trotter.

Piemontaise (Risotto) Rich polaff, mushrooms, tomatoes, pimentos and truffles.

Pigeon (Pigeonneau) Pigeon (young pigeon).

Pilaf (Pilaw) Braised rice in oven.

Piment Pimento (red, green).

Piperade Regional dish: tomatoes, peppers, and eggs beaten to a fluffy consistency.

Piquante (sauce) Sharp (sauce of demi glace, with white wine vinegar, gherkins and herbs).

Pique Studded-narrow strips of fat bacon inserted into lean meat.

Pissenlit Edible dandelion (in salads).

Pistache Pistachio.

Pithiviers (gâteau) Puff pastry gâteau, filled with almond cream.

Plaisirs des dames Petits fours.

Plateau à fromage Cheese board.

Plat (du jour) Dish (of the day).

Plate-côte Flat rib of beef.

Plie Plaice.

Pluvier (Oeufs de) Plovers' eggs.

Poché (pocher) Poached (to poach).

Poêler Cooked in frying pan, also pot roasting.

Pointes d'asperges Asparagus tips.

Poire (avocat) Pear (avocado pear).

Poireau Leek.

Pois (cassés) Peas (split).

Pois chiches Chick-peas.

Poisson (poissonier) Fish (fish cook).

Portefeuille (en) Layers of sliced potatoes and onions, Robert sauce, mashed potatoes on top, glazed.

Poitrine de porc Belly of pork.

Poivrade Sauce for game, usually containing marinade, vinegar, half glaze and herbs.

Poivre (de cayenne) Pepper (cayenne pepper).

Poivron Pepper (pimento).

Pojarski Chopped veal or chicken mixed with butter

and breadcrumbs, cutlet shape, bone stick inserted, breadcrumbed, shallow fried.

Polonaise (chou-fleur) Polish style sautéed and sprinkled with sieved hard white and yolk of egg, fried breadcrumbs, chopped parsley.

Pomerol Claret wine-producing district in Bordeaux.

Pomme Apple.

Pomme de terre Potato.

Pommes noisettes, nature Hazelnut-shaped potatoes, steamed potatoes.

Pompadour (a) Type of ice cream wafer, fan-shaped.

(b) Poached sole, chopped tomatoes, white wine sauce, truffles.

Pont l'Eveque Well known French cheese.

Pont neuf (pomme) Untrimmed thick baton of fried potatoes.

Porc Pork.

Porto Port.

Port Salut French cheese.

Portugaise (a) From Portugal, usually with tomatoes and onions.

(b) Entrée: stuffed tomatoes, château potatoes.

Potage (clair) Soup or broth (consommé). Menu heading for soups.

Pot au feu Beef and pork boiled with vegetables (cabbage, leeks, potatoes).

Pot pourri Stew of various kinds of meats and spices.

Poularde, poule Fattened fowl, hen.

Pouding Pudding.

Pouilly fuissé Dry white wine from the Côte Mâconnaise in Burgundy.

Poule au pot Boiling fowl cooked in a pot with vegetables.

Poulet (de grain, reine) Chicken (corn-fed chicken, young spring chicken).

Pousse de Bambou Bamboo shoot.

Poussin Spring chicken.

Pralin Almond toffee paste used in pastry preparations.

Praire French for type of clam, also called coque rayée or rigatelle.

Praline Nut-flavoured almonds coated with sugar.

Pré sale Salted meadow: lamb and mutton raised on the salt marshes of France-Ardennes and Brittany.

Pressoir Juice extractor.

Princesse Artichoke bottoms filled with asparagus tips, noisette potatoes.

Primeurs Early spring vegetables or fruits.

Printanière With spring vegetables.

Profiterole Round chou pastry usually filled with cream and covered with chocolate.

Provençâle (a) Provence style-chopped tomatoes, garlic, cooked in oil, olives.
(b) Tomatoes, stuffed mushrooms, garlic.

Prune Plum.

Pruneau Prune.

Purée Purée of vegetables, fruit, meat, fish, soups.

Paysanne A cut of vegetable. There are four accepted methods of cutting paysanne:
  1 cm sided triangles;
  1 cm sided squares;
  1 cm rounds;
  1 cm rough-sided rounds.

Paupiettes A fillet of fish filled with a fish stuffing and rolled with the skin side innermost.

Persillé Brushed with melted butter and sprinkled liberally with finely chopped parsley.

Petit pois Flamande Flemish style, a combination of half amount of carrots cut jardinière or macedoine with garden peas.

Polonaise Sprinkled with sieved hard boiled egg white and egg yolk, finely chopped parsley and fried breadcrumbs. Napped with beurre noisette.

Primeurs As for bouquetière but using spring vegetables.

Quartier Quarter.

Quartier d'agneau Quarter of lamb, leg and loin attached.

Quebec (crème) Broad bean soup, garnish of spring vegetables.

Quenelle Chicken, fish or game: forcemeat.

Quenelles Finely sieved chicken, game or fish forcemeat. Seasoned and flavoured accordingly, whisked egg whites and whipping cream added.

Quetsche Elongated plum.

Queue (de boeuf) Tail (oxtail).

Quiche (Lorraine) Tart (filled with egg, bacon, cheese mixture and baked).

Quo vadis (canapé) Soft roes on toast, grilled mushrooms.

Rable (de lièvre, lapin) Loin or saddle of hare or rabbit.

Rachel Artichoke bottoms, slices of poached meat, marrow.

Radis Radish.

Refraichi Refreshed, chilled.

Ragoût Brown stew of beef.

Raie Skate.

Raifort (sauce) Horseradish (sauce).

Raisin (noir, blanc) Grape (black, white).

Raisins de Corinthe (de smyrne) Currants (sultanas).

Raper To grate.

Ratatouille Vegetable stew.

Ravier Oblong deep dish for service of salad or hors d'oeuvre.

Ravigotte (sauce) (a) Velouté sauce, wine and vinegar, shallots, chervil, tarragon and chives. (b) Vinaigrette, capers, parsley, chives, tarragon, onions.

Raton A kind of cheese cake.

Ravioli Small squares of noodle paste filled with minced meat, spinach and cheese, served with a sauce.

Réchauffer To re-heat.

Réduction (réduire) To reduce a liquid by boiling so as to increase or extract the flavour.

Réform (côtelettes d'agneau) Lamb cutlets breadcrumbed and garnished with ham, truffles, beetroot and sauce Robert.

Régence (a) Usually served with various quenelles depending on the dish. (b) For fish: quenelles, oysters, mushrooms, poached soft roes, truffles. (c) Poultry and sweetbread; quenelles, cockscomb, fois gras scallops, mushrooms, truffles, sauce allemande. (d) Game: quenelles, game stuffing, salmis sauce.

Régime alimentaire Diet.

Reine Claude Greengage.

Reine Margot (crème) Chicken soup with milk of almonds, chicken quenelles.

Relevé Spicy, seasoned, and name given to joints of meat on traditional menus.

Rémoulade Mayonnaise sauce, mustard, capers, gherkins, chervil, tarragon, parsley and anchovy.

Renaissance (à la) Garnish of artichoke bottoms, carrots, turnips, French beans, peas, asparagus tips, cauliflower and hollandaise sauce: fondantes potatoes.

Rhubarbe Rhubarb.

Rhum (au) Rum (with).

Richelieu Stuffed tomatoes, stuffed mushrooms, braised lettuce, château potatoes.

Rillettes Meat or poultry cooked and minced, eaten cold as pâté.

Ris (d'agneau, de veau) Sweetbreads (of lamb, of veal).

Rissolée (pommes) Brown roasted potatoes.

Rissoler To brown.

Risotto Braised rice with grated cheese.

Rivière (de) (truite) River (river trout).

Riz Rice.

Robe de chambre (pommes en) Steamed jacket potatoes.

Robert (sauce) Half glaze, white wine, vinegar, chopped onions, mustard.

Rognon Kidney.

Romaine (salade) Cos lettuce.

Romanoff (fraises) (a) Strawberries, whipped cream and curaçao. (b) Meat garnish: stuffed cucumbers, duchess potatoes, croustade filled with celery, rare salpicon and mushrooms, horseradish sauce.

Romarin Rosemary (herb).

Rondelle (de saucisson) Slices of a type of sausage served as an hors d'oeuvre.

Roquefort Famous French blue cheese.

Rosbif Roast beef.

Rossini (a) Foie gras, truffle, half glaze and Madeira wine. (b) For tournedos and noisette: foie gras scallops sautéed in butter, truffles.

Rôti (rotisseur) Roast meat, heading on the menu (roast chef).

Rouennaise Rouen style: half glaze, red wine, duck liver, lemon juice, shallots.

Rouget Red mullet.

Roulade (de saumon, de veau, de porc) Rolled piece (of salmon, of veal, of pork).

Roux (blanc, brun) (a) Fat or butter and flour cooked to various degrees (white, brown). (b) One of the basic ingredients for making sauces.

Royale (a) Poached white of egg, coloured and cut into various shapes, dice, lozenges for consommé. (b) As Régence. (c) Charlotte Royale: bavarois surrounded by slices of Swiss rolls.

Rubane (Bavarois) Ribbons (three flavour bavarois; chocolate, vanilla and strawberry).

Rubens (consommé) Chicken consommé, tomato flavoured, hop shoots.

Russe (salade) Russian salad: mixed diced vegetable salad.

Rutabaga Swede.

Reducing The cooking liquor is strained after use and rapidly boiled. It is then added to the accompanying or coating sauce.

Sabayon Yolk of egg, sugar and white wine or Marsala whipped to a frothy consistency. Also basic sauce for crème anglaise, bavarois.

Sablées (pommes) Diced roast potatoes with breadcrumbs.

Safron Saffron.

Sagou Sago.

Saignant Underdone, term used for cooking of steaks.

Saindoux Lard.

Saint Florentin (pommes) Flat croquette potatoes with chopped ham, rolled in vermicelli, deep fried.

Saint Germain (crème) (a) Fresh pea soup, green peas, croutons, liaison of cream.
(b) Sweetbread garnish: dome shaped purée of fresh peas served in artichoke bottoms.

Saint Honoré (gateau) Shaped like the crown of St Honoré: puff pastry base, profiteroles around, centre filled with pastry cream.

Saint Hubert Game velouté: dice of game and truffles, creme, redcurrant jelly, fine champagne liqueur.

Saint Mande Garnish of peas, French beans, Macaire potatoes.

Saint Paulin French cheese.

Saint Pierre John Dory (fish).

Saison (de) Season (of the).

Salade Salad. *(niçoise)* (mixed: tomatoes, French beans, potatoes, anchovies, black olives, capers, vinaigrette).
(panachée) (lettuce, garnished with ¼ tomatoes, hard boiled eggs, sliced beetroot and French dressing).

Salade de fruits Fruit salad (fresh).

Salamandre Salamander: type of grill.

Salami Salami sausage from Italy served as an hors d'oeuvre.

Salé Salted.

Salpetre Saltpetre used for the pickling of meat.

Salsifis Salsify.

Salpicon Mixture of fruit or vegetable cut into dice and covered with sauce.

Sanglier Wild boar.

Sarah Bernhardt Garnish of demi glace, port wine, meat marrow, croutons, tomatoes, braised lettuce.

Sardine Sardine.

Sarladaise (pomme) (a) Sliced potatoes and truffles cooked in stock in the oven.
(b) Garnish for meat.

Sauce (saucier) Sauce (sauce chef).

Saucisse Sausage.

Saucisson Sausage made with a mixture of raw minced beef, pork and seasoning.

Sauge Sage (herb).

Saumon (fumé, d'Ecosse) Salmon (smoked, Scottish).

Saumonière Salmon kettle.

Saumure Brine.

Sauté (poulet, pommes) Tossed (chicken, potatoes).

Sauter au beurre To toss in butter.

Sauteuse Copper pan used for sautéed dishes.

Sauvage (canard) Wild (duck).

Savarin (aux fruits) Round sponge made with baba paste, fruit salad placed in centre.

Savoyarde (pommes, omelette) Savoy style (potatoes, omelette and cheese).

Saxon (soufflé) Vanilla soufflé served with a sabayon.

Scampi Italian name for Dublin Bay prawn.

Schneider (pommes) Sliced potatoes cooked in milk, cream, meat glaze, butter and chopped parsley.

Schnitzel Term used to denote a thin slice of meat, usually veal.

Sel Salt.

Selle (d'agneau, de mouton) Saddle (of lamb, of mutton).

Semoule Semolina.

Sevigne (creme) Cream of chicken soup, chicken quenelles and julienne of lettuce.

Sicilienne Sicilian style.

Sirop (de groseille, de cassis, de grenadine) Syrup, (redcurrant, blackcurrant, pomegranate).

Soissonnaise With large Soissons (haricot beans). Originally from the town of the same name in Northern France.

Sole Sole.

Solferino (crème) Potato and tomato soup, small balls of carrots and potatoes.

Sorbet (a) Water ice flavoured with wine or liqueur.
(b) A course at banquet between main dishes.

Soubise (sauce) White sauce with onions.

Soufflé (a) A sweet or savoury hot dish in which the egg is incorporated into a thick sauce and the mixture baked.
(b) A usually sweet uncooked dish made by whisking up eggs, cream, sugar, usually fruit juice and gelatine, and leaving the mixture to set.

Soupe (aux choux, à l'oignon) Country style soup (cabbage, onion soup).

Sous chef Second in charge to the head chef.

Sous (la) cendre Originally meat cooked under hot wood, cinders (literally, under ashes). Wrapped in pastry and cooked in oven.

Sous noix Under cushion or nut of veal.

Soya (huile de) Oil from the soya bean.

St Emilion Red wine from the borders of the Pomerol district in Bordeaux.

Strogonoff Strip of fillet of beef cooked with paprika pepper, sherry and sour cream.

Sucre (en poudre, en morceau, cristallisé, glace) Sugar (castor, cube, crystallised, icing sugar).

Suedoise From Sweden.
(a) Cutlets or chops marinaded, breadcrumbed, grilled, served with a suedoise sauce.
(b) Sauce: mayonnaise, horseradish, and apple marmalade cooked in white wine.

Suprêmes A cut from the fillet of a large fish.

Surprise Surprise.
(a) Orange Orange skin scooped out and filled with water ice.
(b) Omelette Omelette: genoise, ice cream covered with meringue, decorated, placed quickly in the oven.

Suzette (crêpe) Flamed pancake with orange, lemon butter, sugar.

Table d'hôte Meal at a set price.

Talleyrand (a) Half glaze, truffle, Madeira wine, foie gras, macaroni and cheese.
(b) Poultry and sweetbread, buttered macaroni, grated cheese, julienne of truffles, dice of foie gras.

Tamiser To sieve.

Tapioca Tapioca used for puddings or soups.

Tartare (a) sauce Mayonnaise with capers, gherkins and parsley.
(b) steak Raw minced steak with egg yolk, capers, onions and various seasonings.

Tarte (tartelette) Tart or pie (small tart).

Tartines beurrées Buttered slices of bread.

Tasse (en) Cup (in a).

Terrine (en) Earthenware dish for cooking and serving in.
  (de lièvre) (hare pâté).

Tête de veau Calf's head.

Tête roulée Pork butcher's speciality made of firm head of pork and served as an hors d'oeuvre.

Thé Tea.

Theodora (salade) Artichoke bottoms, oysters, mushrooms, crayfish, mayonnaise.

Thérèse Poached fillets of fish, noisette potatoes, truffle, white wine sauce.

Thermidor (homard) Lobster in half shell, white wine sauce, with mustard and Mornay sauce.

Thon Tuna fish.

Thym Thyme.

Timbale (a) Small round dish with a double container used for cooking delicate fruit and soufflés.
(b) Presented in timbale dish.

Tisane Infusion.

Tivoli Soft roes, poached oysters, mushrooms, noodles, genoise sauce.

Tomate Tomato.

Topinambour Jerusalem artichoke.

Torta Type of cake made with sponge, fruit and mousse.

Tortue (a) Turtle (turtle soup).
(b) Entrée: quenelles, mushrooms, gherkins, garlic.
(c) Scallop of veal tongue and brain, fried egg, crayfish, croûton, truffles.

Tosca Chicken consommé with tapioca, turtle meat, Madeira, julienne of leek.

Toulousaine (a) Chicken in aspic, Toulouse style, truffles, cocks' kidneys, asparagus tips.
(b) Chicken and sweetbread, chicken quenelle sweetbread scallops, cock's comb, and kidneys, mushrooms, suprême sauce, truffles.

Tourangelle Entrée garnish: French and kidney beans, cooked in velouté.

Tournedos Round, thick piece of steak cut from the middle of the fillet of beef.

Tourner To turn or shape vegetables.

Tourte Round in shape.
(a) Round pastry for entrées or sweets dishes.
(b) Rye brown cottage loaf.

Tranche (mince, épaise) Slice (thin, thick).

Tranche tendre (grasse) Topside of beef (thin flank of beef).

Tranche napolitaine Ice cream with fruit cut into slices.

Trancheur Carver.

Trifle Trifle, also known as soupe anglaise.

Tripe Tripe.

Tronçon Cut through the bone of a flat fish.

Trousser une volaille To truss a chicken.

Truffe Truffle.

Truite (saumonée, au bleu, de rivière) Trout (salmon trout, blue, river).

Turbigo Kidney cut in half sautéed in butter, tomato half glazed on toast, chipolata, mushrooms.

Turque Chicken liver, onions, rice and half glazed.

Tutti frutti Italian ice cream with various fruits.

Tyrolienne (*a*) Sauce Choron with oil.
(*b*) For tournedos and noisettes: fried onion rings, cooked tomatoes.

Vacherin Meringue gâteau with cream, ice cream and fruit.

Vaisselle Crockery (washing up).

Valenciennes Entrée garnish: risotto valencienne (rice cooked in meat stock) and served with croquette potatoes.

Vanille (rocher) Vanilla (spooned out ice cream for serving with fruit).

Vanille Flavoured with vanilla.

Vapeur (pommes) Steamed (potatoes).

Veau Calf: veal.

Velours (crème) Velvet: carrot soup with tapioca.

Velouté (*a*) Smooth thick white sauce made with stock.
(*b*) Type of soup.

Venaison (de cerf, chevreuil, daim, sanglier) Venison (deer, roe buck, buck, wild boar).

Vermicelle Vermicelli used as garnish to soups.

Veronique White wine sauce and white grapes: fish garnish.

Vert pré Grean meadow. Garnish of watercress and straw potatoes with butter 'maitre d'hotel'.

Veuve-Clicquot A champagne shipper.

Viande Meat.

Vichy (*a*) Gaseous mineral water.
(*b*) Carrots cooked in Vichy water, glazed.
(*c*) Garnish of Vichy carrots.

Vichyssoise Soup made with potatoes, leeks, cream and chives — usually eaten cold.

Victoria Fruit slice, macedoine of fruit, cherries, marrons glacés — Madeira wine.

Viennoise (*a*) Veal scallop, breadcrumbed, shallow fried, slice of lemon, olive and anchovy.
(*b*) Meat garnish, noodles croustade filled with leaf spinach, braised celery, new potatoes.

Village Village.

Vin (vinaigre) Wine (vinegar).

Vinaigrette Oil and vinegar dressing or French dressing.

Vin blanc (au) (*a*) White wine.
(*b*) With white wine.
(*c*) White wine sauce.

Vin rouge (au) (*a*) Red wine.
(*b*) With red wine.
(*c*) Red wine sauce.

Viroflay Meat garnish: spinach balls Viroflay style, artichoke quarters, château potatoes.

Viveur (consommé) Beef or duck consommé, garnished with julienne of celery, diablotins with paprika.

Voile Veil of spun sugar.

Voisin (pommes) Anna potatoes with grated cheese.

Voiture (à trancher, à hors d'oeuvre, à entremets) Trolley (carving, hors d'oeuvre, sweet).

Volaille Poultry.

Vol au vent Round puff pastry case which can be filled with such ingredients as chicken or meat in a sauce.

Waldorf (salade) Grated celeriac, mayonnaise, lemon juice in apple topped with walnut.

Waleska Poached fish-scallop of lobster, truffles, and sauce Mornay.

Washington (*a*) Poultry garnish creamed sweetcorn.
(*b*) Fish cooked in butter, lobster scallops, American sauce, truffles.

Waterzoi Waterzootje (Flemish cookery). Similar to bouillabaisse, with butter used instead of oil.

Wellington (filet de boeuf) Larded, cooked in pastry, garnished with tomatoes, braised lettuce, château potatoes, Madeira sauce and foie gras.

Windsor (croute) Ham paste, grilled mushrooms on toast.

Winterthur (à la) Type of lobster dish served with peeled shrimps and a salpicon.

Wladimir Poultry, half sauce bearnaise, half suprême of carrots, julienne of celery, truffles, tarragon leaves, chervil.

Xavier Consommé, peas, chervil.

Xeres (au) With sherry.

Yaourt Yoghurt.

Yvette Scrambled egg with asparagus tips, crayfish tails, truffles, in tartlet, Nantua sauce.

Zabaglione Italian sweet made with a sabayon of yolk of egg, sugar and Marsala wine; finger biscuits.

Zampino Stuffed pig's leg.

Zephir Name given to a light and frothy preparation.

Zeste Zest; 'peel' of the skin of lemon, orange, fruit.

Zingara Tarragon-flavoured half glaze sauce, julienne of ham, tongue, mushrooms, truffles; Madeira.

Zucchini Small vegetable marrow; *see also* Courge.

INDEX